Paige Baltzan

Daniels College of Business, University of Denver

Business Driven Information Systems

SIXTH EDITION

Mc
Graw
Hill
Education

BUSINESS DRIVEN INFORMATION SYSTEMS

2 3 4 5 6 7 8 9 LMN 21 20 19 18

ISBN 978-1-260-09292-9
MHID 1-260-09292-5

Cover Image: © *fuyu Liu/Shutterstock*

To Tony, Hannah, Sophie, and Gus:
What do you always remember?
That I Love You! That I'm Proud of You!

Paige

BRIEF CONTENTS

MODULE 1   **Business Driven MIS**

Chapter 1   Management Information Systems: Business Driven MIS

Chapter 2   Decisions and Processes: Value Driven Business

Chapter 3   Ebusiness: Electronic Business Value

Chapter 4   Ethics and Information Security: MIS Business Concerns

MODULE 2   **Technical Foundations of MIS**

Chapter 5   Infrastructures: Sustainable Technologies

Chapter 6   Data: Business Intelligence

Chapter 7   Networks: Mobile Business

MODULE 3   **Enterprise MIS**

Chapter 8   Enterprise Applications: Business Communications

Chapter 9   Systems Development and Project Management: Corporate Responsibility

APPENDICES

Appendix A   Hardware and Software Basics

Appendix B   Networks and Telecommunications

Appendix C   Designing Databases

Appendix D   Emerging Trends and Technologies

Apply Your Knowledge

Glossary

Notes

Index

CONTENTS

module 1
Business Driven MIS   1

CHAPTER 1
Management Information Systems: Business Driven MIS   2

Opening Case Study: The Internet of Things   3

Section 1.1 Business Driven MIS   5
COMPETING IN THE INFORMATION AGE   5
   Data   6
   Information   9
   Business Intelligence   10
   Knowledge   11
THE CHALLENGE OF DEPARTMENTAL COMPANIES AND THE MIS SOLUTION   13
   The MIS Solution   14
   Systems Thinking   16
   MIS Department Roles and Responsibilities   17
Section 1.2 Business Strategy   19
IDENTIFYING COMPETITIVE ADVANTAGES   20
   Swot Analysis: Understanding Business Strategies   22
THE FIVE FORCES MODEL—EVALUATING INDUSTRY ATTRACTIVENESS   23
   Buyer Power   23
   Supplier Power   24
   Threat of Substitute Products or Services   25
   Threat of New Entrants   25
   Rivalry among Existing Competitors   25
   Analyzing the Airline Industry   26
THE THREE GENERIC STRATEGIES—CHOOSING A BUSINESS FOCUS   27
VALUE CHAIN ANALYSIS—EXECUTING BUSINESS STRATEGIES   29
Learning Outcome Review   32
Opening Case Questions   34
Key Terms   34
Review Questions   34
Closing Case One: Buy Experiences, Not Things   35
Closing Case Two: The World Is Flat: Thomas Friedman   37

Critical Business Thinking   38
Apply Your Knowledge Business Projects   42
AYK Application Projects   46

CHAPTER 2   47
Decisions and Processes: Value Driven Business   47

Opening Case Study: Robots Took My Job   48

Section 2.1 Decision Support Systems   50
MAKING ORGANIZATIONAL BUSINESS DECISIONS   50
   The Decision-Making Process   51
   Decision-Making Essentials   51
MEASURING ORGANIZATIONAL BUSINESS DECISIONS   53
   Efficiency and Effectiveness Metrics   56
USING MIS TO MAKE BUSINESS DECISIONS   58
   Operational Support Systems   58
   Managerial Support Systems   60
   Strategic Support Systems   61
USING AI TO MAKE BUSINESS DECISIONS   64
   Expert Systems   67
   Neural Networks   67
   Genetic Algorithms   68
   Intelligent Agents   69
   Virtual Reality   69
Section 2.2 Business Processes   70
MANAGING BUSINESS PROCESSES   71
   Business Process Modeling   73
USING MIS TO IMPROVE BUSINESS PROCESSES   75
   Operational Business Processes—Automation   76
   Managerial Business Processes—Streamlining   79
   Strategic Business Processes—Reengineering   80
Learning Outcome Review   86
Opening Case Questions   88
Key Terms   88
Review Questions   89
Closing Case One: Business Is Booming for Wearable Technologies   89
Closing Case Two: Defense Advanced Research Projects Agency (DARPA) Grand Challenge   91
Critical Business Thinking   91

Apply Your Knowledge Business Projects   93
AYK Application Projects   97

CHAPTER 3
Ebusiness: Electronic Business Value   98

Opening Case Study: Hello Fresh, Hello Delicious   99

Section 3.1 Web 1.0: Ebusiness   101
DISRUPTIVE TECHNOLOGY   101
    Disruptive versus Sustaining Technology   101
    The Internet and World Wide Web—The Ultimate Business
    Disruptors   102
WEB 1.0: THE CATALYST FOR EBUSINESS   102
    Expanding Global Reach   105
    Opening New Markets   105
    Reducing Costs   105
    Improving Effectiveness   107
THE FOUR EBUSINESS MODELS   108
    Business-to-Business (B2B)   110
    Business-to-Consumer (B2C)   110
    Consumer-to-Business (C2B)   110
    Consumer-to-Consumer (C2C)   110
    Ebusiness Forms and Revenue-Generating
    Strategies   111
EBUSINESS TOOLS FOR CONNECTING AND
COMMUNICATING   112
    Email   114
    Instant Messaging   114
    Podcasting   114
    Videoconferencing   114
    Web Conferencing   114
    Content Management Systems   115
THE CHALLENGES OF EBUSINESS   115
    Identifying Limited Market Segments   115
    Managing Consumer Trust   116
    Ensuring Consumer Protection   116
    Adhering to Taxation Rules   116
Section 3.2 Web 2.0: Business 2.0   116
WEB 2.0: ADVANTAGES OF BUSINESS 2.0   116
    Content Sharing through Open Sourcing   117
    User-Contributed Content   118
    Collaboration Inside the Organization   118
    Collaboration Outside the Organization   119
NETWORKING COMMUNITIES WITH BUSINESS 2.0   120
    Social Tagging   121
BUSINESS 2.0 TOOLS FOR COLLABORATING   122
    Blogs   122

    Wikis   123
    Mashups   124
THE CHALLENGES OF BUSINESS 2.0   125
    Technology Dependence   125
    Information Vandalism   125
    Violations of Copyright and Plagiarism   125
WEB 3.0: DEFINING THE NEXT GENERATION OF ONLINE
BUSINESS OPPORTUNITIES   126
    Egovernment: The Government Moves Online   127
Learning Outcome Review   128
Opening Case Questions   130
Key Terms   130
Review Questions   131
Closing Case One: Slack—Be Less Busy   131
Closing Case Two: Action Finally   133
Critical Business Thinking   134
Apply Your Knowledge Business Projects   136
AYK Application Projects   139

CHAPTER 4
Ethics and Information Security: MIS Business Concerns   140

Opening Case Study: Five Ways Hackers Can Get into Your Business   141

Section 4.1 Ethics   143
INFORMATION ETHICS   143
    Information Does Not Have Ethics, People Do   145
DEVELOPING INFORMATION MANAGEMENT POLICIES   145
    Ethical Computer Use Policy   146
    Information Privacy Policy   148
    Acceptable Use Policy   148
    Email Privacy Policy   149
    Social Media Policy   150
    Workplace Monitoring Policy   151
Section 4.2 Information Security   154
PROTECTING INTELLECTUAL ASSETS   154
    Hackers: A Dangerous Threat to Business   155
    Viruses: A Dangerous Threat to Business   156
THE FIRST LINE OF DEFENSE—PEOPLE   158
THE SECOND LINE OF DEFENSE—TECHNOLOGY   159
    People: Authentication and Authorization   159
    Data: Prevention and Resistance   162
    Attack: Detection and Response   164
Learning Outcome Review   165
Opening Case Questions   166
Key Terms   167
Review Questions   167

Closing Case One: Targeting Target   168
Closing Case Two: To Share—Or Not to Share   169
Critical Business Thinking   172
Apply Your Knowledge Business Projects   175
AYK Application Projects   177

module 2
Technical Foundations of MIS   178

CHAPTER 5
Infrastructures: Sustainable Technologies   179

Opening Case Study: Box Up Your Data   180

Section 5.1 MIS Infrastructures   183
THE BUSINESS BENEFITS OF A SOLID MIS
INFRASTRUCTURE   183
SUPPORTING OPERATIONS: INFORMATION MIS
INFRASTRUCTURE   184
   Backup and Recovery Plan   185
   Disaster Recovery Plan   186
   Business Continuity Plan   188
SUPPORTING CHANGE: AGILE MIS INFRASTRUCTURE   189
   Accessibility   190
   Availability   191
   Maintainability   192
   Portability   192
   Reliability   192
   Scalability   193
   Usability   194
Section 5.2 Building Sustainable MIS Infrastructures   194
MIS AND THE ENVIRONMENT   194
   Increased Electronic Waste   195
   Increased Energy Consumption   196
   Increased Carbon Emissions   196
SUPPORTING THE ENVIRONMENT: SUSTAINABLE MIS
INFRASTRUCTURE   196
   Grid Computing   197
   Virtualized Computing   201
   Cloud Computing   204
   Public Cloud   208
   Private Cloud   209
   Community Cloud   209
   Hybrid Cloud   210
UTILITY COMPUTING   210
   Infrastructure as a Service (IaaS)   211
   Software as a Service (SaaS)   211
   Platform as a Service (PasS)   212

Learning Outcome Review   212
Opening Case Questions   213
Key Terms   214
Review Questions   214
Closing Case One: Etsy   215
Closing Case Two: Interest in Pinterest   216
Critical Business Thinking   218
Apply Your Knowledge Business Projects   220
AYK Application Projects   223

CHAPTER 6
Data: Business Intelligence   224

Opening Case Study: Big Data, Big Business, Big Opportunities   225

Section 6.1 Data, Information, and Databases   227
THE BUSINESS BENEFITS OF HIGH-QUALITY
INFORMATION   227
   Information Type: Transactional and Analytical   227
   Information Timeliness   228
   Information Quality   229
   Information Governance   232
STORING INFORMATION USING A RELATIONAL DATABASE
MANAGEMENT SYSTEM   232
   Storing Data Elements in Entities and Attributes   234
   Creating Relationships through Keys   234
   Coca Cola Relational Database Example   235
USING A RELATIONAL DATABASE FOR BUSINESS
ADVANTAGES   237
   Increased Flexibility   237
   Increased Scalability and Performance   237
   Reduced Information Redundancy   238
   Increased Information Integrity (Quality)   238
   Increased Information Security   238
DRIVING WEBSITES WITH DATA   239
Section 6.2 Business Intelligence   241
SUPPORTING DECISIONS WITH BUSINESS
INTELLIGENCE   241
   Data Marts   243
   Information Cleansing or Scrubbing   244
BUSINESS INTELLIGENCE   247
   The Problem: Data Rich, Information Poor   248
   The Solution: Business Intelligence   248
THE POWER OF BIG DATA ANALYTICS   250
   Distributed Computing   250
   Virtualization   252
   Analyzing Big Data   252
DATA MINING   253
   Data Mining Process Model   254

Data Mining Analysis Techniques   254
Data Mining Modeling Techniques for Predictions   257
DATA ANALYSIS   258
Advanced Data Analytics   259
Data Visualization   260
Learning Outcome Review   263
Opening Case Questions   265
Key Terms   265
Review Questions   266
**Closing Case One: Data Visualization: Stories for the
Information Age   266**
Closing Case Two: Informing Information   268
Critical Business Thinking   271
Apply Your Knowledge Business Projects   274
AYK Application Projects   277

CHAPTER 7
Networks: Mobile Business   278

**Opening Case Study: Disrupting the Taxi:
Uber   279**

**Section 7.1 Connectivity: The Business Value of a
Networked World   281**
OVERVIEW OF A CONNECTED WORLD   281
Network Categories   282
Network Providers   282
Network Access Technologies   283
Network Protocols   286
Network Convergence   288
BENEFITS OF A CONNECTED WORLD   291
CHALLENGES OF A CONNECTED WORLD   293
Security   293
Social, Ethical, and Political Issues   293
**Section 7.2 Mobility: The Business Value of a Wireless
World   294**
WIRELESS NETWORK CATEGORIES   294
Mbusiness: Supporting Anywhere Business   294
Personal Area Networks   295
Wireless LANs   295
Wireless MANs   298
Wireless WAN—Cellular Communication System   298
Wireless WAN—Satellite Communication System   300
Protecting Wireless Connections   300
Managing Mobile Devices   302
BUSINESS APPLICATIONS OF WIRELESS NETWORKS   302
Radio-Frequency Identification (RFID)   303
Global Positioning System (GPS)   304
Geographic Information Systems (GIS)   305
Learning Outcome Review   307

Opening Case Questions   308
Key Terms   309
Review Questions   309
Closing Case One: Wireless Bikes   310
Closing Case Two: Square: Wireless Payments to an iPhone,
Android, or iPad   311
Critical Business Thinking   312
Apply Your Knowledge Business Projects   314
AYK Application Projects   318

module 3
Enterprise MIS   319

CHAPTER 8
**Enterprise Applications: Business
Communications   320**

**Opening Case Study: Dream It, Design It,
3D Print It   321**

Section 8.1 Supply Chain Management   323
**BUILDING A CONNECTED CORPORATION THROUGH
INTEGRATIONS   323**
Integration Tools   324
SUPPLY CHAIN MANAGEMENT   325
Visibility into the Supply Chain   327
TECHNOLOGIES REINVENTING THE SUPPLY CHAIN   329
3D Printing Supports Procurement   331
RFID Supports Logistics   333
Drones Support Logistics   333
Robotics Supports Materials Management   335
The Extended Supply Chain   336
**Section 8.2 Customer Relationship Management and
Enterprise Resource Planning   336**
CUSTOMER RELATIONSHIP MANAGEMENT   337
The Power of the Customer   340
Measuring CRM Success   342
OPERATIONAL AND ANALYTICAL CRM   342
Marketing and Operational CRM   343
Sales and Operational CRM   344
Customer Service and Operational CRM   345
Analytical CRM   346
EXTENDING CUSTOMER RELATIONSHIP MANAGEMENT   347
ENTERPRISE RESOURCE PLANNING   348
The Benefits of ERP   352
Core ERP Components   354
Extended ERP Components   355
Measuring ERP Success   356

ORGANIZATIONAL INTEGRATION WITH ERP   357
    On-Premise ERP   358
    Cloud ERP   358
    Hybrid ERP   361
Learning Outcome Review   363
Opening Case Questions   365
Key Terms   365
Review Questions   366
Closing Case One: Amazon Drone Knocking   366
Closing Case Two: Five Famous ERP Failures   367
Critical Business Thinking   368
Apply Your Knowledge Business Projects   371
AYK Application Projects   375

CHAPTER 9
Systems Development and Project Management:
Corporate Responsibility   376

Opening Case Study: Gamer Delight   377

Section 9.1 Developing Enterprise Applications   379
THE SYSTEMS DEVELOPMENT LIFE CYCLE (SDLC)   379
    Phase 1: Planning   379
    Phase 2: Analysis   381
    Phase 3: Design   382
    Phase 4: Development   384
    Phase 5: Testing   385
    Phase 6: Implementation   386
    Phase 7: Maintenance   388
SOFTWARE DEVELOPMENT METHODOLOGY:
THE WATERFALL   388
AGILE SOFTWARE DEVELOPMENT METHODOLOGIES   390
    Rapid Application Development (RAD) Methodology   390
    Extreme Programming Methodology   391
    Rational Unified Process (RUP) Methodology   391
    Scrum Methodology   391
DEVELOPING A SERVICE-ORIENTED ARCHITECTURE   391
    Service   393
    Interoperability   394
    Loose Coupling   394
Section 9.2 Project Management   395
USING PROJECT MANAGEMENT TO DELIVER SUCCESSFUL
PROJECTS   395
    Unclear or Missing Business Requirements   396
    Skipped Phases   396
    Changing Technology   397
    The Cost of Finding Errors in the SDLC   397
    Balance of the Triple Constraint   398
PRIMARY PROJECT PLANNING DIAGRAMS   399
OUTSOURCING PROJECTS   403
    Outsourcing Benefits   404
    Outsourcing Challenges   405

Learning Outcome Review   407
Opening Case Questions   408
Key Terms   409
Review Questions   409
Closing Case One: Disaster at Denver International
Airport   410
Closing Case Two: Reducing Ambiguity in Business
Requirements   411
Critical Business Thinking   412
Apply Your Knowledge Business Projects   413
AYK Application Projects   417

appendices

APPENDIX A
Hardware and Software Basics   A.1

INTRODUCTION   A.1
HARDWARE BASICS   A.1
    Central Processing Unit   A.2
    Primary Storage   A.3
    Secondary Storage   A.5
    Input Devices   A.7
    Output Devices   A.8
    Communication Devices   A.9
COMPUTER CATEGORIES   A.10
SOFTWARE BASICS   A.10
    System Software   A.12
    Application Software   A.13
    Distributing Application Software   A.13
Key Terms   A.14
Apply Your Knowledge   A.14

APPENDIX B
Networks and Telecommunications   B.1

INTRODUCTION   B.1
NETWORK BASICS   B.1
ARCHITECTURE   B.3
    Peer-to-Peer Networks   B.3
    Client/Server Networks   B.4
TOPOLOGY   B.5
PROTOCOLS   B.6
    Ethernet   B.6
    Transmission Control Protocol/Internet Protocol   B.7
MEDIA   B.8
    Wire Media   B.8
    Wireless Media   B.9

Key Terms   **B.10**
Apply Your Knowledge   **B.10**

APPENDIX C
Designing Databases   C.1

INTRODUCTION   C.1
THE RELATIONAL DATABASE MODEL   C.1
Entities and Attributes   C.2
Business Rules   C.3
DOCUMENTING ENTITY RELATIONSHIP DIAGRAMS   C.3
Basic Entity Relationships   C.4
Relationship Cardinality   C.6
RELATIONAL DATA MODEL AND THE DATABASE   C.7
From Entities to Tables   C.7
Logically Relating Tables   C.8
Key Terms   **C.9**
Apply Your Knowledge   **C.9**

APPENDIX D
Emerging Trends and Technologies   D.1

INTRODUCTION   D.1
TRENDS SHAPING OUR FUTURE   D.2
The World's Population Will Double in the Next
40 Years   D.2

People in Developed Countries Are Living Longer   D.3
The Growth in Information Industries Is Creating a
Knowledge-Dependent Global Society   D.3
The Global Economy Is Becoming More Integrated   D.4
The Economy and Society Are Dominated by
Technology   D.4
Pace of Technological Innovation Is Increasing   D.4
TECHNOLOGIES SHAPING OUR FUTURE   D.5
The Digital Mesh   D.5
Smart Machines   D.6
The New IT Reality   D.6
Key Terms   **D.7**
Apply Your Knowledge   **D.7**

Apply Your Knowledge   **AYK.1**
Glossary   **G.1**
Notes   **N.1**
Index   **I.1**

McGraw-Hill Connect® is a highly reliable, easy-to-use homework and learning management solution that utilizes learning science and award-winning adaptive tools to improve student results.

Homework and Adaptive Learning

- Connect's assignments help students contextualize what they've learned through application, so they can better understand the material and think critically.

- Connect will create a personalized study path customized to individual student needs through SmartBook®.

- SmartBook helps students study more efficiently by delivering an interactive reading experience through adaptive highlighting and review.

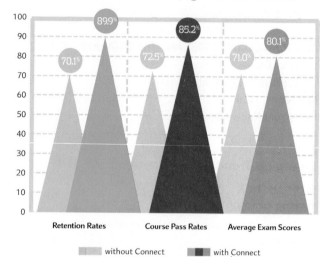

Connect's Impact on Retention Rates, Pass Rates, and Average Exam Scores

Retention Rates: 70.1%, 89.9%
Course Pass Rates: 72.5%, 85.2%
Average Exam Scores: 71.0%, 80.1%

without Connect   with Connect

Over **7 billion questions** have been answered, making McGraw-Hill Education products more intelligent, reliable, and precise.

Using **Connect** improves retention rates by **19.8** percentage points, passing rates by **12.7** percentage points, and exam scores by **9.1** percentage points.

73% of instructors who use **Connect** require it; instructor satisfaction **increases** by 28% when **Connect** is required.

Quality Content and Learning Resources

- Connect content is authored by the world's best subject matter experts, and is available to your class through a simple and intuitive interface.

- The Connect eBook makes it easy for students to access their reading material on smartphones and tablets. They can study on the go and don't need internet access to use the eBook as a reference, with full functionality.

- Multimedia content such as videos, simulations, and games drive student engagement and critical thinking skills.

Robust Analytics and Reporting

- Connect Insight® generates easy-to-read reports on individual students, the class as a whole, and on specific assignments.

- The Connect Insight dashboard delivers data on performance, study behavior, and effort. Instructors can quickly identify students who struggle and focus on material that the class has yet to master.

- Connect automatically grades assignments and quizzes, providing easy-to-read reports on individual and class performance.

©Hero Images/Getty Images

Impact on Final Course Grade Distribution

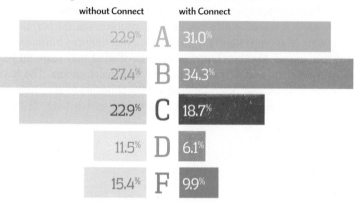

without Connect		with Connect
22.9%	A	31.0%
27.4%	B	34.3%
22.9%	C	18.7%
11.5%	D	6.1%
15.4%	F	9.9%

More students earn **As** and **Bs** when they use **Connect**.

Trusted Service and Support

- Connect integrates with your LMS to provide single sign-on and automatic syncing of grades. Integration with Blackboard®, D2L®, and Canvas also provides automatic syncing of the course calendar and assignment-level linking.

- Connect offers comprehensive service, support, and training throughout every phase of your implementation.

- If you're looking for some guidance on how to use Connect, or want to learn tips and tricks from super users, you can find tutorials as you work. Our Digital Faculty Consultants and Student Ambassadors offer insight into how to achieve the results you want with Connect.

Business Driven Information Systems discusses various business initiatives first and how technology supports those initiatives second. The premise for this unique approach is that business initiatives should drive technology choices. Every discussion first addresses the business needs and then addresses the technology that supports those needs. This text provides the foundation that will enable students to achieve excellence in business, whether they major in operations management, manufacturing, sales, marketing, finance, human resources, accounting, or virtually any other business discipline. *Business Driven Information Systems* is designed to give students the ability to understand how information technology can be a point of strength for an organization.

Common business goals associated with information technology projects include reducing costs, improving productivity, improving customer satisfaction and loyalty, creating competitive advantages, streamlining supply chains, global expansion, and so on. Achieving these results is not easy. Implementing a new accounting system or marketing plan is not likely to generate long-term growth or reduce costs across an entire organization. Businesses must undertake enterprisewide initiatives to achieve broad general business goals such as reducing costs. Information technology plays a critical role in deploying such initiatives by facilitating communication and increasing business intelligence. Any individual anticipating a successful career in business, whether it is in accounting, finance, human resources, or operation management, must understand the basics of information technology that can be found in this text.

We have found tremendous success teaching MIS courses by demonstrating the correlation between business and IT. Students who understand the tight correlation between business and IT understand the power of this course. Students learn 10 percent of what they read, 80 percent of what they personally experience, and 90 percent of what they teach others. The business driven approach brings the difficult and often intangible MIS concepts to the student's level and applies them using a hands-on approach to reinforce the concepts. Teaching MIS with a business driven focus helps:

- Add credibility to IT.
- Open students' eyes to IT opportunities.
- Attract majors.
- Engage students.

FORMAT, FEATURES, AND HIGHLIGHTS

Business Driven Information Systems is state of the art in its discussions, presents concepts in an easy-to-understand format, and allows students to be active participants in learning. The dynamic nature of information technology requires all students—more specifically, business students—to be aware of both current and emerging technologies. Students are facing complex subjects and need a clear, concise explanation to be able to understand and use the concepts throughout their careers. By engaging students with numerous case studies, exercises, projects, and questions that enforce concepts, *Business Driven Information Systems* creates a unique learning experience for both faculty and students.

- **Audience.** *Business Driven Information Systems* is designed for use in undergraduate or introductory MBA courses in management information systems, which are required in many business administration or management programs as part of the common body of knowledge for all business majors.
- **Logical Layout.** Students and faculty will find the text well organized, with the topics flowing logically from one chapter to the next. The definition of each term is provided before it is covered in the chapter, and an extensive glossary is included at the back of the text. Each chapter offers a comprehensive opening case study, learning outcomes, closing case studies, key terms, and critical business thinking questions.

- **Thorough Explanations.** Complete coverage is provided for each topic that is introduced. Explanations are written so that students can understand the ideas presented and relate them to other concepts.

- **Solid Theoretical Base.** The text relies on current theory and practice of information systems as they relate to the business environment. Current academic and professional journals cited throughout the text are found in the Notes at the end of the book—a road map for additional, pertinent readings that can be the basis for learning beyond the scope of the chapters or plug-ins.

- **Material to Encourage Discussion.** All chapters contain a diverse selection of case studies and individual and group problem-solving activities as they relate to the use of information technology in business. Two comprehensive cases at the end of each chapter reinforce content. These cases encourage students to consider what concepts have been presented and then apply those concepts to a situation they might find in an organization. Different people in an organization can view the same facts from different points of view, and the cases will force students to consider some of those views.

- **Flexibility in Teaching and Learning.** Although most textbooks that are text-only leave faculty on their own when it comes to choosing cases, *Business Driven Information Systems* goes much further. Several options are provided to faculty with case selections from a variety of sources, including *CIO, Harvard Business Journal, Wired, Forbes,* and *Time,* to name just a few. Therefore, faculty can use the text alone, the text and a complete selection of cases, or anything in between.

- **Integrative Themes.** Several integrative themes recur throughout the text, which adds integration to the material. Among these themes are value-added techniques and methodologies, ethics and social responsibility, globalization, and gaining a competitive advantage. Such topics are essential to gaining a full understanding of the strategies that a business must recognize, formulate, and in turn implement. In addition to addressing these in the chapter material, many illustrations are provided for their relevance to business practice.

WALKTHROUGH

Learning Outcomes

> **Learning Outcomes.** These outcomes focus on what students should learn and be able to answer upon completion of the chapter.

section 3.1 | Web 1.0: Ebusiness

LEARNING OUTCOMES

3.1 Compare disruptive and sustaining technologies and explain how the Internet and WWW caused business disruption.

3.2 Describe ebusiness and its associated advantages.

3.3 Compare the four ebusiness models.

3.4 Describe the six ebusiness tools for connecting and communicating.

3.5 Identify the four challenges associated with ebusiness.

Chapter Opening Case Study and Opening Case Questions

Chapter Opening Case Study. To enhance student interest, each chapter begins with an opening case study that highlights an organization that has been time-tested and value-proven in the business world. This feature serves to fortify concepts with relevant examples of outstanding companies. Discussion of the case is threaded throughout the chapter.

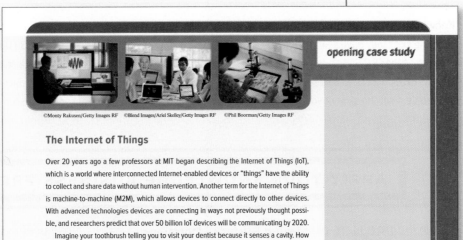

opening case study

©Monty Rakusen/Getty Images RF   ©Blend Images/Ariel Skelley/Getty Images RF   ©Phil Boorman/Getty Images RF

The Internet of Things

Over 20 years ago a few professors at MIT began describing the Internet of Things (IoT), which is a world where interconnected Internet-enabled devices or "things" have the ability to collect and share data without human intervention. Another term for the Internet of Things is machine-to-machine (M2M), which allows devices to connect directly to other devices. With advanced technologies devices are connecting in ways not previously thought possible, and researchers predict that over 50 billion IoT devices will be communicating by 2020.

Imagine your toothbrush telling you to visit your dentist because it senses a cavity. How would you react if your refrigerator placed an order at your local grocery store because your milk and eggs had expired? Predictions indicate that over the next decade almost every device you own—and almost every object imaginable—will be connected to the Internet

Opening Case Questions. Located at the end of the chapter, poignant questions connect the chapter opening case with important chapter concepts.

OPENING CASE QUESTIONS

1. **Knowledge:** Explain the Internet of Things and list three IoT devices.
2. **Comprehension:** Explain why it is important for business managers to understand that data collection rates from IoT devices is increasing exponentially.
3. **Application:** Demonstrate how data from an IoT device can be transformed into information and business intelligence.
4. **Analysis:** Analyze the current security issues associated with IoT devices.
5. **Synthesis:** Propose a plan for how a start-up company can use IoT device data to make better business decisions.

Projects and Case Studies

Case Studies. This text is packed with 27 case studies illustrating how a variety of prominent organizations and businesses have successfully implemented many of this text's concepts. All cases are timely and promote critical thinking. Company profiles are especially appealing and relevant to your students, helping to stir classroom discussion and interest.

Apply Your Knowledge. At the end of each chapter you will find several Apply Your Knowledge projects that challenge students to bring the skills they have learned from the chapter to real business problems. There are also 33 Apply Your Knowledge projects on the OLC that accompanies this text (**www.mhhe.com/baltzan**). These projects ask students to use IT tools such as Excel, Access, and Dreamweaver to solve business problems. These projects help to develop the application and problem-solving skills of your students through challenging and creative business-driven scenarios.

APPLY YOUR KNOWLEDGE BUSINESS PROJECTS

PROJECT I   Making Business Decisions

You are the vice president of human resources for a large consulting company. You are compiling a list of questions that you want each job interviewee to answer. The first question on your list is, "How can MIS enhance your ability to make decisions at our organization?" Prepare a one-page report to answer this question.

PROJECT II   DSS and EIS

Dr. Rosen runs a large dental conglomerate—Teeth Doctors—that employs more than 700 dentists in six states. Dr. Rosen is interested in purchasing a competitor called Dentix that has 150 dentists in three additional states. Before deciding whether to purchase Dentix, Dr. Rosen must consider several issues:

End-of-Chapter Elements

Each chapter contains complete pedagogical support in the form of:

Key Terms. With page numbers referencing where they are discussed in the text.

KEY TERMS

Analytics 10	Feedback 16	Production 16
Big data 7	First-mover advantage 21	Productivity 16
Business analytics 10	Goods 14	Report 9
Business intelligence (BI) 10	Human-generated data 7	Rivalry among existing
Business process 29	Information 9	competitors 25
Business strategy 20	Information age 5	Services 14
Buyer power 23	Internet of Things (IoT) 5	Stakeholder 20
Chief automation officer 19	Knowledge 11	Static report 9

Two Closing Case Studies. Reinforcing important concepts with prominent examples from businesses and organizations. Discussion questions follow each case study.

CLOSING CASE ONE

Buy Experiences, Not Things

Retail is one of the most competitive and stingiest industries in America, boasting some of the most dissatisfied workers across the board. Walmart Stores employees began a week-long strike in Miami, Boston, and the San Francisco Bay Area to publicly display their immense dissatisfaction with the multinational corporation. Employees at Amazon's fulfillment center in Leipzig, Germany, went on strike

Critical Business Thinking. The best way to learn MIS is to apply it to scenarios and real-world business dilemmas. These projects require students to apply critical thinking skills and chapter concepts to analyze the problems and make recommended business decisions.

CRITICAL BUSINESS THINKING

1. Modeling a Business Process
Do you hate waiting in line at the grocery store? Do you get annoyed when the pizza delivery person brings you the wrong order? This is your chance to reengineer the process that drives you crazy. Choose a problem you are currently experiencing and reengineer the process to make it

About the Plug-Ins

Located on the OLC that accompanies this text (**www.mhhe.com/baltzan**), the overall goal of the plug-ins is to provide an alternative for faculty who find themselves in the situation of having to purchase an extra book to support Microsoft Office 2010, 2013, or 2016. The plug-ins presented here offer integration with the core chapters and provide critical knowledge using essential business applications, such as Microsoft Excel, Microsoft Access, Dreamweaver, and Microsoft Project. Each plug-in uses hands-on tutorials for comprehension and mastery.

Plug-In	Description
T1. Personal Productivity Using IT	This plug-in covers a number of things to do to keep a personal computer running effectively and efficiently. The 12 topics covered in this plug-in are: ■ Creating strong passwords. ■ Performing good file management. ■ Implementing effective backup and recovery strategies. ■ Using zip files. ■ Writing professional emails. ■ Stopping spam. ■ Preventing phishing. ■ Detecting spyware. ■ Threads to instant messaging. ■ Increasing PC performance. ■ Using antivirus software. ■ Installing a personal firewall.

End-of-Plug-In Elements

Each plug-in contains complete pedagogical support in the form of:

Plug-In Summary. Revisits the plug-in highlights in summary format.

Making Business Decisions. Small scenario-driven projects that help students focus individually on decision making as they relate to the topical elements in the chapters.

T2. Basic Skills Using Excel	This plug-in introduces the basics of using Microsoft Excel, a spreadsheet program for data analysis, along with a few fancy features. The six topics covered in this plug-in are: ■ Workbooks and worksheets. ■ Working with cells and cell data. ■ Printing worksheets. ■ Formatting worksheets. ■ Formulas. ■ Working with charts and graphics.

T4. Decision Making Using Excel	This plug-in examines a few of the advanced business analysis tools used in Microsoft Excel that have the capability to identify patterns, trends, and rules, and create "what-if" models. The four topics covered in this plug-in are: ■ IF ■ Goal Seek ■ Solver ■ Scenario Manager

Support and Supplemental Material

All of the supplemental material supporting *Business Driven Information Systems* was developed by the author to ensure that you receive accurate, high-quality, and in-depth content. Included is a complete set of materials that will assist students and faculty in accomplishing course objectives.

Video Exercises. Each of the videos that accompany the text is supported by detailed teaching notes on how to turn the videos into classroom exercises to which your students can apply the knowledge they are learning after watching the videos.

Test Bank. This computerized package allows instructors to custom design, save, and generate tests. The test program permits instructors to edit, add, or delete questions from the test banks; analyze test results; and organize a database of tests and students' results.

Instructor's Manual (IM). The IM, written by the author, includes suggestions for designing the course and presenting the material. Each chapter is supported by answers to end-of-chapter questions and problems and suggestions concerning the discussion topics and cases.

PowerPoint Presentations. A set of PowerPoint slides, created by the author, accompanies each chapter and features bulleted items that provide a lecture outline, plus key figures and tables from the text, and detailed teaching notes on each slide.

Image Library. Text figures and tables, as permission allows, are provided in a format by which they can be imported into PowerPoint for class lectures.

Project Files. The author has provided files for all projects that need further support, such as data files.

Tegrity Campus: Lectures 24/7

Tegrity Campus is a service that makes class time available 24/7 by automatically capturing every lecture in a search-able format for students to review when they study and complete assignments. With a simple one-click start-and-stop process, you capture all computer screens and corresponding audio. Students can replay any part of any class with easy-to-use browser-based viewing on a PC or Mac.

Educators know that the more students can see, hear, and experience class resources, the better they learn. In fact, studies prove it. With Tegrity Campus, students quickly recall key moments by using Tegrity Campus's unique search feature. This search helps students efficiently find what they need, when they need it, across an entire semester of class recordings. Help turn all your students' study time into learning moments immediately supported by your lecture.

To learn more about Tegrity, watch a two-minute Flash demo at **http://tegritycampus.mhhe.com.**

Assurance of Learning Ready

Many educational institutions today are focused on the notion of *assurance of learning,* an important element of some accreditation standards. *Business Driven Information Systems* is designed specifically to support your assurance of learning initiatives with a simple, yet powerful solution.

Each test bank question for *Business Driven Information Systems* maps to a specific chapter learning outcome/objective listed in the text. You can use our test bank software, EZ Test and EZ Test Online, or *Connect MIS* to query easily for learning outcomes/objectives that directly relate to the learning objectives for your course. You can then use the reporting features of EZ Test to aggregate student results in similar fashion, making the collection and presentation of assurance of learning data simple and easy.

Aacsb Statement

The McGraw-Hill Companies is a proud corporate member of AACSB International. Understanding the importance and value of AACSB accreditation, *Business Driven Information Systems* recognizes the curricula guidelines detailed in the AACSB standards for business accreditation by connecting selected questions in the test bank to the six general knowledge and skill guidelines in the AACSB standards.

The statements contained in *Business Driven Information Systems* are provided only as a guide for the users of this textbook. The AACSB leaves content coverage and assessment within the purview of individual schools, the mission of the school, and the faculty. Although *Business Driven Information Systems* and the teaching package make no claim of any specific AACSB qualification or evaluation, within *Business Driven Information Systems* we have labeled selected questions according to the six general knowledge and skills areas.

Mcgraw-Hill Customer Care Contact Information

At McGraw-Hill, we understand that getting the most from new technology can be challenging. That's why our services don't stop after you purchase our products. You can email our product specialists 24 hours a day to get product training online. Or you can search our knowledge bank of Frequently Asked Questions on our support website. For Customer Support, call **800-331-5094** or visit **www.mhhe.com/support** where you can look for your question on our FAQ, or you can email a question directly to customer support. One of our technical support analysts will be able to assist you in a timely fashion.

Apply Your Knowledge

Business Driven Information Systems contains 33 projects that focus on student application of core concepts and tools. These projects can be found on the OLC.

Project Number	Project Name	Project Type	Plug-In	Focus Area	Project Level	Skill Set	Page Number
1	Financial Destiny	Excel	T2	Personal Budget	Introductory	Formulas	AYK.4
2	Cash Flow	Excel	T2	Cash Flow	Introductory	Formulas	AYK.4
3	Technology Budget	Excel	T1, T2	Hardware and Software	Introductory	Formulas	AYK.4
4	Tracking Donations	Excel	T2	Employee Relationships	Introductory	Formulas	AYK.4
5	Convert Currency	Excel	T2	Global Commerce	Introductory	Formulas	AYK.5
6	Cost Comparison	Excel	T2	Total Cost of Ownership	Introductory	Formulas	AYK.5
7	Time Management	Excel or Project	T12	Project Management	Introductory	Gantt Charts	AYK.6
8	Maximize Profit	Excel	T2, T4	Strategic Analysis	Intermediate	Formulas or Solver	AYK.6
9	Security Analysis	Excel	T3	Filtering Data	Intermediate	Conditional Formatting, Autofilter, Subtotal	AYK.7
10	Gathering Data	Excel	T3	Data Analysis	Intermediate	Conditional Formatting	AYK.8
11	Scanner System	Excel	T2	Strategic Analysis	Intermediate	Formulas	AYK.8
12	Competitive Pricing	Excel	T2	Profit Maximization	Intermediate	Formulas	AYK.9
13	Adequate Acquisitions	Excel	T2	Break-Even Analysis	Intermediate	Formulas	AYK.9
14	Customer Relations	Excel	T3	CRM	Intermediate	PivotTable	AYK.9
15	Assessing the Value of Information	Excel	T3	Data Analysis	Intermediate	PivotTable	AYK.10
16	Growth, Trends, and Forecasts	Excel	T2, T3	Data Forecasting	Advanced	Average, Trend, Growth	AYK.11
17	Shipping Costs	Excel	T4	SCM	Advanced	Solver	AYK.12
18	Formatting Grades	Excel	T3	Data Analysis	Advanced	If, LookUp	AYK.12

(Continued)

Project Number	Project Name	Project Type	Plug-In	Focus Area	Project Level	Skill Set	Page Number
19	Moving Dilemma	Excel	T2, T3	SCM	Advanced	Absolute vs. Relative Values	AYK.13
20	Operational Efficiencies	Excel	T3	SCM	Advanced	PivotTable	AYK.14
21	Too Much Information	Excel	T3	CRM	Advanced	PivotTable	AYK.14
22	Turnover Rates	Excel	T3	Data Mining	Advanced	PivotTable	AYK.15
23	Vital Information	Excel	T3	Data Mining	Advanced	PivotTable	AYK.15
24	Breaking Even	Excel	T4	Business Analysis	Advanced	Goal Seek	AYK.16
25	Profit Scenario	Excel	T4	Sales Analysis	Advanced	Scenario Manager	AYK.16
26	Electronic Résumés	HTML	T9, T10, T11	Electronic Personal Marketing	Introductory	Structural Tags	AYK.17
27	Gathering Feedback	Dreamweaver	T9, T10, T11	Data Collection	Intermediate	Organization of Information	AYK.17
28	Daily Invoice	Access	T5, T6, T7, T8	Business Analysis	Introductory	Entities, Relationships, and Databases	AYK.17
29	Billing Data	Access	T5, T6, T7, T8	Business Intelligence	Introductory	Entities, Relationships, and Databases	AYK.19
30	Inventory Data	Access	T5, T6, T7, T8	SCM	Intermediate	Entities, Relationships, and Databases	AYK.20
31	Call Center	Access	T5, T6, T7, T8	CRM	Intermediate	Entities, Relationships, and Databases	AYK.21
32	Sales Pipeline	Access	T5, T6, T7, T8	Business Intelligence	Advanced	Entities, Relationships, and Databases	AYK.23
33	Online Classified Ads	Access	T5, T6, T7, T8	Ecommerce	Advanced	Entities, Relationships, and Databases	AYK.23

SIMnet
Keep IT SIMple!

SimNet Online is McGraw-Hill's leading solution for learning Microsoft Office skills and beyond! SimNet is our online training and assessment solution for Microsoft Office skills, computing concepts, Internet Explorer, and Windows content. With no downloads for installation and completely online (requires Adobe Flash Player), SimNet is accessible for today's students through multiple browsers and is easy to use for all. Its consistent user interface and functionality will help save you time and help you be more successful in your course.

Moreover, SimNet offers you lifelong learning. Our codes never expire and the online program is designed with Self-Study and SimSearch features to help you immediately learn isolated Microsoft Office skills on demand. It's more than a resource; it's a tool you can use throughout your entire time at your higher education institution.

Finally, you will see powerful, measurable results with SimNet Online. See results immediately in the student gradebook and generate custom training lessons after an exam to help you determine exactly which content areas you still need to study.

SimNet Online is your solution for mastering Microsoft Office skills!

SIMnet: Keep IT SIMple!

To learn more, visit **www.simnetkeepitsimple.com**

Easy to Use!

SIMnet is McGraw-Hill's leading solution for training and assessment of Microsoft Office skills and beyond! Completely online with no downloads for installation (besides requiring Adobe Flash Player), SIMnet is accessible for today's students through multiple browsers and is easy to use for all! Now, SIMnet offers SIMbook and allows students to go MOBILE for their student learning! Available with videos and interactive "Guide Me" pages to allow students to study MS Office skills on any device! Its consistent, clean user interface and functionality will help save you time and help students be more successful in their course.

Life-Long Learning!

SIMnet offers lifelong learning! SIMnet is designed with self-study and SIMSearch features to help students immediately learn isolated Microsoft Office skills on demand. Students can utilize SIMSearch and Self-Study to learn skills both in and beyond the course. It's more than a resource; it's a tool they can use throughout their entire time at your institution!

Measureable Results!

SIMnet provides powerful, measureable results for you and your students! See results immediately in our various reports and customizable gradebook. Students can also see measurable results by generating a custom training lesson after an exam to help determine exactly which content areas they still need to study! Lastly, instructors can utilize the dashboard to see detailed results of student activity, assignment completion and more! SIMnet Online is your solution for helping students master today's Microsoft Office Skills!

SIMnet for Office 2013 ... Keep IT SIMple!

 Follow our CIT team on Twitter! @mhheCITteam   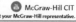 McGraw-Hill CIT
To learn more, visit www.simnetkeepitsimple.com and also contact your McGraw-Hill representative.

McGraw-Hill Higher Education and Blackboard have teamed up. What does this mean for you?

1. **Your life, simplified.** Now you and your students can access McGraw-Hill's Connect™ and Create™ right from within your Blackboard course—all with one single sign-on. Say good-bye to the days of logging on to multiple applications.

2. **Deep integration of content and tools.** Not only do you get single sign-on with Connect™ and Create™, you also get deep integration of McGraw-Hill content and content engines right in Blackboard. Whether you're choosing a book for your course or building Connect™ assignments, all the tools you need are right where you want them—inside of Blackboard.

3. **Seamless gradebooks.** Are you tired of keeping multiple gradebooks and manually synchronizing grades into Blackboard? We thought so. When a student completes an integrated Connect™ assignment, the grade for that assignment automatically (and instantly) feeds your Blackboard grade center.

4. **A solution for everyone.** Whether your institution is already using Blackboard or you just want to try Blackboard on your own, we have a solution for you. McGraw-Hill and Blackboard can now offer you easy access to industry leading technology and content, whether your campus hosts it, or we do. Be sure to ask your local McGraw-Hill representative for details.

Craft your teaching resources to match the way you teach! With McGraw-Hill Create, www.mcgrawhillcreate.com, you can easily rearrange chapters, combine material from other content sources, and quickly upload content you have written, like your course syllabus or teaching notes. Find the content you need in Create by searching through thousands of leading McGraw-Hill textbooks. Arrange your book to fit your teaching style. Create even allows you to personalize your book's appearance by selecting the cover and adding your name, school, and course information. Order a Create book and you'll receive a complimentary print review copy in 3–5 business days or a complimentary electronic review copy (eComp) via email in about one hour. Go to www.mcgrawhillcreate.com today and register. Experience how McGraw-Hill Create empowers you to teach *your* students *your* way.

ACKNOWLEDGMENTS

Working on the sixth edition of *Business Driven Information Systems* has been an involved undertaking, and there are many people whom we want to heartily thank for their hard work, enthusiasm, and dedication.

This text was produced with the help of a number of people at McGraw-Hill, including Brand Manager, Brian Sylvester and Product Developer, David Ploskonka.

In addition, we would like to thank Susan Gouijnstook (Managing Director) for her support and dedication to the success of this text.

Finally, we offer our sincerest gratitude and deepest appreciation to our valuable reviewers whose feedback was instrumental in successfully compiling this text. We could not have done this without you!

Stephen Adams
Lakeland Community College

Adeyemi A. Adekoya
Virginia State University—Petersburg

Joni Adkins
Northwest Missouri State University

Chad Anderson
University of Nevada—Reno

Anne Arendt
Utah Valley University

Laura Atkins
James Madison University

William Ayen
University of Colorado

David Bahn
Metropolitan State University—St. Paul

Nick Ball
Brigham Young University—Provo

Patrick Bateman
Youngstown State University

Terry Begley
Creighton University

Craig Beytien
University of Colorado—Boulder

Sudip Bhattacharjee
University of Connecticut

Meral Binbasioglu
Hofstra University

Joseph Blankenship
Fairmont State College

Beverly Bohn
Park University

Brenda Bradford
Missouri Baptist University

Casey Cegielski
Auburn University—Auburn

Amita Chin
Virginia Commonwealth University

Steve Clements
Eastern Oregon University

Cynthia Corritore
Creighton University

Dan Creed
Normandale Community College

Don Danner
San Francisco State University

Sasha Dekleva
DePaul University

Robert Denker
Baruch College

Hongwei Du
California State University, East Bay

Kevin Duffy
Wright State University—Dayton

Annette Easton
San Diego State University

Barry Floyd
California Polytechnic State University

Valerie Frear
Daytona State College

Laura Frost
Walsh College

Don Gaber
University of Wisconsin—Eau Claire

Biswadip Ghosh
Metropolitan State College of Denver

Richard Glass
Bryant University

Lakshmi Goel
University of North Florida

Mark Goudreau
Johnson & Wales University

Katie Gray
The University of Texas at Austin

Gary Hackbarth
Northern Kentucky University

Shu Han
Yeshiva University

Peter Haried
University of Wisconsin—La Crosse

Rosie Hauck
Illinois State University

Jun He
University of Michigan—Dearborn

James Henson
California State University—Fresno

Terri Holly
Indian River State College

Scott Hunsinger
Appalachian State University

Ted Hurewitz
Rutgers University

Yan Jin
Elizabeth City State University

Brian Jones
Tennessee Technological University

Robert Judge
San Diego State University

B. Kahn
Suffolk University

Virginia Kleist
West Virginia University

Meagan Knoll
Grand Valley State University

Rick Kraas
Kalamazoo Valley Community College

Chetan Kumar
California State University–San Marcos

Guolin Lai
University of Louisiana–Lafayette

Jose Lepervanche
Florida State College–Jacksonville

Norman Lewis
Wayne State University

Mary Lind
North Carolina A&T State University

Steve Loy
Eastern Kentucky University

Joan Lumpkin
Wright State University–Dayton

Linda Lynam
University of Central Missouri

Nicole Lytle-Kosola
California State University–San
Bernardino

Garth MacKenzie
University of Maryland University
College

Michael Martel
Ohio University–Athens

Dana McCann
Central Michigan University

David McCue
University of Maryland

Lynn McKell
Brigham Young University

Patricia McQuaid
California Polytechnic State University

Fiona Nah
University of Nebraska–Lincoln

Eric Nathan
University of Houston Downtown

Bill Neumann
University of Arizona

Richard Newmark
University of Northern Colorado

Kathleen Noce
Pennsylvania State University–Erie

Gisele Olney
University of Nebraska–Omaha

Kevin Parker
Idaho State University–Pocatello

Neeraj Parolia
Towson University

Gang Peng
Youngstown State University

Julie Pettus
Missouri State University

Craig Piercy
University of Georgia

Clint Pires
Hamline University

Jennifer Pitts
Columbus State University

Carol Pollard
Appalachian State University

Lara Preiser-Houy
California State Polytechnic
University–Pomona

John Quigley
East Tennessee State University

Muhammad Razi
Western Michigan University

Lisa Rich
Athens State University

Russell Robbins
University of Pittsburgh

Fred Rodammer
Michigan State University

Steve Ross
Western Washington University

Mark Schmidt
St. Cloud State University

Dana Schwieger
Southeast Missouri State University

Darrell Searcy
Palm Beach Community College

Jay Shah
Texas State University

Vivek Shah
Texas State University

Vijay Shah
West Virginia University–Parkersburg

Jollean Sinclaire
Arkansas State University

Changsoo Sohn
St. Cloud State University

Toni Somers
Wayne State University

Denise Sullivan
Westchester Community College

Yi Sun
California State University–
San Marcos

Mike Tarn
Western Michigan University

Mark Thouin
The University of Texas at Dallas

Lise Urbaczewski
University of Michigan–Dearborn

Hong Wang
North Carolina A&T State University

Barbara Warner
University of South Florida

Connie Washburn
Georgia Perimeter College

Bruce White
Quinnipiac University

Raymond Whitney
University of Maryland University
College

Rosemary Wild
California Polytechnic State University

Marie Wright
Western Connecticut State University

Yajiong Xue
East Carolina University

Ali Yayla
Binghamton University

Grace Zhang
Midwestern State University

Lin Zhao
Purdue University–Calumet

Jeanne Zucker
East Tennessee State University

ABOUT THE AUTHOR

Paige Baltzan

Paige Baltzan teaches in the Department of Business Information and Analytics at the Daniels College of Business at the University of Denver. She holds a B.S.B.A. specializing in Accounting/MIS from Bowling Green State University and an M.B.A. specializing in MIS from the University of Denver. She is a coauthor of several books, including *Business Driven Technology, Essentials of Business Driven Information Systems,* and *I-Series,* and a contributor to *Management Information Systems for the Information Age.*

Before joining the Daniels College faculty in 1999, Paige spent several years working for a large telecommunications company and an international consulting firm, where she participated in client engagements in the United States as well as South America and Europe. Paige lives in Lakewood, Colorado, with her husband, Tony, and daughters, Hannah and Sophie.

Business Driven MIS

MOST COMPANIES TODAY rely heavily on the use of management information systems (MIS) to run various aspects of their businesses. Whether companies need to order and ship goods, interact with customers, or conduct other business functions, management information systems are often the underlying infrastructure performing the activities. Management information systems allow companies to remain competitive in today's fast-paced world and especially when conducting business on the Internet. Organizations must adapt to technological advances and innovations to keep pace with today's rapidly changing environment. Their competitors certainly will!

No matter how exciting technology is, successful companies do not use it simply for its own sake. Companies should have a solid business reason for implementing technology. Using a technological solution just because it is available is not a good business strategy.

The purpose of Module 1 is to raise your awareness of the vast opportunities made possible by the tight correlation between business and technology. Business strategies and processes should always drive your technology choices. Although awareness of an emerging technology can sometimes lead us in new strategic directions, the role of information systems, for the most part, is to support existing business strategies and processes.

MODULE 1:
Business Driven MIS

MODULE 2:
Technical Foundations of MIS

MODULE 3:
Enterprise MIS

Module 1: Business Driven MIS

CHAPTER 1: Management Information Systems: Business Driven MIS

CHAPTER 2: Decisions and Processes: Value Driven Business

CHAPTER 3: Ebusiness: Electronic Business Value

CHAPTER 4: Ethics and Information Security: MIS Business Concerns

1

CHAPTER

Management Information Systems: Business Driven MIS

CHAPTER OUTLINE

SECTION 1.1
Business Driven MIS

- Competing in the Information Age
- The Challenge of Departmental Companies and the MIS Solution

SECTION 1.2
Business Strategy

- Identifying Competitive Advantages
- The Five Forces Model— Evaluating Industry Attractiveness
- The Three Generic Strategies— Choosing a Business Focus
- Value Chain Analysis—Executing Business Strategies

What's in IT for me?

This chapter sets the stage for the textbook. It starts from ground zero by providing a clear description of what information is and how it fits into business operations, strategies, and systems. It provides an overview of how companies operate in competitive environments and why they must continually define and redefine their business strategies to create competitive advantages. Doing so allows them to survive and thrive. Information systems are key business enablers for successful operations in competitive environments.

You, as a business student, must understand the tight correlation between business and technology. You must first recognize information's role in daily business activities and then understand how information supports and helps implement global business strategies and competitive advantages. After reading this chapter, you should have a solid understanding of business driven information systems and their role in managerial decision making and problem solving.

The Internet of Things

Over 20 years ago a few professors at MIT began describing the Internet of Things (IoT), which is a world where interconnected Internet-enabled devices or "things" have the ability to collect and share data without human intervention. Another term for the Internet of Things is machine-to-machine (M2M), which allows devices to connect directly to other devices. With advanced technologies devices are connecting in ways not previously thought possible, and researchers predict that over 50 billion IoT devices will be communicating by 2020.

Imagine your toothbrush telling you to visit your dentist because it senses a cavity. How would you react if your refrigerator placed an order at your local grocery store because your milk and eggs had expired? Predictions indicate that over the next decade almost every device you own—and almost every object imaginable—will be connected to the Internet as people share, store, and manage their lives online. Smoke detectors, alarms, refrigerators, stoves, and windows are just a few home devices already connected to the Internet, sharing information on how to make everything in your life more efficient, effective, safe, and healthy. The Internet of Things is reaching further into our daily lives by combining data from sensors in wearable devices and equipment with analytic programs to help improve the performance of individuals by gaining insights that were traditionally impossible to detect. A few examples of the incredible power of the IoT era include:

- **Smart Yoga Mat:** Smart yoga mats include sensors that provide feedback on yoga postures and calories burned, and can even provide users with guided practice in the comfort of their own home.

- **Smart Thermostats:** IoTs share information in real time to help homeowners manage energy use more efficiently. The system will notify the homeowner if a door is left open, change the temperature in each room when it is occupied, and turn the thermostat up or down depending on the weather and homeowner preferences.

- **Smart Diapers:** Pixie Scientific created disposable diapers with sensors that monitor babies' urine for signs of infection, dehydration, or kidney problems before symptoms appear.

- **Smart Trash Cans:** The city of Allentown, Pennsylvania, connected community trash and recycling cans, allowing them to monitor fill rates, which are then used to recommend the most efficient routes for trash pickup services.

- **Smart Tennis Racket:** Babolat, a French tennis racket manufacturer, created the Play Pure Drive, a $400 smart tennis racket that has the capability to record data on every single shot a user takes and sends the data along with an analysis to the user's smart phone.

- **Smart Frying Pan:** Pantelligent is an innovative sensor-embedded frying pan that actually helps its users learn how to cook by measuring the temperature of the food and communicating with a smart phone when to add ingredients, change heat, flip, and cover, and even when the food is done.

The future of business will focus on big data as IoT devices create, capture, and share massive amounts of data. The business environment is currently collecting more data from IoT devices in one second than all of the data collected from the beginning of time until the year 2000. In fact, over 90 percent of the data in the world was created over the last 2 years. Every minute over 204 million emails are sent and 200 thousand photos are uploaded to Facebook. The terms *analytics, data analysis,* and *business intelligence* are all referring to big data and the massive volumes of data being generated around the globe.

Understanding big data will be a critical skill for knowledge workers in every business, regardless of size, focus, or industry. Future managers will be responsible for analyzing data in ways that were not even possible a decade ago, allowing managers to predict customer behaviors, optimize and improve business processes, and analyze multiple variables for trends and patterns. The total amount of business data roughly doubles every 1.2 years. Big data has created an estimated 6 million new jobs and will assist companies in:

- Understanding consumer behaviors by combining purchasing data with social media data, weather data, competitor data, and economic data.
- Improving the delivery of products by combining delivery process information with current traffic data, vehicle maintenance data, and map data.
- Optimizing health care treatments by capturing diagnosis, tracking pharmaceuticals, and eventually predicting diseases.
- Preventing cyberattacks by analyzing credit card fraud, security system data, and police data.[1]

section 1.1 | Business Driven MIS

LEARNING OUTCOMES

1.1 Describe the information age and the differences among data, information, business intelligence, and knowledge.

1.2 Explain systems thinking and how management information systems enable business communications.

COMPETING IN THE INFORMATION AGE

> LO 1.1: Describe the information age and the differences among data, information, business intelligence, and knowledge.

Did you know that . . .

- The movie *Avatar* took more than 4 years to create and cost $450 million?
- Lady Gaga's real name is Stefani Joanne Angelina Germanotta?
- Customers pay $2.6 million for a 30-second advertising time slot during the Super Bowl?[2]

A *fact* is the confirmation or validation of an event or object. In the past, people primarily learned facts from books. Today, by simply pushing a button, people can find out anything, from anywhere, at any time. We live in the ***information age,*** when infinite quantities of facts are widely available to anyone who can use a computer. The impact of information technology on the global business environment is equivalent to the printing press's impact on publishing and electricity's impact on productivity. College student start-ups were mostly unheard of before the information age. Now, it's not at all unusual to read about a business student starting a multimillion-dollar company from his or her dorm room. Think of Mark Zuckerberg, who started Facebook from his dorm, or Michael Dell (Dell Computers) and Bill Gates (Microsoft), who both founded their legendary companies as college students.

You may think only students well versed in advanced technology can compete in the information age. This is simply not true. Many business leaders have created exceptional opportunities by coupling the power of the information age with traditional business methods. Here are just a few examples:

- Amazon is not a technology company; its original business focus was to sell books, and it now sells nearly everything.
- Netflix is not a technology company; its primary business focus is to rent videos.
- Zappos is not a technology company; its primary business focus is to sell shoes, bags, clothing, and accessories.

Amazon's founder, Jeff Bezos, at first saw an opportunity to change the way people purchase books. Using the power of the information age to tailor offerings to each customer and speed the payment process, he in effect opened millions of tiny virtual bookstores, each with a vastly larger selection and far cheaper product than traditional bookstores. The success of his original business model led him to expand Amazon to carry many other types of products. The founders of Netflix and Zappos have done the same thing for videos and shoes. All these entrepreneurs were business professionals, not technology experts. However, they understood enough about the information age to apply it to a particular business, creating innovative companies that now lead entire industries.

Over 20 years ago a few professors at MIT began describing the ***Internet of Things (IoT),*** a world where interconnected Internet-enabled devices or "things" have the ability to collect and share data without human intervention. Another term commonly associated with the Internet of Things is ***machine-to-machine (M2M),*** which refers to devices that connect directly to other devices. With advanced technologies devices are connecting in ways not previously thought possible, and researchers predict that over 50 billion IoT devices will be communicating by 2020. Kevin Ashton, cofounder and executive director of the Auto-ID Center at MIT, first

BUSINESS DRIVEN DISCUSSION

View from a Flat World

Bill Gates, founder of Microsoft, stated that 20 years ago most people would rather have been a B student in New York City than a genius in China because the opportunities available to students in developed countries were limitless. Today, many argue that the opposite is now true due to technological advances making it easier to succeed as a genius in China than a B student in New York. As a group, discuss whether you agree or disagree with Bill Gate's statement.[4]

mentioned the Internet of Things in a presentation he made to Procter & Gamble. Here's Ashton's explanation of the Internet of Things:

> To date, the 50 petabytes of data available on the Internet has been captured mostly by humans through such methods as typing, recording, and scanning text, photos, and voice recordings. Data entry is the process of gathering data from business documents and entering it into a computer. A vital process for any business. The issue with human data collection is the fact that humans make mistakes! Numbers are frequently transposed, addresses mistyped, and some files are skipped completely. Inaccurate data in a system will lead to incorrect reports and ultimately bad business decisions. Allowing computers to perform the data entry process greatly reduces human error. Computers are precise and accurate and would know when things need replaced, repaired, or recalled saving time and money for companies.[3]

IoT is transforming our world into a living information system as we control our intelligent lighting from our smart phone to a daily health check from our smart toilet. Of course with all great technological advances come unexpected risks and you have to be prepared to encounter various security issues with IoT. Just imagine if your devices are hacked by someone who now has the ability to shut off your water, take control of your car, or unlock the doors of your home from thousands of miles away. We are just beginning to understand the security issues associated with IoT and M2M, and you can be sure that sensitive data leakage from your IoT device is something you will most likely encounter in your life.

Students who understand business along with the power associated with the information age and IoT will create their own opportunities and perhaps even new industries. Realizing the value of obtaining real-time data from connected "things" will allow you to make more informed decisions, identify new opportunities, and analyze customer patterns to predict new behaviors. Our primary goal in this course is to arm you with the knowledge you need to compete in the information age. The core drivers of the information age include:

- Data
- Information
- Business intelligence
- Knowledge (see Figure 1.1)

Data

Data are raw facts that describe the characteristics of an event or object. Before the information age, managers manually collected and analyzed data, a time-consuming and complicated task without which they would have little insight into how to run their business. *Structured data* has a defined length, type, and format and includes numbers, dates, or strings such as Customer Address. Structured data is typically stored in a traditional system such as a relational database or spreadsheet and accounts for about 20 percent of the data that surrounds us. The sources of structured data include:

- *Machine-generated data* is created by a machine without human intervention. Machine-generated structured data includes sensor data, point-of-sale data, and web log data.

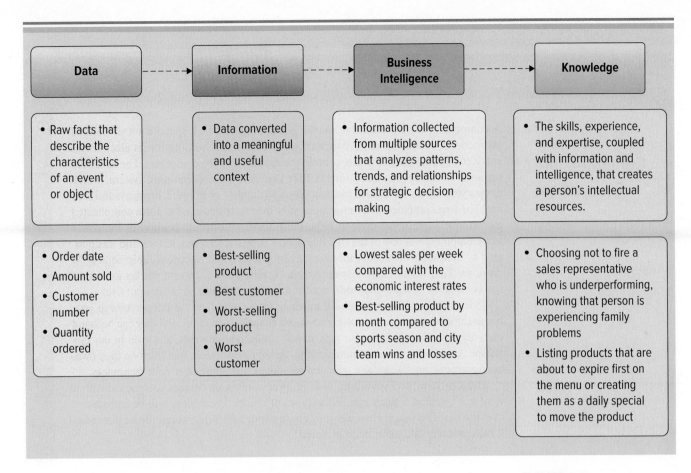

Data	Information	Business Intelligence	Knowledge
• Raw facts that describe the characteristics of an event or object	• Data converted into a meaningful and useful context	• Information collected from multiple sources that analyzes patterns, trends, and relationships for strategic decision making	• The skills, experience, and expertise, coupled with information and intelligence, that creates a person's intellectual resources.
• Order date • Amount sold • Customer number • Quantity ordered	• Best-selling product • Best customer • Worst-selling product • Worst customer	• Lowest sales per week compared with the economic interest rates • Best-selling product by month compared to sports season and city team wins and losses	• Choosing not to fire a sales representative who is underperforming, knowing that person is experiencing family problems • Listing products that are about to expire first on the menu or creating them as a daily special to move the product

FIGURE 1.1

The Differences among Data, Information, Business Intelligence, and Knowledge

■ *Human-generated data* is data that humans, in interaction with computers, generate. Human-generated structured data includes input data, click-stream data, or gaming data.

Unstructured data is not defined and does not follow a specified format and is typically free-form text such as emails, Twitter tweets, and text messages. Unstructured data accounts for about 80 percent of the data that surrounds us. The sources of unstructured data include:

■ Machine-generated unstructured data, including satellite images, scientific atmosphere data, and radar data.

■ Human-generated unstructured data, including text messages, social media data, and emails.

Big data is a collection of large, complex data sets, including structured and unstructured data, which cannot be analyzed using traditional database methods and tools. Lacking data, managers often found themselves making business decisions about how many products to make, how much material to order, or how many employees to hire based on intuition or gut feelings.

Walmart handles over 1 million purchase transactions per hour. Facebook processes over 250 million photo uploads every day. There are over 6 billion cell phone users generating text messages, voice calls, and browsing the web daily. As Google CEO Eric Schmidt has noted, the amount of data currently created every 48 hours is equivalent to the entire amount of data created from the dawn of civilization until the year 2003. In the information age, successful managers must be able to compile, analyze, and comprehend massive amounts of data or big data daily, which helps them make more successful business decisions.

A *snapshot* is a view of data at a particular moment in time. Figure 1.2 shows sales data for Tony's Wholesale Company, a fictitious business that supplies snacks to stores. The data highlight characteristics such as order date, customer, sales representative, product, quantity, and profit. The second line in Figure 1.2, for instance, shows that Roberta Cross sold 90 boxes of Ruffles to Walmart for $1,350, resulting in a profit of $450 (note that Profit = Sales − Costs).

BUSINESS DRIVEN MIS

Computers are Everywhere

A computer is a programmable machine that responds to a specific set of defined instructions. It consists of hardware (the machinery and housing for its electronics) and software (the programs that contain the data used by the computer). The hardware includes a central processing unit (CPU) that controls an operating system, which directs your inputs (keyboard, mouse), outputs (monitor or printer), memory, and storage. The first computers were enormous slow machines designed to solve complicated mathematical questions. Built in 1954, the ENIAC (Electronic Numerical Integrator and Computer) was one of the first digital computers; it weighed 30 tons and was powered by thousands of vacuum tubes, capacitors, relays, and electrical equipment. IBM president Tom Watson famously remarked, "I think there is a world market for maybe five computers." Clearly the world market for computers was far more than five!

Today's computers can do almost anything from controlling the temperature in your house and driving your car, to solving advanced analytical equations, and they can be found everywhere; on our desks, in our laps, in our hands, on our wrists, and even in our eyeglasses. And there is so much more coming, including computers that learn on their own, brain-computer interfacing, and quantum computers that utilize fiber optic technology.

Think of your life 5 years ago, and list three computing devices you use today that were not invented 5 years ago. What types of computing devices will be introduced over the next five years? How will they change your life? What would life be like today if the computer had never been invented?

These data are useful for understanding individual sales; however, they do not provide us much insight into how Tony's business is performing as a whole. Tony needs to answer questions that will help him manage his day-to-day operations such as:

- Who are my best customers?
- Who are my least-profitable customers?
- What is my best-selling product?
- What is my slowest-selling product?
- Who is my strongest sales representative?
- Who is my weakest sales representative?

What Tony needs, in other words, is not data but *information*.

FIGURE 1.2

Tony's Snack Company Data

Order Date	Customer	Sales Representative	Product	Qty	Unit Price	Total Sales	Unit Cost	Total Cost	Profit
4-Jan	Walmart	PJ Helgoth	Doritos	41	$24	$ 984	$18	$738	$246
4-Jan	Walmart	Roberta Cross	Ruffles	90	$15	$1,350	$10	$900	$450
5-Jan	Safeway	Craig Schultz	Ruffles	27	$15	$ 405	$10	$270	$135
6-Jan	Walmart	Roberta Cross	Ruffles	67	$15	$1,005	$10	$670	$335
7-Jan	7-Eleven	Craig Schultz	Pringles	79	$12	$ 948	$ 6	$474	$474
7-Jan	Walmart	Roberta Cross	Ruffles	52	$15	$ 780	$10	$520	$260
8-Jan	Kroger	Craig Schultz	Ruffles	39	$15	$ 585	$10	$390	$195
9-Jan	Walmart	Craig Schultz	Ruffles	66	$15	$ 990	$10	$660	$330
10-Jan	Target	Craig Schultz	Ruffles	40	$15	$ 600	$10	$400	$200
11-Jan	Walmart	Craig Schultz	Ruffles	71	$15	$1,065	$10	$710	$355

Information

Information is data converted into a meaningful and useful context. The simple difference between data and information is that computers or machines need data and humans need information. Data is a raw building block that has not been shaped, processed, or analyzed and frequently appears disorganized and unfriendly. Information gives meaning and context to analyzed data, making it insightful for humans by providing context and structure that is extremely valuable when making informed business decisions.

A *report* is a document containing data organized in a table, matrix, or graphical format allowing users to easily comprehend and understand information. Reports can cover a wide range of subjects or a specific subject for a certain time period or event. A *static report* is created once based on data that does not change. Static reports can include a sales report from last year or salary report from 5 years ago. A *dynamic report* changes automatically during creation. Dynamic reports can include updating daily stock market prices or the calculation of available inventory.

Having the right information at the right moment in time can be worth a fortune. Having the wrong information at the right moment or the right information at the wrong moment can be disastrous. The truth about information is that its value is only as good as the people who use it. People using the same information can make different decisions, depending on how they interpret or analyze the information. Thus information has value only insofar as the people using it do as well.

Tony can analyze his sales data and turn them into information to answer all the preceding questions and understand how his business is operating. Figures 1.3 and 1.4, for instance, show us that Walmart is Roberta Cross's best customer and that Ruffles is Tony's best product

FIGURE 1.3

Tony's Data Sorted by Customer "Walmart" and Sales Representative "Roberta Cross"

Order Date	Customer	Sales Representative	Product	Quantity	Unit Price	Total Sales	Unit Cost	Total Cost	Profit
26-Apr	Walmart	Roberta Cross	Fritos	86	$ 19	$ 1,634	$ 17	$ 1,462	$ 172
29-Aug	Walmart	Roberta Cross	Fritos	76	$ 19	$ 1,444	$ 17	$ 1,292	$ 152
7-Sep	Walmart	Roberta Cross	Fritos	20	$ 19	$ 380	$ 17	$ 340	$ 40
22-Nov	Walmart	Roberta Cross	Fritos	39	$ 19	$ 741	$ 17	$ 663	$ 78
30-Dec	Walmart	Roberta Cross	Fritos	68	$ 19	$ 1,292	$ 17	$ 1,156	$ 136
7-Jul	Walmart	Roberta Cross	Pringles	79	$ 18	$ 1,422	$ 8	$ 632	$ 790
6-Aug	Walmart	Roberta Cross	Pringles	21	$ 12	$ 252	$ 6	$ 126	$ 126
2-Oct	Walmart	Roberta Cross	Pringles	60	$ 18	$ 1,080	$ 8	$ 480	$ 600
15-Nov	Walmart	Roberta Cross	Pringles	32	$ 12	$ 384	$ 6	$ 192	$ 192
21-Dec	Walmart	Roberta Cross	Pringles	92	$ 12	$ 1,104	$ 6	$ 552	$ 552
28-Feb	Walmart	Roberta Cross	Ruffles	67	$ 15	$ 1,005	$ 10	$ 670	$ 335
6-Mar	Walmart	Roberta Cross	Ruffles	8	$ 15	$ 120	$ 10	$ 80	$ 40
16-Mar	Walmart	Roberta Cross	Ruffles	68	$ 15	$ 1,020	$ 10	$ 680	$ 340
23-Apr	Walmart	Roberta Cross	Ruffles	34	$ 15	$ 510	$ 10	$ 340	$ 170
4-Aug	Walmart	Roberta Cross	Ruffles	40	$ 15	$ 600	$ 10	$ 400	$ 200
18-Aug	Walmart	Roberta Cross	Ruffles	93	$ 15	$ 1,395	$ 10	$ 930	$ 465
5-Sep	Walmart	Roberta Cross	Ruffles	41	$ 15	$ 615	$ 10	$ 410	$ 205
12-Sep	Walmart	Roberta Cross	Ruffles	8	$ 15	$ 120	$ 10	$ 80	$ 40
28-Oct	Walmart	Roberta Cross	Ruffles	50	$ 15	$ 750	$ 10	$ 500	$ 250
21-Nov	Walmart	Roberta Cross	Ruffles	79	$ 15	$ 1,185	$ 10	$ 790	$ 395
29-Jan	Walmart	Roberta Cross	Sun Chips	5	$ 22	$ 110	$ 18	$ 90	$ 20
12-Apr	Walmart	Roberta Cross	Sun Chips	85	$ 22	$ 1,870	$ 18	$ 1,530	$ 340
16-Jun	Walmart	Roberta Cross	Sun Chips	55	$ 22	$ 1,210	$ 18	$ 990	$ 220
				1,206	$383	$20,243	$273	$14,385	$5,858

Sorting the data reveals the information that Roberta Cross's total sales to Walmart were $20,243 resulting in a profit of $5,858. (Profit $5,858 = Sales $20,243 − Costs $14,385).

FIGURE 1.4

Information Gained after
Analyzing Tony's Data

Tony's Business Information	Name	Total Profit
Who is Tony's best customer by total sales?	Walmart	$ 560,789
Who is Tony's least-valuable customer by total sales?	Walgreens	$ 45,673
Who is Tony's best customer by profit?	7-Eleven	$ 324,550
Who is Tony's least-valuable customer by profit?	King Soopers	$ 23,908
What is Tony's best-selling product by total sales?	Ruffles	$ 232,500
What is Tony's weakest-selling product by total sales?	Pringles	$ 54,890
What is Tony's best-selling product by profit?	Tostitos	$ 13,050
What is Tony's weakest-selling product by profit?	Pringles	$ 23,000
Who is Tony's best sales representative by profit?	R. Cross	$ 1,230,980
Who is Tony's weakest sales representative by profit?	Craig Schultz	$ 98,980
What is the best sales representative's best-selling product by total profit?	Ruffles	$ 98,780
Who is the best sales representative's best customer by total profit?	Walmart	$ 345,900
What is the best sales representative's weakest-selling product by total profit?	Sun Chips	$ 45,600
Who is the best sales representative's weakest customer by total profit?	Krogers	$ 56,050

measured in terms of total sales. Armed with this information, Tony can identify and then address such issues as weak products and underperforming sales representatives.

A *variable* is a data characteristic that stands for a value that changes or varies over time. For example, in Tony's data, price and quantity ordered can vary. Changing variables allows managers to create hypothetical scenarios to study future possibilities. Tony may find it valuable to anticipate how sales or cost increases affect profitability. To estimate how a 20 percent increase in prices might improve profits, Tony simply changes the price variable for all orders, which automatically calculates the amount of new profits. To estimate how a 10 percent increase in costs hurts profits, Tony changes the cost variable for all orders, which automatically calculates the amount of lost profits. Manipulating variables is an important tool for any business.

Business Intelligence

Business intelligence (BI) is information collected from multiple sources such as suppliers, customers, competitors, partners, and industries that analyzes patterns, trends, and relationships for strategic decision making. BI manipulates multiple variables and in some cases even hundreds of variables, including such items as interest rates, weather conditions, and even gas prices. Tony could use BI to analyze internal data, such as company sales, along with external data about the environment such as competitors, finances, weather, holidays, and even sporting events. Both internal and external variables affect snack sales, and analyzing these variables will help Tony determine ordering levels and sales forecasts. For instance, BI can predict inventory requirements for Tony's business for the week before the Super Bowl if, say, the home team is playing, average temperature is above 80 degrees, and the stock market is performing well. This is BI at its finest, incorporating all types of internal and external variables to anticipate business performance.

Analytics is the science of fact-based decision making. *Business analytics* is the scientific process of transforming data into insight for making better decisions. Analytics is thought of as a broader category than business analytics, encompassing the use of analytical techniques in the sciences and engineering fields as well as business. In this text, we will use the terms *analytics* and *business analytics* as synonymous.

Analytics is used for data-driven or fact-based decision making, helping managers ensure they make successful decisions. A study conducted by MIT's Sloan School of Management and the University of Pennsylvania concluded that firms guided by data-driven decision making have higher productivity and market value along with increased output and profitability. Analytics can range from simple reports to advanced optimization models (models that highlight the best course of actions). *Descriptive analytics* use techniques that describe past

BUSINESS DRIVEN ANALYTICS

The three techniques for business analytics include descriptive analytics, predictive analytics, and prescriptive analytics. For each of the below examples, determine which analytical technique is being used.

Categorizing Analytics

EXAMPLE	DESCRIPTIVE ANALYTICS	PREDICTIVE ANALYTICS	PRESCRIPTIVE ANALYTICS
Which candidate will win the election?			
What price for a product will maximize profit?			
How much money do I need to save each year to have enough money for retirement?			
How many products were sold last year?			
What is the best route for the delivery person to drop off packages to minimize the time needed to deliver all the packages?			
How many Valentine's Day cards should Hallmark print to maximize expected profit?			
How will marketing affect the daily sales of a product?			
How can a company minimize the cost of shipping products from plants to customers?			
What team will win the Superbowl?			
How can I schedule my workforce to minimize operating costs?			
What was the average purchase price for new customers last year?			
How will the placement of a product in a store determine product sales?			
How many customers do we have and where are they located?			

performance and history. *Predictive analytics* use techniques that extract information from data and use it to predict future trends and identify behavioral patterns. *Prescriptive analytics* use techniques that create models indicating the best decision to make or course of action to take. Figure 1.5 displays the three broad categories of analytics.

Knowledge

Knowledge includes the skills, experience, and expertise, coupled with information and intelligence, that create a person's intellectual resources. *Knowledge workers* are individuals valued for their ability to interpret and analyze information. Today's workers are commonly referred to as knowledge workers, and they use BI along with personal experience to make decisions based on both information and intuition, a valuable resource for any company.

Knowledge assets, also called *intellectual capital,* are the human, structural, and recorded resources available to the organization. Knowledge assets reside within the minds of members, customers, and colleagues and include physical structures and recorded media. *Knowledge*

BUSINESS DRIVEN ETHICS AND SECURITY

The Internet of Everything is Everywhere

IoT is transforming our world into a living information system as we control our intelligent lighting from our smart phone to a daily health check from our smart toilet. Of course, with all great technological advances come unexpected risks, and you have to be prepared to encounter various security issues with IoT. Just imagine if your devices are hacked by someone who now can shut off your water, take control of your car, or unlock the doors of your home from thousands of miles away. We are just beginning to understand the security issues associated with IoT and M2M, and you can be sure that sensitive data leakage from your IoT device is something you will most likely encounter in your life.[5] (For more information about IoT, refer to the Opening Case Study.)

In a group, identify a few IoT devices you are using today. These can include fitness trackers that report to your iPhone, sports equipment that provides immediate feedback to an app, or even smart vacuum cleaners. If you are not using any IoT devices today, brainstorm a few you might purchase in the future. How could a criminal or hacker use your IoT to steal your sensitive data? What potential problems or issues could you experience from these types of data thefts? What might be some of the signs that someone had accessed your IoT data illegally? What could you do to protect the data in your device?

facilitators help harness the wealth of knowledge in the organization. Knowledge facilitators help acquire and catalog the knowledge assets in an organization.

Imagine that Tony analyzes his data and finds his weakest sales representative for this period is Craig Schultz. If Tony considered only this information, he might conclude that firing Craig was a good business decision. However, because Tony has knowledge about how the company operates, he knows Craig has been out on medical leave for several weeks; hence, his sales numbers are low. Without this additional knowledge, Tony might have executed a bad business decision, delivered a negative message to the other employees, and sent his best sales representatives out to look for other jobs.

FIGURE 1.5

Three Categories of Analytics

Descriptive Analytics
- Techniques that describes past performance and history.
- Example: Creating a report that includes charts and graphs that explains the data

Predictive Analytics
- Techniques that extract information from data and uses it to predict future trends and identify behavioral patterns.
- Example: Using past sales data to predict future sales

Prescriptive Analytics
- Techniques that create models indicating the best decision to make or course of action to take.
- Example: Airline using past purchasing data as inputs into a model that recommends the best pricing strategy across all flights allowing the company to maximize revenue

FIGURE 1.6

Transformation from Data to Knowledge

DATA: I have one item.

INFORMATION: The item i have is a product that has the most sales during the month of December.

BUSINESS INTELLIGENCE: The month of December this year is going to see interest rates raise by 10 percent and snow stores are expected to cause numerous problems throughout the East coast.

KNOWLEDGE: Given the unexpected financial issues caused by the storms and the interest rate hike we will offer a discount on purchase in November and December to ensure sales levels increase by 10 percent.

The key point in this scenario is that it is simply impossible to collect all the information about every situation, and yet without data, it can be easy to misunderstand the problem. Using data, information, business intelligence, *and* knowledge to make decisions and solve problems is the key to finding success in business. These core drivers of the information age are the building blocks of business systems. Figure 1.6 offers a few different examples of data through knowledge.

THE CHALLENGE OF DEPARTMENTAL COMPANIES AND THE MIS SOLUTION

LO 1.2: Explain systems thinking and how management information systems enable business communications.

Companies are typically organized by department or functional area such as:

- **Accounting:** Records, measures, and reports monetary transactions.
- **Finance:** Deals with strategic financial issues, including money, banking, credit, investments, and assets.
- **Human resources:** Maintains policies, plans, and procedures for the effective management of employees.
- **Marketing:** Supports sales by planning, pricing, and promoting goods or services.
- **Operations management:** Manages the process of converting or transforming resources into goods or services.
- **Sales:** Performs the function of selling goods or services (see Figure 1.7).

Each department performs its own activities. Sales and marketing focus on moving goods or services into the hands of consumers; they maintain transactional data. Finance and accounting focus on managing the company's resources and maintain monetary data. Operations management focuses on manufacturing and maintains production data; human resources focuses on hiring and training people and maintains employee data. Although each department has its own focus and data, none can work independently if the company is to operate as a whole. It is easy to see how a business decision one department makes can affect other departments. Marketing needs to analyze production and sales data to come up with product promotions and advertising strategies. Production needs to understand sales forecasts to determine the company's manufacturing needs. Sales needs to rely on information from operations to understand inventory, place orders, and forecast consumer demand. All departments need to understand the accounting and finance departments' information for budgeting. For the firm to be successful, all departments must work together as a single unit sharing common information and not operate independently or in a silo (see Figure 1.8).

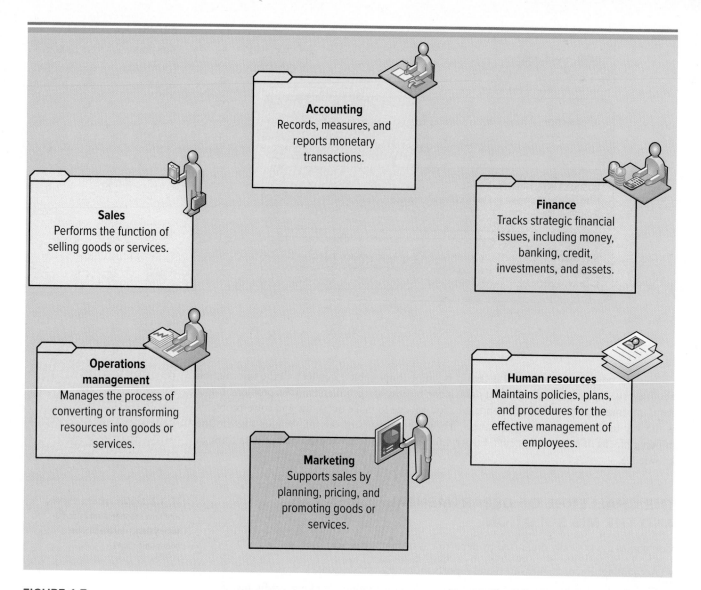

FIGURE 1.7

Departments Working Independently

The MIS Solution

You probably recall the old story of three blind men attempting to describe an elephant. The first man, feeling the elephant's girth, said the elephant seemed very much like a wall. The second, feeling the elephant's trunk, declared the elephant was like a snake. The third man felt the elephant's tusks and said the elephant was like a tree or a cane. Companies that operate departmentally are seeing only one part of the elephant, a critical mistake that hinders successful operation.

Successful companies operate cross-functionally, integrating the operations of all departments. Systems are the primary enabler of cross-functional operations. A *system* is a collection of parts that link to achieve a common purpose. A car is a good example of a system, since removing a part, such as the steering wheel or accelerator, causes the entire system to stop working.

Before jumping into how systems work, it is important to have a solid understanding of the basic production process for goods and services. *Goods* are material items or products that customers will buy to satisfy a want or need. Clothing, groceries, cell phones, and cars are all examples of goods that people buy to fulfill their needs. *Services* are tasks people perform that customers will buy to satisfy a want or need. Waiting tables, teaching, and cutting hair are all examples of services that people pay for to fulfill their needs (see Figure 1.9).

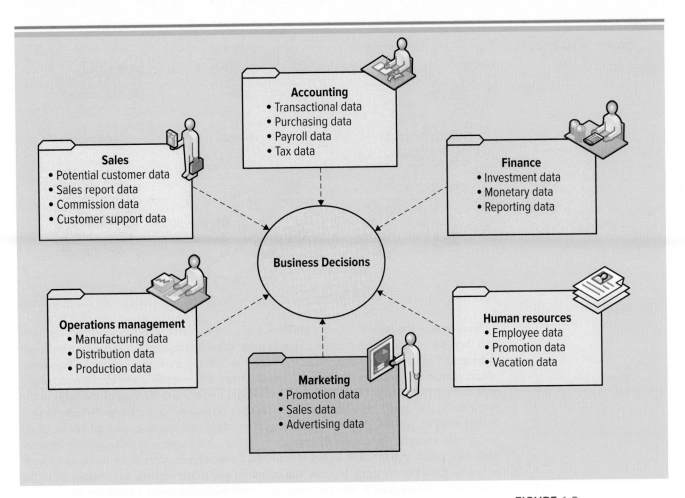

FIGURE 1.8

Departments Working Together

FIGURE 1.9

Different Types of Goods and Services

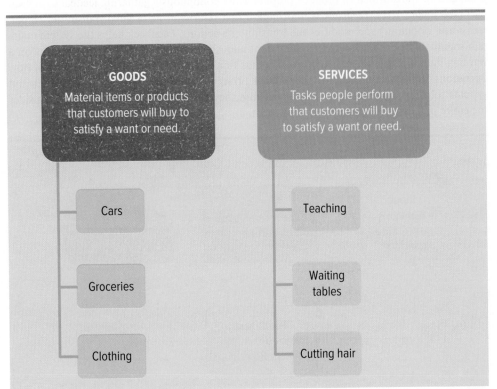

FIGURE 1.10

Input, Process, Output Example

Production is the process where a business takes raw materials and processes them or converts them into a finished product for its goods or services. Just think about making a hamburger (see Figure 1.10). First, you must gather all of the *inputs* or raw materials such as the bun, patty, lettuce, tomato, and ketchup. Second, you *process* the raw materials, so in this example you would need to cook the patty, wash and chop the lettuce and tomato, and place all of the items in the bun. Finally, you would have your *output* or finished product—your hamburger! *Productivity* is the rate at which goods and services are produced based on total output given total inputs. Given our previous example, if a business could produce the same hamburger with less-expensive inputs or more hamburgers with the same inputs, it would see a rise in productivity and possibly an increase in profits. Ensuring the input, process, and output of goods and services work across all of the departments of a company is where systems add tremendous value to overall business productivity.

Systems Thinking

Systems thinking is a way of monitoring the entire system by viewing multiple inputs being processed or transformed to produce outputs while continuously gathering feedback on each part (see Figure 1.11). *Feedback* is information that returns to its original transmitter (input, transform, or output) and modifies the transmitter's actions. Feedback helps the system maintain stability. For example, a car's system continuously monitors the fuel level and turns on a warning light if the gas level is too low. Systems thinking provides an end-to-end view of how operations work together to create a product or service. Business students who understand systems thinking are valuable resources because they can implement solutions that consider the entire process, not just a single component.

FIGURE 1.11

Overview of Systems Thinking

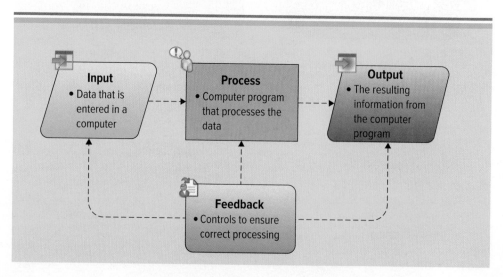

Management information systems (MIS) is a business function, like accounting and human resources, which moves information about people, products, and processes across the company to facilitate decision making and problem solving. MIS incorporates systems thinking to help companies operate cross-functionally. For example, to fulfill product orders, an MIS for sales moves a single customer order across all functional areas, including sales, order fulfillment, shipping, billing, and finally customer service. Although different functional areas handle different parts of the sale, thanks to MIS, to the customer the sale is one continuous process. If one part of the company is experiencing problems, however, then, like the car without a steering wheel, the entire system fails. If order fulfillment packages the wrong product, it will not matter that shipping, billing, and customer service did their jobs right, since the customer will not be satisfied when he or she opens the package.

MIS can be an important enabler of business success and innovation. This is not to say that MIS *equals* business success and innovation or that MIS *represents* business success and innovation. MIS is a tool that is most valuable when it leverages the talents of people who know how to use and manage it effectively. To perform the MIS function effectively, almost all companies, particularly large and medium-sized ones, have an internal MIS department, often called information technology (IT), information systems (IS), or management information systems (MIS). For the purpose of this text, we will refer to it as MIS.

MIS Department Roles and Responsibilities

Management information systems is a relatively new functional area, having been around formally in most organizations only for about 40 years. Job titles, roles, and responsibilities often differ dramatically from organization to organization. Nonetheless, clear trends are developing toward elevating some MIS positions within an organization to the strategic level.

Most organizations maintain positions such as chief executive officer (CEO), chief financial officer (CFO), and chief operations officer (COO) at the strategic level. Recently there are more MIS-related strategic positions such as chief information officer (CIO), chief data officer (CDO), chief technology officer (CTO), chief security officer (CSO), chief privacy officer (CPO), and chief knowledge officer (CKO). See Figure 1.12.

The *chief information officer (CIO)* is responsible for (1) overseeing all uses of information technology and (2) ensuring the strategic alignment of MIS with business goals and objectives. The CIO often reports directly to the CEO. CIOs must possess a solid and detailed understanding of every aspect of an organization coupled with tremendous insight into the capability of MIS. Broad functions of a CIO include:

1. *Manager*—ensure the delivery of all MIS projects, on time and within budget.
2. *Leader*—ensure the strategic vision of MIS is in line with the strategic vision of the organization.
3. *Communicator*—advocate and communicate the MIS strategy by building and maintaining strong executive relationships.

The *chief data officer (CDO)* is responsible for determining the types of information the enterprise will capture, retain, analyze, and share. The difference between the CIO and CDO is that the CIO is responsible for the *information systems* through which data is stored and processed, while the CDO is responsible for the *data,* regardless of the information system.

The *chief technology officer (CTO)* is responsible for ensuring the throughput, speed, accuracy, availability, and reliability of an organization's information technology. CTOs are similar to CIOs, except that CIOs take on the additional responsibility for effectiveness of ensuring that MIS is aligned with the organization's strategic initiatives. CTOs have direct responsibility for ensuring the *efficiency* of MIS systems throughout the organization. Most CTOs possess well-rounded knowledge of all aspects of MIS, including hardware, software, and telecommunications.

With the election of President Barack Obama we saw the appointment of the first-ever national chief technology officer (CTO). The job description, as was listed on Change.gov, stated that the first CTO must "ensure the safety of our networks and lead an interagency effort, working with chief technology and chief information officers of each of the federal agencies, to ensure that they use best-in-class technologies and share best practices." A federal-level CTO demonstrates the ongoing growth of technology positions outside corporate America. In the future expect to see many more technology positions in government and nonprofit organizations.

Chief security officer (CSO)

Responsible for ensuring the security of business systems and developing strategies and safeguards against attacks by hackers and viruses.

Chief knowledge officer (CKO)

Responsible for collecting, maintaining, and distributing company knowledge.

Chief technology officer (CTO)

Responsible for ensuring the speed, accuracy, availability, and reliability of the MIS.

MIS Department Roles and Responsibilities

Chief information officer (CIO)

Responsible for (1) overseeing all uses of MIS and (2) ensuring that MIS strategically aligns with business goals and objectives.

Chief privacy officer (CPO)

Responsible for ensuring the ethical and legal use of information within a company.

Chief data officer (CDO)

Responsible for determining the types of information the enterprise will capture, retain, analyze, and share.

FIGURE 1.12

The Roles and Responsibilities of MIS

The *chief security officer (CSO)* is responsible for ensuring the security of MIS systems and developing strategies and MIS safeguards against attacks from hackers and viruses. The role of a CSO has been elevated in recent years because of the number of attacks from hackers and viruses. Most CSOs possess detailed knowledge of networks and telecommunications because hackers and viruses usually find their way into MIS systems through networked computers.

The *chief privacy officer (CPO)* is responsible for ensuring the ethical and legal use of information within an organization. CPOs are the newest senior executive position in MIS. Recently, 150 of the *Fortune* 500 companies added the CPO position to their list of senior executives. Many CPOs are lawyers by training, enabling them to understand the often complex legal issues surrounding the use of information.

The *chief knowledge officer (CKO)* is responsible for collecting, maintaining, and distributing the organization's knowledge. The CKO designs programs and systems that make it easy for people to reuse knowledge. These systems create repositories of organizational documents, methodologies, tools, and practices, and they establish methods for filtering the information. The CKO must continuously encourage employee contributions to keep the systems up-to-date. The CKO can contribute directly to the organization's bottom line by reducing the learning curve for new employees or employees taking on new roles.

Danny Shaw was the first CKO at Children's Hospital in Boston. His initial task was to unite information from disparate systems to enable analysis of both the efficiency and effectiveness of the hospital's care. Shaw started by building a series of small, integrated information systems that quickly demonstrated value. He then gradually built on those successes, creating a knowledge-enabled organization one layer at a time. Shaw's information systems have enabled administrative and clinical operational analyses.

All the above MIS positions and responsibilities are critical to an organization's success. While many organizations may not have a different individual for each of these positions, they must have leaders taking responsibility for all these areas of concern. The individuals responsible for enterprisewide MIS and MIS-related issues must provide guidance and support to the organization's employees. According to *Fast Company* magazine, a few executive levels you might see created over the next decade include:

- *Chief intellectual property officer* will manage and defend intellectual property, copyrights, and patents. The world of intellectual property law is vast and complicated as new innovations continually enter the market. Companies in the near future will need a core leadership team member who can not only wade through the dizzying sea of intellectual property laws and patents to ensure their own compliance, but also remain vigilant to protect their own company against infringement.

- *Chief automation officer* determines if a person or business process can be replaced by a robot or software. As we continue to automate jobs, a member of the core leadership team of the future will be put in charge of identifying opportunities for companies to become more competitive through automation.

- *Chief user experience officer* will create the optimal relationship between user and technology. User experience used to be an afterthought for hardware and software designers. Now that bulky instruction manuals are largely (and thankfully) a thing of the past, technology companies need to ensure that their products are intuitive from the moment they are activated.

MIS skills gap is the difference between existing MIS workplace knowledge and the knowledge required to fulfill the business goals and strategies. Closing the MIS skills gap by aligning the current workforce with potential future business needs is a complicated proposition. Today, employers often struggle to locate and retain qualified MIS talent, especially individuals with application development, information security, and data analysis skills.

Common approaches to closing an MIS skills gap include social recruiting, off-site training, mentoring services, and partnerships with universities. In many instances, an MIS job will remain unfilled for an extended period of time when an employer needs to hire someone who has a very specific set of skills. In recruiting lingo, such candidates are referred to as purple squirrels. Because squirrels in the real world are not often purple, the implication is that finding the perfect job candidate with exactly the right qualifications, education, and salary expectations can be a daunting—if not impossible—task.

section 1.2 | Business Strategy

LEARNING OUTCOMES

1.3 Explain why competitive advantages are temporary.

1.4 Identify the four key areas of a SWOT analysis.

1.5 Describe Porter's Five Forces Model and explain each of the five forces.

1.6 Compare Porter's three generic strategies.

1.7 Demonstrate how a company can add value by using Porter's value chain analysis.

IDENTIFYING COMPETITIVE ADVANTAGES

Running a company today is similar to leading an army; the top manager or leader ensures all participants are heading in the right direction and completing their goals and objectives. Companies lacking leadership quickly implode as employees head in different directions attempting to achieve conflicting goals. To combat these challenges, leaders communicate and execute business strategies (from the Greek word *stratus* for army and *ago* for leading).

A ***business strategy*** is a leadership plan that achieves a specific set of goals or objectives such as increasing sales, decreasing costs, entering new markets, or developing new products or services. A ***stakeholder*** is a person or group that has an interest or concern in an organization. Stakeholders drive business strategies, and depending on the stakeholder's perspective, the business strategy can change. It is not uncommon to find stakeholders' business strategies have conflicting interests such as investors looking to increase profits by eliminating employee jobs. Figure 1.13 displays the different stakeholders found in an organization and their common business interests.

Good leaders also anticipate unexpected misfortunes, from strikes and economic recessions to natural disasters. Their business strategies build in buffers or slack, allowing the company the ability to ride out any storm and defend against competitive or environmental threats. Of course, updating business strategies is a continuous undertaking as internal and external environments rapidly change. Business strategies that match core company competencies to opportunities result in competitive advantages, a key to success!

FIGURE 1.13

Stakeholders' Interests

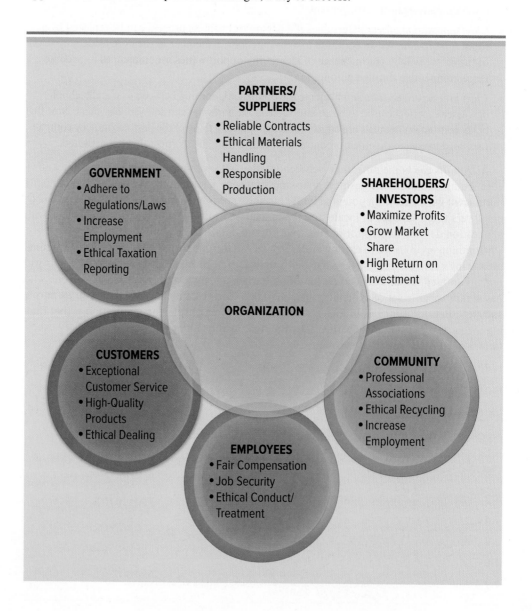

A *competitive advantage* is a feature of a product or service on which customers place a greater value than they do on similar offerings from competitors. Competitive advantages provide the same product or service either at a lower price or with additional value that can fetch premium prices. Unfortunately, competitive advantages are typically temporary because competitors often quickly seek ways to duplicate them. In turn, organizations must develop a strategy based on a new competitive advantage. Ways that companies duplicate competitive advantages include acquiring the new technology, copying the business operations, and hiring away key employees. The introduction of Apple's iPod and iTunes, a brilliant merger of technology, business, and entertainment, offers an excellent example.

In early 2000, Steve Jobs was fixated on developing video editing software when he suddenly realized that millions of people were using computers to listen to music, a new trend in the industry catapulted by illegal online services such as Napster. Jobs was worried that he was looking in the wrong direction and had missed the opportunity to jump on the online music bandwagon. He moved fast, however, and within four months, he had developed the first version of iTunes for the Mac. Jobs's next challenge was to make a portable iTunes player that could hold thousands of songs and be completely transportable. Within nine months, the iPod was born. With the combination of iTunes and iPod, Apple created a significant competitive advantage in the marketplace. Many firms began following Apple's lead by creating portable music players to compete with the iPod. In addition, Apple continues to create new and exciting products to gain competitive advantages, such as its iPad, a larger version of the iPod that functions more as a computer than a music player.[6]

When a company is the first to market with a competitive advantage, it gains a particular benefit, such as Apple did with its iPod. This *first-mover advantage* occurs when a company can significantly increase its market share by being first with a new competitive advantage. FedEx created a first-mover advantage by developing its customer self-service software, which allows people to request parcel pickups, print mailing slips, and track parcels online. Other parcel delivery companies quickly began creating their own online services. Today, customer self-service on the Internet is a standard feature of the parcel delivery business.

Competitive intelligence is the process of gathering information about the competitive environment, including competitors' plans, activities, and products, to improve a company's ability to succeed. It means understanding and learning as much as possible as soon as possible about what is occurring outside the company to remain competitive. Frito-Lay, a premier provider of snack foods such as Cracker Jacks and Cheetos, does not send its sales representatives into grocery stores just to stock shelves; they carry handheld computers and record the product offerings, inventory, and even product locations of competitors. Frito-Lay uses this information to gain competitive intelligence on everything from how well-competing products are selling to the strategic placement of its own products. Managers use four common tools to analyze competitive intelligence and develop competitive advantages as displayed in Figure 1.14.

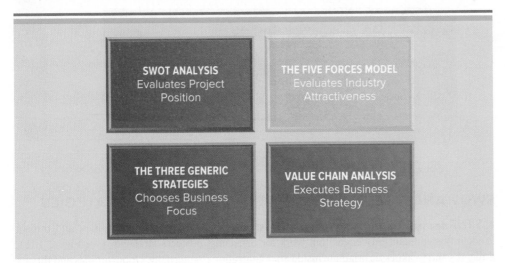

FIGURE 1.14

Business Tools for Analyzing Business Strategies

BUSINESS DRIVEN INNOVATION

SWOT Your Student

What is your dream job? Do you have the right skills and abilities to land the job of your dreams? If not, do you have a plan to acquire those sought-after skills and abilities? Do you have a personal career plan or strategy? Just like a business, you can perform a personal SWOT analysis to ensure your career plan will be successful. You want to know your strengths and recognize career opportunities while mitigating your weaknesses and any threats that can potentially derail your career plans. A key area where many people struggle is technology, and without the right technical skills, you might find you are not qualified for your dream job. One of the great benefits of this course is its ability to help you prepare for a career in business by understanding the key role technology plays in the different industries and functional areas. Regardless of your major, you will all use business driven information systems to complete the tasks and assignments associated with your career.

Perform a personal SWOT analysis for your career plan, based on your current skills, talents, and knowledge. Be sure to focus on your personal career goals, including the functional business area in which you want to work and the potential industry you are targeting, such as health care, telecommunications, retail, or travel.

After completing your personal SWOT analysis, take a look at the table of contents in this text and determine whether this course will eliminate any of your weaknesses or create new strengths. Determine whether you can find new opportunities or mitigate threats based on the material we cover over the next several weeks. For example, Chapter 9 covers project management in detail—a key skill for any business professional who must run a team. Learning how to assign and track work status will be a key tool for any new business professional. Where would you place this great skill in your SWOT analysis? Did it help eliminate any of your weaknesses? When you have finished this exercise, compare your SWOT with your peers to see what kind of competition you will encounter when you enter the workforce.

PERSONAL CAREER SWOT ANALYSIS

STRENGTHS WEAKNESSES

OPPORTUNITES THREATS

SWOT ANALYSIS: UNDERSTANDING BUSINESS STRATEGIES

A *SWOT analysis* evaluates an organization's strengths, weaknesses, opportunities, and threats to identify significant influences that work for or against business strategies (see Figure 1.15). Strengths and weaknesses originate inside an organization or internally. Opportunities and threats originate outside an organization or externally and cannot always be anticipated or controlled.

FIGURE 1.15

Sample SWOT Analysis

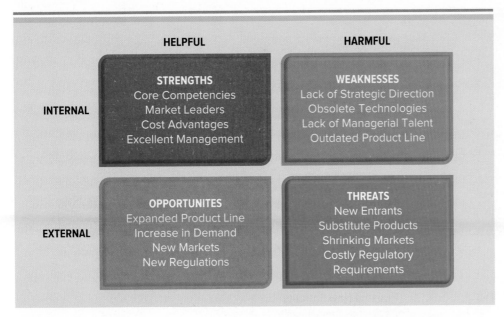

FIGURE 1.15

Sample SWOT Analysis

- **Potential internal strengths (helpful):** Identify all key strengths associated with the competitive advantage including cost advantages, new and/or innovative services, special expertise and/or experience, proven market leader, improved marketing campaigns, and so on.

- **Potential internal weaknesses (harmful):** Identify all key areas that require improvement. Weaknesses focus on the absence of certain strengths, including absence of an Internet marketing plan, damaged reputation, problem areas for service, outdated technology, employee issues, and so on.

- **Potential external opportunities (helpful):** Identify all significant trends along with how the organization can benefit from each, including new markets, additional customer groups, legal changes, innovative technologies, population changes, competitor issues, and so on.

- **Potential external threats (harmful):** Identify all threats or risks detrimental to your organization, including new market entrants, substitute products, employee turnover, differentiating products, shrinking markets, adverse changes in regulations, economic shifts, and so on.[7]

THE FIVE FORCES MODEL—EVALUATING INDUSTRY ATTRACTIVENESS

LO 1.5: Describe Porter's Five Forces Model and explain each of the five forces.

Michael Porter, a university professor at Harvard Business School, identified the following pressures that can hurt potential sales:

- Knowledgeable customers can force down prices by pitting rivals against each other.
- Influential suppliers can drive down profits by charging higher prices for supplies.
- Competition can steal customers.
- New market entrants can steal potential investment capital.
- Substitute products can steal customers.

Formally defined, *Porter's Five Forces Model* analyzes the competitive forces within the environment in which a company operates to assess the potential for profitability in an industry. Its purpose is to combat these competitive forces by identifying opportunities, competitive advantages, and competitive intelligence. If the forces are strong, they increase competition; if the forces are weak, they decrease competition. This section details each of the forces and its associated MIS business strategy (see Figure 1.16).[8]

Buyer Power

Buyer power is the ability of buyers to affect the price they must pay for an item. Factors used to assess buyer power include number of customers, their sensitivity to price, size of orders,

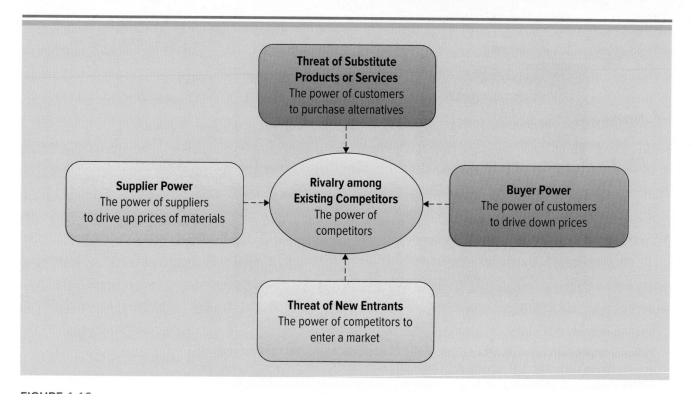

FIGURE 1.16

Porter's Five Forces Model

differences between competitors, and availability of substitute products. If buyer power is high, customers can force a company and its competitors to compete on price, which typically drives prices down.

One way to reduce buyer power is by manipulating *switching costs,* costs that make customers reluctant to switch to another product or service. Switching costs include financial as well as intangible values. The cost of switching doctors, for instance, includes the powerful intangible components of having to build relationships with the new doctor and nurses as well as transferring all your medical history. With MIS, however, patients can store their medical records on DVDs or thumb drives, allowing easy transferability. The Internet also lets patients review websites for physician referrals, which takes some of the fear out of trying someone new.[9]

Companies can also reduce buyer power with *loyalty programs,* which reward customers based on their spending. The airline industry is famous for its frequent-flyer programs, for instance. Because of the rewards travelers receive (free airline tickets, upgrades, or hotel stays), they are more likely to be loyal to or give most of their business to a single company. Keeping track of the activities and accounts of many thousands or millions of customers covered by loyalty programs is not practical without large-scale business systems, however. Loyalty programs are thus a good example of using MIS to reduce buyer power.[10]

Supplier Power

A *supply chain* consists of all parties involved, directly or indirectly, in obtaining raw materials or a product. In a typical supply chain, a company will be both a supplier (to customers) and a customer (of other suppliers), as illustrated in Figure 1.17. *Supplier power* is the suppliers' ability to influence the prices they charge for supplies (including materials, labor, and services). Factors used to appraise supplier power include number of suppliers, size of suppliers,

FIGURE 1.17

Traditional Supply Chain

uniqueness of services, and availability of substitute products. If supplier power is high, the supplier can influence the industry by:

- Charging higher prices.
- Limiting quality or services.
- Shifting costs to industry participants.[11]

Typically, when a supplier raises prices, the buyers will pass on the increase to their customers by raising prices on the end product. When supplier power is high, buyers lose revenue because they cannot pass on the raw material price increase to their customers. Some powerful suppliers, such as pharmaceutical companies, can exert a threat over an entire industry when substitutes are limited and the product is critical to the buyers. Patients who need to purchase cancer-fighting drugs have no power over price and must pay whatever the drug company asks because there are few available alternatives.

Using MIS to find alternative products is one way of decreasing supplier power. Cancer patients can now use the Internet to research alternative medications and practices, something that was next to impossible just a few decades ago. Buyers can also use MIS to form groups or collaborate with other buyers, increasing the size of the buyer group and reducing supplier power. For a hypothetical example, the collective group of 30,000 students from a university has far more power over price when purchasing laptops than a single student.[12]

Threat of Substitute Products or Services

The *threat of substitute products or services* is high when there are many alternatives to a product or service and low when there are few alternatives from which to choose. For example, travelers have numerous substitutes for airline transportation, including automobiles, trains, and boats. Technology even makes videoconferencing and virtual meetings possible, eliminating the need for some business travel. Ideally, a company would like to be in a market in which there are few substitutes for the products or services it offers.

Polaroid had this unique competitive advantage for many years until it forgot to observe competitive intelligence. Then the firm went bankrupt when people began taking digital pictures with everything from video cameras to cell phones.

A company can reduce the threat of substitutes by offering additional value through wider product distribution. Soft-drink manufacturers distribute their products through vending machines, gas stations, and convenience stores, increasing the availability of soft drinks relative to other beverages. Companies can also offer various add-on services, making the substitute product less of a threat. For example, iPhones include capabilities for games, videos, and music, making a traditional cell phone less of a substitute.[13]

Threat of New Entrants

The *threat of new entrants* is high when it is easy for new competitors to enter a market and low when there are significant entry barriers to joining a market. An *entry barrier* is a feature of a product or service that customers have come to expect and entering competitors must offer the same for survival. For example, a new bank must offer its customers an array of MIS-enabled services, including ATMs, online bill paying, and online account monitoring. These are significant barriers to new firms entering the banking market. At one time, the first bank to offer such services gained a valuable first-mover advantage, but only temporarily, as other banking competitors developed their own MIS services.[14]

Rivalry among Existing Competitors

Rivalry among existing competitors is high when competition is fierce in a market and low when competitors are more complacent. Although competition is always more intense in some industries than in others, the overall trend is toward increased competition in almost every industry. The retail grocery industry is intensively competitive. Kroger, Safeway, and Albertsons in the United States compete in many ways, essentially trying to beat or match each other on price. Most supermarket chains have implemented loyalty programs to provide customers special discounts while gathering valuable information about their purchasing habits. In the future, expect to see grocery stores using wireless technologies that track customer movements throughout the store to determine purchasing sequences.

BUSINESS DRIVEN GLOBALIZATION

Sharing Data Around the World

In the past few years, data collection rates have skyrocketed, and some estimate we have collected more data in the past 4 years than since the beginning of time. According to International Data Corporation, data collection amounts used to double every 4 years. With the massive growth of smart phones, tablets, and wearable technology devices, it seems as though data is being collected from everything, everywhere, all the time. It is estimated that data collection is doubling every 2 years, and soon it will double every six months. That is a lot of data! With the explosion of data collection, CTOs, CIOs, and CSOs are facing extremely difficult times as the threats to steal corporate sensitive data also growing exponentially. Hackers and criminals have recently stolen sensitive data from retail giant Target and even the Federal Reserve Bank.

To operate, sensitive data has to flow outside an organization to partners, suppliers, community, government, and shareholders. List 10 types of sensitive data found in a common organization. Review the list of stakeholders; determine which types of sensitive data each has access to and whether you have any concerns about sharing this data. Do you have to worry about employees and sensitive data? How can using one of the four business strategies discussed in this section help you address your data leakage concerns?

Product differentiation occurs when a company develops unique differences in its products or services with the intent to influence demand. Companies can use differentiation to reduce rivalry. For example, although many companies sell books and videos on the Internet, Amazon differentiates itself by using customer profiling. When a customer visits Amazon.com repeatedly, Amazon begins to offer products tailored to that particular customer based on his or her profile. In this way, Amazon has reduced its rivals' power by offering its customers a differentiated service.

To review, the Five Forces Model helps managers set business strategy by identifying the competitive structure and economic environment of an industry. If the forces are strong, they increase competition; if the forces are weak, they decrease it (see Figure 1.18).[15]

Analyzing the Airline Industry

Let us bring Porter's five forces together to look at the competitive forces shaping an industry and highlight business strategies to help it remain competitive. Assume a shipping company is deciding whether to enter the commercial airline industry. If performed correctly, an analysis of the five forces should determine that this is a highly risky business strategy because all five forces are strong. It will thus be difficult to generate a profit.

FIGURE 1.18

Strong and Weak Examples of Porter's Five Forces

	Weak Force: Decreases Competition or Few Competitors	Strong Force: Increases Competition or Lots of Competitors
Buyer Power	An international hotel chain purchasing milk	A single consumer purchasing milk
Supplier Power	A company that makes airline engines	A company that makes pencils
Threat of Substitute Products or Services	Cancer drugs from a pharmaceutical company	Coffee from McDonald's
Threat of New Entrants	A professional hockey team	A dog walking business
Rivalry among Existing Competitors	Department of Motor Vehicles	A coffee shop

FIGURE 1.19

Five Forces Model in the
Airline Industry

	Strong (High) Force: Increases Competition or Lots of Competitors
Buyer Power	Many airlines for buyers to choose from forcing competition based on price.
Supplier Power	Limited number of plane and engine manufacturers to choose from along with unionized workers.
Threat of Substitute Products or Services	Many substitutes, including cars, trains, and buses. Even substitutes to travel such as videoconferencing and virtual meetings.
Threat of New Entrants	Many new airlines entering the market all the time, including the latest sky taxis.
Rivalry among Existing Competitors	Intense competition—many rivals.

- **Buyer power:** Buyer power is high because customers have many airlines to choose from and typically make purchases based on price, not carrier.

- **Supplier power:** Supplier power is high since there are limited plane and engine manufacturers to choose from, and unionized workforces (suppliers of labor) restrict airline profits.

- **Threat of substitute products or services:** The threat of substitute products is high from many transportation alternatives, including automobiles, trains, and boats, and from transportation substitutes such as videoconferencing and virtual meetings.

- **Threat of new entrants:** The threat of new entrants is high because new airlines are continually entering the market, including sky taxies offering low-cost, on-demand air taxi service.

- **Rivalry among existing competitors:** Rivalry in the airline industry is high, and websites such as Travelocity.com force them to compete on price (see Figure 1.19).[16]

THE THREE GENERIC STRATEGIES—CHOOSING A BUSINESS FOCUS

LO 1.6: Compare Porter's three generic strategies.

Once top management has determined the relative attractiveness of an industry and decided to enter it, the firm must formulate a strategy for doing so. If our sample company decided to join the airline industry, it could compete as a low-cost, no-frills airline or as a luxury airline providing outstanding service and first-class comfort. Both options offer different ways of achieving competitive advantages in a crowded marketplace. The low-cost operator saves on expenses and passes the savings along to customers in the form of low prices. The luxury airline spends on high-end service and first-class comforts and passes the costs on to the customer in the form of high prices.

Porter's three generic strategies are generic business strategies that are neither organization nor industry specific and can be applied to any business, product, or service. These three generic business strategies for entering a new market are: (1) broad cost leadership, (2) broad differentiation, and (3) focused strategy. Broad strategies reach a large market segment, whereas focused strategies target a niche or unique market with either cost leadership or differentiation. Trying to be all things to all people is a recipe for disaster because doing so makes projecting a consistent image to the entire marketplace difficult. For this reason, Porter suggests adopting only one of the three generic strategies illustrated in Figure 1.20.[17]

Figure 1.21 applies the three strategies to real companies, demonstrating the relationships among strategies (cost leadership versus differentiation) and market segmentation (broad versus focused).

- **Broad market and low cost:** Walmart competes by offering a broad range of products at low prices. Its business strategy is to be the low-cost provider of goods for the cost-conscious consumer.

- **Broad market and high cost:** Neiman Marcus competes by offering a broad range of differentiated products at high prices. Its business strategy is to offer a variety of specialty and upscale products to affluent consumers.

BUSINESS DRIVEN DEBATE

Is Technology Making Us Dumber or Smarter?

Choose a side and debate the following:

- **Side A:** Living in the information age has made us smarter because we have a huge wealth of knowledge at our fingertips whenever or wherever we need it.
- **Side B:** Living in the information age has caused people to become lazy and dumber because they are no longer building up their memory banks to solve problems; machines give them the answers they need to solve problems.

- **Narrow market and low cost:** Payless competes by offering a specific product, shoes, at low prices. Its business strategy is to be the low-cost provider of shoes. Payless competes with Walmart, which also sells low-cost shoes, by offering a far bigger selection of sizes and styles.

- **Narrow market and high cost:** Tiffany & Co. competes by offering a differentiated product, jewelry, at high prices. Its business strategy allows it to be a high-cost provider of premier designer jewelry to affluent consumers.

FIGURE 1.20

Porter's Three Generic Strategies

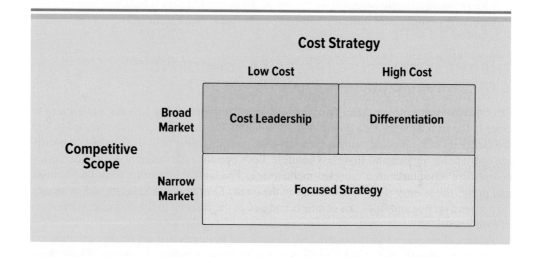

FIGURE 1.21

Examples of Porter's Three Generic Strategies

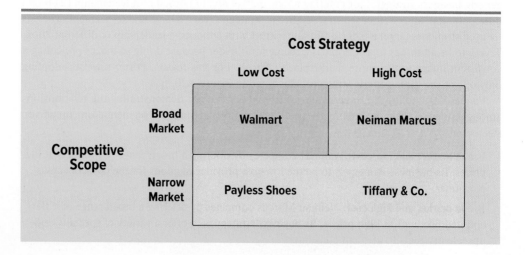

VALUE CHAIN ANALYSIS—EXECUTING BUSINESS STRATEGIES

LO 1.7: Demonstrate how a company can add value by using Porter's value chain analysis.

Firms make profits by applying a business process to raw inputs to turn them into a product or service that customers find valuable. A **business process** is a standardized set of activities that accomplish a specific task, such as processing a customer's order. Once a firm identifies the industry it wants to enter and the generic strategy it will focus on, it must then choose the business processes required to create its products or services. Of course, the firm will want to ensure the processes add value and create competitive advantages. To identify these competitive advantages, Michael Porter created **value chain analysis**, which views a firm as a series of business processes, each of which adds value to the product or service.

Value chain analysis is a useful tool for determining how to create the greatest possible value for customers (see Figure 1.22). The goal of value chain analysis is to identify processes in which the firm can add value for the customer and create a competitive advantage for itself, with a cost advantage or product differentiation.

The *value chain* groups a firm's activities into two categories, primary value activities, and support value activities. **Primary value activities,** shown at the bottom of the value chain in Figure 1.22, acquire raw materials and manufacture, deliver, market, sell, and provide after-sales services.

1. **Inbound logistics** acquires raw materials and resources and distributes to manufacturing as required.
2. **Operations** transforms raw materials or inputs into goods and services.
3. **Outbound logistics** distributes goods and services to customers.
4. **Marketing and sales** promotes, prices, and sells products to customers.
5. **Service** provides customer support after the sale of goods and services.[18]

Support value activities, along the top of the value chain in Figure 1.22, include firm infrastructure, human resource management, technology development, and procurement. Not surprisingly, these support the primary value activities.

- **Firm infrastructure** includes the company format or departmental structures, environment, and systems.
- **Human resource management** provides employee training, hiring, and compensation.
- **Technology development** applies MIS to processes to add value.
- **Procurement** purchases inputs such as raw materials, resources, equipment, and supplies.

It is easy to understand how a typical manufacturing firm transforms raw materials such as wood pulp into paper. Adding value in this example might include using high-quality raw materials or offering next-day free shipping on any order. How, though, might a typical service firm transform raw inputs such as time, knowledge, and MIS into valuable customer service

FIGURE 1.22

The Value Chain

BUSINESS DRIVEN STARTUP

Cool College Start-ups

Not long ago, people would call college kids who started businesses quaint. Now they call them the boss. For almost a decade, *Inc.* magazine has been watching college start-ups and posting a list of the nation's top start-ups taking campuses by storm. Helped in part by low-cost technologies and an increased prevalence of entrepreneurship training at the university level, college students—and indeed those even younger—are making solid strides at founding companies. And they're not just launching local pizza shops and fashion boutiques. They are starting up businesses that could scale into much bigger companies and may already cater to a national audience.[19]

Research *Inc.* magazine and find the year's current Coolest College Startup listing. Choose one of the businesses and perform a Porter's Five Forces analysis and a Porter's three generic strategies analysis. Be sure to highlight each force, including switching costs, product differentiation, and loyalty programs.

knowledge? A hotel might use MIS to track customer reservations and then inform front-desk employees when a loyal customer is checking in so the employee can call the guest by name and offer additional services, gift baskets, or upgraded rooms. Examining the firm as a value chain allows managers to identify the important business processes that add value for customers and then find MIS solutions that support them.

When performing a value chain analysis, a firm could survey customers about the extent to which they believe each activity adds value to the product or service. This step generates responses the firm can measure, shown as percentages in Figure 1.23, to describe how each activity adds (or reduces) value. Then the competitive advantage decision for the firm is

FIGURE 1.23

The Value Chain and Porter's Five Forces Model

MODULE 1:
BUSINESS DRIVEN MIS

	Business Strategy	MIS Topics
Chapter 1: Management Information Systems	Understanding Business Driven MIS	Data Information Business Intelligence Knowledge Systems Thinking Porter's Business Strategies
Chapter 2: Decisions and Processes	Creating Value Driven Businesses	Transaction Processing Systems Decision Support Systems Executive Information Systems Artificial Intelligence Business Process Reengineering
Chapter 3: Ebusiness	Finding Electronic Business Value	eBusiness eBusiness Models Social Networking Knowledge Management Collaboration
Chapter 4: Ethics and Information Security	Identifying MIS Business Concerns	Information Security Policies Authentication and Authorization Prevention and Resistance Detection and Response

MODULE 2:
TECHNICAL FOUNDATIONS OF MIS

	Business Strategy	MIS Topics
Chapter 5: Infrastructures	Deploying Organizational MIS	Grid Computing Cloud Computing Virtualization Sustainable MIS Infrastructures
Chapter 6: Data	Uncovering Business Intelligence	Database Data Management Systems Data Warehousing Data Mining
Chapter 7: Networks	Supporting Mobile Business	Business Networks Web 1.0, Web 2.0, Web 3.0 Mobile MIS Wireless MIS GPS, GIS, and LBS

MODULE 3:
ENTERPRISE MIS

	Business Strategy	MIS Topics
Chapter 8: Enterprise Applications	Enhancing Business Communications	Customer Relationship Management Supply Chain Management Enterprise Resource Planning
Chapter 9: Systems Development and Project Management	Leading MIS Projects	MIS Development Methodologies Project Management Outsourcing

FIGURE 1.24

Overview of *Business Driven Information Systems*

whether to (1) target high value-adding activities to enhance their value further, (2) target low value-adding activities to increase their value, or (3) perform some combination of the two.

MIS adds value to both primary and support value activities. One example of a primary value activity MIS facilitates is the development of a marketing campaign management system that could target marketing campaigns more efficiently, thereby reducing marketing costs. The system would also help the firm pinpoint target market needs better, thereby increasing sales. One example of a support value activity MIS facilitates is the development of a human resources system that could more efficiently reward employees based on performance. The system could also identify employees who are at risk of quitting, allowing managers time to find additional challenges or opportunities that would help retain these employees and thus reduce turnover costs.

Value chain analysis is a highly useful tool that provides hard and fast numbers for evaluating the activities that add value to products and services. Managers can find additional value by analyzing and constructing the value chain in terms of Porter's Five Forces Model (see Figure 1.23). For example, if the goal is to decrease buyer power, a company can construct its value chain activity of "service after the sale" by offering high levels of customer service. This will increase customers' switching costs and reduce their power. Analyzing and constructing support value activities can help decrease the threat of new entrants. Analyzing and constructing primary value activities can help decrease the threat of substitute products or services.[20]

Revising Porter's three business strategies is critical. Firms must continually adapt to their competitive environments, which can cause business strategy to shift. In the remainder of this text, we discuss how managers can formulate business strategies using MIS to create competitive advantages. Figure 1.24 gives an overview of the remaining chapters, along with the relevant business strategy and associated MIS topics.

LEARNING OUTCOME REVIEW

Learning Outcome 1.1: Describe the information age and the differences among data, information, business intelligence, and knowledge.

We live in the information age, when infinite quantities of facts are widely available to anyone who can use a computer. The core drivers of the information age include data, information, business intelligence, and knowledge. Data are raw facts that describe the characteristics of an event or object. Information is data converted into a meaningful and useful context. Business intelligence (BI) is information collected from multiple sources such as suppliers, customers, competitors, partners, and industries that analyzes patterns, trends, and relationships for strategic decision making. Knowledge includes the skills, experience, and expertise, coupled with information and intelligence, that creates a person's intellectual resources. As you move from data to knowledge, you include more and more variables for analysis, resulting in better, more precise support for decision making and problem solving.

Learning Outcome 1.2: Explain systems thinking and how management information systems enable business communications.

A system is a collection of parts that link to achieve a common purpose. Systems thinking is a way of monitoring the entire system by viewing multiple inputs being processed or transformed to produce outputs while continuously gathering feedback on each part. Feedback is information that returns to its original transmitter (input, transform, or output) and modifies the transmitter's actions. Feedback helps the system maintain stability. Management information systems (MIS) is a business function, like accounting and human resources, which moves information about people, products, and processes across the company to facilitate decision making and problem solving. MIS incorporates systems thinking to help companies operate cross-functionally. For example, to fulfill product orders, an MIS for sales moves a single customer order across all functional areas, including sales, order fulfillment, shipping, billing, and finally customer service. Although different functional areas handle different parts of the sale, thanks to MIS, to the customer the sale is one continuous process.

Learning Outcome 1.3: Explain why competitive advantages are temporary.

A competitive advantage is a feature of a product or service on which customers place a greater value than they do on similar offerings from competitors. Competitive advantages provide the same product or service either at a lower price or with additional value that can fetch premium prices. Unfortunately, competitive advantages are typically temporary because competitors often quickly seek ways to duplicate them. In turn, organizations must develop a strategy based on a new competitive advantage. Ways that companies duplicate competitive advantages include acquiring the new technology, copying business processes, and hiring away employees.

Learning Outcome 1.4: Identify the four key areas of a SWOT analysis.

A SWOT analysis evaluates an organization's **s**trengths, **w**eaknesses, **o**pportunities, and **t**hreats to identify significant influences that work for or against business strategies. Strengths and weaknesses originate inside an organization or internally. Opportunities and threats originate outside an organization or externally and cannot always be anticipated or controlled.

Learning Outcome 1.5: Describe Porter's Five Forces Model and explain each of the five forces.

Porter's Five Forces Model analyzes the competitive forces within the environment in which a company operates, to assess the potential for profitability in an industry.

- Buyer power is the ability of buyers to affect the price they must pay for an item.
- Supplier power is the suppliers' ability to influence the prices they charge for supplies (including materials, labor, and services).
- Threat of substitute products or services is high when there are many alternatives to a product or service and low when there are few alternatives from which to choose.
- Threat of new entrants is high when it is easy for new competitors to enter a market and low when there are significant entry barriers to entering a market.
- Rivalry among existing competitors is high when competition is fierce in a market and low when competition is more complacent.

Learning Outcome 1.6: Compare Porter's three generic strategies.

Organizations typically follow one of Porter's three generic strategies when entering a new market: (1) broad cost leadership, (2) broad differentiation, and (3) focused strategy. Broad strategies reach a large market segment. Focused strategies target a niche market. Focused strategies concentrate on either cost leadership or differentiation.

Learning Outcome 1.7: Demonstrate how a company can add value by using Porter's value chain analysis.

To identify competitive advantages, Michael Porter created value chain analysis, which views a firm as a series of business processes, each of which adds value to the product or service. The goal of value chain analysis is to identify processes in which the firm can add value for the customer and create a competitive advantage for itself, with a cost advantage or product differentiation. The value chain groups a firm's activities into two categories—primary value activities and support value activities. Primary value activities acquire raw materials and manufacture, deliver, market, sell, and provide after-sales services. Support value activities, along the top of the value chain in the figure, include firm infrastructure, human resource management, technology development, and procurement. Not surprisingly, these support the primary value activities.

1. **Knowledge:** Explain the Internet of Things and list three IoT devices.

2. **Comprehension:** Explain why it is important for business managers to understand that data collection rates from IoT devices is increasing exponentially.

3. **Application:** Demonstrate how data from an IoT device can be transformed into information and business intelligence.

4. **Analysis:** Analyze the current security issues associated with IoT devices.

5. **Synthesis:** Propose a plan for how a start-up company can use IoT device data to make better business decisions.

6. **Evaluate:** Argue for or against the following statement: "The Internet of Things is just a passing fad and will be gone within a decade."

KEY TERMS

Analytics 10
Big data 7
Business analytics 10
Business intelligence (BI) 10
Business process 29
Business strategy 20
Buyer power 23
Chief automation officer 19
Chief data officer 17
Chief intellectual property officer 19
Chief information officer (CIO) 17
Chief knowledge officer (CKO) 18
Chief privacy officer (CPO) 18
Chief security officer (CSO) 18
Chief technology officer (CTO) 17
Chief user experience officer 19
Competitive advantage 21
Competitive intelligence 21
Data 6
Descriptive analytics 10
Dynamic report 9
Entry barrier 25
Fact 5

Feedback 16
First-mover advantage 21
Goods 14
Human-generated data 7
Information 9
Information age 5
Internet of Things (IoT) 5
Knowledge 11
Knowledge assets 11
Knowledge facilitator 11
Knowledge worker 11
Loyalty program 24
Machine-generated data 6
Machine-to-machine (M2M) 5
MIS skills gap 19
Management information systems (MIS) 17
Porter's Five Forces Model 23
Porter's three generic strategies 27
Predictive analytics 11
Prescriptive analytics 11
Primary value activities 29
Product differentiation 26

Production 16
Productivity 16
Report 9
Rivalry among existing competitors 25
Services 14
Stakeholder 20
Static report 9
Structured data 6
Snapshot 7
Supplier power 24
Supply chain 24
Support value activities 29
Switching costs 24
SWOT analysis 22
System 14
Systems thinking 16
Threat of new entrants 25
Threat of substitute products or services 25
Unstructured data 7
Value chain analysis 29
Variable 10

REVIEW QUESTIONS

1. What is data and why is it important to a business?

2. How can a manager turn data into information?

3. What is the relationship between data, information, business intelligence, and knowledge?

4. Why is it important for a company to operate cross-functionally?

5. Why would a company want to have a CIO, CPO, and CSO?

6. Explain MIS and the role it plays in a company and global business.

7. Do you agree that MIS is essential for businesses operating in the information age? Why or why not?

8. Why is it important for a business major to understand MIS?

9. What type of career are you planning to pursue? How will your specific career use data, information, business intelligence, and knowledge?

10. Explain systems thinking and how it supports business operations.

11. What business strategies would you use if you were developing a competitive advantage for a company?

12. Explain Porter's Five Forces Model and the role it plays in decision making.

13. How could a company use loyalty programs to influence buyer power? How could a company use switching costs to lock in customers and suppliers?

14. What are Porter's three generic strategies and why would a company want to follow only one?

15. How can a company use Porter's value chain analysis to measure customer satisfaction?

CLOSING CASE ONE

Buy Experiences, Not Things

Retail is one of the most competitive and stingiest industries in America, boasting some of the most dissatisfied workers across the board. Walmart Stores employees began a week-long strike in Miami, Boston, and the San Francisco Bay Area to publicly display their immense dissatisfaction with the multinational corporation. Employees at Amazon's fulfillment center in Leipzig, Germany, went on strike demanding higher wages and better benefits. Just search retail strikes and you will find numerous examples of dissatisfied employees doing what they can to improve their situations. However, there is one company that will not appear on the list—Costco Wholesale!

Costco Wholesale, the second-largest retailer in the United States behind Walmart, is an anomaly in a world where retailers are closing their doors due to the inability to compete with online prices. Retail stores such as Aeropostale, Sears, and Macy's are all feeling the pressure of the online marketplaces of today's digital world. Costco requires a $55-a-year membership fee for access to its massive warehouses supplied floor to ceiling with generous portions of everything from olive oil to paper towels. While many businesses are losing customers to the Internet, Costco's sales have grown 40 percent and its stock price has doubled.

Treating employees exceptionally well is the secret to Costco's success. Costco employees make an average of $20 an hour, not including overtime and 88 percent of Costco employees have company-sponsored health insurance. Costco treats its employees well in the belief that a happier work environment will result in a more profitable company. It is obvious Costco is thriving in one of the toughest retail markets in history.

The style of Costco is minimalist with no-frills industrial shelving stocking the 4,000 different products. Products are marked up 14 percent or less over cost. Items such as diapers, suitcases, and tissues, which it sells under its in-house Kirkland Signature brand, get a maximum 15 percent bump. After accounting for expenses such as real estate costs and wages, Costco barely ekes out a profit on many of its products. Eighty percent of its gross profit comes from membership fees; customers renew their memberships at a rate of close to 90 percent.

"They are buying and selling more olive oil, more cranberry juice, more throw rugs than just about anybody," says David Schick, an analyst at Stifel Nicolaus. And that allows Costco to get bulk discounts from its suppliers, often setting the industry's lowest price. Even Amazon can't beat Costco's prices, which means that "showrooming," or browsing in stores but buying online for the better price, isn't much of a concern for Costco.

The company's obsession with selling brand-name merchandise at cut-rate prices occasionally gets it into trouble. Tiffany filed a multimillion-dollar trademark infringement suit against Costco, alleging it improperly labeled merchandise as "Tiffany engagement rings." Costco calls it "an honest mistake" and rebranded the label "Tiffany-style." The suit is pending.

Buying Happiness

When you work hard every single day, you want to spend your hard-earned funds on what science says will make you happy. The Commerce Department released data showing that American consumers are spending their disposable income on eating out, upgrading cars, renovating houses, sports, health, and beauty. Data shows restaurant spending has increased 10 percent over the last year, and automotive sales have increased 7 percent. Analysts say a wider shift is occurring in the mind of the American consumer, spurred by the popularity of a growing body of scientific studies that appear to show that experiences, not objects, bring the most happiness. The Internet is bursting with the "Buy Experiences, Not Things" type of stories that give retailing executives nightmares. Millennials—the 20- and 30-something consumers whom marketers covet—are actively pursuing this new happiness mentality.

A 20-year study conducted by Dr. Thomas Gilovich, a psychology professor at Cornell University, reached a powerful and straightforward conclusion: don't spend your money on things. The trouble with things is that the happiness they provide fades quickly. New possessions quickly become old and what once seemed novel and exciting quickly becomes the norm. The bar is constantly rising and new purchases lead to new expectations. As soon as we get used to a new possession, we look for an even better one. And of course we are always comparing ourselves to the neighbors. By nature, we are always comparing our possessions, and as soon as we buy a new car, a friend buys a better one—and there's always someone with a better one.

Gilovich is not the only person believing experiences make us happier than possessions. Dr. Elizabeth Dunn at the University of British Columbia attributes the temporary happiness achieved by buying things to what she calls "puddles of pleasure." In other words, that kind of happiness evaporates quickly and leaves us wanting more. Things may last longer than experiences, but the memories that linger are what matter most![21]

Questions

1. Imagine you are working for Costco as a manager in its Chicago store. Your boss does not understand the difference between data, information, business intelligence, and knowledge. Using examples of products and services available at Costco, provide examples of each to help your boss understand these important concepts.

2. Explain why it is important for Costco's corporate accounting, marketing, and operations management business units to access and analyze information about your store's sales. What could happen if your store sales were not shared with the different business units at Costco's headquarters?

3. Explain systems thinking and how MIS solves the issue with information silos throughout Costco's entire worldwide organization.

4. Imagine you are working for Costco as a manager in its Chicago store. Using Porter's Five Forces Model, analyze buyer power and supplier power for Costco.

5. Which of the three generic strategies is Costco following?

6. Only members of Costco can purchase products at Costco. Which of Porter's Five Forces did Costco address through the introduction of its members-only program?

The World Is Flat: Thomas Friedman

Christopher Columbus proved in 1492 that the world is round. For centuries, sailors maneuvered the seas, discovering new lands, new people, and new languages as nations began trading goods around the globe. Then Thomas Friedman, a noted columnist for *The New York Times,* published his book *The World Is Flat.*

Friedman argues that the world has become flat due to technological advances connecting people in China, India, and the United States as if we were all next-door neighbors. Physicians in India are reading X-rays for U.S. hospitals, and JetBlue Airways ticket agents take plane reservations for the company from the comfort of their Utah homes. Technology has eliminated some of the economic and cultural advantages developed countries enjoy, making the world a level playing field for all participants. Friedman calls this Globalization 3.0.

Globalization 1.0 started when Christopher Columbus discovered the world is round and the world shrank from large to medium. For the next several hundred years, countries dominated by white men controlled business. Globalization 2.0 began around 1800, during the Industrial Revolution, when the world went from medium to small. In this era, international companies dominated by white men controlled business. Globalization 3.0 began in early 2000, removing distance from the business equation, and the world has gone from small to tiny. In this era, people of all colors from the four corners of the world will dominate business. Farmers in remote villages in Nepal carry an iPhone to access the world's knowledge at, say, Wikipedia or the stock market closing prices at Bloomberg.

Outsourcing, or hiring someone from another country to complete work remotely, will play an enormous role in this era. It has advantages and disadvantages. Outsourcing work to countries where labor is cheap drives down production costs and allows companies to offer lower prices to U.S. consumers. Having an accountant in China complete a U.S. tax return is just as easy as driving to the H&R Block office on the corner and, probably, far cheaper. Calling an 800 number for service can connect consumers to an Indian, Canadian, or Chinese worker on the other end of the line. Of course, outsourcing also eliminates some U.S. manufacturing and labor jobs, causing pockets of unemployment. In fact, the United States has outsourced several million service and manufacturing jobs to offshore, low-cost producers.

Figure 1.25 shows Friedman's list of forces that flattened the world. They converged around the year 2000 and "created a flat world: a global, web-enabled platform for multiple forms of sharing knowledge and work, irrespective of time, distance, geography, and increasingly, language." Three powerful new economies began materializing at this time. In India, China, and the former Soviet Union, more than 3 billion new willing and able participants walked onto the business playing field. Business students will be competing for their first jobs not only against other local students but also against students from around the country and around the globe.[22]

Questions

1. Define Globalization 1.0, 2.0, and 3.0 and provide a sample of the type of business data managers collected during each era.

2. Explain Friedman's flat world and the reasons it is important for all businesses, small or large, to understand.

3. Demonstrate how students competing for jobs in a flat world can create competitive advantages to differentiate themselves in the marketplace.

4. Analyze the current business environment and identify a new flattener not mentioned on Friedman's list.

5. Propose a plan for how a start-up company can use any of Porter's strategies to combat competition in a global world.

6. Argue for or against the following statement: "The world is not flat (in Friedman's sense of the term) because many undeveloped countries are not connected electronically."

FIGURE 1.25

Thomas Friedman's 10 Forces
That Flattened the World

Friedman's 10 Forces That Flattened the World[23]	
1. Fall of the Berlin Wall	The events of November 9, 1989, tilted the worldwide balance of power toward democracies and free markets.
2. Netscape IPO	The August 9, 1995, offering sparked massive investment in fiber-optic cables.
3. Work flow software	The rise of applications from PayPal to virtual private networks (VPNs) enabled faster, closer coordination among far-flung employees.
4. Open sourcing	Self-organizing communities, such as Linux, launched a collaborative revolution.
5. Outsourcing	Migrating business functions to India saved money *and* a Third World economy.
6. Offshoring	Contract manufacturing elevated China to economic prominence.
7. Supply chaining	Robust networks of suppliers, retailers, and customers increased business efficiency.
8. In-sourcing	Logistics giants took control of customer supply chains, helping mom-and-pop shops go global.
9. Informing	Power searching allowed everyone to use the Internet as a personal supply chain of knowledge.
10. Wireless	Wireless technologies pumped up collaboration, making it mobile and personal.

CRITICAL BUSINESS THINKING

1. Focusing on Friedman

Thomas Friedman's newest book is titled *Hot, Flat, and Crowded: Why We Need a Green Revolution—And How It Can Renew America.* Research the Internet to find out as much information as you can about this text. Why would a business manager be interested in reading this text? How will this text affect global business? Do you think *Hot, Flat, and Crowded* will have as great an impact on society as *The World Is Flat* had on business? Why or why not?[24]

2. Pursuing Porter

There is no doubt that Michael Porter is one of the more influential business strategists of the 21st century. Research Michael Porter on the Internet for interviews, additional articles, and new or updated business strategies. Create a summary of your findings to share with your class. How can learning about people such as Thomas Friedman and Michael Porter help prepare you for a career in business? Name three additional business professionals you should follow to help prepare for your career in business.

3. Streaming Movies

The video rental industry is fiercely competitive. Customers have their choice of renting a movie by driving to a store (Redbox), ordering through the mail (Netflix), or watching directly from their television (pay-per-view or Netflix). Using Porter's Five Forces Model (buyer power, supplier power, threat of new entrants, threat of substitute products, and competition), evaluate the attractiveness of entering the movie rental business. Be sure to include product differentiation, switching costs, and loyalty programs in your analysis.

4. Working for the Best

Each year, *Fortune* magazine creates a list of the top 100 companies to work for. Find the most recent list. What types of data do you think *Fortune* analyzed to determine the company ranking? What issues could occur if the analysis of the data was inaccurate? What types of information can you gain by analyzing the list? Create five questions a student performing a job search could answer by analyzing this list.

5. Manipulating Data to Find Your Version of the Truth

How can global warming be real when there is so much snow and cold weather? That's what some people wondered after a couple of massive snowstorms buried Washington, DC. Politicians across the capital made jokes and built igloos as they disputed the existence of climate change. Some concluded the planet simply could not be warming with all the snow on the ground. These comments frustrated Joseph Romm, a physicist and climate expert with the Center for American Progress. He spent weeks turning data into information and graphs to educate anyone who would listen about why this reasoning was incorrect. Climate change is all about analyzing data, turning it into information to detect trends. You cannot observe climate change by looking out the window; you have to review decades of weather data with advanced tools to understand the trends.[25]

Increasingly we see politicians, economists, and newscasters boiling tough issues down to simplistic arguments over what the data mean, each interpreting and spinning the data to support their views and agendas. You need to understand the data and turn them into useful information, or you will not understand when someone is telling the truth and when you are being lied to.

Brainstorm two or three types of data economists use to measure the economy. How do they turn the data into information? What issues do they encounter when attempting to measure the economy? As a manager, what do you need to understand when reading or listening to economic and business reports?

6. Starting Your Own Business

Josh James recently sold his web analytics company, Omniture, to Adobe for $1.8 billion. Yes, James started Omniture from his dorm room! Have you begun to recognize the unbelievable opportunities available to those students who understand the power of MIS, regardless of their major? Answer the following questions.[26]

a. Why is it so easy today for students to create start-ups while still in college?

b. What would it take for you to start a business from your dorm room?

c. How will this course help you prepare to start your own business?

d. Research the Internet and find three examples of college student start-ups.

e. What's stopping you from starting your own business today? You are living in the information age, and with the power of MIS, it is easier than ever to jump into the business game with very little capital investment. Why not start your own business today?

7. Information Issues in the Information Age

We live in the information age, when the collection, storage, and use of data are hot topics. One example of inappropriate data handling occurred at a college where the monitoring of restrooms occurred every 15 seconds to observe the use of toilets, mirrors, and sinks. Students, faculty, and staff began complaining that the data collection was an invasion of their privacy and a violation of their rights.

Another example of inappropriate data handling occurred when a professor of accounting at a college lost a flash drive containing information for more than 1,800 students, including Social Security numbers, grades, and names. Social Security numbers were included because the data went back to before 1993, when the college used Social Security numbers to identify students.

What types of student data does your college collect? What could happen if your professor lost a thumb drive with all of your personal information? What types of issues could you encounter if someone stole your personal data? What can your college do to ensure this type of data storage violation does not occur?

8. 10 Best Things You Will Say to Your Grandchildren

Wired magazine recently posted the top 10 things you will say to your grandchildren. For each expression below, try to identify what it is referring to and why it will be considered outdated.[27]

1. Back in my day, we only needed 140 characters.
2. There used to be so much snow up here, you could strap a board to your feet and slide all the way down.
3. Televised contests gave cash prizes to whoever could store the most data in their head.
4. Well, the screens were bigger, but they only showed the movies at certain times of day.
5. We all had one, but nobody actually used it. Come to think of it, I bet my LinkedIn profile is still out there on the web somewhere.
6. Translation: "English used to be the dominant language. Crazy, huh?"
7. Our bodies were made of meat and supported by little sticks of calcium.
8. You used to keep files right on your computer, and you had to go back to that same computer to access them!
9. Is that the new iPhone 27G? Got multitasking yet?
10. I just can't get used to this darn vat-grown steak. Texture ain't right.

9. IoT in the Room

Each day you are surrounded by millions of bits of data flying around you and you probably have not even noticed! As a collective group, analyze all of the IoT devices currently in your classroom. What types of data are they sending and receiving? How frequently are they sending and receiving the data? What types of IoT device information are you using to manage your life? What types of IoT devices will be in the room in five years and how will they help future students analyze and manage their lives?

10. Teddy The Guardian

Two London-based entrepreneurs are building an Internet of huggable things for sick children to make any hospital visit more like a trip to Disneyland. Teddy The Guardian captures heart rate, temperatures, and blood-oxygen levels when a child grabs it by the paw to give it a cuddle. All measurements are sent wirelessly to nurses and parents mobile devices. The new cute, cuddly teddy bear is packed full of sensors designed to track children's vital signs and help quickly find out potential issues. Teddy The Guardian takes from five to seven seconds to record measurements and is programmed to run five times per hour. Future versions of Teddy The Guardian will be interactive, using machine learning to find out the child's favorite song or bedtime story and then play the related content for a more soothing hospital visit. Big pharmaceutical companies in the United States have already placed over $500,000 in orders and plan to donate the bears to hospitals and clinics.

This is clearly a brilliant idea, and soon we will see Teddy The Guardian in many local hospitals and clinics. Can you identify any additional markets where Teddy The Guardian should focus? Can you think of any ethical issues related to huggable things? Can you think of any security issues related to huggable things?

11. Death of a Product

Porter's Five Forces Model is an essential framework for understanding industries and market forces. Choose one of the categories listed here and analyze what happened to the market using Porter's Five Forces:

- PDA and laptop computer.
- On-demand movies and Blu-ray player.
- Digital camera and Polaroid camera.
- GPS device and a road atlas.
- Digital books and printed books.
- High-definition TV and radio.

12. Applying the Three Generic Strategies

The chapter discussed examples of companies that pursue differentiated strategies so that they are not forced into positions in which they must compete solely on the basis of price. Pick an industry and have your team members find and compare two companies, one that is competing on the basis of price and another that has chosen to pursue a differentiated strategy enabled by the creative use of MIS. Some industries you may want to consider are clothing retailers, grocery stores, airlines, and personal computers. Prepare a presentation for the class on the ways that MIS is being used to help the differentiating company compete against the low-cost provider. Before you begin, spend some class time to make sure each team selects a different industry if at all possible.

13. IoT Time Management

There is no doubt about it, poor time management is one of the leading causes of failure among students. Without being able to manage due dates, deliverables, work, and of course life, students find themselves sinking instead of swimming in the vast college pool. You have decided that enough is enough and you and a few friends are going to take advantage of technology to create an innovative new IoT device to solve this monumental problem. In a group, brainstorm your new time management IoT device and then apply a Porter's Five Forces model. Use the model to determine the chances of success for your new product.

14. Who Really Won the 2014 Winter Olympics?

If you were watching the 2014 Winter Olympics, I bet you were excited to see your country and its amazing athletes compete. As you were following the Olympics day by day, you were probably checking different websites to see how your country ranked. And depending on the website you visited, you could get a very different answer to this seemingly easy question. On the NBC and ESPN networks, the United States ranked second, and on the official Sochie Olympic website, the United States ranked fourth. The simple question of who won the 2014 Winter Olympics changes significantly, depending on whom you asked.[28]

In a group, take a look at the following two charts and brainstorm the reasons each internationally recognized source has a different listing for the top five winners. What measurement is each chart using to determine the winner? Who do you believe is the winner? As a manager, what do you need to understand when reading or listening to business forecasts and reports?

Winter Olympics 2014 Medal Ranking According to NBC News

Rank	Country	Gold	Silver	Bronze	Total
1	Russian Fed.	13	11	9	33
2	United States	9	7	12	28
3	Norway	11	5	10	26
4	Canada	10	10	5	25
5	Netherlands	8	7	9	24

Winter Olympics 2014 Medal Ranking According to Official Sochie Olympic Website

Rank	Country	Gold	Silver	Bronze	Total
1	Russian Fed.	13	11	9	33
2	Norway	11	5	10	26
3	Canada	10	10	5	25
4	United States	9	7	12	28
5	Netherlands	8	7	9	24

PROJECT I Capitalizing on Your Career

Business leaders need to be comfortable with management information systems (MIS) for the following (primary) reasons:

- The sheer magnitude of the dollars spent on MIS must be managed to ensure business value.

- Research has consistently shown that when top managers are active in supporting MIS, they realize a number of benefits, such as gaining a competitive advantage, streamlining business processes, and even transforming entire industries.

- When business leaders are not involved in MIS, systems fail, revenue is lost, and entire companies can even fail because of poorly managed systems.

How do companies get managers involved in MIS? One of the biggest positive factors is managers' personal experience with MIS and MIS education, including university classes and executive seminars. Once managers understand MIS through experience and education, they are more likely to lead their companies in achieving business success through MIS.

1. Search the Internet for examples of the types of technologies currently used in the field or industry that you plan to pursue. For example, if you are planning a career in accounting or finance, you should become familiar with financial systems such as Oracle Financials. For a career in logistics or distribution, research supply chain management systems. If marketing appeals to you, research customer relationship management systems, blogs, emarketing, and social networking.

2. As a competitive tool, MIS can differentiate products, services, and prices from competitors' offerings by improving product quality, shortening product development or delivery time, creating new MIS-based products and services, and improving customer service before, during, and after a transaction. Search the Internet for examples of companies in the industry where you plan to work that have achieved a competitive advantage through MIS.

3. Create a brief report of your findings; include an overview of the type of technologies you found and how companies are using them to achieve a competitive advantage.

PROJECT II Achieving Alignment

Most companies would like to be in the market-leading position of JetBlue, Dell, or Walmart, all of which have used management information systems to secure their respective spots in the marketplace. These companies are relentless about keeping the cost of technology down by combining the best of MIS and business leadership.

The future belongs to those organizations perceptive enough to grasp the significance of MIS and resourceful enough to coordinate their business and management information systems.

1. Use any resource to answer the question, "Why is it challenging for businesses to align MIS and their other operations?" Use the following questions to begin your analysis:

   a. How do companies monitor competitive intelligence and create competitive advantages?
   b. What are some of the greatest MIS challenges for most firms?
   c. What drives MIS decisions?
   d. Who or what is the moving force behind MIS decisions for most companies?

PROJECT III Market Dissection

To illustrate the use of the three generic strategies, consider Figure 1.26. The matrix shown demonstrates the relationships among strategies (cost leadership versus differentiation) and market segmentation (broad versus focused).

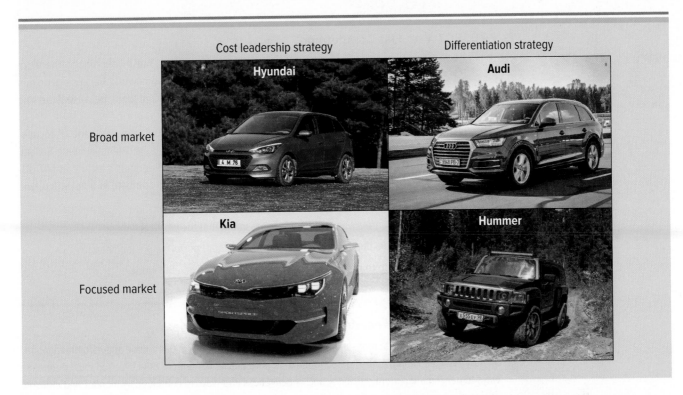

FIGURE 1.26

Porter's Three Generic Strategies

(Hyundai): ©otomobil/Shutterstock. com RF; (Audi): ©Yauhen_D/Shutterstock. com RF; (Kia): ©Zavatskiy Aleksandr/ Shutterstock.com; (Hummer): ©Pavel Vaschenkov/Shutterstock.com RF

- ▪ Hyundai is following a broad cost leadership strategy. It offers low-cost vehicles in each particular model stratification that appeal to a large audience.

- ▪ Audi is pursuing a broad differentiation strategy with its Quattro models available at several price points. Audi's differentiation is safety, and it prices its models higher than Hyundai's to reach a large, stratified audience.

- ▪ Kia has a more focused cost leadership strategy. Kia mainly offers low-cost vehicles in the lower levels of model stratification.

- ▪ Hummer offers the most focused differentiation strategy of any in the industry (including Mercedes-Benz).

Create a similar graph displaying each strategy for a product of your choice. The strategy must include an example of the product in each of the following markets: (1) cost leadership, broad market; (2) differentiation, broad market; (3) cost leadership, focused market; and (4) differentiation, focused market. Potential products include cereal, dog food, soft drinks, computers, shampoo, snack foods, jeans, sneakers, sandals, mountain bikes, TV shows, and movies.

PROJECT IV   Fixing the Post Office

Is there anything more frustrating than waiting in line at the post office? Not only are those lines frustrating, but they are also unprofitable. The U.S. Postal Service has faced multibillion-dollar losses every year for the past few years, making for one of the greatest challenges in its history.

What is killing the post office? Perhaps it is Stamps.com, a website that allows you to customize and print your own stamps 24 hours a day. Getting married? Place a photo of the happy couple right on the stamp for the invitations. Starting a business? Place your business logo on your stamps. Stamps.com even keeps track of a customer's postal spending and can recommend optimal delivery methods. Plus, Stamps.com gives you postage discounts you can't get at the post office or with a postage meter.

Evaluate the U.S. Postal Service, using Porter's Five Forces Model. How could the Postal Service create new products and services to help grow its business? What types of competitive advantages can you identify for the Postal Service?

PROJECT VI   Flat Competition

"When I was growing up in Minneapolis, my parents always said, 'Tom, finish your dinner. There are people starving in China and India.' Today I tell my girls, 'Finish your homework, because people in China and India are starving for your jobs.' And in a flat world, they can have them, because there's no such thing as an American job anymore." Thomas Friedman.

In his book, *The World Is Flat,* Thomas Friedman describes the unplanned cascade of technological and social shifts that effectively leveled the economic world and "accidentally made Beijing, Bangalore, and Bethesda next-door neighbors." The video of Thomas Friedman's lecture at MIT discussing the flat world is available online. If you want to be prepared to compete in a flat world, you must watch this video and answer the following questions:

- Do you agree or disagree with Friedman's assessment that the world is flat?
- What are the potential impacts of a flat world for a student performing a job search?
- What can students do to prepare themselves for competing in a flat world?[29]

PROJECT VII   Measuring Efficiency and Effectiveness

In a group, create a plan to measure the efficiency and effectiveness of this course and recommendations on how you could improve the course to make it more efficient and more effective. You must determine ways to benchmark current efficiency and effectiveness and ways to continuously monitor and measure against the benchmarks to determine if the course is becoming more or less efficient and effective (class quizzes and exams are the most obvious benchmarks). Be sure your plan addresses the following:

- Design of the classroom.
- Room temperature.
- Lighting and electronic capabilities of the classroom.
- Technology available in the classroom.
- Length of class.
- Email and instant messaging.
- Students' attendance.
- Students' preparation.
- Students' arrival time.
- Quizzes and exams (frequency, length, grades).

PROJECT VIII   Adding Value

To identify competitive advantages, Michael Porter created value chain analysis, which views a firm as a series of business processes that each add value to the product or service. Value chain analysis is a useful tool for determining how to create the greatest possible value for customers. The goal of value chain analysis is to identify processes in which the firm can add value for the customer and create a competitive advantage for itself, with a cost advantage or product differentiation.

Starbucks has hired you after your graduation for a temporary position that could turn into a full-time opportunity. With new cafés and juice shops popping up on every corner, coupled with the global recession, Starbucks is worried about losing market share to competitors. Your boss, Heather Sweitzer, is out of ideas for ways to improve the company's profitability. You decide that one of the most useful tools for identifying competitive advantages is Porter's value chain analysis. Of course, you do not yet have the detailed knowledge to complete all of the elements required, but you know enough to get started and plan to take your draft to Sweitzer next week. Using your knowledge of Starbucks, create a value chain analysis. Feel free to make assumptions about operations; just be sure to list any that you make. Also, be sure to write an overview of the tool and its potential value so Sweitzer can understand how it works.

PROJECT IX   Listen to Spider-Man: He Knows What He's Talking About!

Spider-Man's infamous advice—"With great power comes great responsibility"—should be applied to every type of technology you encounter in business. Technology provides countless opportunities for businesses, but it can also lead to countless pitfalls and traps. A great example is how many companies profited from online trading and how many people lost their life savings in online trading scams. For example, Bernard Madoff, the owner of a high-profile New York investment company, was able to forge investment statements and allegedly spent almost $50 billion of his client's money.

Texting and email are great assets for any company that requires instant communication, but they also digitize conversations that can be tracked and retrieved. David Petraeus, director of the CIA, resigned after investigators found evidence from his emails indicating an extramarital affair with his biographer, Paula Broadwell. It should be crystal clear that email is a dangerous tool if it has the ability to take down the director of the CIA.

Craigslist allows anyone to become a provider of goods and services. Unfortunately, Craigslist does not describe exactly what types of goods and services are allowed. Adam Vitale was sentenced to two years in prison after he found a way to bypass Craigslist security and was caught running an online prostitution ring through Craigslist.

When competing in business, you must analyze the good and the bad associated with every technology you encounter. Choose a company that primarily operates online—such as eBay, Netflix, or Amazon—and analyze all of the business opportunities along with the potential pitfalls you might encounter if you were the owner of the company.

PROJECT X   Get the Cow Out of the Ditch

Fortune magazine asked Anne Mulcahy, former chairman and CEO of Xerox, what the best advice she had ever received in business was. She said it occurred at a breakfast meeting in Dallas to which she had invited a group of business leaders. One of them, a plainspoken, self-made, streetwise guy, came up to Mulcahy and said:

> When everything gets really complicated and you feel overwhelmed, think about it this way. *You gotta do three things. First, get the cow out of the ditch. Second, find out how the cow got into the ditch. Third, make sure you do whatever it takes so the cow doesn't go into the ditch again.*

You are working for an international app developer that produces games. For months, you have been collecting metrics on usage by players from all over the world. You notice the metrics on the Asian and European players are falling sharply and sales are dropping. The U.S. and Canada metrics are still growing strongly, and sales are increasing. What can you do to get this cow out of the ditch?

PROJECT XI   I Love TED!

A small nonprofit started in 1984, TED (Technology, Entertainment, and Design) hosts conferences for "ideas worth spreading." TED brings people from all over the globe to share award-winning talks covering the most innovative, informative, and exciting speeches ever given in 20 minutes. You can find TED talks by Al Gore, Bill Gates, Steve Jobs, Douglas Adams, Steven Levitt, Seth Godin, Malcolm Gladwell, and so on.

Visit www.ted.com and peruse the thousands of videos that are available; then answer the following:

- Review the TED website and find three talks you would want to watch. Why did you pick these three and will you make time outside of class to watch them?
- How can you gain a competitive advantage by watching TED?
- How can you find innovative ideas for a start-up by watching TED?
- How can you find competitive intelligence by watching TED?[30]

If you are looking for Excel projects to incorporate into your class, try any of the following after reading this chapter.

Project Number	Project Name	Project Type	Plug-In Focus Area	Project Level	Skill Set	Page Number
1	Financial Destiny	Excel	T2	Personal Budget	Introductory Formulas	AYK.4
2	Cash Flow	Excel	T2	Cash Flow	Introductory Formulas	AYK.4
3	Technology Budget	Excel	T1, T2	Hardware and Software	Introductory Formulas	AYK.4
4	Tracking Donations	Excel	T2	Employee Relationships	Introductory Formulas	AYK.4
5	Convert Currency	Excel	T2	Global Commerce	Introductory Formulas	AYK.5
6	Cost Comparison	Excel	T2	Total Cost of Ownership	Introductory Formulas	AYK.5
7	Time Management	Excel or Project	T12 Project Management	Introductory	Gantt Charts	AYK.6

Decisions and Processes: Value Driven Business

SECTION 2.1
Decision Support Systems

- Making Organizational Business Decisions
- Measuring Organizational Business Decisions
- Using MIS to Make Business Decisions
- Using AI to Make Business Decisions

SECTION 2.2
Business Processes

- Managing Business Processes
- Using MIS to Improve Business Processes

What's in IT for me?

Working faster and smarter has become a necessity for companies. A firm's value chain is directly affected by how well it designs and coordinates its business processes. Business processes offer competitive advantages if they enable a firm to lower operating costs, differentiate, or compete in a niche market. They can also be huge burdens if they are outdated, which impedes operations, efficiency, and effectiveness. Thus, the ability of management information systems to improve business processes is a key advantage.

The goal of Chapter 2 is to provide an overview of specific MIS tools managers can use to support the strategies discussed in Chapter 1. After reading this chapter, you, the business student, should have detailed knowledge of the types of information systems that exist to support decision making and business process reengineering, which in turn can improve organization efficiency and effectiveness and help an organization create and maintain competitive advantages.

©danlefeb/Getty Images RF

©Peppinuzzo/Shutterstock.com RF

©Jabra

Robots Took My Job

Have you ever seen the movie *Terminator* in which machines take over the world? Do you think that scenario could ever come true? Researching the Internet of Things makes you wonder if robots can gain self-consciousness, making the possibility of them taking over the earth a reality. If these are your thoughts, you are not alone. Many prominent people in the field of science and technology are currently debating this hot topic. British physicist Stephen Hawking stated the following:

"The primitive forms of artificial intelligence we already have, have proved very useful. But I think the development of full artificial intelligence could spell the end of the human race," Hawking told the BBC. "Once humans develop artificial intelligence, it would take off on its own and re-design itself at an ever-increasing rate," he said. According to Hawking, the robots may take over the planet if artificial intelligence research is not done properly.

The debate on artificial intelligence has two sides: (1) in agreement with Hawking, stating artificial intelligence will overtake human intelligence; and (2) in disagreement with Hawking, stating that "true" AI—loosely defined as a machine that can pass itself off as a human being or think creatively—is at best decades away. The one truth about AI that is occurring today is that robots are taking over jobs in the workplace. Years ago, the horse was displaced by the automobile. In today's workplace, human labor is being displaced by robots. Oxford University researchers have estimated that 47 percent of U.S. jobs could be automated within the next two decades. But which ones will robots take first? According to Shelly Palmer, CEO of The Palmer Group, the following are the first five jobs robots are replacing, along with the last five jobs robots will replace. (See Figures 2.1 and 2.2,)[1]

FIGURE 2.1

The First Five Jobs Robots
Will Replace

1. Middle Management
If your main job function is taking a number from one box in Excel and putting it in another box in Excel and writing a managerial report, then you are a prime target for a hostile takeover from a robot. Be ready.

2. Salespersons
Robots will dramatically reduce the cost of sales by removing the person from the sales process (request for proposal, quotation, order and fulfillment system), making the entire company far more profitable.

3. Report Writers, Journalists, Authors
Report writing is easy, and robots are being taught to read data, pattern match images or video, or analyze almost any kind of research materials, creating useful managerial reports. Text-to-speech systems are evolving quickly, and even commentators will be replaced by robots.

4. Accountants and Bookkeepers
Machine learning accountants and bookkeepers will operate infinitely better than humans and far cheaper. Robo-accounting is in its infancy, but it is awesome at dealing with accounts payable, accounts receivable, inventory control, auditing, and several other accounting functions.

5. Doctors
Robots make amazing doctors, diagnosticians, and surgeons. IBM's Watson is teaming up with a dozen U.S. hospitals to offer advice on the best treatments for a range of cancers and to help spot early stage skin cancers. And ultra-precise robo-surgeons are currently used for everything from knee replacement surgery to vision correction. This is great news because robotic doctors are going to become a necessity as the world population is expected to reach 11 billion in 2100. With that many people on the earth, even if everyone who ever wanted to be a doctor became one, we still would not have enough doctors.[2]

FIGURE 2.2

The Last Five Jobs Robots
Will Replace

1. Preschool and Elementary School Teacher
Children need to be taught by humans if we want our children to grow up to be human. A robot would be unable to teach a child to be human.

2. Professional Athlete
A robot playing a sport would simply take all of the fun out of the game. Professional athletes need to be human!

3. Politician
As long as fairness and equality are important topics, humans will be the only ones on the political scene.

4. Judge
Judging requires both objective and subjective assessments and simply cannot be replaced by a robot.

5. Mental Health Professional
It takes a great deal of human knowledge to understand mental health issues, and psychologists and psychiatrists will not be replaced by robots due to the delicate nature of humans.[3]

LEARNING OUTCOMES

2.1 Explain the importance of decision making for managers at each of the three primary organization levels along with the associated decision characteristics.

2.2 Define critical success factors (CSFs) and key performance indicators (KPIs) and explain how managers use them to measure the success of MIS projects.

2.3 Classify the different operational support systems, managerial support systems, and strategic support systems and explain how managers can use these systems to make decisions and gain competitive advantages.

2.4 Describe artificial intelligence and identify its five main types.

LO 2.1: Explain the importance of decision making for managers at each of the three primary organization levels along with the associated decision characteristics.

MAKING ORGANIZATIONAL BUSINESS DECISIONS

Porter's strategies outlined in Chapter 1 suggest entering markets with a competitive advantage in overall cost leadership, differentiation, or focus. To achieve these results, managers must be able to make decisions and forecast future business needs and requirements. The most important and most challenging question confronting managers today is how to lay the foundation for tomorrow's success while competing to win in today's business environment. A company will not have a future if it is not cultivating strategies for tomorrow. The goal of this section is to expand on Porter's Five Forces Model, three generic strategies, and value chain analysis to demonstrate how managers can learn the concepts and practices of business decision making to add value. It will also highlight how companies heading into the 21st century are taking advantage of advanced MIS capable of generating significant competitive advantages across the value chain.

As we discussed in Chapter 1, decision making is one of the most important and challenging aspects of management. Decisions range from routine choices, such as how many items to order or how many people to hire, to unexpected ones, such as what to do if a key employee suddenly quits or needed materials do not arrive. Today, with massive volumes of information available, managers are challenged to make highly complex decisions—some involving far more information than the human brain can comprehend—in increasingly short time frames. Figure 2.3 displays the three primary challenges managers face when making decisions.

FIGURE 2.3

Managerial Decision-Making Challenges

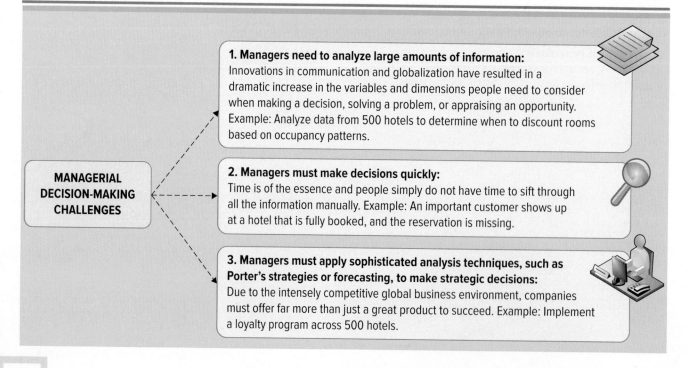

MANAGERIAL DECISION-MAKING CHALLENGES

1. Managers need to analyze large amounts of information:
Innovations in communication and globalization have resulted in a dramatic increase in the variables and dimensions people need to consider when making a decision, solving a problem, or appraising an opportunity. Example: Analyze data from 500 hotels to determine when to discount rooms based on occupancy patterns.

2. Managers must make decisions quickly:
Time is of the essence and people simply do not have time to sift through all the information manually. Example: An important customer shows up at a hotel that is fully booked, and the reservation is missing.

3. Managers must apply sophisticated analysis techniques, such as Porter's strategies or forecasting, to make strategic decisions:
Due to the intensely competitive global business environment, companies must offer far more than just a great product to succeed. Example: Implement a loyalty program across 500 hotels.

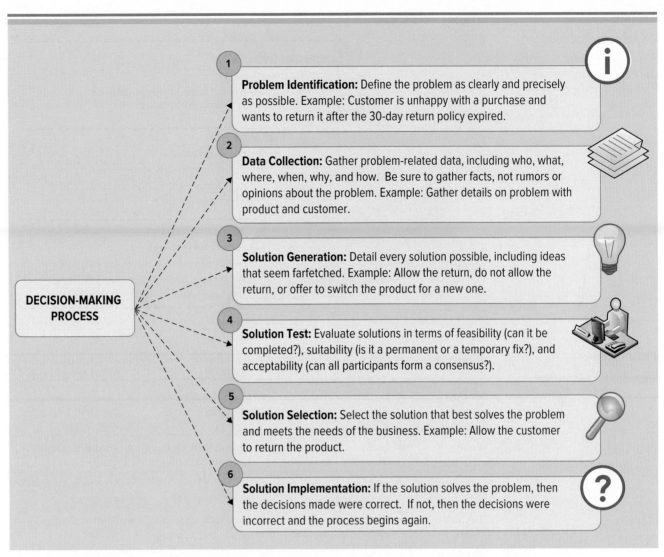

DECISION-MAKING PROCESS

1 **Problem Identification:** Define the problem as clearly and precisely as possible. Example: Customer is unhappy with a purchase and wants to return it after the 30-day return policy expired.

2 **Data Collection:** Gather problem-related data, including who, what, where, when, why, and how. Be sure to gather facts, not rumors or opinions about the problem. Example: Gather details on problem with product and customer.

3 **Solution Generation:** Detail every solution possible, including ideas that seem farfetched. Example: Allow the return, do not allow the return, or offer to switch the product for a new one.

4 **Solution Test:** Evaluate solutions in terms of feasibility (can it be completed?), suitability (is it a permanent or a temporary fix?), and acceptability (can all participants form a consensus?).

5 **Solution Selection:** Select the solution that best solves the problem and meets the needs of the business. Example: Allow the customer to return the product.

6 **Solution Implementation:** If the solution solves the problem, then the decisions made were correct. If not, then the decisions were incorrect and the process begins again.

FIGURE 2.4

The Six-Step Decision-Making Process

The Decision-Making Process

The process of making decisions plays a crucial role in communication and leadership for operational, managerial, and strategic projects. There are numerous academic decision-making models; Figure 2.4 presents just one example.[4]

Decision-Making Essentials

A few key concepts about organizational structure will help our discussion of MIS decision-making tools. The structure of a typical organization is similar to a pyramid, and the different levels require different types of information to assist in decision making, problem solving, and opportunity capturing (see Figure 2.5).

Operational   At the *operational level*, employees develop, control, and maintain core business activities required to run the day-to-day operations. *Operational decisions* affect how the firm is run from day to day; they are the domain of operations managers, who are the closest to the customer. Operational decisions are considered *structured decisions*, which arise when established processes offer potential solutions. Structured decisions are made frequently and are almost repetitive in nature; they affect short-term business strategies. Reordering inventory and creating the employee staffing and weekly production schedules are examples of routine structured decisions. Figure 2.6 highlights the essential elements required for operational decision making. All the elements in the figure should be familiar except metrics, which are discussed in detail below.

FIGURE 2.5

Common Company Structure

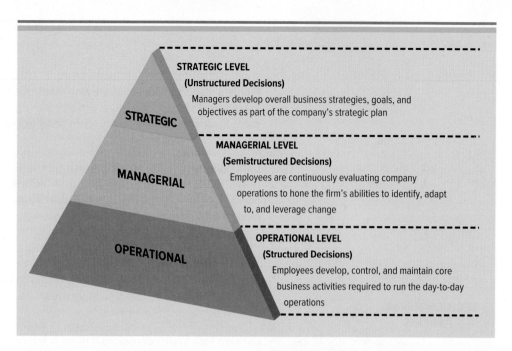

STRATEGIC LEVEL
(Unstructured Decisions)
Managers develop overall business strategies, goals, and objectives as part of the company's strategic plan

MANAGERIAL LEVEL
(Semistructured Decisions)
Employees are continuously evaluating company operations to hone the firm's abilities to identify, adapt to, and leverage change

OPERATIONAL LEVEL
(Structured Decisions)
Employees develop, control, and maintain core business activities required to run the day-to-day operations

FIGURE 2.6

Overview of Decision Making

	STRATEGIC LEVEL	MANAGERIAL LEVEL	OPERATIONAL LEVEL
Employee Types	■ Senior management, presidents, leaders, executives	■ Middle management, managers, directors	■ Lower management, department managers, analysts, staff
Focus	■ External, industry, cross-company	■ Internal, cross-functional (sometimes external)	■ Internal, functional
Time Frame	■ Long term—yearly, multiyear	■ Short term, daily, monthly, yearly	■ Short term, day-to-day operations
Decision Types	■ Unstructured, nonrecurring, one time	■ Semistructured, ad hoc (unplanned) reporting	■ Structured, recurring, repetitive
MIS Types	■ Knowledge	■ Business intelligence	■ Information
Metrics	■ Critical success factors focusing on effectiveness	■ Key performance indicators focusing on efficiency, and critical success factors focusing on effectiveness	■ Key performance indicators focusing on efficiency
Examples	■ How will changes in employment levels over the next 3 years affect the company? ■ What industry trends are worth analyzing? ■ What new products and new markets does the company need to create competitive advantages? ■ How will a recession over the next year affect business? ■ What measures will the company need to prepare for due to new tax laws?	■ Who are our best customers by region, by sales representative, by product? ■ What are the sales forecasts for next month? How do they compare to actual sales for last year? ■ What was the difference between expected sales and actual sales for each month? ■ What was the impact of last month's marketing campaign on sales? ■ What types of ad hoc or unplanned reports might the company require next month?	■ How many employees are out sick? ■ What are next week's production requirements? ■ How much inventory is in the warehouse? ■ How many problems occurred when running payroll? ■ Which employees are on vacation next week? ■ How many products need to be made today?

Managerial   At the *managerial level*, employees are continuously evaluating company operations to hone the firm's abilities to identify, adapt to, and leverage change. A company that has a competitive advantage needs to adjust and revise its strategy constantly to remain ahead of fast-following competitors. Managerial decisions cover short- and medium-range plans, schedules, and budgets along with policies, procedures, and business objectives for the firm. They also allocate resources and monitor the performance of organizational subunits, including departments, divisions, process teams, project teams, and other work groups. *Managerial decisions* concern how the organization should achieve the goals and objectives set by its strategy, and they are usually the responsibility of mid-level management. Managerial decisions are considered *semistructured decisions*; they occur in situations in which a few established processes help to evaluate potential solutions, but not enough to lead to a definite recommended decision. For example, decisions about producing new products or changing employee benefits range from unstructured to semistructured. Figure 2.6 highlights the essential elements required for managerial decision making.

Strategic   At the *strategic level*, managers develop overall business strategies, goals, and objectives as part of the company's strategic plan. They also monitor the strategic performance of the organization and its overall direction in the political, economic, and competitive business environment. *Strategic decisions* involve higher level issues concerned with the overall direction of the organization; these decisions define the organization's overall goals and aspirations for the future. Strategic decisions are highly *unstructured decisions*, occurring in situations in which no procedures or rules exist to guide decision makers toward the correct choice. They are infrequent, extremely important, and typically related to long-term business strategy. Examples include the decision to enter a new market or even a new industry over, say, the next 3 years. In these types of decisions, managers rely on many sources of information, along with personal knowledge, to find solutions. Figure 2.6 highlights the essential elements required for strategic decision making.

MEASURING ORGANIZATIONAL BUSINESS DECISIONS

A *project* is a temporary activity a company undertakes to create a unique product, service, or result. For example, the construction of a new subway station is a project, as is a movie theater chain's adoption of a software program to allow online ticketing. Peter Drucker, a famous management writer, once said that if you cannot measure something, you cannot manage it. How do managers measure the progress of a complex business project?

Metrics are measurements that evaluate results to determine whether a project is meeting its goals. Two core metrics are critical success factors and key performance indicators. *Critical success factors (CSFs)* are the crucial steps companies perform to achieve their goals and objectives and implement their strategies (see Figure 2.7). *Key performance indicators (KPIs)* are the quantifiable metrics a company uses to evaluate progress toward critical success factors. KPIs are far more specific than CSFs.

The purpose of using KPIs is to focus attention on the tasks and processes that management has determined are most important for making progress toward declared goals and targets. KPIs differ per organization. For example, a KPI for a public company may be its stock price, while a KPI in government might be a low unemployment rate. KPIs will also differ for roles people play in the same organization. For example, a chief executive officer (CEO) might consider profitability as the most important KPI, while a sales team manager in the same company might consider successful service level agreement (SLA) delivery numbers as the most important KPI.

It is important to understand the relationship between critical success factors and key performance indicators. CSFs are elements crucial for a business strategy's success. KPIs measure the progress of CSFs with quantifiable measurements, and one CSF can have several KPIs. Of course, both categories will vary by company and industry. Imagine *improve graduation rates* as a CSF for a college. The KPIs to measure this CSF can include:

- Average grades by course and gender.
- Student dropout rates by gender and major.
- Average graduation rate by gender and major.
- Time spent in tutoring by gender and major.

The selection of appropriate KPIs depends, in part, on the organization's ability to actually measure the indicators. Typically, a management team will gather requirements and analyze

LO 2.2: Define critical success factors (CSFs) and key performance indicators (KPIs) and explain how managers use them to measure the success of MIS projects.

BUSINESS DRIVEN MIS

What Level are My Decisions?

For each of the following decisions determine if it is operational, managerial, or strategic.

Decision	Operational Decision	Managerial Decision	Strategic Decision
How many employees are out sick?			
What are the sales forecasts for next month?			
What was the impact of last month's marketing campaign discount on the primary product?			
How will an increase in the interest rate over the next year affect sales?			
How will changes in health insurance laws impact the company over the next 5 years?			
How many paychecks were incorrect during the last payroll run?			
What was the difference between forecast sales and actual sales last month?			
How will new tax laws impact business?			
What are next week's production schedules?			

correlations between metrics, but in the end, they must put the KPIs in practice and observe what behaviors the KPIs encourage. Each KPI should support the level above it so that all levels of the organization are working together toward the same strategic goals.

KPIs can focus on external and internal measurements. A common external KPI is *market share*, or the proportion of the market that a firm captures. We calculate it by dividing the firm's sales by the total market sales for the entire industry. Market share measures a firm's external performance relative to that of its competitors. For example, if a firm's total sales (revenues) are $2 million and sales for the entire industry are $10 million, the firm has captured 20 percent of the total market (2/10 = 20%) or a 20 percent market share.

A common internal KPI is *return on investment (ROI)*, which indicates the earning power of a project. We measure it by dividing the profitability of a project by the costs. This sounds easy, and for many departments where the projects are tangible and self-contained, it is; however, for projects that are intangible and cross departmental lines (such as MIS projects), ROI is challenging to measure. Imagine attempting to calculate the ROI of a fire extinguisher. If the fire extinguisher is never used, its ROI is low. If the fire extinguisher puts out a fire that could have destroyed the entire building, its ROI is astronomically high.

Although monitoring KPIs can help management identify deficiencies within an organization, it is up to management to decide how to correct them. Having too many KPIs can be problematic. It not only dilutes employee attention, it also makes it difficult for managers to prioritize indicators and make sure the key indicators get the attention they deserve.

To that end, many successful companies limit KPI scope to small sets of indicators that evaluate the success of individuals in the organization. Figure 2.8 displays a common approach is to defining KPIs.

Creating KPIs to measure the success of an MIS project offers similar challenges. Think about a firm's email system. How could managers track departmental costs and profits associated with company email? Measuring by volume does not account for profitability because one sales email could land a million-dollar deal, while 300 others might not generate any revenue.

Critical Success Factors

Crucial steps companies perform to achieve their goals and objectives and implement their strategies

- Create high-quality products
- Retain competitive advantages
- Reduce product costs
- Increase customer satisfaction
- Hire and retain the best business professionals

Key Performance Indicators

Quantifiable metrics a company uses to evaluate progress toward critical success factors

- Turnover rates of employees
- Percentage of help desk calls answered in the first minute
- Number of product returns
- Number of new customers
- Average customer spending

FIGURE 2.7

CSF and KPI Metrics

FIGURE 2.8

Method for Defining KPIs

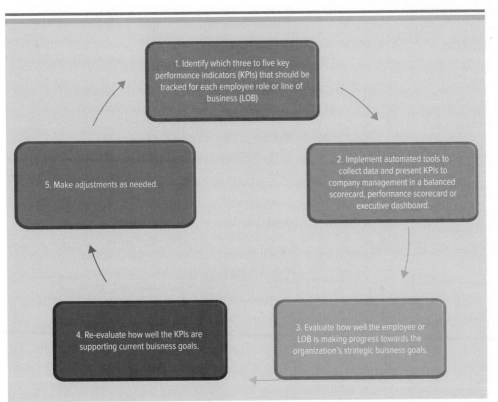

1. Identify which three to five key performance indicators (KPIs) that should be tracked for each employee role or line of business (LOB)

2. Implement automated tools to collect data and present KPIs to company management in a balanced scorecard, performance scorecard or executive dashboard.

3. Evaluate how well the employee or LOB is making progress towards the organization's strategic buisness goals.

4. Re-evaluate how well the KPIs are supporting current buisness goals.

5. Make adjustments as needed.

Nonrevenue-generating departments such as human resources and legal require email but will not be using it to generate profits. For this reason, many managers turn to higher-level metrics, such as efficiency and effectiveness, to measure MIS projects. *Best practices* are the most successful solutions or problem-solving methods that have been developed by a specific organization or industry. Measuring MIS projects helps determine the best practices for an industry.

Efficiency and Effectiveness Metrics

Efficiency MIS metrics measure the performance of MIS itself, such as throughput, transaction speed, and system availability. *Effectiveness MIS metrics* measure the impact MIS has on business processes and activities, including customer satisfaction and customer conversion rates. Efficiency focuses on the extent to which a firm is using its resources in an optimal way, whereas effectiveness focuses on how well a firm is achieving its goals and objectives. Peter Drucker offers a helpful distinction between efficiency and effectiveness: Doing things right addresses efficiency—getting the most from each resource. Doing the right things addresses effectiveness—setting the right goals and objectives and ensuring they are accomplished. Figure 2.9 describes a few of the common types of efficiency and effectiveness MIS metrics. KPIs that measure MIS projects include both efficiency and effectiveness metrics. Of course, these metrics are not as concrete as market share or ROI, but they do offer valuable insight into project performance.[5]

FIGURE 2.9

Common Types of Efficiency and Effectiveness Metrics

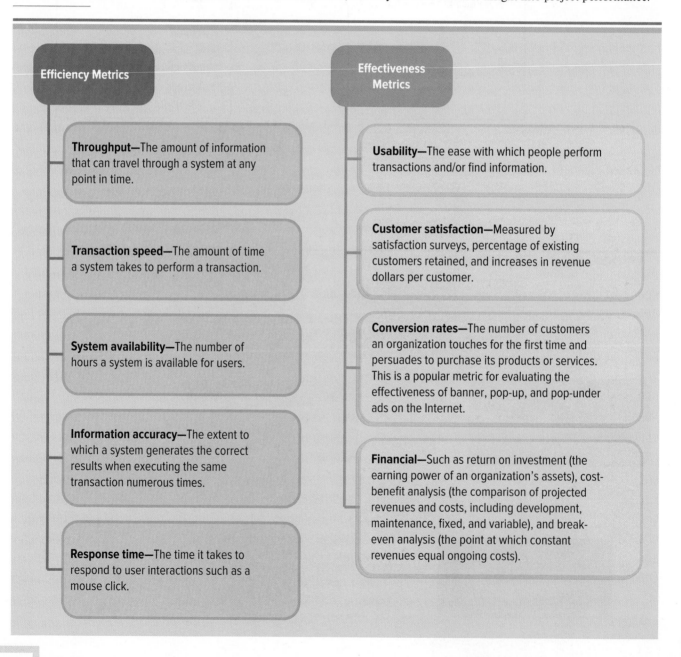

Efficiency Metrics

Throughput—The amount of information that can travel through a system at any point in time.

Transaction speed—The amount of time a system takes to perform a transaction.

System availability—The number of hours a system is available for users.

Information accuracy—The extent to which a system generates the correct results when executing the same transaction numerous times.

Response time—The time it takes to respond to user interactions such as a mouse click.

Effectiveness Metrics

Usability—The ease with which people perform transactions and/or find information.

Customer satisfaction—Measured by satisfaction surveys, percentage of existing customers retained, and increases in revenue dollars per customer.

Conversion rates—The number of customers an organization touches for the first time and persuades to purchase its products or services. This is a popular metric for evaluating the effectiveness of banner, pop-up, and pop-under ads on the Internet.

Financial—Such as return on investment (the earning power of an organization's assets), cost-benefit analysis (the comparison of projected revenues and costs, including development, maintenance, fixed, and variable), and break-even analysis (the point at which constant revenues equal ongoing costs).

BUSINESS DRIVEN DISCUSSION

Making business decisions is a key skill for all managers. Review the following list and, in a group, determine whether the question is focusing on efficiency, effectiveness, or both.

Is It Effective or Is It Efficient?

Business Decision	Efficiency	Effectiveness
What is the best route for dropping off products?		
Should we change suppliers?		
Should we reduce costs by buying lower-quality materials?		
Should we sell products to a younger market?		
Did we make our sales targets?		
What was the turnover rate of employees?		
What is the average customer spending?		
How many new customers purchased products?		
Did the amount of daily transactions increase?		
Is there a better way to restructure a store to increase sales?		

Large increases in productivity typically result from increases in effectiveness, which focus on CSFs. Efficiency MIS metrics are far easier to measure, however, so most managers tend to focus on them, often incorrectly, to measure the success of MIS projects. Consider measuring the success of automated teller machines (ATMs). Thinking in terms of MIS efficiency metrics, a manager would measure the number of daily transactions, the average amount per transaction, and the average speed per transaction to determine the success of the ATM. Although these offer solid metrics on how well the system is performing, they miss many of the intangible or value-added benefits associated with ATM effectiveness. Effectiveness MIS metrics might measure how many new customers joined the bank due to its ATM locations or the ATMs' ease of use. They can also measure increases in customer satisfaction due to reduced ATM fees or additional ATM services such as the sale of stamps and movie tickets, significant time savers and value-added features for customers. Being a great manager means using the added viewpoint offered by effectiveness MIS metrics to analyze all benefits associated with an MIS project.

Efficiency and effectiveness are definitely related. However, success in one area does not necessarily imply success in the other. Efficiency MIS metrics focus on the technology itself. Although these efficiency MIS metrics are important to monitor, they do not always guarantee effectiveness. Effectiveness MIS metrics are determined according to an organization's goals, strategies, and objectives. Here, it becomes important to consider a company's CSFs, such as a broad cost leadership strategy (Walmart, for example), as well as KPIs such as increasing new customers by 10 percent or reducing new-product development cycle times to six months. In the private sector, eBay continuously benchmarks its MIS projects for efficiency and effectiveness. Maintaining constant website availability and optimal throughput performance are CSFs for eBay.

Figure 2.10 depicts the interrelationships between efficiency and effectiveness. Ideally, a firm wants to operate in the upper right-hand corner of the graph, realizing significant increases in both efficiency and effectiveness. However, operating in the upper left-hand corner (minimal effectiveness with increased efficiency) or the lower right-hand corner (significant effectiveness with minimal efficiency) may be in line with an organization's particular strategies. In general, operating in the lower left-hand corner (minimal efficiency and minimal effectiveness) is not ideal for the operation of any organization.

FIGURE 2.10

The Interrelationships between
Efficiency and Effectiveness

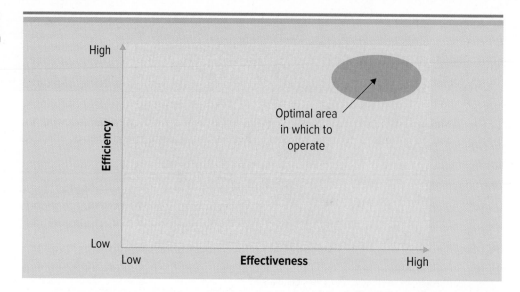

Regardless of what process is measured, how it is measured, and whether it is performed for the sake of efficiency or effectiveness, managers must set *benchmarks*, or baseline values the system seeks to attain. *Benchmarking* is a process of continuously measuring system results, comparing those results to optimal system performance (benchmark values), and identifying steps and procedures to improve system performance. Benchmarks help assess how an MIS project performs over time. For instance, if a system held a benchmark for response time of 15 seconds, the manager would want to ensure response time continued to decrease until it reached that point. If response time suddenly increased to 1 minute, the manager would know the system was not functioning correctly and could start looking into potential problems. Continuously measuring MIS projects against benchmarks provides feedback so managers can control the system.

USING MIS TO MAKE BUSINESS DECISIONS

LO 2.3: Classify the different operational support systems, managerial support systems, and strategic support systems and explain how managers can use these systems to make decisions and gain competitive advantages.

Now that we've reviewed the essentials of decision making, we are ready to understand the powerful benefits associated with using MIS to support managers making decisions.

A *model* is a simplified representation or abstraction of reality. Models help managers calculate risks, understand uncertainty, change variables, and manipulate time to make decisions. MIS support systems rely on models for computational and analytical routines that mathematically express relationships among variables. For example, a spreadsheet program, such as Microsoft Excel, might contain models that calculate market share or ROI. MIS has the capability and functionality to express far more complex modeling relationships that provide information, business intelligence, and knowledge. Figure 2.11 highlights the three primary types of management information systems available to support decision making across the company levels.

Operational Support Systems

Transactional information encompasses all the information contained within a single business process or unit of work, and its primary purpose is to support the performance of daily operational or structured decisions. Transactional information is created, for example, when customers are purchasing stocks, making an airline reservation, or withdrawing cash from an ATM. Managers use transactional information when making structured decisions at the operational level, such as when analyzing daily sales reports to determine how much inventory to carry.

Online transaction processing (OLTP) is the capture of transaction and event information using technology to (1) process the information according to defined business rules, (2) store the information, and (3) update existing information to reflect the new information. During OLTP, the organization must capture every detail of transactions and events. A *transaction processing system (TPS)* is the basic business system that serves the operational level (analysts) and assists in making structured decisions. The most common example of a TPS is an operational accounting system such as a payroll system or an order-entry system.

FIGURE 2.11

Primary Types of MIS Systems
for Decision Making

Unstructured

Semistructured

Structured

Executive
Information
Systems

Decision
Support
Systems

Transaction
Processing
System

Operational   Managerial   Strategic

Using systems thinking, we can see that the inputs for a TPS are *source documents*, the original transaction record. Source documents for a payroll system can include time sheets, wage rates, and employee benefit reports. Transformation includes common procedures such as creating, reading, updating, and deleting (commonly referred to as CRUD) employee records along with calculating the payroll and summarizing benefits. The output includes cutting the paychecks and generating payroll reports. Figure 2.12 demonstrates the systems thinking view of a TPS.[6]

FIGURE 2.12

Systems Thinking Example of
a TPS

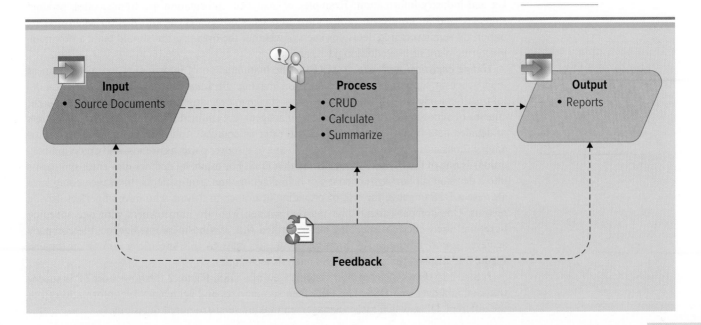

Input
• Source Documents

Process
• CRUD
• Calculate
• Summarize

Output
• Reports

Feedback

BUSINESS DRIVEN ANALYTICS

Will They Stay or Will They Go?

Workplace turnover is a huge issue for business today. Each time an employee walks out the door, the business loses large amounts of capital, including training investments, business process knowledge, and organizational performance history. Anything a business can do to keep employees satisfied and motivated will help the company succeed. Human resource analytics software can analyze employee data to help determine which employees are at risk of leaving the company. The following variables describes the types of data being analyzed to forecast potential employee turnover. Review each variable and explain how it is helping to predict employee turnover. Do you agree this is the best way to determine employee turnover? What other variables would you recommend a business collect to determine employee turnover?

- Time required for next promotion.
- Yearly bonus.
- Time since last raise.
- Employee performance.
- Manager performance.
- Attrition under employee's manager.
- Time off taken.
- Time off not taken.
- Stock grants over time.
- Location of employee.
- Location of employee's team.
- Location of employee's manager.

Managerial Support Systems

Analytical information encompasses all organizational information, and its primary purpose is to support the performance of managerial analysis or semistructured decisions. Analytical information includes transactional information along with other information such as market and industry information. Examples of analytical information are trends, sales, product statistics, and future growth projections. Managers use analytical information when making important semistructured decisions such as whether the organization should build a new manufacturing plant or hire additional sales reps.

Online analytical processing (OLAP) is the manipulation of information to create business intelligence in support of strategic decision making. *Decision support systems (DSSs)* model information using OLAP, which provides assistance in evaluating and choosing among different courses of action. DSSs enable high-level managers to examine and manipulate large amounts of detailed data from different internal and external sources. Analyzing complex relationships among thousands or even millions of data items to discover patterns, trends, and exception conditions is one of the key uses associated with a DSS. For example, doctors may enter symptoms into a decision support system so it can help diagnose and treat patients. Insurance companies also use a DSS to gauge the risk of providing insurance to drivers who have imperfect driving records. One company found that married women who are homeowners with one speeding ticket are rarely cited for speeding again. Armed with this business intelligence, the company achieved a cost advantage by lowering insurance rates to this specific group of customers. Figure 2.13 displays the common DSS analysis techniques.

Figure 2.14 shows the common systems view of a DSS. Figure 2.15 shows how TPSs supply transactional data to a DSS. The DSS then summarizes and aggregates the information from the different TPSs, which assist managers in making semistructured decisions.

FIGURE 2.13

Common DSS Analysis
Techniques

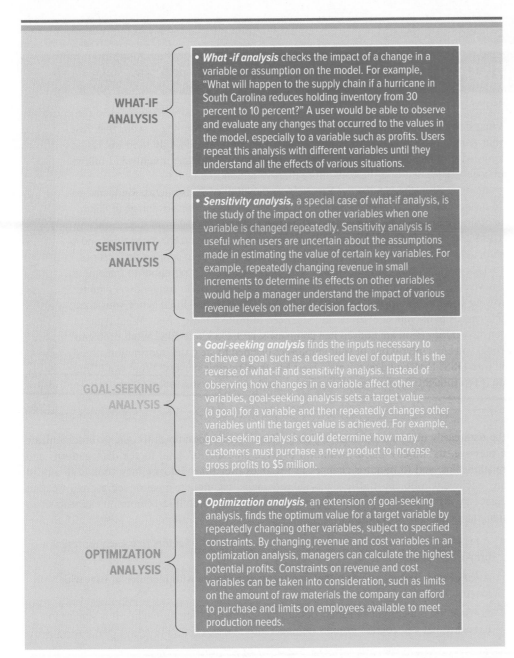

WHAT-IF ANALYSIS

• *What -if analysis* checks the impact of a change in a variable or assumption on the model. For example, "What will happen to the supply chain if a hurricane in South Carolina reduces holding inventory from 30 percent to 10 percent?" A user would be able to observe and evaluate any changes that occurred to the values in the model, especially to a variable such as profits. Users repeat this analysis with different variables until they understand all the effects of various situations.

SENSITIVITY ANALYSIS

• *Sensitivity analysis,* a special case of what-if analysis, is the study of the impact on other variables when one variable is changed repeatedly. Sensitivity analysis is useful when users are uncertain about the assumptions made in estimating the value of certain key variables. For example, repeatedly changing revenue in small increments to determine its effects on other variables would help a manager understand the impact of various revenue levels on other decision factors.

GOAL-SEEKING ANALYSIS

• *Goal-seeking analysis* finds the inputs necessary to achieve a goal such as a desired level of output. It is the reverse of what-if and sensitivity analysis. Instead of observing how changes in a variable affect other variables, goal-seeking analysis sets a target value (a goal) for a variable and then repeatedly changes other variables until the target value is achieved. For example, goal-seeking analysis could determine how many customers must purchase a new product to increase gross profits to $5 million.

OPTIMIZATION ANALYSIS

• *Optimization analysis*, an extension of goal-seeking analysis, finds the optimum value for a target variable by repeatedly changing other variables, subject to specified constraints. By changing revenue and cost variables in an optimization analysis, managers can calculate the highest potential profits. Constraints on revenue and cost variables can be taken into consideration, such as limits on the amount of raw materials the company can afford to purchase and limits on employees available to meet production needs.

Strategic Support Systems

Decision making at the strategic level requires both business intelligence and knowledge to support the uncertainty and complexity associated with business strategies. An *executive information system (EIS)* is a specialized DSS that supports senior-level executives and unstructured, long-term, nonroutine decisions requiring judgment, evaluation, and insight. These decisions do not have a right or wrong answer, only efficient and effective answers. Moving up through the organizational pyramid, managers deal less with the details (finer information) and more with meaningful aggregations of information (coarser information). *Granularity* refers to the level of detail in the model or the decision-making process. The greater the granularity, the deeper the level of detail or fineness of data (see Figure 2.16). A DSS differs from an EIS in that an EIS requires data from external sources to support unstructured decisions (see Figure 2.17). This is not to say that DSSs never use data from external sources, but typically, DSS semistructured decisions rely on internal data only.

Visualization produces graphical displays of patterns and complex relationships in large amounts of data. Executive information systems use visualization to deliver specific key information to top managers at a glance, with little or no interaction with the system. An *infographic* (information graphic) is a representation of information in a graphic format designed to make

BUSINESS DRIVEN ETHICS AND SECURITY

The Criminal in the Cube Next Door

What if the person sitting in the cubicle next to you were running a scam that cost your company $7 billion? An employee at a French bank allegedly used his inside knowledge of business processes to bypass the system and place roughly $73 billion in bogus trades that cost the bank more than $7 billion to unwind.

Findings from the U.S. Secret Service's examination of 23 incidents conducted by 26 insiders determined that 70 percent of the time, insiders took advantage of failures in business process rules and authorization mechanisms to steal from their company. These insiders were authorized and active computer users 78 percent of the time, and a surprising 43 percent used their own user name and password to commit their crimes.[7]

This is a daunting reminder that every employee has the potential to become a knowledgeable insider and, if started on a criminal path, to do tremendous damage to your company. Many DSSs and EISs contain the business intelligence your company needs to operate effectively, and you need to protect these assets. What types of sensitive information are housed in a company's TPS, DSS, and EIS? What problems could you encounter if one of your employees decided to steal the information stored in your DSS? How could you protect your EIS from unethical users? What would you do if you thought the person sharing your cube was a rogue insider?

the data easily understandable at a glance. People use infographics to quickly communicate a message, to simplify the presentation of large amounts of data, to see data patterns and relationships, and to monitor changes in variables over time. Infographics abound in almost any public environment—traffic signs, subway maps, tag clouds, musical scores, and weather charts are just a few examples, among a huge number of possibilities. Common elements of an infographic include the following:

- A *pie chart* a type of graph in which a circle is divided into sectors that each represent a proportion of the whole.

- A *bar chart* is a chart or graph that presents grouped data with rectangular bars with lengths proportional to the values that they represent.

- A *histogram* is a graphical display of data using bars of different heights. It is similar to a bar chart, but a histogram group's numbers into ranges.

FIGURE 2.14

Systems Thinking Example of a DSS

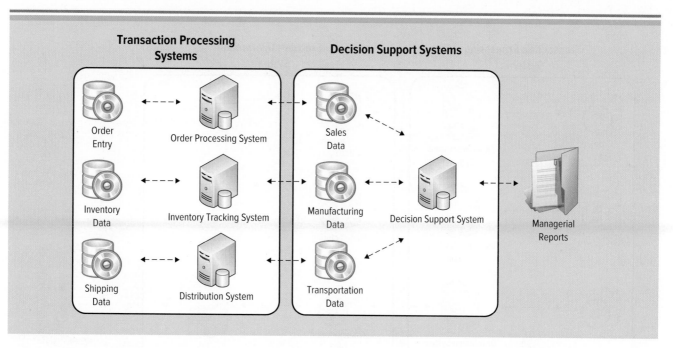

- A *sparkline* is a small embedded line graph that illustrates a single trend. Sparklines are often used in reports, presentations, dashboards, and scoreboards. They do not include axes or labels; context comes from the related content.

- A *time-series chart* is a graphical representation showing change of a variable over time. Time-series charts are used for data that changes continuously, such as stock prices. They allow for a clear visual representation of a change in one variable over a set amount of time (see Figure 2.18).

A common tool that supports visualization is a *digital dashboard*, which tracks KPIs and CSFs by compiling information from multiple sources and tailoring it to meet user needs. Following is a list of potential features included in a dashboard designed for a manufacturing team:

- A hot list of key performance indicators, refreshed every 15 minutes.

- A running line graph of planned versus actual production for the past 24 hours.

FIGURE 2.16

Information Levels throughout an Organization

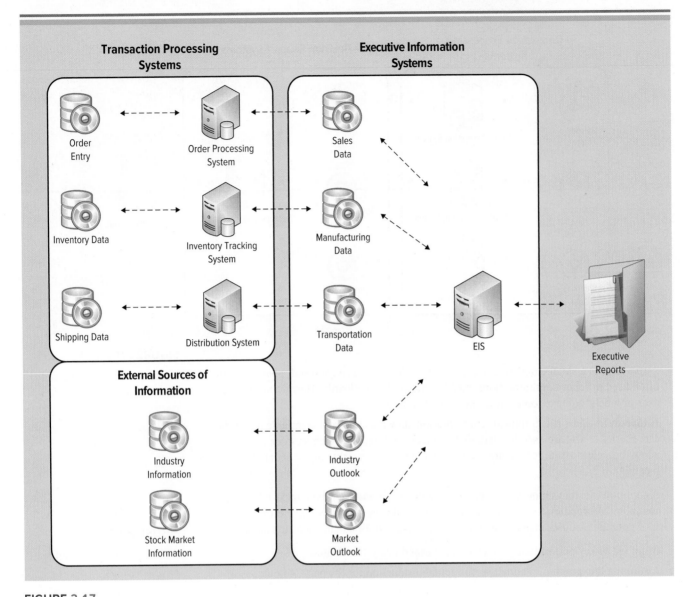

Transaction Processing Systems

Order Entry → Order Processing System

Inventory Data ↔ Inventory Tracking System

Shipping Data ↔ Distribution System

External Sources of Information

Industry Information

Stock Market Information

Executive Information Systems

Sales Data

Manufacturing Data

Transportation Data

Industry Outlook

Market Outlook

EIS

Executive Reports

FIGURE 2.17

Interaction between a TPS and EIS

- A table showing actual versus forecasted product prices and inventories.
- A list of outstanding alerts and their resolution status.
- A graph of stock market prices.

Digital dashboards, whether basic or comprehensive, deliver results quickly. As they become easier to use, more employees can perform their own analyses without inundating MIS staff with questions and requests for reports. Digital dashboards enable employees to move beyond reporting to using information to increase business performance directly. With them, employees can react to information as soon as it becomes available and make decisions, solve problems, and change strategies daily instead of monthly. Digital dashboards offer the analytical capabilities illustrated in Figure 2.19.

One thing to remember when making decisions is the old saying, "Garbage in, garbage out." If the transactional data used in the support system are wrong, then the managerial analysis will be wrong, and the DSS will simply assist in making a wrong decision faster. Managers should also ask, "What is the DSS *not* telling me before I make my final decision?"

LO 2.4: Describe artificial intelligence and identify its five main types.

USING AI TO MAKE BUSINESS DECISIONS

Executive information systems are starting to take advantage of artificial intelligence to facilitate unstructured strategic decision making. *Artificial intelligence (AI)* simulates human thinking and behavior, such as the ability to reason and learn. Its ultimate goal is to build a system

Pie Chart - Sales

Bar Chart - Sales

Histogram - Sales

Sparklines for Sales

Countries	1990	2008	2025	Line chart	Bar chart	Column chart
1 China	1,141	1,333	1,452			
2 India	849	1,140	1,398			
3 United States	250	304	352			
4 Indonesia	178	228	273			
5 Brazil	150	192	223			
6 Pakistan	108	166	226			
7 Bangladesh	116	160	198			
8 Nigeria	94	151	208			
9 Russia	149	143	137			
10 Japan	124	128	126			

Time Series Chart - Sales

that can mimic human intelligence. You might have come across the word *algorithm* if you have been into programming. An **algorithm** refers to a set of instructions that completes a task. In artificial intelligence, an algorithm tells the machines how to figure out answers to different issues or questions.

Intelligent systems are various commercial applications of artificial intelligence. They include sensors, software, and devices that emulate and enhance human capabilities, learn or

FIGURE 2.18

Visualization Chart Types

FIGURE 2.19

Digital Dashboard Analytical Capabilities

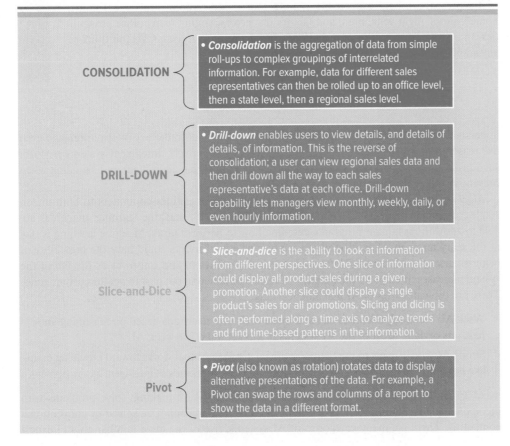

CONSOLIDATION
- **Consolidation** is the aggregation of data from simple roll-ups to complex groupings of interrelated information. For example, data for different sales representatives can then be rolled up to an office level, then a state level, then a regional sales level.

DRILL-DOWN
- **Drill-down** enables users to view details, and details of details, of information. This is the reverse of consolidation; a user can view regional sales data and then drill down all the way to each sales representative's data at each office. Drill-down capability lets managers view monthly, weekly, daily, or even hourly information.

Slice-and-Dice
- **Slice-and-dice** is the ability to look at information from different perspectives. One slice of information could display all product sales during a given promotion. Another slice could display a single product's sales for all promotions. Slicing and dicing is often performed along a time axis to analyze trends and find time-based patterns in the information.

Pivot
- **Pivot** (also known as rotation) rotates data to display alternative presentations of the data. For example, a Pivot can swap the rows and columns of a report to show the data in a different format.

BUSINESS DRIVEN START-UP

Robots are in the House!

What does a classroom look like in 2030? Can you imagine a beautiful steel robot flying around your classroom helping to answer questions and ensure you understand the material? A telepresence robot is a remote-controlled, wheeled device with a display to enable video chat and videoconferencing. Although telepresence robots aren't inexpensive, they are typically much more affordable than the travel costs or fees they might replace. They also enable much more interactivity than regular video chat. In a distance education class, for example, a telepresence robot can move around the room and interact face-to-face with individual students, just as an on-premises instructor might. Here are a few examples of telepresence robots:

- The doctor can see you now—virtually! iRobots are being used in hospitals where they make it possible for doctors to consult with patients, guide staff, and confer with other medical practitioners remotely. The robot travels around the hospital wearing a doctor coat, and on its face is a screen on which the doctor can be seen and see the patients and staff.

- Tired of Skype and long, boring conference calls? No more stagnant monitor in the meeting room. iRobots are being designed for a business environment to enhance telecommuting or teleconferencing. iRobots can sit at the table, write on the whiteboard, and engage in the conversation as if the person were actually at the meeting.

- Afraid your teenager is going to have a party while you are out for the evening or that Grandpa is eating all the sugary food that is bad for his diabetes? iRobots for in-home uses, such as mobile video chat, oversight of children or elderly people, and remote security monitoring are already hitting the market.

Telepresence robots can enable remote tour guides, administrative assistants, home visitors, night watchmen, and factory inspectors, among many other possibilities. In a group, discuss the pros and cons of telepresence robots. Can you think of any additional uses for a telepresence robot?

---

understand from experience, make sense of ambiguous or contradictory information, and even use reasoning to solve problems and make decisions effectively. Intelligent systems perform such tasks as boosting productivity in factories by monitoring equipment and signaling when preventive maintenance is required.

Machine learning is a type of artificial intelligence that enables computers to both understand concepts in the environment, and also to learn. With machine learning, machines are able to act without human programs detailing how to perform tasks. Machine learning is one of the scary terms in AI as it points to a future where AI robots could have the possibility of being smarter than humans. The machine learning comes in and improves as the life of the system increases. It employs the patterns of results obtained in the past to act for current goals. There are two categories of AI machine learning:

- Weak AI: Weak AI machines can still make their own decisions based on reasoning and past sets of data. Most of the AI systems in market today are weak AI.
- Strong AI: *Strong* refers to the field of artificial intelligence that works toward providing brain-like powers to AI machines; in effect, it works to make machines as intelligent as the humans.

AI systems increase the speed and consistency of decision making, solve problems with incomplete information, and resolve complicated issues that cannot be solved by conventional computing. There are many categories of AI systems; five of the most familiar are (1) expert

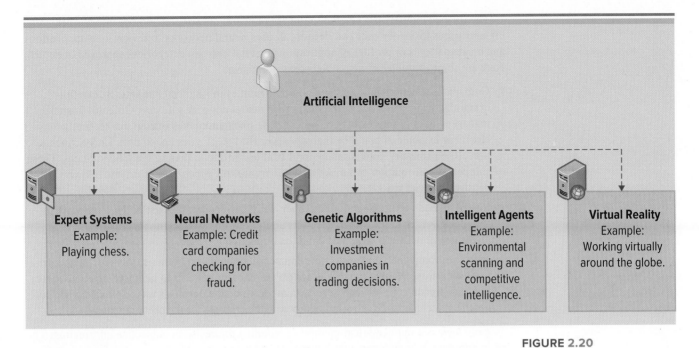

Artificial Intelligence

Expert Systems
Example: Playing chess.

Neural Networks
Example: Credit card companies checking for fraud.

Genetic Algorithms
Example: Investment companies in trading decisions.

Intelligent Agents
Example: Environmental scanning and competitive intelligence.

Virtual Reality
Example: Working virtually around the globe.

FIGURE 2.20

Examples of Artificial Intelligence

systems, (2) neural networks, (3) genetic algorithms, (4) intelligent agents, and (5) virtual reality (see Figure 2.20).

Expert Systems

Expert systems are computerized advisory programs that imitate the reasoning processes of experts in solving difficult problems. Typically, they include a knowledge base containing various accumulated experience and a set of rules for applying the knowledge base to each particular situation. Expert systems are the most common form of AI in the business arena because they fill the gap when human experts are difficult to find or retain or are too expensive. The best-known systems play chess and assist in medical diagnosis. *Case-based reasoning* is a method whereby new problems are solved based on the solutions from similar cases solved in the past. An auto mechanic who fixes an engine by recalling another car that exhibited similar symptoms is using case-based reasoning.

Machine vision is the ability of a computer to "see" by digitizing an image, processing the data it contains, and taking some kind of action. A machine-vision system uses a video camera to capture data and send it to the robot controller. Machine vision is similar in complexity to voice recognition and can be used for handwriting recognition, signature identification, and currency inspection. Two important specifications in any vision system are the sensitivity and the resolution. *Machine vision sensitivity* is the ability of a machine to see in dim light or to detect weak impulses at invisible wavelengths. *Machine vision resolution* is the extent to which a machine can differentiate between objects. In general, the better the resolution, the more confined the field of vision. Sensitivity and resolution are interdependent. All other factors held constant, increasing the sensitivity reduces the resolution, and improving the resolution reduces the sensitivity.

Neural Networks

A *neural network*, also called an artificial neural network, is a category of AI that attempts to emulate the way the human brain works. Neural networks analyze large quantities of information to establish patterns and characteristics when the logic or rules are unknown. Neural networks' many features include:

- Learning and adjusting to new circumstances on their own.
- Lending themselves to massive parallel processing.
- Functioning without complete or well-structured information.
- Coping with huge volumes of information with many dependent variables.
- Analyzing nonlinear relationships in information. (They have been called fancy regression analysis systems.)

The finance industry is a veteran in the use of neural network technology and has been relying on various forms for over two decades. It uses neural networks to review loan applications and create patterns or profiles of applications that fall into two categories—approved or denied. Here are some examples of neural networks in finance:

- Citibank uses neural networks to find opportunities in financial markets. By carefully examining historical stock market data with neural network software, Citibank financial managers learn of interesting coincidences or small anomalies (called market inefficiencies). For example, it could be that whenever IBM stock goes up, so does Unisys stock, or that a U.S. Treasury note is selling for 1 cent less in Japan than in the United States. These snippets of information can make a big difference to Citibank's bottom line in a very competitive financial market.

- Visa, American Express, and many other credit card companies use a neural network to spot peculiarities in individual accounts and follow up by checking for fraud. Visa estimates neural networks save it $50 million annually.

- Insurance companies along with state compensation funds and other carriers use neural network software to identify fraud. The system searches for patterns in billing charges, laboratory tests, and frequency of office visits. A claim for which the diagnosis was a sprained ankle but treatment included an electrocardiogram would be flagged for the account manager.[8]

Fuzzy logic is a mathematical method of handling imprecise or subjective information. The basic approach is to assign values between 0 and 1 to vague or ambiguous information. Zero represents information not included, whereas 1 represents inclusion or membership. For example, fuzzy logic is used in washing machines that determine by themselves how much water to use or how long to wash (they continue washing until the water is clean). In accounting and finance, fuzzy logic allows people to analyze information with subjective financial values (intangibles such as goodwill) that are very important considerations in economic analysis. Fuzzy logic and neural networks are often combined to express complicated and subjective concepts in a form that makes it possible to simplify the problem and apply rules that are executed with a level of certainty.

Deep learning is a process that employs specialized algorithms to model and study complex datasets; the method is also used to establish relationships among data and datasets. To understand deep learning, imagine a toddler whose first word is *dog*. The toddler learns what is (and what is not) a dog by pointing to objects and saying the word *dog*. The parent might say "Yes, that is a dog" or "No, that is not a dog." As the toddler continues to point to objects, he becomes more aware of the features that all dogs possess. What the toddler does, without knowing it, is to clarify a complex abstraction (the concept of dog) by building a hierarchy in which each level of abstraction is created with knowledge that was gained from the preceding layer of the hierarchy.

Genetic Algorithms

A *genetic algorithm* is an artificial intelligence system that mimics the evolutionary, survival-of-the-fittest process to generate increasingly better solutions to a problem. A genetic algorithm is essentially an optimizing system: It finds the combination of inputs that gives the best outputs. *Mutation* is the process within a genetic algorithm of randomly trying combinations and evaluating the success (or failure) of the outcome.

Genetic algorithms are best suited to decision-making environments in which thousands, or perhaps millions, of solutions are possible. Genetic algorithms can find and evaluate solutions with many more possibilities, faster and more thoroughly than a human. Organizations face decision-making environments for all types of problems that require optimization techniques, such as the following:

- Business executives use genetic algorithms to help them decide which combination of projects a firm should invest in, taking complicated tax considerations into account.

- Investment companies use genetic algorithms to help in trading decisions.

- Telecommunication companies use genetic algorithms to determine the optimal configuration of fiber-optic cable in a network that may include as many as 100,000 connection points. The genetic algorithm evaluates millions of cable configurations and selects the one that uses the least amount of cable.

Intelligent Agents

An *intelligent agent* is a special-purpose, knowledge-based information system that accomplishes specific tasks on behalf of its users. Intelligent agents usually have a graphical representation, such as "Sherlock Holmes" for an information search agent.

One of the simplest examples of an intelligent agent is a shopping bot. A *shopping bot* is software that will search several retailer websites and provide a comparison of each retailer's offerings, including price and availability. Increasingly, intelligent agents handle the majority of a company's Internet buying and selling and complete such processes as finding products, bargaining over prices, and executing transactions. Intelligent agents also have the capability to handle all supply chain buying and selling.

Another application for intelligent agents is in environmental scanning and competitive intelligence. For instance, an intelligent agent can learn the types of competitor information users want to track, continuously scan the web for it, and alert users when a significant event occurs.

What do cargo transport systems, book distribution centers, the video game market, and a flu epidemic have in common with an ant colony? They are all complex adaptive systems. By observing parts of Earth's ecosystem, such as ant colonies, artificial intelligence scientists can use hardware and software models that incorporate insect characteristics and behavior to (1) learn how people-based systems behave, (2) predict how they will behave under a given set of circumstances, and (3) improve human systems to make them more efficient and effective. This process of learning from ecosystems and adapting their characteristics to human and organizational situations is called biomimicry.

In the past few years, AI research has made much progress in modeling complex organizations as a whole with the help of multiagent systems. In a multiagent system, groups of intelligent agents can work independently and interact with each other. Agent-based modeling is a way of simulating human organizations by using multiple intelligent agents, each of which follows a set of simple rules and can adapt to changing conditions.

Agent-based modeling systems are being used to model stock market fluctuations, predict the escape routes people seek in a burning building, estimate the effects of interest rates on consumers with different types of debt, and anticipate how changes in conditions will affect the supply chain, to name just a few uses.

Virtual Reality

Virtual reality is a computer-simulated environment that can be a simulation of the real world or an imaginary world. Virtual reality is a fast-growing area of artificial intelligence that had its origins in efforts to build more natural, realistic, multisensory human–computer interfaces. Virtual reality enables telepresence by which users can be anywhere in the world and use virtual reality systems to work alone or together at a remote site. Typically, this involves using a virtual reality system to enhance the sight and touch of a human who is remotely manipulating equipment to accomplish a task. Examples range from virtual surgery, during which surgeon and patient may be on opposite sides of the globe, to the remote use of equipment in hazardous environments such as chemical plants and nuclear reactors.

Augmented reality is the viewing of the physical world with computer-generated layers of information added to it. *Google Glass* is a wearable computer with an optical head-mounted display (OHMD). Developed by Google, it adds an element of augmented reality to the user's world by displaying information in a smart phone–like hands-free format. Google Glass became officially available to the general public in May 2014. Before that, users were required to receive invitations before they could try Google Glass. A *virtual workplace* is a work environment that is not located in any one physical space. It is usually in a network of several places, connected through the Internet, without regard to geographic borders. Employees can interact in a collaborated environment regardless of where they may happen to be in the world. A virtual workplace integrates hardware, people, and online processes. A *haptic interface* uses technology allowing humans to interact with a computer through bodily sensations and movements—for example, a cell phone vibrating in your pocket. A haptic interface is primarily implemented and applied in virtual reality environments and is used in virtual workplaces to enable employees to shake hands, demonstrate products, and collaborate on projects.

Virtual reality (VR) and augmented reality are two sides of the same coin. You could think of augmented reality (AR) as a form of virtual reality with one foot in the real world:

BUSINESS DRIVEN INNOVATION

My Virtual Reality Check

Virtual reality is the use of computer technology to create a simulated environment. Unlike traditional user interfaces, VR places the user inside an experience. Instead of viewing a screen in front of them, users are immersed and able to interact with 3-D worlds. By simulating as many senses as possible, such as vision, hearing, touch, even smell, the computer is transformed into a gatekeeper to this artificial world. The only limits to near-real VR experiences are the availability of content and cheap computing power. Here are a few of the leaders in virtual reality:

1. Soccer training with a virtual reality match.
2. Find your own virtual personal trainer at a simulated gym.
3. Immerse yourself in the Minecraft metaverse.
4. Six Flags is turning to virtual reality to enhance its rollercoaster experience.
5. The U.S. military uses virtual reality therapy to treat post-traumatic stress disorder.
6. Virtual reality can train surgeons for complex operations.
7. Students can attend a virtual field trip.
8. Prospective students can take virtual campus tours.
9. Simulate public speaking—a common phobia for many.
10. Amnesty International uses virtual reality to help people appreciate the ravages of the Syrian conflict.

In a group, create a new product or service using virtual reality. What are the advantages and disadvantages of virtual reality? What potential social problems do you foresee with virtual reality?

augmented reality simulates artificial objects in the real environment; virtual reality creates an artificial environment to inhabit.

In augmented reality, the computer uses sensors and algorithms to determine the position and orientation of a camera. AR technology then renders the 3-D graphics as they would appear from the viewpoint of the camera, superimposing the computer-generated images over a user's view of the real world.

In virtual reality, the computer uses similar sensors and math. However, rather than locating a real camera within a physical environment, the position of the user's eyes are located within the simulated environment. If the user's head turns, the graphics react accordingly. Rather than compositing virtual objects and a real scene, VR technology creates a convincing, interactive world for the user.

section 2.2 | Business Processes

LEARNING OUTCOMES

2.5 Explain the value of business processes for a company and differentiate between customer-facing and business-facing processes.

2.6 Demonstrate the value of business process modeling and compare As-Is and To-Be models.

2.7 Differentiate among automation, streamlining, and reengineering.

MANAGING BUSINESS PROCESSES

Most companies pride themselves on providing breakthrough products and services for customers. But if customers do not receive what they want quickly, accurately, and hassle-free, even fantastic offerings will not prevent a company from annoying customers and ultimately eroding its own financial performance. To avoid this pitfall and protect its competitive advantage, a company must continually evaluate all the business processes in its value chain. Recall from Chapter 1 that a *business process* is a standardized set of activities that accomplish a specific task, such as processing a customer's order. Business processes transform a set of inputs into a set of outputs—goods or services—for another person or process by using people and tools. Understanding business processes helps a manager envision how the entire company operates.

Improving the efficiency and effectiveness of its business processes will improve the firm's value chain. The goal of this section is to expand on Porter's value chain analysis by detailing the powerful value-adding relationships between business strategies and core business processes. Figure 2.21 illustrates several common business processes.

The processes outlined in Figure 2.21 reflect functional thinking. Some processes, such as a programming process, may be contained wholly within a single department. However, most, such as ordering a product, are cross-functional or cross-departmental processes and span the entire organization. The order-to-delivery process focuses on the entire customer order process across functional departments (see Figure 2.22). Another example is product realization,

FIGURE 2.21

Sample Business Processes

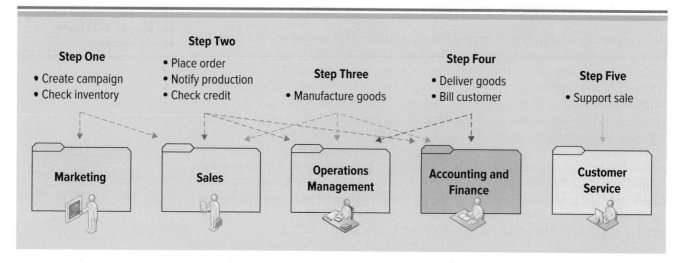

Step One
- Create campaign
- Check inventory

Step Two
- Place order
- Notify production
- Check credit

Step Three
- Manufacture goods

Step Four
- Deliver goods
- Bill customer

Step Five
- Support sale

Marketing **Sales** **Operations Management** **Accounting and Finance** **Customer Service**

FIGURE 2.22

Five Steps in the Order-to-Delivery Business Process

which includes not only the way a product is developed but also the way it is marketed and serviced. Some other cross-functional business processes are taking a product from concept to market, acquiring customers, loan processing, providing postsales service, claim processing, and reservation handling.

Customer-facing processes, also called front-office processes, result in a product or service received by an organization's external customer. They include fulfilling orders, communicating with customers, and sending out bills and marketing information. *Business-facing processes*, also called back-office processes, are invisible to the external customer but essential to the effective management of the business; they include goal setting, day-to-day planning, giving performance feedback and rewards, and allocating resources. Figure 2.23 displays the different categories of customer-facing and business-facing processes along with an example of each.[9]

A company's strategic vision should provide guidance on which business processes are core, that is, which are directly linked to the firm's critical success factors. Mapping these core business processes to the value chain reveals where the processes touch the customers and affect their perceptions of value. This type of map conceptualizes the business as a value delivery system, allowing managers to ensure all core business processes are operating as efficiently and effectively as possible.

A *business process patent* is a patent that protects a specific set of procedures for conducting a particular business activity. A firm can create a value chain map of the entire industry to extend critical success factors and business process views beyond its boundaries. *Core processes* are business processes, such as manufacturing goods, selling products, and providing service, that make up the primary activities in a value chain.

A *static process* uses a systematic approach in an attempt to improve business effectiveness and efficiency continuously. Managers constantly attempt to optimize static process. Examples of static processes include running payroll, calculating taxes, and creating financial statements. A *dynamic process* is continuously changing and provides business solutions to ever-changing business operations. As the business and its strategies change, so do the dynamic processes. Examples of dynamic processes include managing layoffs of employees, changing order levels based on currency rates, and canceling business travel due to extreme weather.

FIGURE 2.23

Customer-Facing, Industry-Specific, and Business-Facing Processes

Customer-Facing Processes
Order processing
Customer service
Sales process
Customer billing
Order shipping

Industry-Specific Customer-Facing Processes
Banking—Loan processing
Insurance—Claims processing
Government—Grant allocation
Hotel—Reservation handling
Airline—Baggage handling

Business-Facing Processes
Strategic planning
Tactical planning
Budget forecasting
Training
Purchasing raw materials

Systems thinking offers a great story to help differentiate between static and dynamic processes. If you throw a rock in the air, you can predict where it will land. If you throw a bird in the air, you can't predict where it will land. The bird, a living dynamic, system, will sense its environment and fly in any direction. The bird gathers and processes input and interacts with its environment. The rock is an example of a static process, and the bird is an example of a dynamic process. Organizations have people and are characteristically dynamic, making it difficult to predict how the business will operate. Managers must anticipate creating and deploying both static and dynamic processes.

BUSINESS PROCESS MODELING

LO 2.6: Demonstrate the value of business process modeling and compare As-Is and To-Be models.

Business process modeling, or *mapping*, is the activity of creating a detailed flowchart or process map of a work process that shows its inputs, tasks, and activities in a structured sequence. A *business process model* is a graphic description of a process, showing the sequence of process tasks, which is developed for a specific purpose and from a selected viewpoint. A set of one or more process models details the many functions of a system or subject area with graphics and text, and its purpose is to:

- Expose process detail gradually and in a controlled manner.
- Encourage conciseness and accuracy in describing the process model.
- Focus attention on the process model interfaces.
- Provide a powerful process analysis and consistent design vocabulary. (See the end of the chapter for business process model examples.)

Business Process Model and Notation (BPMN) is a graphical notation that depicts the steps in a business process. BPMN provides businesses with a graphical view of the end-to-end flow of their business processes. Diagramming business processes allows for easy communication and understanding of how core business processes are helping or hindering the business. Figure 2.24 displays the standard notation from www.BPMN.org, and Figure 2.25 displays a sample BPMN diagram for hiring a taxi cab.[10]

Business process modeling usually begins with a functional process representation of the process problem, or an As-Is process model. *As-Is process models* represent the current state of the operation that has been mapped, without any specific improvements or changes to existing processes. The next step is to build a To-Be process model that displays how the process problem will be solved or implemented. *To-Be process models* show the results of applying change improvement opportunities to the current (As-Is) process model. This approach ensures that the process is fully and clearly understood before the details of a process solution are decided on. The To-Be process model shows how "the what" is to be realized. Figure 2.26 displays the As-Is and To-Be process models for ordering a hamburger.

As-Is and To-Be process models are both integral in business process reengineering projects because these diagrams are very powerful in visualizing the activities, processes, and data flow

FIGURE 2.24

BPMN Notation

BUSINESS PROCESS MODEL AND NOTATION (BPMN)	
EVENT	*BPMN event* is anything that happens during the course of a business process. An event is represented by a circle in a business process model. In Figure 2.25, the events include customer requests, time requests, or the end of the process.
ACTIVITY	*BPMN activity* is a task in a business process. An activity is any work that is being performed in a process. An activity is represented by a rounded-corner rectangle in a business process model. In Figure 2.25, the activities include checking availability, picking up the customers, and confirming the booking.
GATEWAY	*BPMN gateway* is used to control the flow of a process. Gateways handle the forking, merging, and joining of paths within a process. Gateways are represented by a diamond shape in a business process model. In Figure 2.25, the gateways include determining availability status or accepting/declining the request.
FLOW	*BPMN flows* display the path in which the process flows. Flows are represented by arrows in a business process model. In Figure 2.25, the arrows show the path the customer takes through the taxi cab booking process.[11]

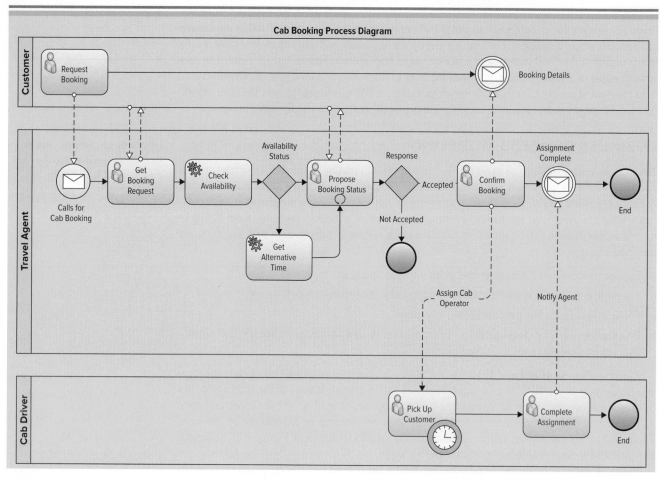

FIGURE 2.25

BPMN Sample Diagram for
Hiring a Taxi Cab

FIGURE 2.26

As-Is and To-Be Process Model
for Ordering a Hamburger

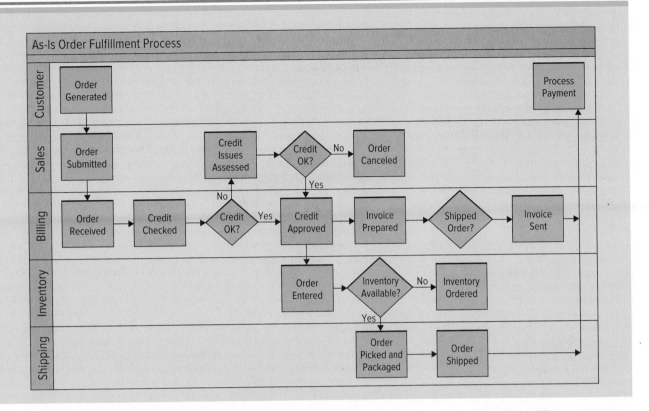

As-Is Order Fulfillment Process

FIGURE 2.27

As-Is Process Model for Order Fulfillment

of an organization. Figure 2.27 illustrates an As-Is process model of the order-to-delivery process, using swim lanes to represent the relevant departments. The *swim lane* layout arranges the steps of a business process into a set of rows depicting the various elements.

You need to be careful not to become inundated in excessive detail when creating an As-Is process model. The primary goal is to simplify, eliminate, and improve the To-Be processes. Process improvement efforts focus on defining the most efficient and effective process identifying all of the illogical, missing, or irrelevant processes.

Investigating business processes can help an organization find bottlenecks, remove redundant tasks, and recognize smooth-running processes. For example, a florist might have a key success factor of reducing delivery time. A florist that has an inefficient ordering process or a difficult distribution process will be unable to achieve this goal. Taking down inaccurate orders, recording incorrect addresses, or experiencing shipping delays can cause errors in the delivery process. Improving order entry, production, or scheduling processes can improve the delivery process.

Business processes should drive MIS choices and should be based on business strategies and goals (see Figure 2.28). Only after determining the most efficient and effective business process should an organization choose the MIS that supports that business process. Of course, this does not always happen, and managers may find themselves in the difficult position of changing a business process because the system cannot support the ideal solution (see Figure 2.28). Managers who make MIS choices and only then determine how their business processes should perform typically fail.

USING MIS TO IMPROVE BUSINESS PROCESSES

LO 2.7: Differentiate among automation, streamlining, and reengineering.

Workflow includes the tasks, activities, and responsibilities required to execute each step in a business process. Understanding workflow, customers' expectations, and the competitive environment provides managers with the necessary ingredients to design and evaluate alternative business processes in order to maintain competitive advantages when internal or external circumstances change. *Workflow control systems* monitor processes to ensure tasks, activities, and responsibilities are executed as specified.

Alternative business processes should be effective (deliver the intended results) and efficient (consume the least amount of resources for the intended value). They should also be adaptable or flexible and support change as customers, market forces, and technology shift.

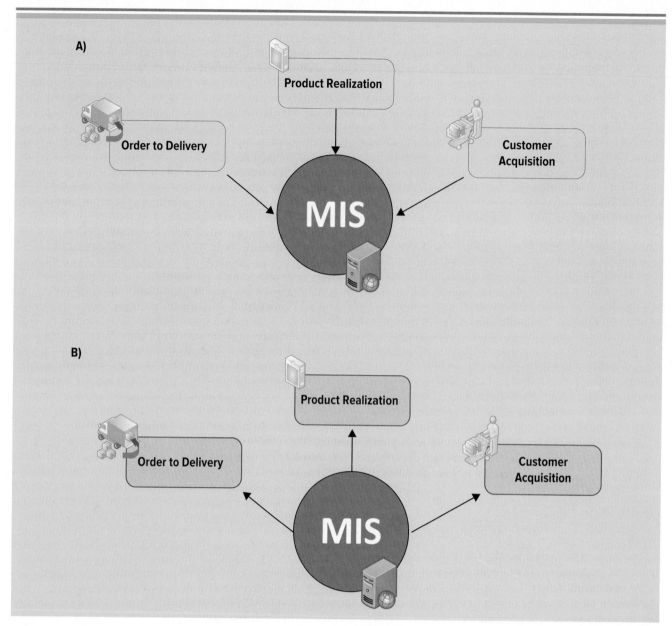

FIGURE 2.28

For Best Results, Business Processes Should Drive MIS Choices

Figure 2.29 shows the three primary types of business process change available to firms and the business areas in which they are most often effective. How does a company know whether it needs to undertake the giant step of changing core business processes? Three conditions indicate the time is right to initiate a business process change:

1. There has been a pronounced shift in the market the process was designed to serve.

2. The company is markedly below industry benchmarks on its core processes.

3. To regain competitive advantage, the company must leapfrog competition on key dimensions.[12]

Operational Business Processes—Automation

Operational business processes are static, routine, daily business processes such as stocking inventory, checking out customers, or daily opening and closing processes. *Operationalized analytics* makes analytics part of a business process. Improving business processes is critical to staying competitive in today's electronic marketplace. Organizations must improve their business processes because customers are demanding better products and services; if customers do not receive what they want from one supplier, often they can simply click a mouse to find many other choices. *Business process improvement* attempts to understand and measure the current process and make performance improvements accordingly. Figure 2.30 displays a typical business process improvement model.[13]

FIGURE 2.29

Primary Types of Business
Process Change

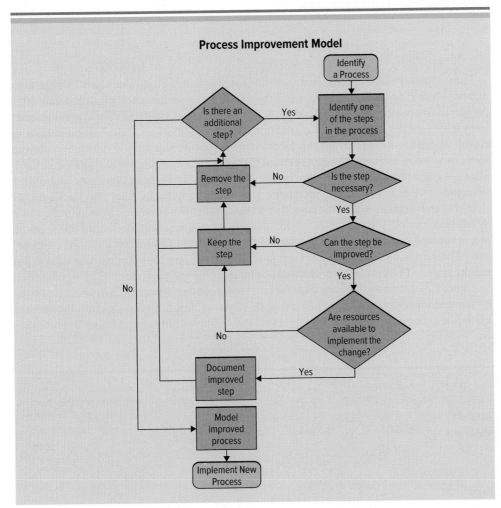

FIGURE 2.30

Business Process Improvement
Model

Process Improvement Model

Identify a Process

Is there an additional step? — Yes → Identify one of the steps in the process

Is the step necessary? — No → Remove the step

Yes

Can the step be improved? — No → Keep the step

Yes

Are resources available to implement the change? — No → Keep the step

Yes → Document improved step

Model improved process

Implement New Process

BUSINESS DRIVEN GLOBALIZATION

IBM Watson taking over the world

Watson is an IBM supercomputer that combines artificial intelligence (AI) and sophisticated analytical software for optimal performance as a "question answering" machine. The supercomputer is named for IBM's founder, Thomas J. Watson.

The Watson supercomputer processes at a rate of 80 teraflops (trillion floating-point operations per second). To replicate (or surpass) a high-functioning human's ability to answer questions, Watson accesses 90 servers with a combined data store of over 200 million pages of information, which it processes against 6 million logic rules. The device and its data are self-contained in a space that could accommodate 10 refrigerators.

To showcase its abilities, Watson challenged two top-ranked players on *Jeopardy!* and beat champions Ken Jennings and Brad Rutter in 2011. The Watson avatar sat between the two other contestants, as a human competitor would, while its considerable bulk sat on a different floor of the building. Like the other contestants, Watson had no Internet access.[14]

In the practice round, Watson demonstrated a humanlike ability for complex wordplay, correctly responding, for example, to "Classic candy bar that's a female Supreme Court justice" with "What is Baby Ruth Ginsburg?" Rutter noted that although the retrieval of information is "trivial" for Watson and difficult for a human, the human is still better at the complex task of comprehension. Nevertheless, machine learning allows Watson to examine its mistakes against the correct answers to see where it erred and so inform future responses.

Early adopters of MIS recognized that they could enhance their value chain through automation, which reduces costs and increases the speed of performing activities. *Automation* is the process of computerizing manual tasks, making them more efficient and effective, and dramatically lowering operational costs. Payroll offers an excellent example. Calculating and tracking payroll for 5,000 employees is a highly labor-intensive process requiring 30 full-time employees. Every two weeks, accounting employees must gather everyone's hours worked, cross-check with wage rates, and then calculate the amount due, minus taxes, and other withholding such as pension contributions and insurance premiums, to create the paychecks. They also track benefits, sick time, and vacation time. If the payroll process is automated, however, one employee can easily calculate payroll, track withholding and deductions, and create paychecks for 5,000 people in a few hours, since everything is performed by the system. Automation improves efficiency and effectiveness and reduces head count, lowering overall operational costs. Transaction processing systems (TPS) are primarily used to automate business processes.

Figure 2.31 illustrates the basic steps for business process improvement. Organizations begin by documenting what they currently do; then they establish a way to measure the process, follow the process, measure the performance, and finally identify improvement opportunities

FIGURE 2.31

Steps in Business Process Improvement

based on the collected information. The next step is to implement process improvements and measure the performance of the new improved process. The loop repeats over and over again as it is continuously improved.[15]

This method of improving business processes is effective for obtaining gradual, incremental improvement. However, several factors have accelerated the need to improve business processes radically. The most obvious is technology. New technologies (such as wireless Internet access) rapidly bring new capabilities to businesses, thereby raising the competitive bar and the need to improve business processes dramatically. For example, Amazon.com reinvented the supply chain for selling books online. After gaining from automation, companies began to look for new ways to use MIS to improve operations, and managers recognized the benefits of pairing MIS with business processes by streamlining. We look at this improvement method next.

Robotic process automation (RPA) is the use of software with artificial intelligence (AI) and machine learning capabilities to handle high-volume, repeatable tasks that previously required a human to perform. Tasks such as running payroll and stocking and reordering inventory will be completely automated with the use of RPA. The difference between RPA and traditional MIS automation is RPA software's ability to be aware and adapt to changing circumstances, exceptions, and new situations. Once RPA software has been trained to capture and interpret the actions of specific processes in existing software applications, it can then manipulate data, activate responses, initiate new actions, and communicate with other systems autonomously. Companies of all sizes will benefit by implementing RPA that can expedite back-office and middle-office tasks in a wide range of industries, including insurance, finance, procurement, supply chain management (SCM), accounting, customer relationship management (CRM), and human resource management (HRM).

RPA software works best when many different, complicated systems are required to work together to perform a business process. For example, if a zip code is missing from an HR form, traditional automation software would flag the form as having an exception, and an employee would correct the problem by finding the right zip code. After completing the form, the employee would send it to payroll, where another employee would enter the correct information into the payroll system. With RPA, the software can adapt, self-learn, and self-correct the error and even interact with the payroll system without human assistance. Though it is expected that automation software will replace up to 140 million full-time employees worldwide by the year 2025, many high-quality jobs will be created for those who are able to maintain and improve RPA software.

Managerial Business Processes—Streamlining

Managerial business processes are semidynamic, semiroutine, monthly business processes such as resource allocation, sales strategy, or manufacturing process improvements. *Streamlining* improves business process efficiencies by simplifying or eliminating unnecessary steps. *Bottlenecks* occur when resources reach full capacity and cannot handle any additional demands; they limit throughput and impede operations. A computer working at its maximum capacity will be unable to handle increased demand and will become a bottleneck in the process. Streamlining removes bottlenecks, an important step if the efficiency and capacity of a business process are being increased. It also eliminates redundancy. *Redundancy* occurs when a task or activity is unnecessarily repeated, for example, if both the sales department and the accounting department check customer credit.

Automating a business process that contains bottlenecks or redundancies will magnify or amplify these problems if they are not corrected first. Here's an example based on a common source of tension in an organization. Increasing orders is a standard KPI for most marketing/sales departments. To meet this KPI, the sales department tends to say yes to any customer request, such as for rush or custom orders. Reducing *cycle time*, the time required to process an order, is a common KPI for operations management. Rush and custom orders tend to create bottlenecks, causing operations to fall below its benchmarked cycle time. Removing these bottlenecks, however, can create master streamlined business processes that deliver both standard and custom orders reliably and profitably. The goal of streamlining is not only to automate but also to improve by monitoring, controlling, and changing the business process.

FedEx streamlined every business process to provide a CSF of speedy and reliable delivery of packages. It created one central hub in Memphis, Tennessee, that processed all its orders. It purchased its own planes to be sure it could achieve the desired level of service. FedEx

BUSINESS DRIVEN MIS

Email Overload—Just Streamline It

The biggest problem with email is that it interferes with workflow. Many employees stop what they are working on and begin checking new email as soon as it arrives. If they do not have the time or capacity to answer it immediately, however, they leave it in the inbox, creating a bottleneck. This process continues all day, and eventually, the inbox is overflowing with hundreds of emails, most of which require a response or action. Employees begin dreading email and feel stressed because their workflow process is off track, and they do not know which tasks need to be completed and when.

To streamline workflow, you can designate certain times for email processing (at the top of the hour or for 30 minutes at three set times a day, for example). Turning off email notification also ensures you are not interrupted during your workflow. When you do begin to check your emails, review them one at a time from top to bottom and deal with each one immediately. Reply, put a note on your to-do list, forward the email, or delete it. Now you are working far more efficiently and effectively, and you are less stressed because your inbox is empty.[16]

Choose a process in your life that is inefficient or ineffective and causing you stress. Using the principles of streamlining, remove the bottlenecks and reduce redundancies. Be sure to diagram the As-Is process and your newly created To-Be process.

combined MIS and traditional distribution and logistics processes to create a competitive advantage. FedEx soon identified another market segment of customers who cared a little less about speed and were willing to trade off early-morning delivery for delivery any time *within* the next day at a significantly lower price. The firm had to reevaluate its strategy and realign its business processes to capture this market segment. Had Federal Express focused only on improving its traditional delivery process to handle increased volume faster and more reliably, it could have missed an entire customer segment.

Strategic Business Processes—Reengineering

Strategic business processes are dynamic, nonroutine, long-term business processes such as financial planning, expansion strategies, and stakeholder interactions. The flat world is bringing more companies and more customers into the marketplace, greatly increasing competition. Wine wholesalers in the United States must now compete globally, for instance, because customers can just as easily order a bottle of wine from a winery in France as from them. Companies need breakthrough performance and business process changes just to stay in the game. As the rate of change increases, companies looking for rapid change and dramatic improvement are turning to *business process reengineering (BPR)*, the analysis and redesign of workflow within and between enterprises.

Figure 2.32 highlights an analogy to process improvement by explaining the different means of traveling along the same route. A company could improve the way it travels by changing from foot to horse and then from horse to car. With a BPR mind-set, however, it would look beyond automating and streamlining to find a completely different approach. It would ignore the road and travel by air to get from point A to point B. Companies often follow the same indirect path for doing business, not realizing there might be a different, faster, and more direct way.

An organization can reengineer its cross-departmental business processes or an individual department's business processes to help meet its CSFs and KPIs. When selecting a business process to reengineer, wise manager's focus on those core processes that are critical to performance, rather than on marginal processes that have little impact. The effort to reengineer a business process as a strategic activity requires a different mind-set than that required in continuous business process improvement programs. Because companies have tended to overlook

———— Better, Faster, Cheaper ————→

FIGURE 2.32

Different Ways to Travel the Same Route

the powerful contribution that processes can make to strategy, they often undertake process improvement efforts by using their current processes as the starting point. Managers focusing on reengineering can instead use several criteria to identify opportunities:

- Is the process broken?
- Is it feasible that reengineering this process will succeed?
- Does it have a high impact on the agency's strategic direction?
- Does it significantly affect customer satisfaction?
- Is it antiquated?
- Does it fall far below best-in-class?
- Is it crucial for productivity improvement?
- Will savings from automation be clearly visible?
- Is the return on investment from implementation high and preferably immediate?

BPR relies on a different school of thought than business process improvement. *In the extreme,* BPR assumes the current process is irrelevant, does not work, or is broken and must be overhauled from scratch. Starting from such a clean slate enables business process designers to disassociate themselves from today's process and focus on a new process. It is as if they are projecting themselves into the future and asking: What should the process look like? What do customers want it to look like? What do other employees want it to look like? How do best-in-class companies do it? How can new technology facilitate the process?

Figure 2.33 displays the basic steps in a business process reengineering effort. It begins with defining the scope and objectives of the reengineering project and then takes the process designers through a learning process with customers, employees, competitors, and new technology. Given this knowledge base, the designers can create a plan of action based on the gap between current processes, technologies, and structures and their vision of the processes of the future. It is then top management's job to implement the chosen solution.[17]

System thinking plays a big role in BPR. Automation and streamlining operate departmentally, whereas BPR occurs at the systems level or companywide level and the end-to-end view of a process.

Creating value for the customer is the leading reason for instituting BPR, and MIS often plays an important enabling role. Fundamentally new business processes enabled Progressive Insurance to slash its claims settlement time from 31 days to four hours, for instance. Typically, car insurance companies follow this standard claims resolution process: The customer gets into an accident, has the car towed, and finds a ride home. The customer then calls the insurance company to begin the claims process, which includes an evaluation of the damage,

FIGURE 2.33

Business Process Reengineering Model

BUSINESS DRIVEN DEBATE

The Battle for Your body

Google Glass and Apple's iWatch have been dominating headlines as the two big products get set to take over the world of wearable technology. The introduction of these two innovative products is creating a great deal of speculation on the future of wearable technology. Supporters for wearable technologies believe "it is the only natural step into our global transformation into constantly connected cyborgs." Critics of wearable technologies believe that the "absurdity of wearing a computer on your face will never be considered mainstream." Do you agree or disagree that the future of technology is wearable?[18]

assignment of fault, and an estimate of the cost of repairs, which usually takes about a month (see Figure 2.34). Progressive Insurance's innovation was to offer a mobile claims process. When a customer has a car accident, he or she calls in the claim on the spot. The Progressive claims adjuster comes to the accident site, surveying the scene and taking digital photographs. The adjuster then offers the customer on-site payment, towing services, and a ride home. A true BPR effort does more for a company than simply improve a process by performing it better, faster, and cheaper. Progressive Insurance's BPR effort redefined best practices for an entire industry.[19] Figures 2.35 through 2.38 provide additional examples of business process modeling.

FIGURE 2.34

Auto Insurance Claims Processes

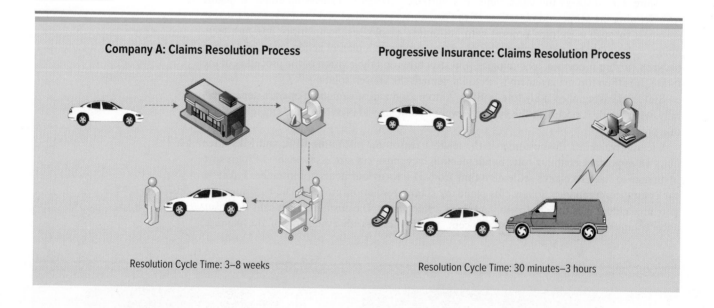

Company A: Claims Resolution Process

Progressive Insurance: Claims Resolution Process

Resolution Cycle Time: 3–8 weeks

Resolution Cycle Time: 30 minutes–3 hours

FIGURE 2.35

Online Sales Process Model

FIGURE 2.36

Online Banking Process Model

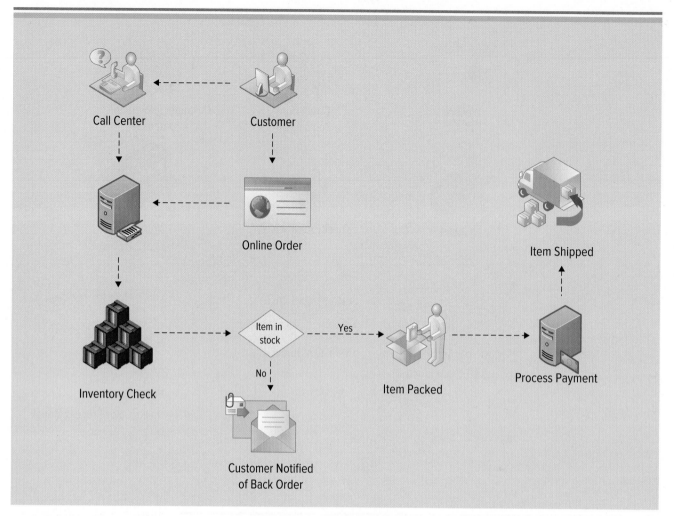

Call Center

Customer

Online Order

Inventory Check

Item in stock

No

Yes

Customer Notified of Back Order

Item Packed

Process Payment

Item Shipped

FIGURE 2.37

Order Fulfillment Process Model

Decides to Purchase Item

Reviews Auction Listing

Places Bid

Wins Bid

Receives Invoice

Pays Invoice

Receives Item

Rates Seller

Ends Sale

Decides to Sell Item

Lists Item on eBay

Sets Initial Price

Sets Auction Length

Invoices Winning Bid

Receives Payment

Ships Item

Rates Buyer

Ends Sale

Learning Outcome 2.1: Explain the importance of decision making for managers at each of the three primary organization levels along with the associated decision characteristics.

Decision-making skills are essential for all business professionals, at every company level, who make decisions that run the business. At the operational level, employees develop, control, and maintain core business activities required to run the day-to-day operations. Operational decisions are considered structured decisions, which arise in situations in which established processes offer potential solutions. Structured decisions are made frequently and are almost repetitive in nature; they affect short-term business strategies.

At the managerial level, employees are continuously evaluating company operations to hone the firm's abilities to identify, adapt to, and leverage change. Managerial decisions cover short- and medium-range plans, schedules, and budgets along with policies, procedures, and business objectives for the firm. These types of decisions are considered semistructured decisions; they occur in situations in which a few established processes help to evaluate potential solutions but not enough to lead to a definite recommended decision.

At the strategic level, managers develop overall business strategies, goals, and objectives as part of the company's strategic plan. They also monitor the strategic performance of the organization and its overall direction in the political, economic, and competitive business environment. Strategic decisions are highly unstructured decisions, occurring in situations in which no procedures or rules exist to guide decision makers toward the correct choice. They are infrequent, extremely important, and typically related to long-term business strategy.

Learning Outcome 2.2: Define critical success factors (CSFs) and key performance indicators (KPIs) and explain how managers use them to measure the success of MIS projects.

Metrics are measurements that evaluate results to determine whether a project is meeting its goals. Two core metrics are critical success factors and key performance indicators. CSFs are the crucial steps companies perform to achieve their goals and objectives and implement their strategies and include creating high-quality products, retaining competitive advantages, and reducing product costs. KPIs are the quantifiable metrics a company uses to evaluate progress toward critical success factors. KPIs are far more specific than CSFs; examples include turnover rates of employees, percentage of help-desk calls answered in the first minute, and number of products returned.

It is important to understand the relationship between critical success factors and key performance indicators. CSFs are elements crucial for a business strategy's success. KPIs measure the progress of CSFs with quantifiable measurements, and one CSF can have several KPIs. Of course, both categories will vary by company and industry. Imagine improved graduation rates as a CSF for a college.

Learning Outcome 2.3: Classify the different operational support systems, managerial support systems, and strategic support systems and explain how managers can use these systems to make decisions and gain competitive advantages.

Being able to sort, calculate, analyze, and slice-and-dice information is critical to an organization's success. Without knowing what is occurring throughout the organization, there is no way that managers and executives can make solid decisions to support the business. The different operational, managerial, and strategic support systems include:

■ Operational: A transaction processing system (TPS) is the basic business system that serves the operational level (analysts) in an organization. The most common example of a TPS is an operational accounting system such as a payroll system or an order-entry system.

- Managerial: A decision support system (DSS) models information to support managers and business professionals during the decision-making process.
- Strategic: An executive information system (EIS) is a specialized DSS that supports senior-level executives within the organization.

Learning Outcome 2.4: Describe artificial intelligence and identify its five main types.

Artificial intelligence (AI) simulates human thinking and behavior, such as the ability to reason and learn. The five most common categories of AI are:

1. Expert systems—computerized advisory programs that imitate the reasoning processes of experts in solving difficult problems.
2. Neural networks—attempts to emulate the way the human brain works.
3. Genetic algorithm—a system that mimics the evolutionary, survival-of-the-fittest process to generate increasingly better solutions to a problem.
4. Intelligent agents—a special-purpose, knowledge-based information system that accomplishes specific tasks on behalf of its users.
5. Virtual reality—a computer-simulated environment that can be a simulation of the real world or an imaginary world.

Learning Outcome 2.5: Explain the value of business processes for a company and differentiate between customer-facing and business-facing processes.

A business process is a standardized set of activities that accomplish a specific task, such as processing a customer's order. Business processes transform a set of inputs into a set of outputs (goods or services) for another person or process by using people and tools. Without processes, organizations would not be able to complete activities. Customer-facing processes result in a product or service that an organization's external customer receives. Business-facing processes are invisible to the external customer but essential to the effective management of the business.

Learning Outcome 2.6: Demonstrate the value of business process modeling and compare As-Is and To-Be models.

Business process modeling (or mapping) is the activity of creating a detailed flowchart or process map of a work process, showing its inputs, tasks, and activities in a structured sequence. A business process model is a graphic description of a process, showing the sequence of process tasks, which is developed for a specific purpose and from a selected viewpoint.

Business process modeling usually begins with a functional process representation of the process problem, or an As-Is process model. As-Is process models represent the current state of the operation that has been mapped, without any specific improvements or changes to existing processes. The next step is to build a To-Be process model that displays how the process problem will be solved or implemented. To-Be process models show the results of applying change improvement opportunities to the current (As-Is) process model. This approach ensures that the process is fully and clearly understood before the details of a process solution are decided on.

Learning Outcome 2.7: Differentiate among automation, streamlining, and reengineering.

Business process improvement attempts to understand and measure the current process and make performance improvements accordingly. Automation is the process of computerizing manual tasks, making them more efficient and effective, and dramatically lowering operational costs. Streamlining improves business process efficiencies by simplifying or eliminating unnecessary steps. Bottlenecks occur when resources reach full capacity and cannot handle any additional demands; they limit throughput and impede operations. Streamlining removes bottlenecks, an important step if the efficiency and capacity of a business process are being increased. Business process reengineering (BPR) is the analysis and redesign of workflow within and between enterprises and occurs at the systems level or companywide level and is the end-to-end view of a process.

1. **Knowledge:** Define the three primary types of decision-making systems and how robots in the workplace could affect each.

2. **Comprehension:** Describe the difference between transactional and analytical information, and determine how robots could improve the process for gathering and manipulating each type for a grocery store such as Safeway.

3. **Application:** Illustrate the business process model used by a robot to perform an analysis on a patient with a cold.

4. **Analysis:** Explain business process reengineering and how robots might dramatically change the current sales process.

5. **Synthesis:** Formulate different metrics that a personal trainer robot for a fitness club could provide a customer.

6. **Evaluation:** Argue for or against the following statement: Robots are better than humans in all business capacities.

KEY TERMS

Algorithm 65
Analytical information 59
Artificial intelligence (AI) 64
As-Is process model 73
Augmented reality 69
Automation 78
Bar chart 62
Benchmarking 58
Benchmarks 58
Best practices 56
Bottlenecks 79
BPMN event 73
BPMN activity 73
BPMN gateway 73
BPMN flow 73
Business-facing process 72
Business process
  improvement 76
Business process model 73
Business process modeling
  (or mapping) 73
Business Process Model and
  Notation (BPMN) 73
Business process patent 72
Business process reengineering
  (BPR) 80
Case-based reasoning 67
Consolidation 65
Core processes 72
Critical success factors (CSFs) 53
Customer-facing process 72
Cycle time 79
Decision support system (DSS) 60
Deep learning 68
Digital dashboard 63
Drill-down 65

Dynamic process 72
Effectiveness MIS metrics 56
Efficiency MIS metrics 56
Executive information system
  (EIS) 61
Expert system 67
Fuzzy logic 68
Genetic algorithm 68
Goal-seeking analysis 61
Google Glass 69
Granularity 61
Haptic interface 69
Histogram 62
Infographics 61
Intelligent agent 69
Intelligent system 65
Key performance indicators
  (KPIs) 53
Machine learning 66
Machine vision 67
Machine vision resolution 67
Machine vision sensitivity 67
Managerial business process 79
Managerial decisions 53
Managerial level 53
Mapping 73
Market share 54
Metrics 53
Model 58
Mutation 68
Neural network 67
Online analytical processing
  (OLAP) 60
Online transaction processing
  (OLTP) 59
Operational business process 76

Operational decisions 51
Operational level 51
Operationalized analytics 76
Optimization analysis 61
Pie chart 62
Project 53
Redundancy 79
Return on investment
  (ROI) 54
Robotic process automation
  (RPA) 79
Semistructured decision 53
Sensitivity analysis 61
Shopping bot 69
Slice-and-dice 65
Source document 59
Sparkline 63
Static process 72
Strategic business process 80
Strategic decisions 53
Strategic level 53
Streamlining 79
Structured decision 51
Swim lane 75
Time-series chart 63
To-Be process model 73
Transaction processing system
  (TPS) 59
Transactional information 59
Unstructured decision 53
Virtual reality 69
Virtual workplace 69
Visualization 61
What-if analysis 61
Workflow 75
Workflow control system 75

1. Why must business professionals understand how MIS supports decision making and problem solving?

2. What is the relationship between critical success factors and key performance indicators? How can a manager use them to understand business operations?

3. What are the three levels of management found in a company? What types of decisions are made at each level?

4. Define transaction processing systems and describe the role they play in a business.

5. Define decision support systems and describe the role they play in a business.

6. Define expert systems and describe the role they play in a business.

7. What are the capabilities associated with digital dashboards?

8. What are the common DSS analysis techniques?

9. How does an electronic spreadsheet program, such as Excel, provide decision support capabilities?

10. What is the difference between the ability of a manager to retrieve information instantly on demand using an MIS and the capabilities provided by a DSS?

11. What is artificial intelligence? What are the five types of AI systems? What applications of AI offer the greatest business value?

12. What is a business process and what role does it play in an organization?

13. Why do managers need to understand business processes? Can you make a correlation between systems thinking and business processes?

14. Why would a manager need to review an As-Is and To-Be process model?

15. How can a manager use automation, streamlining, and business process reengineering to gain operational efficiency and effectiveness?

16. Explain the difference between customer-facing processes and business-facing processes. Which one is more important to an organization?

17. Explain how finding different ways to travel the same road relates to automation, streamlining, and business process reengineering.

CLOSING CASE ONE

Business Is Booming for Wearable Technologies

What will be the next big thing in the world of technology? In the early 1990s, the laptop computer was the big thing, giving users mobility and productivity. Apple gave the world the smart phone in 2007, a device that could fit in the palm of your hand and offered more power than the equipment that NASA used to put men on the moon in the 1960s. Industry analysts are predicting the next big thing will be even smaller and more versatile than the iPhone and similar devices: wearable technology.

Wearable technologies are here, and the applications for both personal and business use are truly inspiring. You can expect them to have a major impact on your everyday lives over the next decade. *Wearable technology* is a device that you wear physically on your body that has tracking technologies to help manage your life. Wearable technologies include smart watches, intelligent glasses, and fitness tracking bands. To be considered a piece of wearable technology, the device must merge with clothing, accessories, or other essentials that are worn on the body rather than be carried.

The current focus of wearable technologies is largely consumer driven, but expect this to change because there are even bigger opportunities in the business world, resulting in improved productivity, reduced job-related injuries, and billions of dollars in savings. Because wearable technologies allow users to go hands-free, there are many ways they will be useful in business, such as wearable devices that connect a customer's data tracking his or her real-time journey through a store or hotel to eliminate the need for credit cards or hotel keys. Emergency personnel and search and rescue teams will receive high-tech mobility and tracking features, ensuring both theirs and the victim's safety. Sales representatives, auto mechanics, and remote service technicians will gain access to real-time data, allowing them to view plans and schematics all hands-free and in real time. Any person requiring real-time access to data—sales representatives, lawyers, doctors, nurses, policemen, firefighters, and military personnel—will benefit from using wearables in the workplace. (See Figure 2.39 for examples of wearable technologies.)[20]

FIGURE 2.39

Wearable Technology Examples

Motorola's HC1 Headset
A hands-free display that resembles the headgear worn by the galactic Marines in James Cameron's *Aliens*, it allows defense, utilities, construction, and aviation workers to access repair manuals and schematics in their line of vision.

XOEye Technologies Safety Glasses
XOEye safety glasses contain blinking LEDs and embedded cameras that can scan barcodes and stream real-time video to offsite technicians. It also tracks biometric markers such as head tilt, which can help employers identify ergonomic issues.

Google Glass
Google Glass is purported to give users an augmented reality experience, supplying information on demand. For example, when a Google Glass wearer walks into an airport, the device might show him detailed information about his flight.

Samsung Galaxy Gear Simband
Galaxy Gear is designed to mimic and sometimes complement the functionality of a traditional smart phone, only on a device that you wear on your wrist like a watch. Using different wavelengths of light beamed at your skin, Simband will track multiple measures of its wearer's health continuously, such as blood pressure, respiration, heart rate, hydration level, and the amount of carbon dioxide in the blood.

Myo Armband
A gesture-based, wireless controller marketed to video gamers; in a factory, it could allow workers to keep their hands free as they operate machinery.

Kapture
An audio-recording wristband; could help workers remember complex instructions or take notes while on a job site.

Questions

1. Define the three primary types of decision-making systems and how wearable technologies in the workplace could affect each.

2. Describe the difference between transactional and analytical information, and determine how wearable technology could affect each for a grocery store.

3. Illustrate the business process model used by a computer service repair technician using wearable technology glasses to fix a broken computer.

4. Explain business process reengineering and how wearable technology might dramatically change the current sales process.

5. Formulate different metrics that a wearable technology for fitness could provide a customer.

6. Argue for or against the following statement: Wearable devices invade consumer privacy.

Defense Advanced Research Projects Agency (DARPA) Grand Challenge

The goal of the DARPA Grand Challenge is to save lives by making one-third of ground military forces autonomous or driverless vehicles. Created in response to a congressional and U.S. Department of Defense (DoD) mandate, the DARPA Grand Challenge brings together individuals and organizations from industry, the research and development (R&D) community, government, the armed services, and academia, and includes students, backyard inventors, and automotive enthusiasts.

The DARPA Grand Challenge 2004

The DARPA Grand Challenge 2004 field test of autonomous ground vehicles ran from Barstow, California, to Primm, Nevada, and offered a $1 million prize. From the qualifying round at the California Speedway, 15 finalists emerged to attempt the Grand Challenge. However, the prize went unclaimed when no vehicles were able to complete the difficult desert route.

The DARPA Grand Challenge 2005

The DARPA Grand Challenge 2005 was held in the Mojave Desert and offered a $2 million prize to the team that completed the 132-mile course in the shortest time under 10 hours. The race, over desert terrain, included narrow tunnels, sharp turns, and a winding mountain pass with a sheer drop-off on one side and a rock face on the other. Five teams completed the course, and "Stanley," the Stanford Racing Team's car, won the $2 million prize with a time of 6 hours, 53 minutes.

DARPA Robotic Challenge 2016

Machines with humanlike abilities have been portrayed in movies and books for a long time. Now they are coming to life at the DARPA Robotics Challenge, a program created to accelerate progress in AI development that would allow them to move in to areas too dangerous for humans along with mitigating natural or human-made disasters. The $2 million first prize was awarded to the Korean team that built robot DRC-Hubo. The $1 million second prize was awarded to the Florida team that built Running Man. The Challenge was a huge success and advances in robotics are being seen in areas around the globe.[21]

Questions

1. How is the DoD using AI to improve its operations and save lives?
2. Why would the DoD use an event like the DARPA Grand Challenge or DARPA Robotic Challenge to further technological innovation?
3. Describe how autonomous vehicles and robots could be used by organizations around the world to improve business efficiency and effectiveness.

1. Modeling a Business Process

Do you hate waiting in line at the grocery store? Do you get annoyed when the pizza delivery person brings you the wrong order? This is your chance to reengineer the process that drives you crazy. Choose a problem you are currently experiencing and reengineer the process to make it more efficient. Be sure to provide As-Is and To-Be process models.

2. Revamping Accounts

The accounting department at your company deals with the processing of critical documents that include invoices, purchase orders, statements, purchase requisitions, financial statements, sales orders, and price quotes. These documents must arrive at their intended destination in a secure and efficient manner.

Processing is currently done manually, which causes a negative ripple effect. Documents tend to be misplaced or delayed, becoming vulnerable to unauthorized changes or exposure of confidential information. In addition, the accounting department incurs costs such as for preprinted forms, inefficient distribution, and storage. Explain automation, streamlining, and business process reengineering and how they can be used to revamp the accounting department.

3. What Type of System Would You Use?

You have been assigned as senior director for a large manufacturing company. Your first assignment is to decide which type of MIS can best support your decision-making needs. For all of the following, determine which type of system you would use to help solve the business problem or make a business decision.

a. You need to analyze daily sales transactions for each region.

b. You need to analyze staffing requirements for each plant.

c. You need to determine which customers are at risk of defaulting on their bills.

d. You need to analyze your competition, including prices, discounts, goods, and services.

e. You need to analyze critical success factors and key performance indicators for status on operations.

f. You need to produce a graphical display of patterns and complex relationships for large amounts of data.

4. Unstructured Communications

You have just received a job as a business analyst for a large sports marketing company. Your boss, Sandy Fiero, wants you to evaluate and improve the current corporate communication process. With the current process, employees receive a great deal of unstructured information in the form of emails, including corporate policies, corporate announcements, and human resource information. You quickly realize that using an email system for communication is causing a great deal of issues, including inaccessible information for any new hires, lost productivity as employees search through hundreds of emails to find information, and miscommunication as global divisions of your organization send out regional human resource policies.

To begin analyzing the processes, create a list of issues you might encounter by using email as a primary communication tool for corporate information. What are the redundancies associated with an email communication process? What are the bottlenecks with an email communication process? Document the As-Is process for sending email communications to employees. Then, reengineer the process and document your suggestions for improving the process and the To-Be communication process.

5. Long-Distance Hugs

Haptic technology digitizes touch. CuteCircuit created the Hug shirt that you can hug and send the exact hug, including strength, pressure, distribution, and even heartbeat, to a long-distance friend who is wearing the partner to your Hug shirt. Ben Hui at Cambridge University is creating hand-squeezes that can be sent by mobile phones. You simply squeeze the phone and your friend feels it, in some form, at the other end. The value of these haptic devices is based on the idea that physical touch is an important element to all human interactions and if you can transfer the physical touch, you can replicate the emotion. In a group, create a new business product that uses a haptic interface. Share your product idea with your peers.

6. Is the Computer Smarter than a Human?

In 2011, the IBM Watson computer defeated the two best contestants in the TV game show *Jeopardy!* What made the achievement so remarkable was that the computer had to read the question, understand what was being asked, search through 200 million pages of text, figure out what the best answer would be, and then hit a buzzer before the other contestants did. It accomplished all these steps in about 3 seconds. IBM predicts that Watson could be the ultimate researcher, helping professionals in various industries find the information they are looking for in a matter of seconds. What do you think about Watson's powerful services? Do you think you could one day have access to this powerful technology on your favorite search engine? How would having an IBM Watson help you in your college career?

7. Searching Telephone Calls

Imagine being able to search a database of customer phone calls to find specific requests or to be able to sort through digital customer complaints to detect the exact moment when the interaction between the customer service representative and the customer went wrong. A new tool called Find It allows the sorting of digital voice records as easily as using Google to sift through documents. Find It is opening limitless business opportunities as organizations begin to understand how they can use this technology to help employees search voice mails or recorded calls for keywords and phrases.

You have recently started your own marketing firm and you want to use the power of Find It to help your customers query all of their unique data records, including digital voice recordings. Now all you need is to prepare your marketing materials to send to potential customers. Create a marketing pitch that you will deliver to customers detailing the business opportunities they could uncover if they purchased Find It. Your marketing pitch can be a one-page document, a catchy tune, a video, or a PowerPoint presentation.

8. Driving Your Business

You have recently opened your own business—choose the business of your dreams and assume you have it up and running. What types of decision will you need to make to operate your business? How can you use MIS to support your decision-making efforts? What types of processes will you find throughout your business? How can you use MIS to revamp your business process for efficiency and effectiveness? Overall, how dependent will your business be on MIS? Do you think you could be just as successful running your business without MIS? Can you name a business that can operate efficiently and effectively without MIS?

APPLY YOUR KNOWLEDGE BUSINESS PROJECTS

PROJECT I   Making Business Decisions

You are the vice president of human resources for a large consulting company. You are compiling a list of questions that you want each job interviewee to answer. The first question on your list is, "How can MIS enhance your ability to make decisions at our organization?" Prepare a one-page report to answer this question.

PROJECT II   DSS and EIS

Dr. Rosen runs a large dental conglomerate—Teeth Doctors—that employs more than 700 dentists in six states. Dr. Rosen is interested in purchasing a competitor called Dentix that has 150 dentists in three additional states. Before deciding whether to purchase Dentix, Dr. Rosen must consider several issues:

- The cost of purchasing Dentix.
- The location of the Dentix offices.

- The current number of customers per dentist, per office, and per state.
- The merger between the two companies.
- The professional reputation of Dentix.
- Other competitors.

Explain how Dr. Rosen and Teeth Doctors can benefit from the use of information systems to make an accurate business decision about whether to purchase Dentix.

PROJECT III Finding Information on Decision Support Systems

You are working on the sales team for a small catering company that maintains 75 employees and generates $1 million in revenues per year. The owner, Pam Hetz, wants to understand how she can use decision support systems to help expand her business. Hetz has an initial understanding of DSS and is interested in learning more about what types are available, how they can be used in a small business, and the costs associated. In a group, research the website www.dssresources.com and compile a presentation that discusses DSSs in detail. Be sure to answer all Hetz's questions on DSS in your presentation.

PROJECT IV Discovering Reengineering Opportunities

In an effort to increase efficiency, your college has hired you to analyze its current business processes for registering for classes. Analyze the current process and determine which steps are:

- Broken
- Redundant
- Antiquated

Be sure to define how you would reengineer the processes for efficiency.

PROJECT V Dashboard Design

Digital dashboards offer an effective and efficient way to view enterprisewide information at near real time. According to Nucleus Research, there is a direct correlation between use of digital dashboards and a company's return on investment (ROI); hence, all executives should be using or pushing the development of digital dashboards to monitor and analyze organizational operations.

Design a digital dashboard for a customer tracking and enterprise operations system. Be sure to address at least four of the following indicators by showing how you would measure it, such as red, yellow, green status; percentage complete status; and so on.

Customer Tracking System	Enterprise Operations
Customers	Accounting
Marketing	Finance
Order entry	Logistics
Collections	Production
Sales	Distribution
Customer service	Manufacturing
Billing	Human resources
Credit limits	Sales
Transportation	Total profit

PROJECT VI Driving Decisions

How do people make decisions? Almost daily, you can read about someone who makes a decision most people would find mind-boggling. Here are a few examples:

- A woman in Ohio was charged with child endangerment after police said she admitted to breast-feeding her child and talking on a cell phone while driving her other children to school.

- A woman in South Florida was caught driving while talking on a cell phone on her left shoulder and eating from a cup of soup in her left hand. The woman would take her right hand off the wheel to spoon soup, driving with no hands while she continued to talk on the phone.

- A man in California was cited for driving while carrying a swimming pool. He drove with one hand while he held his new swimming pool on the roof of his car with the other. His three children were leaning out of the car windows, not wearing seat belts, to help hold the pool.

- A woman in Baltimore was charged with diapering her child in the front seat of the car while driving at 65 miles per hour down the highway.[22]

Find an example of a company that found itself in trouble because its employees made bad decisions. What could the company have done to protect itself from these types of employee blunders?

PROJECT VII iYogi Help Desk Support

It is late at night, and you are working on your final exam when your computer crashes. As your blood pressure climbs and your stress level skyrockets, you call your computer manufacturer's technical support number. Of course, that person tells you the problem has nothing to do with the computer and must have a different source. What are you going to do?

iYogi.net is a 24/7 online support service that allows technicians to take remote control of your computer from Gurgaon, India, and try to fix what ails it. iYogi provides technical support for all Walmart computer customers and sells its services through Walmart.com and Amazon.com. If the thought of turning control over to someone you never met half a world away fills you with terror, it shouldn't. All iYogi technicians are Microsoft, Cisco, and Hewlett-Packard certified.[23]

Describe the types of decisions iYogi technicians are required to make when helping a customer with a computer problem. What would potential CSFs and KPIs for iYogi be? What types of metrics would managers track so they could control operations?

PROJECT VIII Dashboard for Tracking Junk

Do you enjoy kidnapping your rivals' team mascots or toilet-papering their frat houses? If so, you might find your ideal career at College Hunks Hauling Junk. The company hires college students and recent grads to pick up junk and take it away. The founder, Nick Friedman, had a goal of capturing that friendly rivalry so often associated with college life and turning it into profits. When the company launched in 2005, the haulers from Virginia found their truck had been lathered in shaving cream and draped with a University of Maryland flag. The Virginia haulers retaliated, and soon after, dead fish were found on the seats of Maryland's truck. Friedman decided to use this energy as an incentive instead of condemning the unorthodox behavior. "We wanted to harness that competitive, prankster enthusiasm and channel it for good," he says.

Freidman made a bold move and decided that instead of tracking typical key performance indicators such as revenue, average job size, and customer loyalty, he would set up his dashboard to track volume of junk collected and amount donated or recycled. The winning team gains such things as bragging rights and banners, modest monetary prizes, and the right to eat first at the annual company meeting. Most employees check the dashboard daily to view their own and rivals' latest standings.[24]

Why do you think competition is helping College Hunks Hauling Junk exceed its revenue goals? If you were to build a team competition dashboard for your school or your work, what types of metrics would you track? What types of motivators would you use to ensure your team is always in the green?

What types of external information would you want tracked in your dashboard? Could an unethical person use the information from your dashboard to hurt your team or your organization? What can you do to mitigate these risks?

PROJECT IX   Building Robots

Humans are not permitted inside Staples's Denver distribution center. Who is filling all the orders, you ask? Robots! This 100,000-square-foot space belongs to 150 orange robots that resemble over-stuffed ottomans and race around with uncanny accuracy. They're making Staples employees more than twice as productive. The robots, or bots, are built by Kiva Systems, a company with a single critical success factor: Replace the labyrinth of conveyor belts and humans that most distributors rely on to pack items in the online mail-order business. Companies using Kiva bots include Walgreens, Zappos, The Gap, and Amazon.[25]

Robots have captured people's attention for years. From the quirky droids in *Star Wars* to the powerful fighting machines in *Transformers,* they seem to fascinate everyone. Assume your professor has asked you to participate in The Robot Challenge, and you must design a robot that will enhance business operations. It must contain a digital dashboard and provide decision support capabilities for its owners. Be sure to describe your robot, its functions, how the digital dashboard works and supports users, and why customers would purchase your robot. Feel free to include a picture or diagram of how your robot works.

PROJECT X   Educational Processes

Trina Thompson, a New York City resident, is filing a lawsuit against Monroe College, stating that she is unable to find employment after graduating with her bachelor's degree. Thompson is seeking tuition reimbursement of $70,000 and states that she has been unable to find gainful employment since graduating because the school's Office of Career Advancement failed to provide her with the leads and career advice it promised. Monroe College spokesman Gary Axelbank says Thompson's lawsuit is completely without merit and insists it helps its graduates find jobs.[26]

Do you agree that students should be allowed to hold their academic institutions liable for their inability to find a job after graduation? Design the current (As-Is) business process at your school from the time a student begins his or her program until graduation. How could your school reengineer the process to ensure it does not end up in litigation over an individual's expectation of automatically receiving a job after graduation?

PROJECT XI   Wearable Technologies Are Tracking You

With wearable technology, you can track your entire life. Nike's Fuelband and Jawbone's Up track all of your physical activity, caloric burn, and sleep patterns. You can track your driving patterns, tooth-brushing habits, and even laundry status. The question now becomes how to track all of your trackers.

A new company called Exist incorporates tracking devices with weather data, music choices, Netflix favorites, and Twitter activity all in one digital dashboard. Exist wants to understand every area of your life and provide correlation information between such things as your personal productivity and mood. As the different types of data expand, so will the breadth of correlations Exist can point out. For instance, do you tweet more when you are working at home? If so, does this increase productivity? Exist wants to track all of your trackers and analyze the information to help you become more efficient and more effective.[27]

Create a digital dashboard for tracking your life. Choose four areas you want to track and determine three ways you would measure each area. For example, if you track eating habits, you might want to measure calories and place unacceptable levels in red and acceptable levels in green. Once completed, determine whether you can find any correlations among the areas in your life.

If you are looking for Excel projects to incorporate into your class, try any of the following after reading this chapter.

Project Number	Project Name	Project Type	Plug-In Focus Area	Project Focus	Project Skill Set	Page Number
1	Financial Destiny	Excel	T2	Personal Budget	Introductory Formulas	AYK.4
2	Cash Flow	Excel	T2	Cash Flow	Introductory Formulas	AYK.4
3	Technology Budget	Excel	T1, T2	Hardware and Software	Introductory Formulas	AYK.4
4	Tracking Donations	Excel	T2	Employee Relationships	Introductory Formulas	AYK.4
5	Convert Currency	Excel	T2	Global Commerce	Introductory Formulas	AYK.5
6	Cost Comparison	Excel	T2	Total Cost of Ownership	Introductory Formulas	AYK.5
7	Time Management	Excel or Project	T2 or T12	Project Management	Introductory Gantt Charts	AYK.6
8	Maximize Profit	Excel	T2, T4	Strategic Analysis	Intermediate Formulas or Solver	AYK.6
9	Security Analysis	Excel	T3	Filtering Data	Intermediate Conditional Formatting, Autofilter, Subtotal	AYK.7
10	Gathering Data	Excel	T3	Data Analysis	Intermediate Conditional Formatting, PivotTable	AYK.8
11	Scanner System	Excel	T2	Strategic Analysis	Intermediate	AYK.8
12	Competitive Pricing	Excel	T2	Profit Maximization	Intermediate	AYK.9
13	Adequate Acquisitions	Excel	T2	Break-Even Analysis	Intermediate	AYK.9

3

CHAPTER

Ebusiness: Electronic Business Value

SECTION 3.1
WEB 1.0: Ebusiness

- Distruptive Technology
- Web 1.0 : The Catalyst for Ebusiness
- The Four Ebusiness Models
- Ebusiness Tools for Connecting and Communicating
- The Challenges of Ebusiness

SECTION 3.2
Web 2.0: Business 2.0

- Web 2.0: Advantages of Business 2.0
- Networking Communities with Business 2.0
- Business 2.0 Tools for Collaborating
- The Challenges of Business 2.0
- Web 3.0: Defining the Next Generation of Online Business Opportunities

CHAPTER OUTLINE

What's in IT for me?

Internet and communication technologies have revolutionized the way business operates, improving upon traditional methods and even introducing new opportunities and ventures that were simply not possible before. More than just giving organizations another means of conducting transactions, online business provides the ability to develop and maintain customer relationships, supplier relationships, and even employee relationships between and within enterprises.

As future managers and organizational knowledge workers, you need to understand the benefits ebusiness can offer an organization and your career, the challenges that accompany web technologies, and their impact on organizational communication and collaboration. You need to be aware of the strategies organizations can use to deploy ebusiness and the methods of measuring ebusiness success. This chapter will give you this knowledge and help prepare you for success in tomorrow's electronic global marketplace.

Hello Fresh, Hello Delicious

HelloFresh is at the forefront of disrupting a multitrillion-dollar industry at the very beginning of its online transition. HelloFresh is a truly local food product, uniquely suited to individual tastes and meal-time preferences offering delivery of a giant box of delicious food with recipes to enable easy and enjoyable meal preparation for a weekly fee.

HelloFresh aims to provide each and every household in its seven markets with the opportunity to enjoy wholesome home-cooked meals with no planning, no shopping, and no hassle required. Everything required for weeknight meals, carefully planned, locally sourced, and delivered to your door at the most convenient time for each subscriber. Behind the scenes, a huge data driven technology platform puts us in the prime position for disrupting the food supply chain and for fundamentally changing the way consumers shop for food. HelloFresh has local founders across the globe who are able to leverage the global platform and at the same time ensure that the HelloFresh product in each market truly reflects the local community.

HelloFresh offers consumers three different subscription services aimed at vegetarians, families, and couple households that provides them with the ingredients to cook three to five meals during a week. Every week, customers choose their meal plan before Wednesday and select a delivery day between Sunday and Tuesday for their weekly meals to arrive. By keeping it simple on the customer-side of their operations, it liberates HelloFresh to execute in a highly efficient manner with long lead-times and low inventory stock.

HelloFresh is relentless about finding efficiencies in their supply chain and that is most evident in the delivery of their products as they concluded they would be better off not allowing their customers to choose their delivery time slots. By simply omitting this option, it enables HelloFresh to optimise their routes and delivery schedule, which ensures that van drivers can reach the maximum number of homes while travelling the minimum distance and spending the least time on delivery. This has been credited to saving HelloFresh 40 percent in fuel costs and increasing deliveries fourfold with only 50 percent more vans.

Dominik Richter has been CEO since starting HelloFresh in 2011. He has responsibility for keeping a general oversight of the business and strategy. Prior to HelloFresh, Dominik worked with Goldman Sachs in London. Dominik graduated with a degree in International Business in 2009 and from the London School of Economics in 2010 with a master's in Finance. Thomas Griesel has been responsible for the logistics and operations behind HelloFresh since founding it with Dominik in 2011. Previously, Thomas had spent time at OC&C Strategy Consultants and worked on a range of his own businesses and ideas. He graduated from with a degree in International Business Administration in 2009 and from the London Business School in 2010 with a master's in Management.

First Year of Business

All the way back in 2011, Dominik and Thomas arrived in Berlin, intent on starting a new and disruptive business. With a love of healthy food, nutrition, and cooking, and a desire to make access to healthy food as easy as possible for as many people as possible, starting a "food at home" business seemed the natural choice.

Second Year of Business

After examining business models from Sweden to Japan to very local ideas, they and a group of like-minded individuals formulated the recipe for HelloFresh. The team started early in 2012 packing shopping bags in Berlin, Amsterdam, and London with a view to target the highest density population areas in Europe. Quite quickly, they started getting requests from people outside those areas who all wanted to become a part of the HelloFresh family. Wanting to serve as many people as possible, the team developed a logistics model that enabled them to deliver to every single household across a given country.

Third Year of Business

The HelloFresh product started to rapidly gain in popularity, as subscribers shared the excitement about their weekly boxes with friends and colleagues. Subscriber referrals accelerated, as it became clear that HelloFresh had finally solved the "What's for dinner tonight?" problem for its subscribers.

Off to the Races!

Having launched on the East Coast of the United States in December 2012, HelloFresh moved to cover the entire country in September 2014. Over the short time since then, HelloFresh has grown rapidly to become one of the largest players in this market.

Unlike supermarkets that carry between 20,000 and 30,000 items, HelloFresh focuses on 18 to 26 produce items that are sourced from selected local producers. By creating long delivery lead-times through their Wednesday order cut-off date coupled with their low SKUs, HelloFresh is able to forecast their demand over a eight-week time span with 90 to 95 percent accuracy and can subsequently buy wholesale from their suppliers with minimal waste. This business model has the added benefit for setting very clear margin expectations across their products and allowing HelloFresh to set prices at a level where fluctuations won't punish them.[1]

section 3.1 | Web 1.0: Ebusiness

LEARNING OUTCOMES

3.1 Compare disruptive and sustaining technologies and explain how the Internet and WWW caused business disruption.

3.2 Describe ebusiness and its associated advantages.

3.3 Compare the four ebusiness models.

3.4 Describe the six ebusiness tools for connecting and communicating.

3.5 Identify the four challenges associated with ebusiness.

DISRUPTIVE TECHNOLOGY

LO 3.1: Compare disruptive and sustaining technologies and explain how the Internet and WWW caused business disruption.

Polaroid, founded in 1937, produced the first instant camera in the late 1940s. The Polaroid camera, whose pictures developed themselves, was one of the most exciting technological advances the photography industry had ever seen. The company eventually went public, becoming one of Wall Street's most prominent enterprises, with its stock trading above $60 per share in 1997. In 2002, the stock dropped to 8 cents, and the company declared bankruptcy.[2]

How could a company such as Polaroid, which had innovative technology and a captive customer base, go bankrupt? Perhaps company executives failed to use Porter's Five Forces Model to analyze the threat of substitute products or services. If they had, would they have noticed the two threats—one-hour film processing and digital cameras—which eventually stole Polaroid's market share? Would they have understood that their customers, people who want instant access to their pictures, would be the first to try these alternatives? Could the company have found a way to compete with one-hour film processing and the digital camera to save Polaroid?

Many organizations face the same dilemma as Polaroid: what's best for the current business might not be what's best for it in the long term. Some observers of our business environment have an ominous vision of the future—digital Darwinism. *Digital Darwinism* implies that organizations that cannot adapt to the new demands placed on them for surviving in the information age are doomed to extinction.

Disruptive versus Sustaining Technology

A *disruptive technology* is a new way of doing things that initially does not meet the needs of existing customers. Disruptive technologies tend to open new markets and destroy old ones. A *sustaining technology,* on the other hand, produces an improved product customers are eager to buy, such as a faster car or larger hard drive. Sustaining technologies tend to provide us with better, faster, and cheaper products in established markets. Incumbent companies most often lead sustaining technology to market, but they virtually never lead in markets opened by disruptive technologies. Figure 3.1 positions companies expecting future growth from new investments (disruptive technology) and companies expecting future growth from existing investments (sustaining technology).[3]

Disruptive technologies typically enter the low end of the marketplace and eventually evolve to displace high-end competitors and their reigning technologies. Sony is a perfect example. Sony started as a tiny company that built portable, battery-powered transistor radios. The sound quality was poor, but customers were willing to overlook that for the convenience of portability. With the experience and revenue stream from the portables, Sony improved its technology to produce cheap, low-end transistor amplifiers that were suitable for home use and invested those revenues in improving the technology further, which produced still-better radios.

The Innovator's Dilemma, a book by Clayton M. Christensen, discusses how established companies can take advantage of disruptive technologies without hindering existing relationships with customers, partners, and stakeholders. Xerox, IBM, Sears, and DEC all listened to existing customers, invested aggressively in technology, had their competitive antennae up, and still lost their market-dominant positions. They may have placed too much emphasis on satisfying customers' current needs and neglected new disruptive technology to meet customers' future needs, thus losing market share.[4]

FIGURE 3.1

Disruptive and Sustaining
Technologies

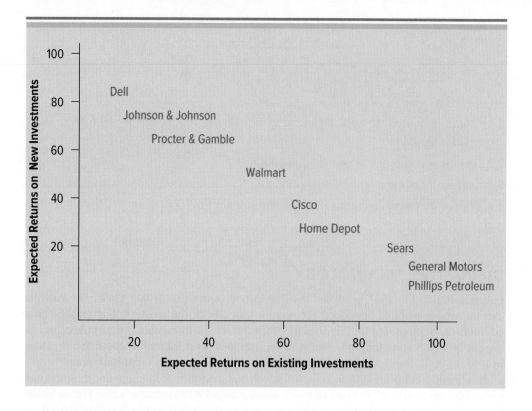

The Internet and World Wide Web—The Ultimate Business Disruptors

The *Internet* is a massive network that connects computers all over the world and allows them to communicate with one another. Computers connected via the Internet can send and receive information, including text, graphics, voice, video, and software. Originally, the Internet was essentially an emergency military communications system operated by the U.S. Department of Defense Advanced Research Project Agency (DARPA), which called the network ARPANET. No one foresaw the dramatic impact it would have on both business and personal communications. In time, all U.S. universities that had defense-related funding installed ARPANET computers, forming the first official Internet network. As users began to notice the value of electronic communications, the purpose of the network started shifting from a military pipeline to a communications tool for scientists.[5]

The Internet and the World Wide Web (WWW) are not synonymous. The WWW is just one part of the Internet, and its primary use is to correlate and disseminate information. The Internet includes the WWW and other forms of communication systems such as email. Figure 3.2 lists the key terms associated with the WWW, and Figure 3.3 lists the reasons for the massive growth of the WWW.[6]

The primary way a user navigates around the WWW is through a *universal resource locator (URL),* which contains the address of a file or resource on the web such as www.apple.com or www.microsoft.com. *URL shortening* is the translation of a long URL into an abbreviated alternative that redirects to the longer URL. Short URLs are preferable for a number of reasons. Long URLs in email messages can break if they fail to wrap properly, long URLs in Twitter tweets can leave no room for a message to accompany it, and long URLs in text messages can make the accompanying message difficult to read. URL shortening services typically provide users with:

- The ability to track, analyze and graph traffic statistics.
- Bookmarklets that enable URL shortening without visiting the site.
- The ability to customize shortened URL extensions.
- A preview function.

WEB 1.0: THE CATALYST FOR EBUSINESS

As people began learning about the WWW and the Internet, they understood that it enabled a company to communicate with anyone, anywhere, at anytime, creating a new way to participate in business. The competitive advantages for first movers would be enormous, thus spurring the beginning

Term	Definition	Example
World Wide Web	Provides access to Internet information through documents, including text, graphics, and audio and video files that use a special formatting language called Hypertext Markup Language	Tim Berners-Lee, a British computer scientist, is considered the inventor of the WWW on March 12, 1989.
Hypertext Markup Language (HTML)	Publishes hypertext on the WWW, which allows users to move from one document to another simply by clicking a hot spot or link	HTML uses tags such as <h1> and </h1> to structure text into headings, paragraphs, lists, hypertext links, and so on.
HTML 5	The current version of HTML delivers everything from animation to graphics and music to movies; it can also be used to build complicated web applications and works across platforms, including a PC, tablet, smart phone, or smart TV.	Includes new tags such as doctype, a simple way to tell the browser what type of document is being looked at: <!DOCTYPE html PUBLIC>
Hypertext Transport Protocol (HTTP)	The Internet protocol web browsers use to request and display web pages using universal resource locators (URLs)	To retrieve the file at the URL http://www.somehost.com/path/file.html
World Wide Web Consortium (W3C)	An international community that develops open standards to ensure the long-term growth of the web (www.w3.org)	Tim Berners-Lee founded the W3C to act as a steward of web standards, which the organization has done for more than 15 years.
Web browser	Allows users to access the WWW	Internet Explorer, Mozilla's Firefox, Google Chrome
Domain name hosting (web hosting)	A service that allows the owner of a domain name to maintain a simple website and provide email capacity	GoDaddy.com, 1&1.com, Web.com
Applet	A program that runs within another application such as a website	The common Hello World applet types "Hello World" across the screen.
Internet Corporation for Assigned Names and Numbers (ICANN)	A nonprofit organization that has assumed the responsibility for Internet Protocol (IP) address space allocation, protocol parameter assignment, domain name system management, and root server system management functions previously performed under U.S. government contract	https://www.icann.org/ Individuals, industry, noncommercial, and government representatives discuss, debate, and develop policies about the technical coordination of the Internet's domain name system.

FIGURE 3.2

Overview of the WWW

of the Web 1.0 Internet boom. *Web 1.0 (or Business 1.0)* is a term to refer to the World Wide Web during its first few years of operation between 1991 and 2003. *Ecommerce* is the buying and selling of goods and services over the Internet. Ecommerce refers only to online transactions. *Ebusiness* includes ecommerce along with all activities related to internal and external business operations such as servicing customer accounts, collaborating with partners, and exchanging real-time information. During Web 1.0, entrepreneurs began creating the first forms of ebusiness.

Ebusiness opened up a new marketplace for any company willing to move its business operations online. A *paradigm shift* occurs when a new, radical form of business enters the market that reshapes the way companies and organizations behave. Ebusiness created a paradigm shift, transforming entire industries and changing enterprisewide business processes that fundamentally rewrote traditional business rules. Deciding not to make the shift to ebusiness proved fatal for many companies (see Figure 3.4 for an overview of industries revamped by the disruption of ebusiness).[7]

FIGURE 3.3

Reasons for Growth of the World Wide Web

The microcomputer revolution made it possible for an average person to own a computer.
Advancements in networking hardware, software, and media made it possible for business computers to be connected to larger networks at a minimal cost.
Browser software such as Microsoft's Internet Explorer and Netscape Navigator gave computer users an easy-to-use graphical interface to find, download, and display web pages.
The speed, convenience, and low cost of email have made it an incredibly popular tool for business and personal communications.
Basic web pages are easy to create and extremely flexible.

BUSINESS DRIVEN ETHICS AND SECURITY

Unethical Disruption

Did you know you can make a living naming things? Eli Altman has been naming things since he was 6 years old and has named more than 400 companies and brands while working for A Hundred Monkeys, a branding consulting company. Altman recently noticed an unfamiliar trend in the industry: nonsensical names such as Flickr, Socializr, Zoomr, Rowdii, Yuuguu, and Oooooc. Why are names like this becoming popular?

The reason is "domain squatting" or "cyber squatting," the practice of buying a domain to profit from a trademarked name. For example, if you wanted to start a business called Drink, chances are a domain squatter has already purchased drink.com and is just waiting for you to pay big bucks for the right to buy it. Domain squatting is illegal and outlawed under the 1999 Anticybersquatting Consumer Protection Act.[8]

Do you agree that domain squatting should be illegal? Why or why not? If you were starting a business and someone were squatting on your domain, what would you do?

FIGURE 3.4

Ebusiness Disruption of Traditional Industries

Industry	Business Changes Due to Technology
Auto	AutoTrader.com is the world's largest used-car marketplace, listing millions of cars from both private owners and dealers. AutoTrader.com actually helps increase used-car dealers' business because it drives millions of qualified leads (potential used-car buyers) to participating automotive dealers and private sellers.
Publishing	With the Internet, anyone can publish online content. Traditionally, publishers screened many authors and manuscripts and selected those that had the best chances of succeeding. Lulu.com turned this model around by providing self-publishing along with print-on-demand capabilities.
Education and Training	Continuing medical education is costly, and just keeping up to date with advances often requires taking training courses and traveling to conferences. Now continuing education in many fields is moving online with over 50 percent of doctors expected to build their skills through online learning. Companies such as Cisco save millions by moving training to the Internet.
Entertainment	The music industry was hit hard by ebusiness, and online music traders such as iTunes average billions of annual downloads. Unable to compete with online music, the majority of record stores closed. The next big entertainment industry to feel the effects of ebusiness will be the multibillion-dollar movie business. Video rental stores are closing their doors as they fail to compete with online streaming and on-demand delivery companies such as Netflix.
Financial Services	Nearly every public efinance company makes money, with online mortgage service Lending Tree leading the pack. Processing online mortgage applications is over 50 percent cheaper for customers.
Retail	Forrester Research predicts ebusiness retail sales will grow at a 10 percent annual growth. It forecasts U.S. online retail sales will be nearly $250 billion, up from $155 billion.
Travel	Travel site Expedia.com is now the biggest leisure-travel agency, with higher profit margins than even American Express. The majority of travel agencies closed as a direct result of ebusiness.

FIGURE 3.5

Ebusiness Advantages

Both individuals and organizations have embraced ebusiness to enhance productivity, maximize convenience, and improve communications. Companies today need to deploy a comprehensive ebusiness strategy, and business students need to understand its advantages, outlined in Figure 3.5. Let's look at each.

Expanding Global Reach

Easy access to real-time information is a primary benefit of ebusiness. *Information richness* refers to the depth and breadth of details contained in a piece of textual, graphic, audio, or video information. *Information reach* measures the number of people a firm can communicate with all over the world. Buyers need information richness to make informed purchases, and sellers need information reach to market and differentiate themselves from the competition properly.

Ebusinesses operate 24 hours a day, 7 days a week. This availability directly reduces transaction costs, since consumers no longer have to spend a lot of time researching purchases or traveling great distances to make them. The faster delivery cycle for online sales helps strengthen customer relationships, improving customer satisfaction and, ultimately, sales.

A firm's website can be the focal point of a cost-effective communications and marketing strategy. Promoting products online allows the company to target its customers precisely whether they are local or around the globe. A physical location is restricted by size and limited to those customers who can get there, but an online store has a global marketplace with customers and information seekers already waiting in line.

Opening New Markets

Ebusiness is perfect for increasing niche-product sales. *Mass customization* is the ability of an organization to tailor its products or services to the customers' specifications. For example, customers can order M&Ms in special colors or with customized sayings such as "Marry Me." *Personalization* occurs when a company knows enough about a customer's likes and dislikes that it can fashion offers more likely to appeal to that person, say by tailoring its website to individuals or groups based on profile information, demographics, or prior transactions. Amazon uses personalization to create a unique portal for each of its customers.

Reducing Costs

Chris Anderson, editor-in-chief of *Wired* magazine, describes niche-market ebusiness strategies as capturing the *long tail,* referring to the tail of a typical sales curve. This strategy demonstrates how niche products can have viable and profitable business models when selling via ebusiness. In traditional sales models, a store is limited by shelf space when selecting products to sell. For this reason, store owners typically purchase products that will be wanted or needed by masses, and the store is stocked with broad products because there isn't room on the shelf for niche products that only a few customers might purchase. Ebusinesses such as Amazon and eBay eliminated the shelf-space dilemma and were able to offer infinite products.

FIGURE 3.6

The Long Tail

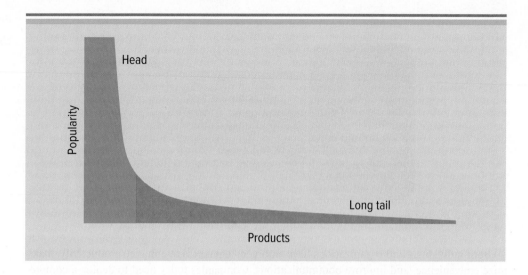

Netflix offers an excellent example of the long tail. Let's assume that an average Blockbuster store maintains 3,000 movies in its inventory, whereas Netflix, without physical shelf limitations, can maintain 100,000 movies in its inventory. Looking at sales data, the majority of Blockbuster's revenue comes from new releases that are rented daily, whereas older selections are rented only a few times a month and don't repay the cost of keeping them in stock. Thus Blockbuster's sales tail ends at title 3,000 (see Figure 3.6) However, Netflix, with no physical limitations, can extend its tail beyond 100,000 (and with streaming video perhaps 200,000). By extending its tail, Netflix increases sales, even if a title is rented only a few times.[9]

Intermediaries are agents, software, or businesses that provide a trading infrastructure to bring buyers and sellers together. The introduction of ebusiness brought about ***disintermediation,*** which occurs when a business sells directly to the customer online and cuts out the intermediary (see Figure 3.7). This business strategy lets the company shorten the order process and add value with reduced costs or a more responsive and efficient service. The disintermediation of the travel agent occurred as people began to book their own vacations online, often at a cheaper rate. At Lulu.com, anyone can publish and sell print-on-demand books, online music, and custom calendars, making the publisher obsolete.[10]

FIGURE 3.7

Business Value of Disintermediation

The more intermediaries that are cut from the distribution chain, the lower the product price. When Dell decided to sell its PCs through Walmart, many were surprised, because Dell's direct-to-customer sales model was the competitive advantage that had kept Dell the market leader for years.

In *reintermediation*, steps are *added* to the value chain as new players find ways to add value to the business process. Levi Strauss originally thought it was a good business strategy to limit all online sales to its own website. A few years later, the company realized it could gain a far larger market share by allowing all retailers to sell its products directly to customers. As ebusiness matures, it has become evident that to serve certain markets in volume, some reintermediation may be desirable. *Cybermediation* refers to the creation of new kinds of intermediaries that simply could not have existed before the advent of ebusiness, including comparison-shopping sites such as Kelkoo and bank account aggregation services such as Citibank.[11]

Operational benefits of ebusiness include business processes that require less time and human effort or can be eliminated. Compare the cost of sending out 100 direct mailings (paper, postage, labor) to the cost of a bulk email campaign. Think about the cost of renting a physical location and operating phone lines versus the cost of maintaining an online site. Switching to an ebusiness model can eliminate many traditional costs associated with communicating by substituting systems, such as Live Help, that let customers chat live with support or sales staff.

Online air travel reservations cost less than those booked over the telephone. Online ordering also offers the possibility of merging a sales order system with order fulfillment and delivery so customers can check the progress of their orders at all times. Ebusinesses can also inexpensively attract new customers with innovative marketing and retain present customers with improved service and support.[12]

One of the most exciting benefits of ebusiness is its low start-up costs. Today, anyone can start an ebusiness with just a website and a great product or service. Even a dog-walking operation can benefit from being an ebusiness.

Improving Effectiveness

Just putting up a simple website does not create an ebusiness. Ebusiness websites must create buzz, be innovative, add value, and provide useful information. In short, they must build a sense of community and collaboration.

MIS measures of efficiency, such as the amount of traffic on a site, don't tell the whole story. They do not necessarily indicate large sales volumes, for instance. Many websites with lots of traffic have minimal sales. The best way to measure ebusiness success is to use *effectiveness* MIS metrics, such as the revenue generated by web traffic, number of new customers acquired by web traffic, and reductions in customer service calls resulting from web traffic.

Interactivity measures advertising effectiveness by counting visitor interactions with the target ad, including time spent viewing the ad, number of pages viewed, and number of repeat visits to the advertisement. Interactivity measures are a giant step forward for advertisers, since traditional advertising methods—newspapers, magazines, radio, and television—provide few ways to track effectiveness. A *heat map* is a two-dimensional representation of data in which values are represented by colors. A simple heat map provides an immediate visual summary of information. More elaborate heat maps allow the viewer to understand complex data. Figure 3.8 displays the ebusiness marketing initiatives allowing companies to expand their reach while measuring effectiveness.[13]

The ultimate outcome of any advertisement is a purchase. Organizations use metrics to tie revenue amounts and number of new customers created directly back to the websites or banner ads. The path the visitor takes though a website is called the clickstream. Through *clickstream data,* they can observe the exact pattern of a consumer's navigation through a site. Clickstream data can include the length of stay on a website, number of abandoned registrations, and number of abandoned shopping carts. When a visitor reaches a website, a hit is generated, and his or her computer sends a request to the site's computer server to begin displaying pages. Each element of a request page is recorded by the website's server log file as a hit. Stickiness is the length of time a visitor spends on a website. Businesses want their websites to be sticky and keep their customer's attention. To interpret such data properly, managers try to benchmark against other companies. For instance, consumers seem to visit their preferred websites regularly, even checking back multiple times during a given session.[14]

TERM	DEFINITION	EXAMPLE
Associate (affiliate) program	Allows a business to generate commissions or referral fees when a customer visiting its website clicks a link to another merchant's website	If a customer to a company website clicks a banner ad to another vendor's website, the company will receive a referral fee or commission when the customer performs the desired action, typically making a purchase or completing a form.
Banner ad	A box running across a website that advertises the products and services of another business, usually another ebusiness	The banner generally contains a link to the advertiser's website. Advertisers can track how often customers click a banner ad resulting in a click-through to their website. Often the cost of the banner ad depends on the number of customers who click the banner ad. Web-based advertising services can track the number of times users click the banner, generating statistics that enable advertisers to judge whether the advertising fees are worth paying.
Click-through	A count of the number of people who visit one site and click an advertisement that takes them to the site of the advertiser	Tracking effectiveness based on click-throughs guarantees exposure to target ads; however, it does not guarantee that the visitor liked the ad, spent any substantial time viewing the ad, or was satisfied with the information contained in the ad.
Cookie	A small file deposited on a hard drive by a website, containing information about customers and their browsing activities	Cookies allow websites to record the comings and goings of customers, usually without their knowledge or consent.
Pop-up ad	A small web page containing an advertisement that appears outside of the current website loaded in the browser	A form of a pop-up ad that users do not see until they close the current web browser screen
Viral marketing	A technique that induces websites or users to pass on a marketing message to other websites or users, creating exponential growth in the message's visibility and effect.	One example of successful viral marketing is Hotmail, which promotes its service and its own advertisers' messages in every user's email notes. Viral marketing encourages users of a product or service supplied by an ebusiness to encourage friends to join. Viral marketing is a word-of-mouth type of advertising program.

FIGURE 3.8

Marketing Benefits from Ebusiness

On a website, *clickstream analytics* is the process of collecting, analyzing and reporting aggregate data about which pages a website visitor visits—and in what order. Clickstream analytics is considered to be most effective when used in conjunction with other, more traditional, market evaluation resources. Since extremely large volumes of data are gathered by clickstream analytics, many businesses rely on big data analytics and related tools to help interpret the data and generate reports for specific areas of interest. There are two levels of clickstream analytics, traffic analytics and ebusiness analytics.

- *Website traffic analytics* uses clickstream data to determine the efficiency of the site for the users and operates at the server level. Traffic analytics tracks data on how many pages are served to the user, how long it takes each page to load, how often the user hits the browser's back or stop button, and how much data is transmitted before the user moves on.

- *Website ebusiness analytics* uses clickstream data to determine the effectiveness of the site as a channel-to-market. Website ebusiness analytics track what pages the shopper lingers on, what the shopper puts in or takes out of a shopping cart, what items the shopper purchases, whether or not the shopper belongs to a loyalty program and uses a coupon code, and the shopper's preferred method of payment.

LO 3.3: Compare the four ebusiness models.

THE FOUR EBUSINESS MODELS

A *business model* is a plan that details how a company creates, delivers, and generates revenues. Some models are quite simple: A company produces a good or service and sells it to customers. If the company is successful, sales exceed costs and the company generates a profit. Other

BUSINESS DRIVEN ANALYTICS

Website Analytics

Stars Inc. is a large clothing corporation that specializes in reselling clothes worn by celebrities. The company's four websites generate 75 percent of its sales. The remaining 25 percent of sales occur directly through the company's warehouse. You have recently been hired as the director of sales. The only information you can find about the success of the four websites is displayed in the table below.

You decide that maintaining four websites is expensive and adds little business value. You propose consolidating to one site. Create a report detailing the business value gained by consolidating to a single website, along with your recommendation for consolidation. Be sure to include your website profitability analysis. Assume that, at a minimum, 10 percent of hits result in a sale; at an average, 30 percent of hits result in a sale; and at a maximum, 60 percent of hits result in a sale.

Website	Classic	Contemporary	New Age	Traditional
Traffic analysis	5,000 hits/day	200 hits/day	10,000 hits/day	1,000 hits/day
Stickiness (average)	20 minutes	1 hour	20 minutes	50 minutes
Number of abandoned shopping carts	400/day	0/day	5,000/day	200/day
Number of unique visitors	2,000/day	100/day	8,000/day	200/day
Number of identified visitors	3,000/day	100/day	2,000/day	800/day
Average revenue per sale	$1,000	$ 1,000	$50	$1,300

models are less straightforward, and sometimes it's not immediately clear who makes money and how much. Radio and network television are broadcast free to anyone with a receiver, for instance; advertisers pay the costs of programming.

The majority of online business activities consist of the exchange of products and services either between businesses or between businesses and consumers. An *ebusiness model* is a plan that details how a company creates, delivers, and generates revenues on the Internet. *Dot-com* was the original term for a company operating on the Internet. Ebusiness models fall into one of the four categories: (1) business-to-business, (2) business-to-consumer, (3) consumer-to-business, and (4) consumer-to-consumer (see Figure 3.9).

FIGURE 3.9

Ebusiness Models

Ebusiness Term	Definition		Business	Consumer
Business-to-business (B2B)	Applies to businesses buying from and selling to each other over the Internet.			
Business-to-consumer (B2C)	Applies to any business that sells its products or services to consumers over the Internet.	Business	B2B	B2C
Consumer-to-business (C2B)	Applies to any consumer that sells a product or service to a business over the Internet.			
Consumer-to-consumer (C2C)	Applies to sites primarily offering goods and services to assist consumers interacting with each other over the Internet.	Consumer	C2B	C2C

Business-to-Business (B2B)

Business-to-business (B2B) applies to businesses buying from and selling to each other over the Internet. Examples include medical billing service, software sales and licensing, and virtual assistant businesses. B2B relationships represent 80 percent of all online business and are more complex with greater security needs than the other types. B2B examples include Oracle and SAP.

Electronic marketplaces, or emarketplaces, are interactive business communities providing a central market where multiple buyers and sellers can engage in ebusiness activities. By tightening and automating the relationship between the two parties, they create structures for conducting commercial exchange, consolidating supply chains, and creating new sales channels.

Business-to-Consumer (B2C)

Business-to-consumer (B2C) applies to any business that sells its products or services directly to consumers online. Carfax offers car buyers detailed histories of used vehicles for a fee. An *eshop,* sometimes referred to as an *estore* or *etailer,* is an online version of a retail store where customers can shop at any hour. It can be an extension of an existing store such as The Gap or operate only online such as Amazon.com. There are three ways to operate as a B2C: brick-and-mortar, click-and-mortar, and pure play (see Figure 3.10).

Consumer-to-Business (C2B)

Consumer-to-business (C2B) applies to any consumer who sells a product or service to a business on the Internet. One example is customers of Priceline.com, who set their own prices for items such as airline tickets or hotel rooms and wait for a seller to decide whether to supply them. The demand for C2B ebusiness will increase over the next few years due to customers' desire for greater convenience and lower prices.

Consumer-to-Consumer (C2C)

Consumer-to-consumer (C2C) applies to customers offering goods and services to each other on the Internet. A good example of a C2C is an auction in which buyers and sellers solicit consecutive bids from each other and prices are determined dynamically. Craigslist and eBay

FIGURE 3.10

Forms of Business-to-Consumer Operations

Brick-and-Mortar Business
A business that operates in a physical store without an Internet presence.
Example: T.J. Maxx

Click-and-Mortar Business
A business that operates in a physical store and on the Internet.
Example: Barnes & Noble

Pure-Play (Virtual) Business
A business that operates on the Internet only without a physical store.
Example: Google

BUSINESS DRIVEN STARTUP

Are Your Ready for your Next Gig?

The word *gig* comes from the music world; a gig is a paid appearance of limited duration. A gig economy is an environment in which temporary employment is common and organizations contract with independent workers for short-term engagements. Today's workforce is expected to change jobs at least seven times before retirement. The gig economy will make workers independent of one company, and job changing will be far easier than ever before.

Forces driving the gig economy include the proliferation of websites and mobile applications designed to help employers and people seeking part-time work find each other. Another important influence is a millennial generation workforce that values work-life balance. Today's workforce is increasingly mobile, and if a job is decoupled from location and work can be done from anywhere, gig workers are free to choose to work a series of jobs that are interesting and enjoyable, rather than making a long-term commitment to a single job that's not interesting or enjoyable, just for the sake of financial security.

From a business perspective, a gig economy can save a company money with lower investments in health insurance, office space, and training expenses. Businesses can also hire experts for individual projects, choosing from the best professionals available without having to maintain high-salaried workers.

A study by Intuit predicted that by 2025, 50 percent of American workers would be independent contractors and members of the gig economy. What are the pros and cons to working in the gig economy? Do you believe you will be part of the gig economy? How can this course help you prepare for work in the gig economy?

are two examples of successful C2C websites, linking like-minded buyers with sellers. Other types of online auctions include forward auctions in which sellers market to many buyers and the highest bid wins, and reverse auctions in which buyers select goods and services from the seller with the lowest bid.

Ebusiness Forms and Revenue-Generating Strategies

As more and more companies began jumping on the ebusiness bandwagon, new forms of ebusiness began to emerge (see Figure 3.11). Many of the new forms of ebusiness went to market

Form	Description	Examples
Content providers	Generate revenues by providing digital content such as news, music, photos, or videos.	Netflix.com, iTunes.com, CNN.com
Infomediaries	Provide specialized information on behalf of producers of goods and services and their potential customers	Edmunds.com, BizRate.com, Bloomberg.com, Zillow.com
Online marketplaces	Bring together buyers and sellers of products and services.	Amazon.com, eBay.com, Priceline.com
Portals	Operate a central website for users to access specialized content and other services.	Google.com, Yahoo.com, MSN.com
Service providers	Provide services such as photo sharing, video sharing, online backup, and storage.	Flickr.com, Mapquest.com, YouTube.com
Transaction brokers	Process online sales transactions.	Etrade.com, Charlesschwab.com, Fidelity.com

FIGURE 3.11

Ebusiness Forms

without clear strategies on how they would generate revenue. Google is an excellent example of an ebusiness that did not figure out a way to generate profits until many years after its launch.[15]

Ebusinesses must have a revenue model, or a model for making money. *Adwords* are keywords that advertisers choose to pay for and appear as sponsored links on the Google results pages. Keywords are chosen by the advertiser and are displayed on the results pages when the search keywords match the advertiser's keywords. The advertiser then pays a fee to Google for the search display.

Google's primary line of business is its search engine; however, the company does not generate revenue from people using its site to search the Internet. It generates revenue from the marketers and advertisers that pay to place their ads on the site. About 200 million times each day, people from all over the world access Google to perform searches. AdWords, a part of the Google site, allows advertisers to bid on common search terms. The advertisers simply enter in the keywords they want to bid on and the maximum amounts they want to pay per click per day. Google then determines a price and a search ranking for those keywords based on how much other advertisers are willing to pay for the same terms. Pricing for keywords can range from 5 cents to $10 a click. Paid search is the ultimate in targeted advertising because consumers type in exactly what they want. A general search term such as *tropical vacation* costs less than a more specific term such as *Hawaiian vacation*. Whoever bids the most for a term appears in a sponsored advertisement link either at the top or along the side of the search-results page.[16]

A *search engine* is website software that finds other pages based on keyword matching similar to Google. *Search engine ranking* evaluates variables that search engines use to determine where a URL appears on the list of search results. *Search engine optimization (SEO)* combines art with science to determine how to make URLs more attractive to search engines resulting in higher search engine ranking. The better the SEO, the higher the ranking for a website in the list of search engine results. SEO is critical because most people only view the first few pages of a search result. After that, a person is more inclined to begin a new search than review pages and pages of search results. Websites can generate revenue through:

- *Pay-per-click:* Generates revenue each time a user clicks a link to a retailer's website.
- *Pay-per-call:* Generates revenue each time a user clicks a link that takes the user directly to an online agent waiting for a call.
- *Pay-per-conversion:* Generates revenue each time a website visitor is converted to a customer.

Figure 3.12 lists the different benefits and challenges of various ebusiness revenue models.[17]

Ebusiness Fraud   As with any great technology, there is always someone using it for unethical practices. When it comes to online advertising and Adword strategies, there are people who purposely click on Google searches just to cost their competitors money. *Click fraud* is the practice of artificially inflating traffic statistics for online advertisements. Some unethical individuals or click fraud scammers even use automated clicking programs called hitbots. *Hitbots* create the illusion that a large number of potential customers are clicking the advertiser's links, when in fact there is no likelihood that any of the clicks will lead to profit for the advertiser.

Affiliate programs allow a business to generate commissions or referral fees when a customer visiting its website clicks a link to another merchant's website. Click fraud scammers often take advantage of the affiliate programs by agreeing to provide exposure to an advertisement in order to receive a portion of the pay-per-click fees the advertiser is paying the affiliate. Instead of placing the ad on legitimate websites, the scammer might place the ad on websites created solely for the purpose of placing the ad. And a site like that, quite naturally, will not have any real, organic traffic. Once the ads are in place, the hitbots generate large volumes of fraudulent clicks, often in a very short time period, for which the scammer bills the owner of the affiliate program. This, of course, costs the company a tremendous amount of money.

LO 3.4: Describe the six ebusiness tools for connecting and communicating.

EBUSINESS TOOLS FOR CONNECTING AND COMMUNICATING

A *cyborg anthropologist* is an individual who studies the interaction between humans and technology, observing how technology can shape humans' lives. Cyborg anthropology as a discipline originated at the 1993 annual meeting of the American Anthropological Association. Cyborg anthropologists study the different online communication methods for businesses, including the technology tools highlighted in Figure 3.13 and covered below in detail.

FIGURE 3.12

Ebusiness Revenue Models

Ebusiness Revenue Model	Benefits	Challenges
Advertising fees	■ Well-targeted advertisements can be perceived as value-added content by trading participants. ■ Easy to implement.	■ Limited revenue potential. ■ Overdone or poorly targeted advertisements can be disturbing elements on the website.
License fees	■ Creates incentives to do many transactions. ■ Customization and back-end integration lead to lock-in of participants.	■ Up-front fee is a barrier to entry for participants. ■ Price differentiation is complicated.
Subscription fees	■ Creates incentives to do transactions. ■ Price can be differentiated. ■ Possibility to build additional revenue from new user groups.	■ Fixed fee is a barrier to entry for participants.
Transaction fees	■ Can be directly tied to savings (both process and price savings). ■ Important revenue source when high level of liquidity (transaction volume) is reached.	■ If process savings are not completely visible, use of the system is discouraged (incentive to move transactions offline). ■ Transaction fees likely to decrease with time.
Value-added services fees	■ Service offering can be differentiated. ■ Price can be differentiated. ■ Possibility to build additional revenue from established and new user groups (third parties).	■ Cumbersome process for customers to evaluate new services continually.

FIGURE 3.13

Ebusiness Tools

Email

Email, short for electronic mail, is the exchange of digital messages over the Internet. No longer do business professionals have to wait for the mail to receive important documents; email single-handedly increased the speed of business by allowing the transfer of documents with the same speed as the telephone. Its chief business advantage is the ability to inform and communicate with many people simultaneously, immediately, and with ease. There are no time or place constraints, and users can check, send, and view emails whenever they require.

An *Internet service provider (ISP)* is a company that provides access to the Internet for a monthly fee. Major ISPs in the United States include AOL, AT&T, Comcast, Earthlink, and Netzero, as well as thousands of local ISPs, including regional telephone companies.

Instant Messaging

Real-time communication occurs when a system updates information at the same rate it receives it. Email was a great advancement over traditional communication methods such as the U.S. mail, but it did not operate in real time. *Instant messaging (IMing)* is a service that enables instant or real-time communication between people. Businesses immediately saw what they could do:

- Answer simple questions quickly and easily.
- Resolve questions or problems immediately.
- Transmit messages as fast as naturally flowing conversation.
- Easily hold simultaneous IM sessions with multiple people.
- Eliminate long-distance phone charges.
- Quickly identify which employees are at their computers.

Web Real-Time Communications (WebRTC) is an open source project that seeks to embed real-time voice, text, and video communications capabilities in web browsers. WebRTC is expected to make audio, video, and data communication between browsers more user-friendly. The goal of WebRTC is to enable communications between browsers. With WebRTC, end-users do not have to download a special software application or use the same client or browser plug-in to communicate directly with each other.

Podcasting

Podcasting converts an audio broadcast to a digital music player. Podcasts can increase marketing reach and build customer loyalty. Companies use podcasts as marketing communication channels discussing everything from corporate strategies to detailed product overviews. The senior executive team can share weekly or monthly podcasts featuring important issues or expert briefings on new technical or marketing developments.

Videoconferencing

A *videoconference* allows people at two or more locations to interact via two-way video and audio transmissions simultaneously as well as share documents, data, computer displays, and whiteboards. Point-to-point videoconferences connect two people, and multipoint conferences connect more than two people at multiple locations.

Videoconferences can increase productivity because users participate without leaving their offices. They can improve communication and relationships because participants see each other's facial expressions and body language, both important aspects of communication that are lost with a basic telephone call or email. They also reduce travel expenses, a big win for firms facing economic challenges. Of course, nothing can replace meeting someone face to face and shaking hands, but videoconferencing offers a viable and cost-effective alternative.

Web Conferencing

Web conferencing, or a *webinar,* blends videoconferencing with document sharing and allows the user to deliver a presentation over the web to a group of geographically dispersed participants. Regardless of the type of hardware or software the attendees are running, every participant can see what is on anyone else's screen. Schools use web conferencing tools such as Illuminate Live to deliver lectures to students, and businesses use tools such as WebEx to demonstrate products. Web conferencing is not quite like being there, but professionals can accomplish more sitting at their desks than in an airport waiting to make travel connections.

A *telepresence robot* is a remote-controlled, wheeled device with a display to enable video chat and videoconferencing. These little robots are tremendously valuable for web conferencing as you feel as though the person is right in the room with you. Here are a few examples of telepresence robots:

- iRobot's Remote Presence Virtual + Independent Telemedicine Assistant (RP-VITA) is designed for use in hospitals where it makes it possible for doctors to consult with patients, guide staff, and confer with other medical practitioners remotely.
- Double Robotics' Double, which consists of a wheeled base integrated with an iPad, is designed for a business environment to enhance telecommuting or teleconferencing.
- Suitable Technologies' Beam+ is designed for in-home uses, such as mobile video chat, oversight of children or elderly people, and remote security monitoring. The vendor's Beam Pro product is designed for the workplace.

Although telepresence robots are expensive, they are typically much more affordable than the travel costs or fees they might replace. They also enable much more interactivity than regular video chat. In a distance education class, for example, a telepresence robot can move around the room and interact face-to-face with individual students, just as an on-premises instructor might.

Content Management Systems

In the fourth century BC, Aristotle catalogued the natural world according to a systematic organization, and the ancient library at Alexandria was reportedly organized by subject, connecting like information with like. Today *content management systems (CMS)* help companies manage the creation, storage, editing, and publication of their website content. CMSs are user-friendly; most include web-based publishing, search, navigation, and indexing to organize information; and they let users with little or no technical expertise make website changes.

A search is typically carried out by entering a keyword or phrase (query) into a text field and clicking a button or a hyperlink. Navigation facilitates movement from one web page to another. Content management systems play a crucial role in getting site visitors to view more than just the home page. If navigation choices are unclear, visitors may hit the Back button on their first (and final) visit to a website. One rule of thumb to remember is that each time a user has to click to find search information, there is a 50 percent chance the user will leave the website instead. A key principle of good website design, therefore, is to keep the number of clicks to a minimum.

Taxonomy is the scientific classification of organisms into groups based on similarities of structure or origin. Taxonomies are also used for indexing the content on the website into categories and subcategories of topics. For example, car is a subtype of vehicle. Every car is a vehicle, but not every vehicle is a car; some vehicles are vans, buses, and trucks. Taxonomy terms are arranged so that narrower/more specific/"child" terms fall under broader/more generic/"parent" terms. Many companies hire information architects to create their website taxonomies. A well-planned taxonomy ensures search and navigation are easy and user-friendly. If the taxonomy is confusing, the site will soon fail.

THE CHALLENGES OF EBUSINESS

LO 3.5: Identify the four challenges associated with ebusiness.

Although the benefits of ebusiness are enticing, developing, deploying, and managing ebusiness systems are not always easy. Figure 3.14 lists the challenges facing ebusiness.[18]

Identifying Limited Market Segments

The main challenge of ebusiness is the lack of growth in some sectors due to product or service limitations. The online food sector has not grown in sales, in part because food products are perishable and consumers prefer to buy them at the supermarket as needed. Other sectors with limited ebusiness appeal include fragile or consumable goods and highly sensitive or confidential businesses such as government agencies.

FIGURE 3.14

Challenges Facing Ebusiness

Managing Consumer Trust

Trust in the ebusiness exchange deserves special attention. The physical separation of buyer and seller, the physical separation of buyer and merchandise, and customer perceptions about the risk of doing business online provide unique challenges. Internet marketers must develop a trustworthy relationship to make that initial sale and generate customer loyalty. A few ways to build trust when working online include being accessible and available to communicate in person with your customers; using customers' testimonials that link to your client website or to provide their contact information; and accepting legitimate forms of payment such as credit cards.

Ensuring Consumer Protection

An organization that wants to dominate with superior customer service as a competitive advantage must not only serve but also protect its customers, guarding them against unsolicited goods and communication, illegal or harmful goods, insufficient information about goods and suppliers, invasion of privacy and misuse of personal information, and online fraud. System security, however, must not make ebusiness websites inflexible or difficult to use.

Adhering to Taxation Rules

Many believe that U.S. tax policy should provide a level playing field for traditional retail businesses, mail-order companies, and online merchants. Yet the Internet marketplace remains mostly free of traditional forms of sales tax, partly because ecommerce law is vaguely defined and differs from state to state. For now, companies that operate online must obey a patchwork of rules about which customers are subject to sales tax on their purchases and which are not.

section 3.2 | Web 2.0: Business 2.0

LEARNING OUTCOMES

3.6 Explain Web 2.0 and identify its four characteristics.

3.7 Explain how Business 2.0 is helping communities network and collaborate.

3.8 Describe the three Business 2.0 tools for collaborating.

3.9 Explain the three challenges associated with Business 2.0.

3.10 Describe Web 3.0 and the next generation of online business.

LO 3.6: Explain Web 2.0 and identify its four characteristics.

WEB 2.0: ADVANTAGES OF BUSINESS 2.0

In the mid-1990s, the stock market reached an all-time high as companies took advantage of ebusiness and Web 1.0, and many believed the Internet was the wave of the future. When new online businesses began failing to meet earning expectations, however, the bubble burst. Some then believed the ebusiness boom was over, but they could not have been more wrong.

BUSINESS DRIVEN GLOBALIZATION

Collaborating for Nonprofits—Kiva

Kiva's mission is to connect people through lending for the sake of alleviating poverty. Kiva is a micro-lending online nonprofit organization that enables individuals to lend directly to entrepreneurs throughout the world. If you want to participate in Kiva, you simply browse the website (www.kiva.org) and choose an entrepreneur that interests you, make a loan, then track your entrepreneur for the next 6 to 12 months while he or she builds the business and makes the funds to repay the loan. When the loan is up, you can relend the money to someone else who is in need.[19]

Kiva is an excellent example of blending ethics and information technology. How is Kiva operating differently than traditional nonprofits? What are the risks associated with investing in Kiva? When you invest in Kiva, you run three primary risks: entrepreneur risk, local field partner risk, and country risk. Analyze each of these risks for potential unethical issues that might arise when donating to Kiva.

Web 2.0 (or *Business 2.0*) is the next generation of Internet use—a more mature, distinctive communications platform characterized by new qualities such as collaboration, sharing, and free. Business 2.0 encourages user participation and the formation of communities that contribute to the content. In Business 2.0, technical skills are no longer required to use and publish information to the World Wide Web, eliminating entry barriers for online business.

Traditional companies tended to view technology as a tool required to perform a process or activity, and employees picked up information by walking through the office or hanging out around the water cooler. Business 2.0 technologies provide a virtual environment that, for many new employees, is just as vibrant and important as the physical environment. Figure 3.15 highlights the common characteristics of Web 2.0.[20]

Content Sharing through Open Sourcing

An *open system* consists of nonproprietary hardware and software based on publicly known standards that allow third parties to create add-on products to plug into or interoperate with the system. Thousands of hardware devices and software applications created and sold by third-party vendors interoperate with computers, such as iPods, drawing software, and mice.

FIGURE 3.15

Four Characteristics of Web 2.0

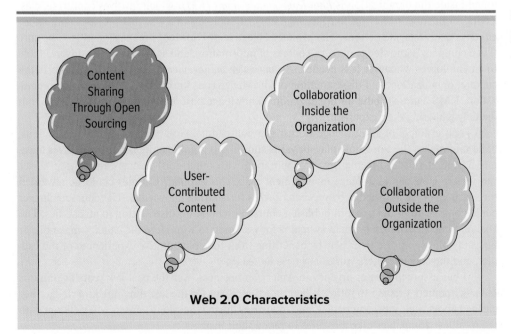

Web 2.0 Characteristics

Source code contains instructions written by a programmer specifying the actions to be performed by computer software. *Closed source* is any proprietary software licensed under exclusive legal right of the copyright holder. *Open source* refers to any software whose source code is made available free (not on a fee or licensing basis as in ebusiness) for any third party to review and modify. Business 2.0 is capitalizing on open source software. Mozilla, for example, offers its Firefox web browser and Thunderbird email software free. Mozilla believes the Internet is a public resource that must remain open and accessible to all; it continuously develops free products by bringing together thousands of dedicated volunteers from around the world. Mozilla's Firefox now holds over 20 percent of the browser market and is quickly becoming a threat to Microsoft's Internet Explorer. How do open source software companies generate revenues? Many people are still awaiting an answer to this very important question.[21]

User-Contributed Content

Ebusiness was characterized by a few companies or users posting content for the masses. Business 2.0 is characterized by the masses posting content for the masses. *User-contributed content* (or *user-generated content*) is created and updated by many users for many users. Websites such as Flickr, Wikipedia, and YouTube, for example, move control of online media from the hands of leaders to the hands of users. Netflix and Amazon both use user-generated content to drive their recommendation tools, and websites such as Yelp use customer reviews to express opinions on products and services. Companies are embracing user-generated content to help with everything from marketing to product development and quality assurance.

Native advertising is an online marketing concept in which the advertiser attempts to gain attention by providing content in the context of the user's experience in terms of its content, format, style, or placement. One of the most popular forms of user-generated content is a *reputation system,* in which buyers post feedback on sellers. eBay buyers voluntarily comment on the quality of service, their satisfaction with the item traded, and promptness of shipping. Sellers comment about prompt payment from buyers or respond to comments left by the buyer. Companies ranging from Amazon to restaurants are using reputation systems to improve quality and enhance customer satisfaction.

Collaboration Inside the Organization

A *collaboration system* is a set of tools that supports the work of teams or groups by facilitating the sharing and flow of information. Business 2.0's collaborative mind-set generates more information faster from a wider audience. *Collective intelligence* is collaborating and tapping into the core knowledge of all employees, partners, and customers. Knowledge can be a real competitive advantage for an organization. The most common form of collective intelligence found inside the organization is *knowledge management (KM),* which involves capturing, classifying, evaluating, retrieving, and sharing information assets in a way that provides context for effective decisions and actions. The primary objective of knowledge management is to be sure that a company's knowledge of facts, sources of information, and solutions are readily available to all employees whenever it is needed. A *knowledge management system (KMS)* supports the capture, organization, and dissemination of knowledge (i.e., know-how) throughout an organization. KMS can distribute an organization's knowledge base by interconnecting people and digitally gathering their expertise.

A great example of a knowledge worker is a golf caddie. Golf caddies give advice such as, "The rain makes the third hole play 10 yards shorter." If a golf caddie is good and gives accurate advice, it can lead to big tips. Collaborating with other golf caddies can provide bigger tips for all. How can knowledge management make this happen? Caddies could be rewarded for sharing course knowledge by receiving prizes for sharing knowledge. The course manager could compile all of the tips and publish a course notebook for distribution to all caddies. The goal of a knowledge management system is for everyone to win. Here the caddies make bigger tips and golfers improve their play by benefiting from the collaborative experiences of the caddies, and the course owners win as business increases.

KM has assumed greater urgency in American business over the past few years as millions of baby boomers prepare to retire. When they punch out for the last time, the knowledge they gleaned about their jobs, companies, and industries during their long careers will walk out with them—unless companies take measures to retain their insights.

BUSINESS DRIVEN START-UP

Using Hashtags

If you have ever seen a word with a # before it in Facebook or Twitter, you have seen a hashtag. A hashtag is a keyword or phrase used to identify a topic and is preceded by a hash or pound sign (#). Hashtags provide an online audience to expand business exposure and directly engage with customers. Customers can type any search keyword in a social media site with a hashtag before the word and the search results will show all related posts. Hashtags can be used to reference promotions, observe market trends, and even provide links to helpful tips.

When you understand hashtags, you can use them to find business ideas and research potential employers. Pick a company you would like to work for and see whether you can find any related hashtags including what they are tweeting and posting. See whether you can find any information on partners and competitors. Which hashtags generate discussion or offer business insights? Check Twitter's and Facebook's trending topics to see whether there are any issues or insights on your career area.

Explicit and Tacit Knowledge Not all information is valuable. Individuals must determine what information qualifies as intellectual and knowledge-based assets. In general, intellectual and knowledge-based assets fall into one of two categories: explicit or tacit. As a rule, *explicit knowledge* consists of anything that can be documented, archived, and codified, often with the help of MIS. Examples of explicit knowledge are assets such as patents, trademarks, business plans, marketing research, and customer lists. *Tacit knowledge* is the knowledge contained in people's heads. The challenge inherent in tacit knowledge is figuring out how to recognize, generate, share, and manage knowledge that resides in people's heads. Although information technology in the form of email, instant messaging, and related technologies can help facilitate the dissemination of tacit knowledge, identifying it in the first place can be a major obstacle.

Collaboration Outside the Organization

The most common form of collective intelligence found outside the organization is *crowdsourcing,* which refers to the wisdom of the crowd. The idea that collective intelligence is greater than the sum of its individual parts has been around for a long time (see Figure 3.16). With

FIGURE 3.16

Crowdsourcing: The Crowd Is Smarter Than the Individual

©Digital Vision/Getty Images RF

Business 2.0, the ability to tap into its power efficiently is emerging. For many years, organizations believed that good ideas came from the top. CEOs collaborated only with the heads of sales and marketing, the quality assurance expert, or the road warrior salesman. The organization chart governed who should work with whom and how far up the chain of command a suggestion or idea would travel. With Business 2.0, this belief is being challenged as firms capitalize on crowdsourcing by opening up a task or problem to a wider group to find better or cheaper results from outside the box.

Crowdfunding sources capital for a project by raising many small amounts from a large number of individuals, typically via the Internet. With Business 2.0, people can be continuously connected, a driving force behind collaboration. Traditional ebusiness communications were limited to face-to-face conversations and one-way technologies that used *asynchronous communications,* or communication such as email, in which the message and the response do not occur at the same time. Business 2.0 brought *synchronous communication,* or communications that occur at the same time, such as IM or chat. Ask a group of college students when they last spoke to their parents. For most the answer is less than hour ago as opposed to the traditional response of a few days ago. In business, too, continuous connections are now expected in today's collaborative world.

NETWORKING COMMUNITIES WITH BUSINESS 2.0

LO 3.7: Explain how Business 2.0 is helping communities network and collaborate.

Social media refers to websites that rely on user participation and user-contributed content, such as Facebook, YouTube, and Digg. A *social network* is an application that connects people by matching profile information. Providing individuals with the ability to network is by far one of the greatest advantages of Business 2.0. *Social networking* is the practice of expanding your business and/or social contacts by constructing a personal network (see Figure 3.17). Social networking sites provide two basic functions. The first is the ability to create and maintain a profile that serves as an online identity within the environment. The second is the ability to create connections between other people within the network. *Social networking analysis (SNA)* maps group contacts (personal and professional) identifying who knows each other and who works together. In a company, it can provide a vision of how employees work together. It can also identify key experts with specific knowledge such as how to solve a complicated programming problem or launch a new product.

Business 2.0 simplifies access to information and improves the ability to share it. Instead of spending $1,000 and two days at a conference to meet professional peers, business people can now use social networks such as LinkedIn to meet new contacts for recruiting, prospecting, and identifying experts on a topic. With executive members from all the *Fortune* 500 companies, LinkedIn has become one of the more useful recruiting tools on the web.

FIGURE 3.17

Social Network Example[22]

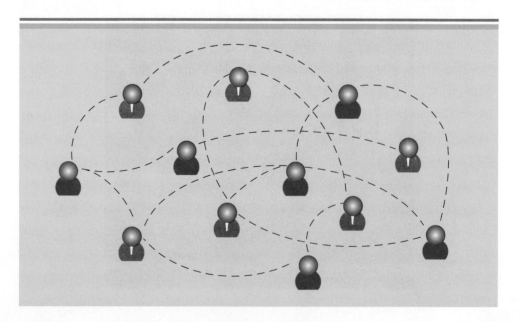

Social graphs represent the interconnection of relationships in a social network. Social networking sites can be especially useful to employers trying to find job candidates with unique or highly specialized skill sets that may be harder to locate in larger communities. Many employers also search social networking sites to find "dirt" and character references for potential employees. Keep in mind that what you post on the Internet stays on the Internet.[23]

Social Tagging

Tags are specific keywords or phrases incorporated into website content for means of classification or taxonomy. An item can have one or more tags associated with it to allow for multiple browsable paths through the items, and tags can be changed with minimal effort (see Figure 3.18). *Social tagging* describes the collaborative activity of marking shared online content with keywords or tags as a way to organize it for future navigation, filtering, or searching. The entire user community is invited to tag, and thus essentially define, the content. Flickr allows users to upload images and tag them with appropriate keywords. After enough people have done so, the resulting tag collection will identify images correctly and without bias. A *hashtag* is a keyword or phrase used to identify a topic and is preceded by a hash or pound sign (#). For example, the hashtag #sandiegofire helped coordinate emergency responses to a fire.

Folksonomy is similar to taxonomy except that crowdsourcing determines the tags or keyword-based classification system. Using the collective power of a community to identify and classify content significantly lowers content categorization costs because there is no complicated nomenclature to learn. Users simply create and apply tags as they wish. For example, although cell phone manufacturers often refer to their products as mobile devices, the folksonomy could include *mobile phone, wireless phone, smart phone, iPhone, BlackBerry,* and so on. All these keywords, if searched, should take a user to the same site. Folksonomies reveal what people truly call things (see Figure 3.19). They have been a point of discussion on the web because the whole point of having a website is for your customers to find it. The majority of websites are found through search terms that match the content.[24]

A *website bookmark* is a locally stored URL or the address of a file or Internet page saved as a shortcut. *Social bookmarking* allows users to share, organize, search, and manage bookmarks. Delicious, a website dedicated to social bookmarking, provides users with a place to store, categorize, annotate, and share favorites. StumbleUpon is another popular social bookmarking website that allows users to locate interesting websites based on their favorite subjects. The more you use the service, the more the system learns about your interests and the better it can show you websites that interest you. StumbleUpon represents a new social networking model in which content finds the users instead of the other way around. Stumble-Upon is all about the users and the content they enjoy.[25]

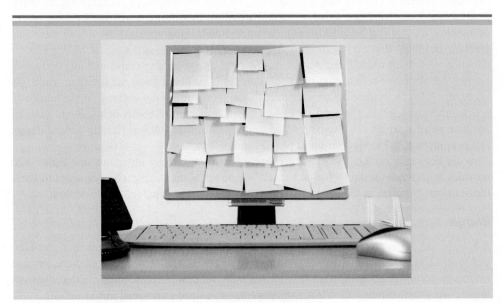

FIGURE 3.18

Social Tagging Occurs When Many Individuals Categorize Content

©Image Source RF

BUSINESS DRIVEN DEBATE

AntiSocial Networking

Before the Internet, angry customers could write letters or make phone calls, but their individual power to find satisfaction or bring about change was relatively weak. Now, disgruntled consumers can create a website or upload a video bashing a product or service, and their efforts can be instantly seen by millions of people. Though many companies monitor the Internet and try to respond to such postings quickly, power has clearly shifted to the consumer. Create an argument for or against the following statement: "Social networking has given power to the consumer that benefits society and creates socially responsible corporations."

FIGURE 3.19

Folksonomy Example: The User-Generated Names for Cellular Phones

©Fotosearch/Getty Images RF.

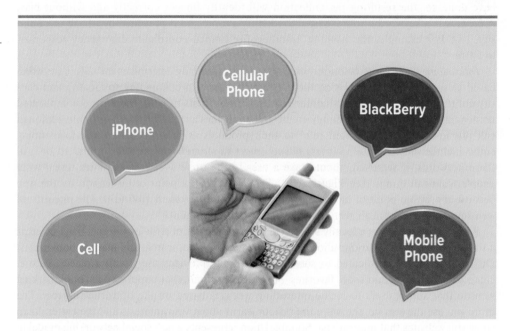

LO 3.8: Describe the three Business 2.0 tools for collaborating.

BUSINESS 2.0 TOOLS FOR COLLABORATING

Snackable content is content that is designed to be easy for readers to consume and to share. Snackable content captures website visitors' attention by offering small consumable pieces of information that can be quickly read and understood. Infographics, photos, and attention-grabbing headlines that ask questions or use humor play a critical part when attracting readers attention who are browsing and don't have the time or patience to consume long, text-heavy articles. Many people believe that snackable content is dumbing down the Internet, while others believe it fits the mobile delivery channel so many consumers use today. To make long-form articles more snackable, they can be broken down into smaller components. Responsive or adaptive website design can also help make content more snackable, as flexible website design makes content easier to view on smart phones and tablets.

Social networking and collaborating are leading businesses in new directions, and Figure 3.20 provides an overview of the tools that harness the power of the people, allowing users to share ideas, discuss business problems, and collaborate on solutions using snackable content.

Blogs

A *blog,* or *web log,* is an online journal that allows users to post their own comments, graphics, and video. Unlike traditional HTML web pages, blog websites let writers communicate—and readers respond—on a regular basis through a simple yet customizable interface that does not require any programming. A *selfie* is a self-photograph placed on a social media website.

FIGURE 3.20

Business 2.0 Communication and Collaboration Tools

BLOG	WIKI	MASHUP
• An online journal that allows users to post their own comments, graphics, and videos	• Collaborative website that allows users to add, remove, and change content	• Content from more than one source to create a new product or service
• Popular business examples include Sweet Leaf Tea, Stoneyfield Farm, Nuts about Southwest, Disney Parks	• Popular business examples include Wikipedia, National Institute of Health, Intelopedia, LexisNexis, Wiki for Higher Education	• Examples include Zillow, Infopedia, Trendsmap, SongDNA, ThisWeKnow

From a business perspective, blogs are no different from marketing channels such as video, print, audio, or presentations. They all deliver results of varying kinds. Consider Sun Microsystem's Jonathan Schwartz and GM's Bob Lutz, who use their blogs for marketing, sharing ideas, gathering feedback, press response, and image shaping. Starbucks has developed a blog called My Starbucks Idea, allowing customers to share ideas, tell Starbucks what they think of other people's ideas, and join discussions. Blogs are an ideal mechanism for many businesses since they can focus on topic areas more easily than traditional media, with no limits on page size, word count, or publication deadline.[26]

Microblogs *Microblogging* is the practice of sending brief posts (140 to 200 characters) to a personal blog, either publicly or to a private group of subscribers who can read the posts as IMs or as text messages. The main advantage of microblogging is that posts can be submitted by a variety of means, such as instant messaging, email, or the web. By far the most popular microblogging tool is Twitter, which allows users to send microblog entries called tweets to anyone who has registered to follow them. Senders can restrict delivery to people they want to follow them or, by default, allow open access.[27]

Real Simple Syndication *Real simple syndication (RSS)* is a web format used to publish frequently updated works, such as blogs, news headlines, audio, and video, in a standardized format. An RSS document or feed includes full or summarized text, plus other information such as publication date and authorship. News websites, blogs, and podcasts use RSS, constantly feeding news to consumers instead of having them search for it. In addition to facilitating syndication, RSS allows a website's frequent readers to track updates on the site.

Wikis

A *wiki* (the word is Hawaiian for "quick") is a type of collaborative web page that allows users to add, remove, and change content, which can be easily organized and reorganized as required. Although blogs have largely drawn on the creative and personal goals of individual authors, wikis are based on open collaboration with any and everybody. Wikipedia, the open encyclopedia that launched in 2001, has become one of the 10 most popular web destinations, reaching an estimated 217 million unique visitors a month.[28]

A wiki user can generally alter the original content of any article, whereas the blog user can only add information in the form of comments. Large wikis, such as Wikipedia, protect the quality and accuracy of their information by assigning users roles such as reader, editor, administrator, patroller, policy maker, subject matter expert, content maintainer, software developer, and system operator. Access to some important or sensitive Wikipedia material is limited to users in these authorized roles.[29]

BUSINESS DRIVEN MIS

Virtual Abandonment

Approximately 35 percent of online shopping carts are abandoned prior to checkout. Abandoned shopping carts relates directly to lost revenues for a business. It is like a customer walking out of the store leaving their cart full of chosen items. Businesses need to focus on why the customers are virtually walking out of their stores. The problem typically lies in the checkout process and can be fixed by the following:

- Make sure the checkout button is easy to find.
- Make sure personal information is safe and the website's security is visible.
- Streamline the checkout process so the customer has as few clicks as possible.
- Do not ask shoppers to create an account prior to checkout, but you can ask them to create an account after checkout.
- Ensure your return policy is visible.[30]

Have you ever abandoned a virtual shopping cart? In a group, visit a website that you or your peers have recently abandoned and review the checkout process. Was it difficult, cumbersome, or lacking security? Then visit Amazon.com and review its checkout process and determine whether Amazon is meeting the preceding recommendations.

The *network effect* describes how products in a network increase in value to users as the number of users increases. The more users and content managers on a wiki, the greater the network effect because more users attract more contributors, whose work attracts more users, and so on. For example, Wikipedia becomes more valuable to users as the number of its contributors increases.

Wikis internal to firms can be vital tools for collecting and disseminating knowledge throughout an organization, across geographic distances, and between functional business areas. For example, what U.S. employees call a "sale" may be called "an order booked" in the United Kingdom, an "order scheduled" in Germany, and an "order produced" in France. The corporate wiki can answer any questions about a business process or definition. Companies are also using wikis for documentation, reporting, project management, online dictionaries, and discussion groups. Of course, the more employees who use the corporate wiki, the greater the network effect and value added for the company.

Mashups

A *mashup* is a website or web application that uses content from more than one source to create a completely new product or service. The term is typically used in the context of music; putting Jay-Z lyrics over a Radiohead song makes something old new. The web version of a mashup allows users to mix map data, photos, video, news feeds, blog entries, and so on to create content with a new purpose. Content used in mashups is typically sourced from an *application programming interface (API),* which is a set of routines, protocols, and tools for building software applications. A programmer then puts these building blocks together.

Most operating environments, such as Microsoft Windows, provide an API so that programmers can write applications consistent with them. Many people experimenting with mashups are using Microsoft, Google, eBay, Amazon, Flickr, and Yahoo APIs, leading to the creation of mashup editors. *Mashup editors* are WYSIWYG, or what-you-see-is-what-you-get tools. They provide a visual interface to build a mashup, often allowing the user to drag and drop data points into a web application. An *ezine* is a magazine published only in electronic form on a computer network. Flipboard is a social-network aggregation, magazine-format application software for multiple devices that collects content from social media and other websites, presents it in magazine format, and allows users to flip through the content.

Whoever thought technology could help sell bananas? Dole Organic now places three-digit farm codes on each banana and creates a mashup using Google Earth and its banana database. Socially and environmentally conscious buyers can plug the numbers into Dole's website and look at a bio of the farm where the bananas were raised. The site tells the story of the farm and its surrounding community, lists its organic certifications, posts some photos, and offers a link to satellite images of the farm in Google Earth. Customers can personally monitor the production and treatment of their fruit from the tree to the grocer. The process assures customers that their bananas have been raised to proper organic standards on an environmentally friendly, holistically minded plantation.[31]

THE CHALLENGES OF BUSINESS 2.0

As much as Business 2.0 has positively changed the global landscape of business, a few challenges remain in open source software, user-contributed content systems, and collaboration systems, all highlighted in Figure 3.21. We briefly describe each one.

Technology Dependence

Many people today expect to be continuously connected, and their dependence on technology glues them to their web connections for everything from web conferencing for a university class or work project to making plans with friends for dinner. If a connection is down, how will they function? How long can people go without checking email, text messaging, listening to free music on Pandora, or watching on-demand television? As society becomes more technology-dependent, outages hold the potential to cause ever-greater havoc for people, businesses, and educational institutions.

Information Vandalism

Open source and sharing are both major advantages of Business 2.0, and ironically they are major challenges as well. Allowing anyone to edit anything opens the door for individuals to damage, destroy, or vandalize website content purposely. One of the most famous examples of wiki vandalism occurred when a false biography entry read that John Seigenthaler, Sr, was assistant to Attorney General Robert F. Kennedy in the early 1960s and was thought to have been directly involved in the assassinations of both Kennedy and his brother, President John F. Kennedy. Seigenthaler did work as an assistant to Robert Kennedy, but he was never involved in the assassinations. Wiki vandalism is a hot issue, and for this reason, wiki software can now store all versions of a web page, tracking updates and changes and ensuring that the site can be restored to its original form if the site is vandalized. It can also color-code the background, ensuring that the user understands which areas have been validated and which areas have not. The real trick to wiki software is to determine which statements are true and which are false, a huge issue when considering how easily and frequently wiki software is updated and changed.[32]

Violations of Copyright and Plagiarism

Online collaboration makes plagiarism as easy as clicking a mouse. Unfortunately, a great deal of copyrighted material tends to find its way to blogs and wikis where, many times, blame

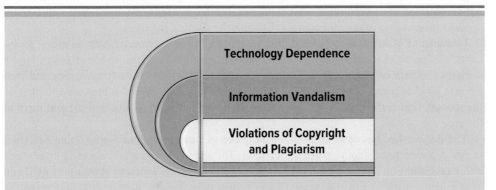

FIGURE 3.21

Challenges of Business 2.0

cannot be traced to a single person. Clearly stated copyright and plagiarism policies are a must for all corporate blogs and wikis. These topics are discussed in detail in Chapter 4.

WEB 3.0: DEFINING THE NEXT GENERATION OF ONLINE BUSINESS OPPORTUNITIES

Although Web 1.0 refers to static text-based information websites and Web 2.0 is about user-contributed content, Web 3.0 is based on intelligent web applications using natural language processing, machine-based learning and reasoning, and intelligent applications. Web 3.0 is the next step in the evolution of the Internet and web applications. Business leaders who explore its opportunities will be the first to market with competitive advantages.

Web 3.0 offers a way for people to describe information so that computers can start to understand the relationships among concepts and topics. To demonstrate the power of Web 3.0, let's look at a few sample relationships: Adam Sandler is a comedian, Lady Gaga is a singer, and Hannah is friends with Sophie. These are all examples of descriptions that can be added to web pages, allowing computers to learn about relationships while displaying the information to humans. With this kind of information in place, interaction between people and machines will be far richer with Web 3.0.

Applying this type of advanced relationship knowledge to a company can create new opportunities. After all, businesses run on information. Whereas Web 2.0 brings people closer together with information by using machines, Web 3.0 brings *machines* closer together by using *information.* These new relationships unite people, machines, and information so a business can be smarter, quicker, more agile, and more successful.

The *deep web,* sometimes called the invisible web, is the large part of the Internet that is inaccessible to conventional search engines. Deep web content includes email messages, chat messages, private content on social media sites, electronic bank statements, electronic health records, and other content that is accessible over the Internet but is not crawled and indexed by search engines such as Google, Yahoo, or Bing.

It is not known how large the deep web is, but many experts estimate that search engines crawl and index less than 1 percent of all the content that can be accessed over the Internet. That part of the Internet that is crawled and indexed by search engines is sometimes referred to as the surface web.

The reasons for not indexing deep web content are varied. It may be that the content is proprietary, in which case the content can only be accessed by approved visitors coming in through a virtual private network. Or the content may be commercial, in which case the content resides behind a member wall and can only be accessed by customers who have paid a fee. Or perhaps the content contains personal identifiable information, in which case the content is protected by compliance regulations and can only be accessed through a portal site by individuals who have been granted access privileges. When mashups have been generated on the fly and components lack a permanent uniform resource location, they also becomes part of the deep web.

The term *deep web* was coined by BrightPlanet in a 2001 white paper entitled "The Deep Web: Surfacing Hidden Value" and is often confused in the media with the term *dark web.* The *dark web* is the portion of the Internet that is intentionally hidden from search engines, uses masked IP addresses, and is accessible only with a special web browser. The key takeaway here is that the dark web is part of the deep web. Like deep web content, dark web content cannot be accessed by conventional search engines, but most often the reason dark web content remains inaccessible to search engines is because the content is illegal.

One goal of Web 3.0 is to tailor online searches and requests specifically to users' preferences and needs. For example, instead of making multiple searches, the user might type a complex sentence or two in a Web 3.0 browser, such as "I want to see a funny movie and then eat at a good Mexican restaurant. What are my options?" The Web 3.0 browser will analyze the request, search the web for all possible answers, organize the results, and present them to the user.

Tim Berners-Lee has described the *semantic web* as a component of Web 3.0 that describes things in a way that computers can understand. The semantic web is not about links between web pages; rather it describes the relationships between *things* (such as A is a part of B and Y is a member of Z) and the properties of things (size, weight, age, price). If information

BUSINESS DRIVEN DISCUSSION

Viral Foxes and Devil Babies

Viral marketing can be a company's greatest success or its worst nightmare. Here are a few popular examples:

- "What Does the Fox Say?" The video created by a pair of Norwegian variety show brothers displays people dressed up as animals dancing around in the woods singing a catchy song. The video received over 400 million views on YouTube and skyrocketed the band Ylvis to virtual stardom.

- The video of a robotic devil baby left in an unattended stroller in the middle of the street in Manhattan attracted over 50 million views in a month. The creators of the devil baby video, Thinkmodo, was creating buzz for the 20th Century Fox movie it was promoting, *Devil's Due.*

- Domino's Pizza employees posted a video showing them making sandwiches with unsanitary ingredients. The video went viral and ended with the arrest of the employees and an apology from the CEO.

Research the web and find an example of a viral video that helped a business achieve success and one that caused a business to fail. Do you think it is important for a business to try to manage its online reputation actively? What can a company do if a negative video goes viral, such as the one concerning Domino's Pizza?

---

about music, cars, concert tickets, and so on is stored in a way that describes the information and associated resource files, semantic web applications can collect information from many sources, combine it, and present it to users in a meaningful way. Although Web 3.0 is still a bit speculative, some topics and features are certain to be included in it, such as:[33]

- Integration of legacy devices: The ability to use current devices such as iPhones, laptops, and so on, as credit cards, tickets, and reservations tools.

- Intelligent applications: The use of agents, machine learning, and semantic web concepts to complete intelligent tasks for users.

- Open ID: The provision of an online identity that can be easily carried to a variety of devices (cell phones, PCs) allowing for easy authentication across different websites.

- Open technologies: The design of websites and other software so they can be easily integrated and work together.

- A worldwide database: The ability for databases to be distributed and accessed from anywhere.

Egovernment: The Government Moves Online

Recent business models that have arisen to enable organizations to take advantage of the Internet and create value are within egovernment. *Egovernment* involves the use of strategies and technologies to transform government(s) by improving the delivery of services and enhancing the quality of interaction between the citizen-consumer and all branches of government.

One example of an egovernment portal, FirstGov.gov, the official U.S. gateway to all government information, is the catalyst for a growing electronic government. Its powerful search engine and ever-growing collection of topical and customer-focused links connect users to millions of web pages, from the federal government, to local and tribal governments, to foreign nations around the world. Figure 3.22 highlights specific egovernment models.

FIGURE 3.22

Extended Ebusiness Models

	Business	Consumer	Government
Business	B2B consint.com	B2C dell.com	B2G lockheedmartin.com
Consumer	C2B priceline.com	C2C ebay.com	C2G egov.com
Government	G2B export.gov	G2C medicare.gov	G2G disasterhelp.gov

LEARNING OUTCOME REVIEW

Learning Outcome 3.1: Compare disruptive and sustaining technologies and explain how the Internet and WWW caused business disruption.

Disruptive technologies offer a new way of doing things that initially does not meet the needs of existing customers. Disruptive technologies redefine the competitive playing fields of their respective markets, open new markets and destroy old ones, and cut into the low end of the marketplace and eventually evolve to displace high-end competitors and their reigning technologies.

Sustaining technologies produce improved products customers are eager to buy, such as a faster car or larger hard drive. Sustaining technologies tend to provide us with better, faster, and cheaper products in established markets and virtually never lead in markets opened by new and disruptive technologies.

The Internet and the World Wide Web caused business disruption by allowing people to communicate and collaborate in ways that were not possible before the information age. The Internet and WWW completely disrupted the way businesses operate, employees communicate, and products are developed and sold.

Learning Outcome 3.2: Describe ebusiness and its associated advantages.

Web 1.0 is a term that refers to the World Wide Web during its first few years of operation, between 1991 and 2003. Ebusiness includes ecommerce along with all activities related to internal and external business operations such as servicing customer accounts, collaborating with partners, and exchanging real-time information. During Web 1.0, entrepreneurs began creating the first forms of ebusiness. Ebusiness advantages include expanding global reach, opening new markets, reducing costs, and improving operations and effectiveness.

Learning Outcome 3.3: Compare the four ebusiness models.

- Business-to-business (B2B) applies to businesses buying from and selling to each other over the Internet.
- Business-to-consumer (B2C) applies to any business that sells its products or services to consumers over the Internet.

- Consumer-to-business (C2B) applies to any consumer who sells a product or service to a business over the Internet.
- Consumer-to-consumer (C2C) applies to sites primarily offering goods and services to assist consumers interacting with each other over the Internet.

The primary difference between B2B and B2C are the customers; B2B customers are other businesses, whereas B2C markets to consumers. Overall, B2B relations are more complex and have higher security needs and are the dominant ebusiness force, representing 80 percent of all online business.

Learning Outcome 3.4: Describe the six ebusiness tools for connecting and communicating.

As firms began to move online, more MIS tools were created to support ebusiness processes and requirements. The ebusiness tools used to connect and communicate include email, instant messaging, podcasting, content management systems, videoconferencing, and web conferencing.

Learning Outcome 3.5: Identify the four challenges associated with ebusiness.

Although the benefits of ebusiness are enticing, developing, deploying, and managing ebusiness systems is not always easy. The challenges associated with ebusiness include identifying limited market segments, managing consumer trust, ensuring consumer protection, and adhering to taxation rules.

Learning Outcome 3.6: Explain Web 2.0 and identify its four characteristics.

Web 2.0, or Business 2.0, is the next generation of Internet use—a more mature, distinctive communications platform characterized by new qualities such as collaboration, sharing, and being free. Web 2.0 encourages user participation and the formation of communities that contribute to the content. In Web 2.0, technical skills are no longer required to use and publish information to the World Wide Web, eliminating entry barriers for online business. The four characteristics of Web 2.0 include:

- Content sharing through open sourcing.
- User-contributed content.
- Collaboration inside the organization.
- Collaboration outside the organization.

Learning Outcome 3.7: Explain how Business 2.0 is helping communities network and collaborate.

A social network is an application that connects people by matching profile information. Providing individuals with the ability to network is by far one of the greatest advantages of Business 2.0. Social networking is the practice of expanding your business and/or social contacts by constructing a personal network. Business 2.0 simplifies the way individuals communicate, network, find employment, and search for information.

Learning Outcome 3.8: Describe the three Business 2.0 tools for collaborating.

The three tools that harness the "power of the people" for Business 2.0 include blogs, wikis, and mashups. A blog, or web log, is an online journal that allows users to post their own comments, graphics, and video. Blog websites let writers communicate—and readers respond—on a regular basis through a simple yet customizable interface that does not require any programming. A wiki is a type of collaborative web page that allows users to add, remove, and change content, which can be easily organized and reorganized as required. Whereas blogs have largely drawn on the creative and personal goals of individual authors, wikis are based on open collaboration with any and everybody. A mashup is a website or web application that uses content from more than one source to create a completely new product or service. A mashup allows users to mix map data, photos, video, news feeds, blog entries, and so on to create content with a new purpose.

Learning Outcome 3.9: Explain the three challenges associated with Business 2.0.

As much as Business 2.0 has positively changed the global landscape of business, a few challenges remain in open source software, user-contributed content systems, and collaboration systems. These challenges include individuals forming unrealistic dependencies on technology, vandalism of information on blogs and wikis, and the violation of copyrights and plagiarism.

Learning Outcome 3.10: Describe Web 3.0 and the next generation of online business.

Web 3.0 is based on intelligent web applications using natural language processing, machine-based learning and reasoning, and intelligent applications. Web 3.0 is the next step in the evolution of the Internet and web applications. Business leaders who explore its opportunities will be the first to market with competitive advantages.

Web 3.0 offers a way for people to describe information in ways that enable computers to understand the relationships among concepts and topics.

OPENING CASE QUESTIONS

1. **Knowledge:** Do you consider HelloFresh a form of disruptive or sustaining technology?
2. **Comprehension:** Is HelloFresh an example of Web 1.0 or Web 2.0?
3. **Application:** Describe the ebusiness model HelloFresh has implemented.
4. **Analysis:** Describe the revenue model HelloFresh has implemented.
5. **Synthesis:** What is HelloFresh's competitive advantage?
6. **Evaluation:** What are the security and trust issues surrounding HelloFresh?

KEY TERMS

Adwords 112
Affiliate program 112
Applet 103
Application programming
    interface (API) 124
Asynchronous communication 120
Blog, or web log 122
Business model 108
Business-to-business (B2B) 110
Business-to-consumer (B2C) 110
Click fraud 112
Clickstream analytics 108
Clickstream data 107
Closed source 118
Collaboration system 118
Collective intelligence 118
Consumer-to-business (C2B) 110
Consumer-to-consumer (C2C) 110
Content management
    system (CMS) 115
Crowdfunding 120
Crowdsourcing 119
Cyborg anthropologist 112
Cybermediation 107

Dark web 126
Deep web 126
Digital Darwinism 101
Disintermediation 106
Disruptive technology 101
Domain name hosting (web
    hosting) 103
Dot-com 109
Ebusiness 103
Ebusiness model 109
Ecommerce 103
Egovernment 127
Eshop (estore or etailer) 110
Explicit knowledge 119
Ezine 124
Folksonomy 121
Hashtag 121
Hitbot 112
Heat map 107
HTML 5 103
Hypertext Markup Language
    (HTML) 103
Hypertext Transport Protocol
    (HTTP) 103

Information reach 105
Information richness 105
Instant messaging (sometimes
    called IM or IMing) 114
Interactivity 107
Intermediaries 106
Internet 102
Internet Corporation for Assigned
    Names and Numbers
    (ICANN) 103
Internet service provider (ISP) 114
Knowledge management
    (KM) 118
Knowledge management system
    (KMS) 118
Long tail 105
Mashup 124
Mashup editor 124
Mass customization 105
Microblogging 123
Native advertising 118
Network effect 124
Open source 118
Open system 117

Paradigm shift 103
Pay-per-call 112
Pay-per-click 112
Pay-per-conversion 112
Personalization 105
Podcasting 114
Real simple syndication
    (RSS) 123
Real-time communication 114
Reintermediation 107
Reputation system 118
Search engine 112
Search engine optimization
    (SEO) 112
Search engine ranking 112
Selfie 122
Semantic web 126
Snackable content 122

Social bookmarking 121
Social graphs 121
Social media 120
Social network 120
Social networking 120
Social networking analysis
    (SNA) 120
Social tagging 121
Source code 118
Sustaining technology 101
Synchronous communication 120
Tacit knowledge 119
Tags 121
Taxonomy 115
Telepresence robot 115
URL shortening 102
Universal resource locator
    (URL) 102

User-contributed content (also
    referred to as user-generated
    content) 118
Videoconference 114
Web 1.0 (or Business 1.0) 103
Web 2.0 (or Business 2.0) 117
Web browser 103
Web conferencing (webinar) 114
Web Real-Time Communications
    (WebRTC) 114
Website bookmark 121
Website ebusiness
    analytics 108
Website traffic analytics 108
Wiki 123
World Wide Web Consortium
    (W3C) 103
World Wide Web (WWW) 103

REVIEW QUESTIONS

1. What is the difference between sustaining and disruptive technology?

2. Do you consider the Internet and World Wide Web forms of sustaining or disruptive technology?

3. How have the Internet and WWW created a global platform for business?

4. What is the difference between ebusiness and ecommerce?

5. What are the benefits and challenges associated with ebusiness?

6. What are the benefits and challenges associated with Business 2.0?

7. Explain business models and their role in a company. How did ebusiness change traditional business models?

8. How can a company use mass customization and personalization to decrease buyer power?

9. How does ebusiness differ from Business 2.0?

10. What are the differences among collective intelligence, knowledge management, and crowdsourcing?

11. Why is knowledge management critical to a business?

12. What are the benefits and challenges associated with wikis?

13. How do disintermediation, reintermediation, and cybermediation differ?

14. What is the semantic web?

CLOSING CASE ONE

Slack—Be Less Busy

Slack is one of the fastest-growing collaboration companies ever started and is used by millions of people every day to collaborate at work. In two short years since its inception, Slack has become a $3 billion company. Slack is like Twitter for businesses. Slack is a centralized group chat platform for the enterprise. With its advanced search and file-sharing functionalities, it can also be linked to third-party apps, such as Google Drive, Dropbox, and Twitter. Slack has long advertised itself as a "freemium" product, where an unlimited number of users can use it for free before deciding to upgrade and pay money for a more robust package with better features.

In time—and it won't be long—Slack will morph into the spinal cord of the office nervous system, connecting numerous third-party business apps and eventually becoming the gateway to a workplace artificial intelligence system that will answer routine questions and proactively seek out information you might otherwise miss.

Slack's founder Stewart Butterfield, also the founder of Flickr, was actually building a gaming company when the team created Slack to help developers and employees communicate. When the gaming company went bankrupt, Butterfield used the opportunity to launch the company's home-grown collaboration tool Slack and the rest is history. And like a game, Slack is fun and engaging and beating up its boring traditional enterprise application competition. Butterfield attributes his company's success to its focus on education, feedback, customer happiness, and metric analysis. Butterfield's vision is for Slack to become the single source of company information.

Slack's AI Vision

The future of Slack is being sketched out by Noah Weiss, Slack's head of search, learning, and intelligence. Weiss envisions Slack communicating with its customers using advanced AI software bots, allowing the application to understand your role inside a company, anticipate your day-to-day needs, and act like a well-trained office assistant.

The information employees share with their colleagues within their many Slack channels creates a valuable trove of a company's collective memory, one that can be mined for training an AI system about how things get done inside that company and even who does what.

"Workers spend about 20 percent of their time looking for information, or looking for a person who has the information they need," Weiss said. "And we've found that a lot of the questions people have are asked over and over again."

Those questions can be basic—"What's the password to the office Wi-Fi network?"—or weightier—"Who's in charge of sales in Berlin?" In time, Slack itself will be smart enough to answer. Combine this with the more than 430 third-party apps that connect to it and Slack becomes the place where you get information and then act on it. Approving expenses and tracking projects are already routine tasks that appear in Slack.

As Slack becomes smarter, it will seek out and present you with information that it thinks you might want to know. This will become especially useful as Slack scales up to work with ever-larger companies. Weiss likens the AI layer to your personal chief of staff. "Slack will know the people you trust and the topics you tend to care about, and over time it will figure out how to better route information to you," he said. "It becomes a robot that's working behind the scenes on your behalf to find things you should know about but might otherwise never see."[34]

Questions

1. Do you consider Slack a form of disruptive or sustaining technology? Why or why not?
2. What types of security and ethical dilemmas are facing Slack?
3. What is the ebusiness model implemented by Slack?
4. What is the revenue model implemented by Slack?
5. Categorize Slack as an example of Web 1.0 (ebusiness) or Web 2.0 (Business 2.0).
6. Explain the four characteristics of Business 2.0 and how each applies to Slack.
7. How could Slack use social networking analysis to help organizations function more efficiently?

Action Finally

Data are all over the Internet! Tons and tons and tons of data! For example, over 152 million blogs are created each year, along with 100 million Twitter accounts resulting in 25 billion tweets, 107 trillion emails are sent, and 730 billion hours of YouTube videos are watched. Known as the social media sector, this arena is by far one of the fastest growing and most influential sectors in business. Companies are struggling to understand how the social media sector impacts them both financially and strategically.

Data are valuable to any company, and the data on the Internet are unique because the information comes directly from customers, suppliers, competitors, and employees. As the social media sector takes off, companies are finding themselves at a disadvantage when attempting to keep up with all of the "online chatter" about their goods and services on the many different social media websites, including Facebook, Twitter, LinkedIn, Yelp, Google, blogs, and so on.

Anytime there is a problem, there is a potential business solution, and Actionly.com chooses to capitalize on the data glut problem. Actionly monitors multiple social media channels through one tracking service, looking for specific keywords for industries, brands, companies, and trends. Actionly customers choose a keyword to monitor—such as a brand, product names, industry terms, or competitor names—and then Actionly constantly collects the data from these social channels and pulls that data into a cohesive digital dashboard. The digital dashboard tracks the desired information, such as marketplace trends, specific companies, competitive brands, entire industries (for example, clean technology), by simultaneously searching Twitter, Facebook, Google, YouTube, Flickr, and blogs. After completing a search, Actionly.com uses Google Analytics to create graphs and charts indicating how frequently each keyword was found throughout the various channels. Additionally, it links each respective channel to the dashboard and filters them with "positive" and "negative" connections, allowing users to respond to any comments.

Actionly.com's business model sets it up for success in this emerging industry. Actionly has a first-mover advantage because it was the first online brand management company offering this service to customers. And the company benefits by using its own services to ensure its brand stays number one on all social media websites. Actionly uses Google Analytics to help transform the data it collects from the various social media websites into valuable business intelligence. Its digital dashboard monitors several key metrics, including:

- **Reputation Management:** Actionly's easy-to-use digital dashboard allows customers to observe and analyze trends and track mentions about brands based on historical data as well as continuously updated data. For example, a customer can view graphs that highlight key trends across 30 days for specific brands, products, or companies.

- **Social ROI:** By connecting to Google Analytics from Actionly, a customer can analyze its campaign performance for individual tweets or Facebook posts to determine which are successful and which are failing. Actionly analyzes every post and click to track page views, visitor information, goal completions, and so on through its digital dashboard, allowing users to customize reports tracking the performance of daily posts.

- **Twitter Analytics:** After adding Twitter accounts to the dashboard, a user can drill down into the data to view graphs of followers, mentions, and retweets. This eliminates the need to manually track a number of Twitter accounts, and a user can view the data in graphs or export the data in Excel for further analysis.

- **Marketing Campaign Tracking:** If a company is launching a big promotion or contest, it can post messages across multiple Facebook or Twitter accounts; all users have to do is select which Twitter or Facebook accounts they want to use and when. Actionly's Campaign Tracking helps a user view which posts are resonating well with customers and measure metrics such as page views, signups, conversions, and revenue by post. Actionly even segments the data by post, account, campaign, or channel, allowing users to measure performance over time.

- **Click Performance:** Actionly tracks performance by hour and day of week, allowing customers to view which clicks are getting the most attention. Actionly's algorithm automatically assigns a sentiment to tweets, allowing the customer to immediately filter positive, negative, or neutral posts to react to information quickly.

- **Sentiment Analysis:** Reviewing positive and negative feedback helps gauge how a brand is doing over time, allowing the client to try to increase the positive sentiment. However, no sentiment scoring is 100 percent accurate due to the complexities of interpretation, culture, sarcasm, and other language nuances. For example, if Actionly is incorrectly tracking a metric, it can change it, allowing users to assign their unique sentiments directly to their tweets. A user can also select to have positive or negative alerts for keywords emailed as soon as the keyword is posted to help manage online brand and company reputations.

- **Competitive Analysis:** Actionly tracks competitor intelligence by watching new-product releases, acquisitions, or customer feedback, allowing a company to stay on top of market entrants, market-related blogs, news, or industry-related seminars/webinars.

- **Find Influencers:** Actionly's digital dashboard allows a user to engage directly with key influencers or people who are driving the online chatter about goods and services. Actionly identifies influencers and determines their relevance to the company, brand, or product. It then compiles a list of influencers based on users with the most followers and who have been most active for the specific searches in the past 30 days.[35]

Questions

1. Would you consider Actionaly Web 1.0 or Web 2.0.
2. Explain why virtual companies such as Actionaly would need to worry about a new social media website.
3. Identify the challenges of ebusiness impacting Actionly.
4. Argue for or against the following statement: Actionly invades consumer privacy by taking data from different websites such as Twitter and Flickr without the consent of the customer who posted the information.

CRITICAL BUSINESS THINKING

1. Anything but Online

Your best friend, Susan Stewart, has started a highly successful custom T-shirt business from your dorm room. Susan is an art major, and each week she creates a limited edition T-shirt focusing on the lyrics from up-and-coming indie bands. You, as an MIS major, see the advantages Susan could reap by porting her business to the Internet. Susan, as an art major, does not like technology and does not believe she needs it to grow her business. Do you agree or disagree that Susan needs to compete online? How can creating an ebusiness benefit Susan? What are the challenges Susan will face as she moves her business to the Internet? How could Susan use Web 2.0 to build loyalty among her followers?

2. The Future of Wikipedia

Wikipedia is a multilingual, web-based, free-content encyclopedia project written collaboratively by volunteers around the world. Since its creation in 2001, it has grown rapidly into one of the largest reference websites. Some people believe Wikipedia will eventually fail under an assault by marketers and self-promoting users. Eric Goldman, a professor at the Santa Clara University

School of Law, argues that Wikipedia will see increasingly vigorous efforts to subvert its editorial process, including the use of automated marketing tools to alter Wikipedia entries to generate online traffic. The site's editors will burn out trying to maintain it, he projects, or Wikipedia will change its open-access architecture and its mission. Do you agree or disagree with Professor Goldman's argument? What can Wikipedia do to combat the challenges of information vandalism and copyright/plagiarism issues?

3. Is Facebook Becoming the Whole World's Social Network?

Facebook's growth, which we already know is massive, is truly a global phenomenon. Nations with the fastest membership growth rates are in South America and Asia. Is Facebook becoming the global phone book? The website www.internetworldstats.com/facebook.htm provides an analysis of the numerical growth rate of members per nation and the penetration Facebook is achieving among each nation's population. Particularly interesting was the monthly growth rate for Indonesia, the Philippines, Mexico, Argentina, and Malaysia—each of which showed about a 10 percent jump in Facebook membership in a single month. In a group, answer the following:

- What potential business opportunities could be created by a worldwide social media network or phone book?
- Facebook, which contains personal data on each member, is becoming the world's phone book. What are the implications of a world phone book for social change?
- What do you think would be the benefits and challenges of global social networking?
- How would tags and crowdsourcing be affected by a global social network?

4. The Toughest College Test You'll Ever Take

If your professor asked you today to kick your social networking habits, do you think you could do it? Can you go without Facebook, cell phones, or the Internet for a week? For a day? A University of Minnesota professor challenged her public relations class to go five days without media or gadgets that didn't exist before 1984. Out of the 43 students in the class, just a handful made it even three days without new technology. Among those who didn't, one student said, "My mother thought I died." How long could you go without any social media? What types of issues might you encounter without constant connections to your friends? How has social media affected society? How has social media affected businesses?[36]

5. Competing with the Big Boys

Provenzo's Rentals is a small, privately owned business that rents sports equipment in Denver, Colorado. The company specializes in winter rentals, including ski, snowboard, and snowmobile equipment. Provenzo's has been in business for 20 years, and for the first time, it is experiencing a decline in rentals. Greg Provenzo, the company's owner, is puzzled by the recent decreases. The snowfall for the past two years has been outstanding, and the ski resorts have opened earlier and closed later than most previous years. Reports say tourism in the Colorado area is up, and the invention of loyalty programs has significantly increased the number of local skiers. Overall, business should be booming. The only reason for the decrease in sales might be the fact that big retailers such as Walmart and Gart's Sports are now renting winter sports equipment. Provenzo would like your team's help in determining how he can use ebusiness and Business 2.0 to help his company increase sales, decrease costs, and compete with these big retailers.

6. Book'em

You are the CIO of Book'em, a company that creates and sells custom book bags. Book'em currently holds 28 percent of market share with over 3,000 employees operating in six countries. You have just finished reading *The Long Tail* by Chris Andersen and *The Innovator's Dilemma* by Clayton Christensen, and you are interested in determining how you can grow your business while reducing costs. Summarize each book and explain how Book'em could implement the strategies explained in each book to create competitive advantages and increase sales.

7. Five Ways Google Docs Speeds Up Collaboration

Google Docs wants you to skip Microsoft Office and collaborate with your group in your browser for free, especially when you're not in the same physical space. Visit Google Docs and answer the following questions.

- What are five ways the new Google Docs can help your team accomplish work more efficiently, even when you're not in the same room together?

- Is Google Docs open source software? What revenue model is Google Docs following?

- Why would putting Google Docs and Microsoft Office on your résumé help differentiate your skills?

- What other applications does Google create that you are interested in learning to help collaborate and communicate with peers and co-workers?

8. Nasty Gal—Eight Years Old and Worth $100 Million

Sophia Amoruso is the founder and CEO of Nasty Gal, an eight-year-old online fashion retail company worth over $100 million. Nasty Gal sells new and vintage clothing, accessories, and shoes online. Amoruso started the company on eBay, selling one-of-a-kind vintage pieces that she sourced, styled, photographed, and shipped herself. The following is excerpted from her new book, *#GIRLBOSS*.

> "I never started a business. I started an eBay store, and ended up with a business. I never would have done it had I known it was going to become this big. I was 22 and, like most 22-year-olds, I was looking for a way to pay my rent and buy my Starbucks chai. Had someone shown me the future of where Nasty Gal would be in 2014, I would have gasped in revulsion, thinking, 'Oh, no, that is way too much work.' There are different kinds of entrepreneurs. There are the ones who start a business because they're educated and choose to, and the ones who do it because it is really the only option. I definitely fall into the latter category. The Internet is a great place to start a business!'

If Sophia Amoruso had started her business in a traditional store, would she have found success? List the advantages Sophia Amoruso gained by selling her items on eBay. If you could start a business on eBay, what would it be and how would you use ebusiness to your advantage?

APPLY YOUR KNOWLEDGE BUSINESS PROJECTS

PROJECT I   Wiki Your Way

Wikis are web-based tools that make it easy for users to add, remove, and change online content. Employees at companies such as Intel, Motorola, IBM, and Sony use them for a host of tasks, from setting internal meeting agendas to posting documents related to new products.

Many companies rely on wikis to engage customers in ongoing discussions about products. Wikis for Motorola and T-Mobile handsets serve as continually updated user guides. TV networks, including ABC and CBS, created fan wikis that let viewers interact with each other as they unraveled mysteries from such shows as *Lost* and *CSI: Crime Scene Investigation*. You would like to implement wikis at your new company, The Consulting Edge, a small computer consulting company catering to mid- and large-sized businesses. Answer the following questions:

- How can a wiki help you attract customers and grow your business?

- How can a wiki help your partners and employees?

- What ethical and security concerns would you have with the wiki?

- What could you do to minimize these concerns?

PROJECT II   Blogging for Dollars

You have purchased a financial investment company, The Financial Level, that caters to individuals and families. You would like to develop a few blogs for your customers, employees, and partners. The goals for your customer blog are to gather honest feedback, provide a place for customers to interact, and help find new opportunities for your businesses. The goals for the employee blog are to gather knowledge, collect employment feedback, and offer a place where employees can post anonymous feedback for issues and concerns so you can manage your staff better.

a. Research the Internet and find several customer blogs and employee blogs.

b. Determine the top three blogs for customers and for employees and critique the blogs for content, ease of use, and overall value.

c. Design a prototype customer blog and a prototype employee blog for The Financial Level, using Word, PowerPoint, or a tool of your choice.

PROJECT III   Is It Web 1.0 or Web 2.0?

Deciding whether a given site is Web 1.0 or Web 2.0 is not as straightforward as it appears. Websites do not have version numbers, and many are dynamic enough to be in permanent beta testing. Facebook and MySpace are good Web 2.0 examples, primarily due to their social networking functions and their reliance on user-generated content. Some sites are easy to identify as Web 1.0 in their approach: Craigslist, for example, emulates an email list server and has no public user profiles or dynamic pages. Many other sites are hard to categorize.

Amazon.com launched in the mid-1990s and has gradually added features over time. The principal content (product descriptions) is not user-created, but much of the site's value is added by user reviews and ratings. Profiles of users do exist, but social features such as friend links, although present, are not widely adopted.

Review the following websites and categorize them as Web 1.0, Web 2.0, or both. Be sure to justify your answer with the characteristics that classify the website as 1.0, 2.0, or both. Why would certain types of businesses choose to remain Web 1.0 and not offer collaboration or open source capabilities?

- www.ebay.com; www.amazon.com; www.facebook.com; www.craigslist.com; www.paypal.com; www.twitter.com; www.irs.gov; www.google.com; www.youtube.com. www.wikipedia.com

- For the following, be sure to use your personal websites as references: your college's website; www.YourVisaCard.com; www.YourBank.com.

PROJECT IV   What Is Accurate on the Internet?

It's a common, if a little morbid, practice for news organizations to prepare obituaries well in advance of celebrities' actual deaths. So *Bloomberg Businessweek* had a 17-page obituary for Apple's Steve Jobs ready to run on his death; unfortunately, the obit was accidently published in 2008 on *Bloomberg Businessweek*'s financial website. The error occurred despite the markers on the story saying "Hold for Release" and "Do Not Use."

In addition to publishing the obituary, *Bloomberg Businessweek* also accidentally published the list of people its reporters should contact when Steve Jobs does die. That list includes Microsoft founder Bill Gates, former Vice President Al Gore (a member of Apple's board of directors), and Google CEO Eric Schmidt. *Bloomberg Businessweek* caught the mistake and pulled the obituary within minutes, but in today's instant information culture, the damage was already done.

Although Jobs was very much alive in 2008, a few stockholders may have gone into cardiac arrest after reading the obituary. What kind of financial impact could a story like this have on Apple? With so many forms of collaboration, how does a company monitor and track each one to ensure that the content is error-free? Once erroneous content is posted to the Internet or written in a text message, what can a company do to rectify the situation? What types of safeguards can a company implement to ensure false information is not posted to a wiki or blog?

PROJECT V   Sticky Wiki

Wiki (Hawaiian for "quick") is software that allows users to create and edit web page content freely, using any web browser. The most common wiki is Wikipedia. Wikis offer a powerful yet flexible collaborative communication tool for developing websites. The best part of a wiki is that it grows and evolves by the collaborative community adding content—the owner of the wiki does not have to add all of the content as is typical in a standard web page.

Many sites offer free wiki software such as Socialtext, a group-editable website. As one of the first wiki companies, Socialtext wikis are designed for anyone who wants to accelerate team communications, enable knowledge sharing better, foster collaboration, and build online communities. Socialtext also offers WikiWidgets, which make it easy for nontechnical business users to create rich, dynamic wiki content. Today, more than 3,000 organizations use Socialtext, including Symantec, Nokia, IKEA, Conde Nast, Ziff-Davis, Kodak, University of Southern California, and Boston College,

Create your own wiki. Wikis can address a variety of needs from student involvement, fraternities and sororities, group activities, sport team updates, local band highlights, and so on. Choose a free wiki software vendor from the following list and create a wiki for something you are involved in or excited about and want to share with others.

- www.socialtext.com—Easy-to-use, business-grade wikis proven by *Fortune* 500 companies.
- www.wetpaint.com—A free, easy-to-use wiki-building site.
- www.CentralDesktop.com—Easy-to-use, a wiki for nontechies.
- www.xwiki.com—Open source and free hosting with professional services.

If you have different wiki software you prefer, feel free to use it to create your wiki.

PROJECT VI   Connectivity Breakdown

When you are considering connectivity services for your business, you need to take continuous access and connectivity seriously. What if one of your employees is about to close a multimillion-dollar deal and loses the Internet connection, jeopardizing the deal? What if a disgruntled employee decides to post your business's collective intelligence on an open source blog or wiki?

What if your patient-scheduling software crashes and you have no idea which patients are scheduled to which operating rooms with which doctors? These are far worse scenarios than a teenage boy not gaining access to his email or Facebook page. What management and technical challenges do you foresee as people and businesses become increasingly dependent on connectivity? What can managers do to meet these challenges and prevent problems?

PROJECT VII   Go for It

Rich Aberman and Bill Clerico found themselves in the difficult position of deciding whether to graduate from college and pursue their dreams of building their own company or head off to graduate school and entry-level jobs. Aberman choose to head off to law school while Clerico choose an entry-level job as an investment banker. After several months, they both decided that it was now or never if they truly wanted to build their dream business because they were both becoming increasingly comfortable with their new lifestyles. Obviously, it would become more difficult to leave their comfortable positions for the uncertainty of being an entrepreneur.

Aberman left law school and Clerico quit his job, and the pair cofounded WePay, an online funds management company. WePay allows individuals and groups all over the world to establish an account and collect money in a variety of ways—from paper checks to credit cards—and then use a debit card to spend the money in the account. WePay collects transaction fees ranging from 50 cents to 3 percent of credit card payments. Luckily, their decision paid off and, a little over a year after founding the company, Aberman and Clerico had raised nearly $2 million from high-profile Internet investors. WePay boasts several thousand customers, ranging from sports teams to fraternities to groups of roommates managing rent and utilities.

Have you thought of starting your own business? What are the advantages and challenges associated with building your own business early in your career? Research the Internet and find three examples of highly successful college start-ups. What do you think were the primary reasons the start-ups found success? What are the advantages of starting your own business while you are still in college? What are a few of the challenges you might face if you choose to start your own business today?

If you are looking for Excel projects to incorporate into your class, try any of the following after reading this chapter.

Project Number	Project Name	Project Type	Plug-In Focus Area	Project Focus	Project Skill Set	Page Number
1	Financial Destiny	Excel	T2	Personal Budget	Introductory Formulas	AYK.4
2	Cash Flow	Excel	T2	Cash Flow	Introductory Formulas	AYK.4
3	Technology Budget	Excel	T1, T2	Hardware and Software	Introductory Formulas	AYK.4
4	Tracking Donations	Excel	T2	Employee Relationships	Introductory Formulas	AYK.4
5	Convert Currency	Excel	T2	Global Commerce	Introductory Formulas	AYK.5
6	Cost Comparison	Excel	T2	Total Cost of Ownership	Introductory Formulas	AYK.5
7	Time Management	Excel or Project	T2 or T12	Project Management	Introductory Gantt Charts	AYK.6
8	Maximize Profit	Excel	T2, T4	Strategic Analysis	Intermediate Formulas or Solver	AYK.6
9	Security Analysis	Excel	T3	Filtering Data	Intermediate Conditional Formatting, Autofilter, Subtotal	AYK.7
10	Gathering Data	Excel	T3	Data Analysis	Intermediate Conditional Formatting, PivotTable	AYK.8
11	Scanner System	Excel	T2	Strategic Analysis	Intermediate	AYK.8
12	Competitive Pricing	Excel	T2	Profit Maximization	Intermediate	AYK.9
13	Adequate Acquisitions	Excel	T2	Break-Even Analysis	Intermediate	AYK.9
24	Electronic Resumes	HTML	T9, T10, T11	Electronic Personal Marketing	Introductory Structural Tags	AYK.16
25	Gathering Feedback	Dreamweaver	T9, T10, T11	Data Collection	Intermediate Organization of Information	AYK.16

4 Ethics and Information Security: MIS Business Concerns

CHAPTER

SECTION 4.1 Ethics	SECTION 4.2 Information Security
■ Information Ethics ■ Developing Information Management Policies	■ Protecting Intellectual Assets ■ The First Line of Defense—People ■ The Second Line of Defense—Technology

What's in IT for me?

This chapter concerns itself with protecting information from potential misuse. Organizations must ensure that they collect, capture, store, and use information in an ethical manner. This means any type of information they collect and use, including about customers, partners, and employees. Companies must ensure that personal information collected about someone remains private. This is not just a nice thing to do. The law requires it. Perhaps more important, information must be kept physically secure to prevent access and possible dissemination and use by unauthorized sources.

You, the business student, must understand ethics and security because they are the top concerns customers voice today. The way they are handled directly influences a customer's likelihood of embracing electronic technologies and conducting business over the web—and thus the company's bottom line. You can find evidence in recent news reports about how the stock price of organizations falls dramatically when information privacy and security breaches are made known. Further, organizations face potential litigation if they fail to meet their ethical, privacy, and security obligations in the handling of information.

©Image Source RF   ©Chad Baker/Ryan McVay/Getty Images RF   ©Mikkel William Nielsen/Getty Images RF

Five Ways Hackers Can Get into Your Business

Hackers don't care what size your business is; they only care if they can get past your defenses and relieve you of your valuables. Hackers actually like small businesses as they tend to have more to steal than an individual person but fewer cyber defenses than a large company. The hard reality is that most small businesses stand at least a 50-50 chance of being targeted for attack by hackers. Did you know:

- Once every three minutes, the average company comes into contact with viruses and malware.
- One in every 291 email messages contains a virus.
- Three things hackers want most are customer data, intellectual property, and bank account information.
- The top five file names used in phishing scams are Details.zip, UPS_document.zip, DCIM. zip, Report.zip, and Scan.zip.
- The average annual cost of a cyberattack on a small or medium-sized business is $188,242.

Cyberthieves are always looking for new ways to gain access to your business data, business networks, and business applications. The best way to protect your business from cybertheft is to build a strong defense and be able to identify vulnerabilities and weak spots. According to John Brandon of *Inc.* magazine, the top five ways hackers will try to gain access to your businesses are highlighted in Figure 4.1. (Please note that there are far more than five ways; these are just the five most common.)

FIGURE 4.1

Five Ways Hackers Gain Access to Your Business

WEAK PASSWORDS
- With a $300 graphics card, a hacker can run 420 billion simple, lowercase, eight-character password combinations a minute.
- Cyberattacks involve weak passwords 80 percent of the time; 55 percent of people use one password for all logins.
- Hackers cracked 6.4 million LinkedIn passwords and 1.5 million eHarmony passwords in separate attacks.

Your Best Defense:
- Use a unique password for each account.
- Aim for at least 20 characters and preferably gibberish, not real words.
- Insert special characters: @#$*&.
- Try a password manager such as LastPass or Dashlane.

FIGURE 4.1

(continued)

MALWARE ATTACKS

- An infected website, USB drive, or application delivers software that can capture keystrokes, passwords, and data.
- An 8 percent increase in malware attacks against small businesses occurs yearly; the average loss from a targeted attack was $92,000.
- Victims of infected mobile developer's websites attacks include Apple, Facebook, and Twitter.

Your Best Defense:

- Run robust malware-detection software such as Norton Toolbar.
- Keep existing software updated.
- Use an iPhone: Android phones are targeted more than any other mobile operating system.

PHISHING EMAILS

- Bogus but official-looking emails prompt you to enter your password or click links to infected websites.
- A 125 percent rise in social-media phishing attacks has occurred since 2012.
- Phishers steal $1 billion from small businesses yearly.
- Many small businesses are targeted with phishing emails designed to look like Better Business Bureau warnings.

Your Best Defense:

- Keep existing software, operating systems, and browsers updated with the latest patches.
- Don't automatically click links in emails to external sites; retype the URL in your browser.

SOCIAL ENGINEERING

- Think 21st-century con artist tactics, e.g., hackers pretending to be you to reset your passwords.
- Twenty-nine percent of all security breaches involve some form of social engineering. Average loss is $25,000 to $100,000 per incident.
- In 2009, social engineers posed as Coca-Cola's CEO, persuading an executive to open an email with software that infiltrated the company's network.

Your Best Defense:

- Rethink what you reveal on social media—it's all fodder for social engineers.
- Develop policies for handling sensitive requests such as password resets over the phone.
- Have a security audit done.

RANSOMWARE

- Hackers hold your website hostage, often posting embarrassing content such as porn, until you pay a ransom.
- Five million dollars is extorted each year. The real cost is the data loss—paying the ransom doesn't mean you get your files back.
- Hackers locked the network at an Alabama ABC TV station, demanding a ransom to remove a red screen on every computer.

Your Best Defense:

- As with malware, do not click suspicious links or unknown websites.
- Regularly back up your data.
- Use software that specifically checks for new exploits.[1]

4.1 Explain the ethical issues in the use of information technology.

4.2 Identify the six epolicies organizations should implement to protect themselves.

INFORMATION ETHICS

LO 4.1: Explain the ethical issues in the use of information technology.

Ethics and security are two fundamental building blocks for all organizations. In recent years, enormous business scandals along with 9/11 have shed new light on the meaning of ethics and security. When the behavior of a few individuals can destroy billion-dollar organizations, the value of ethics and security should be evident.

Copyright is the legal protection afforded an expression of an idea, such as a song, book, or video game. *Intellectual property* is intangible creative work that is embodied in physical form and includes copyrights, trademarks, and patents. A *patent* is an exclusive right to make, use, and sell an invention and is granted by a government to the inventor. As it becomes easier for people to copy everything from words and data to music and video, the ethical issues surrounding copyright infringement and the violation of intellectual property rights are consuming the ebusiness world. Technology poses new challenges for our *ethics*—the principles and standards that guide our behavior toward other people.

The protection of customers' privacy is one of the largest and murkiest ethical issues facing organizations today. *Privacy* is the right to be left alone when you want to be, to have control over your personal possessions, and not to be observed without your consent. Privacy is related to *confidentiality,* which is the assurance that messages and information remain available only to those authorized to view them. Each time employees make a decision about a privacy issue, the outcome could sink the company.

Trust among companies, customers, partners, and suppliers is the support structure of ebusiness. Privacy is one of its main ingredients. Consumers' concerns that their privacy will be violated because of their interactions on the web continue to be one of the primary barriers to the growth of ebusiness.

Information ethics govern the ethical and moral issues arising from the development and use of information technologies as well as the creation, collection, duplication, distribution, and processing of information itself (with or without the aid of computer technologies). Ethical dilemmas in this area usually arise not as simple, clear-cut situations but as clashes among competing goals, responsibilities, and loyalties. Inevitably, there will be more than one socially acceptable or correct decision. The two primary areas concerning software include pirated software and counterfeit software. *Pirated software* is the unauthorized use, duplication, distribution, or sale of copyrighted software. *Counterfeit software* is software that is manufactured to look like the real thing and sold as such. *Digital rights management* is a technological solution that allows publishers to control their digital media to discourage, limit, or prevent illegal copying and distribution. Figure 4.2 contains examples of ethically questionable or unacceptable uses of information technology.[2]

Individuals copy, use, and distribute software.
Employees search organizational databases for sensitive corporate and personal information.
Organizations collect, buy, and use information without checking the validity or accuracy of the information.
Individuals create and spread viruses that cause trouble for those using and maintaining IT systems.
Individuals hack into computer systems to steal proprietary information.
Employees destroy or steal proprietary organization information such as schematics, sketches, customer lists, and reports.

FIGURE 4.2

Ethically Questionable or Unacceptable Information Technology Use

BUSINESS DRIVEN DISCUSSION

Information— Does It Have Ethics?

A high school principal decided it was a good idea to hold a confidential conversation about teachers, salaries, and student test scores on his cellular phone in a local Starbucks. Not realizing that one of the students' parents was sitting next to him, the principal accidentally divulged sensitive information about his employees and students. The irate parent soon notified the school board about the principal's inappropriate behavior, and a committee was formed to decide how to handle the situation.[3]

With the new wave of collaboration tools, electronic business, and the Internet, employees are finding themselves working outside the office and beyond traditional office hours. Advantages associated with remote workers include increased productivity, decreased expenses, and boosts in morale as employees are given greater flexibility to choose their work location and hours. Unfortunately, disadvantages associated with workers working remotely include new forms of ethical challenges and information security risks.

In a group, discuss the following statement: Information does not have any ethics. If you were elected to the committee to investigate the principal's inappropriate Starbucks phone conversation, what types of questions would you want answered? What type of punishment, if any, would you enforce on the principal? What types of policies would you implement across the school district to ensure that this scenario is never repeated? Be sure to highlight how workers working remotely affect business along with any potential ethical challenges and information security issues.

Rule 41 is the part of the United States Federal Rules of Criminal Procedure that covers the search and seizure of physical and digital evidence. Rule 41 originally granted a federal judge magistrate the authority to issue a warrant to search and seize a person or property located within that judge's district if the person or property is part of a criminal investigation or trial. In April 2016, the Judicial Conference of the United States proposed an amendment to Rule 41 that allows a federal judge magistrate to issue a warrant that allows an investigator to gain remote access to a digital device suspected in a crime, even if the device is located outside of the geographic jurisdiction of the judge issuing the warrant. An important goal of the amendment to Rule 41 is to prevent criminals from hiding the location of a computing device with anonymization technology in order to make detection and prosecution more difficult.

Privacy advocates are concerned that the amendment will expand the government's authority to legally hack individuals and organizations and monitor any computer suspected of being part of a botnet. In addition to giving the government the authority to seize or copy the information on a digital device no matter where that device is located, the amendment also allows investigators who are investigating a crime that spans five or more judicial districts to go to one judge for warrants instead of having to request warrants from judges in each jurisdiction.[4]

Unfortunately, few hard and fast rules exist for always determining what is ethical. Many people can either justify or condemn the actions in Figure 4.2, for example. Knowing the law is important, but that knowledge will not always help because what is legal might not always be ethical and what might be ethical is not always legal. For example, Joe Reidenberg received an offer for AT&T cell phone service. AT&T used Equifax, a credit reporting agency, to identify potential customers such as Joe Reidenberg. Overall, this seemed like a good business opportunity between Equifax and AT&T wireless. Unfortunately, the Fair Credit Reporting Act (FCRA) forbids repurposing credit information except when the information is used for "a firm offer of credit or insurance." In other words, the only product that can be sold based on credit information is credit. A representative for Equifax stated, "As long as AT&T Wireless (or any company for that matter) is offering the cell phone service on a credit basis, such as

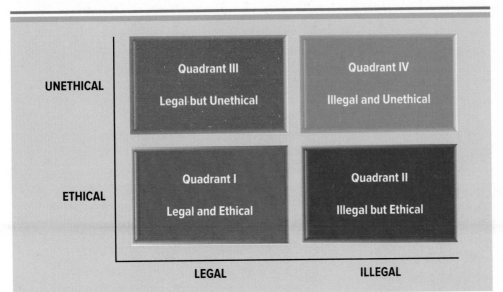

allowing the use of the service before the consumer has to pay, it is in compliance with the FCRA." However, the question remains—is it ethical?[5]

Figure 4.3 shows the four quadrants in which ethical and legal behaviors intersect. The goal for most businesses is to make decisions within quadrant I that are both legal and ethical. There are times when a business will find itself in the position of making a decision in quadrant III, such as hiring child labor in foreign countries, or in quadrant II, such as when a business might pay a foreigner who is getting her immigration status approved because the company is in the process of hiring the person. A business should never find itself operating in quadrant IV. Ethics are critical to operating a successful business today.

Information Does Not Have Ethics, People Do

Information itself has no ethics. It does not care how it is used. It will not stop itself from spamming customers, sharing itself if it is sensitive or personal, or revealing details to third parties. Information cannot delete or preserve itself. Therefore, it falls to those who own the information to develop ethical guidelines about how to manage it.

A few years ago, the ideas of information management, governance, and compliance were relatively obscure. Today, these concepts are a must for virtually every company, both domestic and global, primarily due to the role digital information plays in corporate legal proceedings or litigation. Frequently, digital information serves as key evidence in legal proceedings, and it is far easier to search, organize, and filter than paper documents. Digital information is also extremely difficult to destroy, especially if it is on a corporate network or sent by email. In fact, the only reliable way to obliterate digital information reliably is to destroy the hard drives on which the file was stored. *Ediscovery* (or *electronic discovery*) refers to the ability of a company to identify, search, gather, seize, or export digital information in responding to a litigation, audit, investigation, or information inquiry. As the importance of ediscovery grows, so does information governance and information compliance. The *Child Online Protection Act (COPA)* was passed to protect minors from accessing inappropriate material on the Internet. Figure 4.4 displays the ethical guidelines for information management.

DEVELOPING INFORMATION MANAGEMENT POLICIES

LO 4.2: Identify the six epolicies organizations should implement to protect themselves.

Treating sensitive corporate information as a valuable resource is good management. Building a corporate culture based on ethical principles that employees can understand and implement is responsible management. Organizations should develop written policies establishing employee guidelines, employee procedures, and organizational rules for information. These policies set employee expectations about the organization's practices and standards and protect the organization from misuse of computer systems and MIS resources. If an organization's employees

Information Secrecy

The category of computer security that addresses the protection of data from unauthorized disclosure and confirmation of data source authenticity

Information Governance

A method or system of government for information management or control

Information Management

Examines the organizational resource of information and regulates its definitions, uses, value, and distribution, ensuring that it has the types of data/information required to function and grow effectively

Information Compliance

The act of conforming, acquiescing, or yielding information

Information Property

An ethical issue that focuses on who owns information about individuals and how information can be sold and exchanged

FIGURE 4.4

Ethical Guidelines for Information Management

use computers at work, the organization should, at a minimum, implement epolicies. *Epolicies* are policies and procedures that address information management along with the ethical use of computers and the Internet in the business environment. Figure 4.5 displays the epolicies a firm should implement to set employee expectations.

Ethical Computer Use Policy

In a case that illustrates the perils of online betting, a leading Internet poker site reported that a hacker exploited a security flaw to gain an insurmountable edge in high-stakes, no-limit Texas hold'em tournaments—the ability to see his opponents' hole cards. The cheater, whose

FIGURE 4.5

Overview of Epolicies

BUSINESS DRIVEN ETHICS AND SECURITY

Ethics. It's just one tiny word, but it has monumental impact on every area of business. From the magazines, blogs, and newspapers you read to the courses you take, you will encounter ethics because it is a hot topic in today's electronic world. Technology has provided so many incredible opportunities, but it has also provided those same opportunities to unethical people. Discuss the ethical issues surrounding each of the following situations (yes, these are true stories):

Is IT Really Worth the Risk?

- A student stands up the first day of class before the professor arrives and announces that his fraternity scans textbooks and he has the textbook for this course on his thumb drive, which he will gladly sell for $20. Several students pay on the spot and upload the scanned textbook to their PCs. One student takes down the student information and contacts the publisher about the incident.

- A senior marketing manager is asked to monitor his employee's email because there is a rumor that the employee is looking for another job.

- A vice president of sales asks her employee to burn all of the customer data onto an external hard drive because she made a deal to provide customer information to a strategic partner.

- A senior manager is asked to monitor his employee's email to discover whether she is sexually harassing another employee.

- An employee is looking at the shared network drive and discovers that his boss's entire hard drive, including his email backup, has been copied to the network and is visible to all.

- An employee is accidentally copied on an email listing the targets for the next round of layoffs.

illegitimate winnings were estimated at between $400,000 and $700,000 by one victim, was an employee of AbsolutePoker.com and hacked the system to show that it could be done. Regardless of what business a company operates—even one that many view as unethical—the company must protect itself from unethical employee behavior.[6] *Cyberbullying* includes threats, negative remarks, or defamatory comments transmitted through the Internet or posted on the website. A *threat* is an act or object that poses a danger to assets. *Click-fraud* is the abuse of pay-per-click, pay-per-call, and pay-per-conversion revenue models by repeatedly clicking a link to increase charges or costs for the advertiser. *Competitive click-fraud* is a computer crime in which a competitor or disgruntled employee increases a company's search advertising costs by repeatedly clicking the advertiser's link. Cyberbullying and click-fraud are just a few examples of the many types of unethical computer use found today.

One essential step in creating an ethical corporate culture is establishing an ethical computer use policy. An *ethical computer use policy* contains general principles to guide computer user behavior. For example, it might explicitly state that users should refrain from playing computer games during working hours. This policy ensures that the users know how to behave at work and the organization has a published standard to deal with infractions. For example, after appropriate warnings, the company may terminate an employee who spends significant amounts of time playing computer games at work.

Organizations can legitimately vary in how they expect employees to use computers, but in any approach to controlling such use, the overriding principle should be informed consent. The users should be *informed* of the rules and, by agreeing to use the system on that basis, *consent* to abide by them.

Managers should make a conscientious effort to ensure all users are aware of the policy through formal training and other means. If an organization were to have only one epolicy, it should be an ethical computer use policy because that is the starting point and the umbrella for any other policies the organization might establish.

Part of an ethical computer use policy can include a BYOD policy. A *bring your own device (BYOD)* policy allows employees to use their personal mobile devices and computers to access enterprise data and applications. BYOD policies offer four basic options, including:

- Unlimited access for personal devices.
- Access *only* to nonsensitive systems and data.
- Access but with IT control over personal devices, apps, and stored data.
- Access but preventing local storage of data on personal devices.

Information Privacy Policy

An organization that wants to protect its information should develop an *information privacy policy,* which contains general principles regarding information privacy. Visa created Innovant to handle all its information systems, including its coveted customer information, which details how people are spending their money, in which stores, on which days, and even at what time of day. Just imagine what a sales and marketing department could do if it gained access to this information. For this reason, Innovant bans the use of Visa's customer information for anything outside its intended purpose—billing. Innovant's privacy specialists developed a strict credit card information privacy policy, which it follows.

Innovant has been asked whether it can guarantee that unethical use of credit card information will never occur. In a large majority of cases, the unethical use of information happens not through the malicious scheming of a rogue marketer but, rather, unintentionally. For instance, information is collected and stored for some purpose, such as record keeping or billing. Then, a sales or marketing professional figures out another way to use it internally, share it with partners, or sell it to a trusted third party. The information is "unintentionally" used for new purposes. The classic example of this type of unintentional information reuse is the Social Security number, which started simply as a way to identify government retirement benefits and then was used as a sort of universal personal ID, found on everything from drivers' licenses to savings accounts.

Fair information practices is a general term for a set of standards governing the collection and use of personal data and addressing issues of privacy and accuracy. Different organizations and countries have their own terms for these concerns. The United Kingdom calls it "Data Protection," and the European Union calls it "Personal Data Privacy"; the Organisation for Economic Co-operation and Development (OECD) has written *Guidelines on the Protection of Privacy and Transborder Flows of Personal Data,* which can be found at www.oecd.org/unitedstates.[7]

Acceptable Use Policy

An *acceptable use policy (AUP)* requires a user to agree to follow it to be provided access to corporate email, information systems, and the Internet. *Nonrepudiation* is a contractual stipulation to ensure that ebusiness participants do not deny (repudiate) their online actions. A nonrepudiation clause is typically contained in an acceptable use policy. Many businesses and educational facilities require employees or students to sign an acceptable use policy before gaining network access. When signing up with an email provider, each customer is typically presented with an AUP, which states that the user agrees to adhere to certain stipulations. Users agree to the following in a typical acceptable use policy:

- Not using the service as part of violating any law.
- Not attempting to break the security of any computer network or user.
- Not posting commercial messages to groups without prior permission.
- Not performing any nonrepudiation.

Some organizations go so far as to create a unique information management policy focusing solely on Internet use. An *Internet use policy* contains general principles to guide the proper use of the Internet. Because of the large amounts of computing resources that Internet users can expend, it is essential for such use to be legitimate. In addition, the Internet contains numerous

BUSINESS DRIVEN GLOBALIZATION

The Right to Be Forgotten

The European Commissioner for Justice, Fundamental Rights, and Citizenship, Viviane Reding, announced the European Commission's proposal to create a sweeping new privacy right—the right to be forgotten, allowing individuals to request to have all content that violates their privacy removed. The right to be forgotten addresses an urgent problem in the digital age: the great difficulty of escaping your past on the Internet now that every photo, status update, and tweet lives forever in the cloud. To comply with the European Court of Justice's decision, Google created a new online form by which individuals can request search providers to remove links that violate their online privacy. In the first month, Google received more than 50,000 submissions from people asking the company to remove links. Many people in the United States believe that the right to be forgotten conflicts with the right to free speech. Do people who want to erase their past deserve a second chance? Do you agree or disagree?[8]

materials that some believe are offensive, making regulation in the workplace a requirement. *Cybervandalism* is the electronic defacing of an existing website. *Typosquatting* is a problem that occurs when someone registers purposely misspelled variations of well-known domain names. These variants sometimes lure consumers who make typographical errors when entering a URL. *Website name stealing* is the theft of a website's name that occurs when someone, posing as a site's administrator, changes the ownership of the domain name assigned to the website to another website owner. These are all examples of unacceptable Internet use. *Internet censorship* is government attempts to control Internet traffic, thus preventing some material from being viewed by a country's citizens. Generally, an Internet use policy:

- Describes the Internet services available to users.
- Defines the organization's position on the purpose of Internet access and what restrictions, if any, are placed on that access.
- Describes user responsibility for citing sources, properly handling offensive material, and protecting the organization's good name.
- States the ramifications if the policy is violated.

Email Privacy Policy

An *email privacy policy* details the extent to which email messages may be read by others. Email is so pervasive in organizations that it requires its own specific policy. Most working professionals use email as their preferred means of corporate communications. Although email and instant messaging are common business communication tools, risks are associated with using them. For instance, a sent email is stored on at least three or four computers (see Figure 4.6). Simply deleting an email from one computer does not delete it from the others. Companies can mitigate many of the risks of using electronic messaging systems by implementing and adhering to an email privacy policy.

One major problem with email is the user's expectations of privacy. To a large extent, this expectation is based on the false assumption that email privacy protection exists somehow analogous to that of U.S. first-class mail. Generally, the organization that owns the email system can operate the system as openly or as privately as it wishes. Surveys indicate that the majority of large firms regularly read and analyze employees' email looking for confidential data leaks such as unannounced financial results or the sharing of trade secrets that result in the violation of an email privacy policy and eventual termination of the employee. That means

FIGURE 4.6

Email Is Stored on Multiple
Computers

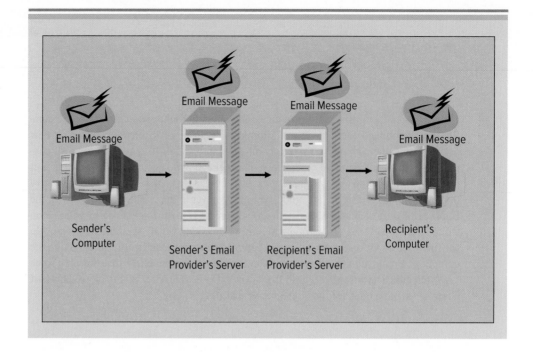

that if the organization wants to read everyone's email, it can do so. Basically, using work email for anything other than work is not a good idea. A typical email privacy policy:

- Defines legitimate email users and explains what happens to accounts after a person leaves the organization.

- Explains backup procedure so users will know that at some point, even if a message is deleted from their computer, it is still stored by the company.

- Describes the legitimate grounds for reading email and the process required before such action is performed.

- Discourages sending junk email or spam to anyone who does not want to receive it.

- Prohibits attempting to mail bomb a site. A *mail bomb* sends a massive amount of email to a specific person or system that can cause that user's server to stop functioning.

- Informs users that the organization has no control over email once it has been transmitted outside the organization.

Spam is unsolicited email. It plagues employees at all levels within an organization, from receptionist to CEO, and clogs email systems and siphons MIS resources away from legitimate business projects. An *anti-spam policy* simply states that email users will not send unsolicited emails (or spam). It is difficult to write anti-spam policies, laws, or software because there is no such thing as a universal litmus test for spam. One person's spam is another person's newsletter. End users have to decide what spam is, because it can vary widely not just from one company to the next, but also from one person to the next. A user can *opt out* of receiving emails by choosing to deny permission to incoming emails. A user can *opt in* to receive emails by choosing to allow permissions to incoming emails. *Teergrubing* is an anti-spamming approach by which the receiving computer launches a return attack against the spammer, sending email messages back to the computer that originated the suspected spam.

Social Media Policy

Did you see the YouTube video showing two Domino's Pizza employees violating health codes while preparing food by passing gas on sandwiches? Millions of people did, and the company took notice when disgusted customers began posting negative comments all over Twitter. Because they did not have a Twitter account, corporate executives at Domino's did not know about the damaging tweets until it was too late. The use of social media can contribute many benefits to an organization, and implemented correctly, it can become a huge opportunity for employees to build brands. But there are also tremendous risks because a few employees

BUSINESS DRIVEN MIS

Identity theft has quickly become the most common, expensive, and pervasive crime in the United States. The identities of more than 15 million U.S. citizens are stolen each year, with financial losses exceeding $50 billion. This means that the identities of almost 10 percent of U.S. adults will be stolen this year, with losses of around $4,000 each, not to mention the 100 million U.S. citizens whose personal data will be compromised due to data breaches on corporate and government databases.

The growth of organized crime can be attributed to the massive amounts of data collection along with the increased cleverness of professional identity thieves. Starting with individually tailored phishing and vishing scams, increasingly successful corporate and government databases hackings, and intricate networks of botnets that hijack millions of computers without a trace, we must wake up to this ever-increasing threat to all Americans.[9]

You have the responsibility to protect yourself from data theft. In a group, visit the Federal Trade Commission's Consumer Information Identity Theft website at http://www.consumer.ftc.gov/features/feature-0014-identity-theft and review what you can do today to protect your identity and how you can ensure that your personal information is safe.

15 Million Identity Theft Victims

representing an entire company can cause tremendous brand damage. Defining a set of guidelines implemented in a social media policy can help mitigate that risk. Companies can protect themselves by implementing a *social media policy* outlining the corporate guidelines or principles governing employee online communications. Having a single social media policy might not be enough to ensure that the company's online reputation is protected. Additional, more specific, social media policies a company might choose to implement include:

- Employee online communication policy detailing brand communication.
- Employee blog and personal blog policies.
- Employee social network and personal social network policies.
- Employee Twitter, corporate Twitter, and personal Twitter policies.
- Employee LinkedIn policy.
- Employee Facebook usage and brand usage policy.
- Corporate YouTube policy.

Social media monitoring is the process of monitoring and responding to what is being said about a company, individual, product, or brand. Social media monitoring typically falls to the *social media manager,* a person within the organization who is trusted to monitor, contribute, filter, and guide the social media presence of a company, individual, product, or brand. Organizations must protect their online reputations and continuously monitor blogs, message boards, social networking sites, and media sharing sites. However, monitoring the hundreds of social media sites can quickly become overwhelming. To combat these issues, a number of companies specialize in online social media monitoring; for example, Trackur.com creates digital dashboards that allow executives to view at a glance the date published, source, title, and summary of every item tracked. The dashboard not only highlights what's being said but also the influence of the particular person, blog, or social media site.

Workplace Monitoring Policy

Increasingly, employee monitoring is not a choice; it is a risk-management obligation. Michael Soden, CEO of the Bank of Ireland, issued a mandate stating that company employees could

BUSINESS DRIVEN DEBATE

Monitoring Employees

Every organization has the right to monitor its employees. Organizations usually inform their employees when workplace monitoring is occurring, especially regarding organizational assets such as networks, email, and Internet access. Employees traditionally offer their consent to be monitored and should not have any expectations of privacy when using organizational assets.

Do you agree or disagree that organizations have an obligation to notify employees about the extent of workplace monitoring, such as how long employees are using the Internet and which websites they are visiting? Do you agree or disagree that organizations have the right to read all employees' email sent or received on an organizational computer, including personal Gmail accounts?

not surf illicit websites with company equipment. Next, he hired Hewlett-Packard to run the MIS department, and illicit websites were discovered on Soden's own computer, forcing Soden to resign. Monitoring employees is one of the biggest challenges CIOs face when developing information management policies.[10]

Physical security is tangible protection such as alarms, guards, fireproof doors, fences, and vaults. New technologies enable employers to monitor many aspects of their employees' jobs, especially on telephones, computer terminals, through electronic and voice mail, and when employees are using the Internet. Such monitoring is virtually unregulated. Therefore, unless company policy specifically states otherwise (and even this is not ensured), your employer may listen, watch, and read most of your workplace communications. **Workplace MIS monitoring** tracks people's activities by such measures as number of keystrokes, error rate, and number of transactions processed (see Figure 4.7 for an overview). The best path for an organization planning to engage in employee monitoring is open communication, including an **employee monitoring policy** stating explicitly how, when, and where the company monitors its employees.

FIGURE 4.7

Internet Monitoring Technologies

Common Internet Monitoring Technologies	
Key logger, or key trapper, software	A program that records every keystroke and mouse click.
Hardware key logger	A hardware device that captures keystrokes on their journey from the keyboard to the motherboard.
Cookie	A small file deposited on a hard drive by a website containing information about customers and their web activities. Cookies allow websites to record the comings and goings of customers, usually without their knowledge or consent.
Adware	Software that generates ads that install themselves on a computer when a person downloads some other program from the Internet.
Spyware (sneakware or stealthware)	Software that comes hidden in free downloadable software and tracks online movements, mines the information stored on a computer, or uses a computer's CPU and storage for some task the user knows nothing about.
Web log	Consists of one line of information for every visitor to a website and is usually stored on a web server.
Clickstream	Records information about a customer during a web surfing session such as what websites were visited, how long the visit was, what ads were viewed, and what was purchased.

BUSINESS DRIVEN ANALYTICS

Many businesses fall into the trap of believing data even when their knowledge or common sense tells them the data is wrong. Studies conducted over decades have found that an alarming 88 percent of spreadsheets suffer from some type of error. Here are a few examples:

Garbage In Is Garbage Out

- London Olympics: A swimming event was oversold when a member of the staff made a single keystroke mistake and entered 20,000 remaining tickets into a spreadsheet instead of 10,000, the actual number of remaining tickets.
- TIBCO Software Company: A spreadsheet error misstated the number of outstanding shares, causing the value of the company to be overstated by $100 million during its acquisition.
- Kodak: The payment of a $11 million severance package to an employee was the result of a faulty spreadsheet.

According to experts and academics who have researched spreadsheet effectiveness, three primary types of errors typically occur in spreadsheet models.

1. **Mechanical error:** Arises from mistakes in typing, cutting and pasting, or other simple manual operations. While a mechanical error may at first appear minor, incorrectly entered data can affect the integrity of an entire model. Furthermore, planning models tend to grow in size and complexity as available computing power increases. As the models grow, the errors created within them increase in both number and severity.

2. **Logic Error:** An inappropriate algorithm is chosen or inappropriate formulas are created to implement the algorithm. The resulting flawed calculations affect not only the worksheet where the error appears but the entire model as well.

3. **Omission Error:** Critical components are left out of a model entirely. Errors of omission are hard to identify. As you work through large spreadsheets, the likelihood is great that a critical item will simply not be inserted and its absence will not be noticed.

Review the list of spreadsheet errors above and rank them in order of easiest to hardest to identify and fix. Have you ever encountered problems in your life due to a data error? What did you do to solve the problem? How did you find the error? What can you do to ensure you do not fall into the trap of believing the data over your own knowledge?

Several common stipulations an organization can follow when creating an employee monitoring policy include:

- Be as specific as possible stating when and what (email, IM, Internet, network activity, etc.) will be monitored.
- Expressly communicate that the company reserves the right to monitor all employees.
- State the consequences of violating the policy.
- Always enforce the policy the same for everyone.

Many employees use their company's high-speed Internet access to shop, browse, and surf the web. Most managers do not want their employees conducting personal business during working hours, and they implement a Big Brother approach to employee monitoring. Many management gurus advocate that organizations whose corporate cultures are based on trust are more successful than those whose corporate cultures are based on mistrust. Before an organization implements monitoring technology, it should ask itself, "What does this say about how we feel about our employees?" If the organization really does not trust its employees, then perhaps it should find new ones. If an organization does trust its employees, then it might want to treat them accordingly. An organization that follows its employees' every keystroke might be unwittingly undermining the relationships with its employees, and it might find the effects of employee monitoring are often worse than lost productivity from employee web surfing.

section 4.2 | Information Security

LEARNING OUTCOMES

4.3 Describe the relationships and differences between hackers and viruses.

4.4 Describe the relationship between information security policies and an information security plan.

4.5 Provide an example of each of the three primary information security areas: (1) authentication and authorization, (2) prevention and resistance, and (3) detection and response.

LO 4.3: Describe the relationships and differences between hackers and viruses.

PROTECTING INTELLECTUAL ASSETS

To reflect the crucial interdependence between MIS and business processes accurately, we should update the old business axiom "Time is money" to say "Uptime is money." *Downtime* refers to a period of time when a system is unavailable. Unplanned downtime can strike at any time for any number of reasons, from tornadoes to sink overflows to network failures to power outages (see Figure 4.8). Although natural disasters may appear to be the most devastating causes of MIS outages, they are hardly the most frequent or most expensive. Figure 4.9 demonstrates that the costs of downtime are not only associated with lost revenues but also with financial performance, damage to reputations, and even travel or legal expenses. A few questions managers should ask when determining the cost of downtime are:[11]

- How many transactions can the company afford to lose without significantly harming business?

- Does the company depend on one or more mission-critical applications to conduct business?

FIGURE 4.8

Sources of Unplanned Downtime

Sources of Unplanned Downtime		
Bomb threat	Frozen pipe	Snowstorm
Burst pipe	Hacker	Sprinkler malfunction
Chemical spill	Hail	Static electricity
Construction	Hurricane	Strike
Corrupted data	Ice storm	Terrorism
Earthquake	Insects	Theft
Electrical short	Lightning	Tornado
Epidemic	Network failure	Train derailment
Equipment failure	Plane crash	Smoke damage
Evacuation	Power outage	Vandalism
Explosion	Power surge	Vehicle crash
Fire	Rodents	Virus
Flood	Sabotage	Water damage (various)
Fraud	Shredded data	Wind

FIGURE 4.9

The Cost of Downtime

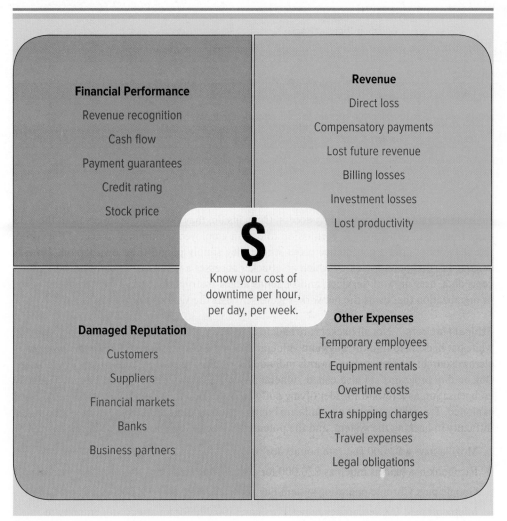

- How much revenue will the company lose for every hour a critical application is unavailable?
- What is the productivity cost associated with each hour of downtime?
- How will collaborative business processes with partners, suppliers, and customers be affected by an unexpected IT outage?
- What is the total cost of lost productivity and lost revenue during unplanned downtime?

The reliability and resilience of MIS systems have never been more essential for success as businesses cope with the forces of globalization, 24/7 operations, government and trade regulations, global recession, and overextended MIS budgets and resources. Any unexpected downtime in today's business environment has the potential to cause both short- and long-term costs with far-reaching consequences.

Information security is a broad term encompassing the protection of information from accidental or intentional misuse by persons inside or outside an organization. Information security is the primary tool an organization can use to combat the threats associated with downtime. Understanding how to secure information systems is critical to keeping downtime to a minimum and uptime to a maximum. Hackers and viruses are two of the hottest issues currently facing information security.

Hackers: A Dangerous Threat to Business

Hackers are experts in technology who use their knowledge to break into computers and computer networks, either for profit or simply for the challenge. Smoking is not just bad for a person's health; it seems it is also bad for company security because hackers regularly use

Common Types of Hackers
■ **Black-hat hackers** break into other people's computer systems and may just look around or may steal and destroy information.
■ **Crackers** have criminal intent when hacking.
■ **Cyberterrorists** seek to cause harm to people or to destroy critical systems or information and use the Internet as a weapon of mass destruction.
■ **Hactivists** have philosophical and political reasons for breaking into systems and will often deface the website as a protest.
■ **Script kiddies** or **script bunnies** find hacking code on the Internet and click-and-point their way into systems to cause damage or spread viruses.
■ **White-hat hackers** work at the request of the system owners to find system vulnerabilities and plug the holes.

FIGURE 4.10

Types of Hackers

smoking entrances to gain building access. Once inside, they pose as employees from the MIS department and either ask for permission to use an employee's computer to access the corporate network or find a conference room where they simply plugin their own laptop. *Drive-by hacking* is a computer attack by which an attacker accesses a wireless computer network, intercepts data, uses network services, and/or sends attack instructions without entering the office or organization that owns the network. Figure 4.10 lists the various types of hackers.

Ethical Hackers   Not all hackers are bad; in fact, it can be a good business strategy to employ white-hat hackers to find the bugs and vulnerabilities in a corporation. A *bug bounty program* is a crowdsourcing initiative that rewards individuals for discovering and reporting software bugs. Bug bounty programs are also called vulnerability rewards programs as they provide financial compensation as a reward for identifying software vulnerabilities that have the potential to be exploited. Typically, payment amounts are commensurate with the size of the organization, the difficulty in hacking the system, and the potential impact of the bug. Here are a few examples:

- Mozilla pays a $3,000 flat rate bounty for bugs.
- Facebook has paid as much as $20,000 for a single bug report.
- Google pays Chrome operating system bug reporters on average $700,000 per year.
- Microsoft paid UK researcher James Forshaw $100,000 for an attack vulnerability in Windows 8.1.
- Apple pays $200,000 for a flaw in the iOS secure boot firmware components.

While the use of white-hat ethical hackers to find bugs is effective, such programs can also be controversial. To limit potential risk, some organizations are offering *closed bug bounty programs* that require an invitation. Apple, for example, has limited bug bounty participation to a few dozen researchers.

Viruses: A Dangerous Threat to Business

One of the most common forms of computer vulnerabilities is a virus. A *virus* is software written with malicious intent to cause annoyance or damage. Some hackers create and leave viruses, causing massive computer damage. *Malware* is software that is intended to damage or disable computers and computer systems. Figure 4.11 shows how a virus is spread.

A *worm* spreads itself not only from file to file but also from computer to computer. The primary difference between a virus and a worm is that a virus must attach to something, such as an executable file, to spread. Worms do not need to attach to anything to spread and can tunnel themselves into computers. Figure 4.12 provides an overview of the most common types of viruses. Two additional computer vulnerabilities include adware and spyware. *Adware* is software that, although purporting to serve some useful function and often fulfilling that function, also allows Internet advertisers to display advertisements without the consent of the computer user. *Spyware* is a special class of adware that collects data about the user and transmits it over the Internet without the user's knowledge or permission. Spyware programs collect specific data about the user, ranging from general demographics such as name, address, and browsing habits, to credit card numbers, Social Security numbers, and user names and passwords. Not all adware programs are spyware, and, used correctly, they can generate revenue for a company, allowing users to receive free products. Spyware is a clear threat to privacy.

FIGURE 4.11

How Computer Viruses Spread

A hacker creates a virus and attaches it to a program, document, or website.

Thinking the file is legitimate, the user downloads it, and the virus infects other files and programs on the computer. Quickly, the virus spreads in email attachments and shared files to co-workers and friends.

FIGURE 4.12

Common Forms of Viruses

Backdoor programs open a way into the network for future attacks.

Denial-of-service attack (DoS) floods a website with so many requests for service that it slows down or crashes.

Distributed denial-of-service attack (DDoS) attacks from multiple computers that flood a website with so many requests for service that it slows down or crashes. A common type is the Ping of Death, in which thousands of computers try to access a website at the same time, overloading it and shutting it down.

Polymorphic viruses and worms change their form as they propagate.

Trojan-horse virus hides inside other software, usually as an attachment or a downloadable file.

Ransomware is a form of malicious software that infects your computer and asks for money. Simplelocker is a new ransomware program that encrypts your personal files and demands payment for the files' decryption keys. Ransomware is malware for data kidnapping, an exploit in which the attacker encrypts the victim's data and demands payment for the decryption key. Ransomware spreads through e-mail attachments, infected programs, and compromised websites. A ransomware malware program may also be called a cryptovirus, cryptotrojan, or cryptoworm. Attackers may use one of several different approaches to extort money from their victims:

- After a victim discovers he cannot open a file, he receives an email ransom note demanding a relatively small amount of money in exchange for a private key. The attacker warns that if the ransom is not paid by a certain date, the private key will be destroyed and the data will be lost forever.

- The victim is duped into believing he is the subject of a police inquiry. After being informed that unlicensed software or illegal web content has been found on his computer, the victim is given instructions for how to pay an electronic fine.

- The malware surreptitiously encrypts the victim's data but does nothing else. In this approach, the data kidnapper anticipates that the victim will look on the Internet for how to fix the problem and makes money by selling anti-ransomware software on legitimate websites.

To protect against data kidnapping, experts urge that users backup data on a regular basis. If an attack occurs, do not pay a ransom. Instead, wipe the disk drive clean and restore data from the backup.

Scareware is a type of malware designed to trick victims into giving up personal information to purchase or download useless and potentially dangerous software. Scareware often takes advantage of vulnerabilities in a computer's browser to generate pop-ups that resemble system error messages. The warnings, which are designed to look authentic, typically alert the user that a large number of infected files have been found on the computing device. The user is then prompted to call a phone number or click on a hyperlink to get the infection cleaned up. If the end user calls the phone number, they are urged to share credit card information in order to make a purchase for bogus software or are sent to a website to download a "clean up" software application that actually contains malware and infects the computer. If the user falls for the scam, he will not only lose the money he paid for the useless software, he may also make his computer unusable. Figure 4.13 displays a few additional weapons hackers use for launching attacks.[12]

Organizational information is intellectual capital. Just as organizations protect their tangible assets—keeping their money in an insured bank or providing a safe working environment for employees—they must also protect their intellectual capital, everything from patents to transactional and analytical information. With security breaches and viruses on the rise and computer hackers everywhere, an organization must put in place strong security measures to survive.

LO 4.4: Describe the relationship between information security policies and an information security plan.

THE FIRST LINE OF DEFENSE—PEOPLE

Organizations today can mine valuable information such as the identity of the top 20 percent of their customers, who usually produce 80 percent of revenues. Most organizations view this type of information as intellectual capital and implement security measures to prevent it from walking out the door or falling into the wrong hands. At the same time, they must enable employees, customers, and partners to access needed information electronically. Organizations address security risks through two lines of defense: the first is people, the second is technology.

Surprisingly, the biggest problem is people because the majority of information security breaches result from people misusing organizational information. *Insiders* are legitimate users who purposely or accidentally misuse their access to the environment and cause some kind of business-affecting incident. For example, many individuals freely give up their passwords or write them on sticky notes next to their computers, leaving the door wide open for hackers. Through *social engineering,* hackers use their social skills to trick people into revealing access credentials or other valuable information. *Dumpster diving,* or looking through people's trash,

FIGURE 4.13

Hacker Weapons

Elevation of privilege is a process by which a user misleads a system into granting unauthorized rights, usually for the purpose of compromising or destroying the system. For example, an attacker might log on to a network by using a guest account and then exploit a weakness in the software that lets the attacker change the guest privileges to administrative privileges.

Hoaxes attack computer systems by transmitting a virus hoax with a real virus attached. By masking the attack in a seemingly legitimate message, unsuspecting users more readily distribute the message and send the attack on to their co-workers and friends, infecting many users along the way.

Malicious code includes a variety of threats such as viruses, worms, and Trojan horses.

Packet tampering consists of altering the contents of packets as they travel over the Internet or altering data on computer disks after penetrating a network. For example, an attacker might place a tap on a network line to intercept packets as they leave the computer. The attacker could eavesdrop or alter the information as it leaves the network.

A **sniffer** is a program or device that can monitor data traveling over a network. Sniffers can show all the data being transmitted over a network, including passwords and sensitive information. Sniffers tend to be a favorite weapon in the hacker's arsenal.

Spoofing consists of forging the return address on an email so that the message appears to come from someone other than the actual sender. This is not a virus but rather a way by which virus authors conceal their identities as they send out viruses.

Splogs (spam blogs) are fake blogs created solely to raise the search engine rank of affiliated websites. Even blogs that are legitimate are plagued by spam, with spammers taking advantage of the comment feature of most blogs to comment with links to spam sites.

Spyware is software that comes hidden in free downloadable software and tracks online movements, mines the information stored on a computer, or uses a computer's CPU and storage for some task the user knows nothing about.

is another way hackers obtain information. *Pretexting* is a form of social engineering in which one individual lies to obtain confidential data about another individual.

Information security policies identify the rules required to maintain information security, such as requiring users to log off before leaving for lunch or meetings, never sharing passwords with anyone, and changing passwords every 30 days. An *information security plan* details how an organization will implement the information security policies. The best way a company can safeguard itself from people is by implementing and communicating its information security plan. This becomes even more important with Web 2.0 as the use of mobile devices, remote workforce, and contractors continue growing. A few details managers should consider surrounding people and information security policies include defining the best practices for:[13]

- Applications allowed to be placed on the corporate network, especially various file sharing applications (Kazaz), IM software, and entertainment or freeware created by unknown sources (iPhone applications).
- Corporate computer equipment used for personal reasons on personal networks.
- Password creation and maintenance including minimum password length, characters to be included while choosing passwords, and frequency for password changes.
- Personal computer equipment allowed to connect to the corporate network.
- Virus protection, including how often the system should be scanned and how frequently the software should be updated. This could also include if downloading attachments is allowed and practices for safe downloading from trusted and untrustworthy sources.

THE SECOND LINE OF DEFENSE—TECHNOLOGY

Once an organization has protected its intellectual capital by arming its people with a detailed information security plan, it can begin to focus on deploying technology to help combat attackers. *Destructive agents* are malicious agents designed by spammers and other Internet attackers to farm email addresses off websites or deposit spyware on machines. Figure 4.14 displays the three areas in which technology can aid in the defense against attacks.

LO 4.5: Provide an example of each of the three primary information security areas: (1) authentication and authorization, (2) prevention and resistance, and (3) detection and response.

People: Authentication and Authorization

Information secrecy is the category of computer security that addresses the protection of data from unauthorized disclosure and confirmation of data source authenticity. *Identity theft* consists of forging someone's identity for the purpose of fraud. The fraud is often financial because thieves apply for and use credit cards or loans in the victim's name. Two means of stealing an identity are phishing and pharming.

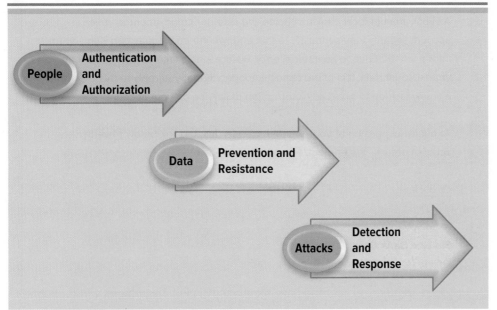

FIGURE 4.14

Three Areas of Information Security

Phishing is a technique to gain personal information for the purpose of identity theft, usually by means of fraudulent emails that look as though they came from legitimate businesses. The messages appear to be genuine, with official-looking formats and logos, and typically ask for verification of important information such as passwords and account numbers, ostensibly for accounting or auditing purposes. Since the emails look authentic, up to one in five recipients responds with the information and subsequently becomes a victim of identity theft and other fraud. Figure 4.15 displays a phishing scam attempting to gain information for Skyline Bank; you should never click emails asking you to verify your identity because companies will never contact you directly asking for your user name or password.[14] A *phishing expedition* is a masquerading attack that combines spam with spoofing. The perpetrator sends millions of spam emails that appear to be from a respectable company. The emails contain a link to a website that is designed to look exactly like the company's website. The victim is encouraged to enter his or her username, password, and sometimes credit card information. *Spear phishing* is a phishing expedition in which the emails are carefully designed to target a particular person or organization. *Vishing (or voice phishing)* is a phone scam that attempts to defraud people by asking them to call a bogus telephone number to confirm their account information.

Pharming reroutes requests for legitimate websites to false websites. For example, if you were to type in the URL to your bank, pharming could redirect to a fake site that collects your information. A *zombie* is a program that secretly takes over another computer for the purpose

FIGURE 4.15

Skyline Bank Phishing Scam

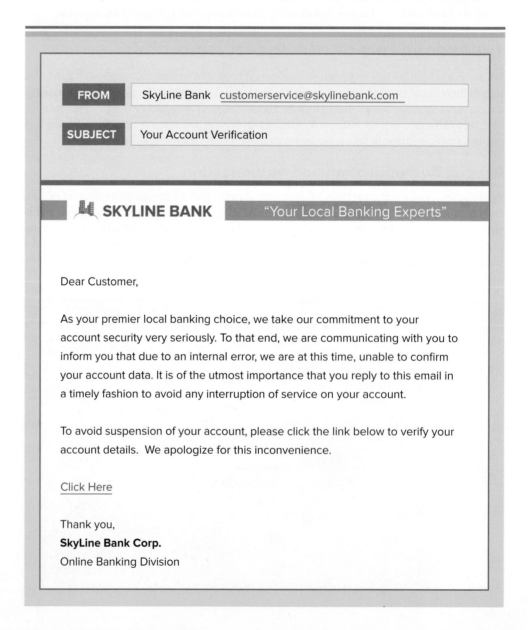

BUSINESS DRIVEN INNOVATION

Beyond the Password

The password, a combination of a user name and personal code, has been the primary way to secure systems since computers first hit the market in the 1980s. Of course, in the 1980s, users had only one password to maintain and remember, and chances are they still probably had to write it down. Today, users have dozens of user names and passwords they have to remember to multiple systems and websites—it is simply no longer sustainable! A few companies are creating new forms of identification, hoping to eliminate the password problem.

- Bionym is developing the Nymi, a wristband with two electrodes that reads your heart's unique electrocardiogram signal and can unlock all your devices.

- Clef is developing the Clef Wave, a free app that generates a unique image on your smart phone that you can point at your webcam, which reads the image and unlocks your websites. The image cannot be stolen because it only stays on your screen for a few seconds. More than 300 websites have enabled the Clef Wave service.

- Illiri is developing an app that emits a unique sound on your smart phone that can be used to unlock other devices, process payments, and access websites. The sound lasts for 10 seconds and can be heard within 1 foot of your device.

In a group, evaluate the three preceding technologies and determine which one you would choose to implement at your school.

---

of launching attacks on other computers. Zombie attacks are almost impossible to trace back to the attacker. A *zombie farm* is a group of computers on which a hacker has planted zombie programs. A *pharming attack* uses a zombie farm, often by an organized crime association, to launch a massive phishing attack.

Sock puppet marketing is the use of a false identity to artificially stimulate demand for a product, brand, or service. A false identity on the Internet is known colloquially as a sock puppet or catfish, depending upon the level of detail attached to the false identity. Typically, a sock puppet has very little (if any) detail attached to it and may simply be a fictional name attached to a new Google or Yahoo email account. Sock puppet marketing is one example of *astroturfing,* the practice of artificially stimulating online conversation and positive reviews about a product, service, or brand. Sock puppets can be created quickly and are frequently used on social media websites that rely on customer reviews. For this reason, many websites only allow customer reviews from a verified customer. Sock puppet marketing is unethical and in some cases, illegal. In the United States, the Federal Trade Commission has the legal authority to levy fines if a company engages in sock puppet marketing.

Authentication and authorization technologies can prevent identity theft, phishing, and pharming scams. *Authentication* is a method for confirming users' identities. Once a system determines the authentication of a user, it can then determine the access privileges (or authorization) for that user. *Authorization* is the process of providing a user with permission, including access levels and abilities such as file access, hours of access, and amount of allocated storage space. Authentication and authorization techniques fall into three categories; the most secure procedures combine all three:

1. **Something the user knows, such as a user ID and password.** The first type of authentication, using something the user knows, is the most common way to identify individual users and typically consists of a unique user ID and password. However, this is actually one of the most *ineffective* ways for determining authentication because passwords are not secure. All it typically takes to crack one is enough time. More than 50 percent of help-desk calls are

password related, which can cost an organization significant money, and a social engineer can coax a password from almost anybody.

2. **Something the user has, such as a smart card or token.** The second type of authentication, using something the user has, offers a much more effective way to identify individuals than a user ID and password. Tokens and smart cards are two of the primary forms of this type of authentication. *Tokens* are small electronic devices that change user passwords automatically. The user enters his or her user ID and token-displayed password to gain access to the network. A *smart card* is a device about the size of a credit card containing embedded technologies that can store information and small amounts of software to perform some limited processing. Smart cards can act as identification instruments, a form of digital cash, or a data storage device with the ability to store an entire medical record.

3. **Something that is part of the user, such as a fingerprint or voice signature.** The third kind of authentication, something that is part of the user, is by far the best and most effective way to manage authentication. *Biometrics* (narrowly defined) is the identification of a user based on a physical characteristic, such as a fingerprint, iris, face, voice, or handwriting. A *voiceprint* is a set of measurable characteristics of a human voice that uniquely identifies an individual. These characteristics, which are based on the physical configuration of a speaker's mouth and throat, can be expressed as a mathematical formula. Unfortunately, biometric authentication such as voiceprints can be costly and intrusive.

Single-factor authentication is the traditional security process, which requires a user name and password. *Two-factor authentication* requires the user to provide two means of authentication, what the user knows (password) and what the user has (security token). *Multifactor authentication* requires more than two means of authentication such as what the user knows (password), what the user has (security token), and what the user is (biometric verification). The goal of multifactor authentication is to make it difficult for an unauthorized person to gain access to a system because, if one security level is broken, the attacker will still have to break through additional levels.

Data: Prevention and Resistance

A *privilege escalation* is a network intrusion attack that takes advantage of programming errors or design flaws to grant the attacker elevated access to the network and its associated data and applications. There are two kinds of privilege escalation:

- *Vertical privilege escalation.* Attackers grant themselves a higher access level such as administrator, allowing the attacker to perform illegal actions such as running unauthorized code or deleting data. For example, an attacker might log on to a network by using a guest account and then exploit a weakness in the software that lets the attacker change the guest privileges to administrative privileges.

- *Horizontal privilege escalation.* Attackers grant themselves the same access levels they already have but assume the identity of another user. For example, someone gaining access to another person's online banking account would constitute horizontal privilege escalation.

Prevention and resistance technologies stop intruders from accessing and reading data by means of content filtering, encryption, and firewalls. *Time bombs* are computer viruses that wait for a specific date before executing their instructions. *Content filtering* occurs when organizations use software that filters content, such as emails, to prevent the accidental or malicious transmission of unauthorized information. Organizations can use content filtering technologies to filter email and prevent emails containing sensitive information from transmitting, whether the transmission was malicious or accidental. It can also filter emails to prevent any suspicious files from transmitting, such as potentially virus-infected files. Email content filtering can also filter for spam, a form of unsolicited email.

Encryption scrambles information into an alternative form that requires a key or password to decrypt. If there were a security breach and the stolen information were encrypted, the thief would be unable to read it. Encryption can switch the order of characters, replace characters with other characters, insert or remove characters, or use a mathematical formula to convert the information into a code. Companies that transmit sensitive customer information over the Internet, such as credit card numbers, frequently use encryption. To *decrypt* information is to decode it and is the opposite of *encrypt*. **Cryptography** is the science that studies encryption, which is the hiding of messages so that only the sender and receiver can read them. The National Institute of Standards and Technology introduced an **advanced encryption standard (AES)** designed to keep government information secure.

Personally identifiable information (PII) is any data that could potentially identify a specific individual. The two types of PII include sensitive PII and nonsensitive PII.

- **Nonsensitive PII** is information transmitted without encryption and includes information collected from public records, phone books, corporate directories, websites, etc. Nonsensitive PII includes information that does not harm an individual such as an address.

- **Sensitive PII** is information transmitted with encryption and, when disclosed, results in a breach of an individual's privacy and can potentially cause the individual harm. Sensitive PII includes biometric information, financial information, medical information, and unique identifiers such as passport or Social Security numbers.

The **HIPAA Security Rule** ensures national standards for securing patient data that is stored or transferred electronically. The HIPAA Security Rule requires the placement of both physical and electronic safeguards on sensitive PII health information. The goal of the HIPAA Security Rule is to protect patient security while still allowing the health care industry to advance technologically. All organizations need to understand and govern PII by:

- Identifying all sources of created, received, maintained, or transmitted PII.
- Evaluating all external sources of PII.
- Identifying all human, natural, and environmental threats to PII.

Some encryption technologies use multiple keys. **Public key encryption (PKE)** uses two keys: a public key that everyone can have and a private key for only the recipient (see Figure 4.16). The organization provides the public key to all customers, whether end consumers or other businesses, who use that key to encrypt their information and send it via the Internet. When it arrives at its destination, the organization uses the private key to unscramble it.

Public keys are becoming popular to use for authentication techniques consisting of digital objects in which a trusted third party confirms correlation between the user and the public key. A **certificate authority** is a trusted third party, such as VeriSign, that validates user identities by means of digital certificates. A **digital certificate** is a data file that identifies individuals or organizations online and is comparable to a digital signature.

A **firewall** is hardware and/or software that guard a private network by analyzing incoming and outgoing information for the correct markings. If they are missing, the firewall prevents the information from entering the network. Firewalls can even detect computers communicating with the Internet without approval. As Figure 4.17 illustrates, organizations typically place a firewall between a server and the Internet. Think of a firewall as a gatekeeper that protects

FIGURE 4.16

Public Key Encryption (PKE)

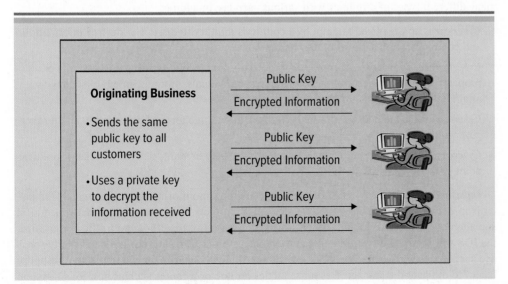

Originating Business

- Sends the same public key to all customers

- Uses a private key to decrypt the information received

Public Key

Encrypted Information

Public Key

Encrypted Information

Public Key

Encrypted Information

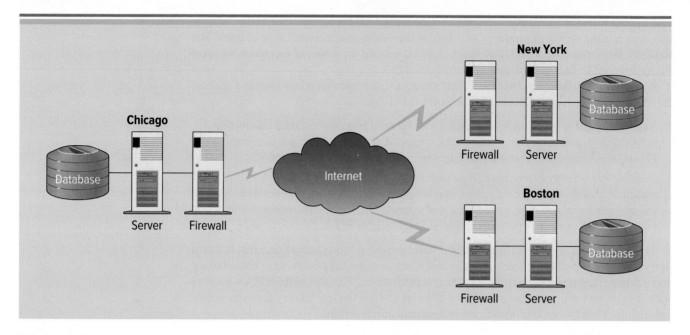

FIGURE 4.17

Sample Firewall Architecture Connecting Systems Located in Chicago, New York, and Boston

computer networks from intrusion by providing a filter and safe transfer points for access to and from the Internet and other networks. It screens all network traffic for proper passwords or other security codes and allows only authorized transmissions in and out of the network.

Firewalls do not guarantee complete protection, and users should enlist additional security technologies such as antivirus software and antispyware software. *Antivirus software* scans and searches hard drives to prevent, detect, and remove known viruses, adware, and spyware. Antivirus software must be frequently updated to protect against newly created viruses.

Attack: Detection and Response

Network behavior analysis gathers an organization's computer network traffic patterns to identify unusual or suspicious operations. Network behavior analysis software tracks critical network characteristics and generates an alarm if an anomaly or strange trend is detected that might indicate the presence of a threat. Trends can include increased traffic volume, bandwidth use and protocol use. With so many intruders planning computer attacks, it is critical for all computer systems to be protected. The presence of an intruder can be detected by watching for suspicious network events such as bad passwords, the removal of highly classified data files, or unauthorized user attempts. Detecting cyber criminals is a difficult job because there are so many different types of criminals with various agendas, including:

- *Cyberwar* is an organized attempt by a country's military to disrupt or destroy information and communication systems of another country.

- *Cyberterrorism* is the use of computer and networking technologies against persons or property to intimidate or coerce governments, individuals, or any segment of society to attain political, religious, or ideological goals.

- *Cyber-espionage* includes governments that are after some form of information about other governments.

- *Cyber-vigilantes* include individuals that seek notoriety or want to make a social or political point such as WikiLeaks.

Intrusion detection software (IDS) features full-time monitoring tools that search for patterns in network traffic to identify intruders. IDS protects against suspicious network traffic and attempts to access files and data. If a suspicious event or unauthorized traffic is identified, the IDS will generate an alarm and can even be customized to shut down a particularly sensitive part of a network. After identifying an attack, an MIS department can implement response tactics to mitigate the damage. Response tactics outline procedures such as how long a system

BUSINESS DRIVEN START-UP

Fingerprints Are the New Keys

Have you ever lost your house key or locked your keys in your home? Technology to the rescue. Keyless entry systems are becoming more and more popular for technology savvy homes. Cutting-edge biometric technology allows users to control home access with a simple fingerprint. These smart keys can open an office, wine cellar, vacation home—really anywhere you would like personalized control, access, and protection. Some systems allow users to program up to 5,000 fingerprints along with customized access times. If your cleaning service professionals always come on Tuesday around noon, no problem. If tampered with, the system can sound the home alarm.[15]

There are a number of reasons to use keyless entry systems, along with just as many reasons not to use keyless systems. List the pros and cons of a keyless entry system. Given the choice, what type of system would you install in your home?

under attack will remain plugged in and connected to the corporate network, when to shut down a compromised system, and how quickly a backup system will be up and running.

Guaranteeing the safety of organization information is achieved by implementing the two lines of defense: people and technology. To protect information through people, firms should develop information security policies and plans that provide employees with specific precautions they should take in creating, working with, and transmitting the organization's information assets. Technology-based lines of defense fall into three categories: authentication and authorization; prevention and resistance; and detection and response.

LEARNING OUTCOME REVIEW

Learning Outcome 4.1: Explain the ethical issues in the use of information technology.

Information ethics govern the ethical and moral issues arising from the development and use of information technologies as well as the creation, collection, duplication, distribution, and processing of information itself (with or without the aid of computer technologies). Ethical dilemmas in this area usually arise not as simple, clear-cut situations but as clashes among competing goals, responsibilities, and loyalties. Inevitably, there will be more than one socially acceptable or correct decision. For this reason, acting ethically and legally are not always the same.

Learning Outcome 4.2: Identify the six epolicies organizations should implement to protect themselves.

1. An ethical computer use policy contains general principles to guide computer user behavior. For example, it might explicitly state that users should refrain from playing computer games during working hours.

2. An information privacy policy contains general principles regarding information privacy.

3. An acceptable use policy (AUP) is a policy that a user must agree to follow to be provided access to corporate email, information systems, and the Internet.

4. An email privacy policy details the extent to which email messages may be read by others.

5. A social media policy outlines the corporate guidelines or principles governing employee online communications.

6. An employee-monitoring policy states explicitly how, when, and where the company monitors its employees.

Learning Outcome 4.3: Describe the relationships and differences between hackers and viruses.

Hackers are experts in technology who use their knowledge to break into computers and computer networks, either for profit or just for the challenge. A virus is software written with malicious intent to cause annoyance or damage. Some hackers create and leave viruses, causing massive computer damage.

Learning Outcome 4.4: Describe the relationship between information security policies and an information security plan.

Information security policies identify the rules required to maintain information security, such as requiring users to log off before leaving for lunch or meetings, never sharing passwords with anyone, and changing passwords every 30 days. An information security plan details how an organization will implement the information security policies. The best way a company can safeguard itself from people is by implementing and communicating its information security plan.

Learning Outcome 4.5: Provide an example of each of the three primary information security areas: (1) authentication and authorization, (2) prevention and resistance, and (3) detection and response.

Authentication and authorization: Authentication is a method for confirming users' identities. Once a system determines the authentication of a user, it can then determine the access privileges (or authorization) for that user. Authorization is the process of providing a user with permission, including access levels and abilities such as file access, hours of access, and amount of allocated storage space.

Prevention and resistance: Content filtering occurs when organizations use software that filters content, such as emails, to prevent the accidental or malicious transmission of unauthorized information. Encryption scrambles information into an alternative form that requires a key or password to decrypt. In a security breach, a thief is then unable to read encrypted information. A firewall is hardware and/or software that guards a private network by analyzing incoming and outgoing information for the correct markings.

Detection and response: Intrusion detection software (IDS) features full-time monitoring tools that search for patterns in network traffic to identify intruders.

OPENING CASE QUESTIONS

1. **Knowledge:** Define information ethics and information security, and explain whether they are important to help prevent hackers from gaining access to an organization.

2. **Comprehension:** Identify two epolicies that a business could implement to ensure the protection of sensitive corporate data from hackers.

3. **Application:** Demonstrate how a business can use authentication and authorization technologies to prevent hackers from gaining access to organizational systems.

4. **Analysis:** Analyze how a business can use prevention and resistance technologies to safeguard its employees from hackers and viruses.

5. **Synthesis:** Explain why hackers want to gain access to organizational data.

6. **Evaluate:** Evaluate additional ways hackers can gain access to organizational data.

Acceptable use policy (AUP) 148
Advanced encryption standard
    (AES) 163
Adware 156
Anti-spam policy 150
Antivirus software 164
Astroturfing 161
Authentication 161
Authorization 161
Biometrics 162
Black-hat hackers 156
Bring your own device (BYOD) 148
Bug bounty program 156
Certificate authority 163
Child Online Protection Act
    (COPA) 145
Click-fraud 147
Competitive click-fraud 147
Confidentiality 143
Content filtering 162
Copyright 143
Counterfeit software 143
Cracker 156
Cryptography 163
Cyber-espionage 164
Cyber-vigilantes 164
Cyberbullying 147
Cyberterrorism 164
Cyberterrorists 156
Cybervandalism 149
Cyberwar 164
Decrypt 162
Destructive agents 159
Digital certificate 163
Digital rights management 143
Downtime 154
Drive-by hacking 156
Dumpster diving 158
Ediscovery (or electronic
    discovery) 145
Email privacy policy 149

Employee monitoring policy 152
Encryption 162
Epolicies 146
Ethical computer use policy 147
Ethics 143
Fair information practices (FIP) 148
Firewall 163
Hackers 155
Hactivists 156
HIPAA Security Rule 163
Horizontal privilege
    escalation 162
Identity theft 159
Information compliance 146
Information ethics 143
Information governance 146
Information management 146
Information property 146
Information privacy policy 148
Information secrecy 159
Information security 155
Information security plan 159
Information security policies 159
Insiders 158
Intellectual property 143
Internet censorship 149
Internet use policy 148
Intrusion detection software
    (IDS) 164
Mail bomb 150
Malware 156
Multifactor authentication 162
Network behavior analysis 164
Nonrepudiation 148
Nonsensitive PII 163
Opt in 150
Opt out 150
Patent 143
Personally identifiable information
    (PII) 163
Pharming 160

Pharming attack 161
Phishing 160
Phishing expedition 160
Physical security 152
Pirated software 143
Pretexting 159
Privacy 143
Privilege escalation 162
Public key encryption (PKE) 163
Ransomware 157
Rule 41 144
Scareware 158
Script kiddies or script
    bunnies 156
Sensitive PII 163
Single-factor authentication 162
Smart card 162
Sock puppet marketing 161
Social engineering 158
Social media manager 151
Social media monitoring 151
Social media policy 151
Spam 150
Spear phishing 160
Spyware 156
Teergrubing 150
Threat 147
Time bomb 162
Tokens 162
Two-factor authentication 162
Typosquatting 149
Vertical privilege escalation 162
Virus 156
Vishing (voice phishing) 160
Voiceprint 162
Website name stealing 149
White-hat hackers 156
Worm 156
Workplace MIS monitoring 152
Zombie 160
Zombie farm 161

1. What are ethics and why are they important to a company?

2. What is the relationship between information management, governance, and compliance?

3. Why are epolicies important to a company?

4. What is the correlation between privacy and confidentiality?

5. What is the relationship between adware and spyware?

6. What are the positive and negative effects associated with monitoring employees?

7. What is the relationship between hackers and viruses?

8. Why is security a business issue, not just a technology issue?

9. What are the growing issues related to employee communication methods, and what can a company do to protect itself?

10. How can a company participating in ebusiness keep its information secure?

11. What technologies can a company use to safeguard information?

12. Why is ediscovery important to a company?

13. What are the reasons a company experiences downtime?

14. What are the costs associated with downtime?

CLOSING CASE ONE

Targeting Target

The biggest retail hack in U.S. history wasn't particularly inventive, nor did it appear destined for success. In the days prior to Thanksgiving 2013, someone installed malware in Target's security and payments system designed to steal every credit card used at the company's 1,797 U.S. stores. At the critical moment—when the Christmas gifts had been scanned and bagged and the cashier asked for a swipe—the malware would step in, capture the shopper's credit card number, and store it on a Target server commandeered by the hackers.

It's a measure of how common these crimes have become, and how conventional the hackers' approach in this case, that Target was prepared for such an attack. Six months earlier, the company began installing a $1.6 million malware detection tool made by the computer security firm FireEye, whose customers also include the CIA and the Pentagon. Target had a team of security specialists in Bangalore to monitor its computers around the clock. If Bangalore noticed anything suspicious, Target's security operations center in Minneapolis would be notified.

On Saturday, November 30, 2013, the hackers had set their traps and had just one thing to do before starting the attack: plan the data's escape route. As they uploaded exfiltration malware to move stolen credit card numbers—first to staging points spread around the United States to cover their tracks, then into their computers in Russia—FireEye spotted them. Bangalore got an alert and flagged the security team in Minneapolis. And then . . . .

Nothing happened.

For some reason, Minneapolis didn't react to the sirens. *Bloomberg Businessweek* spoke to more than 10 former Target employees familiar with the company's data security operation, as well as eight people with specific knowledge of the hack and its aftermath, including former employees, security researchers, and law enforcement officials. The story they tell is of an alert system, installed to protect the bond between retailer and customer that worked beautifully. But then, Target stood by as 40 million credit card numbers—and 70 million addresses, phone numbers, and other pieces of personal information—gushed out of its mainframes.

When asked to respond to a list of specific questions about the incident and the company's lack of an immediate response to it, Target Chairman, President, and Chief Executive Officer Gregg Steinhafel issued an emailed statement: "Target was certified as meeting the standard for the payment card industry (PCI) in September 2013. Nonetheless, we suffered a data breach. As a result, we are conducting an end-to-end review of our people, processes and technology to understand our opportunities to improve data security and are committed to learning from this experience. While we are still in the midst of an ongoing investigation, we have already taken significant steps, including beginning the overhaul of our information security structure and the acceleration of our transition to chip-enabled cards. However, as the investigation is not complete, we don't believe it's constructive to engage in speculation without the benefit of the final analysis."

More than 90 lawsuits have been filed against Target by customers and banks for negligence and compensatory damages. That's on top of other costs, which analysts estimate could run into the billions. Target spent $61 million through February 1, 2014, responding to the breach, according to its fourth-quarter report to investors. It set up a customer response operation, and in an effort to regain lost trust, Steinhafel promised that consumers won't have to pay any fraudulent charges stemming from the breach. Target's profit for the holiday shopping period fell 46 percent from the same quarter the year before; the number of transactions suffered its biggest decline since the retailer began reporting the statistic in 2008.[16]

Questions

1. How did the hackers steal Target's customer data?
2. What types of technology could big retailers use to prevent identity thieves from stealing information?
3. What can organizations do to protect themselves from hackers looking to steal account data?
4. In a team, research the Internet and find the best ways to protect yourself from identity theft.

CLOSING CASE TWO

To Share—Or Not to Share

People love social networks! Social networks are everywhere and a perfect way to share vacation photos, family events, and birthday parties with family, friends, and co-workers. About 40 percent of adults use at least one social media website, and 51 percent of those use more than one website. The majority of users are between the ages of 18 and 24. The Pew Research Center found that 89 percent of social network users primarily use the websites to update friends and family, 57 percent use the websites to make plans with friends, and 49 percent use the websites to make new friends.

Facebook, MySpace, LinkedIn, Friendster, Urban Chat, and Black Planet are just a few of more than 100 websites connecting people around the world who are eager to share everything from photos to thoughts and feelings. But we need to remember that sometimes you can share too much; there can be too much information. Choosing who you share with and what you share is something you want to think about for your personal social networks and corporate social networks. According to Pew Research, more than 40 percent of users allow open access to their social networking profiles, which allows anyone from anywhere to view all of their personal information. The remaining 60 percent restrict access to friends, family, and co-workers. The following are the top 10 things you should consider before posting information to your social networks.

1: If You Don't Want to Share It, Don't Post It

You can select all the privacy settings you want on social networking sites, but the fact is, if you post it, it has the potential to be seen by someone you don't want seeing it. You know all those fun Facebook applications, quizzes, and polls you can't help but fill out? A study performed by the University of Virginia found that of the top 150 applications on Facebook, 90 percent were given access to information they didn't need for the application to function. So when you sign up to find out what sitcom star you most identify with, the makers of that poll now have access to your personal information. It's anybody's guess where it goes from there. Social networking is all about sharing, so something you think is in confidence can easily be shared and then shared again, and before you know it, someone you don't even know has access to something private. "When in doubt, leave it out" is a good motto to follow. And always remember that anything you share has the potential to be leaked in some way.

2: Never Give Out Your Password Hints

Most websites that contain secure personal information require a password and have at least one password hint in case you forget. It typically goes like this: You sign up for something such as online banking; you get a logon and password and then choose a security question for when you forget your password. What's the name of your first pet? What's your mother's maiden name? What was your high school mascot? What's the name of the first street you lived on? Including any of these details on a Facebook wall or status update may not seem like a big deal, but it could provide an identity thief with the last piece of the puzzle needed to hack into your bank account. Think before you post anything that could compromise this information.

3: Never Give Out Your Password

This one really seems like a no-brainer, but if it didn't happen, then Facebook probably wouldn't feel the need to list it in the No. 1 slot on its list of things you shouldn't share. Even sharing the password with a friend so he or she can log on and check something for you can be a risk. This is especially true with couples who feel like there's enough trust to share these kinds of things. Here's another scenario for you: You give your boyfriend your Facebook password because he wants to help you upload some vacation photos. A couple of months later, the relationship sours, he turns into a not-so-nice guy, and then there's a person out there who doesn't like you and has your logon information. Time to cancel your account and get a new one. If you'd kept that information private, you could simply move on with your life. Now you have a compromised profile, and if you link to other sites or profiles, all that information is at risk as well. Keep your password to yourself, no matter what, and you never have to worry about it.

4: Never Provide Personal Financial Information

You would think that nobody would share things like where they do their banking or what their stock portfolio looks like, but it happens. It's easy for an innocent Facebook comment to reveal too much about your personal finances. Consider this scenario: You're posting to a long thread on a friend's wall about the bank crisis. You say something along the lines of, "We don't need to worry because we bank with a teacher's credit union," or even, "We put all our money into blue chip stocks and plan to ride it out." Again, if you're one of the 40 percent who allow open access to your profile, then suddenly identity thieves know where you bank and where you have the bulk of your investments. It's easy to forget that what may seem like a harmless comment on a Facebook wall could reveal a great deal about your personal finances. It's best to avoid that kind of talk.

5: Never Give Out Your Address or Phone Numbers

File this one under security risk. If you share your address and phone number on a social networking site, you open yourself up to threats of identity theft and other personal dangers such as burglaries. If you post that you're going on vacation and you have your address posted, then everyone knows you have an empty house. Identity thieves could pay a visit to your mailbox and open up a credit card in your name. Burglars could rid your home of anything of value. Even just posting your phone number gives people with Internet savvy easy access to your address. Reverse lookup services can supply anyone with your home address in possession of your phone number.

6: Never Share Photos of Your Children

Social networking sites are a common place for people to share pictures of their families, but if you're one of the 40 percent of users who don't restrict access to your profile, then those pictures are there for everyone to see. It's a sad fact, but a lot of predators use the Internet to stalk their prey. If you post pictures of your family and combine that with information like, "My husband is out of town this weekend" or "Little Johnny is old enough to stay at home by himself now," then your children's safety could be at risk. Nobody ever thinks it will happen to them until it does, so safety first is a good default mode when using social networking sites. Just like with other private matters, send family photos only to a select group of trusted friends and colleagues who you know won't share them.

7: Never Provide Company Information

You may be dying to tell the world about your new work promotion, but if it's news that could be advantageous to one of your company's competitors, then it's not something you should share. News of a planned expansion or a big project role and anything else about your workplace should be kept private. Sophos, a security software company, found that 63 percent of companies were afraid of what their employees were choosing to share on social networking sites. If you want to announce it, be selective and send private emails. Many companies are so serious about not being included in social networking sites that they forbid employees from using sites such as Facebook at work. Some IT departments even filter the URLs and block access to these sites so employees aren't tempted to log on.

8: Never Give Links to Websites

With 51 percent of social network users taking advantage of more than one site, there's bound to be some crossover, especially if you have the sites linked. You may post something you find innocuous on Facebook, but then it's linked to your LinkedIn work profile and you've put your job at risk. If you link your various profiles, be aware that what you post in one world is available to the others. In 2009, a case of an employee caught lying on Facebook hit the news. The employee asked off for a weekend shift because he was ill and then posted pictures on his Facebook profile of himself at a party that same weekend. The news got back to his employer easily enough, and he was fired. So if you choose to link your profiles, it's no longer a "personal life" and "work life" scenario.

9: Keep Your Social Plans to Yourself

Sharing your social plans for everybody to see isn't a good idea. Unless you're planning a big party and inviting all the users you're connected to, it will only make your other friends feel left out. Some security issues are also at stake here. Imagine a scenario in which a jealous ex-boyfriend knows that you're meeting a new date that night. What's to keep the ex from showing up and causing a scene or even potentially getting upset or violent? Nothing. If you're planning a party or an outing with a group of friends, send a personal "e-vite" for their eyes only, and nobody is the wiser. If you're trying to cast a wide net by throwing out an idea for a social outing, just remember that anyone who has access to your profile sees it.

10: Do Not Share Personal Conversations

On Facebook, users can send personal messages or post notes, images, or videos to another user's wall. The wall is there for all to see, while messages are between the sender and the receiver, just like an email. Personal and private matters should never be shared on your wall. You wouldn't go around with a bullhorn announcing a private issue to the world, and the same thing goes on the Internet. This falls under the nebulous world of social networking etiquette. There is no official handbook for this sort of thing, but use your best judgment. If it's not something you'd feel comfortable sharing in person with extended family, acquaintances, work colleagues, or strangers, then you shouldn't share it on your Facebook wall.[17]

Questions

1. Define *information ethics* and *information security,* and explain why each is critical to any business.
2. Identify two epolicies that a business could implement to ensure the protection of sensitive corporate data.
3. Demonstrate how a business can use authentication and authorization technologies to prevent information theft.
4. Analyze how a business can use prevention and resistance technologies to safeguard its employees from hackers and viruses.
5. Propose a plan to implement information security plans to ensure your critical information is safe and protected.
6. Evaluate the information security issues facing a business, and identify its three biggest concerns.

1. Information Issues in the Information Age

We live in the information age, in which the collection, storage, and use of data are hot topics. One example of inappropriate data handling occurred at a college where the monitoring of restrooms occurred every 15 seconds to observe the use of toilets, mirrors, and sinks. Students, faculty, and staff began complaining that the data collection was an invasion of their privacy and a violation of their rights.

Another example of inappropriate data handling occurred when a professor of accounting at a college lost a flash drive containing information for more than 1,800 students, including Social Security numbers, grades, and names. Social Security numbers were included because the data went back to before 1993, when the college used Social Security numbers to identify students. What types of student data does your college collect? What could happen if your professor lost a thumb drive containing all of your personal information? What types of issues could you encounter if someone stole your personal data? What can your college do to ensure this type of data storage violation does not occur?

2. WikiBlunders—Thin Ice Reports

According to *PC World*, these false facts all appeared on Wikipedia:

- David Beckham was a Chinese goalkeeper in the 18th century.
- Paul Reiser's dead. (Reiser is an actor.) Sinbad's dead. (Sinbad is an actor.)
- Sergey Brin's dating Jimmy Wales, and both are dead. (Brin founded Google and Wales founded Wikipedia.)
- Tony Blair worships Hitler. (Blair is the former prime minister of the United Kingdom.)
- The Duchess of Cornwall's Christian name is Cow-miller.
- The University of Cincinnati's former president is a lady of the night.
- Conan O'Brien assaults sea turtles while canoeing.

We know that people use information technology to work with information. Knowing this, how could these types of errors occur? What could happen if you decided to use Wikipedia to collect business intelligence for a research paper? What could Wikipedia do to help prevent these types of errors?

3. Yes, I Started the Internet

Imagine that your favorite co-worker is Mary, a hard-working employee who excels at her job and continuously receives outstanding performance reviews. Suddenly, after two years of hard work, Mary is fired and you are wondering what happened. What will you say when you find out that Mary lied on her résumé about having a master's degree? Will you feel that Mary got what she deserved, or should her outstanding job performance have helped management look past this issue? After all, she is excellent at her job.

Every student should know that if dishonesty is discovered, it is often grounds for termination and possibly legal action. Information integrity is a measure of the quality of information. According to Steven D. Levitt, co-author of *Freakonomics* and a renowned economics professor at the University of Chicago, more than 50 percent of people lie on their résumés. Given such repercussions as Mary's fate, you will want to think twice before ever lying on your résumé. The integrity of the information on your résumé is a direct representation of your personal integrity. How would you handle Mary's situation if you were her manager?

4. What Happens on YouTube Stays on YouTube FOREVER!

Are you looking for great career advice? Here it is: Never post anything on publicly accessible websites that you would not feel comfortable showing a recruiter or hiring manager. This includes inappropriate photos; negative comments about jobs, professors, or people; and images of you binge drinking at a holiday party. Future employers will Google you!

The bad news: You have to continue to keep your cyber profile squeaky clean for the rest of your life. Companies can and will fire you for inappropriate online postings. One interesting story occurred when two employees created a private, password-protected group on Facebook where they would complain about their jobs, post derogatory comments about their managers, and highlight new top-secret product information. The managers, being computer savvy, obtained the password and immediately fired the two individuals after reviewing the site. Now one of the individuals is suing the former managers for invasion of privacy.

Do you agree that if you post something online it is open for the world to see? What do you consider is inappropriate material that you should never post to the web? What can you do to remove inappropriate material posted to the web by a friend that identifies you? How do efficiency and effectiveness enter into this scenario? Was social media the most efficient and effective way for the two employees to communicate? What is the potential argument each of these sides might use in order to win the lawsuit?

5. Cheerleader Charged $27,750 for File Sharing 37 Songs

A federal appeals court is ordering a university student to pay the Recording Industry Association of America $27,750—$750 a track—for file sharing 37 songs when she was a high school cheerleader. Have you ever illegally copied or downloaded a song or movie? If you have and you were forced to pay $750 per track, how much would you owe? What is the difference between file sharing and Internet radio streaming? Do you agree or disagree with the appeals court's decision? Why or why not? Why is claiming a lack of copyright knowledge not a good defense against illegally sharing movies or music? If you do not have a good understanding of information laws, what can you do to ensure that you are never named in a federal lawsuit for violating information laws?[18]

6. Police Records Found in Old Copy Machine

Copy machines made after 2002 all contain a hard drive that stores a copy of every document the machine has ever scanned, printed, copied, or faxed. If the hard drive is not erased or scrubbed when the copy machine is resold, all of that digital information is still maintained inside the machine. The Buffalo, New York, Police Sex Crimes Division recently sold several copy machines without scrubbing the hard drives. The hard drives yielded detailed domestic violence complaints and a list of wanted sex offenders. A machine from the Buffalo Police Narcotics Unit contained targets in a major drug raid, and a copier once used by a New York construction company stored 95 pages of pay stubs with names, addresses, and Social Security numbers.[19]

Who do you think should be held responsible for the information issues caused at the Buffalo Police Department? What types of ethical issues and information security issues are being violated? What types of epolicies could a company implement to ensure that these situations do not occur? What forms of information security could a company implement to ensure that these situations do not occur? How does this case support the primary reason that ediscovery is so important to litigation?

7. Discussing the Three Areas of Information Security

Great Granola Inc. is a small business operating out of northern California. The company specializes in selling homemade granola, and its primary sales vehicle is through its website. The company is growing exponentially and expects its revenues to triple this year to $12 million. The company also expects to hire 60 additional employees to support its growth. Joan Martin, the CEO, is aware that if her competitors discover the recipe for her granola or who her primary customers are, it could easily ruin her business. Martin has hired you to draft a document discussing the different areas of information security, along with your recommendations for providing a secure ebusiness environment.

8. Spying on Email

Technology advances now allow individuals to monitor computers that they do not even have physical access to. New types of software can capture an individual's incoming and outgoing email and then immediately forward that email to another person. For example, if you are at work and your child is home from school and she receives an email from John at 3:00 p.m., at 3:01 p.m. you can receive a copy of that email sent to your email address. If she replies to John's email, within seconds you will receive a copy of what she sent to John. Describe two scenarios (other than those described here) for the use of this type of software: one in which the use would be ethical and one in which it would be unethical.

9. Stealing Software

The software industry fights against pirated software on a daily basis. The major centers of software piracy are in places such as Russia and China where salaries and disposable income are comparatively low. People in developing and economically depressed countries will fall behind the industrialized world technologically if they cannot afford access to new generations of software. Considering this, is it reasonable to blame someone for using pirated software when it could cost him or her two months' salary to purchase a legal copy? Create an argument for or against the following statement: Individuals who are economically less fortunate should be allowed access to software free of charge to ensure that they are provided with an equal technological advantage.

10. Censoring Google

The Google debate over operations in China is an excellent example of types of global ethical and security issues U.S. companies face as they expand operations around the world. Google's systems were targeted by highly sophisticated hacker attacks aimed at obtaining proprietary information, including personal data belonging to Chinese human rights activists who use Google's Gmail service.

Google, which originally agreed to filter search results based on Chinese government censorship rules, decided to unfilter search results after what it called an infiltration of its technology and the email accounts of Chinese human-rights activists. China called Google's plan to defy government censorship rules unfriendly and irresponsible and demanded Google to shut down all operations in China.

Why would China want to filter search results? Do you agree or disagree with China's censorship rules? Do you think Google was acting ethically when it agreed to implement China's censorship rules? Why do companies operating abroad need to be aware of the different ethical perspective found in other cultures?

11. Sources Are Not Friends

The Canadian Broadcasting Company (CBC) has issued a social networking policy directing journalists to avoid adding sources or contacts as friends on social networking sites such as Facebook or LinkedIn. Basic rules state that reporters must never allow one source to view what another source says, and reporters must ensure that private conversations with sources remain private. Adding sources as friends can compromise a journalist's work by allowing friends to view other friends in the network. It may also not be in a journalist's best interest to become a friend in a source's network. The CBC also discourages posting any political preferences in personal profiles, comments on bulletin boards, or people's Facebook wall.

This might seem like common sense, but for employees who do not spend countless hours on the Internet, using social networking sites can be confusing and overwhelming. Why is it critical for any new hire to research and review all policies, especially social media policies? Research three companies you would like to work for after graduation, and detail the types of social media policies that the company currently has or should implement.

PROJECT I   Grading Security

Making The Grade is a nonprofit organization that helps students learn how to achieve better grades in school. The organization has 40 offices in 25 states and more than 2,000 employees. The company wants to build a website to offer its services online. Making The Grade's online services will provide parents seven key pieces of advice for communicating with their children to help them achieve academic success. The website will offer information on how to maintain open lines of communication, set goals, organize academics, regularly track progress, identify trouble spots, get to know their child's teacher, and celebrate their children's successes.

You and your team work for the director of information security. Your team's assignment is to develop a document discussing the importance of creating information security policies and an information security plan. Be sure to include the following:

- The importance of educating employees on information security.
- A few samples of employee information security policies specifically for Making The Grade.
- Other major areas the information security plan should address.
- Signs the company should look for to determine whether the website is being hacked.
- The major types of attacks the company should expect to experience.

PROJECT II   Setting Boundaries

Even the most ethical people sometimes face difficult choices. Acting ethically means behaving in a principled fashion and treating other people with respect and dignity. It is simple to say, but not so simple to do because situations are complex or ambiguous. The important role of ethics in our lives has long been recognized. As far back as 44 BC, Cicero said that ethics are indispensable to anyone who wants to have a good career. Having said that, Cicero, along with some of the greatest minds over the centuries, struggled with what the rules of ethics should be.

Our ethics are rooted in our history, culture, and religion, and our sense of ethics may shift over time. The electronic age brings with it a new dimension in the ethics debate—the amount of personal information that we can collect and store and the speed with which we can access and process that information.

In a group, discuss how you would react to the following situations:

a. A senior marketing manager informs you that one of her employees is looking for another job and she wants you to give her access to look through her email.

b. A vice president of sales informs you that he has made a deal to provide customer information to a strategic partner, and he wants you to copy all of the customer information to a thumb drive.

c. You are asked to monitor your employee's email to discover whether he is sexually harassing another employee.

d. You are asked to install a video surveillance system in your office to find out whether employees are taking office supplies home with them.

e. You are looking on the shared network drive and discover that your boss's entire hard drive has been copied to the network for everyone to view. What do you do?

f. You have been accidentally copied on an email from the CEO, which details who will be the targets of the next round of layoffs. What do you do?

PROJECT III   Fired For Smoking on the Weekend

New technologies make it possible for employers to monitor many aspects of their employees' jobs, especially on telephones, computer terminals, through electronic and voice mail, and when employees are using the Internet. Such monitoring is virtually unregulated. Therefore, unless company policy specifically states otherwise (and even this is not ensured), your employer may listen, watch, and read most of your workplace communications.

Employers are taking monitoring activity a step further and monitoring employees, and employees' spouses, at home and on weekends. Yes, you read that correctly. Numerous employees have been fired for smoking cigarettes on the weekend in the privacy of their own home. As health care costs escalate, employers are increasingly seeking to regulate employee behavior—at home as well as in the workplace. Weyco, an insurance benefits administrator in Michigan, initiated a program requiring mandatory breath tests to detect for nicotine, and any employee testing positive would be sent home without pay for one month. If the employee failed the nicotine test a second time, that person would be fired—no matter how long the employee had been with the company.

Weyco's smoking prohibition does not stop with employees but extends to spouses, who must also pass monthly nicotine tests. A positive test means the employee must pay a monthly fee of $80 until the spouse takes a smoking cessation program and tests nicotine-free.

Do you agree that companies have the right to hold employees accountable for actions they perform on weekends in the privacy of their own homes? If you were the CEO of Weyco, what would be your argument supporting its smoking prohibition policies? Do you think Weyco's monitoring practices are ethical? Do you think Weyco's monitoring practices are legal?

PROJECT IV Doodling Passwords

As our online world continues to explode, people are finding the number of user names and passwords they need to remember growing exponentially. For this reason, many users will assign the same password for every logon, choose easy-to-remember names and dates, or simply write down their passwords on sticky notes and attach them to their computers. Great for the person who needs to remember 72 passwords but not so great for system security.

Of course, the obvious answer is to deploy biometrics across the board, but once you start reviewing the costs associated with biometrics, you quickly realize that this is not feasible. What is coming to the rescue to help with the password nightmare we have created? The doodle. Background Draw-a-Secret (BDAS) is a new program created by scientists at Newcastle University in England. BDAS begins by recording the number of strokes it takes a user to draw a doodle and when the user wants to gain access to the system he simply redraws the doodle on a touchpad and it is matched against the stored prototype. If the doodle matches, the user is granted access. Doodles are even described as being far more anonymous, therefore offering greater security than biometrics.

You are probably thinking that you'll end up right back in the same position having to remember all 72 of your password doodles. The good news is that with doodle passwords, you don't have to remember a thing. The doodle password can be displayed to users, and they simply have to redraw it because the system analyzes how the user draws or the user's unique hand strokes, not the actual doodle (similar to handwriting recognition technologies).

If you were going to deploy doodle passwords to your organization, what issues and concerns do you think might occur? Do you agree that doodles are easier to remember than text passwords? Do you agree that doodles offer the most effective way to manage authentication and authorization, even greater than biometrics? What types of unethical issues do you think you might encounter with doodle passwords?

PROJECT V Hacking the Ultimate Hack

Have you ever seen a LifeLock advertisement? If so, you know the Social Security number of LifeLock CEO Todd Davis because he posts it in all ads daring hackers to try to steal his identity. Davis has been a victim of identity theft at least 13 times. The first theft occurred when someone used his identity to secure a $500 loan from a check-cashing company. Davis discovered the crime only after the company called his wife's cell phone to recover the unpaid debt.[20]

If you were starting an identity theft prevention company, do you think it would be a good idea to post your Social Security number in advertisements? Why or why not? What do you think happened that caused Davis's identity to be stolen? What types of information security measures should LifeLock implement to ensure that Davis's Social Security number is not stolen again? If you were LifeLock's CEO, what type of marketing campaign would you launch next?

AYK APPLICATION PROJECTS

If you are looking for Excel projects to incorporate into your class, try any of the following after reading this chapter.

Project Number	Project Name	Project Type	Plug-In Focus Area	Project Focus	Project Skill Set	Page Number
1	Financial Destiny	Excel	T2	Personal Budget	Introductory Formulas	AYK.4
2	Cash Flow	Excel	T2	Cash Flow	Introductory Formulas	AYK.4
3	Technology Budget	Excel	T1, T2	Hardware and Software	Introductory Formulas	AYK.4
4	Tracking Donations	Excel	T2	Employee Relationships	Introductory Formulas	AYK.4
5	Convert Currency	Excel	T2	Global Commerce	Introductory Formulas	AYK.5
6	Cost Comparison	Excel	T2	Total Cost of Ownership	Introductory Formulas	AYK.5
7	Time Management	Excel or Project	T2 or T12	Project Management	Introductory Gantt Charts	AYK.6
8	Maximize Profit	Excel	T2, T4	Strategic Analysis	Intermediate Formulas or Solver	AYK.6
9	Security Analysis	Excel	T3	Filtering Data	Intermediate Conditional Formatting, Autofilter, Subtotal	AYK.7
10	Gathering Data	Excel	T3	Data Analysis	Intermediate Conditional Formatting, PivotTable	AYK.8
11	Scanner System	Excel	T2	Strategic Analysis	Intermediate	AYK.8
12	Competitive Pricing	Excel	T2	Profit Maximization	Intermediate	AYK.9
13	Adequate Acquisitions	Excel	T2	Break-Even Analysis	Intermediate	AYK.9
24	Electronic Resumes	HTML	T9, T10, T11	Electronic Personal Marketing	Introductory Structural Tags	AYK.16
25	Gathering Feedback	Dreamweaver	T9, T10, T11	Data Collection	Intermediate Organization of Information	AYK.16

module 2

Technical Foundations of MIS

MODULE 1:
Business Driven MIS

MODULE 2:
Technical Foundations
of MIS

MODULE 3:
Enterprise MIS

MODULE 2 CONCENTRATES on the technical foundations of MIS. The power of MIS comes from its ability to carry, house, and support information. And information is power to an organization. This module highlights this point and raises awareness of the significance of information to organizational success. Understanding how the MIS infrastructure supports business operations, how business professionals access and analyze information to make business decisions, and how wireless and mobile technologies can make information continuously and instantaneously available are important for strategically managing any company, large or small. Thus, these are the primary learning outcomes of Module 2.

The module begins by reviewing the role of MIS in supporting business growth, operations, and performance. We quickly turn to the need for MIS to be sustainable, given today's focus on being green, and then dive into databases, data warehousing, networking, and wireless technologies—all fundamental components of MIS infrastructures. A theme throughout the module is the need to leverage and yet safeguard the use of information as key to the survival of any company. Information must be protected from misuse and harm, especially with the continued use, development, and exploitation of the Internet and the web.

Module 2: Technical Foundations of MIS

CHAPTER 5: Infrastructures: Sustainable Technologies

CHAPTER 6: Data: Business Intelligence

CHAPTER 7: Networks: Mobile Business

Infrastructures: Sustainable Technologies

5

CHAPTER

SECTION 5.1
MIS Infrastructures

- The Business Benefits of a Solid MIS Infrastructure
- Supporting Operations: Information MIS Infrastructure
- Supporting Change: Agile MIS Infrastructure

SECTION 5.2
Building Sustainable MIS Infrastructures

- MIS and the Environment
- Supporting the Environment: Sustainable MIS Infrastructure
- Utility Computing

CHAPTER OUTLINE

What's in IT for me?

Why do you, as a business student, need to understand the underlying technology of any company? Most people think "that technical stuff" is something they will never personally encounter and for that reason they do not need to know anything about MIS infrastructures. Well, those people will be challenged in the business world. When your database fails and you lose all of your sales history, you will personally feel the impact when you don't receive your bonus. When your computer crashes and you lose all of your confidential information, not to mention your emails, calendars, and messages, then you will understand why everyone needs to learn about MIS infrastructures. You never want to leave the critical task of backing up your data to your MIS department. You want to ensure personally that your information is not only backed up but also safeguarded and recoverable. For these reasons, business professionals in the 21st century need to acquire a base-level appreciation of what MIS can and cannot do for their company. Understanding how MIS supports growth, operations, profitability, and, most recently, sustainability, is crucial whether one is new to the workforce or a seasoned *Fortune* 500 employee. One of the primary goals of this chapter is to create a more level playing field between you as a business professional and the MIS specialists with whom you will work. After reading it, you should have many of the skills you need to assist in analyzing current and even some future MIS infrastructures; in recommending needed changes in processes; and in evaluating alternatives that support a company's growth, operations, and profits.

©ERproductions Ltd/Blend Images LLC RF   ©UpperCut Images/Glow Images RF   ©John Lund/Getty Images RF

Box Up Your Data

What happens when you need a file for a class that you have on your desktop back at home? What happens when you want to share your wedding video with your friends and family around the world? What happens when you want to safeguard the 4,000 selfies you have taken over the past year? Your best bet is to store your data in a Box! Box offers data storage services that:

- Help you securely store, share, and manage your files.
- Store unlimited data at the start.
- Securely send large files online.
- Take advantage of comprehensive security for mobile devices.
- Easily collaborate online with anyone, anywhere.
- Control who can access content.
- Edit documents and files online.

Box is a cloud data-sharing service that can increase your productivity by making it easy to create and collaborate with co-workers by using computers, iPhones, iPads, Androids, or other devices. With a Box site, you can access up to 50GB of files from anywhere. Through a web link, you can invite others to share your files or collaborate on your documents, and you can synchronize files from Box to your desktop and vice versa.

Another College Start-Up Box

Rachel King from InfoWorld interviewed Box founder Aaron Levie on how he and his childhood friends started the company. Box as a platform and company was born in 2005, but even that was well after the establishment of the friendship between Levie and his cofounder and Box's chief financial officer, Dylan Smith. Smith and Levie met as classmates at Islander Middle School on Mercer Island, Washington, a suburb southeast of Seattle, and then went to Mercer Island High School together. "Even back then he started getting me interested in entrepreneurship," Smith recalled. "He was much more interested in technology [than business] back then." Two other key members of the Box team were also childhood friends.

Jeff Queisser, currently vice president of Box's technical operations, met Levie when they were in the fourth and fifth grades, respectively, as neighbors. By high school, Queisser recalled that the two were starting "kinda crazy businesses." "[Levie] was a magician, and I was very much a hard core nerd and doing programming," Queisser laughed.

Sam Ghods, now vice president of technology at Box, joined the group in the tenth grade when his family relocated from Illinois to Mercer Island. The same year in school, Ghods recalled that he and Queisser became friends on the bus to school, eventually hanging out more frequently with Smith and Levie as well and getting involved in various business schemes.

In high school, Levie's parents' hot tub served as the discussion forum. "We would get a call at about 12:30, and it would be Aaron, 'What do you think about this? I think this could be absolutely insane. Like, come over right now. I got towels, just bring shorts, come over,'" Queisser remembers. "This would be at 12:30 and by like 12:40, we were in his hot tub just iterating ideas."

And although he built a lot of websites in high school, Levie doesn't brag about having a strong technical background, admitting, "They weren't very good websites." One example was a search engine dubbed Zizap, which Levie facetiously peddled as "the world's fastest search engine if you have never been to Google." Another project was Fastest, a website that let people buy and sell their homes online. Levie notes sarcastically that it "made sense as a high school senior to launch that company."

These early rumblings of entrepreneurship would soon pay dividends. Levie enrolled at the University of Southern California in 2003 to study business, which is where the idea that was to become Box began to develop. "It's not like a lightning bolt that hits you in the head, and all of a sudden you just get so obsessed with storing files online. It was a series of factors," he explained.

The first piece of the puzzle came from the basic difficulty of getting work done. He and his fellow students were working from lots of computers, collaborating on projects, and accessing files from different places, including libraries, classrooms, and dorm rooms.

"It felt unbelievably kind of painful and taxing to share data across those different systems and with other people. It seemed like there should be a simpler solution," Levie remarked.

A business school project in which students were asked to evaluate a particular industry added another piece to the puzzle. Levie chose the nascent online storage industry and wrote a paper on flaws with existing businesses in the market and what one could do to build a better business effectively. It didn't take long before he realized the massive potential. "It was very obvious that there should be a technology category that solved this problem," he said.

"When we were talking about just the things that we were doing and the stuff we were working on, Box came up," Levie described. "It's very, very early in the process, and Dylan Smith decided to join on board as the other half of the business and product side. He handled the finance and some of the early marketing stuff. That was how we started."[1]

Market Competition

The storage market is increasing as the price and density of storage drops about every 18 months, making it cheaper to offer free storage from big companies that can absorb the costs, such as Apple and Google. There are a number of companies competing in the cloud storage arena, as compared in Figure 5.1.

FIGURE 5.1

Test Center Scorecard

Source: www.inforworld.com

	Ease of Use (20%)	Security and Management (20%)	Third-Party Integrations (20%)	Auditing and Reporting (20%)	Setup (10%)	Value (10%)	Overall Score
Box	9	9	8	9	8	9	8.7 **Very Good**
Citrix ShareFile	8	8	9	8	7	7	8 **Very Good**
Dropbox for Business	9	7	8	5	9	7	7.4 **Good**
Egnyte	9	8	7	8	8	9	8.1 **Very Good**
EMC Syncplicity	9	8	9	8	8	8	8.4 **Very Good**
OwnCloud	7	7	7	7	6	8	7 **Good**

5.1 Explain MIS infrastructure and its three primary types.

5.2 Identify the three primary areas associated with an information MIS infrastructure.

5.3 Describe the characteristics of an agile MIS infrastructure.

THE BUSINESS BENEFITS OF A SOLID MIS INFRASTRUCTURE

LO 5.1: Explain MIS infrastructure and its three primary types.

Management information systems have played a significant role in business strategies, affected business decisions and processes, and even changed the way companies operate. What is the foundation supporting all of these systems that enable business growth, operations, and profits? What supports the volume and complexity of today's user and application requirements? What protects systems from failures and crashes? It is the *MIS infrastructure,* which includes the plans for how a firm will build, deploy, use, and share its data, processes, and MIS assets. A solid MIS infrastructure can reduce costs, improve productivity, optimize business operations, generate growth, and increase profitability.

Briefly defined, *hardware* consists of the physical devices associated with a computer system, and *software* is the set of instructions the hardware executes to carry out specific tasks. In today's business environment, most hardware and software is run via a network. A *network* is a communications system created by linking two or more devices and establishing a standard methodology in which they can communicate. As more companies need to share more information, the network takes on greater importance in the infrastructure. Most companies use a specific form of network infrastructure called a client and server network. A *client* is a computer designed to request information from a server. A *server* is a computer dedicated to providing information in response to requests. A good way to understand this is when someone uses a web browser (this would be the client) to access a website (this would be a server that would respond with the web page being requested by the client). Anyone not familiar with the basics of hardware, software, or networks should review Appendix A, "Hardware and Software Basics," and Appendix B, "Networks and Telecommunications," for more information.

In the physical world, a detailed blueprint would show how public utilities, such as water, electricity, and gas, support the foundation of a building. MIS infrastructure is similar because it shows in detail how the hardware, software, and network connectivity support the firm's processes. Every company, regardless of size, relies on some form of MIS infrastructure, whether it is a few networked personal computers sharing an Excel file or a large multinational company with thousands of employees interconnected around the world.

An MIS infrastructure is dynamic; it continually changes as the business needs change. Each time a new form of Internet-enabled device, such as an iPhone or BlackBerry, is created and made available to the public, a firm's MIS infrastructure must be revised to support the device. This moves beyond just innovations in hardware to include new types of software and network connectivity. An *enterprise architect* is a person grounded in technology, fluent in business, and able to provide the important bridge between MIS and the business. Firms employ enterprise architects to help manage change and dynamically update MIS infrastructure. Figure 5.2 displays the three primary areas on which enterprise architects focus when maintaining a firm's MIS infrastructure.

- **Supporting operations:** *Information MIS infrastructure* identifies where and how important information, such as customer records, is maintained and secured.

- **Supporting change:** *Agile MIS infrastructure* includes the hardware, software, and telecommunications equipment that, when combined, provides the underlying foundation to support the organization's goals.

FIGURE 5.2

MIS infrastructures

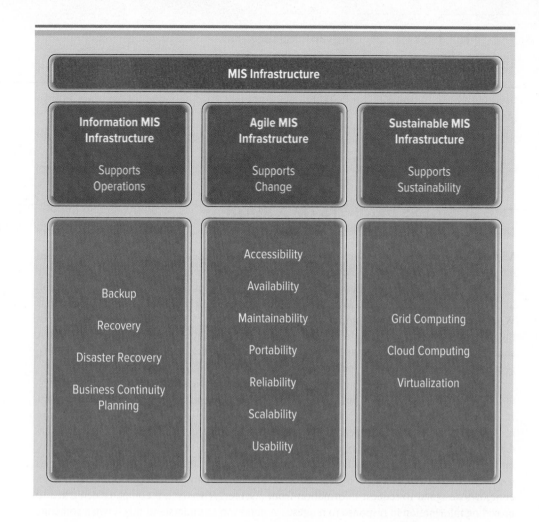

MIS Infrastructure

Information MIS Infrastructure — Supports Operations

Agile MIS Infrastructure — Supports Change

Sustainable MIS Infrastructure — Supports Sustainability

Backup

Recovery

Disaster Recovery

Business Continuity Planning

Accessibility

Availability

Maintainability

Portability

Reliability

Scalability

Usability

Grid Computing

Cloud Computing

Virtualization

■ **Supporting the environment:** *Sustainable MIS infrastructure* identifies ways that a company can grow in terms of computing resources while simultaneously becoming less dependent on hardware and energy consumption.

LO 5.2: Identify the three primary areas associated with an information MIS infrastructure.

SUPPORTING OPERATIONS: INFORMATION MIS INFRASTRUCTURE

Imagine taking a quick trip to the printer on the other side of the room, and when you turn around, you find that your laptop has been stolen. How painful would you find this experience? What types of information would you lose? How much time would it take you to recover all of that information? A few things you might lose include music, movies, emails, assignments, saved passwords, not to mention that all-important 40-page paper that took you more than a month to complete. If this sounds painful, then you want to pay particular attention to this section and learn how to eliminate this pain.

An information MIS infrastructure identifies where and how important information is maintained and secured. An information infrastructure supports day-to-day business operations and plans for emergencies such as power outages, floods, earthquakes, malicious attacks via the Internet, theft, and security breaches to name just a few. Managers must take every precaution to make sure their systems are operational and protected around the clock every day of the year. Losing a laptop or experiencing bad weather in one part of the country simply cannot take down systems required to operate core business processes. In the past, someone stealing company information would have to carry out boxes upon boxes of paper. Today, as data storage technologies grow in capabilities while shrinking in size, a person can simply walk out the front door of the building with the company's data files stored on a thumb drive or external hard drive. Today's managers must act responsibly to protect one of their most valued

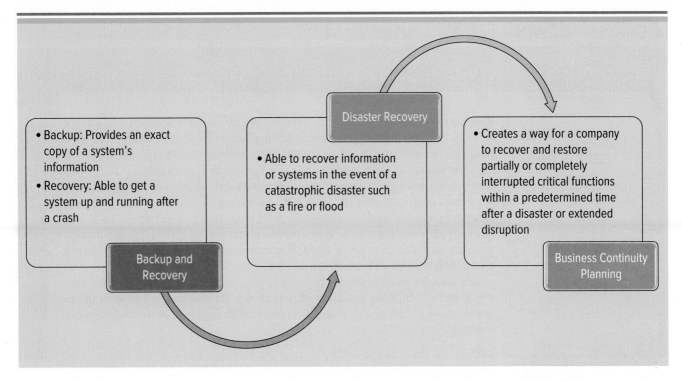

• Backup: Provides an exact copy of a system's information
• Recovery: Able to get a system up and running after a crash

Backup and Recovery

• Able to recover information or systems in the event of a catastrophic disaster such as a fire or flood

Disaster Recovery

• Creates a way for a company to recover and restore partially or completely interrupted critical functions within a predetermined time after a disaster or extended disruption

Business Continuity Planning

FIGURE 5.3

Areas of Support Provided by Information Infrastructure

assets, information. To support continuous business operations, an information infrastructure provides three primary elements:

- Backup and recovery plan
- Disaster recovery plan
- Business continuity plan (see Figure 5.3)

Backup and Recovery Plan

Each year businesses lose time and money because of system crashes and failures. One way to minimize the damage of a system crash is to have a backup and recovery strategy in place. A *backup* is an exact copy of a system's information. *Recovery* is the ability to get a system up and running in the event of a system crash or failure that includes restoring the information backup. Many types of backup and recovery media are available, including maintaining an identical replica or redundant copy of the storage server, external hard drives, thumb drives, and even DVDs. The primary differences between them are speed and cost.

Fault tolerance is the ability for a system to respond to unexpected failures or system crashes as the backup system immediately and automatically takes over with no loss of service. For example, fault tolerance enables a business to support continuous business operations if there is a power failure or flood. Fault tolerance is an expensive form of backup, and only mission-critical applications and operations use it. *Failover,* a specific type of fault tolerance, occurs when a redundant storage server offers an exact replica of the real-time data, and if the primary server crashes, the users are automatically directed to the secondary server or backup server. This is a high-speed and high-cost method of backup and recovery. *Failback* occurs when the primary machine recovers and resumes operations, taking over from the secondary server.

Using DVDs or thumb drives to store your data offers a low-speed and low-cost backup method. It is a good business practice to back up data at least once a week using a low-cost method. This will alleviate the pain of having your laptop stolen or your system crash because you will still have access to your data, and it will only be a few days old.

Deciding how often to back up information and what media to use is a critical decision. Companies should choose a backup and recovery strategy in line with their goals and operational needs. If the company deals with large volumes of critical information, it will require daily, perhaps hourly, backups to storage servers. If it relies on small amounts of noncritical

BUSINESS DRIVEN START-UP

Creating Your BCP Plan

Business disruption costs money. In the event of a disaster or emergency, you will not only lose revenue, you will also incur additional expenses. If you are expecting your insurance to cover your losses, be careful—there are many losses your insurance will not cover such as lost sales, lost business intelligence, and lost customers. To mitigate the risks of a catastrophe, you will want to create a detailed business continuity plan. A business continuity plan (BCP) is not only a good idea but also one of the least expensive plans a company can develop. A BCP will detail how employees will contact each other and continue to keep operations functioning in the event of a disaster or emergency such as a fire or flood. Regrettably, many companies never take the time to develop such a plan until it is too late.

Research the web for sample BCP plans for a small business or a start-up. In a group, create a BCP for a start-up of your choice. Be sure to think of such things as data storage, data access, transaction processing, employee safety, and customer communications.

information, then it might require only weekly backups to external hard drives or thumb drives. A company that backs up on a weekly basis is taking the risk that, if a system crash occurs, it could lose a week's worth of work. If this risk is acceptable, a weekly backup strategy will work. If it is unacceptable, the company needs more frequent backup.

Disaster Recovery Plan

Disasters such as power outages, fires, floods, and hurricanes, and even malicious activities such as hackers and viruses strike companies every day. Disasters can have the following effects on companies and their business operations.

- **Disrupting communications:** Most companies depend on voice and data communications for daily operational needs. Widespread communications outages, from either direct damage to the infrastructure or sudden spikes in usage related to an outside disaster, can be as devastating to some firms as shutting down the whole business.

- **Damaging physical infrastructures:** Fire and flood can directly damage buildings, equipment, and systems, making structures unsafe and systems unusable. Law enforcement officers and firefighters may prohibit business professionals from entering a building, thereby restricting access to retrieve documents or equipment.

- **Halting transportation:** Disasters such as floods and hurricanes can have a deep effect on transportation. Disruption to major highways, roads, bridges, railroads, and airports can prevent business professionals from reporting to work or going home, slow the delivery of supplies, and stop the shipment of products.

- **Blocking utilities:** Public utilities, such as the supply of electric power, water, and natural gas, can be interrupted for hours or days even in incidents that cause no direct damage to the physical infrastructure. Buildings are often uninhabitable and systems unable to function without public utilities.

These effects can devastate companies by causing them to cease operations for hours, days, or longer and risk losing customers whom they cannot then supply. Therefore, to combat these disasters, a company can create a *disaster recovery plan,* which is a detailed process for recovering information or a system in the event of a catastrophic disaster. This plan includes such factors as which files and systems need to have backups and their corresponding frequency and methods along with the strategic location of the storage in a separate physical site that is geographically

Hot Site	Cold Site	Warm Site
A separate and fully equipped facility where the company can move immediately after a disaster and resume business.	A separate facility that does not have any computer equipment but is a place where employees can move after a disaster.	A separate facility with computer equipment that requires installation and configuration.

FIGURE 5.4

Sites to Support Disaster Recovery

dispersed. A company might strategically maintain operations in New York and San Francisco, ensuring that a natural disaster would not have an impact on both locations. A disaster recovery plan also foresees the possibility that not only the computer equipment but also the building where employees work may be destroyed. A *hot site* is a separate and fully equipped facility where the company can move immediately after a disaster and resume business. A *cold site* is a separate facility that does not have any computer equipment but is a place where employees can move after a disaster. A *warm site* is a separate facility with computer equipment that requires installation and configuration. Figure 5.4 outlines these resources that support disaster recovery.

A disaster recovery plan usually has a disaster recovery cost curve to support it. A *disaster recovery cost curve* charts (1) the cost to the company of the unavailability of information and technology and (2) the cost to the company of recovering from a disaster over time. Figure 5.5 displays a disaster recovery cost curve and shows that the best recovery plan in terms of cost and time is where the two lines intersect. Creating such a curve is no small task. Managers must consider the cost of losing information and technology within each department or functional area and across the whole company. During the first few hours of a disaster, those costs may be low, but they rise over time. With those costs in hand, a company must then determine the costs of recovery. Figure 5.6 displays TechTarget's disaster recovery strategies for business.

On April 18, 1906, San Francisco was rocked by an earthquake that destroyed large sections of the city and claimed the lives of more than 3,000 inhabitants. More than a century later, a rebuilt and more durable San Francisco serves as a central location for major MIS corporations as well as a major world financial center. Managers of these corporations are well aware of the potential disasters that exist along the San Andreas Fault and actively update their business continuity plans anticipating such issues as earthquakes and floods. The Union Bank of California is located in the heart of downtown San Francisco and maintains a highly detailed and well-developed business continuity plan. The company employs hundreds of business professionals scattered around the world who coordinate plans for addressing the potential loss of a facility,

FIGURE 5.5

Disaster Recovery Cost Curve

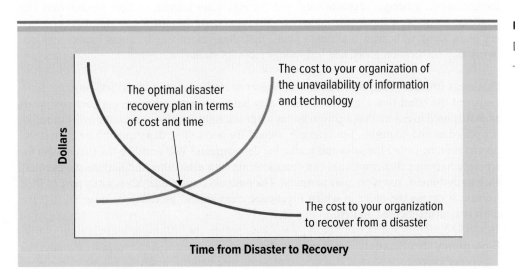

The optimal disaster recovery plan in terms of cost and time

The cost to your organization of the unavailability of information and technology

The cost to your organization to recover from a disaster

Dollars

Time from Disaster to Recovery

FIGURE 5.6

TechTarget's Disaster Recovery
Strategies

DISASTER RECOVERY STRATEGIES	
1. Activate backup and recovery facilities in secondary company data center; transfer production to that site.	Assumes the secondary data center has sufficient resources, e.g., storage capacity, server hardware to accommodate additional processing requirements
2. Activate recovery resources in a cloud-based service; failover critical systems to that site and resume operations.	Ensure that your contract for this service has the ability to flex as your needs dictate; ensure that security of your data can be maintained.
3. Activate backup systems and data at a hot site; transfer operations to that site.	Be sure you know what resources you have available at the hot site, what the declaration rules and fees are, and what your options are if multiple declarations are occurring at the same time.
4. Replace damaged equipment with spare components.	As much as possible, have available spare systems, circuit boards, and power supplies; backup disks with system software; and hard and soft copies of critical documentation
5. Recover virtual machines at an alternate site; assumes VMs have been updated to be current with production VMs.	Create VM clones at an alternate site and keep them updated, and if needed, they can quickly become production VMs.
6. Activate alternate network routes and re-route data and voice traffic away from the failed network service.	Ensure that network infrastructures have diverse routing of local access channels as well as diverse routing of high-capacity circuits.[2]

business professionals, or critical systems so that the company can continue to operate if a disaster happens. Its disaster recovery plan includes hot sites where staff can walk in and start working exactly as if they were in their normal location. It would be a matter of minutes, not hours, for the Union Bank of California to be up and running again in the event of a disaster.[3]

Business Continuity Plan

An *emergency* is a sudden, unexpected event requiring immediate action due to potential threat to health and safety, the environment, or property. *Emergency preparedness* ensures that a company is ready to respond to an emergency in an organized, timely, and effective manner. Natural disasters and terrorist attacks are on the minds of business professionals who take safeguarding their information assets seriously. Disaster recovery plans typically focus on systems and data, ignoring cross-functional and intraorganizational business processes that can be destroyed during an emergency. For this reason, many companies are turning to a more comprehensive and all-encompassing emergency preparedness plan known as *business continuity planning (BCP),* which details how a company recovers and restores critical business operations and systems after a disaster or extended disruption. BCP includes such factors as identifying critical systems, business processes, departments, and the maximum amount of time the business can continue to operate without functioning systems (see Figure 5.7). BCP contains disaster recovery plans along with many additional plans, including prioritizing business impact analysis, emergency notification plans, and technology recovery strategies.

Business Impact Analysis A *business impact analysis* identifies all critical business functions and the effect that a specific disaster may have on them. A business impact analysis is primarily used to ensure that a company has made the right decisions about the order of recovery priorities and strategies. For example, should the accounting department have its systems up and running before the sales and marketing departments? Will email be the first system for recovery to ensure that employees can communicate with each other and outside stakeholders such as customers, suppliers, and partners? The business impact analysis is a key part of BCP because it details the order in which functional areas should be restored, ensuring that the most critical are focused on first.

Emergency Notification Services A business continuity plan typically includes an *emergency notification service,* that is, an infrastructure built for notifying people in the event

FIGURE 5.7

Tech Target's Business
Continuity Strategies

BUSINESS CONTINUITY STRATEGIES	
1. Evacuate existing building and relocate to a prearranged alternate work area.	Assumes the alternate site is ready for occupancy, or can be made ready quickly, based on recovery time objectives; ensure that transportation is available
2. Work from home.	Ensure that staff have broadband and Internet access at home; ensure that there are sufficient network access points to accommodate the increase in usage.
3. Move selected staff to a hot site.	Assumes a hot site program is in place and that space is available at the site for staff
4. Move alternate staff into leadership roles in the absence of key leaders; ensure that they have been cross-trained.	Succession planning is a key strategy in business continuity; it ensures that loss of a senior manager or someone with special expertise can be replaced with minimal disruption to the business.
5. Move staff into local or nearby hotels and set up temporary work space.	Make sure this kind of arrangement is set up with hotels in advance, especially in case of an incident that disrupts many other businesses in the same area.
6. Relocate staff to another company office.	Organizations with multiple offices that have access to the company network as well as work space can be leveraged to temporarily house employees.[4]

of an emergency. Radio stations' occasional tests of the national Emergency Alert System are an example of a very large-scale emergency notification system. A firm will implement an emergency notification service to warn employees of unexpected events and provide them with instructions about how to handle the situation. Emergency notification services can be deployed through the firm's own infrastructure, supplied by an outside service provider on company premises, or hosted remotely by an outside service provider. All three methods provide notification using a variety of methods such as email, voice notification to a cell phone, and text messaging. The notifications can be sent to all the devices selected, providing multiple means in which to get critical information to those who need it.

Technology Recovery Strategies Companies create massive amounts of data vital to their survival and continued operations. A *technology failure* occurs when the ability of a company to operate is impaired because of a hardware, software, or data outage. Technology failures can destroy large amounts of vital data, often causing *incidents,* unplanned interruptions of a service. An *incident record* contains all of the details of an incident. *Incident management* is the process responsible for managing how incidents are identified and corrected. *Technology recovery strategies* focus specifically on prioritizing the order for restoring hardware, software, and data across the organization that best meets business recovery requirements. A technology recovery strategy details the order of importance for recovering hardware, software, data centers, and networking (or connectivity). If one of these four vital components is not functioning, the entire system will be unavailable, shutting down cross-functional business processes such as order management and payroll. Figure 5.8 displays the key areas a company should focus on when developing technology recovery strategies.

SUPPORTING CHANGE: AGILE MIS INFRASTRUCTURE

LO 5.3: Describe the characteristics of an agile MIS infrastructure.

Agile MIS infrastructure includes the hardware, software, and telecommunications equipment that, when combined, provides the underlying foundation to support the organization's goals. If a company grows by 50 percent in a single year, its infrastructure and systems must be able to handle a 50 percent growth rate. If they cannot, they can severely hinder the company's ability not only to grow but also to function.

The future of a company depends on its ability to meet its partners, suppliers, and customers any time of the day in any geographic location. Imagine owning an ebusiness and everyone on the Internet is tweeting and collaborating about how great your business idea is and how successful your company is going to be. Suddenly, you have 5 million global customers interested

BUSINESS DRIVEN MIS

Disaster Recovery

Backup and recovery are essential for any computer system. How painful would it be if someone stole your laptop right now? How much critical information would you lose? How many hours would it take you to re-create your data? Perhaps that will motivate you to implement a backup procedure. How many of you have a disaster recovery plan? Disaster recovery is needed when your best friend dumps a grande latte on your computer or you accidently wash your thumb drive.

Disaster recovery plans are crucial for any business, and you should ensure that your company has everything it needs to continue operations if there is ever a disaster, such as 9/11. You need to decide which disasters are worth worrying about and which ones probably will never occur. For example, if you live in Colorado, chances are good you don't have to worry about hurricanes, but avalanches are another story.

How often does a company need to back up its data? Where should the backup be stored? What types of disasters should companies in your state prepare for in case of an emergency? Why is it important to test the backup? What could happen to a company if it failed to create a disaster recovery plan?

FIGURE 5.8

Key Areas of Technology Recovery Strategies

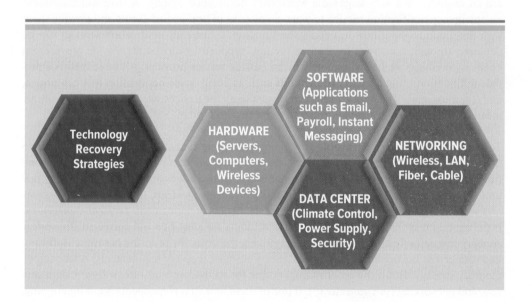

in your website. Unfortunately, you did not anticipate this many customers so quickly, and the system crashes. Users typing in your URL find a blank message stating the website is unavailable and to try back soon. Or even worse, they can get to your website, but it takes three minutes to reload each time they click a button. The buzz soon dies about your business idea as some innovative web-savvy fast follower quickly copies your idea and creates a website that can handle the massive number of customers. The characteristics of agile MIS infrastructures can help ensure that your systems can meet and perform under any unexpected or unplanned changes. Figure 5.9 lists the seven abilities of an agile infrastructure.

Accessibility

Accessibility refers to the varying levels that define what a user can access, view, or perform when operating a system. Imagine the people at your college accessing the main student information

FIGURE 5.9

Agile MIS Infrastructure Characteristics

Accessibility
• Varying levels allow system users to access, view, or perform operational functions.

Availability
• The system is operational during different time frames.

Maintainability
• The system quickly transforms to support environmental changes.

Portability
• The system is available to operate on different devices or software platforms.

Reliability
• The system functions correctly and provides accurate information.

Scalability
• The system can scale up or adapt to the increased demands of growth.

Usability
• The system is easy to learn and efficient and satisfying to use.

system. Each person who accesses the system will have different needs and requirements; for example, a payroll employee will need to access vacation information and salary information, or a student will need to access course information and billing information. Each system user is provided with an access level that details which parts of the system the user can and cannot access and what the user can do when in the system. For example, you would not want your students to be able to view payroll information or a professor's personal information; also, some users can only view information and are not allowed to create or delete information. Top-level MIS employees require *administrator access,* or unrestricted access to the entire system. Administrator access can perform functions such as resetting passwords, deleting accounts, and shutting down entire systems.

Tim Berners-Lee, W3C director and inventor of the World Wide Web, stated, "The power of the web is in its universality. Access by everyone regardless of disability is an essential aspect." *Web accessibility* means that people with disabilities can use the web. The *web accessibility initiative (WAI)* brings together people from industry, disability organizations, government, and research labs from around the world to develop guidelines and resources to help make the web accessible to people with disabilities, including auditory, cognitive, neurological, physical, speech, and visual disabilities. The goal of WAI is to allow people to access the full potential of the web, enabling people with disabilities to participate equally. For example, Apple includes screen magnification and VoiceOver on its iPhone, iPad, and iPod, which allows the blind and visually impaired to use the devices.

Availability

In a 24/7/365 ebusiness environment, business professionals need to use their systems whenever they want from wherever they want. *Availability* refers to the time frames when the system is operational. A system is called *unavailable* when it is not operating and cannot be used. *High availability* occurs when a system is continuously operational at all times. Availability is typically measured relative to "100 percent operational" or "never failing." A widely held but difficult-to-achieve standard of availability for a system is known as "five 9s" (99.999 percent) availability. Some companies have systems available around the clock to support ebusiness operations, global customers, and online suppliers.

Sometimes systems must be taken down for maintenance, upgrades, and fixes, which are completed during downtime. One challenge with availability is determining when to schedule system downtime if the system is expected to operate continuously. Performing maintenance during the evening might seem like a great idea, but evening in one city is morning somewhere else in the world, and business professionals scattered around the globe may not be able to perform specific job functions if the systems they need are unavailable. This is where companies deploy failover systems so they can take the primary system down for maintenance and activate the secondary system to ensure continuous operations.

Maintainability

Companies must watch today's needs, as well as tomorrow's, when designing and building systems that support agile infrastructures. Systems must be flexible enough to meet all types of company changes, environmental changes, and business changes. *Maintainability (or flexibility)* refers to how quickly a system can transform to support environmental changes. Maintainability helps to measure how quickly and effectively a system can be changed or repaired after a failure. For example, when starting a small business, you might not consider that you will have global customers, a common mistake. When building your systems, you might not design them to handle multiple currencies and different languages, which might make sense if the company is not currently performing international business. Unfortunately, when the first international order arrives, which happens easily with ebusiness, the system will be unable to handle the request because it does not have the flexibility to be easily reconfigured for a new language or currency. When the company does start growing and operating overseas, the system will need to be redeveloped, which is not an easy or cheap task, to handle multiple currencies and different languages.

Building and deploying flexible systems allow easy updates, changes, and reconfigurations for unexpected business or environmental changes. Just think what might have happened if Facebook had to overhaul its entire system to handle multiple languages. Another social networking business could easily have stepped in and become the provider of choice. That certainly would not be efficient or effective for business operations.

Portability

Portability refers to the ability of an application to operate on different devices or software platforms, such as different operating systems. Apple's iTunes is readily available to users of Mac computers and PC computers, smart phones, iPods, iPhones, iPads, and so on. It is also a portable application. Because Apple insists on compatibility across its products, both software and hardware, Apple can easily add to its product, device, and service offerings without sacrificing portability. Many software developers are creating programs that are portable to all three devices—the iPhone, iPod, and iPad—which increases their target market and, they hope, their revenue.

Reliability

Reliability (or accuracy) ensures that a system is functioning correctly and providing accurate information. Inaccuracy can occur for many reasons, from the incorrect entry of information to the corruption of information during transmissions. Many argue that the information contained in Wikipedia is unreliable. Because the Wikipedia entries can be edited by any user, there are examples of rogue users inaccurately updating information. Many users skip over Google search findings that correlate to Wikipedia for this reason. Housing unreliable information on a website can put a company at risk of losing customers, placing inaccurate supplier orders, or even making unreliable business decisions. A *vulnerability* is a system weakness, such as a password that is never changed or a system left on while an employee goes to lunch, that can be exploited by a threat. Reliable systems ensure that vulnerabilities are kept at a minimum to reduce risk.

BUSINESS DRIVEN MIS

Ranking the Ab-"ilities"

Do you know how Google makes so much money? Unlike traditional businesses, Google does not make money from the users of its service. Google makes money by charging the companies that want to appear in the sponsored section of a search result. After performing a Google search, you will notice three sections on the resulting page. Along the top and side are the sponsored search results, and the middle lists the organic search results. Google's innovative marketing program, called AdWords, allows companies to bid on common search terms, and the highest bidder is posted first in the sponsored search results. Every time a user clicks a sponsored link, the company that owns the link has to pay Google. This is also called pay-per-click and can cost anywhere from a few cents to a few dollars for each click. A general search term such as "tropical vacation" costs less than a more specific search term such as "Hawaiian vacation." Whichever company bids the most for the search term appears at the top of the sponsored section. Clicking the links in the organic search results does not incur any charges for the company that owns the link.

Rank the agile infrastructure ab-"ilities" for Google from most important to least important in terms of supporting Google's MIS infrastructure and business operations. Be sure to provide the justification behind your ranking.

Scalability

Estimating company growth is a challenging task, in part because growth can occur in a number of forms—the firm can acquire new customers, new product lines, or new markets. *Scalability* describes how well a system can scale up, or adapt to the increased demands of growth. If a company grows faster than anticipated, it might experience a variety of problems, from running out of storage space to taking more time to complete transactions. Anticipating expected and unexpected growth is key to building scalable systems that can support that development.

Performance measures how quickly a system performs a process or transaction. Performance is a key component of scalability as systems that can't scale suffer from performance issues. Just imagine your college's content management system suddenly taking five minutes to return a page after a button is pushed. Now imagine if this occurs during your midterm exam and you miss the two-hour deadline because the system is so slow. Performance issues experienced by firms can have disastrous business impacts causing loss of customers, loss of suppliers, and even loss of help-desk employees. Most users will wait only a few seconds for a website to return a request before growing frustrated and either calling the support desk or giving up and moving on to another website.

Capacity represents the maximum throughput a system can deliver; for example, the capacity of a hard drive represents its size or volume. *Capacity planning* determines future environmental infrastructure requirements to ensure high-quality system performance. If a company purchases connectivity software that is outdated or too slow to meet demand, its employees will waste a great deal of time waiting for systems to respond to user requests. It is cheaper for a company to design and implement agile infrastructure that envisions growth requirements than to update all the equipment after the system is already operational. If a company with 100 workers merges with another company and suddenly 400 people are using the system, performance time could suffer. Planning for increases in capacity can ensure that systems perform as expected. Waiting for a system to respond to requests is not productive.

Web 2.0 is a big driver for capacity planning to ensure that agile infrastructures can meet the business's operational needs. Delivering videos over the Internet requires enough bandwidth to satisfy millions of users during peak periods such as Friday and Saturday evenings. Video transmissions over the Internet cannot tolerate packet loss (blocks of data loss), and allowing one additional user to access the system could degrade the video quality for every user.

BUSINESS DRIVEN DEBATE

Laptop? Notebook? Netbook? Tablet?

Thanks to Moore's law, computing devices are getting smaller, cheaper, and faster every year, allowing innovative companies to create new devices that are smaller and more powerful than current devices. Just look at desktop, laptop, notebook, and tablet computers. These are all different devices allowing users to connect and compute around the globe. Moore's law has been accurate about computing power roughly doubling every 18 months. Do you agree or disagree that Moore's law will continue to apply for the next 20 years? Why or why not?

Usability

Usability is the degree to which a system is easy to learn and efficient and satisfying to use. Providing hints, tips, shortcuts, and instructions for any system, regardless of its ease of use, is recommended. Apple understood the importance of usability when it designed the first iPod. One of the iPod's initial attractions was the usability of the click wheel. One simple and efficient button operates the iPod, making it usable for all ages. And to ensure ease of use, Apple also made the corresponding iTunes software intuitive and easy to use. *Serviceability* is how quickly a third party can change a system to ensure it meets user needs and the terms of any contracts, including agreed levels of reliability, maintainability, or availability. When using a system from a third party, it is important to ensure the right level of serviceability for all users, including remote employees.

---

section 5.2 | Building Sustainable MIS Infrastructures

LEARNING OUTCOMES

5.4 Identify the environmental impacts associated with MIS.

5.5 Explain the three components of a sustainable MIS infrastructure along with their business benefits.

LO 5.4: Identify the environmental impacts associated with MIS.

MIS AND THE ENVIRONMENT

The general trend in MIS is toward smaller, faster, and cheaper devices. Gordon Moore, cofounder of Intel, the world's largest producer of computer chips or microprocessors, observed in 1965 that continued advances in technological innovation made it possible to reduce the size of a computer chip (the brains of a computer, or even a cell phone now) while doubling its capacity every two years. His prediction that this trend would continue has come to be known as *Moore's Law,* which refers to the computer chip performance per dollar doubling every 18 months. Although Moore originally assumed a two-year period, many sources today refer to the 18-month figure.

Moore's Law is great for many companies because they can acquire large amounts of MIS equipment for cheaper and cheaper costs. As ebusinesses continue to grow, companies equip their employees with multiple forms of electronic devices ranging from laptops to cell phones to iPads. This is great for supporting a connected corporation, but significant unintended side effects include our dependence on fossil fuels and increased need for safe disposal of outdated computing equipment. Concern about these side effects has led many companies to turn to an ecological practice known as sustainable MIS. *Sustainable, or green, MIS* describes the production, management, use, and disposal of technology in a way that minimizes damage to the

BUSINESS DRIVEN ETHICS AND SECURITY

Ewaste and the Environment

By some estimates, there may be as many as 1 billion surplus or obsolete computers and monitors in the world. Consider California, where 6,000 computers become surplus every day. If not disposed of properly, this enormous ewaste stream, which can contain more than 1,000 toxic substances, is harmful to human beings and the environment. Beryllium is found in computer motherboards, chromium in floppy disks, lead in batteries and computer monitors, and mercury in alkaline batteries. One of the most toxic chemicals known is cadmium, found in many old laptops and computer chips.

In poorer countries, where the United States and Europe export some of their ewaste, the full impact of the environmental damage is quickly being realized. These areas have little use for obsolete electronic equipment, so local recyclers resell some parts and burn the rest in illegal dumps, often near residential areas, releasing toxic and carcinogenic substances into the air, land, and water.[5]

Have you ever participated in ewaste? What can you do to ensure that you are safely disposing of electronic equipment including batteries? What can governments do to encourage companies to dispose of ewaste safely? What can be done to protect poorer countries from receiving ewaste? Create a list of the ways you can safely dispose of cell phones, computers, printers, ink cartridges, and batteries. What could you do to inform citizens of the issues associated with ewaste and educate them on safe disposal practices?

environment. Sustainable MIS is a critical part of *corporate social responsibility,* that is, companies' acknowledged responsibility to society. *Clean computing,* a subset of sustainable MIS, refers to the environmentally responsible use, manufacture, and disposal of technology products and computer equipment. Although sustainable MIS refers to the environmental impact of computing as a whole, clean computing is specifically focused on the production of environmental waste. A *green personal computer (green PC)* is built using environment-friendly materials and designed to save energy. Building sustainable MIS infrastructures is a core initiative and critical success factor for socially responsible corporations. Figure 5.10 displays the three primary side effects of businesses' expanded use of technology.

Increased Electronic Waste

The fulfillment of Moore's Law has made technological devices smaller, cheaper, and faster, allowing more people from all income levels to purchase computing equipment. This increased demand is causing numerous environmental issues. *Ewaste* refers to discarded, obsolete, or broken electronic devices. Ewaste includes CDs, DVDs, thumb drives, printer cartridges, cell phones, iPods, external hard drives, TVs, VCRs, DVD players, microwaves, and so on. Some say one human year is equivalent to seven years of technological advancements. A personal computer has a life expectancy of only three to five years, and that of a cell phone is less than two years. An *upcycle* reuses or refurbishes ewaste and creates a new product.

Sustainable MIS disposal refers to the safe disposal of MIS assets at the end of their life cycle. It ensures that ewaste does not end up in landfills, causing environmental issues. A single computer contains more than 700 chemicals; some are toxic, such as mercury, lead, and cadmium. If a computer ends up in a landfill, the toxic substances it contains can leach into our land, water, and air. Recycling costs from $15 to $50 for a monitor or computer. Many companies, including public schools and universities, simply can't afford the recycling costs.[6]

Ewaste also occurs when unused equipment stored in attics, basements, and storage facilities never reaches a recycling center. Retrieving the silver, gold, and other valuable metals from these devices is more efficient and less environmentally harmful than removing it from its natural environment.

FIGURE 5.10

Three Pressures Driving
Sustainable MIS Infrastructures

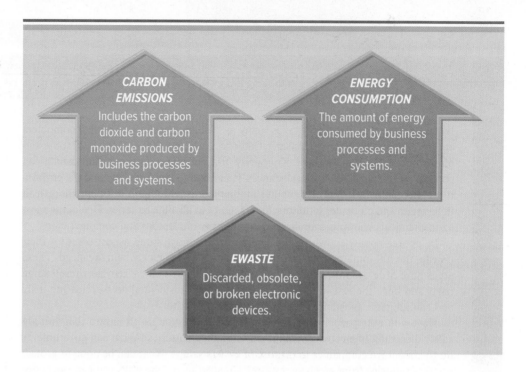

Currently, less than 20 percent of ewaste in the United States is recycled; however, even recycling does not guarantee that the equipment is disposed of safely. Although some recyclers process the material ethically, others ship it to countries such as China and India, where environmental enforcement is weak. This action poses its own global environmental problems.

Increased Energy Consumption

Energy consumption is the amount of energy consumed by business processes and systems. Huge increases in technology use have greatly amplified energy consumption. The energy consumed by a computer is estimated to produce as much as 10 percent of the amount of carbon dioxide produced by an automobile. Computer servers in the United States account for about 1 percent of the total energy needs of the country. Put in perspective, this is roughly equivalent to the energy consumption of Mississippi.

Computers consume energy even when they are not being used. For convenience and to allow for automatic updates and backup, the majority of computer equipment is never completely shut down. It draws energy 24 hours a day.

Increased Carbon Emissions

The major human-generated greenhouse gases, such as carbon emissions from energy use, are very likely responsible for the increases in climatic temperature over the past half a century. Additional temperature increases are projected over the next 100 years, with serious consequences for Earth's environment, if *carbon emissions,* including the carbon dioxide and carbon monoxide produced by business processes and systems, are not reduced.

In the United States, coal provides more than 30 percent of electrical power. When left on continuously, a single desktop computer and monitor can consume at least 100 watts of power per hour. To generate that much energy 24 hours a day for a year would require approximately 714 pounds of coal. When that coal is burned, it releases on average 5 pounds of sulfur dioxide, 5 pounds of nitrogen oxides, and 1,852 pounds (that is almost a ton) of carbon dioxide.[7]

LO 5.5: Explain the three components of a sustainable MIS infrastructure along with their business benefits.

SUPPORTING THE ENVIRONMENT: SUSTAINABLE MIS INFRASTRUCTURE

Combating ewaste, energy consumption, and carbon emissions requires a firm to focus on creating sustainable MIS infrastructures. A sustainable MIS infrastructure identifies ways that a company can grow in terms of computing resources while becoming less dependent on

BUSINESS DRIVEN ANALYTICS

Volkswagen Emissions Scandal

It's been dubbed the "diesel dupe." The U.S. Environmental Protection Agency (EPA) found that many VW cars being sold in America had a "defeat device"—or software—in diesel engines that could detect when they were being tested and change the car's performance accordingly to improve results. The German car giant has since admitted cheating emissions tests in the United States. Full details of how the scheme worked are sketchy, although the EPA has said that the engines had computer software that could sense test scenarios by monitoring speed, engine operation, air pressure, and even the position of the steering wheel.

When the cars were operating under controlled laboratory conditions —which typically involve putting them on a stationary test system—the device appears to have put the vehicle into a sort of safety mode in which the engine ran below normal power and performance. Once on the road, the engines switched out of this test mode. The result? The engines emitted nitrogen oxide pollutants up to 40 times above what is allowed in the United States.

Why is it important that all vehicles adhere to the EPA testing limits? What environmental impacts could occur from Volkswagen's false emission tests? How could the EPA create metrics for testing to ensure cars are operating as expected? How should the EPA handle the Volkswagen scandal?

FIGURE 5.11

Sustainable MIS Infrastructure Components

GRID COMPUTING	VIRTUALIZATION	CLOUD COMPUTING
• A collection of computers, often geographically dispersed, that are coordinated to solve a common problem	• Creates multiple virtual machines on a single computing device	• Stores, manages, and processes data and applications over the Internet rather than on a personal computer or server

hardware and energy consumption. The components of a sustainable MIS infrastructure are displayed in Figure 5.11.

Grid Computing

When a light is turned on, the power grid delivers exactly what is needed, instantly. Computers and networks can now work that way using grid computing. *Grid computing* is a collection of computers, often geographically dispersed, that are coordinated to solve a common problem. With grid computing, a problem is broken into pieces and distributed to many machines, allowing faster processing than could occur with a single system (see Figure 5.12). Computers typically use less than 25 percent of their processing power, leaving more than 75 percent available for other tasks. Innovatively, grid computing takes advantage of this unused processing power

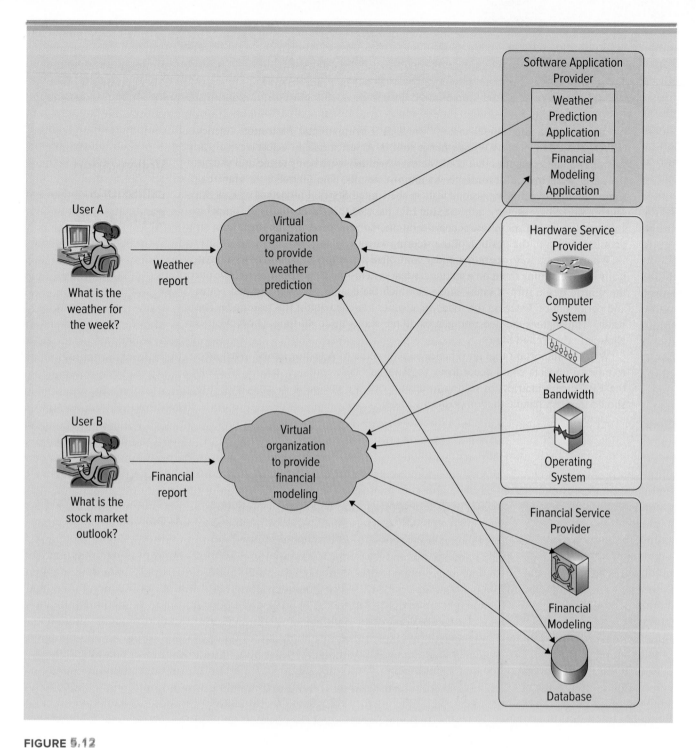

FIGURE 5.12

Virtual Organizations Using Grid Computing

by linking thousands of individual computers around the world to create a virtual supercomputer that can process intensive tasks. Grid computing makes better use of MIS resources, allowing greater scalability because systems can easily grow to handle peaks and valleys in demand, become more cost efficient, and solve problems that would be impossible to tackle with a single computer (see Figure 5.13 and Figure 5.14).[8]

The uses of grid computing are numerous, including the creative environment of animated movies. DreamWorks Animation used grid computing to complete many of its hit films, including *Antz, Shrek, Madagascar,* and *How to Train Your Dragon.* The third *Shrek* film required more than 20 million computer hours to make (compared to 5 million for the first *Shrek* and 10 million for the second). At peak production times, DreamWorks dedicated more than 4,000 computers to its *Shrek* grid, allowing it to complete scenes in days and hours instead of months. With the increased grid computing power, the DreamWork's animators were able to add more realistic

Inevitably, in going about our daily lives—commuting, sheltering our families, eating—each of us contributes to the greenhouse gas emissions that are causing climate change. Yet there are many things each of us, as individuals, can do to reduce our carbon emissions. The choices we make in our homes, our travel, the food we eat, and what we buy and throw away all influence our carbon footprint and can help ensure a stable climate for future generations.[9]

The Nature Conservancy's carbon footprint calculator measures your impact on our climate. Its carbon footprint calculator estimates how many tons of carbon dioxide and other greenhouse gases your choices create each year. Visit the Nature Conservancy's carbon footprint calculator to determine your carbon footprint and what you can do to reduce your emissions (http://www.nature.org/greenliving/carboncalculator/).

How Big Is Your Carbon Footprint?

FIGURE 5.13

Grid Computer Network

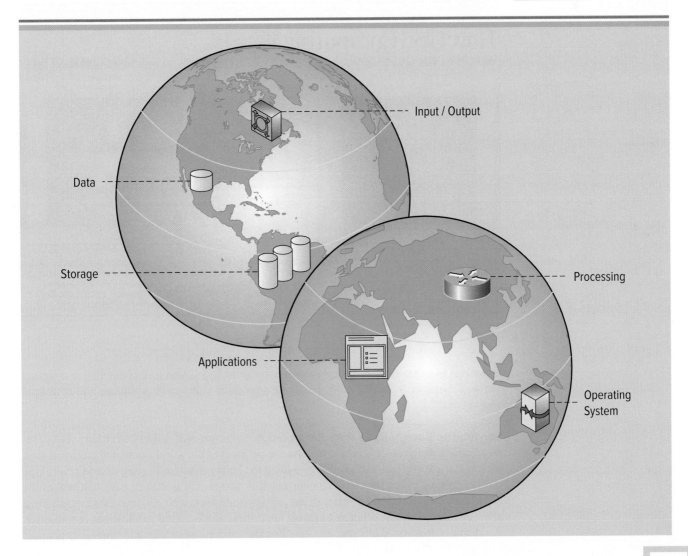

FIGURE 5.14

Grid Computing Example

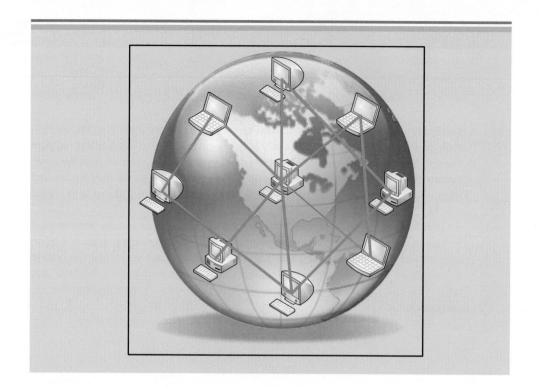

FIGURE 5.15

Making *Shrek 2* with Grid
Computing

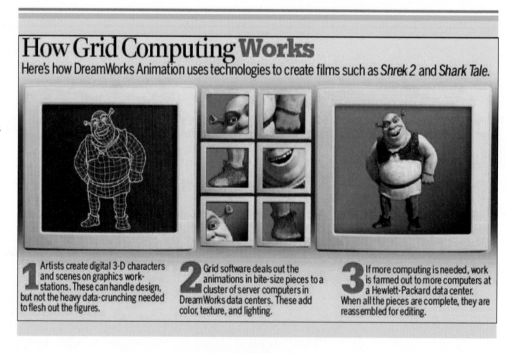

movement to water, fire, and magic scenes (see Figure 5.15). With grid computing, a company can work faster or more efficiently, providing a potential competitive advantage and additional cost savings.[10]

Solving the Energy Issue with Smart Grids   A *smart grid* delivers electricity using two-way digital technology. It is meant to solve the problem of the world's outdated electrical grid, making it more efficient and reliable by adding the ability to monitor, analyze, and control the transmission of power remotely. The current U.S. power grid is said to have outlived its life expectancy by as much as 30 years. Smart grids provide users with real-time usage monitoring, allowing them to choose off-peak times for noncritical or less urgent applications or processes. Residents of Boulder, Colorado, can monitor their use of electricity and control appliances remotely due to the city's large-scale smart grid system. Xcel Energy has installed 21,000 smart grid meters since the $100 million program started several years ago. Energy use by early adopters is down as much as 45 percent.[11]

Virtualized Computing

Most computers and even servers typically run only one operating system, such as Windows or Mac OS, and only one application. When a company invests in a large system such as inventory management, it dedicates a single server to house the system. This ensures that the system has enough capacity to run during peak times and to scale to meet demand. Also, many systems have specific hardware requirements along with detailed software requirements, making it difficult to find two systems with the same requirements that could share the same machine. Through the use of virtualization, computers can run multiple operating systems along with multiple software applications—all at the same time. *Virtualization* creates multiple virtual machines on a single computing device. A good analogy is a computer printer. In the past, you had to purchase a fax machine, copy machine, answering machine, and computer printer separately. This was expensive, required enough energy to run four machines, and created additional amounts of ewaste. Today, you can buy a virtualized computer printer that functions as a fax machine, answering machine, and copy machine all on one physical machine, thereby reducing costs, power requirements, and ewaste. Virtualization is essentially a form of consolidation that can benefit sustainable MIS infrastructures in a variety of ways, for example:

- By increasing availability of applications that can give a higher level of performance, depending on the hardware used.
- By increasing energy efficiency by requiring less hardware to run multiple systems or applications.
- By increasing hardware usability by running multiple operating systems on a single computer.

Originally, computers were designed to run a single application on a single operating system. This left most computers vastly underutilized. (As mentioned earlier, 75 percent of most computing power is available for other tasks.) Virtualization allows multiple virtual computers to exist on a single machine, which allows it to share its resources, such as memory and hard disk space, to run different applications and even different operating systems. Mac computers can run both the Apple operating system and the Windows PC operating system, with the use of virtualization software (see Figure 5.16). Unfortunately, virtualization, at least at the moment, is not available for a PC to run Mac software. There are three basic categories of virtualization:

- *Storage virtualization* combines multiple network storage devices so they appear to be a single storage device.

Apple Macintosh Computer

MAC OS X
Running
Mac
software

WINDOWS 7
Running
Windows 7
software

Sharing memory and hard disk space

FIGURE 5.16

Virtualization Allows an Apple Macintosh Computer to Run OS X and Windows 7

- *Network virtualization* combines networks by splitting the available bandwidth into independent channels that can be assigned in real time to a specific device.
- *Server virtualization* combines the physical resources, such as servers, processors, and operating systems, from the applications. (This is the most common form, and typically, when you hear the term *virtualization,* you can assume server virtualization.)

Virtualization is also one of the easiest and quickest ways to achieve a sustainable MIS infrastructure because it reduces power consumption and requires less equipment that needs to be manufactured, maintained, and later disposed of safely. Managers no longer have to assign servers, storage, or network capacity permanently to single applications. Instead, they can assign the hardware resources when and where they are needed, achieving the availability, flexibility, and scalability a company needs to thrive and grow. Also, by virtually separating the operating system and applications from the hardware, if there is a disaster or hardware failure, it is easy to port the virtual machine to a new physical machine, allowing a company to recovery quickly. One of the primary uses of virtualization is for performing backup, recovery, and disaster recovery. Using virtual servers or a virtualization service provider, such as Google, Microsoft, or Amazon, to host disaster recovery is more sustainable than a single company incurring the expense of having redundant physical systems. Also, these providers' data centers are built to withstand natural disasters and are typically located far away from big cities (see Figure 5.17).

System virtualization is the ability to present the resources of a single computer as if it is a collection of separate computers ("virtual machines"), each with its own virtual CPUs, network interfaces, storage, and operating system.

Virtual machine technology was first implemented on mainframes in the 1960s to allow the expensive systems to be partitioned into separate domains and used more efficiently by more users and applications. As standard PC servers became more powerful in the past decade, virtualization has been brought to the desktop and notebook processors to provide the same benefits.

FIGURE 5.17

Virtualization Architecture

BUSINESS DRIVEN INNOVATION

Upcycle Your Old PCs

Imagine walking into your friend's home and seeing her computer with live fish swimming around inside it. Upon taking a second look, you realize she has upcycled her old Mac into an innovative "macquarium." Some young entrepreneurs are making a fortune by upcycling old Mac desktops as fish tanks. An upcycle reuses or refurbishes ewaste and creates a new product. With the growing problem of ewaste, one alternative is to upcycle your old technology by creating innovative household products or personal accessories. Take a look at one of the devices you are currently using to see whether you can create an upcycled product. Here are a few great ideas to get you started:

- Keyboard magnets
- Computer aquariums
- Mac mailboxes
- Keyboard calendars
- Floppy disk pencil holders
- Circuit board key rings
- RAM key chains
- Circuit earrings
- Cable bracelets
- Motherboard clocks
- Mouse belt buckles

Virtual machines appear both to the user within the system and the world outside as separate computers, each with its own network identity, user authorization and authentication capabilities, operating system version and configuration, applications, and data. The hardware is consistent across all virtual machines: While the number or size of them may differ, devices are used that allow virtual machines to be portable, independent of the actual hardware type on the underlying systems. Figure 5.18 shows an overview of what a system virtualization framework looks like.

Virtual Data Centers   A *data center* is a facility used to house management information systems and associated components, such as telecommunications and storage systems. Data centers, sometimes referred to as server farms, consume power and require cooling and floor space while working to support business growth without disrupting normal business operations and the quality of service. The amount of data a data center stores has grown exponentially over the years as our reliance on information increases. Backups, graphics, documents, presentations, photos, and audio and video files all contribute to the ever-expanding information footprint that requires storage. One of the most effective ways to limit the power consumption and cooling requirements of a data center is to consolidate parts of the physical infrastructure, particularly by reducing the number of physical servers through virtualization. For this reason, virtualization is having a profound impact on data centers as the sheer number of servers a company requires to operate decreases, thereby boosting growth and performance while reducing environmental impact, as shown in Figure 5.19. Google, Microsoft, Amazon, and Yahoo! have all created data centers along the Columbia River in the northwestern United States. In this area, each company can benefit from affordable land, high-speed Internet access, plentiful water for cooling, and even more important, inexpensive electricity. These factors are critical to today's large-scale data centers, whose sheer size and power needs far surpass those of the previous generation.

FIGURE 5.18

System Virtualization

FIGURE 5.19

Ways for Data Centers to
Become Sustainable

The Microsoft data center in Quincy, Washington, is larger than 10 football fields and is pow-ered entirely by hydroelectricity, power generated from flowing water rather than from burning coal or other fossil fuel.[12]

If we take a holistic and integrated approach to overall company growth, the benefits of inte-grating information MIS infrastructures, environmental MIS infrastructures, and sustainable MIS infrastructures become obvious. For example, a company could easily create a backup of its software and important information in one or more geographically dispersed locations using cloud computing. This would be far cheaper than building its own hot and cold sites in different areas of the country. In the case of a security breach, failover can be deployed as a virtual machine in one location of the cloud and be shut down as another virtual machine in a different location on the cloud comes online.

Cloud Computing

Imagine a cyclical business that specializes in Halloween decorations and how its sales trends and orders vary depending on the time of year. The majority of sales occur in September and October, and the remaining 10 months have relatively small sales and small system usage.

The company does not want to invest in massive expensive servers that sit idle 10 months of the year just to meet its capacity spikes in September and October. The perfect solution for this company is cloud computing, which makes it easier to gain access to the computing power that was once reserved for large corporations. Small to medium-size companies no longer have to make big capital investments to access the same powerful systems that large companies run.

According to the National Institute of Standards and Technology, *cloud computing* stores, manages, and processes data and applications over the Internet rather than on a personal computer or server. Cloud computing offers new ways to store, access, process, and analyze information and connect people and resources from any location in the world an Internet connection is available. As shown in Figure 5.20, users connect to the cloud from their personal computers or portable devices by using a client, such as a web browser. To these individual users, the cloud appears as their personal application, device, or document. It is like storing all of your software and documents in the cloud, and all you need is a device to access the cloud. No more hard drives, software, or processing power—that is all located in the cloud, transparent to the users. Users are not physically bound to a single computer or network; they can access their programs and documents from wherever they are, whenever they need to. Just think of having your hard drive located in the sky and being able to access your information and programs using any device from wherever you are. The best part is that even if your machine crashes, is lost, or is stolen, the information hosted in the cloud is safe and always available. (See Figure 5.21 for cloud providers and Figure 5.22 for cloud computing advantages.)

FIGURE 5.20

Cloud Computing Example

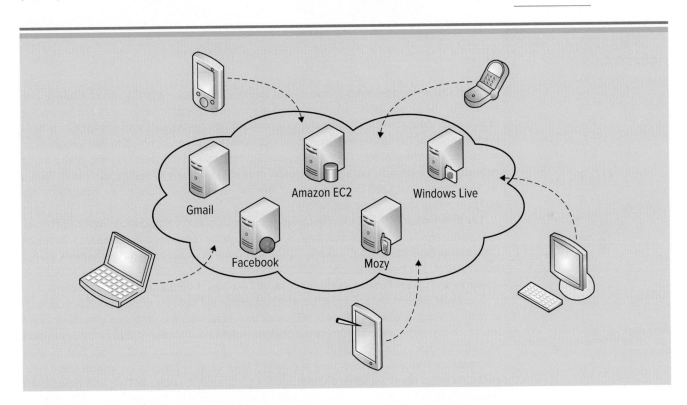

FIGURE 5.21

Overview of Cloud Providers

Cloud Providers	
Amazon—Cloud Drive, Cloud Player, Amazon Prime	Amazon Kindle Fire is sold at a loss to push various types of media through Amazon Prime and Cloud Player, where users can stream videos and music.
Apple—iCloud, iWork, iBooks, iTunes	iCloud brings together iPhones, iPads, and Mac to synchronize data across Apple devices. iWork helps users collaborate.
Google—Google Apps, Google Drive, Gmail, Google Calendar	Google offers a number of cloud services, including Google apps, Gmail, and Google Drive to store data.
Microsoft—Office 365, OneDrive, OneNote, Exchange	OneDrive and Office 365 offer ways to collaborate and share data, photos, email, and documents.

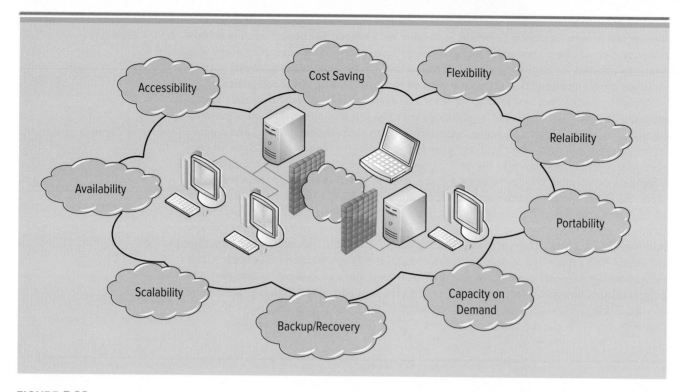

FIGURE 5.22

Cloud Computing Advantages

Multi-tenancy in the cloud means that a single instance of a system serves multiple customers. In the cloud, each customer is called a tenant, and multiple tenants can access the same system. Multi-tenancy helps reduce operational costs associated with implementing large systems because the costs are dispersed across many tenants as opposed to *single-tenancy,* in which each customer or tenant must purchase and maintain an individual system. With a multi-tenancy cloud approach, the service provider only has one place to update its system. With a single-tenancy cloud approach, the service provider would have to update its system in every company where the software was running.

The cloud is a multi-tenant environment, which means that a single architecture hosts multiple customers' applications and data. A *noisy neighbor* refers to a multi-tenancy co-tenant that monopolizes bandwidth, servers, CPUs, and other resources that cause network performance issues. The noisy neighbor effect occurs when one tenant uses the majority of available resources and causes network performance issues for others on the shared infrastructure.

The *cloud fabric* is the software that makes possible the benefits of cloud computing, such as multi-tenancy. A *cloud fabric controller* is an individual who monitors and provisions cloud resources, similar to a server administrator at an individual company. Cloud fabric controllers provision resources, balance loads, manage servers, update systems, and ensure that all environments are available and operating correctly. Cloud fabric is the primary reason cloud computing promotes all of the seven abilities, allowing a business to make its data and applications accessible, available, maintainable, portable, reliable, scalable, and usable. Figure 5.23 displays the top business cloud applications.[13]

The cloud offers a company higher availability, greater reliability, and improved accessibility—all with affordable high-speed access. For flexibility, scalability, and cost efficiency, cloud computing is quickly becoming a viable option for companies of all sizes. With the cloud, you could simply purchase a single license for software such as Microsoft Office or Outlook at a far discounted rate and not worry about the hassle of installing and upgrading the software on your computer. No more worries that you don't have enough memory to run a new program because the hardware is provided in the cloud, along with the software. You simply pay to access the program. Think of this the same way you do your telephone service. You simply pay to access a vendor's service, and you do not have to pay for the equipment required to carry the call around the globe. You also don't have to worry about scalability because the system automatically handles peak loads, which can be spread out among the systems in the cloud. Figure 5.24 displays the characteristics of cloud computing.

BUSINESS DRIVEN GLOBALIZATION

Solving the Ewaste Problem

The United States disposes of more than 384 million units of ewaste yearly and currently recycles less than 20 percent, according to the Electronics TakeBack Coalition. The remaining 80 percent is burned or dumped in landfills, leaking toxic substances such as mercury, lead, cadmium, arsenic, and beryllium into the environment. Reports predict that ewaste will weigh as much as 200 Empire State Buildings by 2017. Solving the **E**waste **P**roblem (**StEP**) Initiative is a group represented by the United Nations organizations, governments, and science organizations, and its mission is to ensure safe and responsible ewaste disposal. StEP predicts ewaste will grow by a third in the next five years with the United States and China being the biggest contributors. Until recently, comprehensive data on global ewaste has been hard to collect because the definition of ewaste differs among countries. For example, the United States only includes consumer electronics such as TVs and computers, whereas Europe includes everything that has a battery or power cord in the ewaste category.[14]

The growth of ewaste is an opportunity for entrepreneurs. Research the web and find examples of schools around the country that are responsibly tackling the ewaste problem. In a group, create a plan for implementing an ewaste recycling program at your school.

FIGURE 5.23

Top Cloud-Based Business Applications

CLOUD APPLICATIONS	
Box box.com	Box is like a file folder that all your gadgets and devices can access. You simply drag a file into Box, and you can instantly access it from anywhere.
Chatter Chatter.com	Chatter is essentially an in-house social network. It allows your employees to share files, collaborate easily on projects, and pose questions to the whole company, which cuts down on meeting times, decreases the number of emails sent, and increases how quickly employees can gather information.
Evernote evernote.com	Evernote makes organizing notes simple. It organizes online all the sticky notes, scribbled-on notepads, and random pictures that you would have cluttering up your desk. It can even recognize writing in images, so if you take a picture of a whiteboard full of notes, you can find that image by searching for one of the phrases in it.
Google Apps Google.com	Google Apps pretty much eliminates the need for many computer programs. You can create and save text documents, spreadsheets, slide shows, and more on Google Docs, and several people can work on one file simultaneously. Google Calendar makes creating and sharing calendars easy, and event reminders can be emailed to invitees. Gmail for Business gives companies personalized email accounts that are easy to set up and amend and that have the flexibility and storage space of Gmail.
MailChimp mailchimp.com	MailChimp is an email publishing platform that allows businesses of all sizes to design and send their email campaigns. Measuring the success of your email campaigns is really easy because the software integrates with Google Analytics for tracking purposes.
Moo uk.moo.com	Moo offers a design and printing service for business cards, postcards, and minicards. Users can customize existing Moo designs, upload their own designs, or import their own images from their Etsy, Facebook, Flickr, Picasa, or SmugMug account.
Mozy mozy.co.uk	Mozy is an online backup service that continuously backs up the files on your computer or server. It gives small businesses the space to back up all their computer and server files for a very reasonable price, so owners know their files are retrievable, even during a data loss crisis.

(continued)

FIGURE 5.23

(continued)

CLOUD APPLICATIONS	
Outright outright.com	Outright is a cloud finance app that helps small businesses with their business accounting. It allows you to track income/expenses, tax obligations, and profits/losses in real time. Ideal for small companies or just entrepreneurs looking to get a hold on their finances
Quickbooks quickbooks.intuit.co.uk	Quickbooks is an online accounting service and can help with all accounting needs, including monitoring cash flow, creating reports, and setting budgets, and is accessible from anywhere in the world.
Skype skype.com	Skype turns your computer into a phone; you can call or chat (with or without video) to other Skype users for free.
Toggl toggl.com	Toggl is a time-tracking application. It allows you to create tasks and projects and assign a certain amount of time to each project. It also logs how long tasks take to complete and how much time you have left to spend in a project.

FIGURE 5.24

Characteristics of Cloud Computing

Because additional cloud resources are always available, companies no longer have to purchase systems for infrequent computing tasks that need intense processing power, such as preparing tax returns during tax season or increased sales transactions during certain holiday seasons. If a company needs more processing power, it is always there in the cloud—and available on a cost-efficient basis. Heroku is the leading cloud platform for building and deploying social and mobile customer applications. Built on open standards, Heroku supports multiple open frameworks, languages, and databases.

With cloud computing, individuals or businesses pay only for the services they need, when they need them, and where, much as we use and pay for electricity. In the past, a company would have to pay millions of dollars for the hardware, software, and networking equipment required to implement a large system such as payroll or sales management. A cloud computing user can simply access the cloud and request a single license to a payroll application. The user does not have to incur any hardware, software, or networking expenses. As the business grows and the user requires more employees to have access to the system, the business simply purchases additional licenses. Rather than running software on a local computer or server, companies can now reach to the cloud to combine software applications, data storage, and considerable computing power. Regardless of which cloud model a business chooses, it can select from four different cloud computing environments—public, private, community, and hybrid (see Figure 5.25).

Public Cloud

Public cloud promotes massive, global, and industrywide applications offered to the general public. In a public cloud, customers are never required to provision, manage, upgrade, or replace

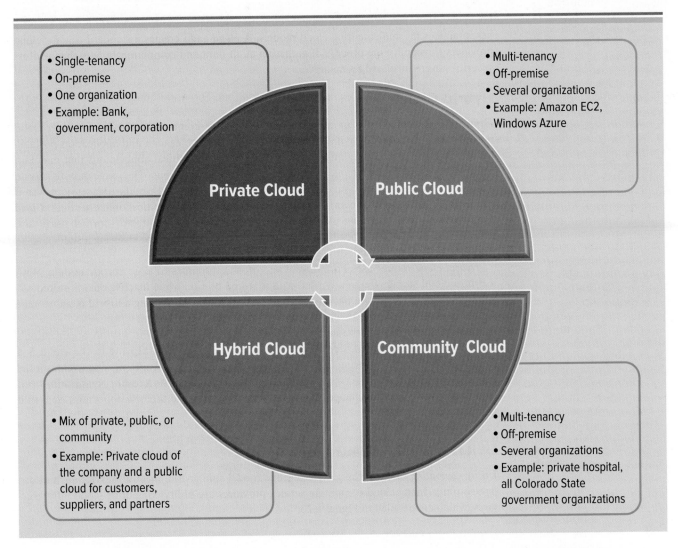

- Single-tenancy
- On-premise
- One organization
- Example: Bank, government, corporation

Private Cloud

- Multi-tenancy
- Off-premise
- Several organizations
- Example: Amazon EC2, Windows Azure

Public Cloud

Hybrid Cloud

- Mix of private, public, or community
- Example: Private cloud of the company and a public cloud for customers, suppliers, and partners

Community Cloud

- Multi-tenancy
- Off-premise
- Several organizations
- Example: private hospital, all Colorado State government organizations

FIGURE 5.25

Cloud Computing Environments

hardware or software. Pricing is utility-style, and customers pay only for the resources they use. Public clouds are the type used by service providers to offer free or paid-for services to the general public. They are open but often have standard restrictions requiring passwords. A few great examples of public cloud computing include Amazon Web Services (AWS), Windows Azure, and Google Cloud Connect.

Private Cloud

Private cloud serves only one customer or organization and can be located on the customer's premises or off the customer's premises. A private cloud is the optimal solution for an organization such as the government that has high data security concerns and values information privacy. Private clouds are far more expensive than public clouds because costs are not shared across multiple customers. Private clouds are mostly used by firms and groups that need to keep data secure. The main downside is that they still require significant investment of time and money to set them up.

Community Cloud

Community cloud serves a specific community with common business models, security requirements, and compliance considerations. Community clouds are emerging in highly regulated industries such as financial services and pharmaceutical companies. Community clouds are private but spread over a variety of groups within one organization. Different sections of the cloud can be set up specifically for each department or group.

The *Cloud Security Alliance (CSA)* is a nonprofit organization that promotes research into best practices for securing cloud computing and cloud delivery models. CSA offers tools, documentation, and reports on cloud computing services, security education, and security best practices for implementing cloud models. A *cloud audit* creates a standard way for cloud providers to simplify the process of gathering audit data and communicate how they address security, governance, and compliance.

Hybrid Cloud

Hybrid cloud includes two or more private, public, or community clouds, but each cloud remains separate and is only linked by technology that enables data and application portability. For example, a company might use a private cloud for critical applications that maintain sensitive data and a public cloud for nonsensitive data applications. The usage of both private and public clouds together is an example of a hybrid cloud. Hybrid clouds offer services even if connectivity faults occur and are often used to provide backup to critical online services. *Cloud bursting* is when a company uses its own computing infrastructure for normal usage and accesses the cloud when it needs to scale for peak load requirements, ensuring a sudden spike in usage does not result in poor performance or system crashes.

Hybrid cloud storage uses both on-site and off-site resources to store corporate data. With a hybrid cloud storage frequently used data is stored on-site, while inactive data is stored off-site in the cloud. Corporate data users are unaware that they are using a hybrid cloud storage system because data retrieval, whether on-site or off-site, is transparent.

Deploying an MIS infrastructure in the cloud forever changes the way an organization's MIS systems are developed, deployed, maintained, and managed. Moving to the cloud is a fundamental shift from moving from a physical world to a logical world, making irrelevant the notion of which individual server applications or data reside on. As a result, organizations and MIS departments need to change the way they view systems and the new opportunities to find competitive advantages.

UTILITY COMPUTING

Utility computing offers a pay-per-use revenue model similar to a metered service such as gas or electricity. Many cloud computing service providers use utility computing cloud infrastructures, which are detailed in Figure 5.26.

FIGURE 5.26

Cloud Service Delivery Models

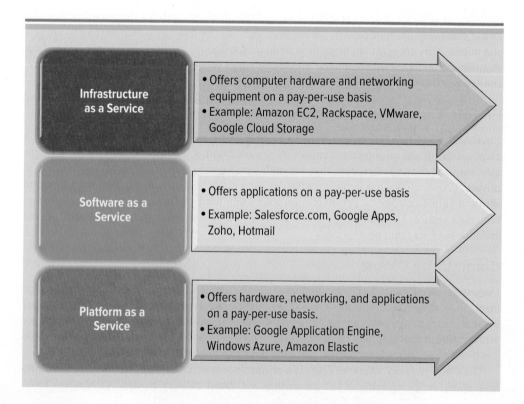

Infrastructure as a Service (IaaS)

Infrastructure as a Service (IaaS) delivers hardware networking capabilities, including the use of servers, networking, and storage, over the cloud using a pay-per-use revenue model. With IaaS, the customer rents the hardware and provides its own custom applications or programs. IaaS customers save money by not having to spend a large amount of capital purchasing expensive servers, which is a great business advantage considering some servers cost more than $100,000. The service is typically paid for on a usage basis, much like a basic utility service such as electricity or gas. IaaS offers a cost-effective solution for companies that need their computing resources to grow and shrink as business demand changes. This is known as *dynamic scaling,* which means the MIS infrastructure can be automatically scaled up or down based on requirements. *Disaster Recovery as a Service (DRaaS)* offers backup services that use cloud resources to protect applications and data from disruption caused by disaster. It gives an organization a total system backup that allows for business continuity in the event of system failure. DRaaS is typically part of a disaster recovery plan or business continuity plan.

Currently the most popular IaaS operation is Amazon's Elastic Compute Cloud, generally known as Amazon EC2, or simply EC2. EC2 provides a web interface through which customers can load and run their own applications on Amazon's computers. Customers control their own operating environment, so they can create, run, and stop services as needed, which is why Amazon describes EC2 as "elastic." IaaS is a perfect fit for companies with research-intensive projects that need to process large amounts of information at irregular intervals, such as those in the scientific or medical fields. Cloud computing services offer these companies considerable cost savings because they can perform testing and analysis at levels that are not possible without access to additional and very costly computing infrastructure.

Software as a Service (SaaS)

Software as a Service (SaaS) delivers applications over the cloud using a pay-per-use revenue model. Before its introduction, companies often spent huge amounts of money implementing and customizing specialized applications to satisfy their business requirements. Many of these applications were difficult to implement, expensive to maintain, and challenging to use. Usability was one of the biggest drivers for creating interest in and success for cloud computing service providers.

SaaS offers a number of advantages; the most obvious is tremendous cost savings. The software is priced on a per-use basis with no up-front costs, so companies get the immediate benefit of reducing capital expenditures. They also get the added benefits of scalability and flexibility to test new software on a rental basis.

Salesforce.com is one of the most popular SaaS providers. It built and delivered a sales automation application, suitable for the typical salesperson, which automates functions such as tracking sales leads and prospects and forecasting. Tapping the power of SaaS can provide access to a large-scale, secure infrastructure, along with any needed support, which is especially valuable for a start-up or small company with few financial resources. A few SaaS extensions include:

- *Data as a Service (DaaS)* facilitates the accessibility of business-critical data in a timely, secure, and affordable manner. DaaS depends on the principle that specified, useful data can be supplied to users on demand, irrespective of any organizational or geographical separation between consumers and providers.

- *Security as a Service (SaaS)* involves applications such as anti-virus software delivered over the Internet with constant virus definition updates that are not reliant on user compliance. Security as a Service is sometimes referred to as cloud security. Security as a Service provides top security expertise that is traditionally better than can be found in an organization. Security as a Service providers include Cisco, McAfee, and Symantec.

- *Unified Communications as a Service (UCaaS)* offers enterprise communication and collaboration services over the Internet such as instant messaging systems, online meetings, and video conferencing. Businesses using UCaaS avoid the large payouts and expenses associated with deploying a unified communications solution on their own. Another advantage of UCaaS is that it provides core business tasks with a high level of availability, flexibility, and scalability. UCaaS include single-tenancy and multi-tenancy implementations. Single-tenancy UCaaS offers a software platform that is integrated with a single enterprise's on-site applications. Multi-tenancy UCaaS offers a single software platform that many enterprises can access. Enterprises can also adopt a hybrid approach, keeping a portion of their unified communications on-site and other applications in the cloud.

Platform as a Service (PaaS)

Platform as a Service (PaaS) supports the deployment of entire systems, including hardware, networking, and applications, using a pay-per-use revenue model. PaaS is a perfect solution for a business because it passes on to the service provider the headache and challenges of buying, managing, and maintaining web development software. With PaaS the development, deployment, management, and maintenance is based entirely in the cloud and performed by the PaaS provider, allowing the company to focus resources on its core initiatives. Every aspect of development, including the software needed to create it and the hardware to run it, lives in the cloud. PaaS helps companies minimize operational costs and increase productivity by providing all the following without up-front investment:

- Increased security.
- Access to information anywhere and anytime.
- Centralized information management.
- Easy collaboration with partners, suppliers, and customers.
- Increased speed to market with significantly less cost.

One of the most popular PaaS services is Google's Application Engine, which builds and deploys web applications for a company. Google's Application Engine is easy to build, easy to maintain, and easy to scale as a company's web-based application needs grow. Google's Application Engine is free and offers a standard storage limit and enough processing power and network usage to support a web application serving about 5 million page views a month. When a customer scales beyond these initial limits, it can pay a fee to increase capacity and performance. This can turn into some huge costs savings for a small business that does not have enough initial capital to buy expensive hardware and software for its web applications. Just think, a two-person company can access the same computing resources as Google. That makes good business sense.

Combining infrastructure as a service, platform as a service, and data as a service we arrive at Big Data as a Service. *Big Data as a Service (BDaaS)* offers a cloud-based Big Data service to help organizations analyze massive amounts of data to solve business dilemmas. BDaaS is a somewhat nebulous term often used to describe a wide variety of outsourcing of various Big Data functions to the cloud. This can range from the supply of data, to the supply of analytical tools with which to interrogate the data (often through a web dashboard or control panel), to carrying out the actual analysis and providing reports. Some BDaaS providers also include consulting and advisory services within their BDaaS packages.

LEARNING OUTCOME REVIEW

Learning Outcome 5.1: Explain MIS infrastructure and its three primary types.

The three primary areas where enterprise architects focus when maintaining a firm's MIS infrastructure are:

- Supporting operations: Information MIS infrastructure identifies where and how important information, such as customer records, is maintained and secured.
- Supporting change: Agile MIS infrastructure includes the hardware, software, and telecommunications equipment that, when combined, provides the underlying foundation to support the organization's goals.
- Supporting the environment: Sustainable MIS infrastructure identifies ways that a company can grow in terms of computing resources while becoming less dependent on hardware and energy consumption.

Learning Outcome 5.2: Identify the three primary areas associated with an information MIS infrastructure.

The three primary areas an information infrastructure provides to support continuous business operations are:

- Backup and recovery: A backup is an exact copy of a system's information. Recovery is the ability to get a system up and running in the event of a system crash or failure that includes restoring the information backup.
- Disaster recovery plan: This plan provides a detailed process for recovering information or a system in the event of a catastrophic disaster.
- Business continuity plan: This details how a company recovers and restores critical business operations and systems after a disaster or extended disruption.

Learning Outcome 5.3: Describe the characteristics of an agile MIS infrastructure.

- Accessibility refers to the varying levels that define what a user can access, view, or perform when operating a system.
- Availability refers to the time frames when the system is operational.
- Maintainability (or flexibility) refers to how quickly a system can transform to support environmental changes.
- Portability refers to the ability of an application to operate on different devices or software platforms, such as different operating systems.
- Reliability (or accuracy) ensures that a system is functioning correctly and providing accurate information.
- Scalability describes how well a system can scale up or adapt to the increased demands of growth.
- Usability is the degree to which a system is easy to learn and efficient and satisfying to use.

Learning Outcome 5.4: Identify the environmental impacts associated with MIS.

Increased energy consumption, increased electronic waste, and increased carbon emissions are all associated with MIS. Ewaste refers to discarded, obsolete, or broken electronic devices. Sustainable MIS disposal refers to the safe disposal of MIS assets at the end of their life cycle.

Learning Outcome 5.5: Explain the three components of a sustainable MIS infrastructure along with their business benefits.

The components of a sustainable MIS infrastructure include:

- Grid computing: A collection of computers, often geographically dispersed, that are coordinated to solve a common problem.
- Cloud computing: The use of resources and applications hosted remotely on the Internet. The term comes (at least in part) from the image of a cloud to represent the Internet or some large networked environment.
- Virtualized computing: The creation of multiple virtual machines on a single computing device.

OPENING CASE QUESTIONS

1. **Knowledge:** List the ways that an agile MIS infrastructure supports Box's business.
2. **Comprehension:** Describe the reasons Box can help a company with its disaster recovery plan and business continuity plan.
3. **Application:** Apply the concepts of cloud computing to Box's business model.

4. **Analysis:** Analyze how Box can benefit from a sustainable MIS infrastructure.

5. **Synthesis:** Develop a way that a company could benefit from grid computing by using Box.

6. **Evaluate:** Assess how Box uses server virtualization to support its growth.

KEY TERMS

Accessibility 190
Administrator access 191
Agile MIS infrastructure 183
Availability 191
Backup 185
Big Data as a Service (BDaaS) 212
Business continuity planning
    (BCP) 188
Business impact analysis 188
Capacity 193
Capacity planning 193
Carbon emissions 196
Clean computing 195
Client 183
Cloud audit 210
Cloud bursting 210
Cloud computing 205
Cloud fabric 206
Cloud fabric controller 206
Cloud Security Alliance (CSA) 209
Cold site 187
Community cloud 209
Corporate social responsibility 195
Data center 203
Data as a Service (DaaS) 211
Disaster recovery cost curve 187
Disaster Recovery as a Service
    (DRaaS) 211
Disaster recovery plan 186
Dynamic scaling 211
Emergency 188
Emergency notification service 188

Emergency preparedness 188
Energy consumption 196
Enterprise architect 183
Ewaste 195
Failback 185
Failover 185
Fault tolerance 185
Green personal computer
    (green PC) 195
Grid computing 197
Hardware 183
High availability 191
Hot site 187
Hybrid cloud 210
Hybrid cloud storage 210
Incident 189
Incident management 189
Incident record 189
Information MIS infrastructure 183
Infrastructure as a Service
    (IaaS) 211
Maintainability (or flexibility) 192
MIS infrastructure 183
Moore's Law 194
Multi-tenancy 206
Network 183
Network virtualization 202
Noisy neighbor 206
Performance 193
Platform as a Service (PaaS) 212
Portability 192
Private cloud 209

Public cloud 208
Recovery 185
Reliability (or accuracy) 192
Scalability 193
Security as a Service (SaaS) 211
Server 183
Server virtualization 202
Serviceability 194
Single-tenancy 206
Smart grid 200
Software 183
Software as a Service (SaaS) 211
Storage virtualization 201
Sustainable MIS disposal 195
Sustainable MIS
    infrastructure 184
Sustainable, or green, MIS 194
System visualization 202
Technology failure 189
Technology recovery strategy 189
Unavailable 191
Unified Communications
    as a Service (UCaaS) 211
Upcycle 195
Usability 194
Utility computing 210
Virtualization 201
Vulnerability 192
Warm site 187
Web accessibility 191
Web accessibility initiative
    (WAI) 191

REVIEW QUESTIONS

1. How often should a business back up its data?

2. Why is it important to ensure that backups are working and can be restored?

3. What is the difference between a disaster recovery plan and a business continuity plan?

4. What are the three forms of MIS infrastructures and what do they support?

5. List the characteristics of an agile MIS infrastructure and explain why they are all critical for supporting change.

6. Explain what capacity planning is and how it can help a business prepare for growth.

7. Explain the difference between fault tolerance and failover.

8. Compare the differences between hot, cold, and warm sites.

9. What is Moore's Law and how does it affect companies?

10. List the business benefits of using grid computing.

11. Identify the benefits and challenges of cloud computing.

12. What is a data center and why would a business develop one?

13. List and describe the three most popular cloud computing delivery models.

14. Why would a company want to use virtualization?

15. Explain why a business today would want to follow sustainable MIS practices.

16. Explain why ebusiness is contributing to the three pressures driving sustainable MIS infrastructures.

CLOSING CASE ONE

Etsy

What do orthopedic surgery and governing a country have in common with knitting socks, scarves, and headbands? Nothing except the salary. Hobbyist Alicia Shaffer is earning $80,000 a month selling her handmade goods on Etsy, which adds up to an annual revenue of $960,000. That is the same amount as an orthopedic surgeon makes and more than twice as much as the U.S. president makes.

Etsy is an online craft makerspace for handmade goods. Etsy is building a human, authentic, and community-centric makerspace that uses the power of business to create a better world. In an Etsy economy, creative entrepreneurs can find meaningful work selling their goods in both global and local markets, where thoughtful consumers can discover those goods and build relationships with the people who make and sell them. It's an ecosystem that connects buyers around the world to the communities where Etsy shop owners live, work, and create. As Etsy grows, it is committed to its mission to ensure its core values are woven into all decisions it makes for the long-term health of its business, from the sourcing of office supplies to employee benefits to the items sold in its marketspace.

Shaffer's company, ThreeBirdNest, is named after her bird tattoo that honors her three children. Shaffer attributes her success to deep-seated motivation and access to a global supply chain through Etsy. ThreeBirdNest launched in 2011, when she made a few headbands for the small women's clothing boutique she ran in Livermore, California. Her headbands were so popular she decided to start selling them online. "I opened an Etsy shop, figuring I'd help pay for my kids' soccer and dance lessons to supplement the boutique's sales," states Shaffer. "I was recovering from the failure of a business I'd run selling baby products—handmade slings, carriers, and blankets. After that business tanked in the recession, I'd lost a little bit of confidence in my ability to be an entrepreneur."

In the first few weeks after its launch, ThreeBirdNest made 90 sales. Shaffer credits much of the traffic to Pinterest, where she pinned her items. Still, she said, "It was absolutely mindboggling. I thought it was a complete fluke." But a few months later, Shaffer found herself hiring a friend to help with shipping as orders began flowing like water. Through its independent website and Etsy shop, ThreeBirdNest receives an average of 150 orders per day, with most orders consisting of three items. Around the holidays, that number goes up to 700 to 1,200 orders per day. Last January, the business raked in a total of $128,000 in sales. Since its launch, it has made 100,000 sales on Etsy alone. ThreeBirdNest is unusually successful on Etsy, as most Etsy shop owners feel lucky to sell 10 pieces a month, and 65 percent of Etsy sellers make less than $100 from their shops in a year. Etsy makerspace crafters usually need day jobs to support their hobbies.[15]

QUESTIONS

1. Why is an agile MIS infrastructure important to Etsy's business?

2. Why is a disaster recovery plan important to Etsy?

3. What are the advantages and disadvantages of using Etsy to sell products?

4. Apply the concepts of cloud computing to Etsy's business model.

5. How is Etsy's business model similar to Software as a Service or utility computing?

Interest in Pinterest

Pinterest has been called the latest addiction for millions of people around the world. Pinterest, a visual social media network, allows users to create "interest boards" where they "pin" items of interests found on the web. Terms you need to understand to use Pinterest include:

- **Pin:** A link to an image from a computer or a website. Pins can include captions for other users. Users upload, or "pin," photos or videos to boards.
- **Board:** Pins live on boards and users can maintain separate boards, which can be categorized by activity or interests, such as cooking, do-it-yourself activities, fitness, music, movies, and so on.
- **Repin:** After pinning an item, it can be repinned by other Pinterest users, spreading the content virally. Repinning allows users to share items they like with friends and family.

"Pinning" is simply done by clicking on a photo or video that captures the attention of a user, whether it be by uploading personal photos or repinning a photo or video from a fellow user. Started in 2010, Pinterest has already attracted over 10 million users with the majority being women between the ages of 25 and 54. Millions of people visit the website each day to find what new items will spark their interest as there are always more and more things to see.

Pinterest is considered a social network, but unlike other social networks, such as Twitter and Facebook, Pinterest is open to invited users only, meaning it is an invitation-only website and users must "ask" for an invitation before gaining access. Upon accepting the invitation, users can gain access to the website and begin inviting their own "friends" with whom they have connections on Facebook or Twitter. Pinterest's mission statement:[16]

> connect everyone in the world through the 'things' they find interesting. We think that a favorite book, toy, or recipe can reveal a common link between two people. With millions of new pins added every week, Pinterest is connecting people all over the world based on shared tastes and interests.

Just like on other social networks, Pinterest users can compile a list of people they want to follow. A user can link a Pinterest board to a Facebook account, allowing instant access to quickly see which of his or her Facebook friends are on the social network. Adding bookmarks allows the user to pin images to other websites such as a book at Barnes & Noble or a set of mugs at Pier 1 Imports. The image is automatically linked to the retailer's website, and if another user clicks on the image, that user receives additional information on the product or service. If users pin a specific image of a plate or sweater, they can add the item's price in the description, which will automatically place a banner ad on the image and show the listed price. If users are unsure of what they are looking for, they can search for a specific event or theme such as "twenty-first birthday party" for a whole array of ideas.

Essentially, Pinterest allows users to paint a visual picture. Just imagine a wedding planner talking to a bride about her upcoming event, and the bride mentions she would like a "classic modernism" wedding. If the wedding planner were confused about what exactly the bride meant by classic modernism, she could quickly visit Pinterest to find an entire suite of photos and videos to spark ideas of how to coordinate the event.

The Business Value of Pinterest

Visual Communication

Pinterest is by far one of the hottest social media spaces available today. Offering all kinds of valuable information from useful cleaning tips to fantastic recipes to beautiful photos and videos, the website is extremely valuable for sharing anything visual. Pinterest is in no way simply a passing fad as companies begin to use the website for social marketing.

One of the best business uses of Pinterest is allowing employees to visually communicate and brainstorm. Visual communication is a new experience for many employees, and the phrase "A picture is worth a thousand words" can help a company perform many tasks, from generating new products to transforming business processes. In fact, many companies are using Pinterest to solicit feedback directly from employees, customers, and suppliers to ensure the company is operating efficiently and effectively. Soliciting feedback directly from customers allows companies to have a customer service support team handle problems before they become mainstream issues. Providing customers with a new channel to post their thoughts and concerns about products or services can provide valuable feedback for any company. Companies typically state that they may not respond to every question or comment but that they take each and every concern into account, demonstrating that they are devoted to creating a bond between themselves and their customers.

Driving Traffic

Pinterest drives traffic—it is that simple! Even though the website operates under an invitation-only model, it has attracted more than 10 million users in less than two years. That number might seem small compared to powerhouses such as Facebook, Twitter, or Google, but it demonstrates there is enough of an audience to send a decent amount of traffic to any business. The images a business pins up should be linked to the relevant page of its website. If users are attracted by it, they may click on it to find out more.

Pinterest also drives traffic by providing higher rankings on search engine optimization as companies appear higher and higher on search lists the more users are pinning to their boards. Linking is one of the key factors search engines consider, and with Pinterest gaining in popularity, it is also growing as a trustworthy domain. The number of Pinterest users combined with its ability to increase search rankings will play an important role when a company is looking to increase visibility and drive traffic to its website. Data from Shareholic found that Pinterest sent more referral traffic to bloggers than Google+, YouTube, and LinkedIn combined, falling just behind Twitter.

Product Branding

Pinterest is an extraordinary branding tool, offering a place where companies can create a presence and community around a product, idea, event, or company. Just like other social networking websites, Pinterest allows a company to reach out and engage its customers, vendors, suppliers, and even employees to communicate about its products and services. Recently the National Football League's Minnesota Vikings began using Pinterest to create a following of favorite photos, statistics, and even game-day recipes!

Pinterest recently deployed an iPhone application that allows users to pin photos and video from their cameras instantly on their boards. Pinterest's unique competitive advantage is its ability to host billions of images and redirect users to the appropriate sources in a user-friendly interface.

Pinterest's Dilemma

Since its inception, Pinterest has been under fire from sites such as Flikr, Photobucket, and Instagram over attributing credit to those who own the images that are pinned. Many users are concerned that they may one day be sued for the improper use of an image they pinned.

The Pinterest Terms of Use state, "If you are a copyright owner, or are authorized to act on behalf of one, or authorized to act under any exclusive right under copyright, please report alleged copyright infringements taking place on or through the Site by completing the following DMCA Notice of Alleged Infringement and delivering it to Pinterest's Designated Copyright Agent."

To protect Pinterest from third-party litigation claims (such as those from authors claiming copyright infringement), Pinterest has incorporated the following statement into its indemnity clause: "You agree to indemnify and hold harmless Pinterest and its officers, directors, employees and agents, from and against any claims, suits, proceedings, disputes, demands, liabilities, damages, losses, costs and expenses, including, without limitation, reasonable legal and accounting fees (including costs of defense of claims, suits or proceedings brought by third parties), arising out of or in any way related to (i) your access to or use of the Services or Pinterest Content, (ii) your User Content, or (iii) your breach of any of these Terms."

Pinterest is well aware of the probability that many of the pinned images might be violating copyright infringement and is attempting to protect itself against any litigation claims resulting from users intentionally or unintentionally breaking the law through its site.[17]

Questions

1. Why do the three different types of MIS infrastructures matter to Pinterest's business model?
2. What types of security and ethical dilemmas are facing Pinterest?
3. How does cloud computing support Pinterest's business model?

CRITICAL BUSINESS THINKING

1. Universities Are Switching to Gmail

Schools around the world are moving to cloud computing applications such as Google Docs & Spreadsheets and Google Calendar. Yale University had planned to move from its own email system to Google Mail but at the last minute decided to cancel the project because school administrators and faculty members did not believe the move could support their business requirements. Do you agree or disagree that Google Gmail would be unable to replace a university's private email system? What are the advantages and disadvantages of a private email system? What are the advantages and disadvantages of using a cloud application such as Google Gmail? What choice would you make if you were the primary decision maker for choosing your school's email system?

2. Desktop Virtualization

Every day users are becoming more comfortable with accessing and storing information in the cloud. This creates increased demand on MIS personnel to help manage, control, and provide access to that information—not just on company-issued computers but on any number of devices, including personal ones. More and more employees want to be able to use their own computing devices—cell phones, netbooks, laptops—instead of company-issued ones. For instance, many students graduating from college have been exposed to Macs and may even own one, yet they are finding PCs as the standard computer of choice for most companies. Do you think it is a good business practice to allow your employees to use their personal devices for work-related business? What are the challenges of allowing users to port business applications to their personal devices? What are the challenges of allowing users to connect to corporate systems with personal devices?

3. I Don't Have a Temperature, But I'm Positive I Have a Virus

Think how horrible it would be to finish your term paper at 4 a.m. and find out that your computer has a virus and you just lost your entire document. Or perhaps you submit your final paper, which is worth 50 percent of your grade, and then head off to Colorado for winter break. You return to find that you failed the course, and you frantically check email to find out what happened. A message from your professor informs you that your document was corrupt and couldn't be opened and that you had 24 hours to resend the file, which you missed because you were skiing down the slopes.

Have you ever experienced having a file corrupted? If so, what could you have done to recover from this situation? Do you think your instructor ever receives corrupted files? How did the file become corrupted? Do you think your instructor would be suspicious if you submitted a corrupted file?

4. Sustainable Departments

Energy prices and global warming are discussed daily in the news as the environmental impact of ewaste is just beginning to be recognized. Sustainability and corporate social responsibility need to be taken seriously by all managers because everyone should take an active role in helping to preserve the environment. List the different departments in a business and the types of environmental issues they typically encounter. Which department do you think creates the most ewaste? Which department uses the greatest amount of electricity or has the largest carbon footprint? What can each department do to help combat its environmental issues? Why do all managers and, for that matter, all employees need to be aware of environmental issues and ways they can create sustainable MIS infrastructures?

5. Facebook's Energy Use

Cheap electricity is great for keeping business costs down, but it often means relying on coal for power. Facebook recently commissioned a new computing facility in Oregon and is using power from PacifiCorp, a utility that gets the majority of its energy from coal-fired power stations, which are major contributors of greenhouse gas emissions. As more and more people subscribe to Facebook, its energy needs are increasing almost exponentially.

Do you agree that Facebook made a wise business decision in selecting a utility provider that uses coal-fired power stations? What alternative sources of energy could Facebook have used to power its computing facility? Do you think Facebook's core customers care about the environment? What types of business challenges might Facebook encounter if it continues using coal-fired power stations?

6. Planning for Disaster Recovery

You are the new senior analyst in the MIS department at Beltz, a large snack food manufacturing company. The company is located on the beautiful shoreline in Charleston, South Carolina. The company's location is one of its best and worst features. The weather and surroundings are beautiful, but the threat of hurricanes and other natural disasters is high. What types of information should be contained in Beltz's disaster recovery plan that will minimize any risks involved with a natural disaster?

7. Comparing Backup and Recovery Systems

Research the Internet to find three vendors of backup and recovery systems. Compare and contrast the three systems, and determine which one you would recommend if you were installing a backup and recovery system for a medium-sized business with 3,500 employees that maintains information on the stock market. Compile your findings in a presentation that you can give to your class that details the three systems' strengths and weaknesses, along with your recommendation.

8. Cool Schools

Very large computers and data centers incur huge energy costs keeping electronic components cooled. Where is your school's data center located? How big is it? What security measures does the facility enforce? Can you get a tour of it? If it is on campus, how is the facility cooled? How is the power supplied? Heating and cooling computer systems are certainly a big issue. Think of ways you could reuse the heat from a data center, such as sending it to a college dorm. Could alternative resources, such as a nearby river or a lake, provide added cooling? What environmental issues could this create?

PROJECT I   Ranking MIS Characteristics

In a group, review the list of MIS infrastructure characteristics that support growth and rank them in order of their impact on a company's success, using 1 to indicate the biggest impact and 7 the least.

MIS Infrastructure Characteristics	Business Impact
Accessibility	
Availability	
Maintainability	
Portability	
Reliability	
Scalability	
Usability	

PROJECT II   Designing a Company Infrastructure

Components of an MIS infrastructure include everything from documentation to business concepts to software and hardware. Deciding which components to implement and how to implement them can be a challenge. New MIS components are released daily, and business needs continually change. An MIS infrastructure that meets your company's needs today may not meet those needs tomorrow. Building an MIS infrastructure that is accessible, available, flexible, reliable, scalable, and usable and performs well is key to your company's growth, operations, and profitability.

You are the manager for a large clothing company called Xedous. You are responsible for developing the initial MIS infrastructure. Create a list of questions you will need answered to develop it. Here are examples of a few of the questions you might ask:

- What are the company's growth expectations?
- Will systems be able to handle additional users?
- How long will information be stored in the systems?
- How much customer history must be stored?
- What are the company's business hours?
- What are the company's backup requirements?

PROJECT III   Recycle Your Cell Phone

For all those excited to get a new iPhone with its numerous applications and cool games, what will you do with your old cell phone? You can help the environment and recycle your phone, PDA, charger, and batteries. Recycling cell phones helps save energy and keep reusable materials out of landfills. Cell phones are made of plastic, copper, and precious metals, which require energy to extract and manufacture. If you decide to recycle your cell phone, be sure to terminate the service, delete any contacts or stored information, and take out the SIM card.

If your old cell phone is still working, you might also want to consider donating it to charity. Many programs will accept working cell phones that they donate to people in need, such as survivors of domestic violence, because old cell phones can still dial 911 even after the service is disconnected. To find local agencies where you can donate your cell phone, visit ncadv.org. Cell phones are only a small percentage of the total computer equipment organizations replace each year. What happens to all of those old laptops, notebooks, servers, and monitors? What is the environmental impact of throwing a computer system into a landfill? What can companies do to recycle their computer equipment? What can the government do to help motivate companies and individuals to recycle?

PROJECT VI Back on Your Feet

You are working for GetSmart, a document creation company for legal professionals. Due to the highly sensitive nature of their work, employees must store all information on the network drive and are not allowed to back up the data to a CD, flash drive, or any other type of external storage, including home computers. The company has been following this policy for the past three years without any problems. You return to work Monday morning after a long weekend to find that the building was struck by lightning, destroying several servers. Unfortunately, the backup network also failed, so all the data from your department have been lost.

Because of this loss, the MIS manager and four colleagues who developed the company backup policy were fired.

You have been placed on a committee with several of your peers to revamp the backup and recovery policies and create a new disaster recovery plan. You must create policies and procedures that will preserve the sensitive nature of the documents while ensuring that the company is safe from disasters. Be sure to address a worst-case scenario in which the entire building is lost.

PROJECT V Growing, Growing, Gone

You are the founder of Black Pearl, a small comic book start-up. The good news is Black Pearl is tremendously successful, with 34 employees in a functional and creative office in downtown Chicago. The comics you produce are of extremely high quality. The artwork is unmatched, and fans find the story lines compelling. Black Pearl comics are quickly becoming classics with extremely loyal customers. You produce all the comics and sell them in your store and via the Internet to individuals all over the United States.

You had a vision when you started Black Pearl. You knew the potential of your business model to revamp the comic industry. You purchased high-end computers and customizable software to support your operations. Now, you are faced with a new dilemma. You have a large international following, and you have decided to pursue international opportunities. You would like to open stores in Japan, France, and Brazil over the next year. To determine whether this is possible, you need to evaluate whether your MIS infrastructure is agile enough to support international requirements. Brainstorm all of the business nuances that will be different when working with international companies and customers. Create a list of questions your MIS department will need to answer to determine whether your system is agile enough to support international business.

PROJECT VI Excuses, Excuses, Excuses

Here are a few examples of the strangest and most unusual excuses employees use when missing work.

- I have a sunburn.
- I'm not sure why but I woke up in Canada.
- I was caught selling an alligator.
- I was locked in the trunk of an abandoned car.
- I have a note from my mom that I could not go to work yesterday.
- I'm just not into it today.
- I was riding my motorcycle and I accidentally hit a nun.
- Some person threw poison ivy at me and now I have a rash on my face.
- I need to stay home as I am convinced I can catch my spouse having an affair.
- I was chasing a seagull and fell down and had to go to the hospital.
- I have a migraine from eating too many jalapeño peppers.

This chapter focuses on MIS infrastructures, the main building blocks that function together to control the entire organization's systems. If your systems cannot operate, then your organization cannot work, similar to how your health controls your ability to work. Attempting to do business with an organization when its systems have crashed, Internet access is down, or the wireless network is malfunctioning is very frustrating. When these types of issues occur, companies do not want to broadcast that they are experiencing technical difficulties because of hackers, an unpaid utility bill, or squirrels got into the data center and ate through all of the wires (yes, that has really happened).

How many times have you called a company and the customer service representative has stated that the system is down or that the system is really slow today? How many times have you missed submitting an assignment because your Internet service was down? Why is it important for an organization's systems to be available 24 hours a day, 7 days a week, and 365 days a year? Why would a company hide the real reason that its systems are malfunctioning? What could happen if customers were informed that the systems were down due to hackers? How can an organization safeguard its systems?

PROJECT VII   Ewaste Not, Want Not

On Earth Day every year, many people, including corporate citizens, devote themselves to recycling and reducing, along with identifying items they can repurpose. Companies such as Dell and Microsoft, two producers of materials that eventually become ewaste, have joined forces with an electronics recycling program run by Goodwill Industries International. Goodwill reports that the program has diverted about 96 million pounds in electronics from landfills.[18]

Assisting in a similar effort are office supply stores Office Depot and Staples, which offer their own sorting and recycling services for used electronics. Apple has even jumped on this bandwagon, allowing customers to turn their old products in to retail locations when they buy something new.

There are so many opportunities to reduce ewaste. Make a list of how the popular technology manufacturers are already trying to reduce ewaste. Would starting a company that helped people locate used computers or other technologies for reuse be a worthwhile venture? Why or why not? Create a list of new alternatives any company could adopt to reuse, recycle, and reduce ewaste.

PROJECT VIII   One Laptop Per Child

The One Laptop Per Child (OLPC) project intends to create a $100 laptop for distribution to the world's poorest children. The machine, called the OLPC or XO laptop, has a rubberized keyboard and an ultra-bright screen readable in daylight; when flipped, it converts to an electronic book reader. To keep the cost as low as possible (at $175, it is currently a bit more than the target), the computer has a host of free software and other tools to support learning opportunities. A special type of networking allows machines within 100 feet or so to communicate with each other and relays a single Internet connection for them to use (where the Internet is available). The XO is targeted at communities where power generation is unreliable or nonexistent; it gets its power via a hand crank, pull cord, or foot pedal.[19]

Do you agree that the One Laptop Per Child project will help educate children around the world? How does the XO computer provide learning opportunities for children in poor regions of the world? What issues could these children encounter if they have an XO laptop? How will cloud computing play an important role in the XO laptop, especially in terms of keeping costs low and data safe? What do you think the typical environment will be like where the XO laptop will be used? What issues will users of the XO laptop encounter that are not common in the United States? What can the creators of the XO laptop do to ensure its functionality even in the most extreme environments?

PROJECT XI   Virtualizing Your Cell Phone

Virtualization is a challenging concept to understand. The formal definition is that it creates multiple virtual machines on a single computing device. OK, let's try that again in English. Imagine you have three cell phones, one for the company you work for, one for a company you are starting on the side, and one for personal calls. For the most part, the phones are idle, and they seldom ever ring at the same time. Since the phones are idle the majority of the time, you notice that it is a waste of time and resources to support idle time, especially when you are paying for cell service on each phone. You decide to use virtualization to help your situation.

Essentially, this would put three virtual cell phones on one device. The individual services and applications for each phone would be independently stored on the one device. From the device's perspective, it sees three virtual phones. This saves time and money in expenses and maintenance.[20]

Virtualization is a hot topic these days because more and more businesses are focusing on social responsibility and attempting to find ways to reduce their carbon footprints. Create an analogy similar to the cell phone that demonstrates virtualization. What are the potential environmental impacts associated with virtualization? What are the business advantages of virtualization? What are the business risks associated with virtualization?

PROJECT X Data Centers on the High Seas

Google is considering constructing a floating data center three to seven miles offshore that could be both powered and cooled by the ocean. It would consist of containers stacked with servers, data storage systems, and networking equipment on barges or other platforms and could be located close to users wherever it is not feasible, cost-effective, or efficient to build on land. Bringing the data closer to the user allows the data to arrive quicker. And since the ocean is a rent-free space, data centers can be as large as 100,000 square feet without real estate fees. The ocean can provide two critical factors that support a sustainable MIS infrastructure—water for cooling and power.[21]

What are the advantages and disadvantages of housing data centers in the ocean? Do you foresee any issues for these data centers with natural disasters? What types of security issues would Google encounter with a floating data center? Do you agree that it is good business sense to house a data center on a barge in the ocean? Why or why not?

AYK APPLICATION PROJECTS

If you are looking for Excel projects to incorporate into your class, try any of the following after reading this chapter.

Project Number	Project Name	Project Type	Plug-In	Focus Area	Project Level	Skill Set	Page Number
8	Book Boxes	Excel	T2, T4	Strategic Analysis	Intermediate	Formulas or Solver	AYK.6
9	Security Analysis	Excel	T3	Filtering Data	Intermediate	Conditional Formatting, Autofilter, Subtotal	AYK.7
10	Gathering Data	Excel	T3	Data Analysis	Intermediate	Conditional Formatting	AYK.8
11	Splashem	Excel	T2	Strategic Analysis	Intermediate	Formulas	AYK.8
12	Bill's Boots	Excel	T2	Profit Maximization	Intermediate	Formulas	AYK.9
13	Adequate Acquisitions	Excel	T2	Break Even Analysis	Intermediate	Formulas	AYK.9
15	Assessing the Value of Information	Excel	T3	Data Analysis	Intermediate	PivotTable	AYK.10
16	Growth, Trends, and Forecasts	Excel	T2, T3	Data Forecasting	Advanced	Average, Trend, Growth	AYK.11
18	Formatting Grades	Excel	T3	Data Analysis	Advanced	If, LookUp	AYK.12
22	Gizmo Turnover	Excel	T3	Data Mining	Advanced	PivotTable	AYK.15
24	Mountain Cycle	Excel	T4	Business Analysis	Advanced	Goal Seek	AYK.16
25	Lutz Motors	Excel	T4	Sales Analysis	Advanced	Scenario Manager	AYK.16

6

CHAPTER

Data: Business Intelligence

CHAPTER OUTLINE

SECTION 6.1 Data, Information, and Databases	**SECTION 6.2** Business Intelligence

▪ The Business Benefits of
  High-Quality Information
▪ Storing Information Using
  a Relational Database
  Management System
▪ Using a Relational Database
  for Business Advantages
▪ Driving Websites with Data
	▪ Supporting Decisions with
	  Business Intelligence
	▪ Business Intelligence
	▪ The Power of Big Data Analytics
	▪ Data Mining
	▪ Data Analytics

What's in IT for me?

This chapter introduces the concepts of information and data and their relative importance to business professionals and firms. It distinguishes between data stored in transactional databases and powerful business intelligence gleaned from data warehouses. Students who understand how to access, manipulate, summarize, sort, and analyze data to support decision making find success. Information has power, and understanding that power will help you compete in the global marketplace. This chapter will provide you with an overview of database fundamentals and the characteristics associated with high-quality information. It will also explain how the various bits of data stored across multiple, operational databases can be transformed in a centralized repository of summarized information in a data warehouse, which can be used for discovering business intelligence.

You, as a business student, need to understand the differences between transactional data and summarized information and the different types of questions you could use a transactional database versus a data warehouse to answer. You need to be aware of the complexity of storing data in databases and the level of effort required to transform operational data into meaningful, summarized information. You need to realize the power of information and the competitive advantage a data warehouse brings an organization in terms of facilitating business intelligence. Armed with the power of information, business students will make smart, informed, and data-supported managerial decisions.

©Image Source/Getty Images RF   ©Maciej Frolow/Getty Images RF   ©C. Zachariasen/PhotoAlto RF

Big Data, Big Business, Big Opportunities

Imagine working 10 years to become the lead marketing executive at a large retail organization to find that your competitor is invading your market share by 20 percent each year. You quickly decided to launch several online marketing promotions while improving your products only to find your efforts are fruitless as your competitor continues to steal your customers, destroying your profits while raising its own.

As you begin to analyze your competitor's business strategy, you find that while you were focused on sales reports, product inventory analysis, and other traditional marketing efforts, your competitor was making a massive investment in upgrading all of its management information systems. This included systems capable of collecting, storing, and analyzing data from every store, product, and sales representative in the market. In fact, your competitor now knows more about your products and sales cycles than you do. The new systems not only collect data throughout its company but also from a group of suppliers, retailers, and distributors around the globe. These new systems provide your competitor with the ability to adjust prices instantly based on daily customer traffic patterns, reorder automatically from every entity in the supply chains, and even move items within a store or between stores for maximum selling efficiencies.

Your competitor has won and not because it had a higher-quality product or better sales and marketing strategies but because it identified the value of management information systems coupled with the ability to instantly access big data within and beyond the organization. You quickly realize that your competitor's agility simply cannot be mimicked, offering it a huge competitive advantage. You sigh as you realize your company is in big trouble because it did not understand the dynamics of the big data age.

We are all familiar with the information age and the improvements made to organizations around the world as they are able to better manage employees, track sales information, and analyze customer purchasing patterns. However, this scenario is an example of the game-changing impact of big data, the massive amounts of data being collected by humans and machines over the last few years. Companies are now capturing hundreds of terabytes of data on everything from operations and finances to weather patterns and stock market trends. Sensors are now embedded in everything from products and machines to store floors, collecting real-time data on operations and customers. Radical customization, continuous experimentation, and information-driven business models are the new trademarks of competition as organizations analyze massive volumes of data. Data volumes are exploding, and more data has been created in the past 2 years than in the entire previous history of the human race. Here are the top 20 facts every manager should know about big data, according to *Forbes* magazine.[1]

- Data is growing faster than ever before, and by the year 2020, about 1.7 megabytes of new information will be created every second for every human being on the planet.

- By 2020, our accumulated digital universe of data will grow from 4.4 zettabytes today to around 44 zettabytes, or 44 trillion gigabytes.

- Every second we create new data. For example, we perform 40,000 search queries every second (on Google alone), which makes it 3.5 searches per day and 1.2 trillion searches per year.

- In 2015, over 1 billion people used Facebook each day.

- Facebook users send on average 31.25 million messages and view 2.77 million videos every minute.

- Every minute, up to 300 hours of video are uploaded to YouTube alone.

- In 2015, a staggering 1 trillion photos will be taken, and billions of them will be shared online. By 2017, nearly 80 percent of photos will be taken on smart phones.

- This year, over 1.4 billion smart phones will be shipped—all packed with sensors capable of collecting all kinds of data, not to mention the data the users create themselves.

- By 2020, we will have over 6.1 billion smart phone users globally (overtaking basic fixed phone subscriptions).

- Within 5 years, there will be over 50 billion smart connected devices in the world, all developed to collect, analyze, and share data.

- By 2020, at least a third of all data will pass through the cloud (a network of servers connected over the Internet).

- Distributed computing (performing computing tasks using a network of computers in the cloud) is very real. Google uses it every day to involve about 1,000 computers in answering a single search query, which takes no more than a second to complete.

- The Hadoop (open source software for distributed computing) market is forecast to grow at a compound annual growth rate of 58 percent, surpassing $1 billion by 2020.

- Estimates suggest that by better integrating big data, health care could save as much as $300 billion a year—that's equal to reducing costs by $1,000 a year for every man, woman, and child.

- The White House has already invested more than $200 million in big data projects.

- For a typical *Fortune* 1000 company, just a 10 percent increase in data accessibility will result in more than $65 million additional net income.

- Retailers who leverage the full power of big data could increase their operating margins by as much as 60 percent.

- Almost 80 percent of organizations have already invested or plan to invest in big data.

- At the moment, less than 0.5 percent of all data is ever analyzed or used.

section 6.1 | Data, Information, and Databases

THE BUSINESS BENEFITS OF HIGH-QUALITY INFORMATION

LO 6.1: Explain the four primary traits that determine the value of information.

Information is powerful. Information can tell an organization how its current operations are performing and help it estimate and strategize about how future operations might perform. The ability to understand, digest, analyze, and filter information is key to growth and success for any professional in any industry. Remember that new perspectives and opportunities can open up when you have the right data that you can turn into information and ultimately business intelligence.

Information is everywhere in an organization. Managers in sales, marketing, human resources, and management need information to run their departments and make daily decisions. When addressing a significant business issue, employees must be able to obtain and analyze all the relevant information so they can make the best decision possible. Information comes at different levels, formats, and granularities. *Information granularity* refers to the extent of detail within the information (fine and detailed or coarse and abstract). Employees must be able to correlate the different levels, formats, and granularities of information when making decisions. For example, a company might be collecting information from various suppliers to make needed decisions, only to find that the information is in different levels, formats, and granularities. One supplier might send detailed information in a spreadsheet, whereas another supplier might send summary information in a Word document, and still another might send a collection of information from emails. Employees will need to compare these differing types of information for what they commonly reveal to make strategic decisions. Figure 6.1 displays the various levels, formats, and granularities of organizational information.

Successfully collecting, compiling, sorting, and finally analyzing information from multiple levels, in varied formats, and exhibiting different granularities can provide tremendous insight into how an organization is performing. Exciting and unexpected results can include potential new markets, new ways of reaching customers, and even new methods of doing business. After understanding the different levels, formats, and granularities of information, managers next want to look at the four primary traits that help determine the value of information (see Figure 6.2).

Information Type: Transactional and Analytical

As discussed previously in the text, the two primary types of information are transactional and analytical. Transactional information encompasses all of the information contained within a single business process or unit of work, and its primary purpose is to support daily operational tasks. Organizations need to capture and store transactional information to perform operational tasks and repetitive decisions such as analyzing daily sales reports and production schedules to determine how much inventory to carry. Consider Walmart, which handles more than 1 million customer transactions every hour, and Facebook, which keeps track of 400 million active users (along with their photos, friends, and web links). In addition, every time a cash register rings up a sale, a deposit or withdrawal is made from an ATM, or a receipt is given at the gas pump, the transactional information must be captured and stored.

Analytical information encompasses all organizational information, and its primary purpose is to support the performance of managerial analysis tasks. Analytical information is useful when making important decisions such as whether the organization should build a new manufacturing plant or hire additional sales personnel. Analytical information makes it possible to do many things that previously were difficult to accomplish, such as spot business trends, prevent diseases,

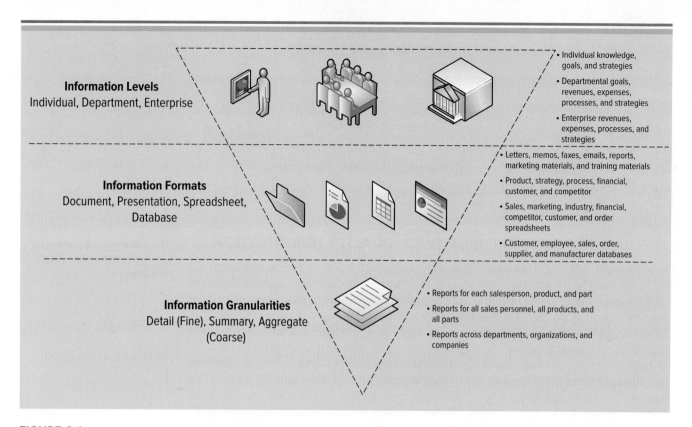

FIGURE 6.1

Levels, Formats, and Granularities of Organizational Information

Information Levels
Individual, Department, Enterprise

- Individual knowledge, goals, and strategies
- Departmental goals, revenues, expenses, processes, and strategies
- Enterprise revenues, expenses, processes, and strategies

Information Formats
Document, Presentation, Spreadsheet, Database

- Letters, memos, faxes, emails, reports, marketing materials, and training materials
- Product, strategy, process, financial, customer, and competitor
- Sales, marketing, industry, financial, competitor, customer, and order spreadsheets
- Customer, employee, sales, order, supplier, and manufacturer databases

Information Granularities
Detail (Fine), Summary, Aggregate (Coarse)

- Reports for each salesperson, product, and part
- Reports for all sales personnel, all products, and all parts
- Reports across departments, organizations, and companies

and fight crime. For example, credit card companies crunch through billions of transactional purchase records to identify fraudulent activity. Indicators such as charges in a foreign country or consecutive purchases of gasoline send a red flag highlighting potential fraudulent activity.

Walmart was able to use its massive amount of analytical information to identify many unusual trends, such as a correlation between storms and Pop-Tarts. Yes, Walmart discovered an increase in the demand for Pop-Tarts during the storm season. Armed with that valuable information, the retail chain was able to stock up on Pop-Tarts that were ready for purchase when customers arrived. Figure 6.3 displays different types of transactional and analytical information.

Information Timeliness

Timeliness is an aspect of information that depends on the situation. In some firms or industries, information that is a few days or weeks old can be relevant, whereas in others, information that is a few minutes old can be almost worthless. Some organizations, such as 911 response centers, stock traders, and banks, require up-to-the-second information. Other organizations, such as insurance and construction companies, require only daily or even weekly information.

FIGURE 6.2

The Four Primary Traits of the Value of Information

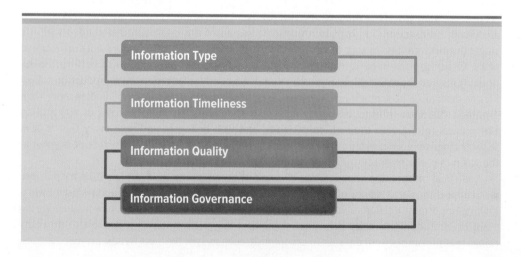

- Information Type
- Information Timeliness
- Information Quality
- Information Governance

FIGURE 6.3

Transactional versus Analytical Information

Transactional Information

- Airline Ticket
- Sales Receipt
- Packing Slip

Database

Analytical Information

- Product Statistics
- Sales Projections
- Future Growth
- Trends

Real-time information means immediate, up-to-date information. *Real-time systems* provide real-time information in response to requests. Many organizations use real-time systems to uncover key corporate transactional information. The growing demand for real-time information stems from organizations' need to make faster and more effective decisions, keep smaller inventories, operate more efficiently, and track performance more carefully. Information also needs to be timely in the sense that it meets employees' needs but no more. If employees can absorb information only on an hourly or daily basis, there is no need to gather real-time information in smaller increments.

Most people request real-time information without understanding one of the biggest pitfalls associated with real-time information—continual change. Imagine the following scenario: Three managers meet at the end of the day to discuss a business problem. Each manager has gathered information at different times during the day to create a picture of the situation. Each manager's picture may be different because of the time differences. Their views on the business problem may not match because the information they are basing their analysis on is continually changing. This approach may not speed up decision making, and it may actually slow it down. Business decision makers must evaluate the timeliness of the information for every decision. Organizations do not want to find themselves using real-time information to make a bad decision faster.

Information Quality

Business decisions are only as good as the quality of the information used to make them. *Information inconsistency* occurs when the same data element has different values. Take, for example, the amount of work that needs to occur to update a customer who had changed her last name due to marriage. Changing this information in only a few organizational systems will lead to data inconsistencies, causing customer 123456 to be associated with two last names. *Information integrity issues* occur when a system produces incorrect, inconsistent, or duplicate data. Data integrity issues can cause managers to consider the system reports invalid and make decisions based on other sources.

To ensure that your systems do not suffer from data integrity issues, review Figure 6.4 for the five characteristics common to high-quality information: accuracy, completeness, consistency, timeliness, and uniqueness. Figure 6.5 provides an example of several problems associated with using low-quality information, including:

1. *Completeness.* The customer's first name is missing.

2. Another issue with *completeness.* The street address contains only a number and not a street name.

3. *Consistency.* There may be a duplication of information since there is a slight difference between the two customers in the spelling of the last name. Similar street addresses and phone numbers make this likely.

FIGURE 6.4

Five Common Characteristics of
High-Quality Information

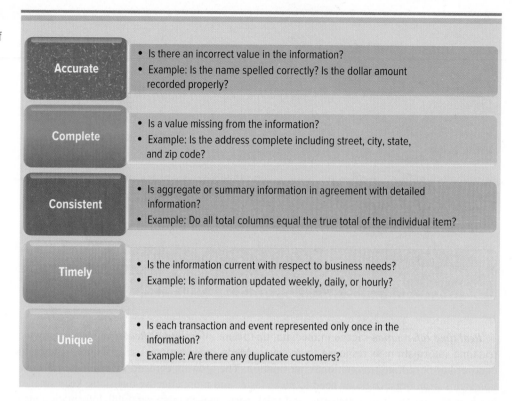

4. *Accuracy.* This may be inaccurate information because the customer's phone and fax numbers are the same. Some customers might have the same number for phone and fax, but the fact that the customer also has this number in the email address field is suspicious.

5. Another issue with *accuracy.* There is inaccurate information because a phone number is located in the email address field.

6. Another issue with *completeness.* The information is incomplete because there is not a valid area code for the phone and fax numbers.

Nestlé uses 550,000 suppliers to sell more than 100,000 products in 200 countries. However, due to poor information, the company was unable to evaluate its business effectively. After some analysis, it found that it had 9 million records of vendors, customers, and materials, half of which were duplicated, obsolete, inaccurate, or incomplete. The analysis discovered that some records abbreviated vendor names, and other records spelled out the vendor names. This created

FIGURE 6.5

Example of Low-Quality
Information

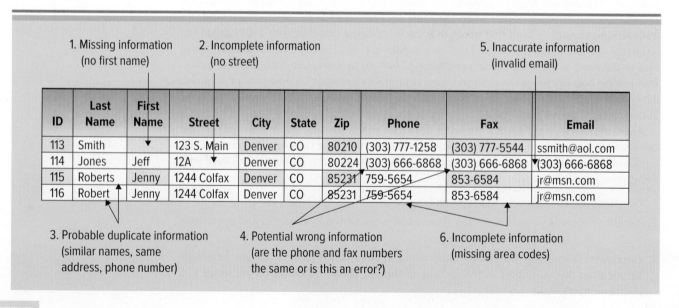

BUSINESS DRIVEN MIS

Determining Information Quality Issues

Real People magazine is geared toward working individuals and provides articles and advice on everything from car maintenance to family planning. The magazine is currently experiencing problems with its distribution list. More than 30 percent of the magazines mailed are returned because of incorrect address information, and each month it receives numerous calls from angry customers complaining that they have not yet received their magazines. Below is a sample of *Real People*'s customer information. Create a report detailing all the issues with the information, potential causes of the information issues, and solutions the company can follow to correct the situation.

ID	First Name	Middle Initial	Last Name	Street	City	State	Zip Code
433	M	J	Jones	13 Denver	Denver	CO	87654
434	Margaret	J	Jones	13 First Ave.	Denver	CO	87654
434	Brian	F	Hoover	Lake Ave.	Columbus	OH	87654
435	Nick	H	Schweitzer	65 Apple Lane	San Francisco	OH	65664
436	Richard	A		567 55th St.	New York	CA	98763
437	Alana	B	Smith	121 Tenny Dr.	Buffalo	NY	142234
438	Trevor	D	Darrian	90 Fresrdestil	Dallas	TX	74532

multiple accounts for the same customer, making it impossible to determine the true value of Nestlé's customers. Without being able to identify customer profitability, a company runs the risk of alienating its best customers.[2]

Knowing how low-quality information issues typically occur can help a company correct them. Addressing these errors will significantly improve the quality of company information and the value to be extracted from it. The four primary reasons for low-quality information are:

1. Online customers intentionally enter inaccurate information to protect their privacy.
2. Different systems have different information entry standards and formats.
3. Data-entry personnel enter abbreviated information to save time or erroneous information by accident.
4. Third-party and external information contains inconsistencies, inaccuracies, and errors.

Understanding the Costs of Using Low-Quality Information Using the wrong information can lead managers to make erroneous decisions. Erroneous decisions in turn can cost time, money, reputations, and even jobs. Some of the serious business consequences that occur due to using low-quality information to make decisions are:

- Inability to track customers accurately.
- Difficulty identifying the organization's most valuable customers.
- Inability to identify selling opportunities.
- Lost revenue opportunities from marketing to nonexistent customers.
- The cost of sending undeliverable mail.
- Difficulty tracking revenue because of inaccurate invoices.
- Inability to build strong relationships with customers.

A **data gap analysis** occurs when a company examines its data to determine if it can meet business expectations, while identifying possible data gaps or where missing data might exist.

Understanding the Benefits of Using High-Quality Information High-quality information can significantly improve the chances of making a good decision and directly increase an organization's bottom line. **Data stewardship** is the management and oversight of an organization's data assets to help provide business users with high-quality data that is easily accessible in a consistent manner. A **data steward** is responsible for ensuring the policies and procedures are implemented across the organization and acts as a liaison between the MIS department and the business. One company discovered that even with its large number of golf courses, Phoenix, Arizona, is not a good place to sell golf clubs. An analysis revealed that typical golfers in Phoenix are tourists and conventioneers who usually bring their clubs with them. The analysis further revealed that two of the best places to sell golf clubs in the United States are Rochester, New York, and Detroit, Michigan. Equipped with this valuable information, the company was able to strategically place its stores and launch its marketing campaigns.

High-quality information does not automatically guarantee that every decision made is going to be a good one, because people ultimately make decisions and no one is perfect. However, such information ensures that the basis of the decisions is accurate. The success of the organization depends on appreciating and leveraging the true value of timely and high-quality information.

Information Governance

Information is a vital resource, and users need to be educated on what they can and cannot do with it. To ensure that a firm manages its information correctly, it will need special policies and procedures establishing rules on how the information is organized, updated, maintained, and accessed. Every firm, large and small, should create an information policy concerning data governance. **Data governance** refers to the overall management of the availability, usability, integrity, and security of company data. **Master data management (MDM)** is the practice of gathering data and ensuring that it is uniform, accurate, consistent, and complete, including such entities as customers, suppliers, products, sales, employees, and other critical entities that are commonly integrated across organizational systems. MDM is commonly included in data governance. A company that supports a data governance program has a defined policy that specifies who is accountable for various portions or aspects of the data, including its accuracy, accessibility, consistency, timeliness, and completeness. The policy should clearly define the processes concerning how to store, archive, back up, and secure the data. In addition, the company should create a set of procedures identifying accessibility levels for employees. Then, the firm should deploy controls and procedures that enforce government regulations and compliance with mandates such as Sarbanes-Oxley.

It is important to note the difference between data governance and data stewardship. Data governance focuses on enterprisewide policies and procedures, while data stewardship focuses on the strategic implementation of the policies and procedures. **Data validation** includes the tests and evaluations used to determine compliance with data governance polices to ensure correctness of data. Data validation helps to ensure that every data value is correct and accurate. In Excel, you can use data validation to control the type of data or the values that users enter into a cell. For example, you may want to restrict data entry to a certain range of dates, limit choices by using a list, or make sure that only positive whole numbers are entered.

<table>
<tr><td>LO 6.2: Describe a database, a database management system, and the relational database model.</td></tr>
</table>

STORING INFORMATION USING A RELATIONAL DATABASE MANAGEMENT SYSTEM

The core component of any system, regardless of size, is a database and a database management system. Broadly defined, a **database** maintains information about various types of objects (inventory), events (transactions), people (employees), and places (warehouses). A **database management system (DBMS)** creates, reads, updates, and deletes data in a database while controlling access and security. Managers send requests to the DBMS, and the DBMS performs the actual manipulation of the data in the database. Companies store their information in databases, and managers access these systems to answer operational questions such as how many customers purchased Product A in December or what the average sales were by region. Two primary

BUSINESS DRIVEN DEBATE

Excel or Access?

Excel is a great tool with which to perform business analytics. Your friend, John Cross, owns a successful publishing company specializing in do-it-yourself books. John started the business 10 years ago and has slowly grown it to 50 employees and $1 million in sales. John has been using Excel to run the majority of his business, tracking book orders, production orders, shipping orders, and billing. John even uses Excel to track employee payroll and vacation dates. To date, Excel has done the job, but as the company continues to grow, the tool is becoming inadequate.

You believe John could benefit from moving from Excel to Access. John is skeptical of the change because Excel has done the job up to now and his employees are comfortable with the current processes and technology. John has asked you to prepare a presentation explaining the limitations of Excel and the benefits of Access. In a group, prepare the presentation that will help convince John to make the switch.

---

tools are available for retrieving information from a DBMS. First is a *query-by-example (QBE) tool* that helps users graphically design the answer to a question against a database. Second is a *structured query language (SQL)* that asks users to write lines of code to answer questions against a database. Managers typically interact with QBE tools, and MIS professionals have the skills required to code SQL. Figure 6.6 displays the relationship between a database, a DBMS, and a user. Some of the more popular examples of DBMS include MySQL, Microsoft Access, SQL Server, FileMaker, Oracle, and FoxPro.

A *data element (or data field)* is the smallest or basic unit of information. Data elements can include a customer's name, address, email, discount rate, preferred shipping method, product name, quantity ordered, and so on. *Data models* are logical data structures that detail the relationships among data elements by using graphics or pictures.

Metadata provides details about data. For example, metadata for an image could include its size, resolution, and date created. Metadata about a text document could contain document length, data created, author's name, and summary. Each data element is given a description, such as Customer Name; metadata is provided for the type of data (text, numeric, alphanumeric, date, image, binary value) and descriptions of potential predefined values such as a certain area code; and finally the relationship is defined. A *data dictionary* compiles all of the metadata about the data elements in the data model. Looking at a data model along with reviewing the data dictionary provides tremendous insight into the database's functions, purpose, and business rules.

DBMS use three primary data models for organizing information: hierarchical, network, and the relational database, the most prevalent. A *relational database model* stores information in the

FIGURE 6.6

Relationship of Database, DBMS, and User

form of logically related two-dimensional tables. A ***relational database management system*** allows users to create, read, update, and delete data in a relational database. Although the hierarchical and network models are important, this text focuses only on the relational database model.

Storing Data Elements in Entities and Attributes

For flexibility in supporting business operations, managers need to query or search for the answers to business questions such as which artist sold the most albums during a certain month. The relationships in the relational database model help managers extract this information. Figure 6.7 illustrates the primary concepts of the relational database model: entities, attributes, keys, and relationships. An ***entity*** (also referred to as a table) stores information about a person, place, thing, transaction, or event. The entities, or tables, of interest in Figure 6.7 are *TRACKS, RECORDINGS, MUSICIANS,* and *CATEGORIES.* Notice that each entity is stored in a different two-dimensional table (with rows and columns).

    Attributes (also called columns or fields) are the data elements associated with an entity. In Figure 6.7, the attributes for the entity *TRACKS* are *TrackNumber, TrackTitle, TrackLength,* and *RecordingID.* Attributes for the entity *MUSICIANS* are *MusicianID, MusicianName, MusicianPhoto,* and *MusicianNotes.* A ***record*** is a collection of related data elements (in the *MUSICIANS* table, these include "3, Lady Gaga, gag.tiff, Do not bring young kids to live shows"). Each record in an entity occupies one row in its respective table.

Creating Relationships through Keys

To manage and organize various entities within the relational database model, you use primary keys and foreign keys to create logical relationships. A ***primary key*** is a field (or group of fields) that uniquely identifies a given record in a table. In the table *RECORDINGS*, the primary key is the field *RecordingID* that uniquely identifies each record in the table. Primary keys are a critical piece of a relational database because they provide a way of distinguishing each record in a table; for instance, imagine you need to find information on a customer named Steve Smith. Simply

FIGURE 6.7

Primary Concepts of the
Relational Database Model

Entities **Foreign keys**

TRACKS

TrackNumber	TrackTitle	TrackLength	RecordingID
1	I Won't	3:45	1
2	Begin Again	4:14	1
3	You Got Me	4:00	1
4	Fallin For you	3:35	1
1	I Gotta Feelin	4:49	2
2	Imma Be	4:17	2
3	Boom Boom Pow	4:11	2
4	Meet Me Halfway	4:44	2

RECORDINGS

RecordingID	RecordingTitle	MuscianID	CategoryID
1	Breakthrough	1	1
2	The E.N.D.	2	1
3	Monkey Business	2	1
4	Elephunk	2	1
5	The Fame Monster	3	1
6	Raymond v. Raymond	4	2

Primary keys

Attributes

MUSICIANS

MusicianID	MusicianName	MusicianPhoto	MusicianNotes
1	Colby Caillat	Colby.jpg	Next concert in Boston 7/1/2011
2	Black Eyed Peas	BYP.bmp	New album due 12/25/2011
3	Lady Gaga	Gaga.tiff	Do not bring young kids to live shows
4	Usher	Usher.bmp	Current album #1 on Billboard

Records

CATEGORIES

CategoryID	CategoryName
1	Pop
2	R&B
3	Rock
4	Country
5	Blues
6	Classical

BUSINESS DRIVEN ANALYTICS

eBay is the world's largest online marketplace, with 97 million global users selling anything to anyone at a yearly total of $62 billion—more than $2,000 every second. Of course, with this many sales, eBay is collecting the equivalent of the Library of Congress worth of data every three days that must be analyzed to run the business successfully. Luckily, eBay discovered Tableau!

Tableau started at Stanford when Chris Stolte, a computer scientist; Pat Hanrahan, an Academy Award–winning professor; and Christian Chabot, a savvy business leader, decided to solve the problem of helping ordinary people understand big data. The three created Tableau, which bridged two computer science disciplines: computer graphics and databases. No more need to write code or understand the relational database keys and categories; users simply drag and drop pictures of what they want to analyze. Tableau has become one of the most successful data visualization tools on the market, winning multiple awards, international expansion, and millions in revenue and spawning multiple new inventions.[3]

Tableau is revolutionizing business analytics, and this is only the beginning. Visit the Tableau website and become familiar with the tool by watching a few of the demos. Once you have a good understanding of the tool, create three questions eBay might be using Tableau to answer, including the analysis of its sales data to find patterns, business insights, and trends.

2 Trillion Rows of Data Analyzed Daily—No Problem

searching the customer name would not be an ideal way to find the information because there might be 20 customers with the name Steve Smith. This is the reason the relational database model uses primary keys to identify each record uniquely. Using Steve Smith's unique ID allows a manager to search the database to identify all information associated with this customer.

A *foreign key* is a primary key of one table that appears as an attribute in another table and acts to provide a logical relationship between the two tables. For instance, Black Eyed Peas in Figure 6.7 is one of the musicians appearing in the *MUSICIANS* table. Its primary key, *MusicianID,* is "2." Notice that *MusicianID* also appears as an attribute in the *RECORDINGS* table. By matching these attributes, you create a relationship between the *MUSICIANS* and *RECORDINGS* tables that states the Black Eyed Peas *(MusicianID 2)* have several recordings, including *The E.N.D., Monkey Business,* and *Elepunk.* In essence, *MusicianID* in the *RECORDINGS* table creates a logical relationship (who was the musician that made the recording) to the *MUSICIANS* table. Creating the logical relationship between the tables allows managers to search the data and turn it into useful information.

Coca Cola Relational Database Example

Figure 6.8 illustrates the primary concepts of the relational database model for a sample order of soda from Coca-Cola. Figure 6.8 offers an excellent example of how data is stored in a database. For example, the order number is stored in the ORDER table, and each line item is stored in the ORDER LINE table. Entities include CUSTOMER, ORDER, ORDER LINE, PRODUCT, and DISTRIBUTOR. Attributes for CUSTOMER include Customer ID, Customer Name, Contact Name, and Phone. Attributes for PRODUCT include Product ID, Description, and Price. The columns in the table contain the attributes.

Consider Hawkins Shipping, one of the distributors appearing in the DISTRIBUTOR table. Its primary key, Distributor ID, is DEN8001. Distributor ID also appears as an attribute in the ORDER table. This establishes that Hawkins Shipping (Distributor ID DEN8001) was responsible for delivering orders 34561 and 34562 to the appropriate customer(s). Therefore, Distributor ID in the ORDER table creates a logical relationship (who shipped what order) between ORDER and DISTRIBUTOR.

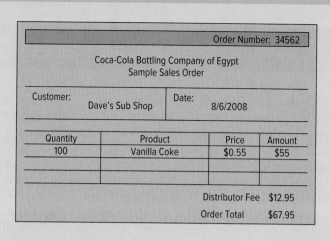

Order Number: 34562

Coca-Cola Bottling Company of Egypt
Sample Sales Order

Customer: Dave's Sub Shop	Date: 8/6/2008

Quantity	Product	Price	Amount
100	Vanilla Coke	$0.55	$55

	Distributor Fee	$12.95
	Order Total	$67.95

CUSTOMER

Customer ID	Customer Name	Contact Name	Phone
23	Dave's Sub Shop	David Logan	(555)333-4545
43	Pizza Palace	Debbie Fernandez	(555)345-5432
765	T's Fun Zone	Tom Repicci	(555)565-6655

ORDER

Order ID	Order Date	Customer ID	Distributor ID	Distributor Fee	Total Due
34561	7/4/2008	23	DEN8001	$22.00	$145.75
34562	8/6/2008	23	DEN8001	$12.95	$67.95
34563	6/5/2008	765	NY9001	$29.50	$249.50

ORDER LINE

Order ID	Line Item	Product ID	Quantity
34561	1	12345AA	75
34561	2	12346BB	50
34561	3	12347CC	100
34562	1	12349EE	100
34563	1	12345AA	100
34563	2	12346BB	100
34563	3	12347CC	50
34563	4	12348DD	50
34563	5	12349EE	100

DISTRIBUTOR

Distributor ID	Distributor Name
DEN8001	Hawkins Shipping
CHI3001	ABC Trucking
NY9001	Van Distributors

PRODUCT

Product ID	Product Description	Price
12345AA	Coca-Cola	$0.55
12346BB	Diet Coke	$0.55
12347CC	Sprite	$0.55
12348DD	Diet Sprite	$0.55
12349EE	Vanilla Coke	$0.55

USING A RELATIONAL DATABASE FOR BUSINESS ADVANTAGES

Many business managers are familiar with Excel and other spreadsheet programs they can use to store business data. Although spreadsheets are excellent for supporting some data analysis, they offer limited functionality in terms of security, accessibility, and flexibility and can rarely scale to support business growth. From a business perspective, relational databases offer many advantages over using a text document or a spreadsheet, as displayed in Figure 6.9.

Increased Flexibility

Databases tend to mirror business structures, and a database needs to handle changes quickly and easily, just as any business needs to be able to do. Equally important, databases need to provide flexibility in allowing each user to access the information in whatever way best suits his or her needs. The distinction between logical and physical views is important in understanding flexible database user views. The *physical view of information* deals with the physical storage of information on a storage device. The *logical view of information* focuses on how individual users logically access information to meet their own particular business needs.

In the database illustration from Figure 6.7, for example, one user could perform a query to determine which recordings had a track length of four minutes or more. At the same time, another user could perform an analysis to determine the distribution of recordings as they relate to the different categories. For example, are there more R&B recordings than rock, or are they evenly distributed? This example demonstrates that although a database has only one physical view, it can easily support multiple logical views that provide for flexibility.

Consider another example: a mail-order business. One user might want a report presented in alphabetical format, in which case, the last name should appear before first name. Another user, working with a catalog mailing system, would want customer names appearing as first name and then last name. Both are easily achievable but different logical views of the same physical information.

Increased Scalability and Performance

In its first year of operation, the official website of the American Family Immigration History Center, www.ellisisland.org, generated more than 2.5 billion hits. The site offers immigration information about people who entered America through the Port of New York and Ellis Island between 1892 and 1924. The database contains more than 25 million passenger names that are correlated to 3.5 million images of ships' manifests.[4]

The database had to be scalable to handle the massive volumes of information and the large numbers of users expected for the launch of the website. In addition, the database needed

FIGURE 6.9

Business Advantages of a Relational Database

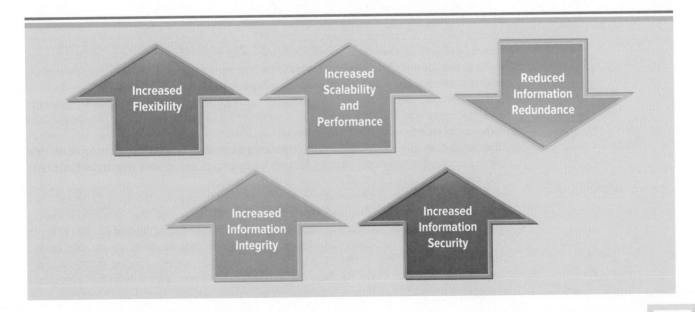

to perform quickly under heavy use. **Data latency** is the time it takes for data to be stored or retrieved. Some organizations must be able to support hundreds or thousands of users including employees, partners, customers, and suppliers, who all want to access and share the same information with minimal data latency. Databases today scale to exceptional levels, allowing all types of users and programs to perform information-processing and information-searching tasks.

Reduced Information Redundancy

Information redundancy is the duplication of data, or the storage of the same data in multiple places. Redundant data can cause storage issues along with data integrity issues, making it difficult to determine which values are the most current or most accurate. Employees become confused and frustrated when faced with incorrect information, causing disruptions to business processes and procedures. One primary goal of a database is to eliminate information redundancy by recording each piece of information in only one place in the database. This saves disk space, makes performing information updates easier, and improves information quality.

Increased Information Integrity (Quality)

Information integrity is a measure of the quality of information. **Integrity constraints** are rules that help ensure the quality of information. The database design needs to consider integrity constraints. The database and the DBMS ensures that users can never violate these constraints. There are two types of integrity constraints: (1) relational and (2) business critical.

Relational integrity constraints are rules that enforce basic and fundamental information-based constraints. For example, a relational integrity constraint would not allow someone to create an order for a nonexistent customer, provide a markup percentage that was negative, or order zero pounds of raw materials from a supplier. A **business rule** defines how a company performs certain aspects of its business and typically results in either a yes/no or true/false answer. Stating that merchandise returns are allowed within 10 days of purchase is an example of a business rule. **Business-critical integrity constraints** enforce business rules vital to an organization's success and often require more insight and knowledge than relational integrity constraints. Consider a supplier of fresh produce to large grocery chains such as Kroger. The supplier might implement a business-critical integrity constraint stating that no product returns are accepted after 15 days past delivery. That would make sense because of the chance of spoilage of the produce. Business-critical integrity constraints tend to mirror the very rules by which an organization achieves success.

The specification and enforcement of integrity constraints produce higher-quality information that will provide better support for business decisions. Organizations that establish specific procedures for developing integrity constraints typically see an increase in accuracy that then increases the use of organizational information by business professionals.

Increased Information Security

Managers must protect information, like any asset, from unauthorized users or misuse. As systems become increasingly complex and highly available over the Internet on many devices, security becomes an even bigger issue. Databases offer many security features, including passwords to provide authentication, access levels to determine who can access the data, and access controls to determine what type of access they have to the information.

For example, customer service representatives might need read-only access to customer order information so they can answer customer order inquiries; they might not have or need the authority to change or delete order information. Managers might require access to employee files, but they should have access only to their own employees' files, not the employee files for the entire company. Various security features of databases can ensure that individuals have only certain types of access to certain types of information.

Identity management is a broad administrative area that deals with identifying individuals in a system (such as a country, a network, or an enterprise) and controlling their access to resources within that system by associating user rights and restrictions with the established identity. Security risks are increasing as more and more databases and DBMS systems are moving to data centers run in the cloud. The biggest risks when using cloud computing are ensuring the security and privacy of the information in the database. Implementing data governance policies and procedures that outline the data management requirements can ensure safe and secure cloud computing.

BUSINESS DRIVEN ETHICS AND SECURITY

Mining large amounts of data can create a number of benefits for business, society, and governments, but it can also create a number of ethical questions surrounding an invasion of privacy or misuse of information. Facebook recently came under fire for its data mining practices as it followed 700,000 accounts to determine whether posts with highly emotional content are more contagious. The study concluded that highly emotional texts are contagious, just as with real people. Highly emotional positive posts received multiple positive replies, whereas highly emotional negative posts received multiple negative replies. Although the study seems rather innocent, many Facebook users were outraged; they felt the study was an invasion of privacy because the 700,000 accounts had no idea Facebook was mining their posts. As a Facebook user, you willingly consent that Facebook owns every bit and byte of data you post, and once you press submit, Facebook can do whatever it wants with your data. Do you agree or disagree that Facebook has the right to do whatever it wants with the data its 1.5 billion users post on its site?[5]

Unethical Data Mining

DRIVING WEBSITES WITH DATA

LO 6.4: Explain the business benefits of a data-driven website.

A *content creator* is the person responsible for creating the original website content. A *content editor* is the person responsible for updating and maintaining website content. *Static information* includes fixed data incapable of change in the event of a user action. *Dynamic information* includes data that change based on user actions. For example, static websites supply only information that will not change until the content editor changes the information. Dynamic information changes when a user requests information. A dynamic website changes information based on user requests such as movie ticket availability, airline prices, or restaurant reservations. Dynamic website information is stored in a *dynamic catalog,* or an area of a website that stores information about products in a database.

Websites change for site visitors depending on the type of information they request. Consider, for example, an automobile dealer. The dealer would create a database containing data elements for each car it has available for sale, including make, model, color, year, miles per gallon, a photograph, and so on. Website visitors might click Porsche and then enter their specific requests such as price range or year made. Once the user hits Go, the website automatically provides a custom view of the requested information. The dealer must create, update, and delete automobile information as the inventory changes.

A *data-driven website* is an interactive website kept constantly updated and relevant to the needs of its customers using a database. Data-driven capabilities are especially useful when a firm needs to offer large amounts of information, products, or services. Visitors can become quickly annoyed if they find themselves buried under an avalanche of information when searching a website. A data-driven website can help limit the amount of information displayed to customers based on unique search requirements. Companies even use data-driven websites to make information in their internal databases available to customers and business partners.

There are a number of advantages to using the web to access company databases. First, web browsers are much easier to use than directly accessing the database by using a custom-query tool. Second, the web interface requires few or no changes to the database model. Finally, it costs less to add a web interface in front of a DBMS than to redesign and rebuild the system to support changes. Additional data-driven website advantages include:

■ **Easy to manage content:** Website owners can make changes without relying on MIS professionals; users can update a data-driven website with little or no training.

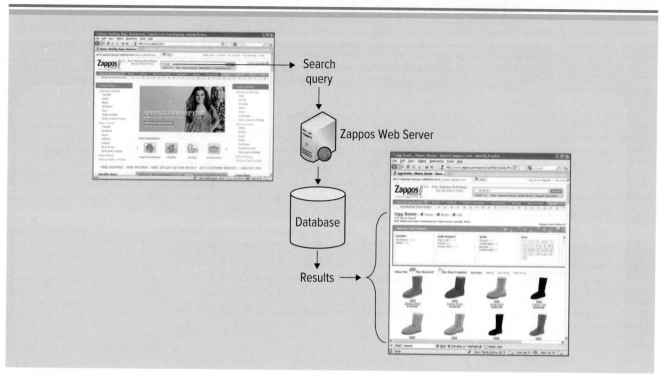

FIGURE 6.10

Zappos.com—A Data-Driven Website

Source: Zappos.com

FIGURE 6.11

BI in a Data-Driven Website

Source: BestMobile.com

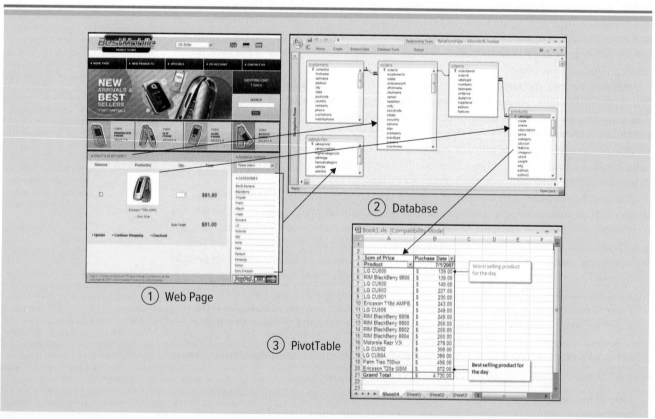

- **Easy to store large amounts of data:** Data-driven websites can keep large volumes of information organized. Website owners can use templates to implement changes for layouts, navigation, or website structure. This improves website reliability, scalability, and performance.

- **Easy to eliminate human errors:** Data-driven websites trap data-entry errors, eliminating inconsistencies while ensuring that all information is entered correctly.

Zappos credits its success as an online shoe retailer to its vast inventory of nearly 3 million products available through its dynamic data-driven website. The company built its data-driven website catering to a specific niche market: consumers who were tired of finding that their most-desired items were always out of stock at traditional retailers. Zappos' highly flexible, scalable, and secure database helped it rank as the most available Internet retailer. Figure 6.10 displays the Zappos data-driven website illustrating a user querying the database and receiving information that satisfies the user's request.[6]

Companies can gain valuable business knowledge by viewing the data accessed and analyzed from their websites. Figure 6.11 displays how running queries or using analytical tools, such as a PivotTable, on the database that is attached to the website can offer insight into the business, such as items browsed, frequent requests, items bought together, and so on.

section 6.2 | Business Intelligence

6.5 Describe the roles and purposes of data warehouses and data marts in an organization.

6.6 Identify the advantages of using business intelligence to support managerial decision making.

6.7 Identify the four common characteristics of big data.

6.8 Explain data mining and identify the three elements of data mining.

6.9 Explain the importance of data analytics and data visualization.

SUPPORTING DECISIONS WITH BUSINESS INTELLIGENCE

LO 6.5: Describe the roles and purposes of data warehouses and data marts in an organization.

Applebee's Neighborhood Grill & Bar posts annual sales in excess of $3.2 billion and is actively using information from its data warehouse to increase sales and cut costs. The company gathers daily information for the previous day's sales into its data warehouse from 1,500 restaurants located in 49 states and seven countries. Understanding regional preferences, such as patrons in Texas preferring steaks more than patrons in New England, allows the company to meet its corporate strategy of being a neighborhood grill appealing to local tastes. The company has found tremendous value in its data warehouse by being able to make business decisions about customers' regional needs. The company also uses data warehouse information to perform the following:

- Base labor budgets on actual number of guests served per hour.
- Develop promotional sale item analysis to help avoid losses from overstocking or understocking inventory.
- Determine theoretical and actual costs of food and the use of ingredients.

In the 1990s, as organizations began to need more timely information about their business, they found that traditional management information systems were too cumbersome to provide relevant information efficiently and effectively. Most of the systems were in the form of operational databases that were designed for specific business functions, such as accounting, order entry, customer service, and sales, and were not appropriate for business analysis for the reasons shown in Figure 6.12.

During the latter half of the 20th century, the numbers and types of operational databases increased. Many large businesses found themselves with information scattered across multiple systems with different file types (such as spreadsheets, databases, and even word processing files), making it almost impossible for anyone to use the information from multiple sources.

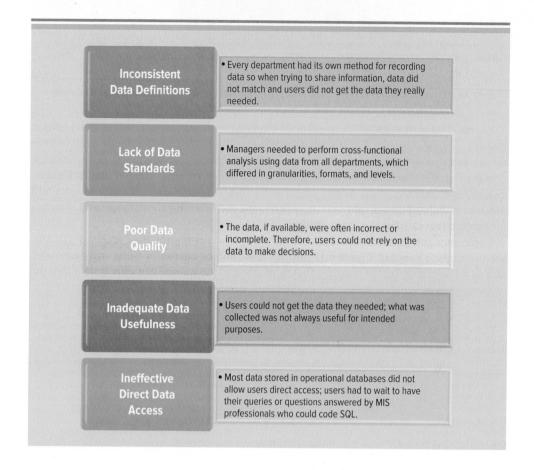

Inconsistent Data Definitions	• Every department had its own method for recording data so when trying to share information, data did not match and users did not get the data they really needed.
Lack of Data Standards	• Managers needed to perform cross-functional analysis using data from all departments, which differed in granularities, formats, and levels.
Poor Data Quality	• The data, if available, were often incorrect or incomplete. Therefore, users could not rely on the data to make decisions.
Inadequate Data Usefulness	• Users could not get the data they needed; what was collected was not always useful for intended purposes.
Ineffective Direct Data Access	• Most data stored in operational databases did not allow users direct access; users had to wait to have their queries or questions answered by MIS professionals who could code SQL.

Completing reporting requests across operational systems could take days or weeks using anti-quated reporting tools that were ineffective for running a business. From this idea, the data warehouse was born as a place where relevant information could be stored and accessed for making strategic queries and reports.

A *repository* is a central location in which data is stored and managed. A ***data warehouse*** is a log-ical collection of information—gathered from many different operational databases—that supports business analysis activities and decision-making tasks. The primary purpose of a data warehouse is to combine information, more specifically, strategic information, throughout an organization into a single repository in such a way that the people who need that information can make decisions and undertake business analysis. A key idea within data warehousing is to collect information from multiple systems in a common location that uses a universal querying tool. This allows operational databases to run where they are most efficient for the business, while providing a common loca-tion using a familiar format for the strategic or enterprisewide reporting information.

Data warehouses go even a step further by standardizing information. Gender, for instance can be referred to in many ways (Male, Female, M/F, 1/0), but it should be standardized on a data warehouse with one common way of referring to each data element that stores gender (M/F). Standardization of data elements allows for greater accuracy, completeness, and con-sistency and increases the quality of the information in making strategic business decisions. The data warehouse then is simply a tool that enables business users, typically managers, to be more effective in many ways, including:

- Developing customer profiles.
- Identifying new-product opportunities.
- Improving business operations.
- Identifying financial issues.
- Analyzing trends.
- Understanding competitors.
- Understanding product performance. (See Figure 6.13.)

Data Warehousing Components

Data Marts

Data aggregation is the collection of data from various sources for the purpose of data processing. One example of a data aggregation is to gather information about particular groups based on specific variables such as age, profession, or income. Businesses collect a tremendous amount of transactional information as part of their routine operations. Marketing, sales, and other departments would like to analyze these data to understand their operations better. Although databases store the details of all transactions (for instance, the sale of a product) and events (hiring a new employee), data warehouses store that same information but in an aggregated form more suited to supporting decision-making tasks. Aggregation, in this instance, can include totals, counts, averages, and the like.

The data warehouse modeled in Figure 6.14 compiles information from internal databases (or transactional and operational databases) and external databases through extraction, transformation, and loading. *Extraction, transformation, and loading (ETL)* is a process that extracts information from internal and external databases, transforms it using a common set of enterprise definitions, and loads it into a data warehouse. The data warehouse then sends portions (or subsets) of the information to data marts. A *data mart* contains a subset of data warehouse information. To distinguish between data warehouses and data marts, think of data

FIGURE 6.14

Data Warehouse Model

Technical Foundations of MIS **Module 2**   243

warehouses as having a more organizational focus and data marts as having a functional focus. Figure 6.14 provides an illustration of a data warehouse and its relationship to internal and external databases, ETL, and data marts.

Lands' End created an organizationwide data warehouse so all its employees could access organizational information. Lands' End soon found out that there could be "too much of a good thing." Many of its employees would not use the data warehouse because it was simply too big, was too complicated, and had too much irrelevant information. Lands' End knew there was valuable information in its data warehouse, and it had to find a way for its employees to easily access the information. Data marts were the perfect solution to the company's information overload problem. Once the employees began using the data marts, they were ecstatic at the wealth of information. Data marts were a huge success for Lands' End.

Information Cleansing or Scrubbing

Maintaining quality information in a data warehouse or data mart is extremely important. The Data Warehousing Institute estimates that low-quality information costs U.S. businesses $600 billion annually. That number may seem high, but it is not. If an organization is using a data warehouse or data mart to allocate dollars across advertising strategies, low-quality information will definitely have a negative impact on its ability to make the right decision.

Dirty data is erroneous or flawed data (see Figure 6.15). The complete removal of dirty data from a source is impractical or virtually impossible. According to Gartner Inc., dirty data is a business problem, not an MIS problem. Over the next 2 years, more than 25 percent of critical data in *Fortune* 1000 companies will continue to be flawed; that is, the information will be inaccurate, incomplete, or duplicated.

Obviously, maintaining quality information in a data warehouse or data mart is extremely important. To increase the quality of organizational information and thus the effectiveness of decision making, businesses must formulate a strategy to keep information clean. *Information cleansing or scrubbing* is a process that weeds out and fixes or discards inconsistent, incorrect, or incomplete information.

Specialized software tools exist that use sophisticated procedures to analyze, standardize, correct, match, and consolidate data warehouse information. This step is vitally important because data warehouses often contain information from several databases, some of which can be external to the organization. In a data warehouse, information cleansing occurs first during

FIGURE 6.15

Dirty Data Problems

Alex Slobodkin/Getty Images RF.

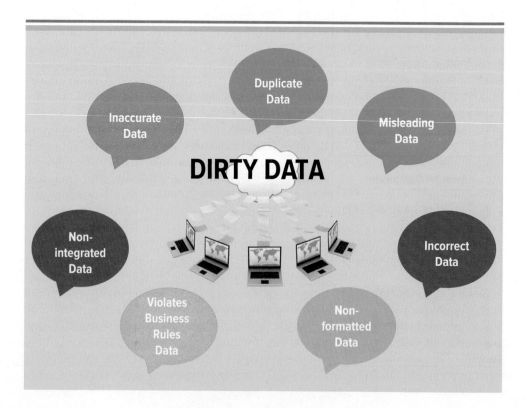

BUSINESS DRIVEN DISCUSSION

Butterfly Effects

The butterfly effect, an idea from chaos theory in mathematics, refers to the way a minor event—such as the movement of a butterfly's wing—can have a major impact on a complex system like the weather. Dirty data can have the same impact on a business as the butterfly effect. Organizations depend on the movement and sharing of data throughout the organization, so the impact of data quality errors are costly and far-reaching. Such data issues often begin with a tiny mistake in one part of the organization, but the butterfly effect can produce disastrous results, making its way through MIS systems to the data warehouse and other enterprise systems. When dirty data or low-quality data enters organizational systems, a tiny error such as a spelling mistake can lead to revenue loss, process inefficiency, and failure to comply with industry and government regulations. Explain how the following errors can affect an organization:

- A cascading spelling mistake.
- Inaccurate customer records.
- Incomplete purchasing history.
- Inaccurate mailing address.
- Duplicate customer numbers for different customers.

---

the ETL process and again once the information is in the data warehouse. Companies can choose information cleansing software from several vendors, including Oracle, SAS, Ascential Software, and Group 1 Software. Ideally, scrubbed information is accurate and consistent.

Looking at customer information highlights why information cleansing is necessary. Customer information exists in several operational systems. In each system, all the details could change—from the customer ID to contact information—depending on the business process the user is performing (see Figure 6.16).

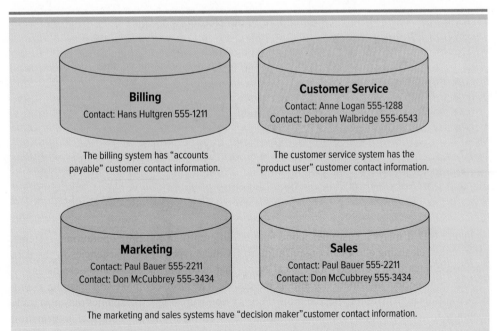

FIGURE 6.16

Contact Information in Operational Systems

Billing
Contact: Hans Hultgren 555-1211

The billing system has "accounts payable" customer contact information.

Customer Service
Contact: Anne Logan 555-1288
Contact: Deborah Walbridge 555-6543

The customer service system has the "product user" customer contact information.

Marketing
Contact: Paul Bauer 555-2211
Contact: Don McCubbrey 555-3434

Sales
Contact: Paul Bauer 555-2211
Contact: Don McCubbrey 555-3434

The marketing and sales systems have "decision maker" customer contact information.

FIGURE 6.17

Standardizing a Customer Name
in Operational Systems

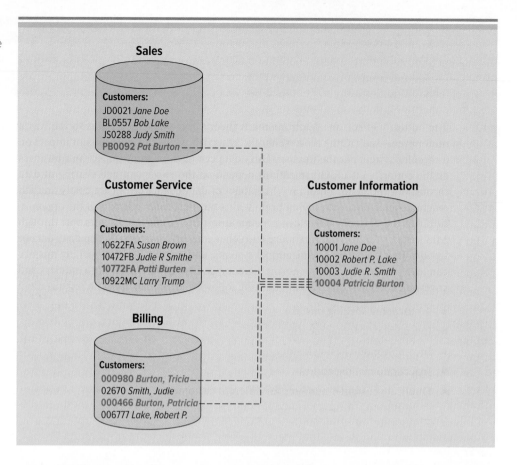

Sales

Customers:

JD0021 *Jane Doe*
BL0557 *Bob Lake*
JS0288 *Judy Smith*
PB0092 *Pat Burton*

Customer Service

Customers:

10622FA *Susan Brown*
10472FB *Judie R Smithe*
10772FA *Patti Burten*
10922MC *Larry Trump*

Customer Information

Customers:

10001 *Jane Doe*
10002 *Robert P. Lake*
10003 *Judie R. Smith*
10004 *Patricia Burton*

Billing

Customers:

000980 *Burton, Tricia*
02670 *Smith, Judie*
000466 *Burton, Patricia*
006777 *Lake, Robert P.*

FIGURE 6.18

Information Cleansing Activities

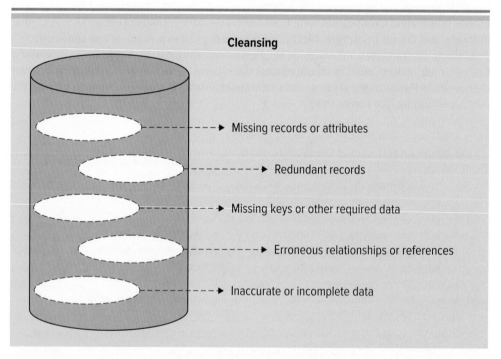

Cleansing

→ Missing records or attributes

→ Redundant records

→ Missing keys or other required data

→ Erroneous relationships or references

→ Inaccurate or incomplete data

Figure 6.17 displays a customer name entered differently in multiple operational systems. Information cleansing allows an organization to fix these types of inconsistencies in the data warehouse. Figure 6.18 displays the typical events that occur during information cleansing.

Achieving perfect information is almost impossible. The more complete and accurate a company wants its information to be, the more it costs (see Figure 6.19). Companies may also trade accuracy for completeness. Accurate information is correct, whereas complete information has no blanks. A birth date of 2/31/10 is an example of complete but inaccurate information

FIGURE 6.19

The Cost of Accurate and
Complete Information

Quality Management

(February 31 does not exist). An address containing Denver, Colorado, without a zip code is an example of accurate information that is incomplete. Many firms complete *data quality audits* to determine the accuracy and completeness of its data. Most organizations determine a percentage of accuracy and completeness high enough to make good decisions at a reasonable cost, such as 85 percent accurate and 65 percent complete.

BUSINESS INTELLIGENCE

Many organizations today find it next to impossible to understand their own strengths and weaknesses, let alone their biggest competitors', because the enormous volume of organizational data is inaccessible to all but the MIS department. A *data point* is an individual item on a graph or a chart. Organizational data includes far more than simple structured data elements in a database; the set of data also includes unstructured data such as voice mail, customer phone calls, text messages, and video clips, along with numerous new forms of data, such as tweets from Twitter.

LO 6.6: **Identify the advantages of using business intelligence to support managerial decision making.**

An early reference to business intelligence occurs in Sun Tzu's book titled *The Art of War.* Sun Tzu claims that to succeed in war, one should have full knowledge of one's own strengths and weaknesses and full knowledge of the enemy's strengths and weaknesses. Lack of either one might result in defeat. A certain school of thought draws parallels between the challenges in business and those of war, specifically:

- Collecting information.
- Discerning patterns and meaning in the information.
- Responding to the resultant information.

Before the start of the information age in the late 20th century, businesses sometimes collected information from nonautomated sources. Businesses then lacked the computing resources to properly analyze the information and often made commercial decisions based primarily on intuition. A *data broker* is a business that collects personal information about consumers and sells that information to other organizations.

As businesses started automating more and more systems, more and more information became available. However, collection remained a challenge due to a lack of infrastructure for information exchange or to incompatibilities between systems. Reports sometimes took months to generate. Such reports allowed informed long-term strategic decision making. However, short-term tactical decision making continued to rely on intuition. In modern businesses, increasing standards, automation, and technologies have led to vast amounts of available information. Data warehouse technologies have set up repositories to store this information. Improved ETL has increased the speedy collecting of information. Business intelligence has now become the art of sifting through large amounts of data, extracting information, and turning that information into actionable knowledge.

A *data lake* is a storage repository that holds a vast amount of raw data in its original format until the business needs it. While a traditional data warehouse stores data in files or folders, a data lake uses a flat architecture to store data. Each data element in a data lake is assigned a unique identifier and tagged with a set of extended metadata tags. When a business question arises, the data lake can be queried for all of the relevant data providing a smaller data set that can then be analyzed to help answer the question.

The Problem: Data Rich, Information Poor

An ideal business scenario would be as follows: As a business manager on his way to meet with a client reviews historical customer data, he realizes that the client's ordering volume has substantially decreased. As he drills down into the data, he notices the client had a support issue with a particular product. He quickly calls the support team to find out all of the information and learns that a replacement for the defective part can be shipped in 24 hours. In addition, he learns that the client has visited the website and requested information on a new product line. Armed with all this information, the business manager is prepared for a productive meeting with his client. He now understands the client's needs and issues, and he can address new sales opportunities with confidence.

For many companies, the above example is simply a pipe dream. Attempting to gather all of the client information would actually take hours or even days to compile. With so much data available, it is surprisingly hard for managers to get information, such as inventory levels, past order history, or shipping details. *Source data* identifies the primary location where data is collected. Source data can include invoices, spreadsheets, time sheets, transactions, and electronic sources such as other databases. Managers send their information requests to the MIS department, where a dedicated person compiles the various reports. In some situations, responses can take days, by which time the information may be outdated and opportunities lost. Many organizations find themselves in the position of being data rich and information poor. Even in today's electronic world, managers struggle with the challenge of turning their business data into business intelligence.

The Solution: Business Intelligence

Employee decisions are numerous and they include providing service information, offering new products, and supporting frustrated customers. A *data set* is an organized collection of data. A *comparative analysis* can compare two or more data sets to identify patterns and trends. Employees can base their decisions on data sets, experience, or knowledge and, preferably a combination of all three. Business intelligence can provide managers with the ability to make better decisions. A few examples of how different industries use business intelligence include:

- **Airlines:** Analyze popular vacation locations with current flight listings.
- **Banking:** Understand customer credit card usage and nonpayment rates.
- **Health care:** Compare the demographics of patients with critical illnesses.
- **Insurance:** Predict claim amounts and medical coverage costs.
- **Law enforcement:** Track crime patterns, locations, and criminal behavior.
- **Marketing:** Analyze customer demographics.
- **Retail:** Predict sales, inventory levels, and distribution.
- **Technology:** Predict hardware failures.

Figure 6.20 displays how organizations using BI can find the cause to many issues and problems simply by asking "Why?" The process starts by analyzing a report such as sales amounts by quarter. Managers will drill down into the report looking for why sales are up or why sales are down. Once they understand why a certain location or product is experiencing an increase in sales, they can share the information in an effort to raise enterprisewide sales. Once they understand the cause for a decrease in sales, they can take effective action to resolve the issue. BI can help managers with *competitive monitoring* where a company keeps tabs of its competitor's activities on the web using software that automatically tracks all competitor website activities such as discounts and new products. Here are a few examples of how managers can use BI to answer tough business questions:

- Where has the business been? Historical perspective offers important variables for determining trends and patterns.

BUSINESS DRIVEN INNOVATION

Gone are the days of staring at boring spreadsheets and trying to understand how the data correlate. With innovative data visualization tools, managers can arrange different ways to view the data, providing new forms of pattern recognition not offered by simply looking at numbers. *Slate,* a news publication, developed a new data visualization tool called News Dots that offers readers a different way of viewing the daily news through trends and patterns. The News Dots tool scans about 500 stories a day from major publications and then tags the content with important keywords such as people, places, companies, and topics. Surprisingly, the majority of daily news overlaps as the people, places, and stories are frequently connected. Using News Dots, you can visualize how the news fits together, almost similar to a giant social network. News Dots uses circles (or dots) to represent the tagged content and arranges them according to size. The more frequently a certain topic is tagged, the larger the dot and its relationship to other dots. The tool is interactive, and users simply click a dot to view which stories mention that topic and which other topics it connects to in the network such as a correlation among U.S. government, Federal Reserve, Senate, bank, and Barack Obama.[7]

How can data visualization help identify trends? What types of business intelligence could you identify if your college used a data visualization tool to analyze student information? What types of business intelligence could you identify if you used a data visualization tool to analyze the industry in which you plan to compete?

News Dots

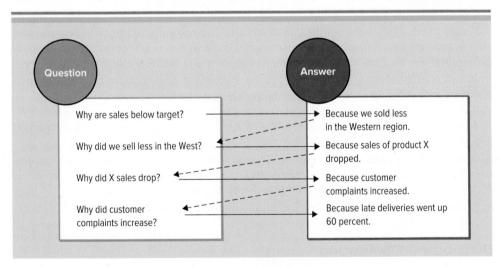

FIGURE 6.20

How BI Can Answer Tough Customer Questions

- Where is the business now? Looking at the current business situation allows managers to take effective action to solve issues before they grow out of control.
- Where is the business going? Setting strategic direction is critical for planning and creating solid business strategies.

Ask a simple question—such as who is my best customer or what is my worst-selling product—and you might get as many answers as you have employees. Databases, data warehouses, and data marts can provide a single source of "trusted" data that can answer questions about customers, products, suppliers, production, finances, fraud, and even employees. A *data map* is a technique for establishing a match, or balance, between the source data and the target data warehouse. This technique identifies data shortfalls and recognizes data issues. Data maps can also alert managers to inconsistencies or help determine the cause and effects of enterprise-wide business decisions.

All business aspects can benefit from the added insights provided by business intelligence, and you, as a business student, will benefit from understanding how MIS can help you make data-driven decisions. *Data-driven decision management* is an approach to business governance that values decisions that can be backed up with verifiable data. The success of the data-driven approach is reliant upon the quality of the data gathered and the effectiveness of its analysis and interpretation.

In the early days of computing, it usually took a specialist with a strong background in technology to mine data for information because it was necessary for that person to understand how databases and data warehouses worked. Today, business intelligence tools often require very little, if any, support from the MIS department. Business managers can customize dashboards to display the data they want to see and run custom reports on the fly. The changes in how data can be mined and visualized allow business executives who have no technology backgrounds to be able to work with analytics tools and make data-driven decisions.

Data-driven decision management is usually undertaken as a way to gain a competitive advantage. A study from the MIT Center for Digital Business found that organizations driven most by data-based decision making had 4 percent higher productivity rates and 6 percent higher profits. However, integrating massive amounts of information from different areas of the business and combining it to derive actionable data in real time can be easier said than done. Errors can creep into data analytics processes at any stage of the endeavor, and serious issues can result when they do.

LO 6.7: Identify the four common characteristics of big data.

THE POWER OF BIG DATA ANALYTICS

Big data is a collection of large, complex data sets, including structured and unstructured data, which cannot be analyzed using traditional database methods and tools. Big data came into fruition primary due to the last 50 years of technology evolution. Revolutionary technological advances in software, hardware, storage, networking, and computing models have transformed the data landscape, making new opportunities for data collection possible. Big data is one of the latest trends emerging from the convergence of technological factors. For example, cell phones generate tremendous amounts of data and much of it is available for use with analytical applications. Big data includes data sources that include extremely large volumes of data, with high velocity, wide variety, and an understanding of the data veracity. The four common characteristics of big data are detailed in Figure 6.21 and Figure 6.22.

The move to big data combines business with science, research, and government activities. A company can now analyze petabytes of data for patterns, trends, and anomalies gaining insights into data in new and exciting ways. A petabyte of data is equivalent to 20 million four-drawer file cabinets filled with text files or 13 years of HDTV content. Big data requires sophisticated tools to analyze all of the structured and unstructured data from millions of customers, devices, and machine interactions (see Figure 6.23). The two primary computing models that have shaped the collection of big data include distributed computing and vitalization.

Distributed Computing

Distributed computing processes and manages algorithms across many machines in a computing environment (see Figure 6.24). A key component of big data is a distributed computing environment that shares resources ranging from memory to networks to storage. With distributed computing, individual computers are networked together across geographical areas and work together to execute a workload or computing processes as if they were one single computing environment. For example, you can distribute a set of programs on the same physical server and use a message service to allow them to communicate and pass information. You can also have a distributed computing environment in which many different systems or servers, each with its own computing memory, work together to solve a common problem.

FIGURE 6.21

Four Common Characteristics of
Big Data

VARIETY
- Different forms of structured and unstructured data
- Data from spreadsheets and databases as well as from email, videos, photos, and PDFs, all of which must be analyzed

VERACITY
- The uncertainty of data, including biases, noise, and abnormalities
- Uncertainty or untrustworthiness of data
- Data must be meaningful to the problem being analyzed
- Must keep data clean and implement processes to keep dirty data from accumulating in systems

VOLUME
- The scale of data
- Includes enormous volumes of data generated daily
- Massive volume created by machines and networks
- Big data tools necessary to analyze zettabytes and brontobytes

VELOCITY
- The analysis of streaming data as it travels around the Internet
- Analysis necessary of social media messages spreading globally

FIGURE 6.22

Big Data Will Create 4.4 Million
Global MIS Jobs

Big Data Will Create 4.4 Million Global MIS Jobs

VOLUME
Scale of Data
- 40 Zettabytes of Data Created by 2020
- 2.5 Quintillion Bytes of Data Created Daily (10 Million Blue-Rays)
- 100 Terabytes of Data per Company
- 6 Billion Cell Phones Creating Data
- 90 Percent of Data has been Created Daily (10 Million Blue-Rays)

VARIETY
Different Forms of Data
- 90 Percent of Data Created is Unstructured
- 400 Million Wireless Monitors
- 4 Billion Hours of Video Created
- 400 Million Tweets
- 30 Billion Pieces of Content Shared on Facebook Monthly

VELOCITY
Analysis of Streaming Data
- Every Minute We Create 72 Hours of You Tube Video, 200,000 Instagram Posts, 205 Million Emails
- 100 Sensors in Every Connetced Cars
- 19 Billion Network Connections

VERACITY
Uncertainty of Data
- 1 in 3 Business Leaders Do Not Trust Data to Make Decisions
- $3.1 Trillion in Poor Data Costs per Year

FIGURE 6.23

Structured and Unstructured
Data Examples

Structured Data	Unstructured Data
Sensor data	Satellite images
Weblog data	Photographic data
Financial data	Video data
Click-stream data	Social media data
Point of sale data	Text message
Accounting data	Voice mail data

FIGURE 6.24

Distributed Computing
Environment

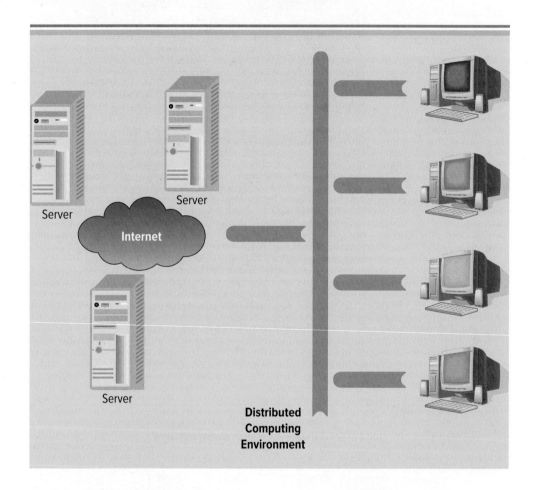

Virtualization

Virtualization is the creation of a virtual (rather than actual) version of computing resources, such as an operating system, a server, a storage device, or network resources (see Figure 6.25). With big data, it is now possible to virtualize data so that it can be stored efficiently and cost-effectively. Improvements in network speed and network reliability have removed the physical limitations of being able to manage massive amounts of data at an acceptable pace. The decrease in price of storage and computer memory allow companies to leverage data that would have been inconceivable to collect only 10 years ago.

Analyzing Big Data

With the onset of big data, organizations are collecting more data than ever. Historically, data were housed in functional systems that were not integrated, such as customer service, finance, and human resources. Today companies can gather all of the functional data together by the petabyte, but finding a way to analyze the data is incredibly challenging. Figure 6.26 displays the three focus areas business are using to dissect, analyze, and understand organizational data.

FIGURE 6.25

Virtualization Example

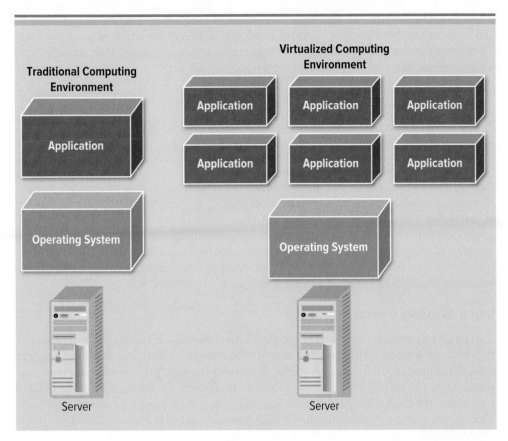

Traditional Computing Environment

Application

Operating System

Server

Virtualized Computing Environment

Application | Application | Application

Application | Application | Application

Operating System

Server

DATA MINING

LO 6.8: Explain data mining and identify the three elements of data mining.

Reports piled on a manager's desk provide summaries of past business activities and stock market data. Unfortunately, these reports don't offer much insight into why these things are happening or what might happen over the next few months. Data mining to the rescue! *Data mining* is the process of analyzing data to extract information not offered by the raw

FIGURE 6.26

Business Focus Areas of Big Data.

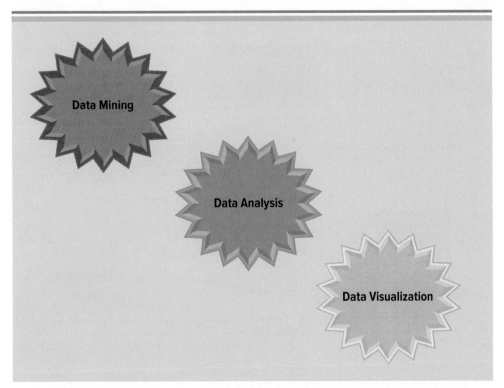

Data Mining

Data Analysis

Data Visualization

data alone. Data mining can also begin at a summary information level (coarse granularity) and progress through increasing levels of detail (drilling down) or the reverse (drilling up). Companies use data mining techniques to compile a complete picture of their operations, all within a single view, allowing them to identify trends and improve forecasts. The three elements of data mining include:

1. **Data:** Foundation for data-directed decision making.
2. **Discovery:** Process of identifying new patterns, trends, and insights.
3. **Deployment:** Process of implementing discoveries to drive success.

One retailer discovered that loyalty program customers spent more over time, so it strategically invested in specific marketing campaigns focusing on these high spenders, thereby maximizing revenue and reducing marketing costs. One manufacturer discovered a sequence of events that preceded accidental releases of toxic chemicals, allowing the factory to remain operational while it prevented dangerous accidents. One insurance company discovered that one of its offices was able to process certain common claim types more quickly than others of comparable size. Armed with this valuable information, the company mimicked this office's best practices across its entire organization, improving customer service.

Data Mining Process Model

Data mining is a continuous process or cycle of activity in which you continually revisit the problems with new projects. This allows past models to be effectively reused to look for new opportunities in the present and future. Data mining allows users to recycle their work to become more effective and efficient on solving future problems. It is similar to creating a household budget and reusing the same basic budget year after year, even though expenses and income change. There are six primary phases in the data mining process, outlined in Figure 6.27 and detailed in Figure 6.28.

Data Mining Analysis Techniques

Data profiling is the process of collecting statistics and information about data in an existing source. Insights extracted from data profiling can determine how easy or difficult it will be to use existing data for other purposes along with providing metrics on data quality. *Data replication* is

FIGURE 6.27

Data Mining Process Model Overview

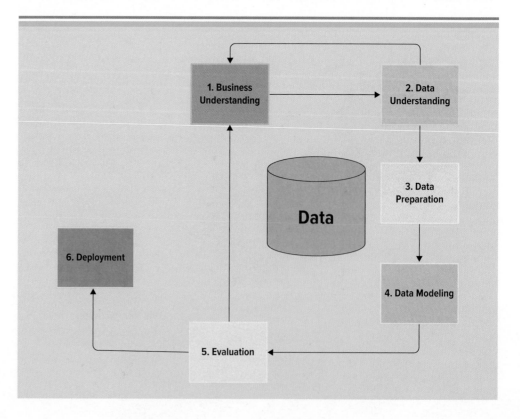

FIGURE 6.28

Data Mining Process Model
Activities

	Phase	Definition	Activities
1.	Business Understanding	Gain a clear understanding of the business problem that must be solved and how it impacts the company.	■ Identify business goals. ■ Assess the situation. ■ Define data mining goals. ■ Create project plan.
2.	Data Understanding	Analyze all current data along with identifying any data quality issues.	■ Gather data. ■ Describe data. ■ Explore data. ■ Verify data quality.
3.	Data Preparation	Gather and organize the data in the correct formats and structures for analysis.	■ Select data. ■ Cleanse data. ■ Integrate data. ■ Format data.
4.	Data Modeling	Apply mathematical techniques to identify trends and patterns in the data.	■ Select modeling technique. ■ Design tests. ■ Build models.
5.	Evaluation	Analyze the trends and patterns to assess the potential for solving the business problem.	■ Evaluate results. ■ Review process. ■ Determine next steps.
6.	Deployment	Deploy the discoveries to the organization for work in everyday business.	■ Plan deployment. ■ Monitor deployment. ■ Analyze results. ■ Review final reports.

the process of sharing information to ensure consistency between multiple data sources. Data mining can determine relationships among such internal factors as price, product positioning, or staff skills, and external factors such as economic indicators, competition, and customer demographics. In addition, it can determine the impact on sales, customer satisfaction, and corporate profits, and drill down into summary information to view detailed transactional data. With data mining, a retailer could use point-of-sale records of customer purchases to send targeted promotions based on an individual's purchase history. By mining demographic data from comment or warranty cards, the retailer could develop products and promotions to appeal to specific customer segments.

A *recommendation engine* is a data mining algorithm that analyzes a customer's purchases and actions on a website and then uses the data to recommend complementary products. Netflix uses a recommendation engine to analyze each customer's film-viewing habits to provide recommendations for other customers with Cinematch, its movie recommendation system. Using Cinematch, Netflix can present customers with a number of additional movies they might want to watch based on the customer's current preferences. Netflix's innovative use of data mining provides its competitive advantage in the movie rental industry. Figure 6.29 displays the common data mining techniques used to perform advanced analytics such as Netflix's Cinematch.

Estimation Analysis   An *estimation analysis* determines values for an unknown continuous variable behavior or estimated future value. Estimation models predict numeric outcomes based on historical data; for example, the percentage of high school students who will graduate based on student-teacher ratio or income levels. An estimate is similar to a guess and is one of the least expensive modeling techniques. Many organizations use estimation analysis to determine the overall costs of a project from start to completion or estimates on the profits from introducing a new product line.

Affinity Grouping Analysis   *Affinity grouping analysis* reveals the relationship between variables along with the nature and frequency of the relationships. Many people refer to affinity

Estimation Analysis

Determines values for an unknown continuous variable behavior or estimated future value.

Affinity Grouping Analysis

Reveals the relationship between variables along with the nature and frequency of the relationships.

Cluster Analysis

A technique used to divide an information set into mutually exclusive groups such that the members of each group are as close together as possible to one another and the different groups are as far apart as possible.

Classification Analysis

The process of organizing data into categories or groups for its most effective and efficient use.

FIGURE 6.29

Data Mining Techniques.

FIGURE 6.30

Market Basket Analysis Example.

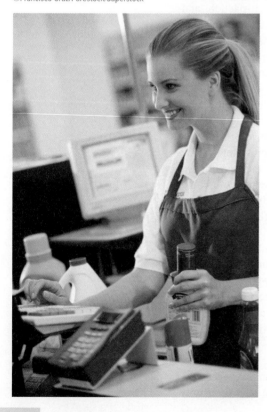

©Francisco Cruz/Purestock/Superstock

grouping algorithms as association rule generators because they create rules to determine the likelihood of events occurring together at a particular time or following each other in a logical progression. Percentages usually reflect the patterns of these events; for example, "55 percent of the time, events A and B occurred together" or "80 percent of the time that items A and B occurred together, they were followed by item C within three days."

One of the most common forms of association detection analysis is market basket analysis. *Market basket analysis* evaluates such items as websites and checkout scanner information to detect customers' buying behavior and predict future behavior by identifying affinities among customers' choices of products and services (see Figure 6.30). Market basket analysis is frequently used to develop marketing campaigns for cross-selling products and services (especially in banking, insurance, and finance) and for inventory control, shelf-product placement, and other retail and marketing applications.

Cluster Analysis *Cluster analysis* is a technique used to divide an information set into mutually exclusive groups such that the members of each group are as close together as possible to one another and the different groups are as far apart as possible. Cluster analysis identifies similarities and differences among data sets, allowing similar data sets to be clustered together. A customer database includes attributes such as name and address, demographic information such as gender and age, and financial attributes such as income and revenue spent. A cluster analysis groups similar attributes together to discover segments or clusters and then examines the attributes and values that define the clusters or segments. Marketing managers can drive promotion strategies that target the specific group identified by the cluster analysis (see Figure 6.31).

A great example of using cluster analysis in business is to create target-marketing strategies based on zip codes. Evaluating customer segments by zip code allows a business to assign a level of importance to each segment. Zip codes offer valuable insight into such things as income levels, demographics, lifestyles, and spending habits. With target marketing, a business can decrease its costs while increasing the success rate of the marketing campaign.

FIGURE 6.31

Example of Cluster Analysis.

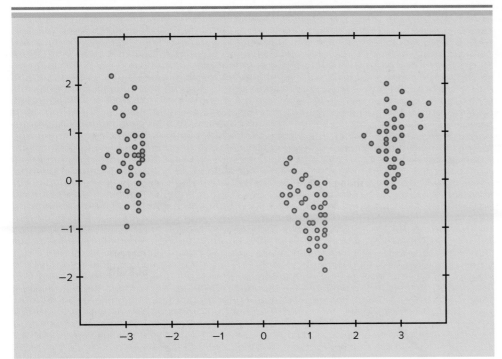

Classification Analysis *Classification analysis* is the process of organizing data into categories or groups for its most effective and efficient use. For example, groups of political affiliation and charity donors. The primary goal of a classification analysis is not to explore data to find interesting segments but to decide the best way to classify records. It is important to note that classification analysis is similar to cluster analysis because it segments data into distinct segments called classes; however, unlike cluster analysis, a classification analysis requires that all classes are defined before the analysis begins. For example, in a classification analysis, the analyst defines two classes: (1) a class for customers who defaulted on a loan; (2) a class for customers who did not default on a loan. Cluster analysis is exploratory analysis and classification analysis is much less exploratory and more grouping. (See Figure 6.32.)

Data Mining Modeling Techniques for Predictions

To perform data mining, users need data mining tools. *Data mining tools* use a variety of techniques to find patterns and relationships in large volumes of information that predict future behavior and guide decision making. Data mining uncovers trends and patterns, which analysts use to build models that, when exposed to new information sets, perform a variety of information analysis functions. Data mining tools for data warehouses help users uncover business intelligence in their data. Data mining uncovers patterns and trends for business analysis such as:

- Analyzing customer buying patterns to predict future marketing and promotion campaigns.
- Building budgets and other financial information.
- Detecting fraud by identifying deceptive spending patterns.
- Finding the best customers who spend the most money.
- Keeping customers from leaving or migrating to competitors.
- Promoting and hiring employees to ensure success for both the company and the individual.

A *prediction* is a statement about what will happen or might happen in the future; for example, predicting future sales or employee turnover. Figure 6.33 displays the three common data mining techniques for predictions. Please note the primary difference between forecasts and predictions. All forecasts are predictions, but not all predictions are forecasts. For example, when you would use regression to explain the relationship between two variables, this is a prediction but not a forecast.

FIGURE 6.32

Classification Analysis Example.

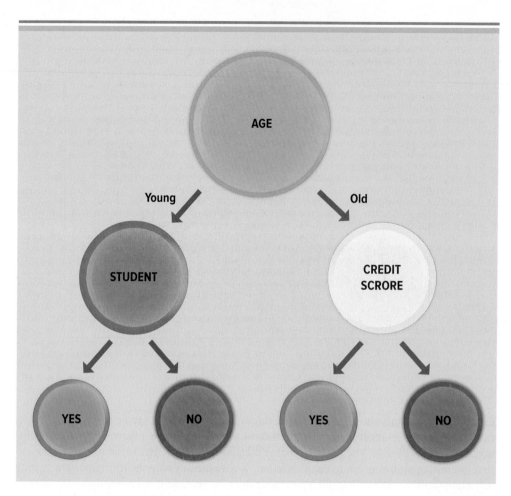

DATA ANALYSIS

LO 6.9: Explain the importance of data analytics and data visualization.

A relational database contains information in a series of two-dimensional tables. With big data, information is multidimensional, meaning it contains layers of columns and rows. A dimension is a particular attribute of information. Each layer in big data represents information according to an additional dimension. An *information cube* is the common term for the representation of

FIGURE 6.33

Data Mining Modeling Techniques for Predictions

Prediction Model	Definition	Example
Optimization model	A statistical process that finds the way to make a design, system, or decision as effective as possible; for example, finding the values of controllable variables that determine maximal productivity or minimal waste.	▪ Determine which products to produce given a limited amount of ingredients. ▪ Choose a combination of projects to maximize overall earnings.
Forecasting model	*Time-series information* is time-stamped information collected at a particular frequency. Forecasts are predictions based on time-series information, allowing users to manipulate the time series for forecasting activities.	▪ Web visits per hour ▪ Sales per month ▪ Customer service calls per day
Regression model	A statistical process for estimating the relation-ships among variables. Regression models include many techniques for modeling and analyzing several variables when the focus is on the relationship between a dependent variable and one or more independent variables.	▪ Predict the winners of a marathon based on gender, height, weight, hours of training. ▪ Explain how the quantity of weekly sales of a popular brand of beer depend on its price at a small chain of supermarkets.

multidimensional information. Figure 6.34 displays a cube (Cube a) that represents store information (the layers), product information (the rows), and promotion information (the columns).

Once a cube of information is created, users can begin to slice and dice the cube to drill down into the information. The second cube (Cube b) in Figure 6.34 displays a slice representing promotion II information for all products at all stores. The third cube (Cube c) in Figure 6.34 displays only information for promotion III, product B, at store 2. By using multidimensional analysis, users can analyze information in a number of different ways and with any number of different dimensions. For example, users might want to add dimensions of information to a current analysis including product category, region, and even forecasts for actual weather. The true value of big data is its ability to provide multidimensional analysis that allows users to gain insights into their information.

Big data is ideal for off-loading some of the querying against a database. For example, querying a database to obtain an average of sales for product B at store 2 while promotion III is under way might create a considerable processing burden for a database, essentially slowing down the time it takes another person to enter a new sale into the same database. If an organization performs numerous queries against a database (or multiple databases), aggregating that information into big data databases could be beneficial.

Advanced Data Analytics

Algorithms are mathematical formulas placed in software that performs an analysis on a data set. *Analytics* is the science of fact-based decision making. Analytics uses software-based algorithms and statistics to derive meaning from data. Advanced analytics uses data patterns to make forward-looking predictions to explain to the organization where it is headed. *Anomaly detection* is the process of identifying rare or unexpected items or events in a data set that do not conform to other items in the data set. One of the key advantages of performing advanced analytics is to detect anomalies in the data to ensure they are not used in models creating false results. An *outlier* is a data value that is numerically distant from most of the other data points in a set of data. Anomaly detection helps to identify outliers in the data that can cause problems with mathematical modeling.

Fast data is the application of big data analytics to smaller data sets in near-real or real-time in order to solve a problem or create business value. The term *fast data* is often associated with business intelligence, and the goal is to quickly gather and mine structured and unstructured data so that action can be taken. As the flood of data from sensors, actuators, and machine-to-machine (M2M) communication in the Internet of Things (IoT) continues to grow, it has become more important than ever for organizations to identify what data is time-sensitive and should be acted upon right away and what data can sit in a data warehouse or data lake until there is a reason to mine it.

FIGURE 6.35

Advanced Data Analytics

Analytics	Description
Behavioral analysis	Using data about people's behaviors to understand intent and predict future actions.
Correlation analysis	Determines a statistical relationship between variables, often for the purpose of identifying predictive factors among the variables.
Exploratory data analysis	Identifies patterns in data, including outliers, uncovering the underlying structure to understand relationships between the variables.
Pattern recognition analysis	The classification or labeling of an identified pattern in the machine learning process.
Social media analysis	Analyzes text flowing across the Internet, including unstructured text from blogs and messages.
Speech analysis	The process of analyzing recorded calls to gather information; brings structure to customer interactions and exposes information buried in customer contact center interactions with an enterprise. Speech analysis is heavily used in the customer service department to help improve processes by identifying angry customers and routing them to the appropriate customer service representative.
Text analysis	Analyzes unstructured data to find trends and patterns in words and sentences. Text mining a firm's customer support email might identify which customer service representative is best able to handle the question, allowing the system to forward it to the right person.
Web analysis	Analyzes unstructured data associated with websites to identify consumer behavior and website navigation.

A *data scientist* extracts knowledge from data by performing statistical analysis, data mining, and advanced analytics on big data to identify trends, market changes, and other relevant information. Figure 6.35 displays the techniques a data scientist will use to perform big data advanced analytics.

Data Visualization

Traditional bar graphs and pie charts are boring and at best confusing and at worst misleading. As databases and graphics collide more and more, people are creating infographics, which display information graphically so it can be easily understood. *Infographics (information graphics)* present the results of data analysis, displaying the patterns, relationships, and trends in a graphical format. Infographics are exciting and quickly convey a story users can understand without having to analyze numbers, tables, and boring charts (see Figure 6.36 and Figure 6.37).

A *data artist* is a business analytics specialist who uses visual tools to help people understand complex data. Great data visualizations provide insights into something new about the underlying patterns and relationships. Just think of the periodic table of elements and imagine if you had to look at an Excel spreadsheet showing each element and the associated attributes in a table format. This would be not only difficult to understand but easy to misinterpret. By placing the elements in the visual periodic table, you quickly grasp how the elements relate and the associated hierarchy. Data artists are experts at creating a story from the information. Infographics perform the same function for business data as the periodic table does for chemical elements.

Analysis paralysis occurs when the user goes into an emotional state of overanalysis (or overthinking) a situation so that a decision or action is never taken, in effect paralyzing the outcome. In the time of big data, analysis paralysis is a growing problem. One solution is to use data visualizations to help people make decisions faster. *Data visualization* describes technologies that allow users to see or visualize data to transform information into a business perspective. Data visualization is a powerful way to simplify complex data sets by placing data in a format that is easily grasped and understood far quicker than the raw data alone. *Data visualization tools* move beyond Excel graphs and charts into sophisticated analysis techniques such as controls, instruments, maps, time-series graphs, and more. Data visualization tools can help uncover correlations and trends in data that would otherwise go unrecognized.

BUSINESS DRIVEN GLOBALIZATION

Congratulations! You have just been hired as a consultant for Integrity Information Inc., a start-up business intelligence consulting company. Your first job is to help work with the sales department in securing a new client, The Warehouse. The Warehouse has been operating in the United States for more than a decade, and its primary business is to sell wholesale low-cost products. The Warehouse is interested in hiring Integrity Information Inc. to clean up the data that are stored in its U.S. database. To determine how good your work is, the client would like your analysis of the following spreadsheet. The Warehouse is also interested in expanding globally and wants to purchase several independent wholesale stores located in Australia, Thailand, China, Japan, and the United Kingdom. Before the company moves forward with the venture, it wants to understand what types of data issues it might encounter as it begins to transfer data from each global entity to the data warehouse. Please create a list detailing the potential issues The Warehouse can anticipate encountering as it consolidates the global databases into a single data warehouse.[8]

Integrity Information Inc.

CUST ID	First Name	Last Name	Address	City	State	Zip	Phone	Last Order Date
233620	Christopher	Lee	12421 W Olympic Blvd	Los Angeles	CA	75080-1100	(972)680-7848	4/18/2014
233621	Bruce	Brandwen	268 W 44th St	New York	PA	10036-3906	(212)471-6077	5/3/2014
233622	Glr	Johnson	4100 E Dry Creek Rd	Littleton	CO	80122-3729	(303)712-5461	5/6/2014
233623	Dave	Owens	466 Commerce Rd	Staunton	VA	24401-4432	(540)851-0362	3/19/2014
233624	John	Coulbourn	124 Action St	Maynard	MA	1754	(978)987-0100	4/24/2014
233629	Dan	Gagliardo	2875 Union Rd	Cheektowaga	NY	14227-1461	(716)558-8191	5/4/2014
23362	Damanceee	Allen	1633 Broadway	New York	NY	10019-6708	(212)708-1576	
233630	Michael	Peretz	235 E 45th St	New York	NY	10017-3305	(212)210-1340	4/30/2014
233631	Jody	Veeder	440 Science Dr	Madison	WI	53711-1064	(608)238-9690 X227	3/27/2014
233632	Michael	Kehrer	3015 SSE Loop 323	Tyler	TX	75701	(903)579-3229	4/28/2014
233633	Erin	Yoon	3500 Carillon Pt	Kirkland	WA	98033-7354	(425)897-7221	3/25/2014
233634	Madeline	Shefferly	4100 E Dry Creek Rd	Littleton	CO	80122-3729	(303)486-3949	3/33/2014
233635	Steven	Conduit	1332 Enterprise Dr	West Chester	PA	19380-5970	(610)692-5900	4/27/2014
233636	Joseph	Kovach	1332 Enterprise Dr	West Chester	PA	19380-5970	(610)692-5900	4/28/2014
233637	Richard	Jordan	1700 N	Philadelphia	PA	19131-4728	(215)581-6770	3/19/2014
233638	Scott	Mikolajczyk	1655 Crofton Blvd	Crofton	MD	21114-1387	(410)729-8155	4/28/2014
233639	Susan	Shragg	1875 Century Park E	Los Angeles	CA	90067-2501	(310)785-0511	4/29/2014
233640	Rob	Ponto	29777 Telegraph Rd	Southfield	MI	48034-1303	(810)204-4724	5/5/2014
233642	Lauren	Butler	1211 Avenue Of The Americas	New York	NY	10036-8701	(212)852-7494	4/22/2014
233643	Christopher	Lee	12421 W Olympic Blvd	Los Angeles	CA	90064-1022	(310)689-2577	3/25/2014
233644	Michelle	Decker	6922 Hollywood Blvd	Hollywood	CA	90028-6117	(323)817-4655	5/8/2014
233647	Natalia	Galeano	1211 Avenue Of The Americas	New York	NY	10036-8701	(646)728-6911	4/23/2014
233648	Bobbie	Orchard	4201 Congress St	Charlotte	NC	28209-4617	(704)557-2444	5/11/2014
233650	Ben	Konfino	1111 Stewart Ave	Bethpage	NY	11714-3533	(516)803-1406	3/19/2014
233651	Lenee	Santana	1050 Techwood Dr NW	Atlanta	GA	30318-KKRR	(404)885-2000	3/22/2014
233652	Lauren	Monks	7700 Wisconsin Ave	Bethesda	MD	20814-3578	(301)771-4772	3/19/2005
233653	Mark	Woolley	10950 Washington Blvd	Culver City	CA	90232-4026	(310)202-2900	4/20/2014

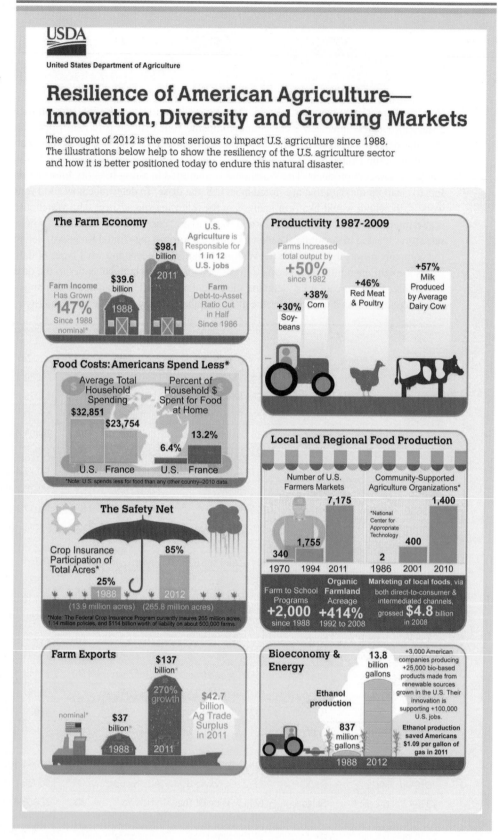

Business intelligence dashboards track corporate metrics such as critical success factors and key performance indicators and include advanced capabilities such as interactive controls, allowing users to manipulate data for analysis. The majority of business intelligence software vendors offer a number of data visualization tools and business intelligence dashboards.

FIGURE 6.37

Infographic Health Example

Big data is one of the most promising technology trends occurring today. Of course, notable companies such as Facebook, Google, and Netflix are gaining the most business insights from big data currently, but many smaller markets are entering the scene, including retail, insurance, and health care. Over the next decade, as big data starts to improve your everyday life by providing insights into your social relationships, habits, and careers, you can expect to see the need for data scientists and data artists dramatically increase.

LEARNING OUTCOME REVIEW

Learning Outcome 6.1: Explain the four primary traits that determine the value of information.

Information is data converted into a meaningful and useful context. Information can tell an organization how its current operations are performing and help it estimate and strategize about how future operations might perform. It is important to understand the different levels, formats, and granularities of information along with the four primary traits that help determine the value of information, which include (1) information type: transactional and analytical; (2) information timeliness; (3) information quality; and (4) information governance.

Learning Outcome 6.2: Describe a database, a database management system, and the relational database model.

A database maintains information about various types of objects (inventory), events (transactions), people (employees), and places (warehouses). A database management system (DBMS) creates, reads, updates, and deletes data in a database while controlling access and security. A DBMS provides methodologies for creating, updating, storing, and retrieving data in a database. In addition, a DBMS provides facilities for controlling data access and security, allowing data sharing and enforcing data integrity. The relational database model allows users to create, read, update, and delete data in a relational database.

Learning Outcome 6.3: Identify the business advantages of a relational database.

Many business managers are familiar with Excel and other spreadsheet programs they can use to store business data. Although spreadsheets are excellent for supporting some data analysis, they offer limited functionality in terms of security, accessibility, and flexibility and can rarely scale to support business growth. From a business perspective, relational databases offer many advantages over using a text document or a spreadsheet, including increased flexibility, increased scalability and performance, reduced information redundancy, increased information integrity (quality), and increased information security.

Learning Outcome 6.4: Explain the business benefits of a data-driven website.

A data-driven website is an interactive website kept constantly updated and relevant to the needs of its customers using a database. Data-driven capabilities are especially useful when the website offers a great deal of information, products, or services because visitors are frequently annoyed if they are buried under an avalanche of information when searching a website. Many companies use the web to make some of the information in their internal databases available to customers and business partners.

Learning Outcome 6.5: Describe the roles and purposes of data warehouses and data marts in an organization.

A data warehouse is a logical collection of information, gathered from many different operational databases, that supports business analysis and decision making. The primary value of a data warehouse is to combine information, more specifically, strategic information, throughout an organization into a single repository in such a way that the people who need that information can make decisions and undertake business analysis.

Learning Outcome 6.6: Identify the advantages of using business intelligence to support managerial decision making.

Many organizations today find it next to impossible to understand their own strengths and weaknesses, let alone their biggest competitors', due to enormous volumes of organizational data being inaccessible to all but the MIS department. Organizational data includes far more than simple structured data elements in a database; the set of data also includes unstructured data such as voice mail, customer phone calls, text messages, and video clips, along with numerous new forms of data, such as tweets from Twitter. Managers today find themselves in the position of being data rich and information poor, and they need to implement business intelligence systems to solve this challenge.

Learning Outcome 6.7: Identify the four common characteristics of big data.

The four Vs of big data include variety, veracity, voluminous, and velocity. Variety includes different forms of structured and unstructured data. Veracity includes the uncertainty of data, including biases, noise, and abnormalities. Voluminous is the scale of data. Velocity is the analysis of streaming data as it travels around the Internet.

Learning Outcome 6.8: Explain data mining and identify the three elements of data mining.

Data mining is the process of analyzing data to extract information not offered by the raw data alone. The three elements of data mining include data, discovery, and deployment.

- Data: Foundation for data-directed decision making.
- Discovery: Process of identifying new patterns, trends, and insights.
- Deployment: Process of implementing discoveries to drive success.

Learning Outcome 6.9: Explain the importance of data analytics and data visualization.

Algorithms are mathematical formulas placed in software that performs an analysis on a data set. Analytics is the science of fact-based decision making. Analytics uses software-based algorithms and statistics to derive meaning from data. Advanced analytics uses data patterns to make forward-looking predictions to explain to the organization where it is headed. Data visualization describes technologies that allow users to see or visualize data to transform information into a business perspective. Data visualization is a powerful way to simplify complex data sets by placing data in a format that is easily grasped and understood far quicker than the raw data alone.

OPENING CASE QUESTIONS

1. **Knowledge:** List the reasons a business would want to display information in a graphic or visual format.
2. **Comprehension:** Explain how issues with low-quality information will impact big data.
3. **Application:** Explain how a marketing department could use data visualization tools to help with the release of a new product.
4. **Analysis:** Categorize the five common characteristics of high-quality information and rank them in order of importance for big data.
5. **Synthesis:** Develop a list of some possible entities and attributes located in a marketing database.
6. **Evaluate:** Asses how a business could use a few of the data analysis techniques to understand how the business is operating.

KEY TERMS

Affinity grouping analysis 255
Algorithms 259
Analysis paralysis 260
Analytics 259
Anomaly detection 259
Attribute 234
Big data 250
Business-critical integrity
    constraint 238
Business rule 238
Business intelligence
    dashboard 262
Classification analysis 257
Cluster analysis 256
Comparative analysis 248
Competitive monitoring 248
Content creator 239
Content editor 239
Data-driven decision
    management 250
Data aggregation 243
Data artist 260
Data broker 247
Data dictionary 233
Data element (or data field) 233
Data gap analysis 232
Data governance 232
Data lake 247
Data latency 238
Data map 249
Data mart 243
Data mining 253
Data mining tools 257

Data model 233
Data point 247
Data profiling 254
Data quality audits   247
Data replication 254
Data scientist 260
Data set 248
Data steward 232
Data stewardship 232
Data validation 232
Data visualization 260
Data visualization tools 260
Data warehouse 242
Database 232
Database management system
    (DBMS) 232
Dirty data 244
Distributed computing 250
Data-driven website 239
Dynamic catalog 239
Dynamic information 239
Entity 234
Estimation analysis 255
Extraction, transformation, and
    loading (ETL) 243
Fast data 259
Foreign key 235
Identity management 238
Infographic (or information
    graphic) 260
Information cleansing or
    scrubbing 244
Information cube 258

Information granularity 227
Information inconsistency 229
Information integrity 238
Information integrity issues 229
Information redundancy 238
Integrity constraint 238
Logical view of information 237
Master data management
    (MDM) 232
Market basket analysis 256
Metadata 233
Outlier 259
Physical view of information 237
Prediction 257
Primary key 234
Query-by-example (QBE)
    tool 233
Real-time information 229
Real-time system 229
Recommendation engine 255
Record 234
Relational database management
    system 234
Relational database model 233
Relational integrity constraint 238
Repository 242
Source data 248
Static information 239
Structured query language
    (SQL) 233
Time-series information 258
Virtualization 252

1. Why does a business need to be concerned with the quality of its data?
2. Why would a company care about the timeliness of its data?
3. What are the five characteristics common to high-quality information?
4. What are the four primary traits that help determine the value of information?
5. What is the difference between an entity and an attribute?
6. What is a data warehouse and why would a business want to implement one?
7. How does ETL help transfer data in and out of the data warehouse?
8. What is the purpose of information cleansing (or scrubbing)?
9. What are the causes of dirty data?
10. What is business intelligence, and how can it help a company achieve success?
11. Why would a business be data rich but information poor?
12. What are the four common characteristics of big data?
13. What is distributed computing, and how has it helped drive the big data era?
14. What is virtualization, and how has it helped drive the big data era?
15. What are the four data-mining techniques?

CLOSING CASE ONE

Data Visualization: Stories for the Information Age

At the intersection of art and algorithm, data visualization schematically abstracts information to bring about a deeper understanding of the data, wrapping it in an element of awe. Although the practice of visually representing information is arguably the foundation of all design, a newfound fascination with data visualization has been emerging. After *The New York Times* and *The Guardian* recently opened their online archives to the public, artists rushed to dissect nearly two centuries' worth of information, elevating this art form to new prominence.

For artists and designers, data visualization is a new frontier of self-expression, powered by the proliferation of information and the evolution of available tools. For enterprises, it is a platform for displaying products and services in the context of the cultural interaction that surrounds them, reflecting consumers' increasing demand for corporate transparency.

"Looking at something ordinary in a new way makes it extraordinary," says Aaron Koblin, one of the more recent pioneers of the discipline. As technology lead of Google's Creative Labs in San Francisco, he spearheaded the search giant's Chrome Experiments series designed to show off the speed and reliability of the Chrome browser.

Forget Pie Charts and Bar Graphs

Data visualization has nothing to do with pie charts and bar graphs. And it's only marginally related to infographics, information design that tends to be about objectivity and clarification. Such representations simply offer another iteration of the data—restating it visually and making it easier to digest. Data visualization, on the other hand, is an interpretation, a different way to look at and think about data that often exposes complex patterns or correlations.

Data visualization is a way to make sense of the ever-increasing stream of information with which we're bombarded and provides a creative antidote to the analysis paralysis that can result from the burden of processing such a large volume of information. "It's not about clarifying data," says Koblin. "It's about contextualizing it."

Today algorithmically inspired artists are reimagining the art-science continuum through work that frames the left-brain analysis of data in a right-brain creative story. Some use data visualization as a bridge between alienating information and its emotional impact: see Chris Jordan's portraits of global mass culture. Others take a more technological angle and focus on cultural utility: the Zoetrope project offers a temporal and historical visualization of the ephemeral web. Still others are pure artistic indulgence—such as Koblin's own Flight Patterns project, a visualization of air traffic over North America.

How Business Can Benefit

There are real implications for business here. Most cell phone providers, for instance, offer a statement of a user's monthly activity. Most often it's an overwhelming table of various numerical measures of how much you talked, when, with whom, and how much it cost. A visual representation of this data might help certain patterns emerge, revealing calling habits and perhaps helping users save money.

Companies can also use data visualization to gain new insight into consumer behavior. By observing and understanding what people do with the data—what they find useful and what they dismiss as worthless—executives can make the valuable distinction between what consumers say versus what they do. Even now, this can be a tricky call to make from behind the two-way mirror of a traditional qualitative research setting.

It's essential to understand the importance of creative vision along with the technical mastery of software. Data visualization isn't about using all the data available but about deciding which patterns and elements to focus on, building a narrative, and telling the story of the raw data in a different, compelling way.

Ultimately, data visualization is more than complex software or the prettying up of spreadsheets. It's not innovation for the sake of innovation. It's about the most ancient of social rituals: storytelling. It's about telling the story locked in the data differently, more engagingly, in a way that draws us in, makes our eyes open a little wider and our jaw drop ever so slightly. And as we process it, it can sometimes change our perspective altogether.[9]

Questions

1. Identify the effects poor information might have on a data visualization project.
2. How does data visualization use database technologies?
3. How could a business use data visualization to identify new trends?
4. What is the correlation between data mining and data visualization?
5. Is data visualization a form of business intelligence? Why or why not?
6. What security issues are associated with data visualization?
7. What might happen to a data visualization project if it failed to cleanse or scrub its data?

Informing Information

Since the beginning of time, humans have been using pictures and images to communicate, moving from cave drawings to hieroglyphics to the Internet. Today, it is easier than ever to paint a picture worth 100,000 words, thanks to technological advances. The primary advantages are databases and data warehouses that capture enormous amounts of data. Informing means accessing large amounts of data from different management information systems. According to a recent analysis of press releases by *PR Newswire,* an article or advertisement that uses visual images can significantly improve the number of views a message generates. This can be a true competitive advantage in the digital age.

An infographic (or information graphic) displays information graphically so it can be more easily understood. Infographics cut straight to the point by presenting complex information in a simple visual format. Infographics can present the results of large data analysis, looking for patterns and relationships that monitor changes in variables over time. Because infographics can easily become overwhelming, users need to be careful not to display too much data, or the resulting infographics can result in information overload. Effective infographics can achieve outstanding results for marketing, advertising, and public relations. According to *PR Newswire,* infographics gain the greatest competitive advantage when they have the following:

- Survey results that are too hard to understand in text format.
- Statistical data that are not interesting for readers.
- Comparison research where the impact can be far more dramatic when presented visually.
- Messages for multilingual audiences.
- Any information that can use a visual element to make it more interesting (see Figures 6.38, 6.39, and 6.40 for examples).[10]

Questions

1. List the reasons a business would want to display information in a graphic or visual format.
2. Describe how a business could use a business intelligence digital dashboard to gain an understanding of how the business is operating.
3. Explain how a marketing department could use data visualization tools to help with the release of a new product.
4. Categorize the five common characteristics of high-quality information and rank them in order of importance for Hotels.com.
5. Develop a list of some possible entities and attributes located in the Hotels.com database.
6. Assess how Hotels.com is using BI to identify trends and change associated business processes.

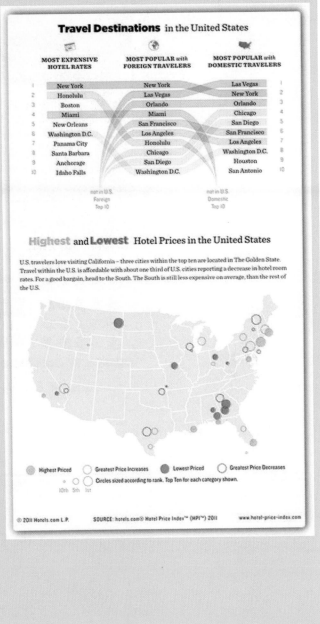

FIGURE 6.38

Hotels.com Travel Infographic

Courtesy of Hotels.com

FIGURE 6.39

Emerson's Food Waste
Infographic

©2015 InSinkErator, InSinkErator® is a
division of Emerson Electric Co.

FIGURE 6.40

Changes in Consumer Action
on the Environment

Source: INFOGRAPHIC: The Road to Fuel
Efficiency," *Department of Energy,*
November 27, 2012. https://energy.gov.

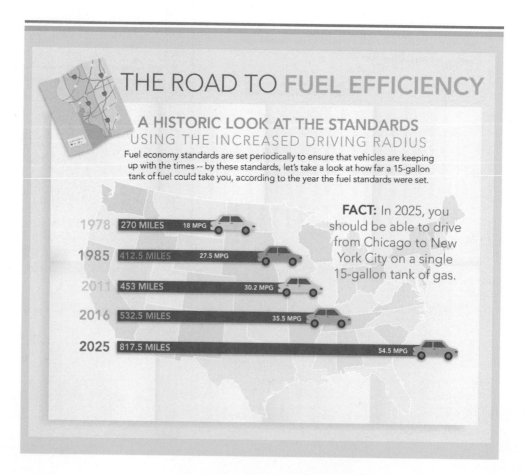

CRITICAL BUSINESS THINKING

1. Improving Information Quality

HangUps Corporation designs and distributes closet organization structures. The company operates five different systems: order entry, sales, inventory management, shipping, and billing. The company has severe information quality issues including missing, inaccurate, redundant, and incomplete information. The company wants to implement a data warehouse containing information from the five different systems to help maintain a single customer view, drive business decisions, and perform multidimensional analysis. Identify how the organization can improve its information quality when it begins designing and building its data warehouse.

2. Information Timeliness

Information timeliness is a major consideration for all organizations. Organizations need to decide the frequency of backups and the frequency of updates to a data warehouse. In a team, describe the timeliness requirements for backups and updates to a data warehouse for:

- Weather tracking systems.
- Car dealership inventories.
- Vehicle tire sales forecasts.
- Interest rates.
- Restaurant inventories.
- Grocery store inventories.

3. Entities and Attributes

Martex Inc. is a manufacturer of athletic equipment, and its primary lines of business include running, tennis, golf, swimming, basketball, and aerobics equipment. Martex currently supplies four primary vendors, including Sam's Sports, Total Effort, The Underline, and Maximum Workout. Martex wants to build a database to help it organize its products. In a group, identify the different types of entity classes and the related attributes that Martex will want to consider when designing the database.

4. Integrating Information

You are currently working for the Public Transportation Department of Chatfield. The department controls all forms of public transportation, including buses, subways, and trains. Each department has about 300 employees and maintains its own accounting, inventory, purchasing, and human resource systems. Generating reports across departments is a difficult task and usually involves gathering and correlating the information from the many different systems. It typically takes about two weeks to generate the quarterly balance sheets and profit-and-loss statements. Your team has been asked to compile a report recommending what the Public Transportation Department of Chatfield can do to alleviate its information and system issues. Be sure that your report addresses the various reasons departmental reports are presently difficult to obtain as well as how you plan to solve this problem.

5. Explaining Relational Databases

You have been hired by Vision, a start-up clothing company. Your manager, Holly Henningson, is unfamiliar with databases and their associated business value. Henningson has asked you to create a report detailing the basics of databases. She would also like you to provide a detailed explanation of relational databases along with their associated business advantages.

6. Gathering Business Intelligence

When considering new business opportunities, you need knowledge about the competition. One of the things many new business owners fail to do is to gather business intelligence on their competitors, such as how many there are and what differentiates each of them. You may find there are too many and that they would be tough competition for you. Or, you may find that there are few competitors and the ones who are out there offer very little value.

Generate a new business idea you could launch on the Internet. Research the Internet to find similar businesses in the area you have chosen. How many sites did you find that are offering the same products or services you are planning to offer? Did you come across any sites from another country that have a unique approach that you did not see on any of the sites in your own country? How would you use this information in pursuing your business idea?

7. Information—Business Intelligence or a Diversion from the Truth?

President Barack Obama used part of his commencement address at Virginia's Hampton University to criticize the flood of incomplete information or downright incorrect information that flows in the 24-hour news cycle. The president said, "You're coming of age in a 24/7 media environment that bombards us with all kinds of content and exposes us to all kinds of arguments, some of which don't always rank all that high on the truth meter. With iPods and iPads and Xboxes and PlayStations—none of which I know how to work—information becomes a distraction, a diversion, a form of entertainment, rather than a tool of empowerment, rather than the means of emancipation."

Do you agree or disagree with President Obama's statement? Who is responsible for verifying the accuracy of online information? What should happen to companies that post inaccurate information? What should happen to individuals who post inaccurate information? What should you remember when reading or citing sources for online information?

8. Google Books

Google is scanning all or parts of the book collections of the University of Michigan, Harvard University, Stanford University, the New York Public Library, and Oxford University as part of its Google Print Library Project. It intends to make those texts searchable on Google. The Authors Guild filed a lawsuit against Google, alleging that its scanning and digitizing of library books constitutes a "massive" copyright infringement. Do you view Google's Print Library Project as a violation of copyright laws? If you were a publisher, how would you feel about Google's project? If you were an author, how would you feel about having your book posted for free on Google Books? What do you think the future of the book publishing industry will look like based on Google's radical new Google Book's website?

9. That Is Not My Mother in the Casket

Information—you simply can't put a value on having the right (or the cost of having the wrong) information. Just look at the mistake made at the Crib Point cemetery in Victoria, Australia, when they were burying Mrs. Ryan, an 85-year-old woman with almost 70 children, grandchildren, and great-grandchildren attending her funeral. The bereaved family of Mrs. Ryan was shocked to lift the lid of her coffin during the funeral to discover another woman lying in her clothes and jewelry. Where was the body of Mrs. Ryan? Mrs. Ryan had been buried earlier that day in the other woman's clothes, jewelry, and plot. What type of information blunder could possibly occur to allow someone to be buried in the wrong clothes, coffin, and plot? What could the cemetery do to ensure its customers are buried in the correct places? Why is the quality of information important to any business? What issues can occur when a business uses low-quality information to make decisions?

10. Data Storage

Information is one of the most important assets of any business. Businesses must ensure information accuracy, completeness, consistency, timeliness, and uniqueness. In addition, business must have a reliable backup service. In part thanks to cloud computing, there are many data storage services on the Internet. These sites offer storage of information that can be accessed from anywhere in the world. These data storage services include Google Docs, Box, and DropBox, to name a few.

Visit a few of these sites along with several others you find through research. Which sites are free? Are there limits to how much you can store? If so, what is the limit? What type of information can you store (video, text, photos, etc.)? Can you allow multiple users with different passwords to access your storage area? Are you contractually bound for a certain duration (annual, etc.)? Does it make good business sense to store business data on the Internet? What about personal data?

11. Sorry, I Didn't Mean to Post Your Social Security Number on the Internet

Programming 101 teaches all students that security is the crucial part of any system. You must secure your data! It appears that some people working for the State of Oklahoma forgot this important lesson when tens of thousands of Oklahoma residents had their sensitive data—including numbers—posted on the Internet for the general public to access. You have probably heard this type of report before, but have you heard that the error went unnoticed for 3 years? A programmer reported the problem, explaining how he could easily change the page his browser was pointing to and grab the entire database for the State of Oklahoma. Also, because of the programming, malicious users could easily tamper with the database by changing data or adding fictitious data. If you are still thinking that isn't such a big deal, it gets worse. The website also posted the Sexual and Violent Offender Registry. Yes, the Department of Corrections employee data were also available for the general public to review.

In a group, discuss the following:

- Why is it important to secure data?
- What can happen if someone accesses your customer database?
- What could happen if someone changes the information in your customer database and adds fictitious data?
- Who should be held responsible for the State of Oklahoma data breach?
- What are the business risks associated with database security?

12. Track Your Life

With wearable technology, you can track your entire life. Nike's Fuelband and Jawbone's Up track all of your physical activity, caloric burn, and sleep patterns. You can track your driving patterns, tooth-brushing habits, and even laundry status. The question now becomes how to track all of your trackers.

A new company called Exist incorporates tracking devices with weather data, music choices, Netflix favorites, and Twitter activity all in one digital dashboard. Exist wants to understand every area of your life and provide correlation information between such things as your personal productivity and mood. As the different types of data expand, so will the breadth of correlations Exist can point out. For instance, do you tweet more when you are working at home? If so, does this increase productivity? Exist wants to track all of your trackers and analyze the information to help you become more efficient and more effective.

Create a digital dashboard for tracking your life. Choose four areas you want to track and determine three ways you would measure each area. For example, if you track eating habits, you might want to measure calories and place unacceptable levels in red and acceptable levels in green. Once completed, determine whether you can find any correlations among the areas in your life.

13. Free Data!

The U.S. Bureau of Labor Statistics states that its role is as the "principal fact-finding agency for the federal government in the broad field of labor economics and statistics." And the data that the bureau provides via its website are available to anyone, free. This can represent a treasure trove of business intelligence and data mining for those who take advantage of this resource.

Visit the website www.bls.gov. What type of information does the site provide? What information do you find most useful? What sort of information concerning employment and wages is available? How is this information categorized? How would this type of information be helpful to a business manager? What type of demographic information is available? How could this benefit a new start-up business?

14. Follow the Data

There is a classic line in the movie *All the President's Men,* which covers the Watergate investigation, where Deep Throat meets with Bob Woodward and coolly advises him to "follow the money." Woodward follows the money, and the Watergate investigation ends with President Richard Nixon's resignation. If you want to find out what is happening in today's data-filled world, you could probably change those words to "follow the data."

One of the newest forms of legal requirements emerging from the data explosion is ediscovery, the legal requirements mandating that an organization must archive all forms of software communications, including email, text messages, and multimedia. Yes, the text message you sent 4 years ago could come back to haunt you.

Organizations today have more data than they know what to do with and are frequently overwhelmed with data management. Getting at such data and presenting them in a useful manner for cogent analysis is a tremendous task that haunts managers. What do you think is involved in data management? What is contained in the zettabytes of data stored by organizations? Why would an organization store data? How long should an organization store its data? What are the risks associated with failing to store organizational data?

APPLY YOUR KNOWLEDGE BUSINESS PROJECTS

PROJECT I   Mining the Data Warehouse

Alana Smith is a senior buyer for a large wholesaler that sells different types of arts and crafts to greeting card stores such as Hallmark. Smith's latest marketing strategy is to send all of her customers a new line of handmade picture frames from Russia. All of her information supports her decision for the new line. Her analysis predicts that the frames should sell an average of 10 to 15 per store per day. Smith is excited about the new line and is positive it will be a success.

One month later, Smith learns the frames are selling 50 percent below expectations, with an average of between five and eight frames sold daily in each store. She decides to access the company's data warehouse information to determine why sales are below expectations. Identify several dimensions of information that Smith will want to analyze to help her decide what is causing the problems with the picture frame sales.

PROJECT II   Different Dimensions

The focus of data warehousing is to extend the transformation of data into information. Data warehouses offer strategic level, external, integrated, and historical information so businesses can make projections, identify trends, and make key business decisions. The data warehouse collects and stores integrated sets of historical information from multiple operational systems and feeds them to one or more data marts. It may also provide end user access to support enterprisewide views of information.

You are currently working on a marketing team for a large corporation that sells jewelry around the world. Your boss has asked you to look at the following dimensions of data to determine which ones you want in your data mart for performing sales and market analysis (see Figure AYK.1). As a team, categorize the different dimensions, ranking them from 1 to 5, with 1 indicating that the dimension offers the highest value and must be in your data mart and 5 indicating that the dimension offers the lowest value and does not need to be in your data mart.

Dimension	Value (1–5)	Dimension	Value (1–5)
Product number		Season	
Store location		Promotion	
Customer net worth		Payment method	
Number of sales personnel		Commission policy	
Customer eating habits		Manufacturer	
Store hours		Traffic report	
Salesperson ID		Customer language	
Product style		Weather	
Order date		Customer gender	
Product quantity		Local tax information	
Ship date		Local cultural demographics	
Current interest rate		Stock market closing	
Product cost		Customer religious affiliation	
Customer political affiliation		Reason for purchase	
Local market analysis		Employee dress code policy	
Order time		Customer age	
Customer spending habits		Employee vacation policy	
Product price		Employee benefits	
Exchange rates		Current tariff information	
Product gross margin			

FIGURE AYK.1

Data Warehouse Data

PROJECT III Understanding Search

Pretend that you are a search engine. Choose a topic to query. It can be anything such as your favorite book, movie, band, or sports team. Search your topic on Google, pick three or four pages from the results, and print them out. On each printout, find the individual words from your query (such as "Boston Red Sox" or "*The Godfather*") and use a highlighter to mark each word with color. Do that for each of the documents that you print out. Now tape those documents on a wall, step back a few feet, and review your documents.

If you did not know what the rest of a page said and could judge only by the colored words, which document do you think would be most relevant? Is there anything that would make a document look more relevant? Is it better for the words to be in a large heading or to occur several times in a smaller font? Do you prefer the words to be at the top or the bottom of the page? How often do the words need to appear? Come up with two or three things you would look for to see whether a document matched a query well. This exercise mimics search engine processes and should help you understand why a search engine returns certain results over others.

PROJECT IV Predicting Netflix

Netflix Inc., the largest online movie rental service, provides more than 12 million subscribers access to more than 100,000 unique DVD titles along with a growing on-demand library in excess of 200,000 choices. Data and information are so important to Netflix that it created The Netflix Prize, an open competition for anyone who could improve the data used in prediction ratings for films (an increase of 10 percent), based on previous ratings. The winner would receive a $1 million prize.

The ability to search, analyze, and comprehend information is vital for any organization's success. It certainly was for Netflix—it was happy to pay anyone $1 million to improve the quality of its information. In a group, explain how Netflix might use databases, data warehouses, and data marts to predict customer movie recommendations. Here are a few characteristics you might want to analyze to get you started:

- Customer demographics.
- Movie genre, rating, year, producer, and type.
- Actor information.
- Internet access.
- Location for mail pickup.

PROJECT V   The Crunch Factory

The Crunch Factory is one of the fourth-largest gym companies operating in Australia, and each gym operates its own system with its own database. Unfortunately, the company failed to develop any data-capturing standards and now faces the challenges associated with low-quality enterprisewide information. For example, one system has a field to capture email addresses, but another system does not. Duplicate customer information among the different systems is another major issue, and the company continually finds itself sending conflicting or competing messages to customers from different gyms. A customer could also have multiple accounts within the company, one representing a membership, another representing additional classes, and yet another for a personal trainer. The Crunch Factory has no way to identify that the different customer accounts are actually for the same customer.

To remain competitive and be able to generate business intelligence, The Crunch Factory has to resolve these challenges. The Crunch Factory has just hired you as its data quality expert. Your first task is to determine how the company can turn its low-quality information into high-quality business intelligence. Create a plan that The Crunch Factory can implement that details the following:

- Challenges associated with low-quality information.
- Benefits associated with high-quality information.
- Recommendations on how the company can clean up its data.

PROJECT VI   Too Much of a Good Thing

The Castle, a premium retailer of clothes and accessories, created an enterprisewide data warehouse so all its employees could access information for decision making. The Castle soon discovered that it is possible to have too much of a good thing. The Castle employees found themselves inundated with data and unable to make any decisions, a common occurrence called analysis paralysis. When sales representatives queried the data warehouse to determine whether a certain product in the size, color, and category was available, they would get hundreds of results showing everything from production orders to supplier contracts. It became easier for the sales representatives to look in the warehouse themselves than to check the system. Employees found the data warehouse was simply too big, too complicated, and contained too much irrelevant information.

The Castle is committed to making its data warehouse system a success and has come to you for help. Create a plan that details the value of the data warehouse to the business, how it can be easier for all employees to use, and the potential business benefits the company can derive from its data warehouse.

PROJECT VII   Twitter Buzz

Technology tools that can predict sales for the coming week, decide when to increase inventory, and determine when additional staff is required are extremely valuable. Twitter is not just for tweeting your whereabouts anymore. Twitter and other social media sites have become great tools for gathering business intelligence on customers, including what they like, dislike, need, and want. Twitter is easy to use, and businesses can track every single time a customer makes a statement about a particular product or service. Good businesses turn this valuable information into intelligence spotting trends and patterns in customer opinion.

Do you agree that a business can use Twitter to gain business intelligence? How many companies do you think are aware of Twitter and exactly how they can use it to gain BI? How do you think Twitter uses a data warehouse? How do you think companies store Twitter information? How would a company use Twitter in a data mart? How would a company use cubes to analyze Twitter data?

AYK APPLICATION PROJECTS

If you are looking for Access projects to incorporate into your class, try any of the following after reading this chapter.

Project Number	Project Name	Project Type	Plug-In	Focus Area	Project Level	Skill Set	Page Number
28	Daily Invoice	Access	T5, T6, T7, T8	Business Analysis	Introductory	Entities, Relationships, and Databases	AYK.17
29	Billing Data	Access	T5, T6, T7, T8	Business Intelligence	Introductory	Entities, Relationships, and Databases	AYK.19
30	Inventory Data	Access	T5, T6, T7, T8	SCM	Intermediate	Entities, Relationships, and Databases	AYK.20
31	Call Center	Access	T5, T6, T7, T8	CRM	Intermediate	Entities, Relationships, and Databases	AYK.21
32	Sales Pipeline	Access	T5, T6, T7, T8	Business Intelligence	Advanced	Entities, Relationships, and Databases	AYK.23
33	Online Classified Ads	Access	T5, T6, T7, T8	Ecommerce	Advanced	Entities, Relationships, and Databases	AYK.23

7

CHAPTER

Networks: Mobile Business

CHAPTER OUTLINE

SECTION 7.1
Connectivity: The Business Value of a Networked World

- Overview of a Connected World
- Benefits of a Connected World
- Challenges of a Connected World

SECTION 7.2
Mobility: The Business Value of a Wireless World

- Wireless Network Categories
- Business Applications of Wireless Networks

What's in IT for me?

The pace of technological change never ceases to amaze. Kindergarten classes are now learning PowerPoint, and many elementary school children have their own cell phones. What used to take hours to download over a dial-up modem connection can now transfer in a matter of seconds through an invisible, wireless network connection from a computer thousands of miles away. We are living in an increasingly wireless present and hurtling ever faster toward a wireless future. The tipping point of ubiquitous, wireless, handheld, mobile computing is approaching quickly.

As a business student, understanding network infrastructures and wireless technologies allows you to take advantage of mobile workforces. Understanding the benefits and challenges of mobility is a critical skill for business executives, regardless of whether you are a novice or a seasoned *Fortune* 500 employee. By learning about the various concepts discussed in this chapter, you will develop a better understanding of how business can leverage networking technologies to analyze network types, improve wireless and mobile business processes, and evaluate alternative networking options.

©fotog/Getty Images RF

©FocusTechnology/Alamy Stock Photo

©Ronnie Kaufman/Blend Images LLC RF

Disrupting the Taxi: Uber

Ray Markovich started driving a taxi in Chicago 3 years ago after shutting his struggling wireless phone store. Driving a cab wasn't particularly gratifying or lucrative—he had to pay $400 a week just to lease his white 2011 Ford Escape. It was predictable, if monotonous, work. Well, there's nothing monotonous about it now. In June, Markovich, a thin, well-dressed man with short brown hair and spots of gray in his mustache and goatee, walked into the local office of Uber, the San Francisco-based taxi technology start-up. Uber put him through an hour of orientation, gave him a free iPhone that carries its car dispatch app and some gear to mount it on the windshield, and sent him on his way.

Since then, Markovich has had to dodge flak from traditional cabbies who complain that they can no longer pick up riders in the city's tonier neighborhoods, and he's receiving a constant flood of emails from Uber itself, offering steep discounts on new cars and other perks to secure his loyalty. At the same time, he has increased his earnings by about 20 percent and says he's simply evolving along with his customers. "No one under the age of 40 with a smart phone is going out and getting a cab anymore," says Markovich. "I say if you can't beat 'em, join 'em."

A battle for the future of transportation is being waged outside our offices and homes. Uber and a growing collection of well-funded start-ups, such as the ride-sharing service Lyft, are trying to make getting a taxi as easy as booking a reservation on OpenTable or checking a price on Amazon—just another thing you do with your smart phone. Flush with Silicon Valley venture capital, these companies have an even grander ambition: they want to make owning a car completely unnecessary. They're battling each other, city regulators, entrenched taxi interests, and critics who claim they are succeeding only because they run roughshod over laws meant to protect public safety. "Being out in front of the taxi industry, putting a bull's-eye on our back, has not been easy," says Travis Kalanick, the chief executive of Uber. "The taxi industry has been ripe for disruption for decades. But only technology has allowed it to really kick in."

In 2009, Uber introduced the idea of allowing passengers to book the nearest town car by smart phone and then track the vehicle on a map as it approaches their location. After the ride, the service automatically compensates the driver from the customer's preloaded credit card—no awkward tipping required. It's a simple experience and a much more pleasant way to get a ride than stepping onto a busy street and waving at oncoming traffic.

Uber has raised $307 million from a group of backers that include Google Ventures, Google's investment arm, and Jeff Bezos, the founder of Amazon. It operates in 270 cities around the world and was on track to book more than $1 billion annually in rides in 2013, according to financial information that leaked to the gossip website Valleywag. Uber has expanded to Dubai; Honolulu; Lyon; Manila; Milwaukee; Pittsburgh; Tucson, Arizona; and Durban, South Africa.

In the process, Uber has managed to become one of the most loved and hated start-ups of the smart phone age. Its customers rave about the reliability and speed of the service even as they bitterly complain about so-called surge pricing, the elevated rates Uber charges during hours of high demand. Uber has also been blocked from operating in several markets by regulators out to protect the interests of consumers or entrenched incumbents, depending on whom you ask. After customers complained about the ban in Austin, Texas, the Austin City Council adopted a regulatory structure for ridesharing, enabling Uber to operate in the city. In Boston and Chicago, taxi operators have sued their cities for allowing unregulated companies to devalue million-dollar operating permits. Things grew especially heated in Paris when incensed taxi drivers shut down highway exits to the main airports and gridlocked city traffic.

Kalanick calls the cab industry a "protectionist scheme." He says these protests are not about the drivers but cab companies "that would prefer not to compete at all and like things the way they are."

His opponents are equally critical. They accuse Uber of risking passengers' lives by putting untested drivers on the road, offering questionable insurance, and lowering prices as part of a long-term conspiracy to kill the competition, among other alleged transgressions. Fueling the anti-Uber cause is the tragic case of a 6-year-old girl in San Francisco who was struck and killed by an Uber driver. "Would you feel comfortable if you had a 21-year-old daughter living alone in the city, using a smart phone app to get in a vehicle for hire, and that vehicle ends up being a 2001 Chevy Astro van with 300,000 miles on it?" says Trevor Johnson, one of the directors of the San Francisco Cab Drivers Association. "I've made it my personal mission to make it as difficult as possible for these guys to operate."

Kalanick calls himself the perfect man for the job of liberating drivers and riders. His previous company, video-streaming start-up Red Swoosh, was well ahead of its time, and Kalanick limped along for years taking no salary before selling it to Akamai Technologies in 2007 for a modest sum. "Imagine hearing 'no' a hundred times a day for 6 years straight," he says. "When you go through an experience like that, you are sort of a hardened veteran. You only persevere if you are really hard-core and fight for what you believe in."[1]

Connectivity: The Business Value of a Networked World

7.1 Explain the five networking elements creating a connected world.

7.2 Identify the benefits and challenges of a connected world.

OVERVIEW OF A CONNECTED WORLD

Computer networks are continuously operating all over the globe, supporting our 24/7/365 always on and always connected lifestyles. You are probably using several networks right now without even realizing it. You might be using a school's network to communicate with teachers, a phone network to communicate with friends, and a cable network to watch TV or listen to the radio. Networks enable telecommunications or the exchange of information (voice, text, data, audio, video). The telecommunication industry has morphed from a government-regulated monopoly to a deregulated market in which many suppliers ferociously compete. Competing telecommunication companies offer local and global telephony services, satellite service, mobile radio, cable television, cellular phone services, and Internet access (all of which are detailed in this chapter). Businesses everywhere are increasingly using networks to communicate and collaborate with customers, partners, suppliers, and employees. As a manager, you will face many communication alternatives, and the focus of this chapter is to provide you with an initial understanding of the different networking elements you will someday need to select (see Figure 7.1).

LO 7.1: Explain the five networking elements creating a connected world.

FIGURE 7.1

Networking Elements Creating a Connected World

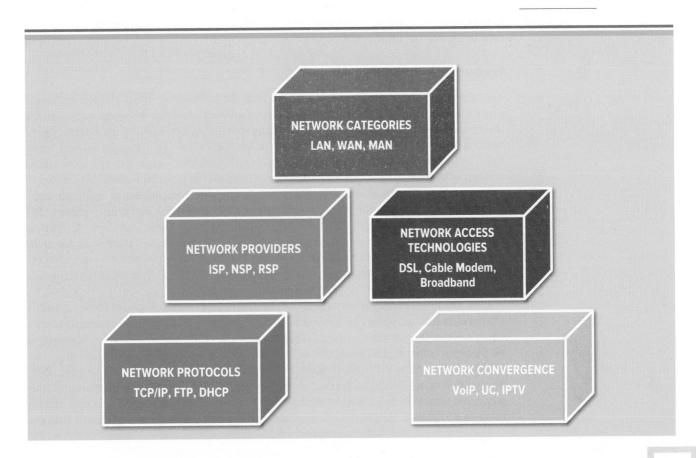

NETWORK CATEGORIES
LAN, WAN, MAN

NETWORK PROVIDERS
ISP, NSP, RSP

NETWORK ACCESS TECHNOLOGIES
DSL, Cable Modem, Broadband

NETWORK PROTOCOLS
TCP/IP, FTP, DHCP

NETWORK CONVERGENCE
VoIP, UC, IPTV

Network Categories

The general idea of a network is to allow multiple devices to communicate at the highest achievable speeds and, very important, to reduce the cost of connecting. How a particular network achieves these goals depends in part on how it is physically constructed and connected. Networks are categorized based on geographic span: local area networks, wide area networks, and metropolitan area networks. Today's business networks include a combination of all three.

A *local area network (LAN)* connects a group of computers in close proximity, such as in an office building, school, or home. LANs allow sharing of files, printers, games, and other resources. A LAN also often connects to other LANs and to wide area networks. A *wide area network (WAN)* spans a large geographic area such as a state, province, or country. Perhaps the best example is the Internet. WANs are essential for carrying out the day-to-day activities of many companies and government organizations, allowing them to transmit and receive information among their employees, customers, suppliers, business partners, and other organizations across cities, regions, and countries and around the world. In networking, *attenuation* represents the loss of a network signal strength measured in decibels (dB) and occurs because the transmissions gradually dissipate in strength over longer distances or because of radio interference or physical obstructions such as walls. A *repeater* receives and repeats a signal to reduce its attenuation and extend its range.

WANs often connect multiple smaller networks, such as local area networks or metropolitan area networks. A *metropolitan area network (MAN)* is a large computer network usually spanning a city. Most colleges, universities, and large companies that span a campus use an infrastructure supported by a MAN. Figure 7.2 shows the relationships and a few differences among a LAN, WAN, and MAN. A cloud image often represents the Internet or some large network environment.

Although LANs, WANs, and MANs all provide users with an accessible and reliable network infrastructure, they differ in many dimensions; two of the most important are cost and performance. It is easy to establish a network between two computers in the same room or building but much more difficult if they are in different states or even countries. This means someone looking to build or support a WAN either pays more or gets less performance, or both. Ethernet is the most common connection type for wired networking and is available in speeds from 10 mbps all the way up to 10,000 Mbps (10 Gbit). The most common wire used for Ethernet networking is Cat5 (Category 5), and the connectors used are RJ45, slightly larger than the RJ11 connectors used by phones, but the same shape.

Network Providers

The largest and most important network, the Internet, has evolved into a global information superhighway. Think of it as a network made up of millions of smaller networks, each with the ability to operate independently of, or in harmony with, the others. Keeping the Internet operational is no simple task. No one owns or runs it, but it does have an organized network topology. The Internet is a hierarchical structure linking different levels of service providers, whose millions of devices, LANs, WANs, and MANs supply all the interconnections. At the top of the hierarchy are *national service providers (NSPs),* private companies that own and maintain the worldwide backbone that supports the Internet. These include Sprint, Verizon, MCI (previously UUNet/WorldCom), AT&T, NTT, Level3, Century Link, and Cable & Wireless Worldwide. Network access points (NAPs) are traffic exchange points in the routing hierarchy of the Internet that connects NSPs. They typically have regional or national coverage and connect to only a few NSPs. Thus, to reach a large portion of the global Internet, a NAP needs to route traffic through one of the NSPs to which it is connected.[2]

One step down in the hierarchy is the regional service provider. *Regional service providers (RSPs)* offer Internet service by connecting to NSPs, but they also can connect directly to each other. Another level down is an Internet service provider (ISP), which specializes in providing management, support, and maintenance to a network. ISPs vary services provided and available bandwidth rates. ISPs link to RSPs and, if they are geographically close, to other ISPs. Some also connect directly to NSPs, thereby sidestepping the hierarchy. Individuals and companies use local ISPs to connect to the Internet, and large companies tend to connect directly using an RSP. Major ISPs in the United States include AOL, AT&T, Comcast, Earthlink, and

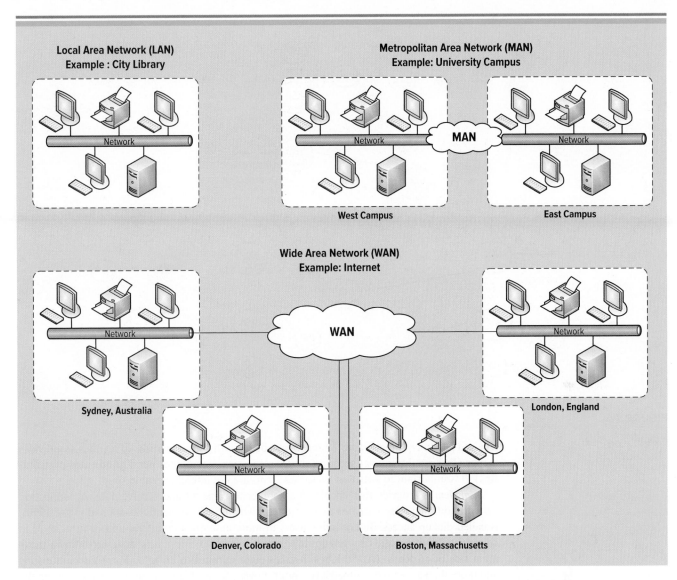

Local Area Network (LAN)
Example : City Library

Metropolitan Area Network (MAN)
Example: University Campus

Network

Network   MAN   Network

West Campus

East Campus

Wide Area Network (WAN)
Example: Internet

Network

WAN

Network

Sydney, Australia

London, England

Network

Network

Denver, Colorado

Boston, Massachusetts

FIGURE 7.2

Network Categories: LAN, WAN, and MAN

NetZero. The further up the hierarchy, the faster the connections and the greater the bandwidth. The backbone shown in Figure 7.3 is greatly simplified, but it illustrates the concept that basic global interconnections are provided by the NSPs, RSPs, and ISPs.[3]

Network Access Technologies

Performance is the ultimate goal of any computer, computer system, or network. Performance is directly related to the network's speed of data transfer and capacity to handle transmission. A network that does not offer adequate performance simply will not get the job done for those who rely on it. Luckily, networks can be upgraded and expanded if performance is inadequate.

We measure network performance in terms of *bandwidth,* the maximum amount of data that can pass from one point to another in a unit of time. Bandwidth is similar to water traveling through a hose. If the hose is large, water can flow through it quickly. Data differs from a hose in that it must travel great distances, especially on a WAN, and not all areas of the network have the same bandwidth. A network essentially has many hoses of unequal capacity connected together, which will restrict the flow of data when one is smaller than the others. Therefore, the speed of transmission of a network is determined by the speed of its smallest bandwidth.

A *bit* (short for binary digit) is the smallest element of data and has a value of either 0 or 1. Bandwidth is measured in terms of *bit rate* (or *data rate*), the number of bits transferred or

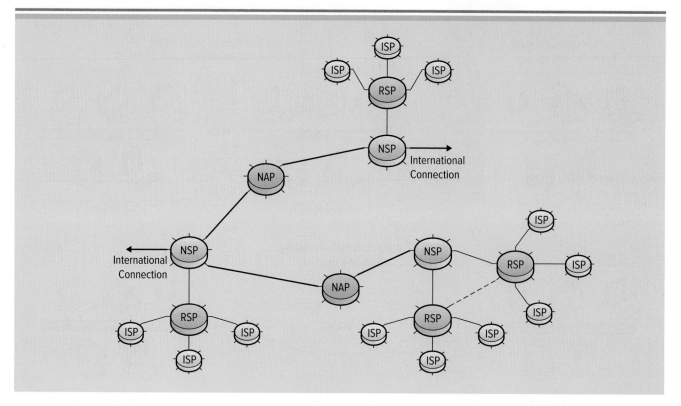

FIGURE 7.3

Internet Topology

received per unit of time. Figure 7.4 represents bandwidth speeds in terms of bit rates. Bandwidth is typically given in bits per second (abbreviated as bps) and bytes per second (abbreviated as Bps). It is important to note that these two terms are not interchangeable.

A *modem* is a device that enables a computer to transmit and receive data. A connection with a traditional telephone line and a modem, which most residential users had in the 1990s, is called dial-up access. Today, many users in underdeveloped countries and in rural areas in developed countries still use dial-up. It has two drawbacks. First, it is slow, providing a maximum rate of 56 Kbps. (At 56 Kbps, it takes eight minutes to download a three-minute song and more than a day to download a two-hour movie.) Second, dial-up modem access ties up the telephone line so the user cannot receive and make phone calls while online. The good news is this is not as big an issue as it once was because many people have cell phones and no longer require the telephone line for making phone calls.[4]

Once the most common connection methods worldwide, dial-up is quickly being replaced by broadband. *Broadband* is a high-speed Internet connection that is always connected. "High-speed" in this case refers to any bandwidth greater than 2 Mbps. Not long ago, broadband speeds were available only at a premium price to support large companies' high-traffic networks. Today, inexpensive access is available for home use and small companies.

The two most prevalent types of broadband access are digital subscriber lines and high-speed Internet cable connections. *Digital subscriber line (DSL)* provides high-speed digital data transmission over standard telephone lines using broadband modem technology, allowing both Internet and telephone services to work over the same phone lines. Consumers typically obtain DSL Internet access from the same company that provides their wired local telephone access,

FIGURE 7.4

Bandwidth Speeds

Bandwidth	Abbreviation	Bits per Second (bps)	Example
Kilobits	Kbps	1 Kbps = 1,000 bps	Traditional modem = 56 Kbps
Megabits	Mbps	1 Mbps = 1,000 Kbps	Traditional Ethernet = 10 MbpsFast Ethernet = 100 Mbps
Gigabits	Gbps	1 Gbps = 1,000 Mbps	Gigabit Ethernet = 1,000 Mbps

such as AT&T or Century Link. Thus, a customer's telephone provider is also its ISP, and the telephone line carries both data and telephone signals using a DSL modem. DSL Internet services are used primarily in homes and small businesses.

DSL has two major advantages over dial-up. First, it can transmit and receive data much faster—in the 1 to 2 Mbps range for downloading and 128 Kbps to 1 Mbps for uploading. (Most high-speed connections are designed to download faster than they upload because most users download more—including viewing web pages—than they upload.) The second major advantage is that because they have an always-on connection to their ISP, users can simultaneously talk on the phone and access the Internet. DSL's disadvantages are that it works over a limited physical distance and remains unavailable in many areas where the local telephone infrastructure does not support DSL technology.[5]

Whereas dial-up and DSL use local telephone infrastructure, *high-speed Internet cable connections* provide Internet access using a cable television company's infrastructure and a special cable modem. A *cable modem (or broadband modem)* is a type of digital modem used with high-speed cable Internet service. Cable modems connect a home computer (or network of home computers) to residential cable TV service; DSL modems connect to residential public telephone service. The ISP typically supplies the cable and DSL modems. Cisco Systems is one of the largest companies producing computer networking products and services, including the Linksys brand of networking components. Typically, broadband or high-speed Internet service has an average transfer rate 10 times faster than conventional dial-up service. *Telecommuting (virtual workforce)* allows users to work from remote locations, such as home or a hotel, using high-speed Internet to access business applications and data.

Unlike DSL, high-speed Internet cable is a shared service, which means everyone in a certain radius, such as a neighborhood, shares the available bandwidth. Therefore, if several users are simultaneously downloading a video file, the actual transfer rate for each will be significantly lower than if only one person were doing so. On average, the available bandwidth using cable can range from 512 Kbps to 50 Mbps for downloading and 786 Kbps for uploading.[6]

Another alternative to DSL or high-speed Internet cable is dedicated communications lines leased from AT&T or another provider. The most common are T1 lines, a type of data connection able to transmit a digital signal at 1.544 Mpbs. Although this speed might not seem impressive and T1 lines are more expensive than DSL or cable, they offer far greater reliability because each is composed of 24 channels, creating 24 connections through one line. If a company has three plants that experience a high volume of data traffic, it might make sense to lease lines for reliability of service.[7]

A company must match its needs with Internet access methods. If it always needs high bandwidth access to communicate with customers, partners, or suppliers, a T1 line may be the most cost-effective method. Figure 7.5 provides an overview of the main methods for Internet access. The bandwidths in the figure represent average speeds; actual speeds vary, depending on the service provider and other factors, such as the type of cabling and speed of the computer.[8]

Broadband over power line (BPL) technology makes possible high-speed Internet access over ordinary residential electrical lines and offers an alternative to DSL or high-speed cable modems. BPL works by transmitting data over electrical lines using signaling frequencies higher than the electrical (or voice in the case of DSL) signals. BPL allows computer data to be sent back and forth across the network with no disruption to power output in the home. Many

FIGURE 7.5

Types of Internet Access

Access Technology	Description	Bandwidth	Comments
Dial-up	On-demand access using a modem and regular telephone line	Up to 56 Kbps	Cheap but slow compared with other technologies
DSL	Always-on connection. Special modem needed	Download: 1 Mbps to 2 Mbps Upload: 128 Kbps to 1 Mbps	Makes use of the existing local telephone infrastructure
Cable	Always-on connection. Special cable modem and cable line required	Download: 512 Kbps to 50 Mbps Upload: 786 Kbps	It is a shared resource with other users in the area
T1	Leased lines for high bandwidth	1.544 Mbps	More expensive than dial-up, DSL, or cable

homeowners are surprised to learn that their electrical system can serve as a home network running speeds between 1 and 3 Mbps with full Internet access. Unfortunately, limitations such as interference and availability have affected BPL's popularity.

Network Protocols

A *packet* is a single unit of binary data routed through a network. Packets directly affect network performance and reliability by subdividing an electronic message into smaller, more manageable packets. *Standard packet formats* include a packet header, packet body containing the original message, and packet footer. The *packet header* lists the destination (for example, in IP packets the destination is the IP address) along with the length of the message data. The *packet footer* represents the end of the packet or transmission end. The packet header and packet footer contain error-checking information to ensure that the entire message is sent and received. The receiving device reassembles the individual packets into the original by stripping off the headers and footers and then piecing together the packets in the correct sequence. *Traceroute* is a utility application that monitors the network path of packet data sent to a remote computer. Traceroute programs send a series of test messages over the network (using the name or IP address) until the last message finally reaches its destination. When finished, traceroute displays the path from the initial computer to the destination computer. A *proxy* is software that prevents direct communication between a sending and receiving computer and is used to monitor packets for security reasons.

A *protocol* is a standard that specifies the format of data as well as the rules to be followed during transmission. Computers using the same protocol can communicate easily, providing accessibility, scalability, and connectability between networks. *File transfer protocol (FTP)* is a simple network protocol that allows the transfer of files between two computers on the Internet. To transfer files with FTP, the FTP client program initiates a connection to a remote computer running FTP server software. After completing the connection, the client can choose to send and/or receive files electronically. Network access technologies use a standard Internet protocol called *transmission control protocol/Internet protocol (TCP/IP),* which provides the technical foundation for the public Internet as well as for large numbers of private networks. One of the primary reasons for developing TCP/IP was to allow diverse or differing networks to connect and communicate with each other, essentially allowing LANs, WANs, and MANs to grow with each new connection. An *IP address* is a unique number that identifies where computers are located on the network. IP addresses appear in the form of xxx.xxx.xxx.xxx, though each grouping can be as short as a single digit.

TCP (the TCP part of TCP/IP) verifies the correct delivery of data because data can become corrupt when traveling over a network. TCP ensures that the size of the data packet is the same throughout its transmission and can even retransmit data until delivered correctly. IP (the IP part of TCP/IP) verifies that the data are sent to the correct IP address, numbers represented by four strings of numbers ranging from 0 to 255 separated by periods. For example, the IP address of www.apple.com is 97.17.237.15.

Here is another way to understand TCP/IP. Consider a letter that needs to go from the University of Denver to Apple's headquarters in Cupertino, California. TCP makes sure the envelope is delivered and does not get lost along the way. IP acts as the sending and receiving labels, telling the letter carrier where to deliver the envelope and who it was from. The Postal Service mainly uses street addresses and zip codes to get letters to their destinations, which is really what IP does with its addressing method. Figure 7.6 illustrates this example. However,

FIGURE 7.6

Example of TCP/IP

BUSINESS DRIVEN DISCUSSION

Net Neutrality

Net neutrality—the great debate has been raging for some time now, with the battle lines clearly drawn. *Net neutrality* is about ensuring that everyone has equal access to the Internet. It is the founding principle that all consumers should be able to use the Internet and be free to access its resources without any form of discrimination.

On one side of the debate are the ISPs, such as Comcast, that are building the Internet infrastructure and want to charge customers relative to their use, namely, the amount of bandwidth they consume. The ISPs argue that more and more users accessing bandwidth-intense resources provided by the likes of YouTube and Netflix place huge demands on their networks. They want Internet access to move from a flat-rate pricing structure to a metered service.

On the other hand, content providers, such as Google, support the counterargument that if ISPs move toward metered schemes, this may limit the usage of many resources on the Internet such as iTunes and Netflix. A metered service may also stifle the innovative opportunities the open Internet provides.

The U.S. Court of Appeals for the District of Columbia Circuit struck down the Federal Communications Commission's net neutrality rules, which would have required Internet service providers to treat all Web traffic equally. The ruling will allow ISPs to charge companies such as Netflix and Amazon fees for faster content delivery.

Do you agree that the government should control the Internet? Should website owners be legally forced to receive or transmit information from competitors or other websites they find objectionable? Provide examples of when net neutrality might be good for a business and when net neutrality might be bad for a business. Overall, is net neutrality good or bad for business?[9]

---

unlike the Postal Service, which allows multiple people to share the same physical address, each device using an IP address to connect to the Internet must have a unique address or else it could not detect which individual device a request should be sent to.

One of the most valuable characteristics of TCP/IP is how scalable its protocols have proven to be as the Internet has grown from a small network with just a few machines to a huge internetwork with millions of devices. Although some changes have been required periodically to support this growth, the core of TCP/IP is the same as it was more than 25 years ago.[10] *Dynamic host configuration protocol (DHCP)* allows dynamic IP address allocation so users do not have to have a preconfigured IP address to use the network. DHCP allows a computer to access and locate information about a computer on the server, enabling users to locate and renew their IP address. ISPs usually use DHCP to allow customers to join the Internet with minimum effort. DHCP assigns unique IP addresses to devices, then releases and renews these addresses as devices leave and return to the network.

If there is one flaw in TCP/IP, it is the complexity of IP addresses. This is why we use a *domain name system (DNS)* to convert IP addresses into *domains,* or identifying labels that use a variety of recognizable naming conventions. Therefore, instead of trying to remember 97.17.237.15, users can simply specify a domain name to access a computer or website, such as www.apple.com. Figure 7.7 lists the most common Internet domains.[11]

The list of domain names is expected to expand in the coming years to include entities such as .pro (for accountants, lawyers, and physicians), .aero (for the air-transport industry), and .museum (for museums). The creation of an .xxx domain was recently approved for pornographic content. Countries also have domain names such as .au (Australia), .fr (France), and .sp (Spain).

Websites with heavy traffic often have several computers working together to share the load of requests. This offers load balancing and fault tolerance, so when requests are made to a

Domain Name	Use
.biz	Reserved for businesses
.com	Reserved for commercial organizations and businesses
.edu	Reserved for accredited postsecondary institutions
.gov	Reserved for U.S. government agencies
.info	Open to any person or entity but intended for information providers
.mil	Reserved for U.S. military
.net	Open to any person or entity
.org	Reserved for nonprofit organizations

FIGURE 7.7

Internet Domains

popular site such as www.facebook.com, they will not overload a single computer and the site does not go down if one computer fails. A single computer can also have several host names; for instance, if a company is hosting several websites on a single server, much as an ISP works with hosting.

Domain names are essentially rented, with renewable rights, from a domain name registrar, such as godaddy.com. Some registrars only register domain names, whereas others provide hosting services for a fee. ICANN (Internet Corporation for Assigned Names and Numbers) is a nonprofit governance and standards organization that certifies all domain name registrars throughout the world. With the certification, each registrar is authorized to register domain names, such as .com, .edu, or .org.[12]

Network Convergence

In part due to the explosive use of the Internet and connectivity of TCP/IP, there is a convergence of network devices, applications, and services. Consumers, companies, educational institutions, and government agencies extensively engage in texting, web surfing, videoconference applications, online gaming, and ebusiness. *Network convergence* is the efficient coexistence of telephone, video, and data communication within a single network, offering convenience and flexibility not possible with separate infrastructures. Almost any type of information can be converted into digital form and exchanged over a network. Network convergence then allows the weaving together of voice, data, and video. The benefits of network convergence allow for multiple services, multiple devices, but one network, one vendor, and one bill, as suggested by Figure 7.8.

One of the challenges associated with network convergence is using the many tools efficiently and productively. Knowing which communication channel—PC, text message, videoconference—to use with each business participant can be a challenge. *Unified communications (UC)* is the integration of communication channels into a single service. UC integrates communication

FIGURE 7.8

The Benefits of Network Convergence

channels, allowing participants to communicate using the method that is most convenient for them. UC merges instant messaging, videoconferencing, email, voice mail, and voice over IP. This can decrease the communication costs for a business while enhancing the way individuals communicate and collaborate.

One area experiencing huge growth in network convergence is the use of the Internet for voice transmission. *Voice over IP (VoIP)* uses IP technology to transmit telephone calls. For the first time in more than 100 years, VoIP is providing an opportunity to bring about significant change in the way people communicate using the telephone. VoIP service providers—specialists as well as traditional telephone and cable companies and some ISPs—allow users to call anyone with a telephone number, whether local, long distance, cellular, or international.

Two ways to use VoIP for telephone calls are through a web interface that allows users to make calls from their computer and through a phone attached to a VoIP adapter that links directly to the Internet through a broadband modem. Figure 7.9 illustrates these two ways along with the use of VoIP-enabled phones, bypassing the need for an adapter.

VoIP services include fixed-price unlimited local and long-distance calling plans (at least within the United States and Canada), plus a range of interesting features, such as:

- The ability to have more than one phone number, including numbers with different area codes.

- Integration of email and voice mail so users can listen to their voice mail by using their computer.

- The ability to receive personal or business calls via computer, no matter where the user is physically located.[13]

The biggest benefit of VoIP is its low cost. Because it relies on the Internet connection, however, service can be affected if the bandwidth is not appropriate or Internet access is not available.

Skype is a perfect example of IP applied to telephone use. Unlike typical VoIP systems that use a client and server infrastructure, Skype uses a peer-to-peer network. *Peer-to-peer (P2P)* is a computer network that relies on the computing power and bandwidth of the participants in the network rather than a centralized server. Skype's user directory is distributed among the users in its network, allowing scalability without a complex and expensive centralized infrastructure. Peer-to-peer networks became an overnight sensation years ago through a service called Napster that distributed digital music illegally. Skype has found a way to use this resource to provide value to its users.[14]

As the popularity of VoIP grows, governments are becoming more interested in regulating it as they do traditional telephone services. In the United States, the Federal Communications Commission requires compliance among VoIP service providers comparable to those for traditional telephone providers such as support for local number portability, services for the disabled, and law enforcement for surveillance, along with regulatory and other fees.

An exciting and new convergence is occurring in the area of television with *Internet Protocol TV (IPTV)*, which distributes digital video content using IP across the Internet and private

FIGURE 7.9

VoIP Connectivity

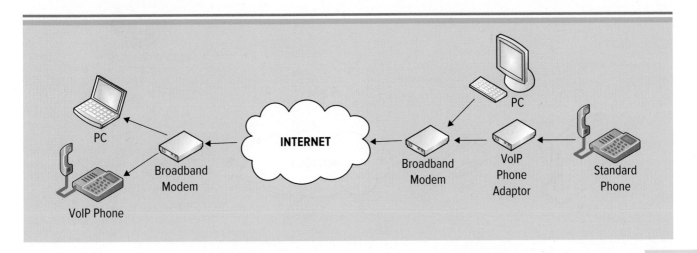

BUSINESS DRIVEN DEBATE

Should Airlines Allow Cellphone Calls During Flights?

The Federal Communications Commission has proposed allowing passengers to use their mobile wireless devices, including cell phones, while flying above 10,000 feet. Cell phones on airplanes would not be using the traditional cellular networks because they are not designed to operate at 35,000 feet. Rather, calls would be batched and bounced down to the ground through a satellite or specialized air-to-ground cellular system, forcing airlines to charge much more per minute than standard carrier rates.

Supporters say that cell phone use does not interfere with aviation safety and that on foreign airlines where it is permitted, passengers' calls tend to be short and unobtrusive.

Critics argue that allowing voice calls in flight would compromise flight attendants' ability to maintain order in an emergency, increase cabin noise and tension among passengers, and add unacceptable risk to aviation security. They also point out that a majority of the traveling public want the cell phone ban maintained. Do you agree or disagree with the use of cell phones on airlines?[15]

IP networks. Comcast provides an example of a private IP network that also acts as a cable TV provider. Traditional television sends all program signals simultaneously to the television, allowing the user to select the program by selecting a channel. With IPTV, the user selects a channel and the service provider sends only that single program to the television. Like cable TV, IPTV uses a box that acts like a modem to send and receive the content (see Figure 7.10). A few IPTV features include:

- **Support of multiple devices:** PCs and televisions can access IPTV services.
- **Interactivity with users:** Interactive applications and programs are supported by IPTV's two-way communication path.
- **Low bandwidth:** IPTV conserves bandwidth because the provider sends only a single channel.
- **Personalization:** Users can choose not only what they want to watch but also when they want to watch it.[16]

FIGURE 7.10

IPTV Components

HDTV   IPTV Set-Top Box   INTERNET   World TV Broadcasts   IPTV Service Provider

BENEFITS OF A CONNECTED WORLD

Before networks, transferring data between computers was time-consuming and labor-intensive. People had to copy data physically from machine to machine using a disk.

Resource sharing makes all applications, equipment (such as a high-volume printer), and data available to anyone on the network, without regard to the physical location of the resource or the user. Sharing physical resources also supports a sustainable MIS infrastructure, allowing companies to be agile, efficient, and responsible at the same time. Cloud computing (see Chapter 5) and virtualization consolidate information as well as systems that enhance the use of shared resources. By using shared resources, cloud computing, and virtualization allow for collective computing power, storage, and software on demand.

Perhaps even more important than sharing physical resources is sharing data. Most companies, regardless of size, depend not just on their customer records, inventories, accounts receivable, financial statements, and tax information but also on their ability to share these, especially with operations in remote locations. Networking with a LAN, WAN, or MAN allows employees to share data quickly and easily and to use applications such as databases and collaboration tools that rely on sharing. By sharing data, networks have made business processes more efficient. For example, as soon as an order is placed, anyone in the company who needs to view it—whether in marketing, purchasing, manufacturing, shipping, or billing—can do so.

Intranets and extranets let firms share their corporate information securely. An *intranet* is a restricted network that relies on Internet technologies to provide an Internet-like environment within the company for information sharing, communications, collaboration, web publishing, and the support of business processes, as suggested in Figure 7.11. This network is protected by security measures such as passwords, encryption, and firewalls, and thus only authorized users can access it. Intranets provide a central location for all kinds of company-related information such as benefits, schedules, strategic directions, and employee directories.[17]

An *extranet* is an extension of an intranet that is available only to authorized outsiders, such as customers, partners, and suppliers. Having a common area where these parties can share information with employees about, for instance, order and invoice processing can be a major competitive advantage in product development, cost control, marketing, distribution, and supplier relations. Companies can establish direct private network links among themselves or create private, secure Internet access, in effect a private tunnel within the Internet, called a *virtual private network (VPN)*. Figure 7.12 illustrates using a VPN to connect to a corporate server.

Extranets enable customers, suppliers, consultants, subcontractors, business prospects, and others to access selected intranet websites and other company network resources that allow

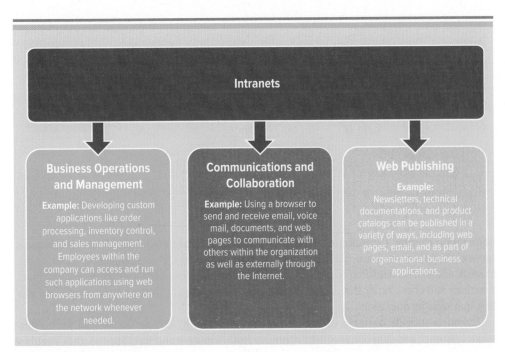

FIGURE 7.11

Intranet Uses

BUSINESS DRIVEN START-UP

Where Would You GoPro?

Just imagine a beautiful white-tailed eagle soaring high above the French Alps. Well, you can soar right along with this beautiful creature, getting a true bird's eye view from the streaming wireless video sent from a GoPro camera attached to its back. The incredible footage went viral, and now everybody from new fathers to Olympic athletes is sharing their GoPro footage. Wil Tidman, who runs GoPro's 40-person production team, stated, "We want to show the cameras' diverse uses and give the users the ability to edit and share videos online." Currently, the company is averaging three GoPro-hashtagged videos uploaded to YouTube per minute.

Who's Shooting All That Action Footage

- People with dramatic jobs, from soldiers to oil riggers, use GoPro in their work, and Tidman's team scours the web for potential hits. He found footage of a firefighter rescuing a cat from a burning building, and the resulting YouTube post got 18 million views.

- "A father sent us footage of him throwing his baby into the air," says Tidman. "The child had a camera on his head, and you saw the excitement of their relationship." GoPro aired it as a 30-second spot during last year's Super Bowl.

- GoPro equipped the Rolling Stones with 40 cameras for their 2013 tour. Tidman's team also helps indies, some of whose clips have earned them a degree of fame, proof of a GoPro bump.[18]

In a group, choose one of your favorite products or services and create a marketing strategy using GoPro.

FIGURE 7.12

Using a VPN

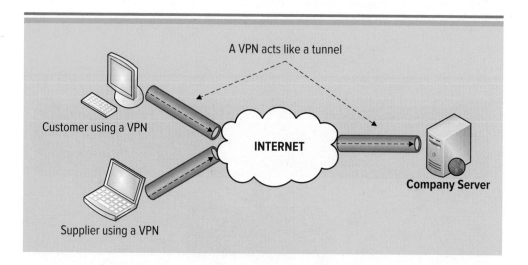

information sharing. Consultants and contractors can facilitate the design of new products or services. Suppliers can ensure that the raw materials necessary for the company to function are in stock and can be delivered in a timely fashion. Customers can access ordering and payment functions and check order status. The extranet links the company to the outside world in a way that improves its operations.

Extranets provide business value in several ways. First, by relying on web browsers, they make customer and supplier access to company resources easy and fast. Second, they enable a company to customize interactive web-enabled services for the intended audience to build and strengthen strategic relationships with customers and suppliers. Finally, extranets can allow and improve collaboration with customers and other business partners.

CHALLENGES OF A CONNECTED WORLD

Networks have created a diverse yet globally connected world. By eliminating time and distance, networks make it possible to communicate in ways not previously imaginable. Even though networks provide many business advantages, they also create increased challenges in (1) security and (2) social, ethical, and political issues.

Security

Networks are a tempting target for mischief and fraud. A company first has to ensure proper identification of users and authorization of network access. Outside suppliers might be allowed to access production plans via the company's extranet, for example, but they must not be able to see other information such as financial records. The company should also preserve the integrity of its data; only qualified users should be allowed to change and update data and only well-specified data. Security problems intensify on the Internet, where companies need to guard against fraud, invalid purchases, and misappropriation of credit card information.

Two methods for encrypting network traffic on the web are secure sockets layer and secure hypertext transfer protocol. *Secure sockets layer (SSL)* is a standard security technology for establishing an encrypted link between a web server and a browser, ensuring that all data passed between them remain private. Millions of websites use SSL to protect their online transactions with their customers.

To create an SSL connection, a web server requires an *SSL certificate,* an electronic document that confirms the identity of a website or server and verifies that a public key belongs to a trustworthy individual or company. (Public key is described in Chapter 4.) Typically, an SSL certificate will contain a domain name, the company name and address, and the expiration date of the certificate and other details. Verisign is the leading Internet certification authority that issues SSL certificates. When a browser connects to a secure site, it retrieves the site's SSL certificate, makes sure it has not expired, and confirms that a certification authority has issued it. If the certificate fails on any one of these validation measures, the browser will display a warning to the end user that the site is not secure. If a website is using SSL, a lock icon appears in the lower right-hand corner of the user's web browser.

Secure hypertext transfer protocol (SHTTP or HTTPS) is a combination of HTTP and SSL to provide encryption and secure identification of an Internet server. HTTPS protects against interception of communications, transferring credit card information safely and securely with special encryption techniques. When a user enters a web address using https://, the browser will encrypt the message. However, the server receiving the message must be configured to receive HTTPS messages.

In summary, each company needs to create a network security policy that specifies aspects of data integrity availability and confidentiality or privacy as well as accountability and authorization. With a variety of security methods, such as SSL and SHTTP, a company can protect its most important asset, its data.

Social, Ethical, and Political Issues

Only a small fraction of the world's population has access to the Internet, and some people who have had access in the past have lost it due to changes in their circumstances such as unemployment or poverty. Providing network access to those who want or need it helps to level the playing field and removes the *digital divide,* a worldwide gap giving advantage to those with access to technology. Organizations trying to bridge the divide include the Boston Digital Bridge Foundation, which concentrates on local schoolchildren and their parents, helping to make them knowledgeable about computers, programs, and the Internet. Other organizations provide inexpensive laptops and Internet access in low-income areas in developing countries.[19]

Another social issue with networking occurs with newsgroups or blogs where like-minded people can exchange messages. If the topics are technical in nature or sports related such as cycling, few issues arise. Problems can begin when social media feature topics people can be sensitive about, such as politics, religion, or sex, or when someone posts an offensive message to someone else. Different countries have different and even conflicting laws about Internet use, but because the Internet knows no physical boundaries, communication is hard to regulate, even if anyone could. Some people believe network operators should be responsible for the content they carry, just as newspapers and magazines are. Operators, however, feel that like the post office or phone companies, they cannot be expected to police what users say. If they censored messages, how would they avoid violating users' rights to free speech?

Many employers read and censor employee emails and limit employee access to distracting entertainment such as YouTube and social networks such as Facebook. Spending company time playing is not a good use of resources, they believe.

Social issues can even affect the government and its use of networks to snoop on citizens. The FBI has installed a system at many ISPs to scan all incoming and outgoing email for nuggets of interest. The system was originally called Carnivore, but bad publicity caused it to be renamed DCS1000. Although the name is much more generic, its goal is the same: locate information on illegal activities by spying on millions of people. A common conception associated with networking technologies is "Big Brother is watching!" People are wary of how much information is available on the Internet and how easily it can fall into the wrong hands.[20]

---

section 7.2 | Mobility: The Business Value of a Wireless World

LEARNING OUTCOMES

7.3 Describe the different wireless network categories.

7.4 Explain the different wireless network business applications.

LO 7.3: Describe the different wireless network categories.

WIRELESS NETWORK CATEGORIES

Mbusiness: Supporting Anywhere Business

Internet-enabled mobile devices are quickly outnumbering personal computers. *Mobile business* (or *mbusiness, mcommerce*) is the ability to purchase goods and services through a wireless Internet-enabled device. The emerging technology behind mbusiness is a mobile device equipped with a web-ready micro-browser that can perform the following services:

- Mobile entertainment—downloads for music, videos, games, voting, and ring tones as well as text-based messaging services.

- Mobile sales/marketing—advertising, campaigns, discounts, promotions, and coupons.

- Mobile banking—manage accounts, pay bills, receive alerts, and transfer funds.

- Mobile ticketing—purchase tickets for entertainment, transportation, and parking, including the ability to feed parking meters automatically.

- Mobile payments—pay for goods and services, including in-store purchases, home delivery, vending machines, taxis, gas, and so on.

Organizations face changes more extensive and far-reaching in their implications than anything since the modern industrial revolution occurred in the early 1900s. Technology is a primary force driving these changes. Organizations that want to survive must recognize the immense power of technology, carry out required organizational changes in the face of it, and learn to operate in an entirely different way.

As far back as 1896, Italian inventor Guglielmo Marconi demonstrated a wireless telegraph, and in 1927, the first radiotelephone system began operating between the United States and Great Britain. Automobile-based mobile telephones were offered in 1947. In 1964, the first communications satellite, Telstar, was launched, and soon after, satellite-relayed telephone service and television broadcasts became available. Wireless networks have exploded since then, and newer technologies are now maturing that allow companies and home users alike to take advantage of both wired and wireless networks.[21]

Before delving into a discussion of wireless networks, we should distinguish between *mobile* and *wireless,* terms that are often used synonymously but actually have different meanings. *Mobile* means the technology can travel with the user; for instance, users can download software, email messages, and web pages onto a laptop or other mobile device for portable reading or reference. Information collected while on the road can be synchronized with a PC or company server. *Wireless,* on the other hand, refers to any type of operation accomplished without the use of a hard-wired connection. There are many environments in which the network devices are wireless but not mobile, such as wireless home or office networks with stationary PCs and printers. Some forms of mobility do not require a wireless connection; for instance, a worker can use a wired laptop at home, shut down the laptop, drive to work, and attach the laptop to the company's wired network.

In many networked environments today, users are both wireless and mobile; for example, a mobile user commuting to work on a train can maintain a VoIP call and multiple TCP/IP connections at the same time. Figure 7.13 categorizes wireless networks by type.

Personal Area Networks

A *personal area network (PAN)* provides communication for devices owned by a single user that work over a short distance. PANs are used to transfer files, including email, calendar appointments, digital photos, and music. A PAN can provide communication between a wireless headset and a cell phone or between a computer and a wireless mouse or keyboard. Personal area networks generally cover a range of less than 10 meters (about 30 feet). *Bluetooth* is a wireless PAN technology that transmits signals over short distances among cell phones, computers, and other devices. The name is borrowed from Harald Bluetooth, a king in Denmark more than 1,000 years ago. Bluetooth eliminates the need for wires, docking stations, or cradles, as well as all the special attachments that typically accompany personal computing devices. Bluetooth operates at speeds up to 1 Mbps within a range of 33 feet or less. Devices that are Bluetooth-enabled communicate directly with each other in pairs, like a handshake. Up to eight can be paired simultaneously. And Bluetooth is not just for technology devices. An array of Bluetooth-equipped appliances, such as a television set, a stove, and a thermostat, can be controlled from a cell phone—all from a remote location.[22]

Wireless LANs

A *wireless LAN (WLAN)* is a local area network that uses radio signals to transmit and receive data over distances of a few hundred feet. An *access point (AP)* is the computer or network device that serves as an interface between devices and the network. Each computer initially connects to the access point and then to other computers on the network. A *wireless access point (WAP)* enables devices to connect to a wireless network to communicate with each other. WAPs with *multiple-in/multiple-out (MIMO) technology* have multiple transmitters and receivers, allowing them to send and receive greater amounts of data than traditional networking devices. *Wireless fidelity (Wi-Fi)* is a means by which portable devices can connect wirelessly

FIGURE 7.13

Wireless Communication Network Categories

BUSINESS DRIVEN ETHICS AND SECURITY

Teddy The Guardian

Two London-based entrepreneurs are building an Internet of huggable things for sick children to make any hospital visit more like a trip to Disneyland. Teddy The Guardian captures heart rate, temperatures, and blood-oxygen levels when a child grabs it by the paw to give it a cuddle. All measurements are sent wirelessly to nurses' and parents' mobile devices. The cute, cuddly teddy bear is packed full of sensors designed to track children's vital signs and help quickly find out potential issues. Teddy The Guardian takes from 5 to 7 seconds to record measurements and is programmed to run five times per hour. Future versions of Teddy The Guardian will be interactive, using machine learning to find out the child's favorite song or bedtime story and then play the related content for a more soothing hospital visit. Big pharmaceutical companies in the United States have already placed over $500,000 in orders and plan to donate the bears to hospitals and clinics.

This is clearly a brilliant idea, and soon we will see Teddy The Guardian in many local hospitals and clinics. Can you identify any additional markets on which Teddy The Guardian should focus? Can you think of any ethical issues related to huggable things? Can you think of any security issues related to huggable things?

to a local area network, using access points that send and receive data via radio waves. Wi-Fi has a maximum range of about 1,000 feet in open areas such as a city park and 250 to 400 feet in closed areas such as an office building. *Wi-Fi infrastructure* includes the inner workings of a Wi-Fi service or utility, including the signal transmitters, towers, or poles and additional equipment required to send out a Wi-Fi signal. Most WLANs use a Wi-Fi infrastructure in which a wireless device, often a laptop, communicates through an access point or base station by means of, for instance, wireless fidelity.

Areas around access points where users can connect to the Internet are often called hotspots. *Hotspots* are designated locations where Wi-Fi access points are publicly available. Hotspots are found in places such as restaurants, airports, and hotels—places where business professionals tend to gather. Hotspots are extremely valuable for those business professionals who travel extensively and need access to business applications. By positioning hotspots at strategic locations throughout a building, campus, or city, network administrators can keep Wi-Fi users continuously connected to a network or the Internet, no matter where they roam.[23]

In a Wi-Fi network, the user's laptop or other Wi-Fi-enabled device has a wireless adapter that translates data into a radio signal and transmits it to the wireless access point. The wireless access point, which consists of a transmitter with an antenna that is often built into the hardware, receives the signal and decodes it. The access point then sends the information to the Internet over a wired broadband connection, as illustrated in Figure 7.14. When receiving data, the wireless access point takes the information from the Internet, translates it into a radio signal, and sends it to the computer's wireless adapter. If too many people try to use the Wi-Fi network at one time, they can experience interference or dropped connections. Most laptop computers come with built-in wireless transmitters and software to enable computers to discover the existence of a Wi-Fi network automatically.

Wi-Fi operates at considerably higher frequencies than cell phones use, which allows greater bandwidth. The bandwidths associated with Wi-Fi are separated according to several wireless networking standards, known as 802.11, for carrying out wireless local area network communication. The *Institute of Electrical and Electronics Engineers (IEEE)* researches and institutes electrical standards for communication and other technologies. *IEEE 802.11n (or Wireless-N)* is the newest standard for wireless networking. Compared with earlier standards such as 802.11b, Wireless-N offers faster speeds, more flexibility, and greater range. The organization denotes different versions of the standard—for example, Wireless-G and Wireless-N—by

Sports Sensors

A sensor is a device that detects or measures a physical property such as heat, light, sound, or motion and records, indicates, or otherwise reacts to it in a particular way. With wireless apps and sensors, a number of new, high-tech tools for amateurs provide coach-quality feedback to athletes of all levels, including:

- **Tennis (Sony):** Sony recently created a tennis-tracking device and app that will let users collect the kind of game-play data that used to be available only to professionals.

- **Golf (Swingbyte):** The ultralight sensor clips to the club and monitors speed, acceleration, arc, and other statistics.

- **Hockey (Fwd Powershot):** The ultralight sensor fits into the handle end of the stick and measures swing speed, angle, and acceleration.

- **Basketball (94Fifty Smart Sensor):** Embedded in a standard ball, the sensor tracks shot speed, arc, and backspin plus dribble speed and force.

- **Baseball (Zepp):** Stuck to the knob of the bat, the sensor tracks the speed and plane of a swing and the angle of impact.[24]

In a group, create a product that takes advantage of sensors, including what the sensor would measure and how it would deliver the feedback to the user.

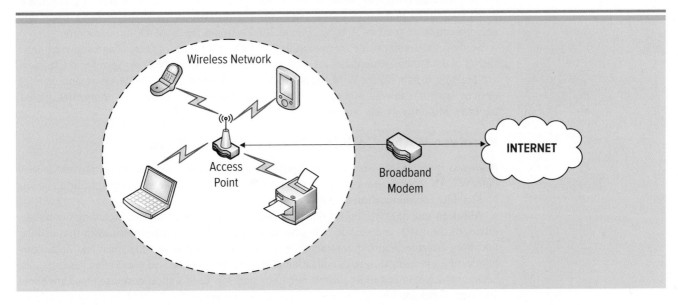

FIGURE 7.14

Wi-Fi Networks

a lowercase letter at the end of this number. Figure 7.15 outlines the bandwidths associated with a few of these standards.[25]

An increasing number of digital devices, including most laptops, netbooks, tablets such as the iPad, and even printers are incorporating Wi-Fi technology into their design. Cell phones are incorporating Wi-Fi so they can automatically switch from the cell network to a faster Wi-Fi network where available for data communications. BlackBerrys and iPhones can connect to an access point for data communications such as email and web browsing, but not for voice unless they use the services of Skype or another VoIP.

FIGURE 7.15

Wi-Fi Standards and Bandwidths

Wi-Fi Standard	Bandwidth
802.11a	54 Mbps
802.11b	11 Mbps
802.11g	54 Mbps
802.11n	140 Mbps

Wireless MANs

A *wireless MAN (WMAN)* is a metropolitan area network that uses radio signals to transmit and receive data. WMAN technologies have not been highly successful to date, mainly because they are not widely available, at least in the United States. One with the potential for success is *Worldwide Interoperability for Microwave Access (WiMAX),* a communications technology aimed at providing high-speed wireless data over metropolitan area networks. In many respects, WiMAX operates like Wi-Fi, only over greater distances and with higher bandwidths. A WiMAX tower serves as an access point and can connect to the Internet or another tower. A single tower can provide up to 3,000 square miles of coverage, so only a few are needed to cover an entire city. WiMAX can support data communications at a rate of 70 Mbps. In New York City, for example, one or two WiMAX access points around the city might meet the heavy demand more cheaply than hundreds of Wi-Fi access points. WiMAX can also cover remote or rural areas where cabling is limited or nonexistent and where it is too expensive or physically difficult to install wires for the relatively few users.[26]

WiMAX can provide both line-of-sight and non-line-of-sight service. A non-line-of-sight service uses a small antenna on a mobile device that connects to a WiMAX tower less than 6 miles away where transmissions are disrupted by physical obstructions. This form of service is similar to Wi-Fi but has much broader coverage area and higher bandwidths. A line-of-sight option offers a fixed antenna that points at the WiMAX tower from a rooftop or pole. This option is much faster than non-line-of-sight service, and the distance between the WiMAX tower and antenna can be as great as 30 miles. Figure 7.16 illustrates the WiMAX infrastructure.[27]

Some cellular companies are evaluating WiMAX as a means of increasing bandwidth for a variety of data-intensive applications such as those used by smart phones. Sprint and Clearwire are building a nationwide WiMAX network in the United States. WiMAX-capable gaming devices, laptops, cameras, and even cell phones are being manufactured by companies, including Intel, Motorola, Nokia, and Samsung.[28]

Wireless WAN—Cellular Communication System

A *wireless WAN (WWAN)* is a wide area network that uses radio signals to transmit and receive data. WWAN technologies can be divided into two categories: cellular communication systems and satellite communication systems.

Although mobile communications have been around for generations, including the walkie-talkies of the 1940s and mobile radiophones of the 1950s, it was not until 1983 that cellular telephony became available commercially. A cell phone is a device for voice and data, communicating wirelessly through a collection of stationary ground-based sites called base stations, each of which is linked to its nearest neighbor stations. Base station coverage areas are about 10 square miles and are called cells, as Figure 7.17 illustrates.[29]

The first cell phone was demonstrated in 1973 by Motorola (it weighed almost 2 pounds), but it took 10 years for the technology to become commercially available. The Motorola DynaTAC, marketed in 1983, weighed 1 pound and cost about $4,000. Cellular technology has come a long way since then.[30]

Cellular systems were originally designed to provide voice services to mobile customers and thus were designed to interconnect cells to the public telephone network. Increasingly, they provide data services and Internet connectivity. There are more cell phones than landline phones in many countries today, and it is no longer uncommon for cell phones to be the only phones people have.

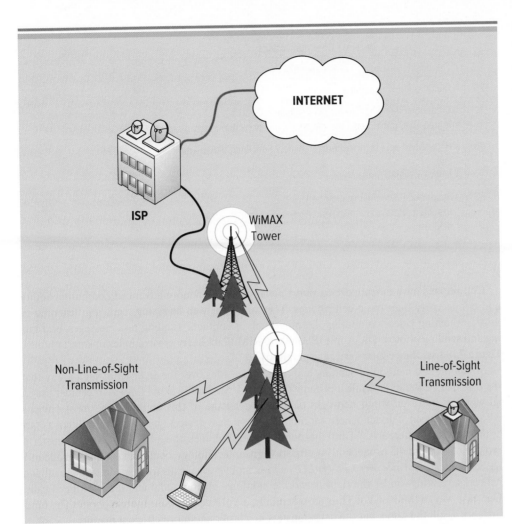

FIGURE 7.16

WiMAX Infrastructure

Sources: "Rip Curl Turns to Skype for Global Communications," www. voipinbusiness.co.uk/rip_curl_turns_to_skype_for_gl.asp July 07, 2006, accessed January 21, 2008; "Navigating the Mobility Wave," www.busmanagement.com, accessed February 2, 2008; "Sprint Plans Launch of Commercial WiMAX Service in Q2 2008," www.intomobile.com, accessed February 10, 2008; Deepak Pareek, *WiMAX: Taking Wireless to the MAX,* Boca Raton, FL: CRC Press, 2006. wimax.com, accessed February 9, 2008.

FIGURE 7.17

Cell Phone Communication System Overview

Sources: "Rip Curl Turns to Skype for Global Communications," www. voipinbusiness.co.uk/rip_curl_turns_to_skype_for_gl.asp July 07, 2006, accessed January 21, 2008; "Navigating the Mobility Wave," www.busmanagement.com, accessed February 2, 2008; "Sprint Plans Launch of Commercial WiMAX Service in Q2 2008," www.intomobile.com, accessed February 10, 2008; Deepak Pareek, *WiMAX: Taking Wireless to the MAX,* Boca Raton, FL: CRC Press, 2006. wimax.com, accessed February 9, 2008.

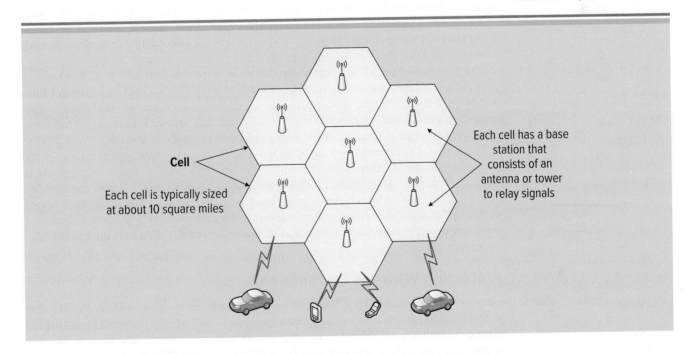

FIGURE 7.18

Cell Phone Generations

Wireless Communications		Speed
1G	– The original analog cell phone network	14.4 Kbps
2G	– Digital cell phone service	10 Kbps - 144 Kbps
3G	– Broadband Internet services over cellular networks – Added MMS (multimedia message services) or picture message services	144 Kbps - 4 Mbps
4G	– High-speed access, anywhere, anytime, to anything digital—audio, video, text – Improved video transmissions	100 Mbps
5G	– Superior data communication rate – Expected to provide artificial intelligence capabilities on wearable devices	1.5 Gbps over a distance of 90 meters

Cell phones have morphed into *smart phones* that offer more advanced computing ability and connectivity than basic cell phones. They allow for web browsing, emailing, listening to music, watching video, computing, keeping track of contacts, sending text messages, and taking and sending photos. The Apple iPhone and RIM BlackBerry are examples of smart phones. Figure 7.18 lists the cellular service generations.

Streaming is a method of sending audio and video files over the Internet in such a way that the user can view the file while it is being transferred. Streaming is not limited to cellular usage; all wireless and even wired networks can take advantage of this method. The most obvious advantage is speed, a direct benefit for mobile and wireless devices since they are still not as fast as their wired counterparts.[31] Until this point, all smart phones, though equipped with long-term evolution (LTE) or 4G broadband-based data transfer technology, could not support broadband-based phone calls. *Voice over LTE (VoLTE)* allows mobile voice calls to be made over broadband networks, creating—under the right network conditions—clearer audio and fewer dropped calls. One easy way to think of VoLTE is as, essentially, a VoIP call on your mobile phone. The functionality is still the same, but the data transfers in a faster and more efficient manner.

Wireless WAN—Satellite Communication System

The other wireless WAN technology is a satellite communication system. A *satellite* is a space station that orbits Earth, receiving and transmitting signals from Earth-based stations over a wide area. When satellite systems first came into consideration in the 1990s, the goal was to provide wireless voice and data coverage for the entire planet, without the need for mobile phones to roam between many provider networks. But by the time satellite networks were ready for commercial use, they had already been overtaken by cellular systems.

The devices used for satellite communication range from handheld units to mobile base stations to fixed satellite dish receivers. The peak data transmission speeds range from 2.4 Kbps to 2 Mbps. For the everyday mobile professional, satellite communication may not provide a compelling benefit, but for people requiring voice and data access from remote locations or guaranteed coverage in local locations, satellite technology is a viable solution.

Conventional communication satellites move in stationary orbits approximately 22,000 miles above Earth. A newer satellite medium, the low-orbit satellite, travels much closer to Earth and can pick up signals from weak transmitters. Low-orbit satellites also consume less power and cost less to launch than conventional satellites. With satellite networks, business-people almost anywhere in the world have access to full communication capabilities, including voice, videoconferencing, and Internet access. Figure 7.19 briefly illustrates the satellite communication system.[32]

Protecting Wireless Connections

Network intrusions can occur if access codes or passwords are stored on a device that is lost or stolen. However, any time a wireless network connects to a wired one, the wireless network can serve as a conduit for a hacker to gain entry into an otherwise secure wired network. This risk is especially high if the wireless network is not sufficiently secured in its own right.

BUSINESS DRIVEN GLOBALIZATION

Wi-Fi for Fishes

Not too long ago, the Seattle Aquarium decided it needed to take a deep dive into its network infrastructure and deploy wireless across its facilities. Now, a year and half in, the aquarium has found Wi-Fi to be a tool that not only lets it serve visitors in unique ways but enriches the exchanges possible between staff members and the community, says Pam Lamon, the aquarium's web and social media coordinator. For instance, there are long stretches when Umi, the aquarium's 40-pound giant Pacific octopus, doesn't move at all. Now, staff members armed with tablets can roam around the exhibit showing visitors videos of Umi feeding while they field questions.

Wireless even lets the aquarium interact with people who can't visit in person. For instance, during a recent Google + Hangout on Air, a young boy from an East Coast school asked an aquarium diver how many fish were swimming in the tank with her. The diver, wearing a wetsuit and a facemask with a microphone and speaker, began pointing out fish. "One, two, three, four, five, six, seven," she counted off, before giving up and telling him there were 500, give or take a few. "It's a little bit hard to know for sure because they just don't hold still while we count them," she joked.

The Seattle Aquarium is far from alone among businesses and organizations that are tapping into wireless to expand or improve services. As wireless has morphed from a pleasant perk to a necessity for employees and clients across industries, many businesses are finding they can no longer make do without wireless or with limited Wi-Fi services. Today, not only is there incentive to find better solutions, but companies also have access to more sophisticated equipment to help them pinpoint network problems. From next-generation access points to cloud-based management systems, wireless tools can provide expanded capabilities, are easy to manage, and are available in a range of prices.[33]

In a group, choose a business in your area that could benefit from wireless technology, like the Seattle Aquarium, and create a plan detailing the additional services it could offer its customers.

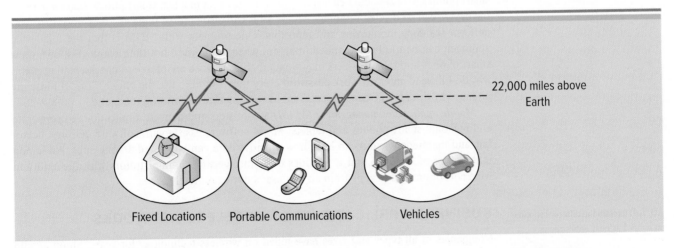

22,000 miles above Earth

Fixed Locations   Portable Communications   Vehicles

FIGURE 7.19

Satellite Communication System

Before the emergence of the Internet, hackers generally had to be physically present within the corporate complex to gain access to a wired network. The thousands, if not millions, of access points enabled by the Internet now allow hackers to work from a distance. This threat has spawned a variety of security techniques, from firewalls to VPNs to SSL and HTTPS.

Several techniques can secure wireless networks from unauthorized access whether used separately or in combination. One method is authenticating Wi-Fi access points. Because Wi-Fi communications are broadcast, anyone within listening distance can intercept communications. Every time someone uses an unsecured website via a public Wi-Fi access point, his or her logon name and password are sent over the open airwaves with a high risk that someone might eavesdrop or capture logon names, passwords, credit card numbers, and other vital information. *Wired equivalent privacy (WEP)* is an encryption algorithm designed to protect wireless transmission data. If you are using a Wi-Fi connection, WEP encrypts the data by using a key that converts the data to a nonhuman readable form. The purpose of WEP was to provide wireless networks with the equivalent level of security as wired networks. Unfortunately, the technology behind WEP has been demonstrated to be relatively insecure compared to newer protocols such as WPA. WLANs that use Wi-Fi have a built-in security mechanism called *Wi-Fi protected access (WPA),* a wireless security protocol to protect Wi-Fi networks. It is an improvement on the original Wi-Fi security standard, Wired Equivalent Privacy (WEP), and provides more sophisticated data encryption and user authentication. Anyone who wants to use an access point must know the WPA encryption key to access the Wi-Fi connection.

War chalking is the practice of tagging pavement with codes displaying where Wi-Fi access is available. The codes for war chalking tell other users the kind of access available, the speed of the network, and if the network is secured. *War driving* is deliberately searching for Wi-Fi signals while driving by in a vehicle. Many individuals who participate in war driving simply map where Wi-Fi networks are available. Other individuals have a more malicious intent and use war driving to hack or break into these networks. War driving has been a controversial practice since its inception and has raised the awareness of the importance of wireless network security.

Managing Mobile Devices

IT consumerization is the blending of personal and business use of technology devices and applications. Today's workforce grew up with the Internet, and its members do not differentiate between corporate and personal technology. Employees want to use the same technology they have at home in the office. This blending of personal and business technology is having a significant impact on corporate MIS departments, which traditionally choose all of the technology for the organization. Today, MIS departments must determine how to protect their networks and manage technology that they did not authorize or recommend. Two ways an MIS department can manage IT consumerization is through mobile device management and mobile application management.

Mobile device management (MDM) remotely controls smart phones and tablets, ensuring data security. MIS departments implement MDM by requiring passcodes on organizational smart phones to ensure data encryption and, in the event of a lost smart phone, that all data on the device can be deleted remotely. MDM tools can also enforce policies, track inventory, and perform real-time monitoring and reporting. One problem with MDM is that the full-device approach can be too heavy-handed in an era when employees, not their employers, own their smart phones and tablets. Users may wonder, "If I only use my phone to check email at night, why do I have to enter my work password every time I want to use the phone?" or, "If I lose my phone, why does my IT department want to wipe pictures of my dog remotely?"

Mobile application management (MAM) administers and delivers applications to corporate and personal smart phones and tablets. MAM software assists with software delivery, licensing, and maintenance and can limit how sensitive data can be shared among apps. An important feature of MAM is that it provides corporate network administrators with the ability to wipe corporate mobile apps from an end user's device remotely.

LO 7.4: Explain the different wireless network business applications.

BUSINESS APPLICATIONS OF WIRELESS NETWORKS

Companies of all types and sizes have relied on wireless technology for years. Shipping and trucking companies developed some of the earliest wireless applications to help track vehicles and valuable cargo, optimize the logistics of their global operations, perfect their delivery capabilities, and reduce theft and damage. Government agencies such as the National Aeronautics and Space Administration and the Department of Defense have relied on satellite technologies for decades to track the movement of troops, weaponry, and military assets; to receive and broadcast data; and to communicate over great distances.

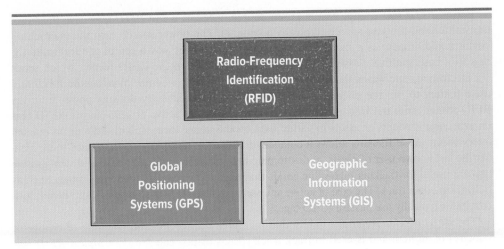

FIGURE 7.20

Wireless Business Applications

Radio-Frequency
Identification
(RFID)

Global
Positioning
Systems (GPS)

Geographic
Information
Systems (GIS)

Wireless technologies have also aided the creation of new applications. Some build upon and improve existing capabilities. UPS, for example, is combining several types of wireless network technologies from Bluetooth to WWANs and deploying scanners and wearable data-collection terminals to automate and standardize package management and tracking across all its delivery centers. Figure 7.20 displays the three business applications taking advantage of wireless technologies.

Radio-Frequency Identification (RFID)

Radio-frequency identification (RFID) uses electronic tags and labels to identify objects wirelessly over short distances. It holds the promise of replacing existing identification technologies such as the bar code. RFID wirelessly exchanges information between a tagged object and a reader/writer. An *RFID tag* is an electronic identification device that is made up of a chip and antenna. An *RFID reader (RFID interrogator)* is a transmitter/receiver that reads the contents of RFID tags in the area. A RFID system is composed of one or more RFID tags, one or more RFID readers, two or more antennas (one on the tag and one on each reader), RFID application software, and a computer system or server, as Figure 7.21 illustrates. Tags, often smaller than a grain of rice, can be applied to books or clothing items as part of an adhesive bar-code label or included in items such as ID cards or packing labels. Readers can be stand-alone devices, such as for self-checkout in a grocery store, integrated with a mobile device for portable use, or built in as in printers. The reader sends a wireless request that is received by all tags in the area that have been programmed to listen to wireless signals. Tags receive the signal via their antennas and respond by transmitting their stored data. The tag can hold many types of data, including a product number, installation instructions, and history of activity (such as the date the item was shipped). The reader receives a signal from the tag using its antenna, interprets the information sent, and transfers the data to the associated computer system or server.

FIGURE 7.21

Elements of an RFID system

Network

RFID
Reader/
Writer

Computer
System or
Server

Tagged
Products

Passive RFID tags do not have a power source, whereas *active RFID tags* have their own transmitter and a power source (typically a battery). The power source runs the microchip's circuitry and broadcasts a signal to the reader (similar to the way a cell phone transmits signals to a base station). Passive RFID tags draw power from the RFID reader, which sends out electromagnetic waves that induce a current in the tag's antenna. *Semi-passive RFID tags* use a battery to run the microchip's circuitry but communicate by drawing power from the RFID reader. *Asset tracking* occurs when a company places active or semi-passive RFID tags on expensive products or assets to gather data on the items' location with little or no manual intervention. Asset tracking allows a company to focus on its supply chain, reduce theft, identify the last known user of assets, and automate maintenance routines. Active and semi-passive tags are useful for tracking high-value goods that need to be scanned over long ranges, such as railway cars on a track. The cost of active and semi-passive RFID tags is significant; hence, low-cost items typically use passive RFID tags.

The *RFID accelerometer* is a device that measures the acceleration (the rate of change of velocity) of an item and is used to track truck speeds or taxi cab speeds. *Chipless RFID tags* use plastic or conductive polymers instead of silicon-based microchips, allowing them to be washed or exposed to water without damaging the chip. Examples of the innovative uses of RFID include:

- RFID chips injected under the skin of animals by using a syringe to help ranchers meet regulations, track wild animals for ecological studies, and return lost pets to their owners.

- Retail stores using RFID to track and monitor inventory. Hospitals and pharmaceutical companies meet government regulations and standards with RFID. Even local libraries are using RFID to control theft and speed up the checkout process.

- RFID antitheft systems installed by car manufacturers. Toll roads use RFID to collect payments from passing cars.

- Hospitals tracking patients', doctors', and nurses' locations to facilitate help in emergency situations and ensure safety. RFID also tracks equipment location to ensure quick response times during an emergency.

- American Express and MasterCard using RFID for automatic payments.

- Walmart and other large retailers using RFID to maintain inventory, stop shoplifting, and speed customer checkout processes.[34]

Global Positioning System (GPS)

A *global positioning system (GPS)* is a satellite-based navigation system providing extremely accurate position, time, and speed information. The U.S. Department of Defense developed the technology in the early 1970s and later made it available to the public. GPS uses 24 global satellites that orbit Earth, sending signals to a receiver that can communicate with three or four satellites at a time. A GPS receiver can be a separate unit connected to a mobile device using cable or wireless technology such as Bluetooth, or it can be included in devices such as mobile phones or vehicle navigation systems. *Automatic vehicle location (AVL)* uses GPS tracking to track vehicles. AVL systems use a GPS receiver in the vehicle that links to a control center. Garmin is one of the more popular manufacturers of GPS tracking systems, offering vehicle tracking, phone and laptop integration, and hiker navigation for water and air.

The satellites broadcast signals constantly; the receiver measures the time it takes for the signals to reach it. This measurement, which uses the speed of the signal to determine the distance, is taken from three distinct satellites to provide precise location information. The time measurements depend on high-powered clocks on each satellite and must be precise because an error of one-thousandth of a second can result in a location variation of more than 200 miles. GPS can produce very accurate results, typically within 5 to 50 feet of the actual location (military versions have higher accuracy). GPS also provides latitude, longitude, and elevation information.[35] *Latitude* represents a north/south measurement of position. *Longitude* represents an east/west measurement of position. *Geocache* is a GPS technology adventure game that posts the longitude and latitude location for an item on the Internet for users to find. GPS users find the geocache and typically sign a guest book or take an item and leave an item for the next adventure players to find. Caches are often placed in locations that are interesting or challenging for people to discover. A *geocoin,* a round coin-sized object, is uniquely numbered

BUSINESS DRIVEN ANALYTICS

THE MAGIC MOBILITY OF DISNEY

The Walt Disney Company offers a MagicBand to all customers vising their parks. The MagicBand is a wristband with an RFID chip that transmits over 40 feet to track real-time information on customer locations throughout its park. The magic of this data is how Disney analyzes the data to help provide its customers with the ultimate service and convenience while in the park. Armed with customer and location data, park employees can personally greet customers at restaurants and rides, offer products and shows customers will favor, inform customers of wait times for rides, and even connect to their credit cards so there is no need to carry cash.

What security concerns would you have when using the MagicBand? What ethical concerns would you have knowing your personal and location data is being tracked and monitored in real time? What other businesses could benefit from using a device similar to Disney's MagicBand?

and hidden in geocache. Geocoins can also be shaped to match a theme such as the state of Colorado or a birthday party hat. Geocoins are often decorative or commemorative, making them collectible and highly valuable for technology adventures.

GPS applications are in every kind of company vehicle these days—from police cars to bulldozers, from dump trucks to mayoral limousines. Emergency response systems use GPS to track each of their vehicles and so dispatch those closest to the scene of an accident. If a vehicle is missing, its GPS locator can help locate it. *Estimated time of arrival (ETA)* is the time of day of an expected arrival at a certain destination and is typically used for navigation applications. *Estimated time en route (ETE)* is the time remaining before reaching a destination using the present speed and is typically used for navigation applications.

Geographic Information Systems (GIS)

GPS provides the foundation for geographic information systems. A *geographic information system (GIS)* stores, views, and analyzes geographic data, creating multidimensional charts or maps. For example, GISs are monitoring global warming by measuring the speed of glaciers melting in Canada, Greenland, and Antarctica. *Cartography* is the science and art of making an illustrated map or chart. GIS allows users to interpret, analyze, and visualize data in different ways that reveal patterns and trends in the form of reports, charts, and maps. *Edge matching (warping, rubber sheeting)* occurs when paper maps are laid edge to edge and items that run across maps but do not match are reconfigured to match. Edge matching is a critical component of creating a GIS database because map misalignments occur frequently for many reasons, including survey error and cartographic errors. *GIS map automation* links business assets to a centralized system where they can be tracked and monitored over time.

Spatial data (geospatial data or geographic information) identifies the geographic location of features and boundaries on Earth, such as natural or constructed features, oceans, and more. Spatial data can be mapped and is stored as coordinates and topology. A GIS accesses, manipulates, and analyzes spatial data. *Geocoding* in spatial databases is a coding process that assigns a digital map feature to an attribute that serves as a unique ID (tract number, node number) or classification (soil type, zoning category). GIS professionals are certified in geocoding practices to ensure that industry standards are met when classifying spatial data.

Companies that deal in transportation combine GISs with database and GPS technology. Airlines and shipping companies can plot routes with up-to-the-second information about the location of all their transport vehicles. Hospitals can locate their medical staff with GIS and sensors that pick up transmissions from ID badges. Automobiles have GPSs linked to GIS maps that display the car's location and driving directions on a dashboard screen. GM offers the

OnStar system, which sends a continuous stream of information to the OnStar center about the car's exact location.

Some mobile phone providers combine GPS and GIS capabilities so they can locate users within a geographical area about the size of a tennis court to assist emergency services such as 911. Farmers can use GIS to map and analyze fields, telling them where to apply the proper amounts of seed, fertilizer, and herbicides.

A GIS can find the closest gas station or bank or determine the best way to get to a particular location. But it is also good at finding patterns, such as finding the most feasible location to hold a conference according to where the majority of a company's customers live and work. GIS can present this information in a visually effective way (see Figure 7.22).

A GIS can provide information and insight to both mobile users and people at fixed locations. Google Earth combines satellite imagery, geographic data, and Google's search capabilities to create a virtual globe that users can download to a computer or mobile device. Not only does this provide useful business benefits, but it also allows for many educational opportunities. Instead of just talking about the Grand Canyon, an instructor can use Google Earth to view that region.

GPS and GIS both use *location-based services (LBS),* applications that use location information to provide a service. LBS is designed to give mobile users instant access to personalized local content and range from 911 applications to buddy finders ("Let me know when my friend is within 1,000 feet") to games (treasure hunts) to location-based advertising ("Visit the Starbucks on the corner and get $1.00 off a latte"). Many LBS applications complement GPS and GIS, such as:

- Emergency services
- Field service management
- Find-it services
- Mapping
- Navigation
- Tracking assets
- Traffic information
- Vehicle location
- Weather information
- Wireless advertising[36]

FIGURE 7.22

GIS Uses

GRAPHICAL INFORMATION SYSTEMS USES	
Finding what is nearby	Given a specific location, the GIS finds sources within a defined radius. These might be entertainment venues, medical facilities, restaurants, or gas stations. Users can also use GIS to locate vendors that sell a specific item they want and get the results as a map of the surrounding area or an address.
Routing information	Once users have an idea where they want to go, GIS can provide directions to get there using either a map or step-by-step instructions. Routing information can be especially helpful when combined with search services.
Sending information alerts	Users may want to be notified when information relevant to them becomes available near their location. A commuter might want to know that a section of the highway has traffic congestion, or a shopper might want to be notified when a favorite store is having a sale on a certain item.
Mapping densities	GIS can map population and event densities based on a standard area unit, such as square miles, making it easy to see distributions and concentrations. Police can map crime incidents to determine where additional patrolling is required, and stores can map customer orders to identify ideal delivery routes.
Mapping quantities	Users can map quantities to find out where the most or least of a feature may be. For example, someone interested in opening a specialty coffee shop can determine how many others are already in the area, and city planners can determine where to build more parks

BUSINESS DRIVEN INNOVATION

Snapping a Theftie

Has your smart phone ever been stolen? If so, you are not alone; more than 3 million Americans' phones were stolen in 2013, which is twice the number in 2012, according to a *Consumer Reports* survey. Of course, every good entrepreneur can spot an opportunity, and a new antitheft app is one step ahead of criminals who are targeting smart phones.

Lookout is among the latest additions to the growing antitheft industry, and the app features some smart ways of helping you get one step ahead of thieves. A smart phone's front-facing camera is often regarded as merely a portal to endless selfie photographs. But Lookout puts the camera to good use by capturing a photo of you—or of any would-be thief—when someone inputs your phone's password incorrectly three times. That photo, or theftie, is instantly emailed to the phone's owner, along with the device's approximate location. The antitheft app is free to download, but this handy photo feature is not available on iPhones due to Apple restrictions and comes with an annual charge of $30.[37]

Lookout's team has been adding new features to the app's alerts, based on the methods thieves use to steal phones undetected. The app also will send emails to its owner if anyone attempts to remove the phone's SIM card, enables airplane mode, or turns off the device. From that point, the owner can choose to lock or wipe the phone remotely.

Do you agree that antitheft apps are smart business? Are any ethical issues involved in taking thefties? How would you feel if company security policy required you to install Lookout on your cell phone? If you could add a new feature to Lookout, how would it work and what would it do to deter smart phone theft?

Just as Facebook and Twitter helped fuel the Web 2.0 revolution, applications such as Foursquare, Gowalla, and Loopt are bringing attention to LBS. Each application is a mobile phone service that helps social media users find their friends' location. Facebook and Twitter have added location-based services to complement their applications.

LEARNING OUTCOME REVIEW

Learning Outcome 7.1: Explain the five networking elements creating a connected world.

- **Network categories:**

  Networks are categorized based on geographic span: local area networks, wide area networks, and metropolitan area networks.

- **Network providers:**

  At the top of the hierarchy are national service providers (NSPs), private companies that own and maintain the worldwide backbone that supports the Internet. Regional service providers (RSPs) offer Internet service by connecting to NSPs, but they also can connect directly to each other. Another level down are the Internet service providers (ISPs); recall from Chapter 3 that an ISP provides access to the Internet for a monthly fee.

- **Network access technologies:**

  A modem is a device that enables a computer to transmit and receive data. Broadband is a high-speed Internet connection that is always connected. A Digital subscriber line (DSL) allows high-speed digital data transmission over standard telephone lines. Internet cable connections provide Internet access using a cable television company's infrastructure and a special cable modem. A T1 line is a type of data connection able to transmit a digital signal at 1.544 Mpbs.

■ **Network protocols:**

A protocol is a standard that specifies the format of data as well as the rules to be followed during transmission. Network access technologies use a standard Internet protocol called transmission control protocol/Internet protocol (TCP/IP); it provides the technical foundation for the public Internet as well as for large numbers of private networks.

■ **Network convergence:**

Network convergence is the efficient coexistence of telephone, video, and data communication within a single network, offering convenience and flexibility not possible with separate infrastructures. Voice over IP (VoIP) uses IP technology to transmit telephone calls. Internet protocol TV (IPTV) distributes digital video content using IP across the Internet and private IP networks.

Learning Outcome 7.2: Identify the benefits and challenges of a connected world.

Before networks, transferring data between computers was time-consuming and labor-intensive. People had to copy data physically from machine to machine using a disk. Networks offer many advantages for a business, including:

■ Sharing resources

■ Providing opportunities

■ Reducing travel

Networks have created a diverse yet globally connected world. By eliminating time and distance, networks make it possible to communicate in ways not previously imaginable. Even though networks provide many business advantages, they also create increased challenges in (1) security and (2) social, ethical, and political issues.

Learning Outcome 7.3: Describe the different wireless network categories.

There are four types of wireless networks—PAN, WLAN, WMAN, and WWAN. A PAN provides communication over a short distance that is intended for use with devices that are owned and operated by a single user. A WLAN is a local area network that uses radio signals to transmit and receive data over distances of a few hundred feet. A WMAN is a metropolitan area network that uses radio signals to transmit and receive data, and a WWAN is a wide area network that uses radio signals to transmit and receive data.

Learning Outcome 7.4: Explain the different wireless network business applications.

Mobile and wireless business applications and services are using satellite technologies. These technologies are GPS, GIS, and LBS. GPS is a satellite-based navigation system providing extremely accurate position, time, and speed information. GIS is location information that can be shown on a map. LBSs are applications that use location information to provide a service that both GPS and GIS use.

OPENING CASE QUESTIONS

1. **Knowledge:** List the ways Uber is using networks to improve its competitive advantage in the taxi market.

2. **Comprehension:** Describe the different types of networks Uber is using to run its business.

3. **Application:** Explain how challenges with wireless networking could affect Uber's business model.

4. **Analysis:** Explain why some market segments are not included in Uber's business model.

5. **Synthesis:** Develop a use for LBS that Uber customers can benefit from using when looking for a taxi.

6. **Evaluate:** Evaluate the security dilemmas that Uber faces in using the various forms of wireless technology.

KEY TERMS

Access point (AP) 295
Active RFID tag 304
Asset tracking 304
Attenuation 282
Automatic vehicle location
    (AVL) 304
Bandwidth 283
Bit 283
Bit rate (or data rate) 283
Bluetooth 295
Broadband 284
Broadband over power line
    (BPL) 285
Cable modem (or broadband
    modem) 285
Cartography 305
Chipless RFID tag 304
Digital divide 293
Digital subscriber line (DSL) 284
Domain name system (DNS) 287
Dynamic host configuration
    protocol (DHCP) 287
Edge matching (warping, rubber
    sheeting) 305
Estimated time en route (ETE) 305
Estimated time of arrival
    (ETA) 305
Extranet 291
File transfer protocol (FTP) 286
Geocache 304
Geocoding 305
Geocoin 304
Geographic information system
    (GIS) 305
GIS map automation 305
Global positioning system
    (GPS) 304
High-speed Internet cable
    connection 285

Hotspot 296
IEEE 802.11n (or Wireless-N) 296
Institute of Electrical and
    Electronics Engineers
    (IEEE) 296
Internet Protocol TV (IPTV) 289
Intranet 291
IP address 286
IT consumerization 302
Latitude 304
Local area network (LAN) 282
Location-based service (LBS) 306
Longitude 304
Mobile business (or mbusiness,
    mcommerce) 294
Metropolitan area network
    (MAN) 282
Mobile application management
    (MAM) 302
Mobile device management
    (MDM) 302
Modem 284
Multiple-in/multiple-out (MIMO)
    technology 295
National service provider
    (NSP) 282
Network convergence 288
Packet 286
Packet footer 286
Packet header 286
Passive RFID tag 304
Peer-to-peer (P2P) 289
Personal area network (PAN) 295
Protocol 286
Proxy 286
Radio-frequency identification
    (RFID) 303
Regional service provider
    (RSP) 282

Repeater 282
RFID accelerometer 304
RFID reader (RFID
    interrogator) 303
RFID tag 303
Satellite 300
Secure hypertext transfer protocol
    (SHTTP or HTTPS) 293
Secure sockets layer (SSL) 293
Semi-passive RFID tag 304
Smart phones 300
Spatial data (geospatial data or
    geographic information) 305
SSL certificate 293
Standard packet format 286
Streaming 300
Telecommuting (virtual
    workforce) 285
Traceroute 286
Transmission control protocol/
    Internet protocol (TCP/IP) 286
Unified communications (UC) 288
Virtual private network (VPN) 291
Voice over IP (VoIP) 289
Voice over LTE (VoLTE) 300
War chalking 302
War driving 302
Wide area network (WAN) 282
Wi-Fi infrastructure 296
Wi-Fi protected access (WPA) 302
Wired equivalent privacy (WEP) 302
Wireless access point (WAP) 295
Wireless fidelity (Wi-Fi) 295
Wireless LAN (WLAN) 295
Wireless MAN (WMAN) 298
Wireless WAN (WWAN) 298
Worldwide Interoperability
    for Microwave Access
    (WiMAX) 298

REVIEW QUESTIONS

1. Why would a manager be concerned with bandwidth? How is bandwidth measured?

2. How have networks contributed to the digital divide?

3. What are the different levels of service providers that supply the interconnections to the Internet?

4. What are the different Internet access technologies you can use to connect to the Internet?

5. What is network convergence and why is it important to a business?

6. What is VoIP and how can it benefit a business?

7. What is the difference between an intranet and an extranet?

8. How do SSL and SHTTP provide security for networks?

9. What is a personal area network?

10. How does Wi-Fi work?

11. What are GIS, GPS, and LBS? How are businesses using these applications to compete?

12. What is RFID and how could it help a large retailer track inventory?

13. What are the advantages of mobile business?

14. How does a domain name system work?

15. What is the difference between VoIP and IPTV?

CLOSING CASE ONE

Wireless Bikes

Bike-sharing programs have been a popular trend in many foreign countries for years but have just started in the United States, driven mainly by the desire to provide zero-emissions transportation for commuters and tourists in urban areas. A new Denver, Colorado, company, Denver B-cycle, offers one of the largest bike-sharing programs in the United States. The company has more than 500 bikes, all made by Trek, that are available through more than 50 bike stations, or B-stations as they are called, in the Denver metropolitan area. Each B-station is fully operated by using a variety of wireless technologies, such as RFID, GPS, and Wi-Fi, which have a number of locking docks that hold as few as five bikes or as many as 25. The number of bikes at each location depends on the amount of use expected.

There are several methods by which a user can access a bike. One method is to use the B-station kiosk machine that allows users to unlock bikes with a credit card. This method is preferred for those who seek infrequent usage for short-term rentals. Here, the user receives a day pass that is good for a 24-hour rental. Another option for those planning to use bikes on a regular basis is to purchase a 7-day, 30-day, or annual membership online or at the B-station kiosk. Members receive an RFID-enabled card that allows them to retrieve any of the available bikes from the B-stations located around the city. Members can also download an iPhone app with the added convenience of using the device to unlock and locate bikes.

Once a user selects a bike by using the day pass, RFID-enabled membership card, or iPhone application, the transaction must be validated before the bike is unlocked. This is all done using RFID readers and Wi-Fi-enabled devices that validate the transaction with the company's main database. An RFID reader collects the ID number encoded to an RFID tag attached to the bike. The device then forwards the ID number, using Wi-Fi to the company's central database, so that the system knows which particular bike to associate with which user. Once validated, the user is then alerted with a beep and a green light, indicating the selected bike is unlocked and available for use. When a user wants to return a bicycle, he or she only needs to find an empty dock at any B-station to roll the bike into the locking position. A beep and green light will signal that the bike has been securely locked, and the RFID reader records the tag ID from the bike and sends this information to the company database to complete the transaction.

In addition to having an RFID tag on each bike, embedded GPS units record the routes that a user travels. When a user returns the bike, the GPS information is uploaded to the company database, along with that bike's tag ID number. These data help Denver B-cycle understand the most common routes that its users take in addition to allowing the company to collaborate with Denver merchants to target product or service offerings to members, based on their daily routes. For example, a coffee shop might email a coupon to a user who rides by each day. The GPS units also help to protect the company in case a user does not return a bike or a bike is stolen. B-cycle can use LBS to help find the missing bike.[38]

Questions

1. What advantages does a wireless network provide Denver B-cycle?
2. What challenges does a wireless network create for Denver B-cycle?
3. What information not described in the case can Denver B-cycle use with RFID and LBS data?
4. How could Denver B-cycle use other wired or wireless network technologies to gain a competitive advantage?

CLOSING CASE TWO

Square: Wireless Payments to an iPhone, Android, or iPad

Square is a little device that magically transforms a smart phone into a credit/debit card machine. It's changing the game for electronic payments and the way we traditionally send and receive money. Square allows you to buy, sell, and send money by using any Apple or Android mobile device. With three free mobile apps—Square Register, Square Wallet, and Square Cash—Square is designed to help small businesses and sole proprietorships accept credit card payments and help consumers transition to a cashless lifestyle. Here is how Square works:

- **Request your free reader:** Sign up and Square will send you a free Square Reader to take payments on an iPhone, iPad, or Android. Activate your account and process payments in minutes.
- **Download Square Register:** Square Register is a free app that works with Square Reader to turn a smart phone or iPad into a mobile point of sale. Payments, sales reports, and hardware—Square Register does all this and more.
- **Go places. Sell things:** Plug in Square Reader, sign in to Square Register, and start swiping. Send receipts via email or text message. Request more free Square Readers so staff can sell for your business, too.

Square is amazing technology, but the question you have to ask is whether Square is really changing how we process payments. If you own a small business and could traditionally only accept cash, then the answer is yes! Just think of vendors at farmer's markets, street fairs, or flea markets. Unfortunately, small business does not always equate to large profits. These types of customers have low volume and minimal transactions, which equate to low profits for a payment processor like Square, which makes its money by taking 2.75 percent of the total purchase. If you purchase $100 worth of t-shirts at the local street fair with your Visa card, Square collects $2.75 and has to pay Visa $2.20, making a mere $0.55. Square has to run its business on these profits, including expenses for marketing, sales, customer service, employees, accounting, and so on. For a viable business, Square needs to scale its way to massive payment volumes, and with PayPal and Intuit quickly building card readers of their own, the competition is growing.[39]

Questions

1. Would you categorize Square as a disruptive technology?
2. How is Square using wireless networks to gain a competitive advantage?
3. What can Square do to maintain its competitive advantage and become more profitable?
4. If you were given $1 million dollars to invest in Square, would you do it?

CRITICAL BUSINESS THINKING

1. Building Nationwide Broadband

The Federal Communications Commission is proposing a nationwide broadband plan, a sweeping initiative to provide—among other things—100 megabit per second Internet access to 100 million people by 2020. The FCC also proposes to deliver 1 gigabit per second access to places such as schools, libraries, and government buildings. "The national broadband plan is a 21st-century roadmap to spur economic growth and investment, create jobs, educate our children, protect our citizens, and engage in our democracy," said FCC Chairman Julius Genachowski.[40]

How will implementing nationwide broadband create technology jobs? Identify three new products or services you could create based on nationwide broadband. Will a nationwide broadband plan eliminate the digital divide in the United States?

2. Foursquare Cheating

Foursquare is one of the latest social networking sites that use location-based services. Users check in to places they visit, such as a bar, restaurant, or library. The main goal in using Foursquare is to earn badges and Mayor titles for favorite establishments by checking in more than friends or other Foursquare users. However, users were found to be cheating, recording check-ins to places they had not been. In an effort to make it more difficult to cheat, the company introduced a new cheater code, which uses a smart phone GPS—where available—to validate the users' true location.[41]

Why is GPS important to Foursquare? How could individuals cheat on providing locations? Why would individuals cheat about their locations? What did Foursquare implement to halt cheating? Do you think Foursquare users will still find ways to cheat?

3. Pandora Makes Users' Music Public

Pandora, the online music company, lets users create personalized music stations that they can stream online, but it also makes those stations viewable to anyone on the Internet who knows someone's email address. For example, someone with the email address sergey@google.com likes a band called Rise Against. Using the email address of Steve Jobs implies he likes country music legend Willie Nelson and jazz trumpeter Chris Botti.[42]

Do you view your music selection as private or public information? How could someone use this information unethically? Do you see this as a threat for Pandora? Do you think customers will stop using the service? What can Pandora do to ensure customer privacy?

4. Wireless Network Vulnerability

Empty cans of Pringles could be helping malicious hackers spot wireless networks that are open to attack. Security companies have demonstrated that by using a simple Pringles can to create a homemade antenna, someone can easily identify wireless networks. Known as the PringlesCantenna, these networks are rapidly becoming popular because they are cheap (under $10) and easy to set up.

Wireless network security is a big concern of network managers. Because companies and home users have increasingly adopted wireless technology, security precautions need to be enforced. After all, the very nature of using wireless technology deliberately puts information on the airwaves, and anyone within range and equipped with an appropriate receiver (e.g., PringlesCantenna) can grab this information. This is why many wireless networks should apply authentication and encryption mechanisms to provide a trusted level of security.[43]

Create a report based on Internet research that discusses the tips, techniques, and best practices to protect against this type of amateur hacking. Include a summary on the types of detection and prevention technology available, specifically the use of firewalls and built-in wireless security mechanisms.

5. Cars Hacked

Who would have thought that a car could be hacked? But that is exactly what happened in Austin, Texas. About a hundred cars were broken into, not by the usual method of either picking the lock or smashing a window but instead through a Wi-Fi connection. A local dealership, where all the cars were purchased, had installed a Wi-Fi-enabled black box under the dashboard that could disable the car and set off the horn if the owner did not make payments. However, in this case, the owners were not in arrears but, rather, the victims of a recently laid-off employee at the dealership who was seeking revenge by using the web-based system to disable the cars one by one. After someone at the dealership figured out the cars had been hacked, the password that allowed authorization to the black boxes was quickly changed.

Is the black box a good idea? Do you consider this an ethical business practice? If you had bought a car with a black box, would you have it removed? How many customers do you think will consider buying another car from that dealership?

6. Wireless Fitness

Sandifer's Fitness Club is located in central South Carolina. Rosie Sandifer has owned and operated the club for 20 years. The club has three outdoor pools, two indoor pools, 10 racquetball courts, 10 tennis courts, an indoor and outdoor track, and a two-story exercise equipment and massage therapy building. Sandifer has hired you as a summer intern specializing in MIS. The extent of Sandifer's current technology includes a few PCs in the accounting department and two PCs with Internet access for the rest of the staff. Your first assignment is to create a report detailing networks and wireless technologies. The report should explain how the club could gain a business advantage by implementing a wireless network. If Sandifer likes your report, she will hire you as the full-time employee in charge of MIS. Be sure to include all the uses for wireless devices the club could implement to improve its operations.

7. Google TV

As more Internet-related services move beyond delivering content just to the computer, Google wants to bring that content into the living room. In a joint venture, Google is teaming with Sony and Intel to introduce IPTV services either through new Internet-accessible TVs or a new set-top box allowing consumers to search for content, browse the web, view photo albums, and more. Google would provide the needed software along with advertisement opportunities, Sony would manufacture the new TVs, and Intel would supply the processors that make it all happen. Although consumers can already watch TV shows on their computers as well as on a TV, porting Internet content to an HDTV screen seems like the next logical step, which is the magic of IPTV. However, this is a very crowded playing field with many firms competing for the living room space. Google is competing with the likes of VUDU, TiVo, Yahoo! Connected TV, Netflix, Roku, Rovi, DivX, Apple TV, Xbox 360, Boxee, CinemaNow, Popbox, and many others, with no clear winner, at least not at the moment. Brainstorm the advantages and disadvantages associated with IPTV. Do you think Google TV will be successful? Why or why not?

8. Could the Domain Name System Be Hacked?

Is it possible for someone to hack the DNS? If so, it would be a disaster! By hacking the DNS, someone could change a website's IP address, thereby redirecting someone to a fictitious or look-alike site that could collect passwords and even credit card information. This scenario really happened. A Brazilian ISP, NET Virtua, was hacked using a method called DNS *cache poisoning,* which takes advantage of a hole in DNS software that redirects users to websites they did not request. The NET Virtua users were trying to access Bradesco, a bank in Brazil, but were sent to a fraudulent website that tried to install malware and steal users' passwords. Luckily, the hack was detected before too much damage was done.[44]

How can the DNS be protected from cache poisoning? Because every ISP maintains its own DNS, is this impossible?

9. Shipment Routes

Mary Conzachi works in the logistics department for Loadstar, a large trucking company and barge operator in the Midwest. She has looked into a variety of systems to keep track of the location of trucks and barges so that the company can route shipments better and answer customer inquiries faster. Conzachi's major concern is with the trucks; the barges have commodities and take weeks to move something. She states that it is much harder to keep up with trucking. She needs to know the exact location of the truck at any given time. You have been hired to assist her in recommending a solution. What solution would you recommend? Why?

10. Google Collected Public Wi-Fi Data . . . By Mistake

Google has admitted to collecting data sent over unsecured Wi-Fi networks mistakenly, using its Street View cars. Google photographs homes from public streets, using a fleet of company cars. Google said it was trying to gather information about the location, strength, and configuration of Wi-Fi networks so it could improve the accuracy of location-based services such as Google Maps and driving directions. However, in the process, the cars were also collecting snippets of emails and other Internet activity from unprotected wireless networks in the homes. Google blamed this on a programming error, temporarily halted the Street View data collection, and announced it would stop collecting all Wi-Fi data.[45] Do you believe this was a mistake by Google? If home users do not protect their wireless networks, what is to stop a neighbor from collecting the same information? Who is really at fault here?

APPLY YOUR KNOWLEDGE BUSINESS PROJECTS

PROJECT I   GoGo Gadgets

Now that Wi-Fi and other types of high-speed wireless networks are becoming common, devices using that technology are multiplying rapidly. Wireless gadgets run the gamut from cell phones to kitchen appliances and digital cameras. Here are some of the hottest new wireless broadband gadgets.

■ Samsung's $2,100 Zipel refrigerator features a touch screen with Wi-Fi to browse the Internet, stream media, take notes, and even pull up nutritional information for more than 500 types of food. It will also show Google Calendar entries and weather reports as well as news alerts and other articles.

■ Toshiba's UX600 LED TV is a Wi-Fi-enabled HDTV that can stream content straight to its display without network cables.

■ HTC EVO 4G mobile phone has the ultrafast WiMAX technology, enabling users to surf the web and download beyond broadband speeds with increased reliability. Users can enjoy VoD and IPTV and download music or electronic books, all delivered on a 3.8-inch WVGA screen.

■ Sony's Cybershot is a digital camera with Wi-Fi capabilities, allowing users to share their snapshots wirelessly using a built-in web browser.[46]

New wireless technologies promise to make today's wireless fidelity networks seem like slow modem dial-up connections. New technologies will provide greater reach geographically of wireless networks along with new personal and business uses. Search the Internet and discover new wireless devices that entrepreneurs and established companies can use to improve their business.

- Explain how companies can use these devices to create competitive advantages, streamline production, and improve productivity.

PROJECT II   WAP

Wireless Internet access is quickly gaining popularity among people seeking high-speed Internet connections when they are away from their home or office. The signal from a typical wireless access point (WAP) extends only about 300 feet in any direction, so the user must find a hotspot to access the Internet while on the road. Sometimes hotspots are available for free or for a small fee. You work for a sales company, SalesTek, which has a sales force of 25 representatives and customers concentrated in Denver, Colorado; Salt Lake City, Utah; and Santa Fe, New Mexico. Your sales representatives are constantly on the road, and they require 24/7 Internet access.

You have been asked to find hotspots for your colleagues to connect while they are on the road. It is critical for your sales force to access the Internet 24/7 to connect with customers, suppliers, and the corporate office. Create a document detailing how your mobile workforce can stay connected to the Internet while traveling. Here are a few tips to get you started:

- Use websites such as www.wifinder.com and www.jiwire.com to determine which commercial hotspots would be the most appropriate for your sales force and the commercial network service that these hotspots use.

- Search the websites of two or three commercial networks that seem most appropriate to discover more about pricing and services. (Hint: T-Mobile is one example.)

- Use www.wifinder.com and www.wififreespot.com to determine how many free public hotspots are available in these cities. Are there enough for your company to rely on them, or should you use a commercial Wi-Fi system? If so, which one?

- You might also research www.fon.com to see alternative methods of using home broadband connections.

PROJECT III   Securing Your Home Wireless Network

Wireless networks are so ubiquitous and inexpensive that anyone can easily build one with less than $100 worth of equipment. However, wireless networks are exactly that—wireless—they do not stop at walls. Living in an apartment, dorm, or house means that your neighbors can access your network.

It is one thing to let neighbors borrow sugar or a cup of coffee, but problems occur when you allow them to borrow your wireless network. There are several good reasons for not sharing a home wireless network, including:

- Slowing of Internet performance.

- Potential for others to view files on your computers and spread dangerous software such as viruses.

- Possibility for others to monitor the websites you visit, read your email and instant messages as they travel across the network, and copy your user names and passwords.

- Availability for others to send spam or perform illegal activities with your Internet connection.

Securing a home wireless network makes it difficult for uninvited guests to connect through your wireless network. Create a document detailing how you can secure a home wireless network.

PROJECT IV   Weather Bots

Warren Jackson designed a GPS-equipped robot when he was a graduate student at the University of Pennsylvania. The robot was created to bring weather balloons back down to Earth, allowing them to land in a predetermined location. The National Weather Service has collected most of its information using weather balloons that carry a device to measure items such as air pressure, wind, and humidity. When the balloon reaches about 100,000 feet and pressure causes it to pop, the device falls and lands a substantial distance from its launch point. The weather service and researchers sometimes look for the $200 device, but of the 80,000 sent up annually, they write off many as lost.

Jackson's idea was so inventive that Penn's Weiss Tech House—a university organization that encourages students to innovate and bring their ideas to market—awarded Jackson and some fellow graduate engineering students first prize in its third annual PennVention Contest. Jackson won $5,000 and access to expert advice on prototyping, legal matters, and branding.[47]

GPS and GIS can be used in all sorts of devices, in many industries, for multiple purposes. You want to compete, and win first prize, in the PennVention next year. Create a product, using a GPS or GIS, that is not currently in the market today that you will present at the next PennVention.

PROJECT V   Free Wi-Fi in Africa

Covering Africa with free and low-cost Wi-Fi may not seem like a smart thing, but that is exactly what Paul English, the cofounder of travel search engine Kayak.com, plans to do. English has created a hybrid nonprofit/for-profit company, JoinAfrica, to explore the creation of two tiers of Wi-Fi access in Africa. The first tier will be free and offer basic email service (from Gmail, Yahoo!, etc.) and web browsing (Wikipedia, BBC, etc.). The second tier will be fee-based and offer additional capabilities, including audio, video, and high-quality images.[48]

Although many countries in Africa struggle to have proper drinking water or even efficient electrical power, English and the JoinAfrica initiative believe having access to the Internet is just as important. JoinAfrica will work with for-profit telecommunication companies in Africa to first branch out with existing connections in villages, providing residents with the first-tier services, and residents can pay money to upgrade to the second tier. More bandwidth-intensive services such as streaming video and pornography will be throttled to ensure a basic level of service for all as the networks grow.

- List 10 ways wireless access could hurt remote villages in Africa.
- What other infrastructure requirements will JoinAfrica need to implement to ensure the project's success?
- How will changes in technology over the next decade affect the JoinAfrica project?
- What types of security and ethical issues will JoinAfrica face?
- If you were given $1 million, would you invest it in JoinAfrica?

PROJECT VI   Never Run with Your iPod

Jennifer Goebel was disqualified from her first-place spot in the Lakefront Marathon in Milwaukee after race officials spotted her using an iPod. A controversial 2007 rule banned portable music devices by all U.S. Track and Field participants because music could give a runner a competitive advantage and cause safety issues if the runner can't hear announcements. The officials for the Lakefront Marathon took action after viewing online photos of Goebel using her iPod; ironically, the photos were posted by Goeble herself on her own website.[49]

Do you agree with the USTAF's decision to disqualify Jennifer Goebel? How could an iPod give a runner a competitive advantage? With so many wireless devices entering the market, it is almost impossible to keep up with the surrounding laws. Do you think Goebel was aware of the headphone ban? In your state, what are the rules for using wireless devices while driving? Do you agree with these rules? How does a business keep up with the numerous, ever-changing rules surrounding wireless devices? What could happen to a company that fails to understand the laws surrounding wireless devices?

PROJECT VII   Ding-a-Ling Took My $400!

A satellite television customer requested her service to be disconnected due to poor reception. Soon after disconnecting the service, the customer noticed a direct bank withdrawal for a $430 early-termination fee from the satellite provider. To make matters worse, the unplanned charge caused hundreds of dollars in overdraft charges. To top it all off, a customer service representative apparently named Ding-A-Ling called the customer to see if she would consider reconnecting the service.[50]

Never give any company your checking account number or direct access to your bank account. If you want to establish a good relationship with a company, give it your credit card number. When a relationship with a supplier turns sour, the last thing you want is for that company to have direct access to your checking account.

Do you think what the satellite provider did was ethical? What could the customer do when disconnecting her service to avoid this type of issue? Can credit card companies enter your bank account and take out as much money as you owe at any time they want? Why is it important to never give a supplier direct access to your business checking account?

PROJECT VIII   911 McNuggets

Cellular technologies have changed the way we do business, and it is hard to imagine life without them. There are many wonderful advantages of using wireless technologies in business, but there are also some serious disadvantages, like the ability to make a bad decision faster.

A woman in Florida called 911 three times after McDonald's employees told her they were out of Chicken McNuggets. The woman stated that this is an emergency and if she had known they didn't have any McNuggets, then she would not have given them any money. The woman said McDonald's offered her a McDouble, but that she didn't want one. The woman was cited on a charge of misuse of 911.[51]

It is so easy to pick up the phone, from anywhere, at any time, and make a bad call. How many times do you see people making calls on their cell phones from inappropriate locations? If this woman had to wait in line to use a pay phone, do you think it would have given her time to calm down and rethink her decision? With technology and the ability to communicate at our fingertips, do you agree that it is easier than ever to make a bad decision? What can you do to ensure that you think before you communicate?

PROJECT IX   Wireless Networks and Streetlights

Researchers at Harvard University and BBN Technologies are designing CitySense, a wireless network attached to streetlights that can report real-time data across the entire city of Cambridge, Massachusetts. The CitySense network mounts each node on a municipal streetlight, where it draws power from city electricity. Each node includes a Wi-Fi interface, weather sensors, and download and uploading data capabilities.[52]

You are responsible for deploying a CitySense network around your city. What goals would you have for the system besides monitoring urban weather and pollution? What other benefits could a CitySense network provide? How could local businesses and citizens benefit from the network? What legal and ethical concerns should you understand before deploying the network? What can you do to protect your network and your city from these issues?

If you are looking for Excel projects to incorporate into your class, try any of the following after reading this chapter.

Project Number	Project Name	Project Type	Plug-In	Focus Area	Project Level	Skill Set	Page Number
9	Security Analysis	Excel	T3	Filtering Data	Intermediate	Conditional Formatting, Autofilter, Subtotal	AYK.7
10	Gathering Data	Excel	T3	Data Analysis	Intermediate	Conditional Formatting	AYK.8
11	Scanner System	Excel	T2	Strategic Analysis	Intermediate	Formulas	AYK.8
12	Competitive Pricing	Excel	T2	Profit Maximization	Intermediate	Formulas	AYK.9
13	Adequate Acquisitions	Excel	T2	Break Even Analysis	Intermediate	Formulas	AYK.9
15	Assessing the Value of Information	Excel	T3	Data Analysis	Intermediate	PivotTable	AYK.10
16	Growth, Trends, and Forecasts	Excel	T2, T3	Data Forecasting	Advanced	Average, Trend, Growth	AYK.11
18	Formatting Grades	Excel	T3	Data Analysis	Advanced	If, LookUp	AYK.12
22	Turnover Rates	Excel	T3	Data Mining	Advanced	PivotTable	AYK.15
23	Vital Information	Excel	T3	Data Mining	Advanced	PivotTable	AYK.15
24	Breaking Even	Excel	T4	Business Analysis	Advanced	Goal Seek	AYK.16
25	Profit Scenario	Excel	T4	Sales Analysis	Advanced	Scenario Manager	AYK.16

Enterprise MIS

ORGANIZATIONS USE VARIOUS types of information systems to help run their daily operations. These primarily transactional systems concentrate on the management and flow of low-level data items for basic business processes such as purchasing and order delivery. The data are often rolled up and summarized into higher-level decision support systems to help firms understand what is happening in their organizations and how best to respond. To achieve seamless and efficient handling of data and informed decision making, organizations must ensure that their enterprise systems are tightly integrated, providing an end-to-end view of operations.

This module introduces various types of enterprise information systems and their role in helping firms reach their strategic goals, including supply chain management, customer relationship management, and enterprise resource planning. Organizations that can correlate and summarize enterprisewide information are prepared to meet their strategic business goals and outperform their competitors.

This module then dives into how enterprise systems can be built to support global businesses, the challenges in that process, and how well things turn out if systems are built according to good design principles, sound management practices, and flexibility to support ever-changing business needs. Making this happen requires not only extensive planning, but also well-honed people skills.

MODULE 1:
Business Driven MIS

MODULE 2:
Technical Foundations of MIS

MODULE 3:
Enterprise MIS

Module 3: Enterprise MIS

CHAPTER 8: Enterprise Applications: Business Communications

CHAPTER 9: Systems Development and Project Management: Corporate
Responsibility

8

CHAPTER

Enterprise Applications: Business Communications

CHAPTER OUTLINE

SECTION 8.1
Supply Chain Management

- Building a Connected Corporation Through Integrations
- Supply Chain Management
- Technologies Reinventing the Supply Chain

SECTION 8.2
Customer Relationship Management and Enterprise Resource Planning

- Customer Relationship Management
- Organizational and Analytical CRM
- Extending Customer Relationship Management
- Enterprise Resource Planning
- Organizational Integration with ERP

What's in IT for me?

This chapter introduces high-profile strategic initiatives an organization can undertake to help it gain competitive advantages and business efficiencies—supply chain management, customer relationship management, and enterprise resource planning. At the simplest level, organizations implement enterprise systems to gain efficiency in business processes, effectiveness in supply chains, and an overall understanding of customer needs and behaviors. Successful organizations recognize the competitive advantage of maintaining healthy relationships with employees, customers, suppliers, and partners. Doing so has a direct and positive effect on revenue and greatly adds to a company's profitability.

You, as a business student, must understand the critical relationship your business will have with its employees, customers, suppliers, and partners. You must also understand how to analyze your organizational data to ensure that you are not just meeting but exceeding expectations. Enterprises are technologically empowered as never before to reach their goals of integrating, analyzing, and making intelligent business decisions.

©MakerBot®   Courtesy of 3D Systems, Inc.   Courtesy of 3D Systems, Inc.

Dream It, Design It, 3D Print It

Have you ever lost a beloved pet? No worries, just draw a picture of your pet and print a plastic replica from your 3D desktop printer so your cat or dog can sit on your desk forever. Can you imagine printing your drawing in 3D? Well, there is no need to imagine this because you can do it today for as little as $300. Just think of all the problems you can solve by having your own 3D printer. Did you recently lose the key to your car's roof rack? No worries, just download the specifications and print one. Did you forgot your girlfriend's birthday? No worries, just download and customize a silver bracelet with her initials, and in less than 30 minutes, you'll have the beautiful custom piece of jewelry on her wrist—without ever leaving your apartment.

Welcome to the wonderful world of 3D printing. For almost 30 years, 3D printing has been used by large manufacturing companies to create everything from custom parts to working prototypes. The medical industry uses 3D printing to create custom hearing aids, artificial limbs, and braces, and art designers and architects use 3D printers to create models and prototypes of statues and buildings. Traditionally, 3D printing was only available to large corporations and engineers who could code the intricate devices. Today, the first generation of consumer 3D printers is hitting the market at affordable prices with software easy enough for children to use.

The disruption occurring in the 3D printing world can, of course, be attributed to Moore's law as the technology has increased in capacity and processing power while decreasing in size and costs. Now you can purchase your own 3D printer for as little as $300 to $5,000; simply connect it to your Wi-Fi network and begin downloading files to create your own 3D objects. Current 3D printers offer a wide range of colors and materials, including plastics, metal, glass, and even chocolate. That's right—you can custom print your own valentine chocolates! The only barrier to 3D printing is that the software used to control the printer is still rather difficult for the average person to use, but you can expect that to change because software makers, such as Autodesk, are quickly releasing new, user-friendly applications. Autodesk just released 123D, a suite of free applications that enables ordinary people to design and customize objects on their PCs or even their iPads and then send them to a 3D printer.

3D printers work by first creating a digital computer aided design (CAD) file, produced with a 3D modeling program or scanned into a 3D modeling program with a 3D scanner. To get from this digital file to instructions that the 3D printer understands, software then slices the design into hundreds or thousands of horizontal layers. Typically, the 3D printer uses either a fused deposition modeling printer, which applies the tiny layers of material, or a laser sintering process by which a laser fuses the material together. Names such as 3DSystems, Afinia, and MakerBot produce 3D printers for just a few thousand dollars for consumers and small businesses alike. Figure 8.1 represents a few of the best 3D printed objects according to *PC Magazine* and *Wired*.[1]

FIGURE 8.1

3D Printed Objects

Acoustic guitar
Why print a guitar? Well, a little-known fact is that the supplies of exotic woods are running considerably low, so manufacturers of instruments need to start researching for alternative materials. Scott Summit, cofounder of Bespoke Innovations, says that the good news is that there is no gold standard for guitars compared to other stringed instruments such as the violin, so they can be made of anything. In addition, guitarists prefer to have their own unique sound in addition to a customized guitar face, something that will be available with a truly original, 3D-printed guitar.

Bikinis
The N12 is named after Nylon 12, the material in which the bikini was 3D printed by Continuum Fashion. Nylon 12 makes an ideal swimsuit material because it is innately waterproof. As well as being the first 3D printed bikini, it is also the first bikini that actually becomes more comfortable when it gets wet.

Bionic ear
To construct the ear, Princeton University researchers print the polymer gel onto an approximate ear shape and implant calf cells onto the matrix. The silver nanoparticles fuse to create an antenna, which picks up radio signals before being transferred to the cochlea, which translates the sound into brain signals. Despite all of this, researchers have yet to draw up plans to attach the ear to the human head.

Cars
In 2010, Stratasys and Kor Ecologic teamed up to develop Urbee, the first car ever to have its entire body 3D printed by printing layers of material on top of each other until a finished product appeared.

Car parts for Jay Leno
Comedian and car nut Jay Leno had a 1907 White Steamer with a badly damaged feedwater heater, a part that bolts onto the cylinders. Using a NextEngine 3D scanner and Dimension 3D printer, he was able to whip up a new one in 33 hours. "It's an amazingly versatile technology," Leno said on his website. "My EcoJet supercar needed air-conditioning ducts. We used plastic parts we designed, right out of the 3D copier. We didn't have to make these scoops out of aluminum—plastic is what they use in a real car. And the finished ones look like factory production pieces."

Chocolate heads
Some people give roses, some people give 3D-printed jewelry, some people give their undying love. But in Japan, you can give your lover your chocolate head so they can bite into your brain as the ultimate expression of love.

Clothes
Dutch designer Iris van Herpen was at Fashion Week in Paris, accompanied by MIT Media Lab's Neri Oxman, to showcase a dress that was fabricated using 3D printing technology. It was printed on an Objet Connex500 multimaterial 3D printer. Most 3D printers require creations to be printed using only one type of fabric or material, but the Connex500 allows mixing of different types of material.

Google Glasses
Chinese entrepreneur Sunny Gao printed a fully functioning pair of Google Glasses at a hackathon event in Shanghai. Unfortunately, the 3D printed version of the glasses doesn't boast Wi-Fi or Bluetooth support, unlike the real thing—but they are identical in every other way.

Meat (yes, meat)
U.S. start-up Modern Meadow believes it can make artificial raw meat using a 3D bioprinter, the BBC reported. Peter Thiel, one of Silicon Valley's most prominent venture capitalists, PayPal cofounder, and early Facebook investor, has just backed the company with $350,000. The team reportedly has a prototype, but it's "not ready for consumption."

Robotic prosthetic
Easton LaChappelle, a 17-year-old high school student from Colorado, used free online resources for 3D printers to construct a fully functional prosthetic arm and hand. The high school student found inspiration from one of his past projects, which involved building a robotic hand made entirely of LEGOs when he was 14. His creation was able to open and close its fingers using two things: fishing line and servomotors.[2]

section 8.1 | Supply Chain Management

LEARNING OUTCOMES

8.1 Explain integrations and the role they play in connecting a corporation.

8.2 Describe supply chain management along with its impact on business.

8.3 Identify the three technologies that are reinventing the supply chain.

BUILDING A CONNECTED CORPORATION THROUGH INTEGRATIONS

LO 8.1: Explain integrations and the role they play in connecting a corporation.

Until the 1990s, each department in the United Kingdom's Ministry of Defense and Army headquarters had its own information system, and each system had its own database. Sharing information was difficult, requiring employees to input the same information manually into different systems multiple times. Often, management could not even compile the information it needed to answer questions, solve problems, and make decisions.

To combat this challenge, the ministry integrated its systems, or built connections among its many databases. These connections, or *integrations*, allow separate systems to communicate directly with each other, eliminating the need for manual entry into multiple systems. Building integrations allows information sharing across databases along with dramatic increases in quality. The army can now generate reports detailing its state of readiness and other essential intelligence, tasks that were nearly impossible before the integrations. *Eintegration* is the use of the Internet to provide customers with the ability to gain personalized information by querying corporate databases and their information sources. *Application integration* is the integration of a company's existing management information systems. *Data integration* is the integration of data from multiple sources, which provides a unified view of all data.

Two common methods are used for integrating databases. The first is to create forward and backward integrations that link processes (and their underlying databases) in the value chain. A *forward integration* sends information entered into a given system automatically to all downstream systems and processes. A *backward integration* sends information entered into a given system automatically to all upstream systems and processes. Figure 8.2 demonstrates how this method works across the systems or processes of sales, order entry, order fulfillment, and billing. In the order entry system, for example, an employee can update the customer's information. Via the integrations, that information is sent upstream to the sales system and downstream to the order fulfillment and billing systems. Ideally, an organization wants to build

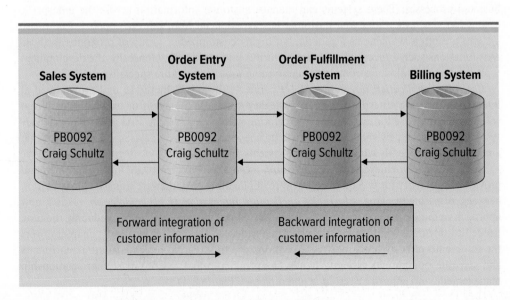

FIGURE 8.2

A Forward and Backward Customer Information Integration Example

FIGURE 8.3

Integrating Customer
Information Among Databases

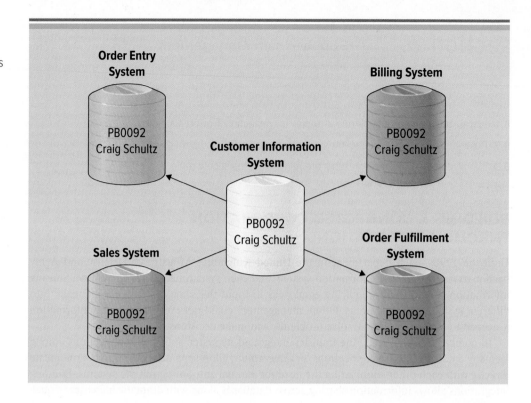

both forward and backward integrations, which provide the flexibility to create, update, and delete information in any of the systems. However, integrations are expensive and difficult to build and maintain, causing most organizations to invest in forward integrations only.

The second integration method builds a central repository for a particular type of information. Figure 8.3 provides an example of customer information integrated using this method across four systems in an organization. Users can create, update, and delete customer information only in the central customer database. As users perform these tasks, integrations automatically send the new and/or updated customer information to the other systems. The other systems limit users to read-only access of the customer information stored in them. Neither integration method entirely eliminates information redundancy, but both do ensure information consistency among multiple systems.

Integration Tools

Enterprise systems provide enterprisewide support and data access for a firm's operations and business processes. These systems can manage customer information across the enterprise, letting you view everything your customer has experienced from sales to support. Enterprise systems are often available as a generic, but highly customizable, group of programs for business functions such as accounting, manufacturing, and marketing. Generally, the development tools for customization are complex programming tools that require specialist capabilities.

Enterprise application integration (EAI) connects the plans, methods, and tools aimed at integrating separate enterprise systems. A legacy system is a current or existing system that will become the base for upgrading or integrating with a new system. EAI reviews how legacy systems fit into the new shape of the firm's business processes and devises ways to reuse what already exists efficiently while adding new systems and data.

Integrations are achieved using *middleware* —several types of software that sit between and provide connectivity for two or more software applications. Middleware translates information between disparate systems. *Enterprise application integration (EAI) middleware* takes a new approach to middleware by packaging commonly used applications together, reducing the time needed to integrate applications from multiple vendors. The remainder of this chapter covers the three enterprise systems most organizations use to integrate their disparate departments and separate operational systems: supply chain management (SCM), customer relationship management, and enterprise resource planning (see Figure 8.4).

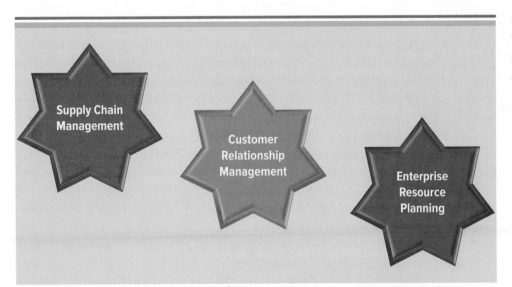

FIGURE 8.4

The Three Primary Enterprise Systems

SUPPLY CHAIN MANAGEMENT

The average company spends nearly half of every dollar it earns on suppliers and raw materials to manufacture products. It is not uncommon to hear of critical success factors focusing on getting the right products to the right place at the right time at the right cost. For this reason, tools that can help a company source raw materials, manufacture products, and deliver finished goods to retailers and customers are in high demand. A *supply chain* consists of all parties involved, directly or indirectly, in obtaining raw materials or a product. Figure 8.5 highlights the five basic supply chain activities a company undertakes to manufacture and distribute products. To automate and enable sophisticated decision making in these critical areas, companies are turning to systems that provide demand forecasting, inventory control, and information flows between suppliers and customers.

Supply chain management (SCM) is the management of information flows between and among activities in a supply chain to maximize total supply chain effectiveness and corporate profitability. In the past, manufacturing efforts focused primarily on quality improvement efforts within the company; today these efforts reach across the entire supply chain, including customers, customers' customers, suppliers, and suppliers' suppliers. Today's supply chain is an intricate network of business partners linked through communication channels and relationships. Supply chain management systems manage and enhance these relationships with the primary goal of creating a fast, efficient, and low-cost network of business relationships that take products from concept to market. SCM systems create the integrations or tight process and information linkages between all participants in the supply chain. Supply chain management performs three main business processes (see Figure 8.6):

1. Materials flow from suppliers and their upstream suppliers at all levels.

2. Materials are transformed into semifinished and finished products—the organization's own production processes.

3. Products are distributed to customers and their downstream customers at all levels.[3]

Consider a customer purchasing a mountain bike from a dealer. Dozens of steps are required to complete this transaction from beginning to end. The customer places an order with the dealer. The dealer purchases the bike from the manufacturer. The manufacturer purchases the raw materials required to make the bike such as aluminum, rubber tires, brakes, accessories, and packaging from different suppliers. The raw materials are stored in the manufacturer's warehouse until a production order requires the bike to be built, at which time the finished product is sent to the dealer or, in some cases, directly to the customer. The supply chain for a bike manufacturer includes all processes and people required to fulfill the customer's order (see Figure 8.7).

Walmart and Procter & Gamble (P&G) have implemented a successful SCM system that links Walmart's distribution centers directly to P&G's manufacturing centers (see Figure 8.8). The customer generates order information by purchasing a product from Walmart. Walmart supplies

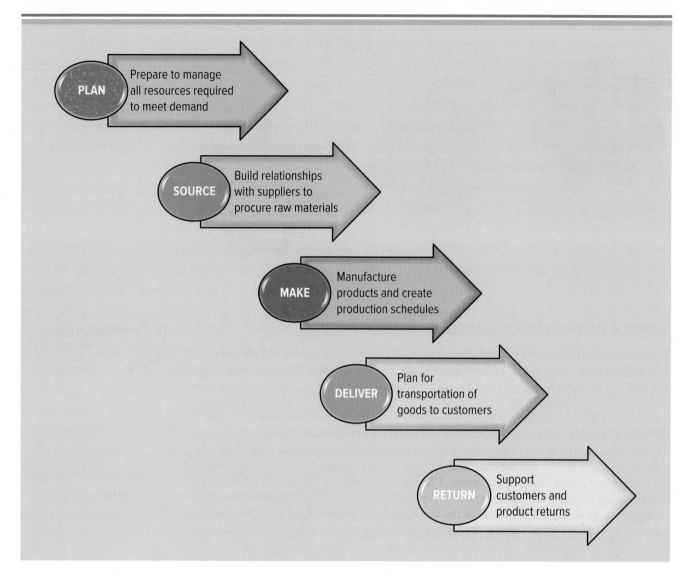

FIGURE 8.5

The Five Basic Supply Chain Activities

the order information to its warehouse or distributor. The warehouse or distributor transfers the order information to P&G, which provides pricing and availability information to the store and replenishes the product to the distributor. Payment is transferred electronically. Effective and efficient supply chain management systems can enable an organization to have these impacts on Porter's Five Forces Model[4]:

- Decrease the power of its buyers.
- Increase its supplier power.
- Increase buyers' switching costs to reduce the threat of substitute products or services.
- Create entry barriers to reduce the threat of new entrants.
- Increase efficiencies while seeking a competitive advantage through cost leadership (see Figure 8.9).

Supply chain management systems can increase profitability across an organization. For example, a manufacturing plant manager might focus on keeping the inventory of Product A as low as possible, which will directly reduce the manufacturing costs and make the plant manager look great. However, the plant manager and the business might not realize that these savings are causing increased costs in other areas, such as having to pay more to procure raw materials for immediate production needs or increasing costs due to expedited shipping services. Only an end-to-end view or an integrated supply chain would uncover these issues, allowing a firm to adjust business strategies to increase profitability across the enterprise.

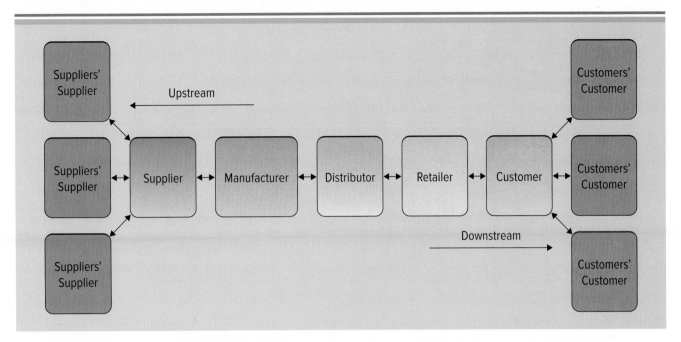

FIGURE 8.6

A Typical Supply Chain

The supply chain is only as strong as its weakest link. Companies use supply chain management metrics to measure the performance of supply chains to identify weak links quickly. A few of the common supply chain management metrics include:

- **Back order:** An unfilled customer order for a product that is out of stock.
- **Inventory cycle time:** The time it takes to manufacture a product and deliver it to the retailer.
- **Customer order cycle time:** The agreed upon time between the purchase of a product and the delivery of the product.
- **Inventory turnover:** The frequency of inventory replacement.

Visibility into the Supply Chain

Supply chain design determines how to structure a supply chain, including the product, selection of partners, the location and capacity of warehouses, transportation methods, and supporting

FIGURE 8.7

Supply Chain for a Bike Manufacturer

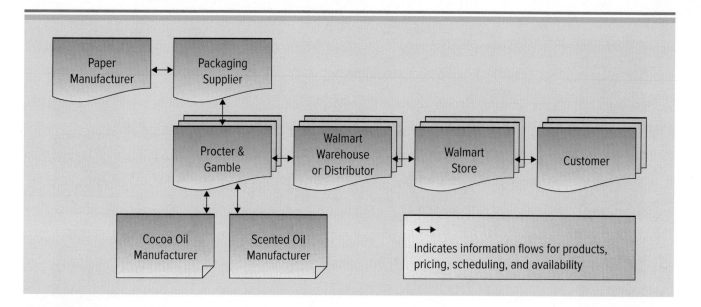

FIGURE 8.8

Supply Chain for a Product
Purchased from Walmart

management information systems. Considerable evidence shows that this type of supply chain design results in superior supply chain capabilities and profits.

Supply chain visibility is the ability to view all areas up and down the supply chain in real time. The goal of supply chain visibility is to improve and strengthen the supply chain by making data readily available to all stakeholders, including the customer. To react to demand, an organization needs to know all customer events triggered upstream and downstream and so must their suppliers and their suppliers' suppliers. Without this information, supply chain participants are blind to the supply and demand needs occurring in the marketplace, a factor required to implement successful business strategies.

Supply chain visibility has become more important as companies have outsourced parts of their supply chains and lost control and visibility over what used to be part of their own operations. Supply chain visibility technology promotes quick response to change by allowing privileged users to take action and reshape demand or redirect supply. To improve visibility across the supply chain, firms can use supply chain planning systems and supply chain execution systems.

Supply chain planning systems use advanced mathematical algorithms to improve the flow and efficiency of the supply chain while reducing inventory. To yield accurate results, however, supply chain planning systems require information inputs that are correct and up-to-date regarding customers, orders, sales, manufacturing, and distribution capabilities.

Ideally, the supply chain consists of multiple firms that function as efficiently and effectively as a single firm, with full information visibility. *Supply chain execution systems* ensure supply chain cohesion by automating the different activities of the supply chain. For example, a supply chain execution system might electronically route orders from a manufacturer to a supplier using *electronic data interchange (EDI)*, a standard format for the electronic exchange of information between supply chain participants. Figure 8.10 details how supply chain planning and supply chain execution systems interact with the supply chain.

FIGURE 8.9

Effective and Efficient Supply
Chain Management's Effect on
Porter's Five Forces

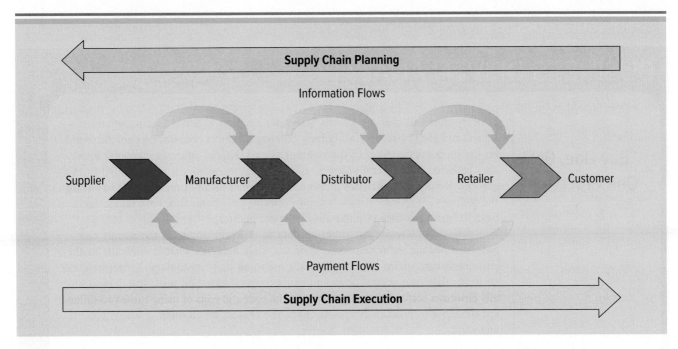

FIGURE 8.10

Supply Chain Planning's and
Supply Chain Execution's Roles
in the Supply Chain

A good example of inventory issues that occur when a company does not have a clear vision of its entire supply chain is the bullwhip effect. The *bullwhip effect* occurs when distorted product-demand information ripples from one partner to the next throughout the supply chain. The misinformation regarding a slight rise in demand for a product could cause different members in the supply chain to stockpile inventory. These changes ripple throughout the supply chain, magnifying the issue and creating excess inventory and costs for all. For example, if a car dealership is having a hard time moving a particular brand of car, it might offer significant discounts to try to move the inventory. Without this critical information, the car manufacturer might see a rise in demand for this particular brand of car and increase production orders, not realizing that the dealerships are actually challenged with selling the inventory. Today, integrated supply chains provide managers with the visibility to see their suppliers' and customers' supply chains, ensuring that supply always meets demand.

TECHNOLOGIES REINVENTING THE SUPPLY CHAIN

LO 8.3: **Identify the three technologies that are reinventing the supply chain.**

Optimizing the supply chain is a critical business process for any successful organization. Just think of the complexity of Walmart's supply chain and the billions of products being sent around the world, guaranteeing every shelf is fully stocked. The three components of supply chain management on which companies focus to find efficiencies include procurement, logistics, and materials management (see Figure 8.11) .

Procurement is the purchasing of goods and services to meet the needs of the supply chain. The procurement process is a key supply chain strategy because the capability to purchase input materials at the right price is directly correlated to the company's ability to operate. Without the right inputs, the company simply can't create cost-effective outputs. For example, if McDonald's could not procure potatoes or had to purchase potatoes at an outrageous price, it would be unable to create and sell its famous french fries. In fact, procuring the right-size potatoes that can produce the famous long french fries is challenging in some countries where locally grown potatoes are too small. Procurement can help a company answer the following questions:

- What quantity of raw materials should we purchase to minimize spoilage?
- How can we guarantee that our raw materials meet production needs?
- At what price can we purchase materials to guarantee profitability?
- Can purchasing all products from a single vendor provide additional discounts?

Logistics includes the processes that control the distribution, maintenance, and replacement of materials and personnel to support the supply chain. Recall from the value chain analysis in

BUSINESS DRIVEN ANALYTICS

Buy One, Get One Groceries

Grocery stores all over the United States use coupons as a way to compete for customers and keep customer loyalty high. Safeway produces coupons on demand based on the products currently in the customer's cart. Kroger analyzes customer loyalty data gathered over several years. Knowing most customers throw junk mail in the garbage, Kroger uses analytics to mine the customer loyalty program data to ensure the coupons are specific for each family, offering only items they have bought in the past. Kroger mails over 15 million coupons per quarter.

Safeway and Kroger are gathering data at different points in the supply chain. Safeway does not gather customer data and only analyzes what is currently in the customer's cart, giving coupons in real time to all daily customers. Kroger gathers customer data over several years and mails coupons based on historical data to loyalty customer cardholders only. What are the pros and cons of using these two different strategies to produce coupons? Given the choice, which method would you use and why?

Chapter 1 that the primary value activities for an organization include inbound and outbound logistics. *Inbound logistics* acquires raw materials and resources and distributes them to manufacturing as required. *Outbound logistics* distributes goods and services to customers. Logistics controls processes inside a company (warehouse logistics) and outside a company (transport logistics) and focuses on the physical execution part of the supply chain. Logistics includes the increasingly complex management of processes, information, and communication to take

FIGURE 8.11

The Three Business Areas of Supply Chain Management

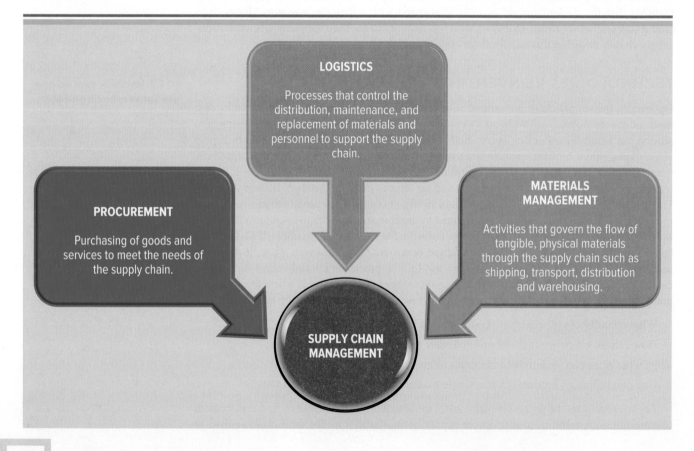

BUSINESS DRIVEN GLOBALIZATION

3D Printing for Poverty

Thirty-three-year-old Kodjo Afate Grikou wanted to help his community in West Africa to print necessities that they can't source locally, such as kitchen utensils for cooking. The structure of the 3D printer he had in mind uses very little in terms of new parts because it is mostly made up of ewaste and scrap metal. Before building this printer, he set up his project on the European social funding website, ulule. The project received more than $10,000, despite the printer costing only $1,000, mostly through purchasing new parts that he couldn't find locally. Grikou hopes that his innovation will inspire teenagers and young people in his community to attend school and gain an education so they can make further life-changing developments that will benefit not only their lives but also others around them. In a group, brainstorm ways 3D printing can help rural communities fight poverty.[5]

a product from cradle to grave. *Cradle to grave* provides logistics support throughout the entire system or life of the product. Logistics can help a company answer the following questions:

- What is the quickest way to deliver products to our customers?
- What is the optimal way to place items in the warehouse for picking and packing?
- What is the optimal path to an item in the warehouse?
- What path should the vehicles follow when delivering the goods?
- What areas or regions are the trucks covering?

Materials management includes activities that govern the flow of tangible, physical materials through the supply chain such as shipping, transport, distribution, and warehousing. In materials management, you focus on quality and quantity of materials as well as on how you will plan, acquire, use, and dispose of such materials. It can include the handling of liquids, fuel, produce, plants, and a number of other potentially hazardous items. Materials management focuses on handling all materials safely, efficiently, and in compliance with regulatory requirements and disposal requirements. Materials management can help a company answer the following concerns:

- What are our current inventory levels?
- What items are running low in the warehouse?
- What items are at risk of spoiling in the warehouse?
- How do we dispose of spoiled items?
- What laws need to be followed for storing hazardous materials?
- Which items must be refrigerated when being stored and transported?
- What are the requirements to store or transport fragile items?

As with all other areas of business, disruptive technologies are continuously being deployed to help businesses find competitive advantages in each component of the supply chain, as outlined in Figure 8.12.

3D Printing Supports Procurement

The process of *3D printing* (additive manufacturing) builds—layer by layer in an additive process—a three-dimensional solid object from a digital model. The additive manufacturing process of 3D printing is profoundly different from traditional manufacturing processes. The *Financial Times* and other sources are stating that 3D printing has the potential to be vastly more disruptive to business than the Internet. That is a bold statement! The reason people are betting on 3D printing

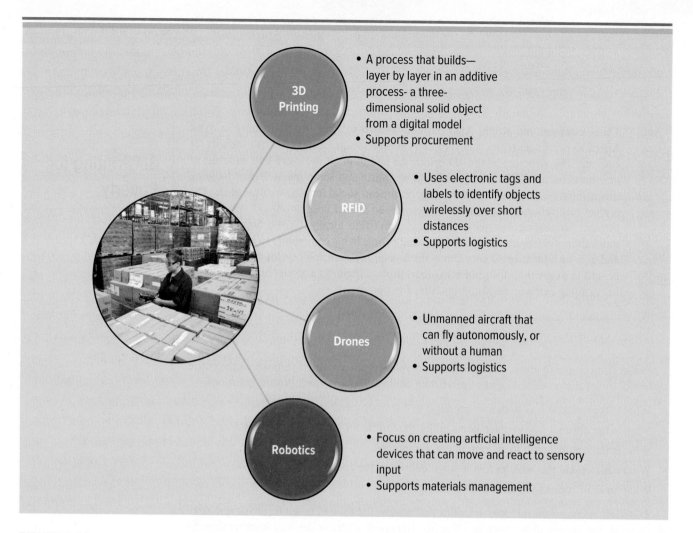

3D Printing
- A process that builds— layer by layer in an additive process- a three-dimensional solid object from a digital model
- Supports procurement

RFID
- Uses electronic tags and labels to identify objects wirelessly over short distances
- Supports logistics

Drones
- Unmanned aircraft that can fly autonomously, or without a human
- Supports logistics

Robotics
- Focus on creating artficial intelligence devices that can move and react to sensory input
- Supports materials management

FIGURE 8.12

Disruptive Business Technologies

to disrupt business is that it brings production closer to users, thus eliminating steps in the supply chain similar to disintermediation by the Internet. Three-dimensional printing also promotes mass customization, small production batches, and reduction in inventory. Traditionally, the costs associated with 3D printing made it accessible only to large corporations. Now with inexpensive printers, scanners, and applications, the technology is accessible to small and mid-sized businesses and home users. With the advances in 3D printing, the need to procure materials will become far easier because businesses can simply print the parts and components required for the production process. There is no doubt about it: 3D printing will affect the production process and supply chains and cause business disruption. These printers are creating auto parts, cell phone covers, jewelry, toys, bicycles, and manufacturing prototypes for testing purposes.[6]

To print a 3D product, users create a digital model that is sliced into thin cross-sections called layers. During the printing process, the 3D printer starts at the bottom of the design and adds successive layers of material to complete the project. *Computer-aided design/ computer-aided manufacturing (CAD/CAM)* systems are used to create the digital designs and then manufacture the products. For example, a user creates a design with a CAD application and then manufactures the product by using CAM systems. Before 3D printers existed, creating a prototype was time-consuming and expensive, requiring skilled craftsmen and specific machinery. Instead of sending modeling instructions to a production company, advances in 3D printing allow users to create prototypes and products on demand from their desks. Shipping required parts from around the world could become obsolete because the spare parts can now be 3D printed on demand. This could have a major impact on how businesses large and small operate and interact on a global scale in the future.

The *maker movement* is a cultural trend that places value on an individual's ability to be a creator of things as well as a consumer of things. In this culture, individuals who create things are called "makers." The movement is growing rapidly and is expected to be economically disruptive; as ordinary people become more self-sufficient, they will be able to make their own products instead of procuring brand-name products from retail stores. Makers come from all walks of life, with diverse skill sets and interests. The thing they have in common is creativity, an interest in design, and access to tools and raw materials that make production possible. The growth of the maker movement is often attributed to the rise of community *makerspaces*, a community center that provides technology, manufacturing equipment, and educational opportunities to the public that would otherwise be inaccessible or unaffordable. Although the majority of makers are hobbyists, entrepreneurs and small manufacturers are also taking advantage of the classes and tools available in makerspaces.[7]

In the future, expect to see 4D printing transforming the supply chain. *4D printing* is additive manufacturing that prints objects capable of transformation and self-assembly. When using 3D printing, a product is printed and then manually assembled. With the invention of 4D printing, a product will be printed and then be capable of changing form or self-assembling with minimal human interaction. The business benefits of 4D printing will include assemble-at-home products that will greatly reduce transportation costs.

RFID Supports Logistics

A television commercial shows a man in a uniform quietly moving through a family home. The man replaces the empty cereal box with a full one just before a hungry child opens the cabinet; he then opens a new sack of dog food as the hungry bulldog eyes him warily, and, finally, he hands a full bottle of shampoo to the man in the shower whose bottle had just run out. The next wave in supply chain management will be home-based supply chain fulfillment. Walgreens is differentiating itself from other national chains by marketing itself as the family's just-in-time supplier. Consumers today are becoming incredibly comfortable with the idea of going online to purchase products when they want, how they want, and at the price they want. Walgreens is developing custom websites for each household, which allow families to order electronically and then at their convenience go to the store to pick up their goods at a special self-service counter or the drive-through window. Walgreens is making a promise that goes beyond low prices and customer service and extends right into the home.

Radio-frequency identification (RFID) uses electronic tags and labels to identify objects wirelessly over short distances. It holds the promise of replacing existing identification technologies such as the bar code. RFID tags are evolving, too, and the advances will provide more granular information to enterprise software. Today's tags can store an electronic product code. In time, tags could hold more information, making them portable mini-databases. *RFID's electronic product code (RFID EPC)* promotes serialization or the ability to track individual items by using the unique serial number associated with each RFID tag. Although a bar code might identify a product such as a bottle of salad dressing, an RFID EPC tag can identify each specific bottle and allow item-level tracking to determine whether the product has passed its expiration date. Businesses can tell automatically where all its items are in the supply chain just by gathering the data from the RFID chips. The possibilities of RFID are endless, and one area it is affecting is logistics. RFID tags for applications such as highway toll collection and container tracking remain in continuous use for several years. Like regular electronic components, the tags are adhered to rigid substrates and packaged in plastic enclosures. In contrast, tags on shipping cartons are used for a much shorter time and are then destroyed. Disposable tags are adhered to printed, flexible labels pasted onto the carton, and these smart labels contain an RFID chip and antenna on the back. A thermal printer/encoder prints alphanumeric and bar code data on the labels while encoding the chip at the same time. Figures 8.13 and 8.14 display how an RFID system works in the supply chain.

Drones Support Logistics

A *drone* is an unmanned aircraft that can fly autonomously, or without a human. Amazon.com is piloting drone aircraft for package deliveries. Amazon is now working on small drones that could someday deliver customers' packages in half an hour or less. UPS and FedEx have also been experimenting with their own versions of flying parcel carriers. Drones are already here and use GPS to help coordinate the logistics of package delivery. The problems with drones include Federal Aviation Administration (FAA) approval and the advanced ability to detect and avoid objects. GPS coordinates can easily enable the drone to find the appropriate package

FIGURE 8.13

RFID Components

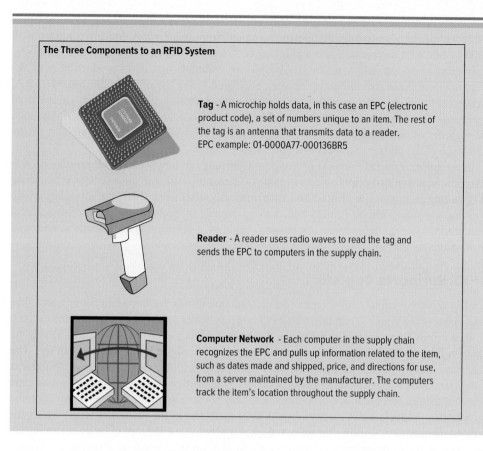

The Three Components to an RFID System

Tag - A microchip holds data, in this case an EPC (electronic product code), a set of numbers unique to an item. The rest of the tag is an antenna that transmits data to a reader. EPC example: 01-0000A77-000136BR5

Reader - A reader uses radio waves to read the tag and sends the EPC to computers in the supply chain.

Computer Network - Each computer in the supply chain recognizes the EPC and pulls up information related to the item, such as dates made and shipped, price, and directions for use, from a server maintained by the manufacturer. The computers track the item's location throughout the supply chain.

FIGURE 8.14

RFID in the Supply Chain

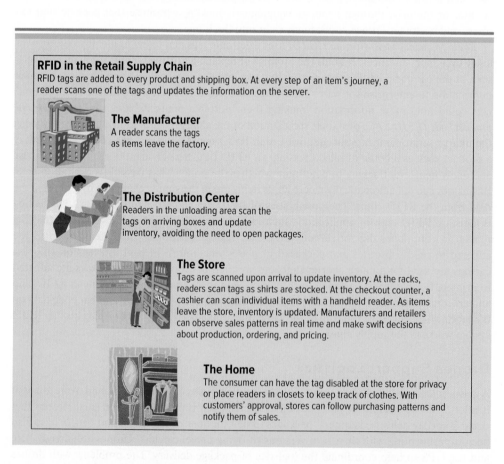

RFID in the Retail Supply Chain
RFID tags are added to every product and shipping box. At every step of an item's journey, a reader scans one of the tags and updates the information on the server.

The Manufacturer
A reader scans the tags as items leave the factory.

The Distribution Center
Readers in the unloading area scan the tags on arriving boxes and update inventory, avoiding the need to open packages.

The Store
Tags are scanned upon arrival to update inventory. At the racks, readers scan tags as shirts are stocked. At the checkout counter, a cashier can scan individual items with a handheld reader. As items leave the store, inventory is updated. Manufacturers and retailers can observe sales patterns in real time and make swift decisions about production, ordering, and pricing.

The Home
The consumer can have the tag disabled at the store for privacy or place readers in closets to keep track of clothes. With customers' approval, stores can follow purchasing patterns and notify them of sales.

BUSINESS DRIVEN ETHICS AND SECURITY

In 1976, the big movie studios sued Sony for releasing the first VCR because it advertised it as "a way of recording feature-length movies from TV to VHS tape for watching and taking over to friends' houses." Over the next 8 years, Universal Studios, along with other powerful media groups, fought Sony over creating the device because it could allow users to violate copyright laws. The courts went back and forth for years attempting to determine whether Sony would be held liable for creating a device that enabled users to break copyright laws. In 1984, the U.S. Supreme Court ruled in favor of Sony: "If a device is capable of sustaining a substantial noninfringing use, then it is lawful to make and sell that device. That is, if the device is merely capable of doing something legit, it is legal to make no matter how it is used in practice."[8]

Just think of cars, knives, guns, and computers as they are all used to break the law, and nobody would be allowed to produce them if they were held responsible for how people used them. Do you agree that if you make a tool and sell it to someone who goes on to break the law, you should be held responsible? Do you agree that 3D printers will be used to infringe copyright, trademark, and patent protections? If so, should 3D printers be illegal?

3D Printing Weapons

delivery location, but objects not included in the GPS, such as cars, dogs, and children, will need to be detected and avoided.

FedEx founder Fred Smith stated that his drones are up and running in the lab; all he requires to move his fleet of drones from the lab to production is approval from regulators. "We have all this stuff working in the lab right now, we don't need to reinvent the wheel," remarks Smith. "We need a set of rules from the FAA. It's just a matter of getting the laws in place so companies can begin building to those specifications and doing some real field testing."[9]

Robotics Supports Materials Management

Robotics focuses on creating artificial intelligence devices that can move and react to sensory input. The term *robot* was coined by Czech playwright Karl Capek in his play *R.U.R.* (*Rossum's Universal Robots*), which opened in Prague in 1921. *Robota* is the Czech word for "forced labor." The term *robotics* was introduced by writer Isaac Asimov; in his science fiction book *I, Robot,* published in 1950, he presented three laws of robotics:

1. A robot may not injure a human being, or, through inaction, allow a human being to come to harm.

2. A robot must obey the orders given it by human beings except where such orders would conflict with the First Law.

3. A robot must protect its own existence as long as such protection does not conflict with the First or Second Law.[10]

You can find robots in factories performing high-precision tasks, in homes vacuuming the floor and the pool, and in dangerous situations such as cleaning toxic wastes or defusing bombs. Amazon alone has more than 10,000 robots in its warehouses, picking, packing, and managing materials to fulfill customer orders. The robots are made by Kiva Systems, a company Amazon bought for $775 million in 2012. Kiva pitches its robots—which can cost between a few million dollars and as much as roughly $20 million—as simplifying and reducing costs via materials management. The robots are tied into a complex grid that optimizes item placement in the warehouse and allows the robots to pick the inventory items and bring them to the workers for packing. Watching an order fulfillment center equipped with Kiva robots is amazing; the operators stand still while the products come to them. Inventory pods store the products that

FIGURE 8.15

Extending the Supply Chain

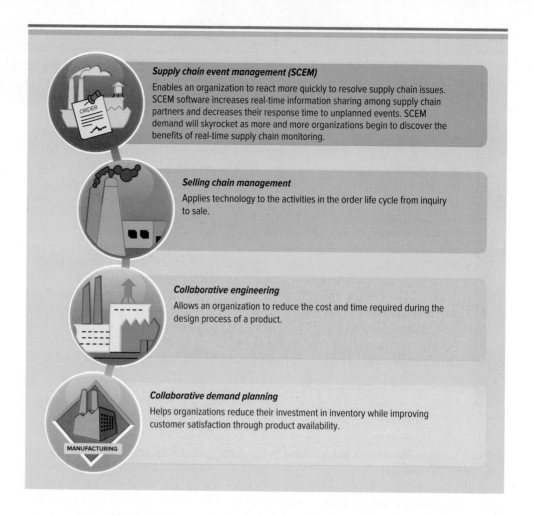

Supply chain event management (SCEM)

Enables an organization to react more quickly to resolve supply chain issues. SCEM software increases real-time information sharing among supply chain partners and decreases their response time to unplanned events. SCEM demand will skyrocket as more and more organizations begin to discover the benefits of real-time supply chain monitoring.

Selling chain management

Applies technology to the activities in the order life cycle from inquiry to sale.

Collaborative engineering

Allows an organization to reduce the cost and time required during the design process of a product.

Collaborative demand planning

Helps organizations reduce their investment in inventory while improving customer satisfaction through product availability.

MANUFACTURING

are carried and transferred by a small army of little orange robots, eliminating the need for traditional systems such as conveyors and sorters. Though assessing the costs and benefits of robots versus human labor can be difficult, Kiva boasts that a packer working with its robots can fulfill three to four times as many orders per hour. Zappos, Staples, and Amazon are just a few of the companies taking advantage of the latest innovation in warehouse management by replacing traditional order fulfillment technologies such as conveyor belts with Kiva's little orange robots.[11]

The Extended Supply Chain

As the supply chain management market matures, it is becoming even more sophisticated and incorporating additional functionality such as marketing, customer service, and even product development to its extended supply chain. Advanced communications tools, easy-to-use decision support systems, and building trust among participants when sharing information are all making the home-based supply chain possible. A few of the fastest-growing extensions for supply chain management are included in Figure 8.15.

section 8.2 | **Customer Relationship Management and Enterprise Resource Planning**

LEARNING OUTCOMES

8.4 Explain operational and analytical customer relationship management.

8.5 Identify the core and extended areas of enterprise resource planning.

8.6 Discuss the current technologies organizations are integrating in enterprise resource planning systems.

CUSTOMER RELATIONSHIP MANAGEMENT

Today, most competitors are simply a mouse-click away. This intense marketplace has forced organizations to switch from being sales focused to being customer focused. *Customer relationship management (CRM)* involves managing all aspects of a customer's relationship with an organization to increase customer loyalty and retention and an organization's profitability. CRM allows an organization to gain insights into customers' shopping and buying behaviors in order to develop and implement enterprisewide strategies. The key players in CRM initiatives are outlined in Figure 8.16. CRM strategic goals include:

- Identify sales opportunities.
- Classify low-value customers and create marketing promotions to increase consumer spending.
- Classify high-value customers and create marketing promotions to increase consumer loyalty.
- Analyze marketing promotions by product, market segment, and sales region.
- Identify customer relationship issues along with strategies for quick resolution.

FIGURE 8.16

Customer Relationship Management Key Players

Lead: A Person or company that is unknown to your business.

Account: An existing business relationship exists and can include customers, prospects, partners, and competitors.

Contact: Specific individual representing the account.

Sales Opportunity: An opportunity exists for a potential sale of goods or services related to an account or contact.

FIGURE 8.17

Customer Contact Points

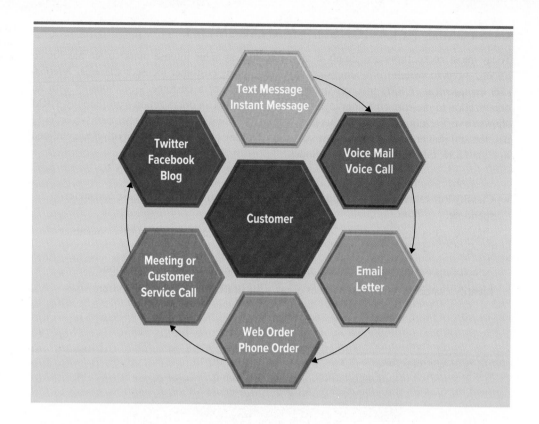

The complicated piece of the CRM puzzle is identifying customers and the many communication channels they use to contact companies, including call centers, web access, email, sales representatives, faxes, and cell phones. A single customer may access an organization multiple times through many different channels (see Figure 8.17). CRM systems can help to collect all of the points of customer contact along with sales and financial information to provide a complete view of each customer (see Figure 8.18.) CRM systems track every communication between the customer and the organization and provide access to cohesive customer information for all business areas from accounting to order fulfillment. Understanding all customer communications allows the organization to communicate effectively with each customer. It gives the organization a detailed understanding of each customer's products and services record regardless of the customer's preferred communication channel. For example, a customer service representative can easily view detailed account information and history through a CRM system when providing information to a customer such as expected delivery dates, complementary product information, and customer payment and billing information.

Companies that understand individual customer needs are best positioned to achieve success. Of course, building successful customer relationships is not a new business practice; however, implementing CRM systems allows a company to operate more efficiently and effectively in the area of supporting customer needs. CRM moves far beyond technology by identifying customer needs and designing specific marketing campaigns tailored to each. This enables a firm to treat customers as individuals, gaining important insights into their buying preferences and shopping behaviors. Firms that treat their customers well reap the rewards and generally see higher profits and highly loyal customers. Identifying the most valuable customers allows a firm to ensure that these customers receive the highest levels of customer service and are offered the first opportunity to purchase new products. *Customer analytics* involves gathering, classifying, comparing, and studying customer data to identify buying trends, at-risk customers, and potential future opportunities. *Sales analytics* involves gathering, classifying, comparing, and studying company sales data to analyze product cycles, sales pipelines, and competitive intelligence. Software with advanced analytics capabilities helps you attract and retain loyal and profitable customers and gives you the insight you need to increase revenues, customer satisfaction, and customer loyalty.

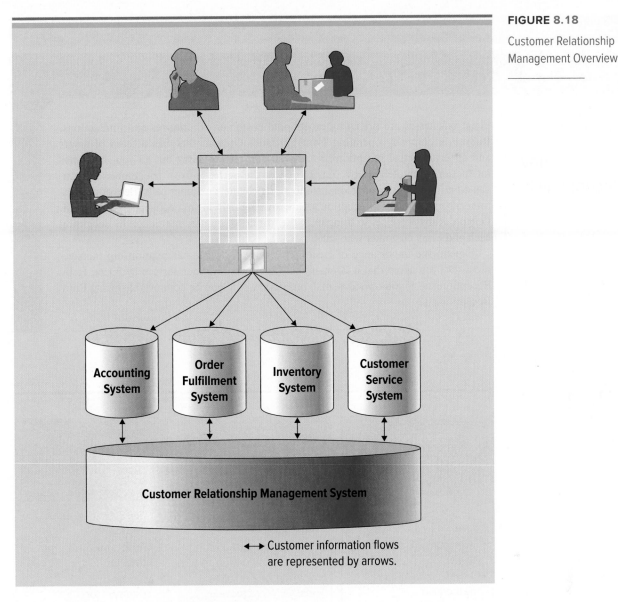

FIGURE 8.18

Customer Relationship Management Overview

Customer information flows are represented by arrows.

Firms can find their most valuable customers by using the RFM formula—recency, frequency, and monetary value. In other words, an organization must track:

- How *recently* a customer purchased items.
- How *frequently* a customer purchases items.
- The *monetary value* of each customer purchase.

After gathering this initial CRM information, the firm can analyze it to identify patterns and create marketing campaigns and sales promotions for different customer segments. For example, if a customer buys only at the height of the season, the firm should send a special offer during the off-season. If a certain customer segment purchases shoes but never accessories, the firm can offer discounted accessories with the purchase of a new pair of shoes. If the firm determines that its top 20 percent of customers are responsible for 80 percent of the revenue, it can focus on ensuring that these customers are always satisfied and receive the highest levels of customer service.

There are three phases in the evolution of CRM: (1) reporting, (2) analyzing, and (3) predicting. **CRM reporting technologies** help organizations identify their customers across other applications. **CRM analysis technologies** help organizations segment their customers into categories such as best and worst customers. **CRM predicting technologies** help organizations predict customer behavior, such as which customers are at risk of leaving. Figure 8.19 highlights a few of the important questions an organization can answer in these areas by using CRM technologies.

BUSINESS DRIVEN START-UP

Ruby Receptionists

Great businesses are driven by exceptional customer experiences and interactions. Ruby is a company operating from Portland, Oregon, that has a team of smart and cheerful virtual receptionists that you can hire to carry out all your customer interactions—remotely. Ruby aims to deliver the perfect mix of friendliness, charm, can-do attitude, and professionalism to all its clients' customer calls. Best of all, customers believe the Ruby receptionists are working right in your office, not in Portland, Oregon. Ruby promises to bring back the lost art of human interaction by delighting each and every customer who calls.[12]

Explain the importance of customer service for customer relationship management. Do you agree that a company can improve customer service by hiring Ruby Receptionists? If you owned a small business, would you be comfortable hiring Ruby Receptionists?

FIGURE 8.19

Evolution of CRM

REPORTING Customer Identification: Asking What Happened	ANALYZING Customer Segmentation: Asking Why It Happened	PREDICTING Customer Prediction: Asking What Will Happen
• What is the total revenue by customer? • How many units did we make? • What were total sales by product? • How many customers do we have? • What are the current inventory levels?	• Why did sales not meet forecasts? • Why was production so low? • Why did we not sell as many units as previous years? • Who are our customers? • Why was revenue so high? • Why are inventory levels low?	• What customers are at risk of leaving? • Which products will our customers buy? • Who are the best customers for a marketing campaign? • How do we reach our customers? • What will sales be this year? • How much inventory do we need to preorder?

The Power of the Customer

A standard rule of business states that the customer is always right. Although most businesses use this as their motto, they do not actually mean it. Ebusiness firms, however, must adhere to this rule as the power of the customer grows exponentially in the information age. Various websites and videos on YouTube reveal the power of the individual consumer (see Figure 8.20). A decade ago if you had a complaint against a company, you could make a phone call or write a letter. Now you can contact hundreds or thousands of people around the globe and voice your complaint or anger with a company or product. You—the customer—can now take your power directly to millions of people, and companies have to listen.

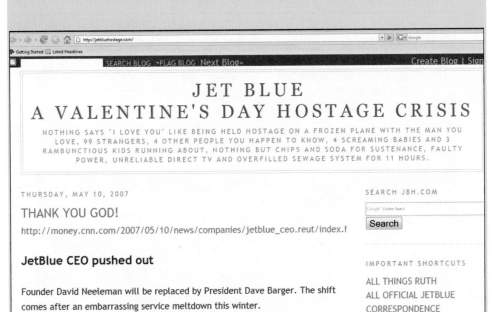

FIGURE 8.20

The Power of the Customer

Source: www.dontbuydodgechrysler vehicles.com
Source: www.jetbluehostage.com

Measuring CRM Success

Using CRM metrics to track and monitor performance is a best practice for many companies. Figure 8.21 displays a few common CRM metrics a manager can use to track the success of the system. Just remember that you only want to track between five and seven of the hundreds of CRM metrics available.

OPERATIONAL AND ANALYTICAL CRM

The two primary components of a CRM strategy are operational CRM and analytical CRM. *Operational CRM* supports traditional transactional processing for day-to-day front-office operations or systems that deal directly with the customers. *Analytical CRM* supports back-office operations and strategic analysis and includes all systems that do not deal directly with the customers. Figure 8.22 provides an overview of the two.

Figure 8.23 shows the different technologies marketing, sales, and customer service departments can use to perform operational CRM.

FIGURE 8.21

CRM Metrics

Sales Metrics	Customer Service Metrics	Marketing Metrics
Number of prospective customers	Cases closed same day	Number of marketing campaigns
Number of new customers	Number of cases handled by agent	New customer retention rates
Number of retained customers	Number of service calls	Number of responses by marketing campaign
Number of open leads	Average number of service requests by type	Number of purchases by marketing campaign
Number of sales calls	Average time to resolution	Revenue generated by marketing campaign
Number of sales calls per lead	Average number of service calls per day	Cost per interaction by marketing campaign
Amount of new revenue	Percentage compliance with service-level agreement	Number of new customers acquired by marketing campaign
Amount of recurring revenue	Percentage of service renewals	Customer retention rate
Number of proposals given	Customer satisfaction level	Number of new leads by product

FIGURE 8.22

Operational CRM and Analytical CRM

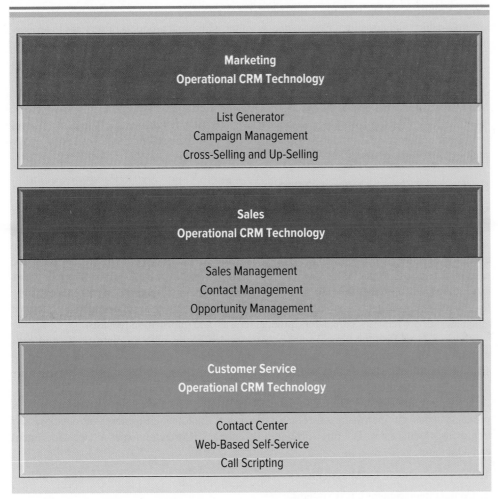

FIGURE 8.23

Operational CRM Technologies

Marketing and Operational CRM

Companies are no longer trying to sell one product to as many customers as possible; instead, they are trying to sell one customer as many products as possible. Marketing departments switch to this new way of doing business by using CRM technologies that allow them to gather and analyze customer information to tailor successful marketing campaigns. In fact, a marketing campaign's success is directly proportional to the organization's ability to gather and analyze the right customer information. The three primary operational CRM technologies a marketing department can implement to increase customer satisfaction are:

1. List generator.
2. Campaign management.
3. Cross-selling and up-selling.

List Generator *List generators* compile customer information from a variety of sources and segment it for different marketing campaigns. These sources include website visits, questionnaires, surveys, marketing mailers, and so on. After being compiled, the customer list can be filtered based on criteria such as household income, gender, education level, political facilitation, age, or other factors. List generators provide the marketing department with valuable information on the type of customer it must target to find success for a marketing campaign.

Campaign Management *Campaign management systems* guide users through marketing campaigns by performing such tasks as campaign definition, planning, scheduling, segmentation, and success analysis. These advanced systems can even calculate the profitability and track the results for each marketing campaign.

Cross-Selling and Up-Selling Two key sales strategies a marketing campaign can deploy are cross-selling and up-selling. *Cross-selling* is selling additional products or services to an existing customer. For example, if you were to purchase Tim Burton's movie *Alice in Wonderland* on Amazon, you would also be asked whether you want to purchase the movie's soundtrack or the original book. Amazon is taking advantage of cross-selling by offering customers goods across its book, movie, and music product lines. *Up-selling* is increasing the value of the sale. McDonald's performs up-selling by asking customers whether they would like to super-size their meals for an extra cost. CRM systems offer marketing departments all kinds of information about customers and products, which can help identify up-selling and cross-selling opportunities to increase revenues.

Sales and Operational CRM

Sales departments were the first to begin developing CRM systems. They had two primary motivations to track customer sales information electronically. First, sales representatives were struggling with the overwhelming amount of customer account information they were required to maintain and track. Second, managers found themselves hindered because much of their vital customer and sales information remained in the heads of their sales representatives, even if the sales representative left the company. Finding a way to track customer information became a critical success factor for many sales departments. *Customer service and support (CSS)* is a part of operational CRM that automates service requests, complaints, product returns, and information requests.

Figure 8.24 depicts the typical sales process, which begins with an opportunity and ends with billing the customer for the sale. Leads and potential customers are the lifeblood of all sales organizations, whether they sell computers, clothing, consulting, or cars. How leads are handled can make the difference between revenue growth and decline.

Sales force automation (SFA) automatically tracks all the steps in the sales process. SFA products focus on increasing customer satisfaction, building customer relationships, and improving product sales. The three primary operational CRM technologies a sales department can adopt are:

1. Sales management CRM systems.

FIGURE 8.24

A Typical Sales Process

2. Contact management CRM systems.

3. Opportunity management CRM systems.

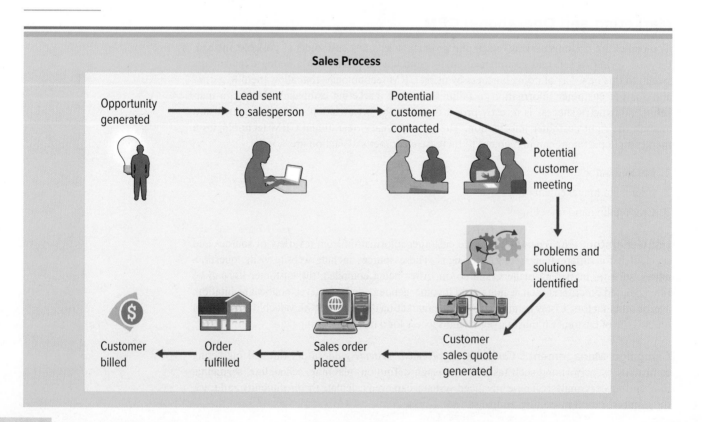

Sales Process

Opportunity generated → Lead sent to salesperson → Potential customer contacted → Potential customer meeting → Problems and solutions identified

Customer billed ← Order fulfilled ← Sales order placed ← Customer sales quote generated

Sales Management CRM Systems *Sales management CRM systems* automate each phase of the sales process, helping individual sales representatives coordinate and organize all their accounts. Features include calendars, reminders for important tasks, multimedia presentations, and document generation. These systems can even provide an analysis of the sales cycle and calculate how each sales representative is performing during the sales process.

Contact Management CRM Systems A *contact management CRM system* maintains customer contact information and identifies prospective customers for future sales, using tools such as organizational charts, detailed customer notes, and supplemental sales information. For example, a contact management system can take an incoming telephone number and automatically display the person's name along with a comprehensive history, including all communications with the company. This allows the sales representative to personalize the phone conversation and ask such things as, "How is your new laptop working, Sue?" or "How was your family vacation to Colorado?" The customer feels valued since the sales associate knows her name and even remembers details of their last conversation.

Opportunity Management CRM Systems *Opportunity management CRM systems* target sales opportunities by finding new customers or companies for future sales. They determine potential customers and competitors and define selling efforts, including budgets and schedules. Advanced systems can even calculate the probability of a sale, which can save sales representatives significant time and money when qualifying new customers. The primary difference between contact management and opportunity management is that contact management deals with existing customers and opportunity management with new or potential customers.

Customer Service and Operational CRM

Most companies recognize the importance of building strong customer relationships during the marketing and sales efforts, but they must continue this effort by building strong post-sale relationships also. A primary reason firms lose customers is due to negative customer service experiences. Providing outstanding customer service is challenging, and many CRM technologies can assist organizations with this important activity. The three primary ones are:

1. Contact center.
2. Web-based self-service.
3. Call scripting.

Contact Center A *contact center* or *call center* is where customer service representatives answer customer inquiries and solve problems, usually by email, chat, or phone. It is one of the best assets a customer-driven organization can have because maintaining a high level of customer support is critical to obtaining and retaining customers. Figure 8.25 highlights a few of the services contact center systems offer.

Contact centers also track customer communication histories along with problem resolutions—information critical for providing a comprehensive customer view to the service representative. Representatives who can quickly comprehend the customer's concerns provide tremendous value to the customer and to the company. Nothing makes frustrated customers happier than not having to explain their problems all over again to yet another customer service representative.

Web-Based Self-Service *Web-based self-service systems* allow customers to use the web to find answers to their questions or solutions to their problems. FedEx uses web-based self-service systems to let customers electronically track packages without having to talk to a customer service representative. Another feature of web-based self-service is *click-to-talk* functions, which allow customers to click a button and talk with a representative via the Internet. Powerful customer-driven features such as these add value to any organization by providing customers with real-time information that helps resolve their concerns.

Call Scripting Companies that market and sell highly technical products have a difficult time finding competent customer service representatives. *Call scripting systems* gather product details and issue resolution information that can be automatically generated into a script for the representative to read to the customer. These systems even provide questions the representative

BUSINESS DRIVEN INNOVATION

Nice Emotions

New emotion-detection software called Perform, created by Nice Systems, helps firms improve customer service by identifying callers who are displeased or upset. Perform determines a baseline of emotion and can detect emotional issues during the first few seconds of a call; any variation from the baseline activates an alert. When an elderly person who was highly distressed over medical costs hung up during a phone call to the insurance company, Perform identified the customer's frustration and automatically emailed a supervisor. The supervisor was able to review a recording of the conversation and immediately called the customer back suggesting ways to lower the costs.[13]

How do you think emotion-detection software will affect customer relationships? What other departments or business processes could benefit from its use? Create a new product that uses emotion-detection software. What business problem would your product solve and who would be your primary customers?

FIGURE 8.25

Contact Center Services

can ask the customer to troubleshoot the problem and find a resolution. This feature not only helps reps answer difficult questions quickly but also presents a uniform response so customers don't receive different answers.

Analytical CRM

Analytical CRM provides information about customers and products that was once impossible to locate, such as which type of marketing and sales campaign to launch and which customers to target and when. Unlike operational CRM, which automates call centers and sales forces with the aim of enhancing customer service, analytical CRM works by using business intelligence to identify patterns in product sales and customer behaviors. *Uplift modeling* is a form of predictive analytics for marketing campaigns that attempts to identify target markets or people who could be convinced to buy products. The "uplift" refers to the increased sales that can follow after this form of analytical CRM analysis. Analytical CRM provides priceless customer information, supports important business decisions, and plays a vital role in your organization's success.

Analytical CRM tools can slice and dice vast amounts of information to create custom views of customers, products, and market segments, highlighting opportunities for cross-selling and up-selling. Analytical CRM provides *customer segmentation*, which divides a market into categories that share similar attributes such as age, location, gender, habits, and so on. By segmenting customers into groups, it becomes easier to create targeted marketing and sales campaigns, ensuring that you are not wasting resources marketing products to the wrong customers. *Website personalization* occurs when a website has stored enough data about a person's likes and dislikes to fashion offers more likely to appeal to that person. Many marketers use CRM to personalize customer communications and decide which customers are worth pursuing. Here are a few examples of the information insights analytical CRM can help an organization gain.

BUSINESS DRIVEN START-UP

Straightjacket Customer Service

You might not want to put the fact that you won the Straightjacket Award on your résumé unless you worked for Rackspace, a Texas company that specializes in hosting websites. At Rackspace, the coveted Straightjacket Award is won by the employee who best delivers "fanatical customer support," one of the firm's critical success factors. The company motivates its customer service representatives by dividing them into teams, each responsible for its own profitability. The company then measures such things as customer turnover, up-selling, cross-selling, and referrals. The team with the highest scores wins the Straightjacket Award, and each member receives a 20 percent bonus.[14]

Assume your professor has hired you as the employee relationship manager for your class. What type of award would you create to help increase class participation? What type of award would you create to help increase the overall average on exams? What type of award would you create to help increase student collaboration? Be sure to name your awards and describe their details. Also, what type of metrics would you create to measure your awards? How could a CRM system help you implement your awards?

■ **Find new profitable customers:** Analytical CRM could highlight that the most profitable market segment consists of women between 35 and 45 years old who drive SUVs and live within 30 miles of the city limits. The firm could then find a way to locate these customers for mailings and other opportunities.

■ **Exceed customer expectations:** Analytical CRM helps a firm move past the typical "Dear Mr. Smith" greeting by personalizing communications. For example, if the firm knows the customer's favorite brand and size of shoe, it can notify the customer that a pair of size 12 Nike cross trainers is available for him to try on the next time he visits the store.

■ **Discover the activities the firm performs the best:** Analytical CRM can determine what an organization does better than its competitors. If a restaurant caters more lunches to midsized companies than its competition does, it can purchase a specialized mailing targeting these customers for future mailings.

■ **Eliminate competition:** Analytical CRM can determine sales trends, enabling the company to provide customers with special deals and outsmarting its competition. A sports store might identify its best customers for outdoor apparel and invite them to a private sale right before the competition runs its sale.

■ **Care about customers:** Analytical CRM can determine what customers want and need, so a firm can contact them with an invitation to a private sale, remind them that a product needs a tune-up, or send them a personalized letter along with a discount coupon to help spark a renewed relationship.

EXTENDING CUSTOMER RELATIONSHIP MANAGEMENT

Organizations are discovering a wave of other key business areas where it is beneficial to build strong relationships beyond customers. These include supplier relationship management (SRM), partner relationship management (PRM), and employee relationship management (ERM) as outlined in Figure 8.26.

Supplier relationship management (SRM) focuses on keeping suppliers satisfied by evaluating and categorizing suppliers for different projects. SRM applications help companies analyze suppliers based on a number of key variables, including prices, inventory availability, and business focus or strategies. It can then determine the best supplier to collaborate with and develop strong relationships with to streamline processes, outsource services, and provide products the firm could not offer alone.

FIGURE 8.26

Extending Customer
Relationship Management

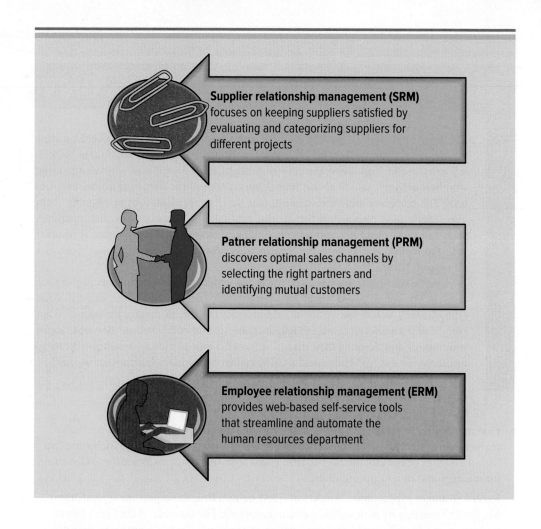

Supplier relationship management (SRM)
focuses on keeping suppliers satisfied by
evaluating and categorizing suppliers for
different projects

Patner relationship management (PRM)
discovers optimal sales channels by
selecting the right partners and
identifying mutual customers

Employee relationship management (ERM)
provides web-based self-service tools
that streamline and automate the
human resources department

Partner relationship management (PRM) discovers optimal sales channels by selecting the right partners and identifying mutual customers. A PRM system offers real-time sales channel information about such things as inventory availability, pricing strategies, and shipping information, allowing a company to expand its market by offering specialized products and services.

Employee relationship management (ERM) provides web-based self-service tools that streamline and automate the human resources department. Employees are the backbone of an enterprise and the communication channel to customers, partners, and suppliers. Their relationship with the company is far more complex and long-lasting than the relationship with customers, thus many enterprises are turning to ERM systems to help retain key employees.

An important part of ERM is *candidate relationship management,* a proactive approach to building, filling, and maintaining a company's talent pipeline for recruiting and hiring. Candidate relationship management maintains a pool of potential employees that can be hired on demand. LinkedIn is a popular tool for candidate relationship management, allowing a company to keep important information on potential hires.

LO 8.5 Identify the core and extended areas of enterprise resource planning.

ENTERPRISE RESOURCE PLANNING

Today's business leaders need significant amounts of information to be readily accessible with real-time views into their businesses so that decisions can be made when they need to be, without the added time of tracking data and generating reports. *Enterprise resource planning (ERP)* integrates all departments and functions throughout an organization into a single IT system (or integrated set of IT systems) so employees can make decisions by viewing enterprisewide information about all business operations. To truly understand the complexity of ERP systems, you must think about the many different functional business areas and their associated business processes as well as cross-functional business processes such as supply chain management and customer relationship management and beyond. At its most basic level, ERP software integrates these various business functions into one complete system to streamline business processes and information across the entire organization. Essentially, ERP helps employees do their jobs more efficiently by breaking down barriers between business units.

Many organizations fail to maintain consistency across business operations. If a single department, such as sales, decides to implement a new system without considering the other departments, inconsistencies can occur throughout the company. Not all systems are built to talk to each other and share data, and if sales suddenly implements a new system that marketing and accounting cannot use or is inconsistent in the way it handles information, the company's operations become siloed. Figure 8.27 displays sample data from a sales database, and Figure 8.28 displays samples from an accounting database. Notice the differences in data formats, numbers, and identifiers. Correlating this data would be difficult, and the inconsistencies would cause numerous reporting errors from an enterprisewide perspective.

The two key components of an ERP system help to resolve these issues and include a common data repository and modular software design. A *common data repository* allows every department of a company to store and retrieve information in real time, allowing information to be more reliable and accessible. *Module software design* divides the system into a set of functional units (named modules) that can be used independently or combined with other modules for increased business flexibility. Module software design allows customers to mix and match modules so they purchase only the required modules. If a company wants to implement the system slowly, it can begin with just one module, such as accounting, and then incorporate additional modules such as purchasing and scheduling.

ERP systems share data supporting business processes within and across departments. In practice, this means that employees in different divisions—for example, accounting and sales—can rely on the same information for their specific needs. ERP software also offers some degree of synchronized reporting and automation. Instead of forcing employees to maintain separate databases and spreadsheets that have to be manually merged to generate reports, some ERP solutions allow staff to pull reports from one system. For instance, with sales orders automatically flowing into the financial system without any manual rekeying, the order management department can process orders more quickly and accurately, and the finance department can close the books faster. Other common ERP features include a portal or dashboard to enable employees to quickly understand the business's performance on key metrics.

FIGURE 8.27

Sales Information Sample

	OrderDate	ProductName	Quantity	Unit Price	Unit Cost	Customer ID	SalesRep ID
2	Monday, January 04, 2022	Mozzarella cheese	41.5	$ 24.15	$ 15.35	AC45	EX-107
3	Monday, January 04, 2022	Romaine lettuce	90.65	$ 15.06	$ 14.04	AC45	EX-109
4	Tuesday, January 05, 2022	Red onions	27.15	$ 12.08	$ 10.32	AC67	EX-104
5	Wednesday, January 06, 2022	Romaine lettuce	67.25	$ 15.16	$ 10.54	AC96	EX-109
6	Thursday, January 07, 2022	Black olives	79.26	$ 12.18	$ 9.56	AC44	EX-104
7	Thursday, January 07, 2022	Romaine lettuce	46.52	$ 15.24	$ 11.54	AC32	EX-104
8	Thursday, January 07, 2022	Romaine lettuce	52.5	$ 15.26	$ 11.12	AC84	EX-109
9	Friday, January 08, 2022	Red onions	39.5	$ 12.55	$ 9.54	AC103	EX-104
10	Saturday, January 09, 2022	Romaine lettuce	66.5	$ 15.98	$ 9.56	AC4	EX-104
11	Sunday, January 10, 2022	Romaine lettuce	58.26	$ 15.87	$ 9.50	AC174	EX-104
12	Sunday, January 10, 2022	Pineapple	40.15	$ 33.54	$ 22.12	AC45	EX-104
13	Monday, January 11, 2022	Pineapple	71.56	$ 33.56	$ 22.05	AC4	EX-104
14	Thursday, January 14, 2022	Romaine lettuce	18.25	$ 15.00	$ 10.25	AC174	EX-104
15	Thursday, January 14, 2022	Romaine lettuce	28.15	$ 15.26	$ 10.54	AC44	EX-107
16	Friday, January 15, 2022	Pepperoni	33.5	$ 15.24	$ 10.25	AC96	EX-109
17	Friday, January 15, 2022	Parmesan cheese	14.26	$ 8.05	$ 4.00	AC96	EX-104
18	Saturday, January 16, 2022	Parmesan cheese	72.15	$ 8.50	$ 4.00	AC103	EX-109
19	Monday, January 18, 2022	Parmesan cheese	41.5	$ 24.15	$ 15.35	AC45	EX-107
20	Monday, January 18, 2022	Romaine lettuce	90.65	$ 15.06	$ 14.04	AC45	EX-109
21	Wednesday, January 20, 2022	Tomatoes	27.15	$ 12.08	$ 10.32	AC67	EX-104
22	Thursday, January 21, 2022	Peppers	67.25	$ 15.16	$ 10.54	AC96	EX-109
23	Thursday, January 21, 2022	Mozzarella cheese	79.26	$ 12.18	$ 9.56	AC44	EX-104
24	Saturday, January 23, 2022	Black olives	46.52	$ 15.24	$ 11.54	AC32	EX-104
25	Sunday, January 24, 2022	Mozzarella cheese	52.5	$ 15.26	$ 11.12	AC84	EX-109
26	Tuesday, January 26, 2022	Romaine lettuce	39.5	$ 12.55	$ 9.54	AC103	EX-104
27	Wednesday, January 27, 2022	Parmesan cheese	66.5	$ 15.98	$ 9.56	AC4	EX-104
28	Thursday, January 28, 2022	Peppers	58.26	$ 15.87	$ 9.50	AC174	EX-104
29	Thursday, January 28, 2022	Mozzarella cheese	40.15	$ 33.54	$ 22.12	AC45	EX-104
30	Friday, January 29, 2022	Tomatoes	71.56	$ 33.56	$ 22.05	AC4	EX-104
31	Friday, January 29, 2022	Peppers	18.25	$ 15.00	$ 10.25	AC174	EX-104

FIGURE 8.28

Accounting Information Sample

	OrderDate	ProductName	Quantity	Unit Price	Total Sales	Unit Cost	Total Cost	Profit	Customer	SalesRep
2	04-Jan-22	Mozzarella cheese	41	24	984	18	738	246	The Station	Debbie Fernandez
3	04-Jan-22	Romaine lettuce	90	15	1,350	14	1,260	90	The Station	Roberta Cross
4	05-Jan-22	Red onions	27	12	324	8	216	108	Bert's Bistro	Loraine Schultz
5	06-Jan-22	Romaine lettuce	67	15	1,005	14	938	67	Smoke House	Roberta Cross
6	07-Jan-22	Black olives	79	12	948	6	474	474	Flagstaff House	Loraine Schultz
7	07-Jan-22	Romaine lettuce	46	15	690	14	644	46	Two Bitts	Loraine Schultz
8	07-Jan-22	Romaine lettuce	52	15	780	14	728	52	Pierce Arrow	Roberta Cross
9	08-Jan-22	Red onions	39	12	468	8	312	156	Mamm'a Pasta Palace	Loraine Schultz
10	09-Jan-22	Romaine lettuce	66	15	990	14	924	66	The Dandelion	Loraine Schultz
11	10-Jan-22	Romaine lettuce	58	15	870	14	812	58	Carmens	Loraine Schultz
12	10-Jan-22	Pineapple	40	33	1,320	28	1,120	200	The Station	Loraine Schultz
13	11-Jan-22	Pineapple	71	33	2,343	28	1,988	355	The Dandelion	Loraine Schultz
14	14-Jan-22	Romaine lettuce	18	15	270	14	252	18	Carmens	Loraine Schultz
15	14-Jan-22	Romaine lettuce	28	15	420	14	392	28	Flagstaff House	Debbie Fernandez
16	15-Jan-22	Pepperoni	33	53	1,749	35	1,155	594	Smoke House	Roberta Cross
17	15-Jan-22	Parmesan cheese	14	8	112	4	56	56	Smoke House	Loraine Schultz
18	16-Jan-22	Parmesan cheese	72	8	576	4	288	288	Mamm'a Pasta Palace	Roberta Cross
19	18-Jan-22	Parmesan cheese	10	8	80	4	40	40	Mamm'a Pasta Palace	Loraine Schultz
20	18-Jan-22	Romaine lettuce	42	15	630	14	588	42	Smoke House	Roberta Cross
21	20-Jan-22	Tomatoes	48	9	432	7	336	96	Two Bitts	Loraine Schultz
22	21-Jan-22	Peppers	29	21	609	12	348	261	The Dandelion	Roberta Cross
23	21-Jan-22	Mozzarella cheese	10	24	240	18	180	60	Mamm'a Pasta Palace	Debbie Fernandez
24	23-Jan-22	Black olives	98	12	1,176	6	588	588	Two Bitts	Roberta Cross
25	24-Jan-22	Mozzarella cheese	45	24	1,080	18	810	270	Carmens	Loraine Schultz
26	26-Jan-22	Romaine lettuce	58	15	870	14	812	58	Two Bitts	Loraine Schultz
27	27-Jan-22	Parmesan cheese	66	8	528	4	264	264	Flagstaff House	Loraine Schultz
28	28-Jan-22	Peppers	85	21	1,785	12	1,020	765	Pierce Arrow	Loraine Schultz
29	28-Jan-22	Mozzarella cheese	12	24	288	18	216	72	The Dandelion	Debbie Fernandez
30	29-Jan-22	Tomatoes	40	9	360	7	280	80	Pierce Arrow	Roberta Cross

Figure 8.29 shows how an ERP system consolidates and correlates data from across the enterprise and generates enterprisewide organizational reports. Original ERP implementations promised to capture all information onto one true "enterprise" system, with the ability to touch all the business processes within the organization. Unfortunately, ERP solutions have fallen short of these promises, and typical implementations have penetrated only 15 to 20 percent of the organization. The issue ERP intends to solve is that knowledge within a majority of organizations currently resides in silos that are maintained by a select few, without the ability to be shared across the organization, causing inconsistency across business operations.

The heart of an ERP system is a central database that collects information from and feeds information into all the ERP system's individual application components (called modules),

FIGURE 8.29

Enterprise Resource Planning
System Overview

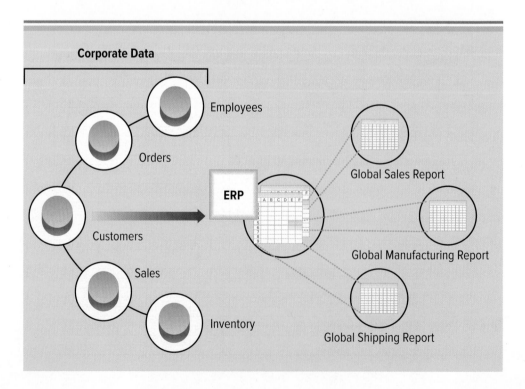

supporting diverse business functions such as accounting, manufacturing, marketing, and human resources. When a user enters or updates information in one module, it is immediately and automatically updated throughout the entire system, as illustrated in Figure 8.30.

ERP automates business processes such as order fulfillment—taking an order from a customer, shipping the purchase, and then billing for it. With an ERP system, when a customer service representative takes an order from a customer, he or she has all the information necessary to complete the order (the customer's credit rating and order history, the company's inventory levels, and the delivery schedule). Everyone else in the company sees the same information and has access to the database that holds the customer's new order. When one department finishes with the order, it is automatically routed via the ERP system to the next department. To find out where the order is at any point, a user need only log in to the ERP system and track it down, as illustrated in Figure 8.31.

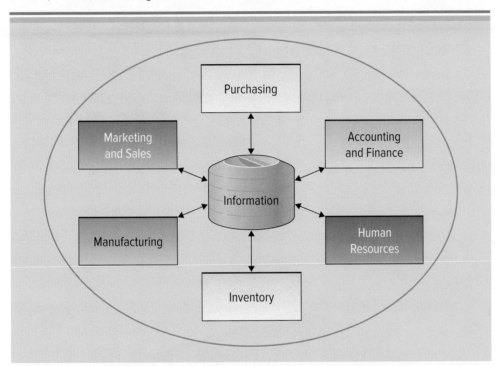

FIGURE 8.30

ERP Integration Data Flow

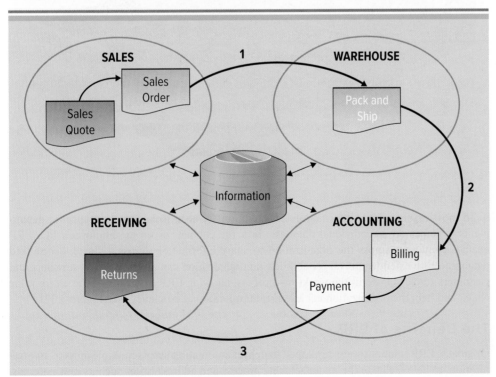

FIGURE 8.31

ERP Process Flow

FIGURE 8.32

The Organization before and after ERP

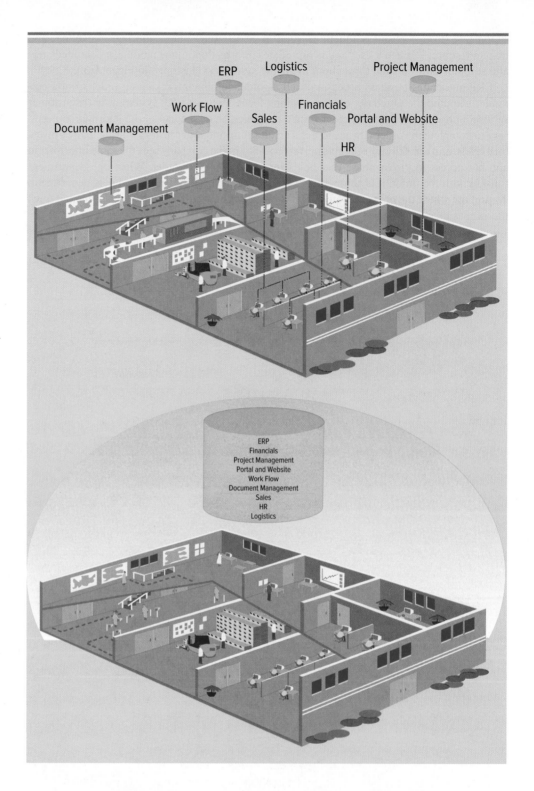

In most organizations, information has traditionally been isolated within specific departments, whether on an individual database, in a file cabinet, or on an employee's PC. ERP enables employees across the organization to share information across a single, centralized database. With extended portal capabilities, an organization can also involve its suppliers and customers to participate in the workflow process, allowing ERP to penetrate the entire value chain, and help the organization achieve greater operational efficiency (see Figure 8.32).

The Benefits of ERP

Originally, ERP solutions were developed to deliver automation across multiple units of an organization, to help facilitate the manufacturing process and address issues such as raw materials,

Classic Cars Inc. operates high-end automotive dealerships that offer luxury cars along with luxury service. The company is proud of its extensive inventory, top-of-the-line mechanics, and especially its exceptional service, which includes operating a cappuccino bar at each dealership.

Classic Cars

The company currently has 40 sales representatives at four locations. Each location maintains its own computer systems, and all sales representatives have their own contact management systems. This splintered approach to operations causes numerous problems in customer communication, pricing strategy, and inventory control, such as:

- A customer can get different quotes at different dealerships for the same car.

- Sales representatives frequently steal each other's customers and commissions.

- Sales representatives send their customers to other dealerships to see specific cars that turn out not to be on the lot.

- Marketing campaigns are typically generic and not designed to target specific customers.

- If a sales representative quits, all his or her customer information is lost.

You work for Customer One, a small consulting company that specializes in enterprisewide strategies. The owner of Classic Cars Inc. has hired you to help him formulate a strategy to put his company back on track. Develop a proposal detailing how an ERP system can alleviate the company's problems and create new sales opportunities.

---

inventory, order entry, and distribution. However, ERP was unable to extend to other functional areas of the company such as sales, marketing, and shipping. It could not tie in any CRM capabilities that would allow organizations to capture customer-specific information, nor did it work with websites or portals used for customer service or order fulfillment. Call center or quality assurance staff could not tap into the ERP solution, nor could ERP handle document management, such as cataloging contracts and purchase orders.

ERP has grown over the years to become part of the extended enterprise. From its beginning as a tool for materials planning, it has extended to warehousing, distribution, and order entry. With its next evolution, ERP expands to the front office including CRM. Now administrative, sales, marketing, and human resources staff can share a tool that is truly enterprisewide. To compete on a functional level today, companies must adopt an enterprisewide approach to ERP that utilizes the Internet and connects to every facet of the value chain. Figure 8.33 shows how ERP has grown to accommodate the needs of the entire organization.

Applications such as SCM, CRM, and ERP are the backbone of ebusiness. Integration of these applications is the key to success for many companies. Integration allows the unlocking of information to make it available to any user, anywhere, anytime.

Most organizations today have no choice but to piece their SCM, CRM, and ERP applications together since no one vendor can respond to every organizational need; hence, customers purchase applications from multiple vendors. As a result, organizations face the challenge of integrating their systems. For example, a single organization might choose its CRM components from Siebel, SCM components from i2, and financial components and HR management components from Oracle. Figure 8.34 displays the general audience and purpose for each of these applications that have to be integrated.

The current generation of ERP, ERP-II, is composed of two primary components—core and extended. *Core ERP components* are the traditional components that are included in most ERP systems and primarily focus on internal operations. *Extended ERP components* are the extra

FIGURE 8.33

The Evolution of ERP

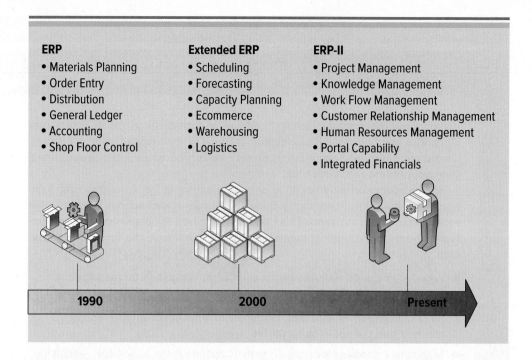

ERP	Extended ERP	ERP-II
• Materials Planning • Order Entry • Distribution • General Ledger • Accounting • Shop Floor Control	• Scheduling • Forecasting • Capacity Planning • Ecommerce • Warehousing • Logistics	• Project Management • Knowledge Management • Work Flow Management • Customer Relationship Management • Human Resources Management • Portal Capability • Integrated Financials

1990   2000   Present

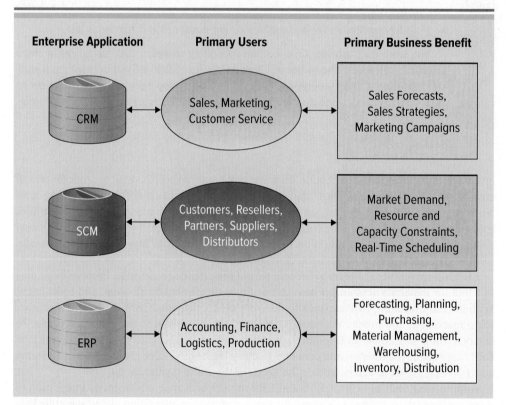

Enterprise Application	Primary Users	Primary Business Benefit
CRM	Sales, Marketing, Customer Service	Sales Forecasts, Sales Strategies, Marketing Campaigns
SCM	Customers, Resellers, Partners, Suppliers, Distributors	Market Demand, Resource and Capacity Constraints, Real-Time Scheduling
ERP	Accounting, Finance, Logistics, Production	Forecasting, Planning, Purchasing, Material Management, Warehousing, Inventory, Distribution

components that meet organizational needs not covered by the core components and primarily focus on external operations. Figure 8.35 provides an example of an ERP system with its core and extended components.

Core ERP Components

The three most common core ERP components focusing on internal operations are:

1. Accounting and finance.

2. Production and materials management.

3. Human resources.

FIGURE 8.35

Core ERP Components and
Extended ERP Components

Core ERP Components

Accounting and Finance

Production and Materials Management

Human Resources

Enterprise Resource Planning Software

Business Intelligence

Customer Relationship Management

Supply Chain Management

Ebusiness

Extended ERP Components

Accounting and Finance ERP Components *Accounting and finance ERP components* manage accounting data and financial processes within the enterprise with functions such as general ledger, accounts payable, accounts receivable, budgeting, and asset management. One of the most useful features of an ERP accounting/finance component is credit management. Most organizations manage their relationships with customers by setting credit limits, or limits on how much a customer can owe at any one time. ERP financial systems correlate customers' orders with their account balances to determine credit availability. They also perform all types of advanced profitability modeling techniques.

Production and Materials Management ERP Components *Production and materials management ERP components* handle production planning and execution tasks such as demand forecasting, production scheduling, job cost accounting, and quality control. Demand forecasting helps determine production schedules and materials purchasing. A company that makes its own product prepares a detailed production schedule, and a company that buys products for resale develops a materials requirement plan.

Human Resources ERP Components *Human resources ERP components* track employee information, including payroll, benefits, compensation, and performance assessment and ensure compliance with all laws. They even allow the organization to perform detailed employee analysis, such as identifying who is likely to leave the company unless additional compensation or benefits are provided and whether the most talented people are working in areas where they can have the greatest impact. Human resources components can also identify which employees are using which resources, such as online training and long-distance telephone services.

Extended ERP Components

Extended ERP components meet the organizational needs not covered by the core components and primarily focus on external operations. Many are Internet-enabled and require interaction with customers, suppliers, and business partners outside the organization. The four most common extended ERP components are:

1. Business intelligence.
2. Customer relationship management.
3. Supply chain management.
4. Ebusiness.

Business Intelligence ERP Components   Many organizations have found that ERP tools can provide even greater value with the addition of powerful business intelligence systems. The business intelligence components of ERP systems typically collect information used throughout the organization (including data used in many other ERP components), organize it, and apply analytical tools to assist managers with decisions. Data warehouses are one of the most popular extensions to ERP systems.

Customer Relationship Management ERP Components   ERP vendors now include additional functionality that provides services formerly found only in CRM systems. The CRM components in ERP systems include contact centers, sales force automation, and advanced marketing functions. The goal is to provide an integrated view of customer data, enabling a firm to manage customer relationships effectively by responding to customer needs and demands while identifying the most (and least) valuable customers so the firm can better allocate its marketing resources.

Supply Chain Management ERP Components   ERP vendors are expanding their systems to include SCM functions that manage the information flows between and among supply chain stages, maximizing total supply chain effectiveness and profitability. SCM components allow a firm to monitor and control all stages in the supply chain from the acquisition of raw materials to the receipt of finished goods by customers.

Ebusiness ERP Components   The newest extended ERP components are the ebusiness components that allow companies to establish an Internet presence and fulfill online orders. Two of the primary features of ebusiness components are elogistics and eprocurement. *Elogistics* manages the transportation and storage of goods. *Eprocurement* is the business-to-business (B2B) online purchase and sale of supplies and services. A common mistake many businesses make is jumping into online business without properly integrating the entire organization on the ERP system. One large toy manufacturer announced less than a week before Christmas that it would be unable to fulfill any of its online orders. The company had all the toys in the warehouse, but it could not organize the basic order processing function to deliver the toys to consumers on time.

Measuring ERP Success

There is no guarantee of success for an ERP system. It is difficult to measure the success of an ERP system because one system can span an entire organization, including thousands of employees across the globe. ERPs focus on how a corporation operates internally, and optimizing these operations takes significant time and energy.

Two of the primary forces driving ERP failure include software customization and ERP costs. *Software customization* modifies existing software according to the business's or user's requirements. Since ERP systems must fit business processes, many enterprises choose to customize their ERP systems to ensure that they meet business and user needs. Figure 8.36 displays the different forms of software customization a business will undertake to ensure the success of an ERP implementation. Heavy customization leads to complex code that must be continuously maintained and upgraded. It should be noted that customizing an ERP system is costly and complex and should only be done when there is a specific business advantage. According to Meta Group, it takes the average company 8 to 18 months to see any benefits from an ERP system. The primary risk for an ERP implementation includes the associated costs displayed in Figure 8.37.

One of the best methods of measuring ERP success is the balanced scorecard, created by Dr. Robert Kaplan and Dr. David Norton, both from the Harvard Business School. The *balanced scorecard* is a management system, as well as a measurement system, that a firm uses

FIGURE 8.36

Software Customization
Examples

SOFTWARE CUSTOMIZATION	
Business Processes or Workflows	Software can be customized to support the needs of business process work-flows unique to each business or department.
Code Modifications	The most expensive customization occurs when application code is changed and should only be done if the code changes provide specific competitive advantages.
Integrations	Data integration is key for business process support that spans functional areas and legacy systems.
Reports, Documents, Forms	Customization to reports, documents, and forms can consist of simple layout or design changes or complex logic programming rules for specific business requirements.
User-Interface Changes	An ERP system can be customized to ensure that each user has the most efficient and effective view of the application.

FIGURE 8.37

ERP Costs

ERP COSTS	
Software Costs	Purchasing the software can cost millions of dollars for a large enterprise.
Consulting Fees	Hiring external experts to help implement the system correctly can cost millions of dollars.
Process rework	Redefine processes to ensure that the company is using the most efficient and effective processes.
Customization	If the software package does not meet all of the company's needs, customizing the software may be required.
Integration	Ensuring that all software products, including disparate systems not part of the ERP system, are working together or are integrated.
Testing	Testing that all functionality works correctly along with testing all integrations.
Training	Training all new users and creating the training user manuals.
Data warehouse integration and data conversions	Moving data from an old system into the new ERP system.

to translate business strategies into executable tasks. It provides feedback for both internal and external business processes, allowing continuous improvement. Kaplan and Norton describe the balanced scorecard as follows: "The balanced scorecard retains traditional financial measures. But financial measures tell the story of past events, an adequate story for industrial age companies for which investments in long-term capabilities and customer relationships were not critical for success. These financial measures are inadequate, however, for guiding and evaluating the journey that information age companies must make to create future value through investment in customers, suppliers, employees, processes, technology, and innovation."[15] The balanced scorecard uses four perspectives to monitor an organization:

1. The learning and growth perspective.
2. The internal business process perspective.
3. The customer perspective.
4. The financial perspective (see Figure 8.38).

ORGANIZATIONAL INTEGRATION WITH ERP

LO 8.6: Discuss the current technologies organizations are integrating in enterprise resource planning systems.

The goal of ERP is to integrate all of the organizational systems into one fully functioning, high-performance system that is capable of meeting all business needs and user requirements. Traditional ERP systems were typically accessed from a computer on the customers' premises or office. Tomorrow's ERP systems will enhance the ability of organizations to apply context

FIGURE 8.38

The Four Primary Perspectives
of the Balanced Scorecard

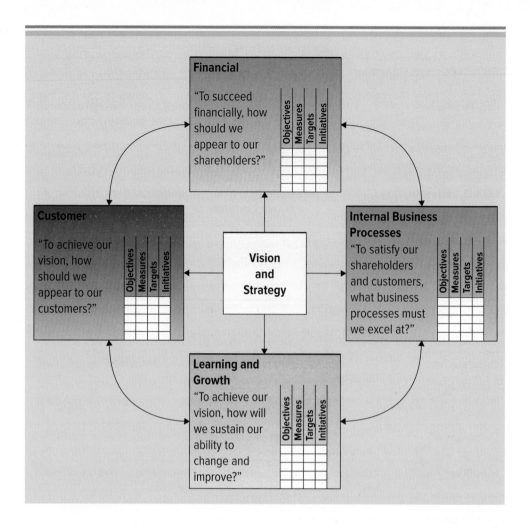

to decision making and adapt more easily to changing events. ERP systems in the future will focus on usability, ubiquity, accessibility, and mobility, drawing many advantages, including:

- Drive cost efficiencies.
- Faster time to market.
- Better enable mobile workforce.
- Better leverage data to provide insights.
- New product development.

Of course, ERP of the future will have many challenges, including data management, source record management, and coordinating integrations and support activities. Figure 8.39 displays the three primary ERP implementation choices driving the next generation of business operations.

On-Premise ERP

Until a decade ago, virtually all ERP systems were installed on-premise. *On-premise systems* include a server at a physical location using an internal network for internal access and firewalls for remote users' access. Remote users had to access the ERP system through a firewall, which protected the system against unauthorized access. These systems are known as on-premise systems, and they are still in wide use today. The ERP, SCM, and CRM systems that run on-premise are referred to as legacy systems. *Legacy system* is an old system that is fast approaching or beyond the end of its useful life with in an organization.

Cloud ERP

The cloud has changed the legacy model of ERP implementation. According to the National Institute of Standards and Technology (NIST), *cloud computing* stores, manages, and processes

FIGURE 8.39

ERP Implementation Choices

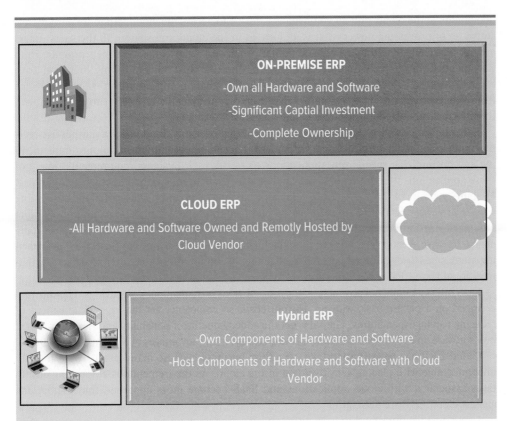

data and applications over the Internet rather than on a personal computer or server. Cloud computing offers new ways to store, access, process, and analyze information and connect people and resources from any location in the world where an Internet connection is available. As shown in Figure 8.40, users connect to the cloud from their personal computers or portable devices by using a client, such as a web browser. To these individual users, the cloud appears as their personal application, device, or document. It is like storing all of your software and

FIGURE 8.40

Cloud Computing Example.

documents in the cloud, and all you need is a device to access the cloud. No more hard drives, software, or processing power—that is all located in the cloud, transparent to the users. Users are not physically bound to a single computer or network; they can access their programs and documents from wherever they are, whenever they need to. Just think of having your hard drive located in the sky and being able to access your information and programs using any device from wherever you are. The best part is that even if your machine crashes, is lost, or is stolen, the information hosted in the cloud is safe and always available.

Software as a Service (SaaS) delivers applications over the cloud using a pay-per-use revenue model. Before its introduction, companies often spent huge amounts of money implementing and customizing specialized applications to satisfy their business requirements. Many of these applications were difficult to implement, expensive to maintain, and challenging to use. Usability was one of the biggest drivers for creating interest in and success for cloud computing service providers. SaaS ERP uses the cloud platform to enable organizations not only to unite around business processes but also to gather cloud data across supplier networks and supply chains to drive greater efficiency in manufacturing projects. The move to SaaS ERP is attracting many small and midsized businesses that simply cannot afford the costs associated with a traditional large ERP implementation.

SaaS offers a number of advantages; the most obvious is tremendous cost savings. The software is priced on a per-use basis with no up-front costs, so companies get the immediate benefit of reducing capital expenditures. They also get the added benefits of scalability and flexibility to test new software on a rental basis. Figure 8.41 displays the many advantages of SaaS implementations.

Cloud ERP has been slow to take off across business because many people were initially uncomfortable with placing sensitive data in the cloud. As the tremendous cost-saving advantages associated with cloud applications and SaaS become more apparent, the reservations against cloud ERP are dissipating.

Large organizations tend to have difficulty adjusting to cloud solutions simply because they want greater levels of control over their enterprise applications. Smaller, less complex organizations that lack sophisticated MIS departments are more likely to gravitate toward the cloud because it is easy for them to change business processes to fit the software. SaaS ERP can provide a company with the flexibility of on-premise software and the added benefits of a vendor maintaining and housing the applications off the premises. The biggest concerns for organizations interested in cloud ERP solutions is data security and potential vendor outages causing business downtime. Without an on-premises MIS department, the organization is truly at the

FIGURE 8.41

Advantages of SaaS Implementations

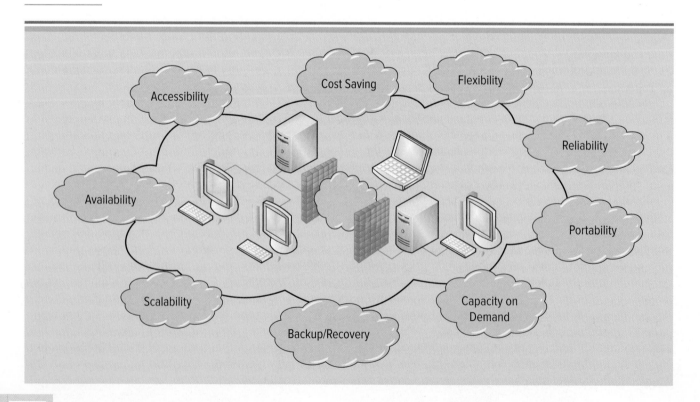

mercy of the vendor during any system outage, and for critical organizational systems such as ERP, this could be an unacceptable risk.

Hybrid ERP

It is conventional wisdom that a diversified stock portfolio is a very effective hedge against investment risk. For the same reason, companies that are not comfortable with the risk and/or loss of control associated with moving wholesale into ERP cloud computing but still want to explore this evolving infrastructure might find a hybrid ERP approach to be the perfect answer. By "hybrid ERP approach," we mean mostly on site but with some carefully selected hosted applications.

Building an all-encompassing ERP system traditionally ended in expensive failures. Nike, K-Mart, and Hershey all lost over $100 million in failed ERP implementations. Based on the need to avoid expensive failures along with the emergence of cloud computing, enterprises can now adopt hybrid ERP architectures. The idea behind *hybrid ERP* is to split the ERP functions between an on-premises ERP system and one or more functions handled as Software as a Service in the cloud. Typically, the on-premise legacy application operates at the corporate headquarters, whereas cloud-based specific applications support business needs such as mobility and web-based functionality. It is also becoming increasingly popular. In fact, many analysts are predicting that hybrid ERP will become a mainstay in the ERP market in the next few years.

Often a hybrid ERP system is implemented when the legacy system becomes very large and costly to customize, maintain, and upgrade or when mergers and acquisitions leave an organization with multiple ERP solutions that it is unable to consolidate to a single ERP system. Hybrid ERP architectures also support organizations with multiple operations based in multiple geographic locations. The following scenarios are common in organizations that use hybrid architectures of ERP:

- A business with a very specific local focus—single-site or multisite within a single country or region.
- A business with operations geared strongly toward a specific industry that doesn't feature strongly at corporate headquarters.
- A newly acquired operation with a mismatch of multiple outdated, unsupported ERPs.
- A small subsidiary with no formal ERP in place.

Managing the data across the enterprise is one of the biggest concerns for organizations deploying hybrid ERP architectures. It is critical for the business to have absolutely no duplication of effort between the two ERP systems. Consistency is required for any hybrid application to ensure that there is always a single source of information for accounting, financials, customer service, production, and other business areas. Hundreds of ERP vendors offer best-of-breed ERP applications or vertical market solutions to meet the unique requirements of specific industries such as manufacturing, distribution, retail, and others. Figure 8.42 displays an overview of ERP vendors by business size. Figure 8.43 displays the important factors driving the future of ERP.

ERP VENDORS BY TIER		
	Enterprise Size	**ERP Vendor**
Tier I	Large Enterprise	■ SAP ■ Oracle ■ Microsoft
Tier II	Midsized Business	■ Infor ■ Lawson ■ Epicor ■ Sage
Tier III	Small Business	■ Exact Globe ■ Syspro ■ NetSuite ■ Consona

FIGURE 8.42

ERP Vendors by Tier

BUSINESS DRIVEN DISCUSSION

Bean Integration

At Flavors, a premium coffee shop, customers receive more than just a great cup of coffee. They also get exposure to music, art, literature, and town events. Flavors offers the following:

- Music center—information about all live music events occurring in the area and an open microphone two nights a week for local musicians.
- Art gallery—a space in the store filled with great pieces from local artists.
- Book clubs—a way for customers to meet to discuss current and classic literature.
- Coffee sampler—free tastings in which experts showcase coffees from around the world.
- Community calendar—weekly meetings to help customers find ways to become more involved in their community.
- Brewing courses—lessons in the finer details of the brewing, grinding, and blending using equipment for sale in Flavor stores, from the traditional press to a digital espresso machine. Also includes a trouble-shooting guide developed by brewing specialists.

Flavors's sales are great and profits are soaring; however, operations need an overhaul. The following is a quick look at Flavors's current nonfood offerings.

- Flavors does not receive any information about how many customers attend live events in the music center. Musicians typically maintain a fan email list and CD sales records for the event; however, they don't always provide this information to the store.
- The art gallery is run by several local artists who pay Flavors a small commission on each sale. Flavors has no input about the art displayed in the store or information about who purchases it.
- Book club events are booked and run through the local bookstore, Pages Up, which runs a tab during the meetings and pays Flavors with a check at the end of each month. Flavors has no access to book club customer information or sales information.
- Coffee sampler events are run through Flavors's primary operations.
- Community event information is open to all members of the community. Each event is run by a separate organization, which provides monthly event feedback to Flavors in a variety of formats from Word to Access files.
- Brewing and machine resource courses are run by the equipment manufacturers, and all customer and sales information is provided to Flavors in a Word document at the end of each year.

Flavors's owners want to revamp the way the company operates so they can take advantage of enterprise systems, and they have hired you as an integration expert. They also want to gain a better understanding of how the different events they host affect the different areas of their business. For example, should they have more open-microphone nights and fewer book clubs? The other way around? Currently, they have no way to tell which events result in higher sales. Create an integration strategy so Flavors can take advantage of CRM, SCM, and ERP across the company.

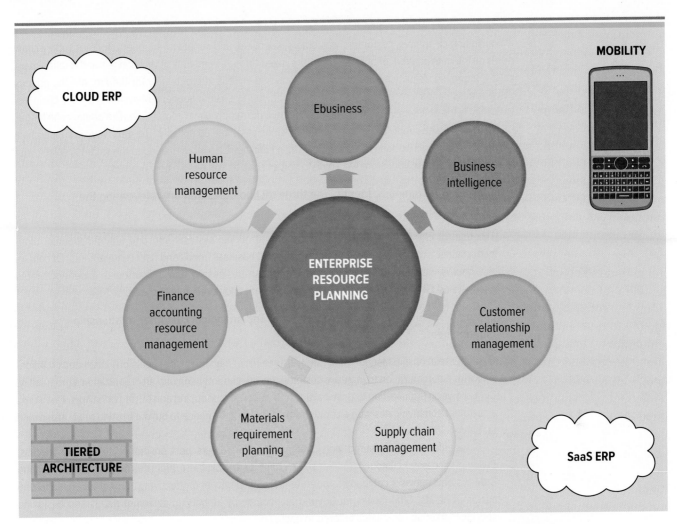

CLOUD ERP

Ebusiness

Human resource management

Business intelligence

ENTERPRISE RESOURCE PLANNING

Finance accounting resource management

Customer relationship management

Materials requirement planning

Supply chain management

TIERED ARCHITECTURE

SaaS ERP

FIGURE 8.43

Organizational Integration of ERP

Learning Outcome 8.1: Explain integrations and the role they play in connecting a corporation.

Integrations allow separate systems to communicate directly with each other, eliminating the need for manual entry into multiple systems. Building integrations allows information sharing across databases along with dramatic increase of quality.

Learning Outcome 8.2: Describe supply chain management along with its impact on business.

A supply chain consists of all parties involved, directly or indirectly, in obtaining raw materials or a product. To automate and enable sophisticated decision making in these critical areas, companies are turning to systems that provide demand forecasting, inventory control, and information flows between suppliers and customers. Supply chain management (SCM) is the management of information flows between and among activities in a supply chain to maximize total supply chain effectiveness and corporate profitability. In the past, manufacturing efforts focused primarily on quality improvement efforts within the company; today these efforts reach across the entire supply chain, including customers, customers' customers, suppliers, and suppliers' suppliers. Today's supply chain is an intricate network of business partners linked through communication channels and relationships.

Improved visibility across the supply chain and increased profitability for the firm are the primary business benefits received when implementing supply chain management systems. Supply chain visibility is the ability to view all areas up and down the supply chain in real time. The primary challenges associated with supply chain management include costs and complexity. The next wave in supply chain management will be home-based supply chain fulfillment. No more running to the store to replace your products because your store will come to you as soon as you need a new product.

Learning Outcome 8.3: Identify the three technologies that are reinventing the supply chain.

The goal of ERP is to integrate all of the organizational systems into one fully functioning, high-performance system that is capable of meeting all business needs and user requirements. Of course, this goal is incredibly difficult to achieve because businesses and technologies experience rapid change, and ERP must support mobility, cloud, SaaS, and tiered architectures.

Learning Outcome 8.4: Explain operational and analytical customer relationship management.

Customer relationship management (CRM) is a means of managing all aspects of a customer's relationship with an organization to increase customer loyalty and retention and an organization's profitability. CRM allows an organization to gain insights into customers' shopping and buying behaviors. Every time a customer communicates with a company, the firm has the chance to build a trusting relationship with that particular customer.

Companies that understand individual customer needs are best positioned to achieve success. Building successful customer relationships is not a new business practice; however, implementing CRM systems allows a company to operate more efficiently and effectively in the area of supporting customer needs. CRM moves far beyond technology by identifying customer needs and designing specific marketing campaigns tailored to each.

The two primary components of a CRM strategy are operational CRM and analytical CRM. Operational CRM supports traditional transactional processing for day-to-day front-office operations or systems that deal directly with the customers. Analytical CRM supports back-office operations and strategic analysis and includes all systems that do not deal directly with the customers.

Learning Outcome 8.5: Identify the core and extended areas of enterprise resource planning.

Enterprise resource planning (ERP) integrates all departments and functions throughout an organization into a single IT system (or integrated set of IT systems) so employees can make decisions by viewing enterprisewide information about all business operations. The current generation of ERP, ERP-II, is composed of two primary components—core and extended. Core ERP components are the traditional components included in most ERP systems and primarily focus on internal operations. Extended ERP components are the extra components that meet organizational needs not covered by the core components and primarily focus on external operations .

Learning Outcome 8.6: Discuss the current technologies organizations are integrating in enterprise resource planning systems.

The goal of ERP is to integrate all of the organizational systems into one fully functioning, high-performance system that is capable of meeting all business needs and user requirements. Of course, this goal is incredibly difficult to achieve because businesses and technologies experience rapid change, and ERP must support mobility, cloud, SaaS, and tiered architectures.

1. **Knowledge:** Define 3D printing and its impact on business.

2. **Comprehension:** Explain CRM and how 3D printing could affect customer relations.

3. **Application:** Provide an example of how 3D printing might affect the global economy.

4. **Analysis:** Analyze how 3D printing is affecting supply chains.

5. **Synthesis:** Propose a plan for how a company can use 3D printing to increase sales and customer satisfaction.

6. **Evaluate:** Argue for or against the following statement: "3D printing will be more disruptive to business than the Internet."

KEY TERMS

Accounting and finance ERP component 355
Analytical CRM 342
Application integration 323
Backward integration 323
Balanced scorecard 356
Bullwhip effect 329
Call scripting system 345
Campaign management system 343
Candidate relationship management 348
Click-to-talk 345
Cloud computing 358
Common data repository 349
Computer-aided design/computer-aided manufacturing (CAD/CAM) 332
Contact center or call center 345
Contact management CRM system 345
Core ERP component 353
Cradle to grave 331
CRM analysis technologies 339
CRM predicting technologies 339
CRM reporting technologies 339
Cross-selling 344
Customer analytics 338
Customer relationship management (CRM) 337
Customer segmentation 346
Customer service and support (CSS) 344

3D printing 331
4D printing 333
Data integration 323
Drone 333
Eintegration 323
Electronic data interchange (EDI) 328
Elogistics 356
Employee relationship management (ERM) 348
Enterprise application integration (EAI) 324
Enterprise application integration (EAI) middleware 324
Enterprise resource planning (ERP) 348
Enterprise system 324
Eprocurement 356
Extended ERP component 353
Forward integration 323
Human resources ERP component 355
Hybrid ERP 361
Integration 323
Legacy system 358
List generator 343
Logistics 329
Maker movement 332
Makerspace 333
Materials management 331
Middleware 324
Module software design 349
On-premise system 358

Operational CRM 342
Opportunity management CRM system 345
Partner relationship management (PRM) 348
Procurement 329
Production and materials management ERP component 355
Radio-frequency identification (RFID) 333
RFID's electronic product code (RFID EPC) 333
Robotics 335
Sales analytics 338
Sales force automation (SFA) 344
Sales management CRM system 345
Software customization 356
Supplier relationship management (SRM) 347
Supply chain 325
Supply chain design 327
Supply chain execution system 328
Supply chain management (SCM) 325
Supply chain planning system 328
Supply chain visibility 328
Uplift modeling 346
Up-selling 344
Web-based self-service system 345
Website personalization 346

1. How do integrations connect a corporation?
2. What is the difference between forward and backward integrations?
3. What are the five primary activities in a supply chain?
4. What is the bullwhip effect and how can it affect a supply chain and a firm's profitability?
5. Why are customer relationships important to an organization? Do you agree that every business needs to focus on customers to survive in the information age?
6. What is the difference between operational and analytical CRM?
7. How can a sales department use CRM to improve operations?
8. How can a marketing department use CRM to improve operations?
9. What are the differences among customer relationship management, supplier relationship management, and employee relationship management?
10. What is an enterprise resource planning system?
11. What are the components in a core ERP system?
12. What are the components in an extended ERP system?
13. What does a company need to integrate to become connected?

CLOSING CASE ONE

Amazon Drone Knocking

Using drones to drop off packages could be great for buyers who might want to get certain items as fast as humanly possible. Back in 2013, when Amazon revealed plans to begin delivering packages via flying drones through Prime Air, some seemed skeptical about the reality of deploying such a system. Recently, Amazon doubled down on those claims by releasing information on one of its new drones in action, and it is seriously impressive.

A new video presented by former *Top Gear* host Jeremy Clarkson (who is working on a show for Amazon) takes us through the entire process, from ordering, to warehouse launch, to delivery. The new drone looks a lot different from the one Amazon showed us a couple of years ago. This one has a more commercial and streamlined look, and instead of showing the package hanging in open air, the new drone hides the item in a square compartment. Just Google "Amazon Prime Air Drone video with Jeremy Clarkson" to see for yourself this amazing new drone that will dramatically impact the supply chain.

According to Amazon, the drone reaches a height of about 400 feet in vertical mode and then switches to horizontal mode to travel up to 15 miles away from the warehouse. During the flight, the drone uses what Amazon calls "sense and avoid technology" to avoid collisions with other objects in its flight path.

Toward the end of the video, the drone alights atop an Amazon logo in the yard of a consumer and spits out the package (in this case, shoes) and then takes off in a matter of seconds. The delivery process, which Amazon is careful to note is real and not a simulation, comes off seamlessly, making the prospect of drone deliveries seem like something that will be viable just a few months from now.

However, despite the encouraging footage, Amazon is still holding off on announcing exactly when its drones will take to the skies. On the updated Prime Air page featuring the new flight footage, a message reads, "Putting Prime Air into service will take some time, but we will deploy when we have the regulatory support needed to realize our vision."

The FAA's Unmanned Aircraft Systems Registration Task Force Aviation Rulemaking Committee is still hammering out rules for private and commercial drone use in U.S. air space, so Amazon's lack of a specific launch timeline for Prime Air is understandable. But based on the video, it's becoming increasingly clear that Prime Air might not be a mere marketing stunt but a real look at the future of Amazon deliveries.

Retailers Racing to the Drone Games

Walmart recently applied to U.S. regulators for permission to test drones for home delivery, curbside pickup, and checking warehouse inventories, a sign it plans to go head-to-head with Amazon in using drones to fill and deliver online orders.

Walmart wants to start using drones in an effort to create a more efficient supply chain and connect their network of stores, distribution centers, fulfillment centers, and transportation fleet. The world's largest retailer by revenue has for several months been conducting indoor tests of small unmanned aircraft systems (drones) and is now seeking for the first time to test the machines outdoors. In addition to having drones take inventory of trailers outside its warehouses and perform other tasks aimed at making its distribution system more efficient, Walmart is asking the FAA for permission to research drone use in "deliveries to customers at Walmart facilities, as well as to consumer homes." The move comes as Amazon, Google, and other companies test drones in the expectation that the FAA will soon establish rules for their widespread commercial use.[16]

Questions

1. How will drones impact the supply chain?
2. Why are big retailers racing to be the first to market with drone home delivery?
3. How can a CRM system help communicate issues in the supply chain between customers and drones?
4. What types of jobs can be taken over by drones?
5. What are the pros and cons of using a drone to deliver packages?

CLOSING CASE TWO

Five Famous ERP Failures

The world of ERP may seem boring to those caught up in the hysteria over Twitter and iPhone applications, but there's plenty of drama to be found: Troubled multimillion-dollar software deals that produce spectacular failures and huge spending nightmares; vendor marketing bravado that breeds cutthroat competition and contempt; and embarrassing and costly lawsuits over botched implementations and intellectual property breaches. Consider CIO.com's brief and semichronological history of five ERP scandals as a warning if you're contemplating an upgrade or implementation.

1. **Definitely Not a Sweet Experience for Hershey.** Could a failed technology implementation take down a *Fortune* 500 company (in this case, Hershey Foods)? Well, it certainly didn't help Hershey's operations during the Halloween season in 1999 or make Wall Street investors thrilled. In the end, Hershey's ghastly problems with its SAP ERP, Siebel CRM, and Manugistics supply chain applications prevented it from delivering $100 million worth of Kisses for Halloween that year and caused the stock to dip 8 percent. So I guess a failed technology project can't actually take down a *Fortune* 500 company for good, but it can certainly knock it around a bit.

2. **Just Do It: Fix Our Supply Chain System.** What did a $400 million upgrade to Nike's supply chain and ERP systems get the world-renowned shoe- and athletic gear maker? Well, for starters,

$100 million in lost sales, a 20 percent stock dip, and a collection of class-action lawsuits. This was all back in 2000, and the horrendous results were due to a bold ERP, supply chain, and CRM project that aimed to upgrade the systems into one superstar system. Nike's tale is both of woe and warning.

3. **HP's "Perfect Storm" of ERP Problems.** The epic tale of HP's centralization of its disparate North American ERP systems onto one SAP system proves that one can never be too pessimistic when it comes to ERP project management. You see, in 2004, HP's project managers knew all of the things that could go wrong with their ERP rollout. But they just didn't plan for so many of them to happen at once. The project eventually cost HP $160 million in order backlogs and lost revenue—more than five times the project's estimated cost. Said Gilles Bouchard, then-CIO of HP's global operations: "We had a series of small problems, none of which individually would have been too much to handle. But together they created the perfect storm."

4. **A New Type of Freshman Hazing.** Pity the college freshman at the University of Massachusetts in fall 2004: The last thing they needed was some computer program to haunt their lives and make their new collegiate experience even more uncertain. But more than 27,000 students at the University of Massachusetts as well as Stanford University and Indiana University were forced to do battle with buggy portals and ERP applications that left them at best unable to find their classes and at worst unable to collect their financial aid checks. Said one UMass senior at the time: "The freshmen were going crazy because they didn't know where to go." After a couple of tense days and weeks, however, everyone eventually got their checks and class schedules.

5. **Waste Management Trashes Its "Fake" ERP Software.** Garbage-disposal giant Waste Management is still embroiled in an acrimonious $100 million legal battle with SAP over an 18-month installation of its ERP software. The initial deal began in 2005, but the legal saga commenced in March 2008, when Waste Management filed suit and claimed SAP executives participated in a fraudulent sales scheme that resulted in the massive failure. Several months later, SAP fired back, claiming that Waste Management allegedly violated its contractual agreement with SAP in several ways, including by "failing to timely and accurately define its business requirements" and not providing "sufficient, knowledgeable, decision-empowered users and managers" to work on the project. In the fall of 2008, accusations were still flying about documentation, depositions, and delays in bringing the case before a judge. And that proposed 18-month implementation now sounds like a dream scenario.[17]

Questions

1. Why do you think it is so difficult to find successful ERP implementation?
2. How do you think cloud computing will help ERP implementations find success?
3. What advice would you give a company deciding to implement an ERP system?
4. How can integrating SCM, CRM, and ERP help improve business operations at your school?

CRITICAL BUSINESS THINKING

1. Political Supply Chains

The U.S. government brokered a deal with the United Arab Emirates (UAE) allowing the UAE government–owned firm Dubai Ports World (DPW) to operate six major U.S. ports (New York, New Jersey, Baltimore, New Orleans, Miami, Philadelphia) after DPW purchased the current United Kingdom–based port operator, P&O, the fourth largest port company in the world.

Some citizens are worried that the federal government may be outsourcing U.S. port operations to a company prone to terrorist infiltration by allowing a firm from the United Arab Emirates to run port operations within the United States. People involved in terrorism have come from the United Arab Emirates. Some of its financial institutions laundered the money for the 9/11 terrorists. You have been called in on an investigation to determine the potential effects on U.S. businesses' supply chains if these ports were shut down due to terrorist activities. Create an argument for or against outsourcing these ports to the UAE. Be sure to detail the effect on U.S. businesses' supply chains if these ports are subjected to terrorist acts.[18]

2. Analyzing Dell's Supply Chain Management System

Dell's supply chain strategy is legendary. If you want to build a successful SCM system, your best bet is to model your SCM system after Dell's. In a team, research Dell's supply chain management strategy on the web and create a report discussing any new SCM updates and strategies the company is currently using that were not discussed in this text. Be sure to include a graphical presentation of Dell's current supply chain model.

3. Total Recall

The Firestone Tire Company issued a recall for all tires issued on a certain brand of Ford's sport-utility vehicles. The tire treads on some SUVs separated during use, which could cause a fatal accident because the defect caused vehicles to roll over. In the beginning, Firestone denied it had a tire problem, stating that Ford had incorrectly matched its SUVs with the wrong brand of tires. It also suggested that the shock absorbers might have been rubbing against the tires, causing the defect. Firestone soon recalled the tires because the company received more and more pressure from government and consumer advocacy groups. Interestingly, all of the defective tires were manufactured at the same tire factory, and the company soon shut down that facility. Information was soon found that Firestone had recalled the identical type of tire in South America and had already settled a lawsuit for an accident caused by the tread defect. Discuss each of the following factors in relation to this case: quality, inventory, ethics, supply chain visibility, profitability, and customer loyalty.[19]

4. Finding Shelf Space at Walmart

Walmart's business strategy of being a low-cost provider by managing its supply chain down to the minutia has paid off greatly. Each week, approximately 100 million customers, or one-third of the U.S. population, visit Walmart's U.S. stores. Walmart is currently the world's largest retailer and the second-largest corporation behind ExxonMobil. It was founded by Sam Walton in 1962 and is the largest private employer in the United States and Mexico. Walmart is also the largest grocery retailer in the United States, with an estimated 20 percent of the retail grocery and consumables business, and the largest toy seller in the United States, with an estimated 45 percent of the retail toy business, having surpassed Toys "R" Us in the late 1990s.

Walmart's business model is based on selling a wide variety of general merchandise at "always low prices." The reason Walmart can offer such low prices is due to its innovative use of information technology tools to create its highly sophisticated supply chain. Walmart has famously invited its major suppliers to develop powerful supply chain partnerships jointly. These are designed to increase product flow efficiency and, consequently, Walmart's profitability.[20]

You are the owner of a high-end collectible toy company. You create everything from authentic sports figure replicas to famous musicians and movie characters, including Babe Ruth, Hulk Hogan, Mick Jagger, Ozzy Osbourne, Alien, and the Terminator. It would be a huge win for your company if you could get your collectibles into Walmart. Compile a strategic plan highlighting the steps required to approach Walmart as your supply chain partner. Be sure to address the pros and cons of partnering with the chain, including the cost to revamp your current supply chain to meet Walmart's tough supply chain requirements.

5. Customer Relationship Management Strategies

On average, it costs an organization six times more to sell to a new customer than to sell to an existing customer. As the co-owner of a medium-sized sports equipment distributor, you have recently been notified that sales for the past three months have decreased by an average of 20 percent. The reasons for the decline in sales are numerous, including a poor economy and some negative publicity your company received regarding a defective product line. In a group, explain how implementing a CRM system can help you understand and combat the decline in sales. Be sure to justify why a CRM system is important to your business and its future growth.

Also, search the Internet for at least one recent and authoritative article that compares or ranks customer relationship management systems. Select two packages from the list and compare their functions and features as described in the article(s) you found as well as on each company's website. Find references in the literature where companies that are using each package have reported their experiences, both good and bad. Draw on any other comparisons you can find. Prepare a presentation for delivery in class on the strengths and weaknesses of each package, which one you favor, and why.

6. Searching for Employee Loyalty

You are the CEO of Razz, a start-up web-based search company that is planning to compete directly with Google. The company had an exceptional first year and is currently receiving over 500,000 hits a day from customers all over the world. You have hired 250 people in the past four months, doubling the size of your organization. With so many new employees starting so quickly, you are concerned about how your company's culture will evolve and whether your employees are receiving enough attention. You are already familiar with customer relationship management and how CRM systems can help an organization create strong customer relationships. However, you are unfamiliar with employee relationship management and you are wondering what ERM systems might be able to offer your employees and your company. Research the web, create a report detailing features and functions of ERM systems, and determine what value will be added to your organization if you decide to implement an ERM solution.

7. Driving Up Profits with Loyalty (or Driving Down?)

The Butterfly Café is located in downtown San Francisco and offers specialty coffee, teas, and organic fruits and vegetables. The café holds a number of events to attract customers such as live music, poetry readings, book clubs, charity events, and local artist's nights. A listing of all participants attending each event is tracked in the café's database. The café uses the information for marketing campaigns and offers customers who attend multiple events additional discounts. A marketing database company, InTheKnow.com, has offered to pay the Butterfly Café a substantial amount of money for access to its customer database, which it will then sell to other local businesses. The owner of the Butterfly Café, Penny Dirks, has come to you for advice. She is not sure whether her customers would appreciate her selling their personal information and how it might affect her business. However, the amount of money InTheKnow.com is offering is enough to finance her much-needed new patio for the back of the café. InTheKnow.com has promised that the sale will be completely confidential. What should Dirks do?

8. Supporting Customers

Creative.com is an ebusiness that sells craft materials and supplies over the Internet. You have just started as the vice president of customer service, and you have a team of 45 customer service representatives. Currently, the only form of customer service is the toll-free number, and the company is receiving a tremendous number of calls regarding products, orders, and shipping information. The average wait time for a customer to speak to a customer service representative is 35 minutes. Orders are being canceled, and Creative.com is losing business due to its lack of customer service. Create a strategy to revamp the customer service center and get the company back on track.

9. Implementing an ERP System

Blue Dog Inc. is a leading manufacturer in the high-end sunglasses industry, reaching record revenue levels of more than $250 million last year. Blue Dog is currently deciding on the possibility of implementing an ERP system to help decrease production costs and increase inventory control. Many of the executives are nervous about making such a large investment in an ERP system due to its low success rates. As a senior manager at Blue Dog Inc., you have been asked to compile a list of the potential benefits and risks associated with implementing an ERP system along with your recommendations for the steps the company can take to ensure a successful implementation. Be sure also to explain why ERP systems include CRM and SCM components and the advantages the company can gain by implementing all of the components for a connected corporation.

PROJECT I   Shipping Problems

Entrepreneurship is in Alyssa Stuart's blood. Stuart has been starting businesses since she was 10 years old, and she finally has the perfect business of custom-made furniture. Customers who visit her shop can choose from a number of fabrics and 50 styles of couch and chair designs to create their custom-made furniture. Once the customer decides on a fabric pattern and furniture design, the information is sent to China, where the furniture is built and shipped to the customer via the West Coast. Stuart is excited about her business; all of her hard work has finally paid off because she has more than 17,000 customers and 875 orders currently in the pipe.

Stuart's business is booming. Her high-quality products and outstanding customer service have created an excellent reputation for her business. But the business is at risk of losing everything, and she has come to you for help solving her supply chain issues. The parcel delivery companies such as FedEx and UPS are on strike, and Alyssa is not sure how her raw materials or finished products will be delivered. What strategies do you recommend for Alyssa's business to continue working and overcome the strike?

PROJECT II   Great Stories

When customers have an unpleasant customer experience, the company no longer has to worry about them telling a few friends and family; the company now has to worry about them telling everyone. Internet service providers are giving frustrated consumers another means of fighting back. Free or low-cost computer space for Internet websites is empowering consumers to tell not only their friends but also the world about the way they have been treated. A few examples of disgruntled customer stories from the Internet include:

- A bike-riding tourist requires stitches after being bitten on the leg by a dog. The tourism company is banned from renting bikes and in turn bars the tourist from taking any future tours.

- A customer leaving Best Buy refuses to show the receipt voluntarily to the guard at the door. The Best Buy employees try to seize the customer's cart and then decide to park a car behind the customer's vehicle.

- Enterprise Rent-A-Car operates a high-stress business, and frequently its customers find that the company did not honor reservations, did not have cars ready for reservations, rented cars with empty tanks of gas, and charged higher rates to corporate account holders.

The pervasive nature of the Internet is increasing customer power and changing business from product-focused to customer-focused. Explain the difference between product-focused business and customer-focused business and why CRM is more important than ever before.

PROJECT III   JetBlue on YouTube

JetBlue took an unusual and interesting CRM approach by using YouTube to apologize to its customers. JetBlue's founder and former CEO, David Neeleman, apologized to customers via YouTube after a very bad week for the airline: 1,100 flights were canceled due to snowstorms, causing thousands of passengers to be stranded at airports around the country. Neeleman's unrehearsed, unrefined, and sincere YouTube apology made customers understand the issues and accept the company's apology.

You are the founder and CEO of GoodDog, a large pet food manufacturing company. Recently, at least 16 pet deaths have been tied to tainted pet food, fortunately not manufactured by your company. A recall of potentially deadly pet food has dog and cat owners studying their animals for even the slightest hint of illness and swamping veterinarians nationwide with calls about symptoms. Create a strategy for using YouTube as a vehicle to communicate with your customers as they fear for their pets' lives. Be sure to highlight the pros and cons of using YouTube as a customer communication vehicle. Are there any other new technologies you could use as a customer communication vehicle that would be more effective than YouTube? With all the new advances in technology and the many ways to reach customers, do you think using YouTube is a smart approach? What else could you do to help gain back customers' trust?

PROJECT IV Gaining Business Intelligence from Strategic Initiatives

You are a new employee in the customer service department at Premier One, a large office supply distributor. The company has been in business for 3 years and focuses on providing top of the line office supplies at a low cost. The company currently has 90 employees and operates in seven states.

Sales over the past 3 years have tripled, and the manual systems currently in place are no longer sufficient to run the business. Your first task is to meet with your new team and create a presentation for the president and chief executive officer describing supply chain management, customer relationship management, and enterprise resource planning. The presentation should highlight the main benefits Premier One can receive from these enterprise systems along with any additional added business value that can be gained from the systems.

PROJECT V Zappos Passion

Tony Hsieh's first entrepreneurial effort began at the age of 12, when he started his own custom button business. Realizing the importance of advertising, Hsieh began marketing his business to other kids through directories, and soon his profits soared to a few hundred dollars a month. Throughout his adolescence, Hsieh started several businesses, and by the time he was in college, he was making money selling pizzas out of his Harvard dorm room. Another entrepreneurial student, Alfred Lin, bought pizzas from Hsieh and resold them by the slice, making a nice profit. Hsieh and Lin quickly became friends.

After Harvard, Hsieh founded LinkExchange in 1996, a company that helped small businesses exchange banner ads. A mere 2 years later, Hsieh sold LinkExchange to Microsoft for $265 million. Using the profits from the sale, Hsieh and Lin formed a venture capital company that invested in start-up businesses. One investment that caught their attention was Zappos, an online etailer of shoes. Both entrepreneurs viewed the $40 billion shoe market as an opportunity they could not miss, and in 2000, Hsieh took over as Zappos' CEO with Lin as his chief financial officer.

Today, Zappos is leading its market and offering an enormous selection of more than 90,000 styles of handbags, clothing, and accessories from more than 500 brands. One reason for Zappos' incredible success was Hsieh's decision to use the advertising and marketing budget for customer service, a tactic that would not have worked before the Internet. Zappos' passionate customer service strategy encourages customers to order as many sizes and styles of products as they want, ships them for free, and offers free return shipping. Zappos encourages customer communication, and its call center receives more than 5,000 calls a day with the longest call to date lasting more than four hours.

Zappos' extensive inventory is stored in a warehouse in Kentucky right next to a UPS shipping center. Only available stock is listed on the website, and orders as late as 11 P.M. are still guaranteed next-day delivery. To facilitate supplier and partner relationships, Zappos built an extranet that provides its vendors with all kinds of product information, such as items sold, times sold, price, customer, and so on. Armed with these kinds of details, suppliers can quickly change manufacturing schedules to meet demand.

Zappos Culture

Along with valuing its partners and suppliers, Zappos also places a great deal of value on its employee relationships. Zappos employees have fun, and walking through the offices, you will see all kinds of things not normally seen in business environments—bottle-cap pyramids, cotton-candy machines, and bouncing balls. Building loyal employee relationships is a critical success factor at Zappos, and to facilitate this relationship, the corporate headquarters are located in the same building as the call center (where most employees work) in Las Vegas. All employees receive 100 percent company-paid health insurance along with a daily free lunch.

Of course, the Zappos culture does not work for everyone, and the company pays to find the right employees through "The Offer," which extends to new employees the option of quitting and receiving payment for time worked plus an additional $1,000 bonus. Why the $1,000 bonus for quitting? Zappos management believes that is a small price to pay to find those employees who do not have the sense of commitment Zappos requires. Less than 10 percent of new hires take The Offer.

Zappos' unique culture stresses the following:

1. Delivering WOW through service.
2. Embracing and driving change.
3. Creating fun and a little weirdness.
4. Being adventurous, creative, and open-minded.
5. Pursuing growth and learning.
6. Building open and honest relationships with communication.
7. Building a positive team and family spirit.
8. Doing more with less.
9. Being passionate and determined.
10. Being humble.

Zappos' Sale to Amazon

Amazon purchased Zappos for $880 million. Zappos employees shared $40 million in cash and stock, and the Zappos management team remained in place. Having access to Amazon's world-class warehouses and supply chain is sure to catapult Zappos' revenues, though many wonder whether the Zappos culture will remain. It'll be interesting to watch![21]

Questions

1. Define SCM and how it can benefit Zappos.
2. Explain CRM and why Zappos would benefit from the implementation of a CRM system.
3. Demonstrate why Zappos would need to implement SCM, CRM, and ERP for a connected corporation.
4. Analyze the merger between Zappos and Amazon and assess potential issues for Zappos customers.
5. Propose a plan for how Zappos can use Amazon's supply chain to increase sales and customer satisfaction.
6. Argue for or against the following statement: "In the electronic age, customer relationships are more important than ever, and Zappos provides the new benchmark that all corporations should follow."

PROJECT VI   Searching Telephone Calls

Imagine being able to search a database of customer phone calls to find specific requests or to be able to sort through digital customer complaints to detect the exact moment when the interaction between the customer service representative and the customer went wrong. A new tool called Find It allows the sorting of digital voice records as easily as using Google to sift through documents. Find It is opening limitless business opportunities as organizations begin to understand how they can use this technology to help employees search voice mails or recorded calls for keywords and phrases.

You have recently started your own marketing firm and you want to use the power of Find It to help your customers query all of their unique data records, including digital voice recordings. Now all you need is to prepare your marketing materials to send to potential customers. Create a marketing pitch that you will deliver to customers detailing the business opportunities they could uncover if they purchase Find It. Your marketing pitch can be a one-page document, a catchy tune, a video, or a PowerPoint presentation.

PROJECT VII   Sharptooth Incorporated

Stephen Kern is the founder and CEO of Sharptooth, a small business that buys and sells comic strips to magazines and newspapers around the country. Some of Sharptooth's artists have made it big and are syndicated in hundreds of magazines and newspapers, whereas others are new to the industry. Kern started in the business as an artist and began contracting other artists when he realized he had a knack for promoting and marketing comic materials. His artistic background is great for spotting talented young artists but not so great for running the business.

Kern recently began selling comics to new forms of media such as blogs, websites, and other online tools. He has hired you to build him a new system to track all online comic sales. You quickly notice that Kern has a separate system for each of his lines of business, including newspaper sources, magazine sources, billboard sources, and now online sources. You notice that each system works independently to perform its job of creating, updating, and maintaining sales information, but you are wondering how he operates his business as a whole. Create a list of issues Kern will encounter if he continues to run his business with four systems performing the same operations. What could happen to the business if he cannot correlate the details of each? Be sure to highlight at least 10 issues by which separate systems could cause problems.

PROJECT VIII   Eating In

Having been employed by the same company for more than 20 years, Mary Lou Lively was shocked when she was suddenly terminated along with about 900 of her co-workers. It took Lively a few weeks to recover from the shock, and then she finally began focusing her efforts on searching for a new job. Lively was sure her loyal employment history and strong skill set would land her a new job in no time; however, after several months of searching, she wasn't having any luck. With her emergency funds quickly being depleted, Lively knew she had to find a new job soon or she'd need to start selling her assets or cashing in her retirement savings.

The one positive aspect of having so much free time was that she could focus on her true passion, cooking. Mary Lou began making a little money by catering lunches and dinners for local businesses and neighbors. One day she overheard a neighbor remark that she was hosting a large party and didn't have enough time to prepare the meal. Almost jokingly, Lively asked her how much she'd be willing to pay for a catered event. Soon Lively was catering for numerous neighbors and small businesses, and she knew she had to make a decision about whether she would go into business for herself or continue searching for other employment.

After a year in the catering business, Lively was earning a good living and building a stellar reputation. She began catering for all types of events, including weddings, and business was so good that she hired several employees to help grow her business. As Lively begins to plan her expansion, she has asked for your help in answering the following questions:

1. How important is customer loyalty for Lively's business? What can she do to ensure that her customers remain loyal? How could one disgruntled customer hurt business? What can she do to combat this challenge?

2. Research the business Yelp.com. What service does Yelp.com perform? Would a small business see Yelp.com as an opportunity or a threat? What are the pros and cons a customer should be aware of when using Yelp.com?

3. Lively's responsibilities include forecasting, inventory control, scheduling, and ensuring high-quality products. What types of forecasts would she require to run her business? What types of inventory would she want to track? What might happen if her inventory tracking tool was off by 50 percent? What types of schedules does Lively need to generate? What things might occur to

disrupt schedules and cause her to reschedule? How can a supply chain management system help run the business?

4. Lively wants to create a business based on loyal customers and loyal employees. She offers her employees bonuses for new ideas, recipes, or business referrals. What risks is Lively encountering by offering these bonuses? One employee idea that she has implemented is turning out to be a competitive advantage for her business; however, the employee has quit and is now working for a competitor. Should Lively still pay the employee the bonus? What should she do to ensure that she is building strong employee relationships?

5. Lively overheard one of her customers talking about enterprise systems such as CRM, SCM, and ERP. However, she is sure they are available only to big companies that have lots of capital. Research the Internet and find examples of enterprise systems for small business. Do you think she should invest in these types of systems to run her business? Why or why not?

AYK APPLICATION PROJECTS

If you are looking for Excel projects to incorporate into your class, try any of the following after reading this chapter.

Project Number	Project Name	Project Type	Plug-In	Focus Area	Project Level	Skill Set	Page Number
9	Security Analysis	Excel	T3	Filtering Data	Intermediate	Conditional Formatting, Autofilter, Subtotal	AYK.7
10	Gathering Data	Excel	T3	Data Analysis	Intermediate	Conditional Formatting, PivotTable	AYK.8
11	Scanner System	Excel	T2	Strategic Analysis	Intermediate	Formulas	AYK.8
12	Competitive Pricing	Excel	T2	Profit Maximization	Intermediate	Formulas	AYK.9
13	Adequate Acquisitions	Excel	T2	Break-Even Analysis	Intermediate	Formulas	AYK.9
15	Assessing the Value of Information	Excel	T3	Data Analysis	Intermediate	PivotTable	AYK.10
16	Growth, Trends, and Forecasts	Excel	T2, T3	Data Forecasting	Advanced	Average, Trend, Growth	AYK.11
18	Formatting Grades	Excel	T3	Data Analysis	Advanced	If, LookUp	AYK.12
22	Turnover Rates	Excel	T3	Data Mining	Advanced	PivotTable	AYK.15
23	Vital Information	Excel	T3	Data Mining	Advanced	PivotTable	AYK.15
24	Breaking Even	Excel	T4	Business Analysis	Advanced	Goal Seek	AYK.16
25	Profit Scenario	Excel	T4	Sales Analysis	Advanced	Scenario Manager	AYK.16

9
CHAPTER

Systems Development and Project Management: Corporate Responsibility

SECTION 9.1
Developing Enterprise Applications

- The Systems Development Life Cycle (SDLC)
- Software Development Methodology: The Waterfall
- Agile Software Development Methodologies
- Developing a Service-Oriented Architecture

SECTION 9.2
Project Management

- Using Project Management to Deliver Successful Projects
- Primary Project Planning Diagrams
- Outsourcing Projects

CHAPTER OUTLINE

What's in IT for me?

This chapter provides an overview of how organizations build information systems. As a business student, you need to understand this process because information systems are the underlying foundations of company operations. Your understanding of the principles of building information systems will make you a more valuable employee. You will be able to identify trouble spots early and make suggestions during the design process that will result in a better information systems project—one that satisfies both you and your business.

Building an information system is like constructing a house. You could sit back and let the developers do all the design work, construction, and testing, and hope the finished product will satisfy your needs. However, participating in the process helps guarantee that your needs are not only heard but also met. It is good business practice to have direct user input steering the development of the finished product. Your knowledge of the systems development process will allow you to participate and ensure that you are building flexible enterprise architectures that support not only current business needs but also future ones.

©Jason Reed/Ryan McVay/Getty
Images RF

©BananaStock/Jupiterimages/
Thinkstock RF

©Janis Christie/Getty Images RF

Gamer Delight

It is a dream come true when you can make an incredible salary doing what you love, and that is exactly what is happening in the gaming industry. To the gamer's delight, profitable careers can be found for people with design, development, and programming skills. Video programmers are finding success in technology companies, marketing corporations, advertising agencies, and video game development companies. In fact, video games are a $30 billion industry in the United States, especially as more people play games on their mobile phones, according to Reuters. Companies around the globe are paying application programmers, developers, and designers incredible salaries for their skills and capabilities.

Video Game Programmer

Video game programmers are software engineers who work on games for console or handheld video gaming systems. In addition to understanding computer languages and structures, they must also be familiar with the specific target systems on which their games will be played, as well as the development platforms used to create games

Video game programming experts specializing in networking or graphic engines are seeing starting salaries as high as $100,000. One of the great benefits of the video game industry is that it is hardly affected by depression or bad economies. New college graduates without any industry experience are offered $60,000 annually.

Technical Directors

Technical directors for a game development company get high salaries even at the entry level. Those having the least experience are said to get an average of $60,000 every year, and that increases to more than $70,000 for individuals who have more than 3 years of know-how. The highest compensation for this particular job description was $195,500 annually.

Video Games Designer

Video game designers work with a team developing and designing video games. Game designers are an important part of a comprehensive team of designers and developers that coordinate the complex task of creating a new video game. Game designers have duties such as designing characters, levels, puzzles, art, and animation. They may also write code, using various computer programming languages. Depending on their career duties, they may also be responsible for project management tasks and testing early versions of video games.

Video game designers also receive comparatively high compensation whether the knowledge comes from experience or formal education. The designer with fewer than 3 years of experience normally starts at $50,000 each year, which increases to $75,000 after the third year. Once the video game design expert earns more than 6 years of on-the-job experience, this can go up to $100,000 annually. The creative director or lead designer earns up to $180,000 every year after getting substantial experience in the industry.

Video Game Producer

Video game producers supervise all aspects of creating a video game and are held liable for decisions from start to finish. These individuals coordinate the work of different departments involved and ensure that deadlines are met and the project remains within the budget. The minimum salary for producers is $62,000, while those with over 6 years of experience can earn up to $180,000 a year.

Video Game Artists and Animators

The artists and animators for video game development companies earn an average salary of $50,000 annually. Senior lead artists earn anywhere from $80,000 to $215,000 annually. Earning high income is quite easy in the video game industry if you have a good education, experience, determination, and creativity.[1]

9.1 Describe the seven phases of the systems development life cycle.

9.2 Summarize the different software development methodologies.

9.3 Explain why a company would implement a service-oriented architecture.

THE SYSTEMS DEVELOPMENT LIFE CYCLE (SDLC)

LO 9.1: Describe the seven phases of the systems development life cycle.

The multimillion-dollar Nike SCM system failure is legendary; as Nike CEO Philip Knight famously stated, "This is what we get for our $400 million?" Nike partnered with i2 to implement an SCM system that never came to fruition. i2 blamed the failed implementation on the fact that Nike failed to use the vendor's implementation methodology and templates. Nike blamed the failure on faulty software.[2]

It is difficult to get an organization to work if its systems do not work. In the information age, software success or failure can lead directly to business success or failure. Companies rely on software to drive business operations and ensure that work flows throughout the company. As more and more companies rely on software to operate, so do the business-related consequences of software successes and failures.

The potential advantages of successful software implementations provide firms with significant incentives to manage software development risks. However, an alarmingly high number of software development projects come in late or over budget, and successful projects tend to maintain fewer features and functions than originally specified. Understanding the basics of software development, or the systems development life cycle, will help organizations avoid potential software development pitfalls and ensure that software development efforts are successful.

Before jumping into software development, it is important to understand a few key terms. A *legacy system* is an old system that is fast approaching or beyond the end of its useful life within an organization. *Conversion* is the process of transferring information from a legacy system to a new system. *Software customization* modifies software to meet specific user or business requirements. *Off-the-shelf application software* supports general business processes and does not require any specific software customization to meet the organization's needs.

The *systems development life cycle (SDLC)* is the overall process for developing information systems, from planning and analysis through implementation and maintenance. The SDLC is the foundation for all systems development methods, and hundreds of activities are associated with each phase. These activities typically include determining budgets, gathering system requirements, and writing detailed user documentation.

The SDLC begins with a business need, proceeds to an assessment of the functions a system must have to satisfy the need, and ends when the benefits of the system no longer outweigh its maintenance costs. This is why it is referred to as a life cycle. The SDLC is composed of seven distinct phases: planning, analysis, design, development, testing, implementation, and maintenance (see Figure 9.1).

Phase 1: Planning

The *planning phase* establishes a high-level plan of the intended project and determines project goals. Planning is the first and most critical phase of any systems development effort, regardless of whether the effort is to develop a system that allows customers to order products online, determine the best logistical structure for warehouses around the world, or develop a strategic information alliance with another organization. Organizations must carefully plan the activities (and determine why they are necessary) to be successful. A *change agent* is a person or event that is the catalyst for implementing major changes for a system to meet business changes. *Brainstorming* is a technique for generating ideas by encouraging participants to offer as many ideas as possible in a short period without any analysis until all the ideas have been exhausted. Many times, new business opportunities are found as the result of a brainstorming session.

FIGURE 9.1

The SDLC and Its Associated
Activities

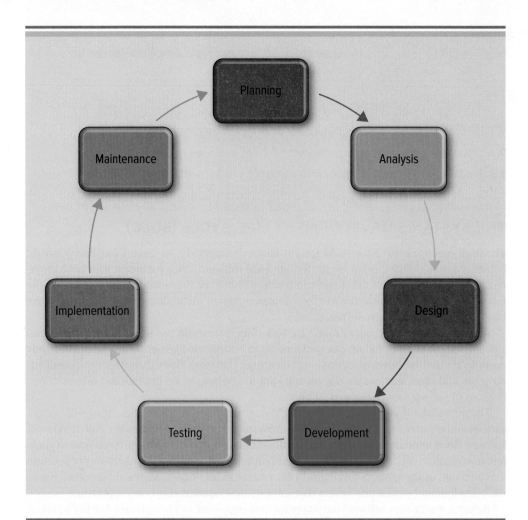

Phase	Associated Activity
Planning	■ Brainstorm issues and identify opportunities for the organization. ■ Prioritize and choose projects for development. ■ Set the project scope. ■ Develop the project plan.
Analysis	■ Gather the business requirement for the system. ■ Define any constraints associated with the system.
Design	■ Design the technical architecture required to support the system. ■ Design the system models.
Development	■ Build the technical architecture. ■ Build the database. ■ Build the applications.
Testing	■ Write the test conditions. ■ Perform system testing.
Implementation	■ Write detailed user documentation. ■ Provide training for the system users.
Maintenance	■ Build a help desk to support the system users. ■ Provide an environment to support system changes.

The Project Management Institute (PMI) develops procedures and concepts necessary to support the profession of project management (www.pmi.org). PMI defines a *project* as a temporary activity a company undertakes to create a unique product, service, or result. *Project management* is the application of knowledge, skills, tools, and techniques to project activities to

BUSINESS DRIVEN START-UP

Just Ask TED

You'll remember this day because it is the day you were introduced to TED (www.ted.com). TED is a nonprofit devoted to "ideas worth spreading." The company hosts a yearly conference focusing on technology, entertainment, and design (TED). It gathers the world's innovative minds and challenges them to give the talk of their lives in just 18 minutes. Each talk is posted to the TED website and includes such famous speakers as:

- Chris Anderson, editor of *Wired* and author of *The Long Tail: Why the Future of Business Is Selling Less of More.*
- Tim Berners-Lee, inventor of the World Wide Web.
- Jeff Bezos, founder of Amazon.com.
- Richard Branson, founder of Virgin Group.
- Bill Clinton, former president of the United States.
- Peter Diamandis, chairman of the X Prize Foundation.
- Sergey Brin and Larry Page, cofounders of Google.
- Malcolm Gladwell, author of *Blink* and *The Tipping Point.*
- Bill Gates, founder of Microsoft.
- Seth Godin, a marketing guru.
- Steven Levitt, author of *Freakonomics.*[3]

As you brainstorm your future start-up, hoping to become the next Bill Gates or Steve Jobs, how can you use TED to generate ideas? Review the TED website and choose three talks that could help lead to the next great business idea.

meet project requirements. A *project manager* is an individual who is an expert in project planning and management, defines and develops the project plan, and tracks the plan to ensure that the project is completed on time and on budget. The project manager is the person responsible for executing the entire project and defining the project scope that links the project to the organization's overall business goals. The *project scope* describes the business need (the problem the project will solve) and the justification, requirements, and current boundaries for the project. The *project plan* is a formal, approved document that manages and controls the entire project.

Phase 2: Analysis

In the *analysis phase,* the firm analyzes its end-user business requirements and refines project goals into defined functions and operations of the intended system. *Business requirements* are the specific business requests the system must meet to be successful, so the analysis phase is critical because business requirements drive the entire systems development effort. A sample business requirement might state, "The CRM system must track all customer inquiries by product, region, and sales representative." The business requirement will state what the system must accomplish to be considered successful. If a system does not meet the business requirements, it will be deemed a failed project. For this reason, the organization must spend as much time, energy, and resources as necessary to gather accurate and detailed business requirements. (Figure 9.2 displays ways to gather business requirements.)

Requirements management is the process of managing changes to the business requirements throughout the project. Projects are typically dynamic in nature, and change should be expected and anticipated for successful project completion. A *requirements definition document* prioritizes all of the business requirements by order of importance to the company. *Sign-off* is the users' actual signatures, indicating they approve all of the business requirements.

FIGURE 9.2

Methods for Gathering Business
Requirements

Methods for Gathering Business Requirements
Conduct a *joint application development (JAD)* session where employees meet, sometimes for several days, to define or review the business requirements for the system.
Interview individuals to determine current operations and current issues.
Compile questionnaires to survey employees to discover issues.
Make observations to determine how current operations are performed.
Review business documents to discover reports, policies, and how information is used throughout the organization.

Once a business analyst takes a detailed look at how an organization performs its work and its processes, the analyst can recommend ways to improve these processes to make them more efficient and effective. *Process modeling* involves graphically representing the processes that capture, manipulate, store, and distribute information between a system and its environment. One of the most common diagrams used in process modeling is the data flow diagram. A *data flow diagram (DFD)* illustrates the movement of information between external entities and the processes and data stores within the system (see Figure 9.3). Process models and data flow diagrams establish the specifications of the system. *Computer-aided software engineering (CASE)* tools are software suites that automate systems analysis, design, and development. Process models and data flow diagrams can provide the basis for the automatic generation of the system if they are developed using a CASE tool.

Phase 3: Design

The *design phase* establishes descriptions of the desired features and operations of the system, including screen layouts, business rules, process diagrams, pseudocode, and other documentation. During the analysis phase, end users and MIS specialists work together to gather the detailed business requirements for the proposed project from a logical point of view. That is, during analysis, business requirements are documented without respect to technology or the

FIGURE 9.3

Sample Data Flow Diagram

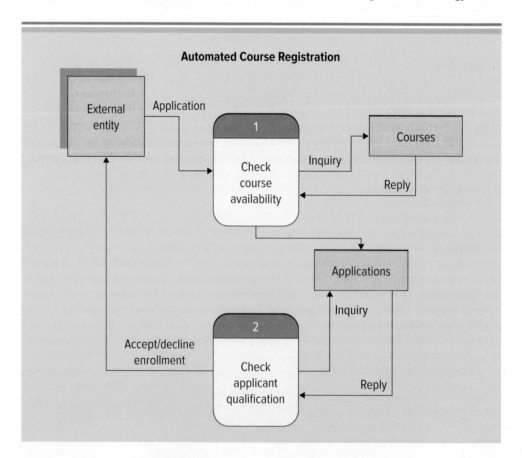

BUSINESS DRIVEN DEBATE

Flawed Development

Data must be secure! A computer programming course would teach you that security is a critical component that must be included in every system. Apparently, the employees that developed the new system for the state of Oklahoma were out sick during this important class. The new system mistakenly posted confidential data, including Social Security numbers, for thousands of Oklahoma residents on the state's website. The really unfortunate part of this systems blunder is that the error went unnoticed for more than 3 years. A programmer found the error when he realized that by changing his web browser, he could redirect his page to the entire database for the state. To make matters even worse, due to development issues, a hacker could have easily changed all the data in the database or added false data to elements such as the state's Sexual and Violent Offender Registry.[4]

Why is it important to secure data? What can happen if someone accesses your customer database? What could happen if someone changes the information in your customer database and adds fictitious data? What phases in the systems development life cycle should have found these errors? How could these errors go unnoticed for over 3 years? Who should be held responsible for the system issues?

technical infrastructure that will support the system. Moving into the design phase turns the project focus to the physical or technical point of view, defining the technical architecture that will support the system, including data models, screen designs, report layouts, and database models (see Figure 9.4).

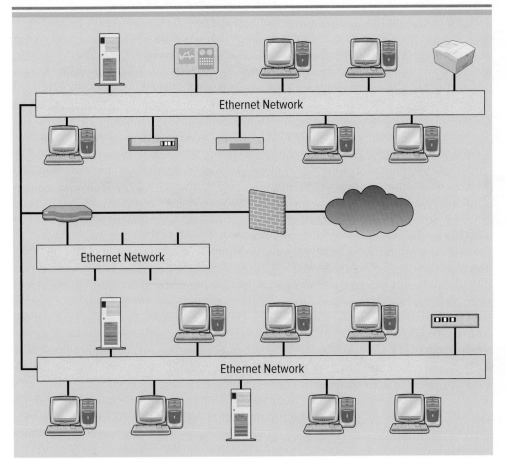

FIGURE 9.4

Sample Technical Architecture

The graphical user interface (GUI) is the interface to an information system. GUI screen design is the ability to model the information system screens for an entire system by using icons, buttons, menus, and submenus. Data models represent a formal way to express data relationships to a database management system (DBMS). Entity relationship diagrams document the relationships between entities in a database environment (see Figure 9.5). *Pseudocode*, meaning fake code, is an informal description of how the computer program should work. Pseudocode is intended for human reading rather than machine reading.

Phase 4: Development

The *development phase* transforms all the detailed design documents from the design phase into the actual system. In this phase, the project transitions from preliminary designs to actual physical

FIGURE 9.5

Sample Entity Relationship Diagram

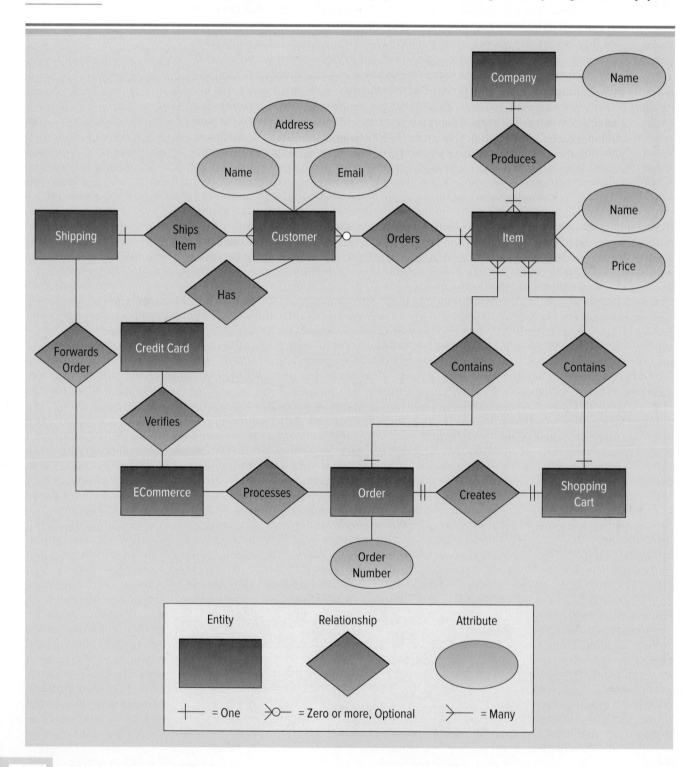

implementation. During development, the company purchases and implements the equipment necessary to support the architecture. *Software engineering* is a disciplined approach for constructing information systems through the use of common methods, techniques, or tools. Software engineers use computer-aided software engineering (CASE) tools, which provide automated support for the development of the system. *Control objects for information and related technology (COBIT)* is a set of best practices that helps an organization maximize the benefits of an information system, at the same time establishing appropriate controls to ensure minimum errors.

Coders are the people who write the programs that operate computers. The term *programming language* refers to a unique set of keywords (words that it understands) along with a special syntax for organizing program instructions that execute computer commands. During development, the team defines the programming language it will use to build the system. There is a huge range of programming languages to choose from, and each one can be used for different purposes. The most common languages include:

- C: A powerful language used primarily for operating hardware.
- C++: Based on C using an object-oriented approach.
- Ada: Used to control spacecraft, satellites, and airplanes.
- Java: Works on computers, cell phones, and tablets.
- MATLAB: Ideal for mathematical computations.
- PHP: Creates interactive websites.
- Python: A text-based language that can be used to build computer programs.
- Scratch: A visual language that is ideal for learning programming.
- Ruby: Automatically turns lots of information into web pages.
- Javascript: Builds interactive websites.
- XML: Used to manipulate Excel files and workbooks.

A *scripting language* is a programming method that provides for interactive modules to a website. *Object-oriented languages* group data and corresponding processes into objects. *Fourth-generation languages (4GL)* are programming languages that look similar to human languages. For example, a typical 4GL command might state, "FIND ALL RECORDS WHERE NAME IS 'SMITH'." Programming languages are displayed in Figure 9.6.

Phase 5: Testing

The *testing phase* brings all the project pieces together into a special testing environment to eliminate errors and bugs and verify that the system meets all the business requirements defined in the analysis phase. *Bugs* are defects in the code of an information system. *Test conditions* detail the steps the system must perform along with the expected result of each step (see Figure 9.7). Testers execute test conditions and compare the expected results with the actual results to verify that the system functions correctly. Each time the actual result is different from the expected result, a bug is generated, and the system must be fixed in development. A typical

FIGURE 9.6

Overview of Programming Languages

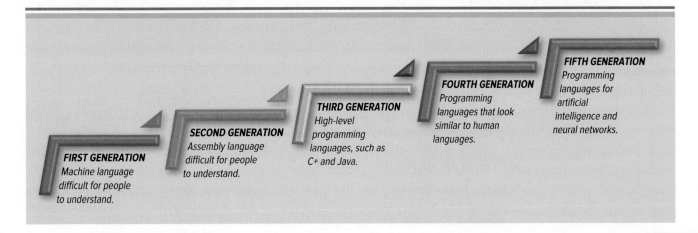

FIRST GENERATION Machine language difficult for people to understand.

SECOND GENERATION Assembly language difficult for people to understand.

THIRD GENERATION High-level programming languages, such as C+ and Java.

FOURTH GENERATION Programming languages that look similar to human languages.

FIFTH GENERATION Programming languages for artificial intelligence and neural networks.

FIGURE 9.7

Sample Test Conditions

Test Condition Number	Date Tested	Tested	Test Condition	Expected Result	Actual Result	Pass/ Fail
1	1/1/09	Emily Hickman	Click system Start button.	Main menu appears.	Same as expected result	Pass
2	1/1/09	Emily Hickman	Click Logon button in main menu.	Logon screen appears asking for user name and password.	Same as expected result	Pass
3	1/1/09	Emily Hickman	Type Emily Hickman in the user name field.	Emily Hickman appears in the user name field.	Same as expected result	Pass
4	1/1/09	Emily Hickman	Type Zahara 123 in the password field.	XXXXXXXXX appears in the password field.	Same as expected result	Pass
5	1/1/09	Emily Hickman	Click OK button.	User logon request is sent to database, and user name and password are verified.	Same as expected result	Pass
6	1/1/09	Emily Hickman	Click Start.	User name and password are accepted, and the system main menu appears.	Screen appeared stating logon failed and user name and password were incorrect.	Fail

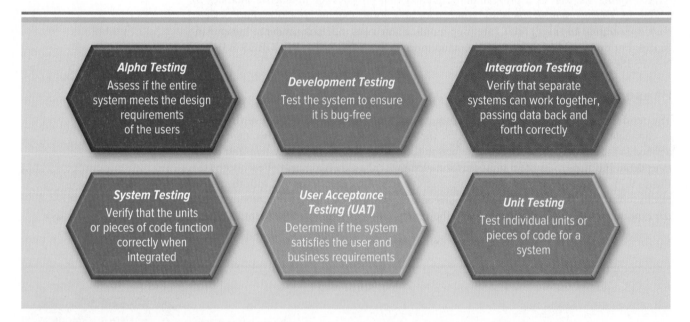

FIGURE 9.8

Different Forms of System Testing

systems development effort has hundreds or thousands of test conditions that must be verified against the business requirements to ensure that the system is operating as expected. Figure 9.8 displays the different types of tests typically included in a systems development effort.

Phase 6: Implementation

In the *implementation phase*, the organization places the system into production so users can begin to perform actual business operations with it. In this phase, the detailed *user documentation* is created that highlights how to use the system and how to troubleshoot issues

BUSINESS DRIVEN ANALYTICS

Bugs Everywhere

Bug reports are an important part of software development. All bugs must be logged, fixed, and tested. There are three common types of bugs programmers look for when building a system.

- Syntax errors: a mistake in the program's words or symbols.

- Runtime errors: A mistake that causes the program to crash, such as dividing by 0 or adding together two strings.

- Logic errors: A mistake that causes the output of the program to be wrong, such as adding instead of subtracting, using < instead of >, or using the wrong data in an equation.

Rank the three types of bugs by which one is the easiest to identify and which one is the most difficult to identify. What happens if metrics are not tracked on bug identification and bug fixes? What happens if a bug is not caught during development and goes live in production?

Imagine the following scenario: a tester creates a new bug report for a problem that was already identified as a bug; however, it is not detected as a duplicate. What happens to the project? This is a particularly common issue with large, complex system development efforts. How can you mitigate the problem of different users reporting the same bug or problem about the same system?

or problems. Training is also provided for the system users and can take place online or in a classroom. **Online training** runs over the Internet or on a CD or DVD, and employees complete the training on their own time at their own pace. **Workshop training** is held in a classroom environment and led by an instructor. One of the best ways to support users is to create a **help desk** or a group of people who respond to users' questions. Figure 9.9 displays the different implementation methods an organization can choose to ensure success.

FIGURE 9.9

System Implementation Methods

Parallel Implementation
Uses both the legacy system and new system until all users verify that the new system functions correctly

Plunge Implementation
Discards the legacy system and immediately migrates all users to the new system

Pilot Implementation
Assigns a small group of people to use the new system until it is verified to work correctly; then the remaining users migrate to the new system

Phased Implementation
Installs the new system in phases (for example, by department) until it is verified to work correctly

FIGURE 9.10

Examples of System Reports

Report	Examples
Internal report	Presents data that are distributed inside the organization and intended for employees within an organization. Internal reports typically support day-to-day operations monitoring that supports managerial decision making.
Detailed internal report	Presents information with little or no filtering or restrictions of the data.
Summary internal report	Organizes and categorizes data for managerial perusal. A report that summarizes total sales by product for each month is an example of a summary internal report. The data for a summary report are typically categorized and summarized to indicate trends and potential problems.
Exception reporting	Highlights situations occurring outside of the normal operating range for a condition or standard. These internal reports include only exceptions and might highlight accounts that are unpaid or delinquent or identify items that are low in stock.
Information system control report	Ensures the reliability of information, consisting of policies and their physical implementation, access restrictions, or record keeping of actions and transactions.
Information systems audit report	Assesses a company's information system to determine necessary changes and to help ensure the information systems' availability, confidentiality, and integrity.
Post-implementation report	Presents a formal report or audit of a project after it is up and running.

Phase 7: Maintenance

Maintaining the system is the final sequential phase of any systems development effort. In the *maintenance phase*, the organization performs changes, corrections, additions, and upgrades to ensure that the system continues to meet business goals. This phase continues for the life of the system because the system must change as the business evolves and its needs change, which means conducting constant monitoring, supporting the new system with frequent minor changes (for example, new reports or information capturing), and reviewing the system to be sure it is moving the organization toward its strategic goals. *Corrective maintenance* makes system changes to repair design flaws, coding errors, or implementation issues. *Preventive maintenance* makes system changes to reduce the chance of future system failure. During the maintenance phase, the system will generate reports to help users and MIS specialists ensure that it is functioning correctly (see Figure 9.10).

SOFTWARE DEVELOPMENT METHODOLOGY: THE WATERFALL

Today, systems are so large and complex that teams of architects, analysts, developers, testers, and users must work together to create the millions of lines of custom-written code that drive enterprises. For this reason, developers have created a number of systems development life cycle methodologies. A *methodology* is a set of policies, procedures, standards, processes, practices, tools, techniques, and tasks that people apply to technical and management challenges. Firms use a methodology to manage the deployment of technology with work plans, requirements documents, and test plans, for instance. A formal methodology can include coding standards, code libraries, development practices, and much more.

The oldest and the best known is the *waterfall methodology*, a sequence of phases in which the output of each phase becomes the input for the next (see Figure 9.11). In the SDLC, this means the steps are performed one at a time, in order, from planning through implementation and maintenance. The traditional waterfall method no longer serves most of today's development efforts, however; it is inflexible and expensive, and it requires rigid adherence to the sequence of steps. Its success rate is only about 1 in 10. Figure 9.12 explains some issues related to the waterfall methodology.[5]

Today's business environment is fierce. The desire and need to outsmart and outplay competitors remains intense. Given this drive for success, leaders push internal development teams

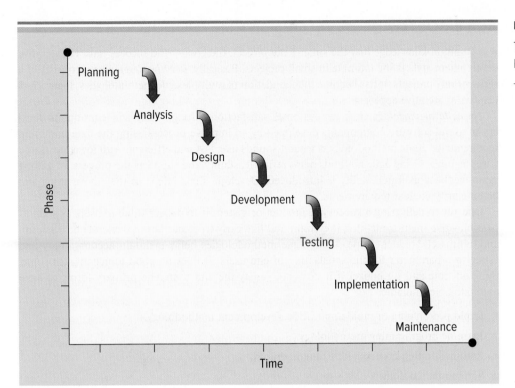

FIGURE 9.11

The Traditional Waterfall
Methodology

FIGURE 9.12

Disadvantages of the Waterfall
Methodology

Issues Related to the Waterfall Methodology	
The business problem	Any flaws in accurately defining and articulating the business problem in terms of what the business users actually require flow onward to the next phase.
The plan	Managing costs, resources, and time constraints is difficult in the waterfall sequence. What happens to the schedule if a programmer quits? How will a schedule delay in a specific phase affect the total cost of the project? Unexpected contingencies may sabotage the plan.
The solution	The waterfall methodology is problematic in that it assumes users can specify all business requirements in advance. Defining the appropriate IT infrastructure that is flexible, scalable, and reliable is a challenge. The final IT infrastructure solution must meet not only current but also future needs in terms of time, cost, feasibility, and flexibility. Vision is inevitably limited at the head of the waterfall.

and external vendors to deliver agreed-upon systems faster and cheaper so they can realize benefits as early as possible. Even so, systems remain large and complex. The traditional waterfall methodology no longer serves as an adequate systems development methodology in most cases. Because this development environment is the norm and not the exception anymore, development teams use a new breed of alternative development methods to achieve their business objectives.

Prototyping is a modern design approach by which the designers and system users use an iterative approach to building the system. *Discovery prototyping* builds a small-scale representation or working model of the system to ensure that it meets the user and business requirements. The following are advantages of prototyping:

- Prototyping encourages user participation.
- Prototypes evolve through iteration, which supports change better.
- Prototypes have a physical quality allowing users to see, touch, and experience the system as it is developed.
- Prototypes tend to detect errors earlier.
- Prototyping accelerates the phases of the SDLC, helping to ensure success.

AGILE SOFTWARE DEVELOPMENT METHODOLOGIES

It is common knowledge that the smaller the project, the greater the success rate. The iterative development style is the ultimate in small projects. Basically, *iterative development* consists of a series of tiny projects. It has become the foundation of multiple agile methodologies. Figure 9.13 displays an iterative approach.

An *agile methodology* aims for customer satisfaction through early and continuous delivery of useful software components developed by an iterative process using the bare minimum requirements. Agile methodology is what it sounds like: fast and efficient, with lower costs and fewer features. Using agile methods helps refine feasibility and supports the process for getting rapid feedback as functionality is introduced. Developers can adjust as they move along and better clarify unclear requirements.[6]

One key to delivering a successful product or system is to deliver value to users as soon as possible—give them something they want and like early to create buy-in, generate enthusiasm, and, ultimately, reduce scope. Using agile methodologies helps maintain accountability and establish a barometer for the satisfaction of end users. It does no good to accomplish something on time and on budget if it does not satisfy the end user. The primary forms of agile methodologies include:

- Rapid prototyping or rapid application development methodology.
- Extreme programming methodology.
- Rational unified process (RUP) methodology.
- Scrum methodology.

It is important not to get hung up on the names of the methodologies—some are proprietary brand names, others are generally accepted names. It is more important to know how these alternative methodologies are used in today's business environment and the benefits they can deliver.

Rapid Application Development (RAD) Methodology

In response to the faster pace of business, rapid application development has become a popular route for accelerating systems development. *Rapid application development (RAD) methodology* (also called *rapid prototyping*) emphasizes extensive user involvement in the rapid and

FIGURE 9.13

The Iterative Approach

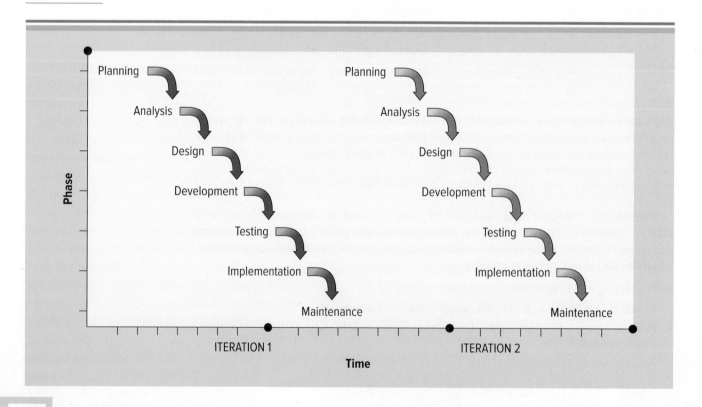

Fundamentals of RAD
Focus initially on creating a prototype that looks and acts like the desired system.
Actively involve system users in the analysis, design, and development phases.
Accelerate collecting the business requirements through an interactive and iterative construction approach.

FIGURE 9.14

Fundamentals of RAD

evolutionary construction of working prototypes of a system, to accelerate the systems development process. Figure 9.14 displays the fundamentals of RAD.

Extreme Programming Methodology

Extreme programming (XP) methodology, like other agile methods, breaks a project into four phases, and developers cannot continue to the next phase until the previous phase is complete. The delivery strategy supporting XP is that the quicker the feedback, the more improved the results. XP has four basic phases: planning, designing, coding, and testing. Planning can include user interviews, meetings, and small releases. During design, functionality is not added until it is required or needed. During coding, the developers work together soliciting continuous feedback from users, eliminating the communication gap that generally exists between developers and customers. During testing, the test requirements are generated before any code is developed. Extreme programming saves time and produces successful projects by continuously reviewing and revamping needed and unneeded requirements.[7]

Customer satisfaction is the primary reason XP finds success because developers quickly respond to changing business requirements, even late in the life cycle. XP encourages managers, customers, and developers to work together as a team to ensure the delivery of high-quality systems. XP is similar to a puzzle; there are many small pieces, and individually the pieces make no sense, but when they are pieced together, they can create a new system.

Rational Unified Process (RUP) Methodology

The *rational unified process (RUP) methodology*, owned by IBM, provides a framework for breaking down the development of software into four gates. Each gate consists of executable iterations of the software in development. A project stays in a gate waiting for the stakeholder's analysis, and then it either moves to the next gate or is canceled. The gates include:[8]

- **Gate one: inception.** This phase ensures that all stakeholders have a shared understanding of the proposed system and what it will do.
- **Gate two: elaboration.** This phase expands on the agreed-upon details of the system, including the ability to provide an architecture to support and build it.
- **Gate three: construction.** This phase includes building and developing the product.
- **Gate four: transition.** Primary questions answered in this phase address ownership of the system and training of key personnel.

Because RUP is an iterative methodology, the user can reject the product and force the developers to go back to gate one. RUP helps developers avoid reinventing the wheel and focuses on rapidly adding or removing reusable chunks of processes addressing common problems.

Scrum Methodology

Another agile methodology, *scrum methodology*, uses small teams to produce small pieces of software using a series of sprints, or 30-day intervals, to achieve an appointed goal. In rugby, a scrum is a team pack and everyone in the pack works together to move the ball down the field. In scrum methodology, each day ends or begins with a stand-up meeting to monitor and control the development effort.

DEVELOPING A SERVICE-ORIENTED ARCHITECTURE

One of the latest trends in systems development is creating a service-oriented architecture. *Service-oriented architecture (SOA)* is a business-driven enterprise architecture that supports

LO 9.3: Explain why a company would implement a service-oriented architecture.

BUSINESS DRIVEN ETHICS AND SECURITY

Planning for the Unexpected

Unexpected situations happen all the time, and the more you plan for them, the better prepared you'll be when developing software. Your employees will get into accidents, contract viruses and diseases, and experience other life issues. All of these scenarios lead to unplanned absenteeism, which can throw your project plan into a tailspin. What can happen to a project when a key employee suddenly quits or is forced to go on short-term disability? When reviewing all the different SDLC methodologies, which one offers the greatest flexibility for unplanned employee downtime? If you could choose when your employee was absent, which phase in the SDLC would be the safest for your project to still continue and achieve success? What can you do to ensure that you are preparing for unplanned absenteeism on your project plan?

integrating a business as linked, repeatable activities, tasks, or services. SOA ensures that MIS systems can adapt quickly, easily, and economically to support rapidly changing business needs. SOA promotes a scalable and flexible enterprise architecture that can implement new or reuse existing MIS components, creating connections among disparate applications and systems. It is important to understand that SOA is not a concrete architecture; it is thought that leads to a concrete architecture. It might be described as a style, paradigm, concept, perspective, philosophy, or representation. That is, SOA is an approach, a way of thinking, a value system that leads to decisions that design a concrete architecture allowing enterprises to plug in new services or upgrade existing services in a granular approach. Figure 9.15 discusses the problems that can be addressed by implementing SOA. Figure 9.16 displays the three key technical concepts of SOA.

FIGURE 9.15

Business Issues and SOA Solutions

Service-Oriented Architecture Solutions	
■ Agents unable to see policy coverage information remotely. ■ Calls/faxes used to get information from other divisions. ■ Clinical patient information stored on paper. ■ Complex access to supplier design drawings.	Integrate information to make it more accessible to employees.
■ High cost of handling customer calls. ■ Reconciliation of invoice deductions and rebates. ■ Hours on hold to determine patient insurance eligibility. ■ High turnover leading to excessive hiring and training costs.	Understand how business processes interact to manage administrative costs better.
■ Decreasing customer loyalty due to incorrect invoices. ■ Customers placed on hold to check order status. ■ Inability to update policy endorsements quickly. ■ Poor service levels.	Improve customer retention and deliver new products and services through reuse of current investments.
■ Time wasted reconciling separate databases. ■ Manual processes such as handling trade allocations. ■ Inability to detect quality flaws early in cycle. ■ High percentage of scrap and rework.	Improve people productivity with better business integration and connectivity.

FIGURE 9.16

SOA Concepts

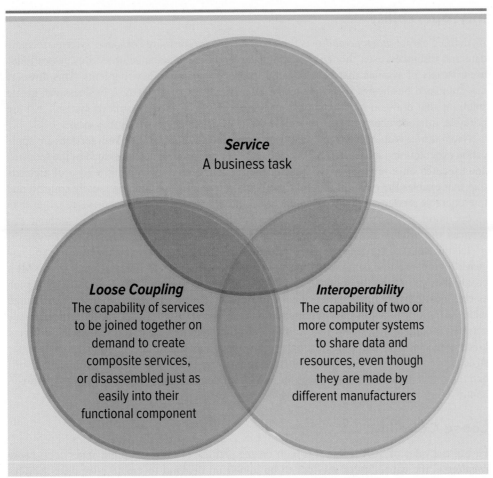

Service

Service-oriented architecture begins with a service—an SOA *service* being simply a business task, such as checking a potential customer's credit rating when opening a new account. It is important to stress that this is part of a business process. Services are like software products; however, when describing SOA, do not think about software or MIS. Think about what a company does on a day-to-day basis and break up those business processes into repeatable business tasks or components.

SOA works with services that are not just software or hardware but, rather, business tasks. It is a pattern for developing a more flexible kind of software application that can promote loose coupling among software components while reusing existing investments in technology in new, more valuable ways across the organization. SOA is based on standards that enable interoperability, business agility, and innovation to generate more business value for those who use these principles.

SOA helps companies become more agile by aligning business needs and the MIS capabilities that support these needs. Business drives requirements for MIS; SOA enables the MIS environment to respond to these requirements effectively and efficiently. SOA is about helping companies apply reusability and flexibility that can lower cost (of development, integration, and maintenance), increase revenue, and obtain sustainable competitive advantage through technology.

It is very important to note that SOA is an evolution. Although its results are revolutionary, it builds on many technologies used in the marketplace, such as web services, transactional technologies, information-driven principles, loose coupling, components, and object-oriented design. The beauty of SOA is that these technologies exist together in SOA through standards, well-defined interfaces, and organizational commitments to reuse key services instead of reinventing the wheel. SOA is not just about technology but about how technology and business link themselves for a common goal of business flexibility.

Interoperability

As defined earlier, *interoperability* is the capability of two or more computer systems to share data and resources, even though they are made by different manufacturers. Businesses today use a variety of systems that have resulted in diverse operating environments. This diversity has inundated businesses with the lack of interoperability. With SOA, a business can create solutions that draw on functionality from these existing, previously isolated systems that are portable, interoperable, or both, regardless of the environment in which they exist.

A *web service* is an open-standards way of supporting interoperability. Web services are application programming interfaces (API) that can be accessed over a network, such as the Internet, and executed on a remote system hosting the requested services. SOA is a style of architecture that enables the creation of applications that are built by combining loosely coupled and interoperable services. In SOA, since the basic unit of communication is a message rather than an operation, web services are usually loosely coupled. Although SOA can exist without web services, the best-practice implementation of SOA for flexibility always involves web services.

Technically, web services are based on *Extensible Markup Language (XML)*, a markup language for documents, containing structured information. The technical specifics of XML's capabilities go beyond the scope of this book, but for our purposes, they support things such as ebusiness transactions, mathematical equations, and a thousand other kinds of structured data. XML is a common data representation that can be used as the medium of exchange between programs that are written in different programming languages and execute different kinds of machine instructions. In simple terms, think about XML as the official translator for structured information. Structured information is both the content (word, picture, and so on) and the role it plays. XML is the basis for all web service technologies and the key to interoperability; every web service specification is based on XML.

Loose Coupling

Part of the value of SOA is that it is built on the premise of loose coupling of services. *Loose coupling* is the capability of services to be joined on demand to create composite services or disassembled just as easily into their functional components. Loose coupling is a way of ensuring that the technical details such as language, platform, and so on are decoupled from the service. For example, look at currency conversion. Today all banks have multiple currency converters, all with different rate refreshes at different times. By creating a common service, conversion of currency, that is loosely coupled to all banking functions that require conversion, the rates, times, and samplings can be averaged to ensure floating the treasury in the most effective manner possible. Another example is common customer identification. Most businesses lack a common customer ID and, therefore, have no way to determine who the customers are and what they buy for what reason. Creating a common customer ID that is independent of applications and databases allows loosely coupling the service, customer ID, to data and applications without the application or database ever knowing who it is or where it is.

The difference between traditional, tightly bound interactions and loosely coupled services is that, before the transaction occurs, the functional pieces (services) operating within the SOA are dormant and disconnected. When the business process initiates, these services momentarily interact with each other. They do so for just long enough to execute their piece of the overall process, and then they go back to their dormant state, with no long-standing connection to the other services with which they just interacted.

The next time the same service is called, it could be as part of a different business process with different calling and destination services. A great way to understand this is through the analogy of the telephone system. At the dawn of widespread phone usage, operators had to plug in a wire physically to create a semipermanent connection between two parties. Callers were "tightly bound" to each other. Today you pick up your cell phone and put it to your ear, and there's no dial tone—it's disconnected. You enter a number and push "Talk," and only then does the process initiate, establishing a loosely coupled connection just long enough for your conversation. Then when the conversation is over, your cell phone goes back to dormant mode until a new connection is made with another party. As a result, supporting a million cell phone subscribers does not require the cell phone service provider to support a million live connections; it requires supporting only the number of simultaneous conversations at any given time. It allows for a much more flexible and dynamic exchange.

LEARNING OUTCOMES

9.4 Explain project management and identify the primary reasons projects fail.

9.5 Identify the primary project planning diagrams.

9.6 Identify the three types of outsourcing along with their benefits and challenges.

USING PROJECT MANAGEMENT TO DELIVER SUCCESSFUL PROJECTS

No one would think of building an office complex by turning loose 100 construction teams to build 100 rooms with no single blueprint or agreed-upon vision of the completed structure. Yet this is precisely the situation in which many large organizations find themselves when managing information technology projects. Organizations routinely overschedule their resources (human and otherwise), develop redundant projects, and damage profitability by investing in nonstrategic efforts that do not contribute to the organization's bottom line. Business leaders face a rapidly moving and unforgiving global marketplace that will force them to use every possible tool to sustain competitiveness; project management is one of those tools. For this reason, business personnel must anticipate being involved in some form of project management during their career. Figure 9.17 displays a few examples of the different types of projects organizations encounter.

Tangible benefits are easy to quantify and typically measured to determine the success or failure of a project. *Intangible benefits* are difficult to quantify or measure (see Figure 9.18 for examples). One of the most difficult decisions managers make is identifying the projects in which to invest time, energy, and resources. An organization must choose what it wants to do—justifying it, defining it, and listing expected results—and how to do it, including project budget, schedule, and analysis of project risks. *Feasibility* is the measure of the tangible and intangible

LO 9.4: Explain project management and identify the primary reasons projects fail.

FIGURE 9.17

Types of Organizational Projects

(left): ©John Giustina/Getty Images RF; (left-middle): ©George Doyle/Getty Images RF; (middle): ©iStockphoto.com/teekid RF; (right-middle): ©Ingram Publishing RF; (right): ©Image Source RF

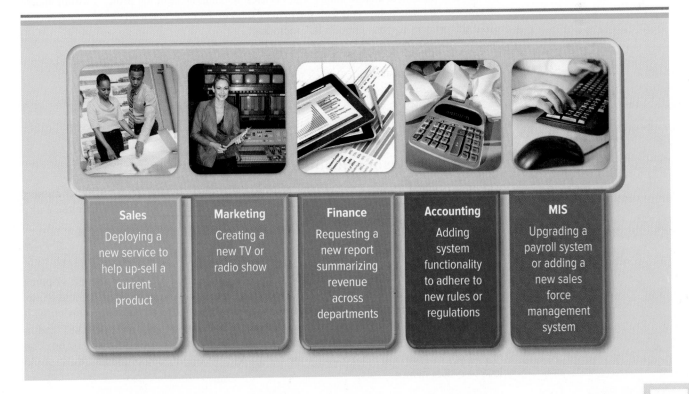

Sales	Marketing	Finance	Accounting	MIS
Deploying a new service to help up-sell a current product	Creating a new TV or radio show	Requesting a new report summarizing revenue across departments	Adding system functionality to adhere to new rules or regulations	Upgrading a payroll system or adding a new sales force management system

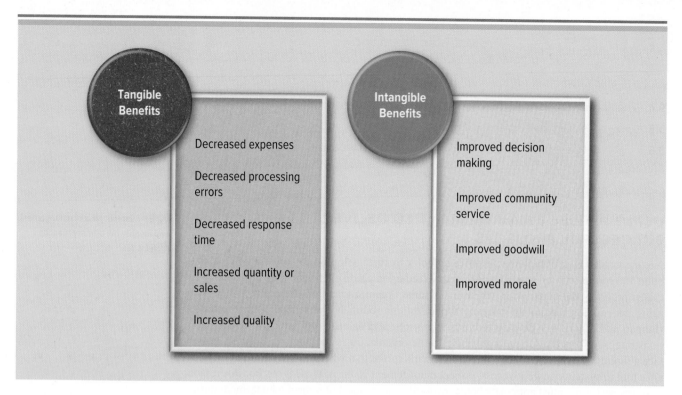

FIGURE 9.18

Examples of Tangible and Intangible Benefits

benefits of an information system. Figure 9.19 displays several types of feasibility studies business analysts can use to determine the projects that best fit business goals.

With today's volatile economic environment, many businesses are being forced to do more with less. Businesses today must respond quickly to a rapidly changing business environment by continually innovating goods and services. Effective project management provides a controlled way to respond to changing market conditions, to foster global communications, and to provide key metrics to enable managerial decision making. Developing projects within budget and on time is challenging, and with the help of solid project management skills, managers can avoid the primary reasons projects fail, including:

- Unclear or missing business requirements.
- Skipped SDLC phases.
- Changing technology.
- The cost of finding errors.
- Balance of the triple constraints.

Unclear or Missing Business Requirements

The most common reason systems fail is because the business requirements are either missing or incorrectly gathered during the analysis phase. The business requirements drive the entire system. If they are not accurate or complete, the system will not be successful.

Skipped Phases

The first thing individuals tend to do when a project falls behind schedule is to start skipping phases in the SDLC. For example, if a project is three weeks behind in the development phase, the project manager might decide to cut testing from six weeks to three weeks. Obviously, it is impossible to perform all the testing in half the time. Failing to test the system will lead to unfound errors, and chances are high that the system will fail. It is critical for an organization to perform all phases in the SDLC during every project. Skipping any of the phases is sure to lead to system failure.

FIGURE 9.19

Types of Feasibility Studies

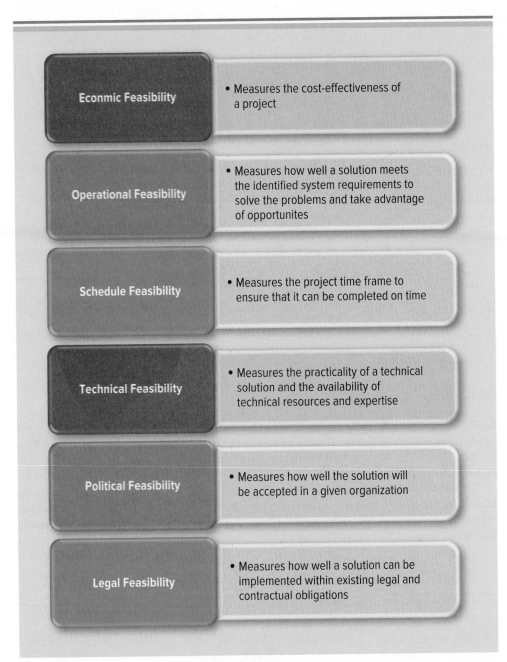

Econmic Feasibility	• Measures the cost-effectiveness of a project
Operational Feasibility	• Measures how well a solution meets the identified system requirements to solve the problems and take advantage of opportunites
Schedule Feasibility	• Measures the project time frame to ensure that it can be completed on time
Technical Feasibility	• Measures the practicality of a technical solution and the availability of technical resources and expertise
Political Feasibility	• Measures how well the solution will be accepted in a given organization
Legal Feasibility	• Measures how well a solution can be implemented within existing legal and contractual obligations

Changing Technology

Many real-world projects have hundreds of business requirements, take years to complete, and cost millions of dollars. As Moore's law states, technology changes at an incredibly fast pace; therefore, it is possible that an entire project plan will need to be revised in the middle of a project as a result of a change in technology. Technology changes so fast that it is almost impossible to deliver an information system without feeling the pain of updates.

The Cost of Finding Errors in the SDLC

It is important to discuss the relationship between the SDLC and the cost for the organization to fix errors. An error found during the analysis and design phase is relatively inexpensive to fix. All that is typically required is a change to a Word document. However, exactly the same error found during the testing or implementation phase will cost the organization an enormous amount to fix because it has to change the actual system. Figure 9.20 displays how the cost to fix an error grows exponentially the later the error is found in the SDLC.

FIGURE 9.20

The Cost of Fixing Errors

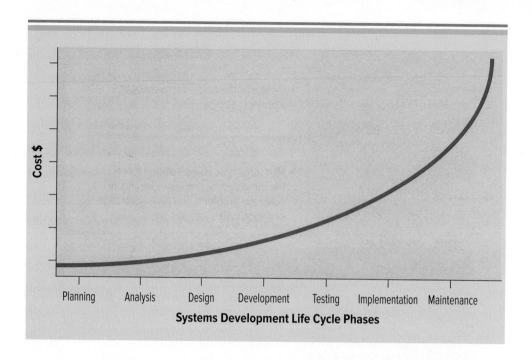

Systems Development Life Cycle Phases

Balance of the Triple Constraint

Figure 9.21 displays the relationships among the three primary and interdependent variables in any project—time, cost, and scope. All projects are limited in some way by these three constraints. The Project Management Institute calls the framework for evaluating these competing demands *the triple constraint*.

The relationship among these variables is such that if any one changes, at least one other is likely to be affected. For example, moving up a project's finish date could mean either increasing costs to hire more staff or decreasing the scope to eliminate features or functions. Increasing a project's scope to include additional customer requests could extend the project's time to

FIGURE 9.21

The Triple Constraint: Changing One Changes All

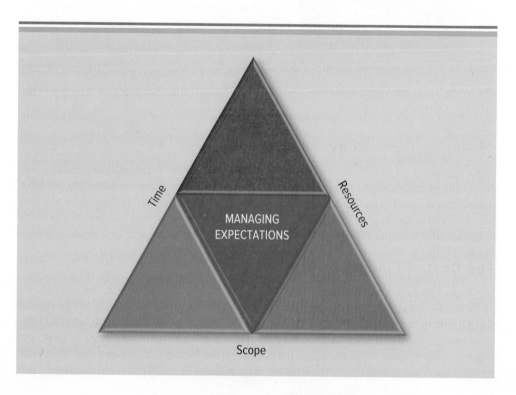

Tool	Description
Communication plan	Defines the how, what, when, and who regarding the flow of project information to stakeholders and is key for managing expectations.
Executive sponsor	The person or group who provides the financial resources for the project.
Project assumption	Factors considered to be true, real, or certain without proof or demonstration. Examples include hours in a workweek or time of year the work will be performed.
Project constraint	Specific factors that can limit options, including budget, delivery dates, available skilled resources, and organizational policies.
Project deliverable	Any measurable, tangible, verifiable outcome, result, or item that is produced to complete a project or part of a project. Examples of project deliverables include design documents, testing scripts, and requirements documents.
Project management office (PMO)	An internal department that oversees all organizational projects. This group must formalize and professionalize project management expertise and leadership. One of the primary initiatives of the PMO is to educate the organization on techniques and procedures necessary to run successful projects.
Project milestone	Represents key dates when a certain group of activities must be performed. For example, completing the planning phase might be a project milestone. If a project milestone is missed, then chances are the project is experiencing problems.
Project objectives	Quantifiable criteria that must be met for the project to be considered a success.
Project requirements document	Defines the specifications for product/output of the project and is key for managing expectations, controlling scope, and completing other planning efforts.
Project scope statement	Links the project to the organization's overall business goals. It describes the business need (the problem the project will solve) and the justification, requirements, and current boundaries for the project. It defines the work that must be completed to deliver the product with the specified features and functions, and it includes constraints, assumptions, and requirements—all components necessary for developing accurate cost estimates.
Project stakeholder	Individuals and organizations actively involved in the project or whose interests might be affected as a result of project execution or project completion.
Responsibility matrix	Defines all project roles and indicates what responsibilities are associated with each role.
Status report	Periodic reviews of actual performance versus expected performance.

FIGURE 9.22

PMBOK Elements of Project Management

completion or increase the project's cost—or both—to accommodate the changes. Project quality is affected by the project manager's ability to balance these competing demands. High-quality projects deliver the agreed-upon product or service on time and on budget. Project management is the science of making intelligent trade-offs between time, cost, and scope. Benjamin Franklin's timeless advice— *by failing to prepare, you prepare to fail* —applies to many of today's software development projects.

The Project Management Institute created the *Project Management Body of Knowledge (PMBOK)* for the education and certification of project managers. Figure 9.22 summarizes the key elements of project planning according to *PMBOK*.

PRIMARY PROJECT PLANNING DIAGRAMS

LO 9.5: Identify the primary project planning diagrams.

Project planning is the process of detailed planning that generates answers to common operational questions such as why we are doing this project or what the project will accomplish for the business. Some of the key questions project planning can help answer include:

- How are deliverables being produced?
- What activities or tasks need to be accomplished to produce the deliverables?
- Who is responsible for performing the tasks?
- What resources are required to perform the tasks?
- When will the tasks be performed?

- How long will it take to perform each task?
- Do any tasks depend on other tasks being completed before they can begin?
- How much does each task cost?
- What skills and experience are required to perform each task?
- How is the performance of the task being measured including quality?
- How are issues being tracked?
- How is change being addressed?
- How is communication occurring and when?
- What risks are associated with each task?

The project objectives are among the most important areas to define because they are essentially the major elements of the project. When an organization achieves the project objectives, it has accomplished the major goals of the project and the project scope is satisfied. Project objectives must include metrics so that the project's success can be measured. The metrics can include cost, schedule, and quality metrics. Figure 9.23 lists the SMART criteria—useful reminders about how to ensure that the project has created understandable and measurable objectives.

The project plan is a formal, approved document that manages and controls project execution. The project plan should include a description of the project scope, a list of activities, a schedule, time estimates, cost estimates, risk factors, resources, assignments, and responsibilities. In addition to these basic components, most project professionals also include contingency plans, review and communications strategies, and a *kill switch* —a trigger that enables a project manager to close the project before completion.

A good project plan should include estimates for revenue and strategic necessities. It also should include measurement and reporting methods and details for how top leadership will engage in the project. It also informs stakeholders of the benefits of the project and justifies the investment, commitment, and risk of the project as it relates to the overall mission of the organization.

Managers need to monitor projects continuously to measure their success. If a project is failing, the manager must cancel the project and save the company any further project costs.

FIGURE 9.23

SMART Criteria for Successful Objective Creation

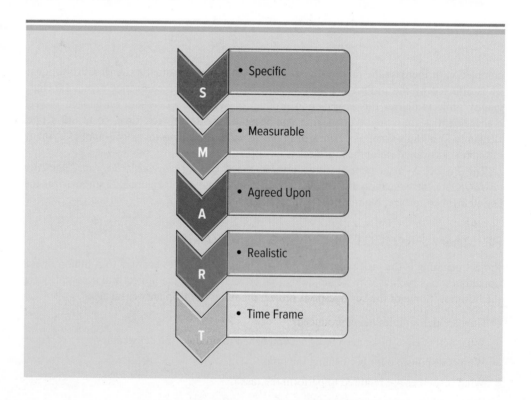

- Specific
- Measurable
- Agreed Upon
- Realistic
- Time Frame

S
M
A
R
T

BUSINESS DRIVEN MIS

SharePoint

Life is good when you can complete all your projects by the due date and under budget. Life is not good when you miss your deadlines, exceed your budget, and fail to meet the business requirements. One tool that can help ensure that your life always stays good is Microsoft SharePoint. With SharePoint, you can connect with employees enterprisewide to collaborate, share ideas, and reinvent the way work flows. Whether working as a team or an individual, SharePoint helps you organize information, people, and projects. SharePoint can make any manager's life easier by organizing teamwork around common milestones. You can make sure that work is completed by assigning people tasks that can be tracked and prioritized. You can keep an eye on important details with real-time summaries of your projects that warn you about delays and keep next steps and milestones on your radar. Explain why using a project management/collaboration tool such as SharePoint can help ensure that you never fail as a manager. Be sure to explain any project management terms such as deliverables, dependencies, and milestones.[9]

Canceling a project is not necessarily a failure as much as it is successful resource management because it frees resources that can be used on other projects that are more valuable to the firm.

The most important part of the plan is communication. The project manager must communicate the plan to every member of the project team and to any key stakeholders and executives. The project plan must also include any project assumptions and be detailed enough to guide the execution of the project. A key to achieving project success is earning consensus and buy-in from all key stakeholders. By including key stakeholders in project plan development, the project manager allows them to have ownership of the plan. This often translates to greater commitment, which in turn results in enhanced motivation and productivity. The two primary diagrams most frequently used in project planning are PERT and Gantt charts.

A *dependency* is a logical relationship that exists between the project tasks, or between a project task and a milestone. A *PERT (Program Evaluation and Review Technique) chart* is a graphical network model that depicts a project's tasks and the relationships between them. PERT charts define dependency between project tasks before those tasks are scheduled. A *critical path analysis* is a project diagramming method used to predict total project duration. This important tool will help ensure you complete your project on-time and within your budget. A *critical path* for a project is the series of activities that determine the earliest time by which the project can be completed. In other words, it represents the longest path through the project and the maximum amount of time it will take you to finish. *Slack* is the amount of time an activity may be delayed without delaying a succeeding activity or the project finish date. The critical path has the least amount of slack. There are normally several tasks done in parallel on projects, and most projects have multiple paths they can take to complete the project. You are not finished with the project until you have finished all the tasks. The longest path or path containing the critical tasks is what is driving the completion date for the entire project. Figure 9.24 displays the critical path for the project.

A *Gantt chart* is a simple bar chart that lists project tasks vertically against the project's time frame, listed horizontally. A Gantt chart works well for representing the project schedule. It also shows actual progress of tasks against the planned duration. Figure 9.25 displays a software development project using a Gantt chart.

FIGURE 9.24

Critical Path Example

FIGURE 9.25

Microsoft Project, a Gantt Chart Example

Source: Microsoft

OUTSOURCING PROJECTS

LO 9.6: Identify the three types of outsourcing along with their benefits and challenges.

In the high-speed global business environment, an organization needs to increase profits, grow market share, and reduce costs. Two basic options are available to organizations wishing to develop and maintain their information systems: in-sourcing or outsourcing.

In-sourcing (in-house development) uses the professional expertise within an organization to develop and maintain its information technology systems. In-sourcing has been instrumental in creating a viable supply of IT professionals and in creating a better quality workforce combining both technical and business skills.

Outsourcing is an arrangement by which one organization provides a service or services for another organization that chooses not to perform them in-house. In some cases, the entire MIS department is outsourced, including planning and business analysis as well as the design, development, and maintenance of equipment and projects. Outsourcing can range from a large contract under which an organization such as IBM manages all MIS services for another company, to hiring contractors and temporary staff on an individual basis. Common reasons companies outsource include:

- **Core competencies.** Many companies have recently begun to consider outsourcing as a way to acquire best-practices and the business process expertise of highly skilled technology resources for a low cost. Technology is advancing at such an accelerated rate that companies often lack the technical resources required to keep current.

- **Financial savings.** It is far cheaper to hire people in China and India than pay the required salaries for similar labor in the United States.

- **Rapid growth.** Firms must get their products to market quickly and still be able to react to market changes. By taking advantage of outsourcing, an organization can acquire the resources required to speed up operations or scale to new demand levels.

- **The Internet and globalization.** The pervasive nature of the Internet has made more people comfortable with outsourcing abroad as India, China, and the United States become virtual neighbors.

Outsourcing MIS enables organizations to keep up with market and technology advances—with less strain on human and financial resources and more assurance that the IT infrastructure will keep pace with evolving business priorities (see Figure 9.26). The three forms of outsourcing options available for a project are:

1. *Onshore outsourcing* —engaging another company within the same country for services.

2. *Nearshore outsourcing* —contracting an outsourcing arrangement with a company in a nearby country. Often this country will share a border with the native country.

3. *Offshore outsourcing* —using organizations from developing countries to write code and develop systems. In offshore outsourcing, the country is geographically far away.

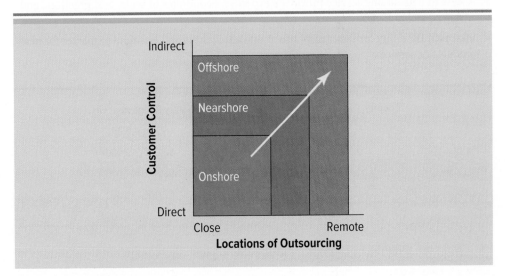

FIGURE 9.26

Outsourcing Models

BUSINESS DRIVEN INNOVATION

Scratch

Scratch is a visual programming language that is perfect for anyone learning to code. Scratch creates programs by connecting blocks of code by using a drag-and-drop GUI so users do not have to type programming languages. Users can simply select colored blocks of code that, when joined, create a script or a set of computer instructions that can make objects such as people and animals move and speak. Users can create interactive stories, games, and animations with the click of a button.

Scratch is a free project created by the Lifelong Kindergarten Group at the MIT Media Lab and currently has more than 8 million users. The goal of Scratch is to help young people learn to think creatively, reason systematically, and work collaboratively—essential skills for life in the 21st century.[10]

In a group, visit the Scratch website at http://scratch.mit.edu/. What type of system development methodology is Scratch using? What skills can young people learn from creating Scratch programs?

Since the mid-1990s, major U.S. companies have been sending significant portions of their software development work offshore—primarily to vendors in India but also to vendors in China, eastern Europe (including Russia), Ireland, Israel, and the Philippines. The big selling point for offshore outsourcing is inexpensive but good work. The overseas counterpart to an American programmer who earns as much as $63,000 per year is paid as little as $5,000 per year (see Figure 9.27). Developing countries in Asia and South Africa offer some outsourcing services but are challenged by language difference, inadequate telecommunication equipment, and regulatory obstacles. India is the largest offshore marketplace because it promotes English along with a technologically advanced population. Infosys, NIIT, Mahindra Satyam, Tata Consultancy Services, and Wipro are among the biggest Indian outsourcing service providers, each of which has a large presence in the United States.[11]

Outsourcing Benefits

The many benefits associated with outsourcing include:

- Increased quality and efficiency of business processes.
- Reduced operating expenses for head count and exposure to risk for large capital investments.
- Access to outsourcing service provider's expertise, economies of scale, best practices, and advanced technologies.
- Increased flexibility for faster response to market changes and less time to market for new products or services.

FIGURE 9.27

Typical Salary Ranges for Computer Programmers

Country	Salary Range per Year
China	$5,000–9,000
India	$6,000–10,000
Philippines	$6,500–11,000
Russia	$7,000–13,000
Ireland	$21,000–28,000
Canada	$25,000–50,000
United States	$60,000–90,000

BUSINESS DRIVEN GLOBALIZATION

DUI in a Golf Cart

Swedish police stopped Bill Murray and charged him with drunk driving when he attempted to drive his golf cart around the city. A golf cart hits top speed at 3 miles per hour, and although it might seem odd that you can be issued a DUI for driving one, many countries have laws against such practices. A few other culture blunders you want to avoid include the following:

- One American company learned that the name of the cooking oil they were marketing translated as "jackass oil" in Spanish.

- A deodorant marketing campaign displayed images of a strong, courageous man washing his dog. The campaign failed in Islamic countries, where dogs are considered unclean.

- A sports equipment company packaged golf balls in groups of four for sales throughout Japan. Sales plummeted because the word *four* pronounced in Japanese sounds the same as the word for *death* and items packaged in fours are considered unlucky.[12]

Companies that are expanding globally are looking for opportunities, not problems. Yet local laws and procedures that come into play when setting up shop abroad—everything from hiring and firing to tax filings—can be a minefield. What types of culture, language, and legal issues should a company expect to encounter when dealing with outsourcing to another country? What can a company do to mitigate these risks?

Outsourcing Challenges

Outsourcing comes with several challenges. These arguments are valid and should be considered when a company is thinking about outsourcing. Many challenges can be avoided with proper research. The challenges include:

- **Length of contract.** Most companies look at outsourcing as a long-term solution with a time period of several years. Training and transferring resources around the globe is difficult and expensive; hence, most companies pursuing offshore outsourcing contract for multiple years of service. The following are a few of the challenges facing the length of the contract:

  1. It can be difficult to break the contract.
  2. Forecasting business needs for the next several years is challenging, and the contract might not meet future business needs.
  3. Recreating an internal MIS department if the outsource provider fails is costly and challenging.

- **Threat to competitive advantage.** Many businesses view MIS as a competitive advantage and view outsourcing as a threat because the outsourcer could share the company's trade secrets.

- **Loss of confidentiality.** Information on pricing, products, sales, and customers can be a competitive asset and often critical for business success. Outsourcing could place confidential information in the wrong hands. Although confidentiality clauses contained in the contracts are supposed to protect the company, the potential risk and costs of a breach must be analyzed.

Every type of organization in business today relies on software to operate and solve complex problems or create exciting opportunities. Software built correctly can support nimble organizations and transform with them as they and their businesses transform. Software that effectively meets employee needs will help an organization become more productive and enhance decision making. Software that does not meet employee needs might have a damaging effect on productivity and can even cause a business to fail. Employee involvement in software development, along with the right implementation, is critical to the success of an organization.

BUSINESS DRIVEN DISCUSSION

Death March

Edward Yourdon's book *Death March* describes the complete software developer's guide to surviving "mission impossible" projects. MIS projects are challenging, and project managers are expected to achieve the impossible by pulling off a successful project even when pitted against impossible challenges. In *Death March,* famous software developer Edward Yourdon presents his project classification displayed here. Yourdon measures projects based on the level of pain and chances for success.

- **Mission Impossible Project:** This project has a great chance of success, and your hard work will pay off as you find happiness and joy in the work. For example, this is the type of project where you work all day and night for a year and become the project hero as you complete the mission impossible and reap a giant promotion as your reward.

- **Ugly Project:** This project has a high chance of success but is very painful and offers little happiness. For example, you work day and night to install a new accounting system, and although successful, you hate accounting and dislike the company and its products.

- **Kamikaze Project:** This is a project that has little chance of success, but you are so passionate about the content that you find great happiness working on the project. For example, you are asked to build a website to support a cancer foundation, a cause near to your heart, but the company is nonprofit and doesn't have any funds to help buy the software you need to get everything working. You patch the system together and implement many manual work-arounds just to keep the system functioning.

- **Suicide Project:** This project has no chance of success and offers you nothing but pain. This is the equivalent of your worst nightmare project. Word of caution: avoid suicide projects![13]

Analyze your school and work projects and find a project that would fit in each box. What could you have done differently on your suicide project to ensure its success? What can you do to avoid being placed on a suicide project? Given the choice, which type of project would you choose to work on and why?

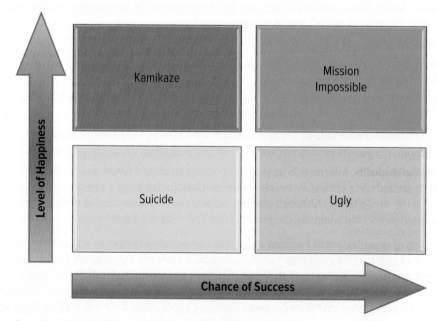

Source: From Edward Yourdon, *Death March,* 2nd edition, Prentice Hall, 2004.

Learning Outcome 9.1: Describe the seven phases of the systems development life cycle.

The seven phases in the SDLC are:

- Planning—involves establishing a high-level plan of the intended project and determining project goals.

- Analysis—involves analyzing end-user business requirements and refining project goals into defined functions and operations of the intended system.

- Design—involves describing the desired features and operations of the system, including screen layouts, business rules, process diagrams, pseudocode, and other documentation.

- Development—involves transforming all the detailed design documents from the design phase into the actual system.

- Testing—involves bringing all the project pieces together into a special testing environment to test for errors, bugs, and interoperability and verifying that the system meets all the business requirements defined in the analysis phase.

- Implementation—involves placing the system into production so users can begin to perform actual business operations with the system.

- Maintenance—involves performing changes, corrections, additions, and upgrades to ensure that the system continues to meet the business goals.

Learning Outcome 9.2: Summarize the different software development methodologies.

The oldest and the best known project management methodology is the waterfall methodology, a sequence of phases in which the output of each phase becomes the input for the next. In the SDLC, this means the steps are performed one at a time, in order, from planning through implementation and maintenance. The traditional waterfall method no longer serves most of today's development efforts, however; it is inflexible and expensive, and it requires rigid adherence to the sequence of steps. Its success rate is only about 1 in 10.

There are a number of software development methodologies:

- Agile methodology aims for customer satisfaction through early and continuous delivery of useful software components developed by an iterative process with a design point that uses the bare minimum requirements.

- Waterfall methodology follows an activity-based process in which each phase in the SDLC is performed sequentially from planning through implementation and maintenance.

- Rapid application development (RAD) methodology emphasizes extensive user involvement in the rapid and evolutionary construction of working prototypes of a system to accelerate the systems development process.

- Extreme programming (XP) methodology breaks a project into tiny phases, and developers cannot continue on to the next phase until the first phase is complete.

- Rational unified process (RUP) provides a framework for breaking down the development of software into four gates.

- Scrum uses small teams to produce small pieces of deliverable software by using sprints, or 30-day intervals, to achieve an appointed goal.

Learning Outcome LO 9.3 Explain why a company would implement a service-oriented architecture.

Service-oriented architecture (SOA) is a business-driven enterprise architecture that supports integrating a business as linked, repeatable activities, tasks, or services. SOA ensures that MIS systems can adapt quickly, easily, and economically to support rapidly changing business needs. SOA promotes a scalable and flexible enterprise architecture that can implement new or reuse existing MIS components, creating connections among disparate applications and systems. It is important to understand that SOA is not a concrete architecture; it is a way of thinking that leads to a concrete architecture.

Learning Outcome 9.4: Explain project management and identify the primary reasons projects fail.

A project is a temporary or short-term endeavor undertaken to create a unique product, service, or result, such as developing a custom ecommerce site or merging databases. Project management is the application of knowledge, skills, tools, and techniques to project activities to meet project requirements. A project manager is an individual who is an expert in project planning and management, defines and develops the project plan, and tracks the plan to ensure that the project is completed on time and on budget. The primary reasons projects fail include unclear or missing business requirements, skipped phases, changing technology, the cost of finding errors in the SDLC, and imbalance of the triple constraints.

Learning Outcome 9.5: Identify the primary project planning diagrams.

A PERT (Program Evaluation and Review Technique) chart is a graphical network model that depicts a project's tasks and the relationships between those tasks. A dependency is a logical relationship that exists between the project tasks or between a project task and a milestone. A Gantt chart is a simple bar chart that depicts project tasks against a calendar. In a Gantt chart, tasks are listed vertically and the project's time frame is listed horizontally. A Gantt chart works well for representing the project schedule. It also shows actual progress of tasks against the planned duration.

Learning Outcome 9.6: Identify the three types of outsourcing along with their benefits and challenges.

- Onshore outsourcing—engaging another company within the same country for services.
- Nearshore outsourcing—contracting an outsourcing arrangement with a company in a nearby country.
- Offshore outsourcing—using organizations from developing countries to write code and develop systems.

The many benefits associated with outsourcing include increased quality and efficiency of a process, service, or function; reduction of operating expenses and exposure to risks involved with large capital investments; and access to the outsourcing service provider's expertise, economies of scale, best practices, and advanced technologies. Outsourcing comes with several challenges, including length of contracts, losing competitive advantages, and risking a breach of confidential information.

OPENING CASE QUESTIONS

1. **Knowledge:** What are the three interdependent variables shaping project management? Why are these variables important to a video game software development project?

2. **Comprehension:** If you were consulting to a business that wanted to build a video game for the iPhone, which development methodology would you recommend and why?

3. **Application:** Illustrate the triple constraints role when building a new game. Why is the cost of finding errors important to a business when developing and designing video games?

4. **Analysis:** What is a prototype and why would a new game benefit from building one?

5. **Synthesis:** Which phase in the systems development life cycle is the most critical when building a video game? Which phase in the systems development life cycle is the least critical when building a video game?

6. **Evaluate:** What are the ethical and security issues associated with outsourcing the development of a video game to India or China?

Agile methodology 390
Alpha testing 386
Analysis phase 381
Brainstorming 379
Bugs 385
Business requirement 381
Change agent 379
Communication plan 399
Computer-aided software engineering (CASE) 382
Control objects for information and related technology (COBIT) 385
Conversion 379
Corrective maintenance 388
Critical path 401
Critical path analysis 401
Data flow diagram (DFD) 382
Dependency 401
Design phase 382
Development phase 384
Development testing 386
Discovery prototyping 389
Executive sponsor 399
Extensible Markup Language (XML) 394
Extreme programming (XP) methodology 391
Feasibility 395
Fourth-generation languages (4GL) 385
Gantt chart 401
Help desk 387
Implementation phase 386
Interoperability 394
Intangible benefits 395
Integration testing 386
In-sourcing (in-house development) 403

Iterative development 390
Joint application development 382
Kill switch 400
Legacy system 379
Loose coupling 394
Maintenance phase 388
Methodology 388
Nearshore outsourcing 403
Object-oriented languages 385
Offshore outsourcing 403
Off-the-shelf application software 379
Online training 387
Onshore outsourcing 403
Outsourcing 403
Parallel implementation 387
PERT (Program Evaluation and Review Technique) chart 401
Phased implementation 387
Pilot implementation 387
Planning phase 379
Plunge implementation 387
Preventive maintenance 388
Process modeling 382
Programming language 385
Project 380
Project assumption 399
Project constraint 399
Project deliverable 399
Project management 380
Project management office (PMO) 399
Project manager 381
Project milestone 399
Project objectives 399
Project plan 381
Project requirements document 399

Project scope 381
Project scope statement 399
Project stakeholder 399
Prototyping 389
Pseudocode 384
Rapid application development (RAD) methodology (also called rapid prototyping) 390
Rational unified process (RUP) methodology 391
Requirements definition document 381
Requirements management 381
Responsibility matrix 399
Scripting language 385
Scrum methodology 391
Service 393
Service-oriented architecture (SOA) 391
Sign-off 381
Slack 401
Software customization 379
Software engineering 385
Status report 399
Systems development life cycle (SDLC) 379
System testing 386
Tangible benefits 395
Test conditions 385
Testing phase 385
Unit testing 386
User acceptance testing (UAT) 386
User documentation 386
Waterfall methodology 388
Web service 394
Workshop training 387

1. What role does project management play in the systems development effort?

2. What role does the project manager play in determining a project's success?

3. Why would a project require an executive sponsor?

4. Which phase in the systems development life cycle is the most important?

5. If you had to skip a phase during the development of a system, which phase would it be and why?

6. Which phase in the systems development life cycle contains the most risk? Be sure to explain your answer.

7. Which project management methodology would you choose to run your software development project?

8. If you started on a new software development project and the project plan was using the waterfall methodology, would you remain on the project? What could you do to prepare your project better for success?

9. Explain the different types of feasibility studies a project manager can use to prioritize project importance.

10. Why should end users be involved in the systems development effort?

11. Why would a project manager use Gantt and PERT charts?

12. Why is gathering business requirements a challenge for most projects?

13. What are the different types of outsourcing available for a project?

14. What are the risks associated with outsourcing?

15. Explain the goals of the Project Management Institute and identify three key terms associated with *PMBOK*.

CLOSING CASE ONE

Disaster at Denver International Airport

One good way to learn how to develop successful systems is to review past failures. One of the most infamous system failures is Denver International Airport's (DIA) baggage system. When the automated baggage system design for DIA was introduced, it was hailed as the savior of modern airport design. The design relied on a network of 300 computers to route bags and 4,000 cars to carry luggage across 21 miles of track. Laser scanners were to read bar-coded luggage tags, and advanced scanners tracked the movement of toboggan-like baggage carts.

When DIA finally opened its doors for reporters to witness its revolutionary baggage handling system, the scene was rather unpleasant. Bags were chewed up, lost, and misrouted in what has since become a legendary systems nightmare.

One of the biggest mistakes made in the baggage handling system fiasco was that not enough time was allowed to develop the system properly. In the beginning of the project, DIA assumed it was the responsibility of individual airlines to find their own way of moving the baggage from the plane to the baggage claim area. The automated baggage system was not involved in the initial planning of the DIA project. By the time the DIA developers decided to create an integrated baggage system, the time frame for designing and implementing such a complex and huge system was not possible.

Another common mistake that occurred during the project was that the airlines kept changing their business requirements. This caused numerous issues, including the implementation of power supplies that were not properly updated for the revised system design, which caused overloaded motors and mechanical failures. Besides the power supply design problem, the optical sensors did not read the bar codes correctly, causing issues with baggage routing.

Finally, BAE, the company that designed and implemented the automated baggage system for DIA, had never created a baggage system of this size before. BAE had created a similar system in an airport in Munich, Germany, where the scope was much smaller. Essentially, the baggage system had an inadequate IT infrastructure because it was designed for a much smaller system.

DIA simply could not open without a functional baggage system so the city had no choice but to delay the opening date for more than 16 months, costing taxpayers roughly $1 million per day, which totaled around $500 million.[14]

Questions

1. One problem with DIA's baggage system was inadequate testing. Why is testing important to a project's success? Why do so many projects decide to skip testing?

2. Evaluate the different systems development methodologies. Which one would have most significantly increased the chances of the project's success?

3. How could more time spent in the analysis and design phase have saved Colorado taxpayers hundreds of millions of dollars?

4. Why could BAE not take an existing IT infrastructure and simply increase its scale and expect it to work?

CLOSING CASE TWO

Reducing Ambiguity in Business Requirements

The main reason projects fail is bad business requirements. Business requirements are considered bad because of ambiguity or insufficient involvement of end users during analysis and design.

A requirement is unambiguous if it has the same interpretation for all parties. Different interpretations by different participants will usually result in unmet expectations. Here is an example of an ambiguous requirement and an example of an unambiguous requirement:

Ambiguous requirement: The financial report must show profits in local and U.S. currencies.

Unambiguous requirement: The financial report must show profits in local and U.S. currencies, using the exchange rate printed in *The Wall Street Journal* for the last business day of the period being reported.

Ambiguity is impossible to prevent completely because it is introduced into requirements in natural ways. For example:

- Requirements can contain technical implications that are obvious to the IT developers but not to the customers.

- Requirements can contain business implications that are obvious to the customer but not to the IT developers.

- Requirements may contain everyday words whose meanings are "obvious" to everyone, yet different for everyone.

- Requirements are reflections of detailed explanations that may have included multiple events, multiple perspectives, verbal rephrasing, emotion, iterative refinement, selective emphasis, and body language—none of which are captured in the written statements.

Tips for Reviewing Business Requirements

When reviewing business requirements, always look for the following words to help reduce ambiguity dramatically:

- *And* and *or* have well-defined meanings and ought to be completely unambiguous, yet they are often understood only informally and interpreted inconsistently. For example, consider the statement "The alarm must ring if button T is pressed and if button F is pressed." This statement may be intended to mean that to ring the alarm, both buttons must be pressed, or it may be intended to mean that either one can be pressed. A statement like this should never appear in a requirement because the potential for misinterpretation is too great. A preferable approach is to be very explicit; for example, "The alarm must ring if both buttons T and F are pressed simultaneously. The alarm should not ring in any other circumstance."

- *Always* might really mean "most of the time," in which case it should be made more explicit. For example, the statement "We always run reports A and B together" could be challenged with "In other words, there is never any circumstance in which you would run A without B and B without A?" If you build a system with an "always" requirement, you are actually building the system never to run report A without report B. If a user suddenly wants report B without report A, you will need to make significant system changes.

- *Never* might mean rarely, in which case it should be made more explicit. For example, the statement "We never run reports A and B in the same month" could be challenged with, "So that means that if I see that A has been run, I can be absolutely certain that no one will want to run B." Again, if you build a system that supports a "never" requirement, the system users can never perform that requirement. For example, the system would never allow a user to run reports A and B in the same month, no matter what the circumstances.

- Boundary conditions are statements about the line between true and false and do and do not. These statements may or may not be meant to include end points. For example, "We want to use method X when there are up to 10 pages, but method Y otherwise." If you were building this system, would you include page 10 in method X or in method Y? The answer to this question will vary causing an ambiguous business requirement.[15]

Questions

1. Why are ambiguous business requirements the leading cause of system development failures?
2. Why do the words *and* and *or* tend to lead to ambiguous requirements?
3. Research the web and determine other reasons for bad business requirements.
4. What is wrong with the following business requirement: "The system must support employee birthdays because every employee always has a birthday every year"?

CRITICAL BUSINESS THINKING

1. Selecting a Systems Development Methodology

Exus Incorporated is an international billing outsourcing company. Exus currently has revenues of $5 billion, more than 3,500 employees, and operations on every continent. You have recently been hired as the CIO. Your first task is to increase the software development project success rate, which is currently at 20 percent. To ensure that future software development projects are successful, you want to standardize the systems development methodology across the entire enterprise. Currently, each project determines which methodology it uses to develop software.

Create a report detailing three system development methodologies that were covered in this text. Compare each of these methodologies to the traditional waterfall approach. Finally, recommend which methodology you want to implement as your organizational standard. Be sure to highlight any potential roadblocks you might encounter when implementing the new standard methodology.

2. Understanding Project Failure

You are the director of project management for Stello, a global manufacturer of high-end writing instruments. The company sells to primarily high-end customers, and the average price for one of its fine writing instruments is about $350. You are currently implementing a new customer relationship management system, and you want to do everything you can to ensure a successful systems development effort. Create a document summarizing the primary reasons this project could fail, along with your strategy to eliminate the possibility of system development failure on your project.

3. Missing Phases in the Systems Development Life Cycle

Hello Inc. is a large concierge service for executives operating in Chicago, San Francisco, and New York. The company performs all kinds of services from dog walking to airport transportation. Your manager, Dan Martello, wants to skip the testing phase during the company's financial ERP implementation. He feels that because the system came from a vendor, it should work correctly. Draft a memo explaining the importance of following the SDLC and the ramifications to the business if the financial system is not tested.

4. Refusing to Sign Off

You are the primary client on a large extranet development project. After carefully reviewing the requirements definition document, you are positive that there are missing, ambiguous, inaccurate, and unclear requirements. The project manager is pressuring you for your sign-off because he has already received sign-off from five of your co-workers. If you fail to sign off on the requirements, you are going to put the entire project at risk because the time frame is nonnegotiable. What would you do? Why?

5. Saving Failing Systems

Crik Candle Company manufactures low-end candles for restaurants. The company generates more than $40 million in annual revenues and has more than 300 employees. You are in the middle of a large, multimillion-dollar supply chain management implementation. Your project manager has just come to you with the information that the project might fail for the following reasons:

- Several business requirements were incorrect, and the scope has to be doubled.
- Three developers recently quit.
- The deadline has been moved up a month.

Develop a list of options that your company can follow to ensure that the project remains on schedule and within budget.

6. Explaining Project Management

Prime Time Inc. is a large consulting company that specializes in outsourcing people with project management capabilities and skills. You are in the middle of an interview for a job with Prime Time. The manager performing the interview asks you to explain why managing a project plan is critical to a project's success. The manager also wants you to explain scope creep and feature creep and your tactics for managing them on a project. Finally, the manager wants you to elaborate on your strategies for delivering successful projects and reducing risks. Create a document explaining your answers to these important questions.

7. Applying Project Management Techniques

You have been hired by a medium-sized airline company, Sun Best. Sun Best currently flies more than 300 routes in the East. The company is experiencing tremendous issues coordinating its 3,500 pilots, 7,000 flight attendants, and 2,000 daily flights. Determine how Sun Best could use a Gantt chart to help it coordinate pilots, flight attendants, and daily flights. Using Excel, create a sample Gantt chart highlighting the different types of activities and resources Sun Best could track with the tool.

APPLY YOUR KNOWLEDGE BUSINESS PROJECTS

PROJECT I   Methods Behind Methodologies

Signatures Inc. specializes in producing personalized products such as coffee mugs and pens with company logos. The company generates more than $40 million in annual revenues and has more than 300 employees. The company is in the middle of a large, multimillion-dollar SCM implementation, and it has just hired your project management outsourcing firm to take over the project management efforts.

On your first day, your team is told that the project is failing for the following reasons:

- The project is using the traditional waterfall methodology.
- The SDLC was not followed, and the developers decided to skip the testing phase.
- A project plan was developed during the analysis phase, but the old project manager never updated or followed the plan.

Determine what your first steps would be to get this project back on track.

PROJECT II   The Travel Store

The Travel Store is facing a dilemma because it tripled in size over the past 3 years and finds its online sales escalating beyond a billion dollars. The company is having a hard time continuing with operations because its business processes can't scale to meet the new demand. In the past six months, sales and profits have dropped and the stock price is plummeting.

The Travel Store is determined to take quick and decisive action to restore profitability and improve its credibility in the marketplace. One of its top priorities is to overhaul its inventory management system in an effort to create optimal levels of inventory to support sales demand. This would prevent higher-volume stores from running out of key sale items while also ensuring that lower-sales stores would not be burdened with excess inventory that could be moved only at closeout prices. The company would like to outsource this function but is worried about the challenges of transferring the responsibility of this important business function as well as the issues surrounding confidentiality and scope definition. List the competitive advantages outsourcing could give the Travel Store and recommendations for addressing the company's outsourcing concerns.

PROJECT III   GEM Athletic Center

First Information Corporation is a large consulting company that specializes in systems analysis and design. The company has more than 2,000 employees, and its first-quarter revenues reached $15 million. The company prides itself on maintaining an 85 percent success rate for all project implementations. The primary reason attributed to the unusually high project success rate is the company's ability to define accurate, complete, and high-quality business requirements.

The GEM Athletic Center located in Cleveland, Ohio, is interested in implementing a new payroll system. The current payroll process is manual and takes three employees two days each month to complete. The GEM Athletic Center does not have an IT department and is outsourcing the entire procurement, customization, and installation of the new payroll system to First Information Corporation.

You have been working for First Information for a little over one month. Your team has just been assigned the GEM Athletic Center project, and your first task is to define the initial business requirements for the development of the new payroll system.

  a. Review the testimony of three current GEM Athletic Center accounting employees who detail the current payroll process, along with their wish list for the new system. Figure 9.28 presents the testimonies of Maggie Cleaver, Anne Logan, and Jim Poulos.

  b. Review Closing Case Two, "Reducing Ambiguity in Business Requirements," and highlight several techniques you can use to develop solid business requirements.

  c. After careful analysis, create a report detailing the business requirements for the new system. Be sure to list any assumptions, issues, or questions in your document.

PROJECT IV   Confusing Coffee

Business requirements are the detailed set of business requests that any new system must meet to be successful. A sample business requirement might state, "The system must track all customer sales by product, region, and sales representative." This requirement states what the system must do from the business perspective, giving no details or information about how the system will meet this requirement.

You have been hired to build an employee payroll system for a new coffee shop. Review the following business requirements and highlight any potential issues.

- All employees must have a unique employee ID.

- The system must track employee hours worked based on employee's last name.

- Employees must be scheduled to work a minimum of eight hours per day.

- Employee payroll is calculated by multiplying the employee's hours worked by $7.25.

- Managers must be scheduled to work morning shifts.

- Employees cannot be scheduled to work more than eight hours per day.

- Servers cannot be scheduled to work morning, afternoon, or evening shifts.

- The system must allow managers to change and delete employees from the system.

FIGURE 9.28

Employee Testimonies

Jim Poulos, Director of Sales

Each week I have to review all of the new memberships sold in our club. Each of my seven sales representatives receives $50 from a new sale for the initiation fee. They also receive 10 percent of the type of membership sold. Membership types include:

- Adult, $450/month
- Youth, $300/month
- Family, $750/month
- Senior, $300/month

Each sales representative is also paid $4.50/hour and receives a 25 percent bonus for working overtime and holidays. If the sales representative sells over 200 percent of expected sales, they receive an additional 25 percent bonus on their commissions. If the membership is sold during a promotion, the commission rate decreases. The payroll department uses time sheets to track my sales representatives' hourly pay. I have to sign all time sheets once they are completed by the payroll department. I check my sales representatives' schedule to validate the times on the employee time sheets. I then have to submit a separate listing of each employee and their corresponding commissions for initiation fees and memberships sold. I track all of my sales representatives' vacation and sick time. If they are over their vacation or sick time, I have them sign a form stating that if they quit, they will pay back all negative vacation or sick time.

I would like a system that can automatically calculate commissions and be able to handle sales forecasting and "what if" analysis on my sales representatives' commission rates. I would like to be able to walk up to my sales representatives and tell them that if they sell four more family memberships and one adult, they will receive their bonus. I would also like to be able to design promotions for our best customers. These types of things would really help boost sales at our club.

Maggie Cleaver, Payroll Manager

The first thing I do each week is collect the time sheets. I review each time sheet to ensure that the employee punched in and out correctly. If the employee forgot to clock out, I contact that person's director to find the time that the employee should have clocked out. I then calculate all regular hours, overtime hours, and holiday hours and total these on the time sheet. I also track sick time and vacation time and total these on the time sheet. Once completed, I send the time sheet to the directors of each department for approval.

When I receive the signed time sheets back, I begin to calculate payments. First, I calculate regular pay, then overtime pay, and finally holiday pay. I then add in the sales representatives' commissions, which I receive from the director of sales. I then calculate payment amounts for aerobics instructors because they are paid by class, not by hour. I receive the aerobics class schedule from the fitness coordinator. I then total the entire pay and send a sheet with payment amounts to my co-worker Anne, who calculates taxes. I then calculate all sick time and vacation time and track this in a separate document. I then print labels that state each employee's name, department, and the pay period. I place the labels on a new time sheet, which is returned to the employee punch clock.

I would like a system that automatically tracks employee sick time and vacation time. I would also like a system that can automatically calculate regular pay, overtime pay, and holiday pay. I don't know if there is a system that can validate employee time sheets, but if there is, that would be great.

Anne Logan, Tax Manager

I receive the payment amounts from Maggie. I then calculate all city, state, and federal taxes. I also deduct health benefits and retirement plan benefits. I then cut the check to the employee and the corresponding checks for the taxes to the government. I manually calculate W2s and all quarterly taxes. I'm also responsible for correcting personal information such as a change of address. I'm also responsible for cutting checks if an incorrect amount was issued. I also track amounts owed by employees that have gone over their sick time or vacation time. I also generate checks for all salaried employees.

The part of my job that takes the longest is correlating the total cash debit for all checks and the total amount calculated for all checks. It's amazing how many times these two figures do not match, which indicates that a check was written for the wrong amount.

I would like a system that determines taxes automatically, along with quarterly tax filing statements. I would also like a system that can perform audits.

PROJECT V   Picking Projects

You are a project management contractor attempting to contract work at a large telecommunications company, Hex Incorporated. Your interview with Debbie Fernandez, the senior vice president of IT, went smoothly. The last thing she wants to see from you before she makes her final hiring decision

FIGURE 9.29

CRM Project Plan

_____

Source: Microsoft

is a prioritized list of the following projects. You are sure to land the job if Fernandez is satisfied with your prioritization.

Create a report prioritizing the following projects, and be sure to include the business justifications for your prioritization.

- Upgrade accounting system.
- Develop employee vacation tracking system.
- Enhance employee intranet.
- Cleanse and scrub data warehouse information.
- Performance-test all hardware to ensure 20 percent growth scalability.
- Implement changes to employee benefits system.
- Develop backup and recovery strategy.
- Implement supply chain management system.
- Upgrade customer relationship management system.
- Build executive information system for CEO.

PROJECT VI   Keeping Time

Time Keepers Inc. is a small firm that specializes in project management consulting. You are a senior project manager, and you have recently been assigned to the Tahiti Tanning Lotion account. The Tahiti Tanning Lotion company is currently experiencing a 10 percent success rate (90 percent failure rate) on all internal IT projects. Your first assignment is to analyze one of the current project plans being used to develop a new CRM system (see Figure 9.29).

Review the project plan and create a document listing the numerous errors in the plan. Be sure to provide suggestions on how to fix the errors.

If you are looking for Excel projects to incorporate into your class, try any of the following after reading this chapter.

Project Number	Project Name	Project Type	Plug-In	Focus Area	Project Level	Skill Set	Page Number
9	Security Analysis	Excel	T3	Filtering Data	Intermediate	Conditional Formatting, Autofilter, Subtotal	AYK.7
10	Gathering Data	Excel	T3	Data Analysis	Intermediate	Conditional Formatting, PivotTable	AYK.8
11	Scanner System	Excel	T2	Strategic Analysis	Intermediate	Formulas	AYK.8
12	Competitive Pricing	Excel	T2	Profit Maximization	Intermediate	Formulas	AYK.9
13	Adequate Acquisitions	Excel	T2	Break-Even Analysis	Intermediate	Formulas	AYK.9
15	Assessing the Value of Information	Excel	T3	Data Analysis	Intermediate	PivotTable	AYK.10
16	Growth, Trends, and Forecasts	Excel	T2, T3	Data Forecasting	Advanced	Average, Trend, Growth	AYK.11
18	Formatting Grades	Excel	T3	Data Analysis	Advanced	If, LookUp	AYK.12
22	Turnover Rates	Excel	T3	Data Mining	Advanced	PivotTable	AYK.15
23	Vital Information	Excel	T3	Data Mining	Advanced	PivotTable	AYK.15
24	Breaking Even	Excel	T4	Business Analysis	Advanced	Goal Seek	AYK.16
25	Profit Scenario	Excel	T4	Sales Analysis	Advanced	Scenario Manager	AYK.16

Hardware and Software Basics

APPENDIX A

LEARNING OUTCOMES

A.1 Describe the six major categories of hardware and provide an example of each.

A.2 Identify the different computer categories and explain their potential business uses.

A.3 Identify the two main types of software.

INTRODUCTION

LO A.1: Describe the six major categories of hardware and provide an example of each.

Managers need to determine what types of hardware and software will satisfy their current and future business needs, the right time to buy the equipment, and how to protect their investments. This does not imply that managers need to be experts in all areas of technology; however, building a basic understanding of hardware and software can help them make the right investment choices.

Information technology can be an important enabler of business success and innovation. Information technology can be composed of the Internet, a personal computer, a cell phone that can access the web, a personal digital assistant, or presentation software. All of these technologies help perform specific information processing tasks. There are two basic categories of information technology: hardware and software. *Hardware* consists of the physical devices associated with a computer system. *Software* is the set of instructions the hardware executes to carry out specific tasks. Software, such as Microsoft Excel, and various hardware devices, such as a keyboard and a monitor, interact to create a spreadsheet or a graph. This appendix covers the basics of computer hardware and software, including terminology, characteristics, and the associated managerial responsibilities for building a solid enterprise architecture.

HARDWARE BASICS

In many industries, exploiting computer hardware is key to gaining a competitive advantage. Frito-Lay gained a competitive advantage by using handheld devices to track the strategic placement and sale of items in convenience stores. Sales representatives could track sale price, competitor information, the number of items sold, and item location in the store, all from their handheld device.[1]

A *computer* is an electronic device operating under the control of instructions stored in its own memory that can accept, manipulate, and store data. Figure A.1 displays the two primary components of a computer—hardware and software. A computer system consists of six hardware components (see Figure A.2). Figure A.3 displays how these components work together to form a computer system.

Central Processing Unit

The dominant manufacturers of CPUs today include Intel (with its Celeron and Pentium lines for personal computers) and Advanced Micro Devices (AMD) (with its Athlon series).[2]

The *central processing unit (CPU)* (or *microprocessor*) is the actual hardware that interprets and executes the program (software) instructions and coordinates how all the other hardware devices work together. The CPU is built on a small flake of silicon and can contain the equivalent of several million transistors. CPUs are unquestionably one of the 20th century's greatest technological advances.

A CPU contains two primary parts: control unit and arithmetic/logic unit. The *control unit* interprets software instructions and literally tells the other hardware devices what to do, based on the software instructions. The *arithmetic-logic unit (ALU)* performs all arithmetic operations (for example, addition and subtraction) and all logic operations (such as sorting and comparing numbers). The control unit and ALU perform different functions. The control unit obtains instructions from the software. It then interprets the instructions, decides which tasks other devices perform, and finally tells each device to perform the task. The ALU responds to the control unit and does whatever it dictates, performing either arithmetic or logic operations.

FIGURE A.1

Hardware and Software Overview

HARDWARE

The physical devices associated with a computer system

CENTRAL PROCESSING UNIT

CPU: The computer's "brain"

RAM: Integrated circuits; works with the CPU

INPUT DEVICE

• Keyboard; mouse; scanner

OUTPUT DEVICE

• Monitor; printer; headphones

STORAGE DEVICE

• DVD; memory stick; hard drive

COMMUNICATION DEVICE

• Modem; wireless card

CONNECTING DEVICE

• Cables; USB port

SOFTWARE

The set of instructions the hardware executes to carry out specific tasks

SYSTEM SOFTWARE

Controls how the various tools work together with application software

OPERATING SYSTEM SOFTWARE

• Windows; Mac OS; Linux

UTILITY SOFTWARE

• Antivirus; screen savers; data recovery

APPLICATION SOFTWARE

Performs specific information processing needs

WORD PROCESSING SOFTWARE

• Microsoft Word

SPREADSHEET SOFTWARE

• Microsoft Excel

CPU	• The actual hardware that interprets and executes the program (software) instructions and coordinates how all the other hardware devices work together
Primary Storage	• The computer's main memory, which consists of the random access memory (RAM), the cache memory, and the read-only memory (ROM) that is directly accessible to the central processing unit (CPU)
Secondary Storage	• Equipment designed to store large volumes of data for long-term storage (diskette, CD, DVD, memory stick)
Input Devices	• Equipment used to capture information and commands (mouse, keyboard, scanner)
Output Devices	• Equipment used to see, hear, or otherwise accept the results of information processing requests (monitor, printer, microphone)
Communication Device	• Equipment used to send information and receive it from one location to another (modem, wireless card)

The number of CPU cycles per second determines how fast a CPU carries out the software instructions; more cycles per second means faster processing, and faster CPUs cost more than their slower counterparts. CPU speed is usually quoted in megahertz and gigahertz. *Megahertz (MHz)* is the number of millions of CPU cycles per second. *Gigahertz (GHz)* is the number of billions of CPU cycles per second. Figure A.4 displays the factors that determine CPU speed.

Advances in CPU Design   Chip makers are pressing more functionality into CPU technology. Most CPUs are *complex instruction set computer (CISC) chips*, which is a type of CPU that can recognize as many as 100 or more instructions, enough to carry out most computations directly. *Reduced instruction set computer (RISC) chips* limit the number of instructions the CPU can execute to increase processing speed. The idea of RISC is to reduce the instruction set to the bare minimum, emphasizing the instructions used most of the time and optimizing them for the fastest possible execution. An RISC processor runs faster than a CISC processor.

Primary Storage

Primary storage is the computer's main memory, which consists of the random access memory (RAM), cache memory, and read-only memory (ROM) that is directly accessible to the CPU.

©Fuse/Getty Images RF

©George Doyle/Stockbyte/Getty Images RF

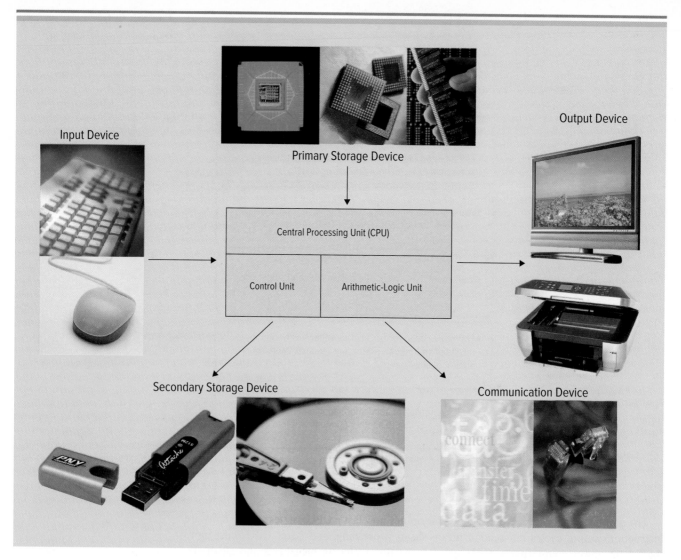

FIGURE A.3

How the Hardware Components Work Together

Random Access Memory *Random access memory (RAM)* is the computer's primary working memory, in which program instructions and data are stored so that they can be accessed directly by the CPU via the processor's high-speed external data bus.

RAM is often called read/write memory. In RAM, the CPU can write and read data. Most programs set aside a portion of RAM as a temporary workspace for data so that one can modify (rewrite) as needed until the data are ready for printing or storage on secondary storage media, such as a hard drive or memory key. RAM does not retain its contents when the power

FIGURE A.4

Factors That Determine CPU Speed

CPU Speed Factors
Clock speed—the speed of the internal clock of a CPU that sets the pace at which operations proceed within the computer's internal processing circuitry.
Word length—number of bits (0s and 1s) that the CPU can process at any one time. Computers work in terms of bits and bytes using electrical pulses that have two states: on and off.
Bus width—the size of the internal electrical pathway along which signals are sent from one part of the computer to another. A wider bus can move more data, hence producing faster processing.
Chip line width—the distance between transistors on a chip. The shorter the chip line width, the faster the chip since more transistors can be placed on a chip and the data and instructions travel shorter distances during processing.

to the computer is switched off; hence, users should save their work frequently. When the computer is turned off, everything in RAM is wiped clean. *Volatility* refers to a device's ability to function with or without power. RAM is *volatile*, meaning it must have constant power to function; its contents are lost when the computer's electric supply fails.

Cache Memory *Cache memory* is a small unit of ultra-fast memory that stores recently accessed or frequently accessed data so that the CPU does not have to retrieve this data from slower memory circuits such as RAM. Cache memory that is built directly into the CPU's circuits is called primary cache. Cache memory contained on an external circuit is called secondary cache.

©Nick Rowe/Getty Images RF

Read-Only Memory *Read-only memory (ROM)* is the portion of a computer's primary storage that does not lose its contents when one switches off the power. ROM is *nonvolatile*, meaning it does not require constant power to function. ROM contains essential system programs that neither the user nor the computer can erase. Since the computer's internal memory is blank during start-up, the computer cannot perform any functions unless given start-up instructions. These instructions are stored in ROM.

Flash memory is a special type of rewritable read-only memory (ROM) that is compact and portable. *Memory cards* contain high-capacity storage that holds data such as captured images, music, or text files. Memory cards are removable; when one is full, the user can insert an additional card. Subsequently, the data can be downloaded from the card to a computer. The card can then be erased and used again. Memory cards are typically used in digital devices such as cameras, cellular phones, and personal digital assistants (PDA). *Memory sticks* provide nonvolatile memory for a range of portable devices, including computers, digital cameras, MP3 players, and PDAs.

Secondary Storage

Storage is a hot area in the business arena as organizations struggle to make sense of exploding volumes of data. *Secondary storage* consists of equipment designed to store large volumes of data for long-term storage. Secondary storage devices are nonvolatile and do not lose their contents when the computer is turned off. Some storage devices, such as a hard disk, offer easy update capabilities and a large storage capacity. Others, such as CD-ROMs, offer limited update capabilities but possess large storage capacities.

Storage capacity is expressed in bytes, with megabytes being the most common. A *megabyte (MB or M or Meg)* is roughly 1 million bytes. Therefore, a computer with 256 MB of RAM translates into the RAM being able to hold roughly 256 million characters of data and software instructions. A *gigabyte (GB)* is roughly 1 billion bytes. A *terabyte (TB)* is roughly 1 trillion bytes (refer to Figure A.5).[3]

A typical double-spaced page of pure text is roughly 2,000 characters. Therefore, a 40 GB (40 gigabyte or 40 billion characters) hard drive can hold approximately 20 million pages of text.

Common storage devices include:

- Magnetic medium
- Optical medium

Magnetic medium *Magnetic medium* is a secondary storage medium that uses magnetic techniques to store and retrieve data on disks or tapes coated with magnetically sensitive materials. Like iron filings

©Keith Eng 2007 RF

Term	Size
Kilobyte (KB)	1,024 bytes
Megabyte (MB)	1,024 KB 1,048,576 bytes
Gigabyte (GB)	1,024 MB (10^9 bytes)
Terabyte (TB)	1,024 GB (10^{12} bytes) 1 TB = Printing of 1 TB would require 50,000 trees to be made into paper and printed.
Petabyte (PB)	1,024 TB (10^{15} bytes) 200 PB = All production of digital magnetic tape in 1995
Exabyte (EB)	1,024 PB (10^{18} bytes) 2 EB = Total volume of information generated worldwide annually 5 EB = All words ever spoken by human beings

on a sheet of waxed paper, these materials are reoriented when a magnetic field passes over them. During write operations, the read/write heads emit a magnetic field that orients the magnetic materials on the disk or tape to represent encoded data. During read operations, the read/write heads sense the encoded data on the medium.

One of the first forms of magnetic medium developed was magnetic tape. *Magnetic tape* is an older secondary storage medium that uses a strip of thin plastic coated with a magnetically sensitive recording medium. The most popular type of magnetic medium is a hard drive. A *hard drive* is a secondary storage medium that uses several rigid disks coated with a magnetically sensitive material and housed together with the recording heads in a hermetically sealed mechanism. Hard drive performance is measured in terms of access time, seek time, rotational speed, and data transfer rate.

A *solid state drive* is an all-electronic storage device that is an alternative to a hard disk and is faster than a hard disk because there is zero latency (no read/write head to move). Instead of storing data magnetically like traditional hard drives, solid state drives store data using flash memory and have no moving parts so they do not need to "spin up" while in a sleep state and they don't need to move a drive head to different parts of the drive to access data. Therefore, solid state drives can access data faster than traditional hard drives and are far more rugged and reliable, offering greater protection in hostile environments.

Optical Medium   Optical medium is a secondary storage medium for computers on which information is stored at extremely high density in the form of tiny pits. The presence or absence of pits is read by a tightly focused laser beam. Optical medium types include:

- **Compact disk-read-only memory (CD-ROM) drive**—an optical drive designed to read the data encoded on CD-ROMs and to transfer this data to a computer.

©Daisuke Morita/Getty Images RF

- **Compact disk-read-write (CD-RW) drive**—an optical drive that enables users to erase existing data and write new data repeatedly to a CD-RW.

- **Digital video disk (DVD)**—a CD-ROM format capable of storing up to a maximum of 17 GB of data; enough for a full-length feature movie.

- **DVD-ROM drive**—a read-only drive designed to read the data encoded on a DVD and transfer the data to a computer.

- **Digital video disk-read/write (DVD-RW)**—a standard for DVD discs and player/recorder mechanisms that enables users to record in the DVD format.

CD-ROMs and DVDs offer an increasingly economical medium for storing data and programs. The overall trend in secondary storage is toward more direct-access methods, higher capacity with lower costs, and increased portability.

Input Devices

An *input device* is equipment used to capture information and commands. A keyboard is used to type in information, and a mouse is used to point and click buttons and icons. A *stylus* is used as a penlike device that taps the screen to enter commands. Numerous input devices are available in many environments, some of which have applications that are more suitable in a personal setting than a business setting. A keyboard, mouse, and scanner are the most common forms of input devices (see Figure A.6).

©Stockbyte/Getty Images RF

New forms of input devices allow people to exercise and play video games at the same time. The Kilowatt Sport from Powergrid Fitness lets people combine strength training with their favorite video games. Players can choose any PlayStation or Xbox game that uses a joystick to run the

FIGURE A.6

Input Devices

MANUAL INPUT DEVICES		AUTOMATED INPUT DEVICES	
KEYBOARD	• Provides a set of alphabetic, numeric, punctuation, symbol, and control keys	IMAGE SCANNER	• Captures images, photos, graphics, and text that already exist on paper
MOUSE	• One or more control buttons housed in a palm-sized case and designed so that one can move it about on the table next to the keyboard	BAR CODE SCANNER	• Captures information that exists in the form of vertical bars whose width and distance apart determine a number
TOUCH PAD	• Form of a stationary mouse on which the movement of a finger causes the pointer on the screen to move; typically found below the space bar on laptops	BIOMETRIC SCANNER	• Captures human physical attributes such as a fingerprint or iris for security purposes
TOUCH SCREEN	• Allows the use of a finger to point at and touch a monitor to execute commands	OPTICAL MARK READER	• Detects the presence or absence of a mark in a predetermined place (popular for multiple-choice exams)
POINTING DEVICE	• Devices used to navigate and select objects on a display screen	OPTICAL CHARACTER READER	• Converts text into digital format for computer input
GAME CONTROLLER	• Devices used for games to obtain better control screen action	DIGITAL STILL CAMERA	• Digitally captures still images in varying resolutions
		DIGITAL VIDEO CAMERA	• Digitally captures video
		WEBCAM	• Digitally captures video and uploads it directly to the Internet
		MICROPHONE	• Captures sounds such as a voice for voice-recognition software
		POINT-OF-SALE (POS)	• Captures information at the point of a transaction, typically in a retail environment

elliptical trainer. After loading the game, participants stand on a platform while pushing and pulling a resistance rod in all directions to control what happens in the game. The varied movement targets muscle groups on the chest, arms, shoulders, abdomen, and back. The machine's display shows information such as pounds lifted and current resistance level, and players can use one-touch adjustment to vary the degree of difficulty.[4] *Adaptive computer devices* are input devices designed for special applications for use by people with different types of special needs. An example is a keyboard with tactile surfaces, which can be used by the visually impaired.

Another new input device is a stationary bicycle. A computer design team of graduate and undergraduate students at MIT built the Cyclescore, an integrated video game and bicycle. The MIT students tested current games on the market but found users would stop pedaling to concentrate on the game. To engage users, the team is designing games that interact with the experience of exercise itself, for example, monitoring heart rate and adjusting the difficulty of the game according to the user's bicycling capabilities. In one game, the player must pedal to make a hot-air balloon float over mountains while collecting coins and shooting at random targets.[5]

Output Devices

An *output device* is equipment used to see, hear, or otherwise accept the results of information processing requests. Among output devices, printers and monitors are the most common; however, speakers and plotters (special printers that draw output on a page) are widely used (see Figure A.7). In addition, output devices are responsible for converting computer-stored information into a form that can be understood.

FIGURE A.7

Output Devices

©Yasuhide Fumoto/Digital Vision/ Getty Images RF

©Stephen VanHorn/Alamy Stock Photo RF

MONITORS		PRINTERS	
CATHODE-RAY TUBE (CRT)	• A vacuum tube that uses an electron gun (cathode) to emit a beam of electrons that illuminates phosphors on a screen as the beam sweeps across the display repeatedly	INK-JET PRINTER	• Printer that makes images by forcing ink droplets through nozzles
LIQUID CRYSTAL DISPLAY (LCD)	• Low-powered displays used in laptop computers where rod-shaped crystal molecules change their orientation when an electrical current flows through them	LASER PRINTER	• Printer that forms images using an electrostatic process, the same way a photocopier works
LIGHT-EMITTING DIODE (LED)	• Tiny bulb used for backlight to improve the image on the screen	MULTIFUNCTION PRINTER	• Printer that can scan, copy, fax, and print all in one device
ORGANIC LIGHT-EMITTING DIODE (OLED)	• Displays use many layers of organic material emitting a visible light and therefore eliminating the need for backlighting	PLOTTER	• Printer that uses computer-directed pens for creating high-quality images, blueprints, schematics, etc.
		3-D PRINTER	• Printer that can produce solid, three-dimensional objects

A new output device based on sensor technology aims to translate American Sign Language (ASL) into speech, enabling the millions of people who use ASL to better communicate with those who do not know the rapid gesturing system. The AcceleGlove is a glove lined on the inside with sensors embedded in rings. The sensors, called accelerometers, measure acceleration and can categorize and translate finger and hand movements. Additional, interconnected attachments for the elbow and shoulder capture ASL signs that are made with full arm motion. When users wear the glove while signing ASL, algorithms in the glove's software translate the hand gestures into words. The translations can be relayed through speech synthesizers or read on a PDA-size computer screen. Inventor Jose L. Hernandez-Rebollar started with a single glove that could translate only the ASL alphabet. Now, the device employs two gloves that contain a 1,000-word vocabulary.[6]

Other new output devices are being developed every day. Needapresent.com, a British company, has developed a vibrating USB massage ball that plugs into a computer's USB port to generate a warm massage for sore body parts during those long evenings spent coding software or writing papers. Needapresent.com also makes a coffee cup warmer that plugs into the USB port.[7]

Communication Devices

A *communication device* is equipment used to send information and receive it from one location to another. A telephone modem connects a computer to a phone line to access another computer. The computer works in terms of digital signals, whereas a standard telephone line works with analog signals. Each digital signal represents a bit (either 0 or 1). The modem must convert the digital signals of a computer into analog signals so they can be sent across the telephone line. At the other end, another modem translates the analog signals into digital signals, which can then be used by the other computer. Figure A.8 displays the different types of modems.

©Ingram Publishing RF

Carrier Technology	Description	Speed	Comments
Dial-up access	On-demand access using a modem and regular telephone line (POT).	2400 bps to 56 Kbps	■ Cheap but slow.
Cable	Special cable modem and cable line required.	512 Kbps to 20 Mbps	■ Must have existing cable access in area. ■ Bandwidth is shared.
DSL (digital subscriber line)	This technology uses the unused digital portion of a regular copper telephone line to transmit and receive information. A special modem and adapter card are required.	128 Kbps to 8 Mbps	■ Doesn't interfere with normal telephone use. ■ Bandwidth is dedicated. ■ Must be within 5 km (3.1 miles) of telephone company switch.
Wireless (LMCS)	Access is gained by connection to a high-speed cellular-like local multipoint communications system (LMCS) network via wireless transmitter/receiver.	30 Mbps or more	■ Can be used for high-speed data, broadcast TV, and wireless telephone service.
Satellite	Newer versions have two-way satellite access, removing the need for a phone line.	6 Mbps or more	■ Bandwidth is not shared. ■ Some connections require an existing Internet service account. ■ Setup fees can range from $500 to $1,000.

FIGURE A.8

Comparing Modems

COMPUTER CATEGORIES

Supercomputers today can hit processing capabilities of well over 200 teraflops—the equivalent of everyone on Earth performing 35,000 calculations per second (see Figure A.9). For the past 20 years, federally funded supercomputing research has given birth to some of the computer industry's most significant technology breakthroughs, including:

- Clustering, which allows companies to chain together thousands of PCs to build mass-market systems.
- Parallel processing, which provides the ability to run two or more tasks simultaneously and is viewed as the chip industry's future.
- Mosaic browser, which morphed into Netscape and made the web a household name.

Federally funded supercomputers have also advanced some of the country's most dynamic industries, including advanced manufacturing, gene research in the life sciences, and real-time financial-market modeling.[8]

Computers come in different shapes, sizes, and colors. And they meet a variety of needs. An *appliance* is a computer dedicated to a single function, such as a calculator or computer game. An *ebook* is an electronic book that can be read on a computer or special reading device. Some are small enough to carry around; others are the size of a telephone booth. Size does not always correlate to power, speed, and price (see Figure A.10).

MIT's Media Lab is developing a laptop that it will sell for $100 each to government agencies around the world for distribution to millions of underprivileged schoolchildren. Using a simplified sales model and reengineering the device helped MIT reach the $100 price point. Almost half the price of a current laptop comprises marketing, sales, distribution, and profit. Of the remaining costs, the display panel and backlight account for roughly half, while the rest covers the operating system. The low-cost laptop will use a display system that costs less than $25, a 500 MHz processor from AMD, a wireless LAN connection, 1 GB of storage, and the Linux operating system. The machine will automatically connect with others. China and Brazil have already ordered 3 million and 1 million laptops, respectively. MIT's goal is to produce around 150 million laptops per year.[9]

SOFTWARE BASICS

Hardware is only as good as the software that runs it. Over the years, the cost of hardware has decreased while the complexity and cost of software have increased. Some large software applications, such as customer relationship management systems, contain millions of lines of code, take years to develop, and cost millions of dollars. The two main types of software are system software and application software.

FIGURE A.9

Supercomputer

©Photodisc/Getty Images RF

Computer Category	Description
Smart phone	A cellular telephone with a keypad that runs programs, music, photos, and email, and includes many features of a PDA.
Personal digital assistant (PDA)	A small, handheld computer that performs simple tasks such as taking notes, scheduling appointments, and maintaining an address book and a calendar. The PDA screen is touch-sensitive, allowing a user to write directly on the screen, capturing what is written.
Handheld (ultra portable, pocket) computer	Computer that is portable enough to fit in a purse or pocket and has its own power source or battery.
Laptop (portable, notebook) computer	Computer that is portable enough to fit on a lap or in a bag and has its own power source or battery. Laptops come equipped with all of the technology that a personal desktop computer has, yet weigh as little as 2 pounds.
Tablet computer	Computer with a flat screen that uses a mouse or fingertip for input instead of a keyboard. Similar to PDAs, tablet PCs use a writing pen or stylus to write notes on the screen and touch the screen to perform functions such as clicking a link while visiting a website.
Personal computer (microcomputer)	Computer that is operated by a single user who can customize the functions to match personal preferences.
Desktop computer	Computer that sits on, next to, or under a user's desk and is too large to carry around. The computer box is where the CPU, RAM, and storage devices are held with a monitor on top, or a vertical system box (called a tower) usually placed on the floor within a work area.
Workstation computer	Similar to a desktop but has more powerful mathematical and graphics processing capabilities and can perform more complicated tasks in less time. Typically used for software development, web development, engineering, and ebusiness tools.
Minicomputer (server)	Designed to meet the computing needs of several people simultaneously in a small to medium-sized business environment. A common type of minicomputer is a server and is used for managing internal company applications, networks, and websites.
Mainframe computer	Designed to meet the computing needs of hundreds of people in a large business environment. Mainframe computers are a step up in size, power, capability, and cost from minicomputers.
Supercomputer	The fastest, most powerful, and most expensive type of computer. Organizations such as NASA that are heavily involved in research and number crunching employ supercomputers because of the speed with which they can process information. Other large, customer-oriented businesses such as General Motors and AT&T employ supercomputers just to handle customer information and transaction processing.

System Software

System software controls how the various technology tools work together along with the application software. System software includes both operating system software and utility software.

Operating System Software   Linus Torvalds, a Finnish programmer, may seem an unlikely choice to be one of the world's top managers. However, Linux, the software project he created while a university student, is now one of the most powerful influences on the computer world. Linux is an operating system built by volunteers and distributed for free and has become one of the primary competitors to Microsoft. Torvalds coordinates Linux development with a few dozen volunteer assistants and more than 1,000 programmers scattered around the globe. They contribute code for the kernel—or core piece—of Linux. He also sets the rules for dozens of technology companies that have lined up behind Linux, including IBM, Dell, Hewlett-Packard, and Intel.

Although basic versions of Linux are available for free, Linux is having a considerable financial impact.[10]

Operating system software controls the application software and manages how the hardware devices work together. When using Excel to create and print a graph, the operating system software controls the process, ensures that a printer is attached and has paper, and sends the graph to the printer along with instructions on how to print it. Some computers are configured with two operating systems so they can *dual boot*—provide the user with the option of choosing the operating system when the computer is turned on. An *embedded operating system* is used in computer appliances and special-purpose applications, such as an automobile, ATM, or media player, that are used for a single purpose. An iPod has a single-purpose, embedded operating system.

Operating system software also supports a variety of useful features, one of which is multitasking. *Multitasking* allows more than one piece of software to be used at a time. Multitasking is used when creating a graph in Excel and simultaneously printing a word processing document. With multitasking, both pieces of application software are operating at the same time. There are different types of operating system software for personal environments and for organizational environments (see Figure A.11).

Utility Software   *Utility software* provides additional functionality to the operating system. Utility software includes antivirus software, screen savers, and antispam software. Operating systems are customized by using the *control panel*, which is a Windows feature that provides options that set default values for the Windows operating system. For example, the *system clock* works like a wristwatch and uses a battery mounted on the motherboard to provide power when the computer is turned off. If the user moves to a different time zone, the system clock can be

FIGURE A.11

Operating System Software

Operating System Software	
Linux	An open source operating system that provides a rich environment for high-end workstations and network servers. Open source refers to any program whose source code is made available for use or modification as users or other developers see fit.
Mac OS X	The operating system of Macintosh computers.
Microsoft Windows	Generic name for the various operating systems in the Microsoft Windows family, including Microsoft Windows CE, Microsoft Windows, Microsoft Windows ME, Microsoft Windows, Microsoft Windows XP, Microsoft Windows NT, and Microsoft Windows Server.
MS-DOS	The standard, single-user operating system of IBM and IBM-compatible computers, introduced in 1981. MS-DOS is a command-line operating system that requires the user to enter commands, arguments, and syntax.
UNIX	A 32-bit multitasking and multiuser operating system that originated at AT&T's Bell Laboratories and is now used on a wide variety of computers, from mainframes to PDAs.

Types of Utility Software	
Crash-proof	Helps save information if a computer crashes.
Disk image for data recovery	Relieves the burden of reinstalling applications if a hard drive crashes or becomes irretrievably corrupted.
Disk optimization	Organizes information on a hard disk in the most efficient way.
Encrypt data	Protects confidential information from unauthorized eyes.
File and data recovery	Retrieves accidental deletion of photos or documents.
Uninstaller	Can remove software that is no longer needed.

adjusted in the control panel. *Safe mode* occurs if the system is failing and will load only the most essential parts of the operating system and will not run many of the background operating utilities. *System restore* enables a user to return to the previous operating system. Figure A.12 displays a few types of available utility software.

Application Software

Application software is used for specific information processing needs, including payroll, customer relationship management, project management, training, and many others. Application software is used to solve specific problems or perform specific tasks. From an organizational perspective, payroll software, collaborative software such as videoconferencing (within groupware), and inventory management software are all examples of application software (see Figure A.13). *Personal information management (PIM) software* handles contact information, appointments, task lists, and email. *Course management software* contains course information such as a syllabus and assignments and offers drop boxes for quizzes and homework, along with a grade book.

Distributing Application Software

After software has been deployed to its users, it is not uncommon to find bugs or additional errors that require fixing. *Software updates (software patch)* occur when the software vendor releases updates to software to fix problems or enhance features. *Software upgrade* occurs when

Types of Application Software	
Browser	Enables the user to navigate the World Wide Web.
Communication	Turns a computer into a terminal for transmitting data to and receiving data from distant computers through the telephone system.
Data management	Provides the tools for data retrieval, modification, deletion, and insertion.
Desktop publishing	Transforms a computer into a desktop publishing workstation.
Email	Provides email services for computer users, including receiving mail, sending mail, and storing messages.
Groupware	Increases the cooperation and joint productivity of small groups of co-workers.
Presentation graphics	Creates and enhances charts and graphs so that they are visually appealing and easily understood by an audience.
Programming	Possesses an artificial language consisting of a fixed vocabulary and a set of rules (called syntax) that programmers use to write computer programs.
Spreadsheet	Simulates an accountant's worksheet on-screen and lets users embed hidden formulas that perform calculations on the visible data.
Word processing	Transforms a computer into a tool for creating, editing, proofreading, formatting, and printing documents.

the software vendor releases a new version of the software, making significant changes to the program. Application software can be distributed using one of the following methods:

- *Single user license*—restricts the use of the software to one user at a time.
- *Network user license*—enables anyone on the network to install and use the software.
- *Site license*—enables any qualified users within the organization to install the software, regardless of whether the computer is on a network. Some employees might install the software on a home computer for working remotely.
- *Application service provider license*—specialty software paid for on a license basis or per-use basis or usage-based licensing.

KEY TERMS

Adaptive computer device A.8
Appliance A.10
Application service provider license A.14
Application software A.13
Arithmetic-logic unit (ALU) A.2
Cache memory A.5
Central processing unit (CPU) (or microprocessor) A.2
Communication device A.9
Complex instruction set computer (CISC) chip A.3
Computer A.2
Control panel A.12
Control unit A.2
Course management software A.13
Dual boot A.12
Ebook A.10
Embedded operating system A.12

Flash memory A.5
Gigabyte (GB) A.5
Gigahertz (GHz) A.3
Hard drive A.6
Hardware A.1
Input device A.7
Magnetic medium A.5
Magnetic tape A.6
Megabyte (MB, M, or Meg) A.5
Megahertz (MHz) A.3
Memory card A.5
Memory stick A.5
Microprocessor A.2
Multitasking A.12
Network user license A.14
Nonvolatile A.5
Operating system software A.12
Output device A.8
Personal information management (PIM) software A.13
Primary storage A.3

Random access memory (RAM) A.4
Read-only memory (ROM) A.5
Reduced instruction set computer (RISC) chip A.3
Safe mode A.13
Secondary storage A.5
Single-user license A.14
Site license A.14
Solid state drive A.6
Software A.1
Software updates (software patch) A.13
Software upgrade A.13
Stylus A.7
System clock A.12
System restore A.13
System software A.12
Terabyte (TB) A.5
Utility software A.12
Volatile A.5
Volatility A.5

APPLY YOUR KNOWLEDGE

PROJECT # 1. A Computer

Dell is considered the fastest company on Earth and specializes in computer customization. Connect to Dell's website at www.dell.com. Go to the portion of Dell's site that allows you to customize either a laptop or a desktop computer. First, choose an already prepared system and note its price and capability in terms of CPU speed, RAM size, monitor quality, and storage capacity. Now, customize that system to increase CPU speed, add more RAM, increase monitor size and quality, and add more storage capacity. What is the difference in price between the two? Which system is more in your price range? Which system has the speed and capacity you need?

PROJECT #   2. Small Business Computers

Many types of computers are available for small businesses. Use the Internet to find three vendors of laptops or notebooks that are good for small businesses. Find the most expensive and the least expensive that the vendor offers and create a table comparing the different computers based on the following:

- CPU
- Memory
- Hard drive
- Optical drive
- Operating system
- Utility software
- Application software
- Support plan

   Determine which computer you would recommend for a small business looking for an inexpensive laptop. Determine which computer you would recommend for a small business looking for an expensive laptop.

Networks and Telecommunications

B

APPENDIX

LEARNING OUTCOMES

B.1 Compare LANs, WANs, and MANs.

B.2 Compare the two types of network architectures.

B.3 Explain topology and the different types found in networks.

B.4 Describe protocols and the importance of TCP/IP.

B.5 Identify the different media types found in networks.

INTRODUCTION

LO B.1: Compare LANs, WANs, and MANs.

Change is everywhere in the information technology domain, but nowhere is change more evident and more dramatic than in the realm of networks and telecommunications. Most management information systems today rely on digital networks to communicate information in the form of data, graphics, video, and voice. Companies large and small from all over the world are using networks and the Internet to locate suppliers and buyers, to negotiate contracts with them, and to provide bigger, better, and faster services than ever before. *Telecommunication systems* enable the transmission of data over public or private networks. A *network* is a communications system created by linking two or more devices and establishing a standard methodology by which they can communicate. The world's largest and most widely used network is the Internet. The Internet is a global network of networks that uses universal standards to connect millions of networks around the world. Telecommunication systems and networks are traditionally complicated and historically inefficient. However, businesses can benefit from today's network infrastructures that provide reliable global reach to employees and customers.

NETWORK BASICS

Networks range from small two-computer networks to the biggest network of all, the Internet. A network provides two principal benefits: the ability to communicate and the ability to share.

Today's corporate digital networks include a combination of local area networks, wide area networks, and metropolitan area networks. A *local area network (LAN)* is designed to connect a group of computers in proximity to each other, such as in an office building, a school, or a home. A LAN is useful for sharing resources such as files, printers, games, or other applications. A LAN in turn often connects to other LANs and to the Internet or wide area networks. A *wide area network (WAN)* spans a large geographic area, such as a state, province, or country. WANs often connect multiple smaller networks, such as local area networks or metropolitan area networks. The world's most popular WAN is the Internet. A *metropolitan area network (MAN)* is a large computer network usually spanning a city. Figure B.1 highlights the three types of networks, and Figure B.2 illustrates each network type.

Direct data communication links between a company and its suppliers or customers, or both, have been successfully used to give the company a strategic advantage. The SABRE airline reservation system is a classic example of a strategic management information system that depends on communication provided through a network. SABRE Airline Solutions pioneered technological advances for the industry in areas such as revenue management, pricing, flight scheduling, cargo, flight operations, and crew scheduling. In addition, not only did SABRE help invent ecommerce for the travel industry, the company also holds claim to progressive solutions that defined—and continue to revolutionize—the travel and transportation marketplace.

A network typically includes four things (besides the computers themselves):

1. **Protocol**—a set of communication rules to make sure that everyone speaks the same language.
2. **Network interface card (NIC)**—a card that plugs into the back (or side) of your computers and lets them send and receive messages from other computers.
3. **Cable**—the medium to connect all of the computers.
4. **Hub (switch or router)**—hardware to perform traffic control.

We will continue to define many of these terms and concepts in the sections that follow. Networks are differentiated by the following:

- Architecture—peer-to-peer, client/server.
- Topology—bus, star, ring, hybrid, wireless.
- Protocols—Ethernet, transmission control protocol/Internet protocol (TCP/IP).
- Media—coaxial, twisted-pair, fiber-optic.

FIGURE B.1

Network Types

Network Types	
Local area network (LAN)	Designed to connect a group of computers in proximity to each other, such as in an office building, a school, or a home. A LAN is useful for sharing resources such as files, printers, games, or other applications. A LAN in turn often connects to other LANs and to the Internet or wide area networks.
Wide area network (WAN)	Spans a large geographic area, such as a state, province, or country. WANs often connect multiple smaller networks, such as local area networks (LANs) or metropolitan area networks (MANs).
Metropolitan area network (MAN)	A large computer network usually spanning a city. Most colleges, universities, and large companies that span a campus use an infrastructure supported by a MAN.

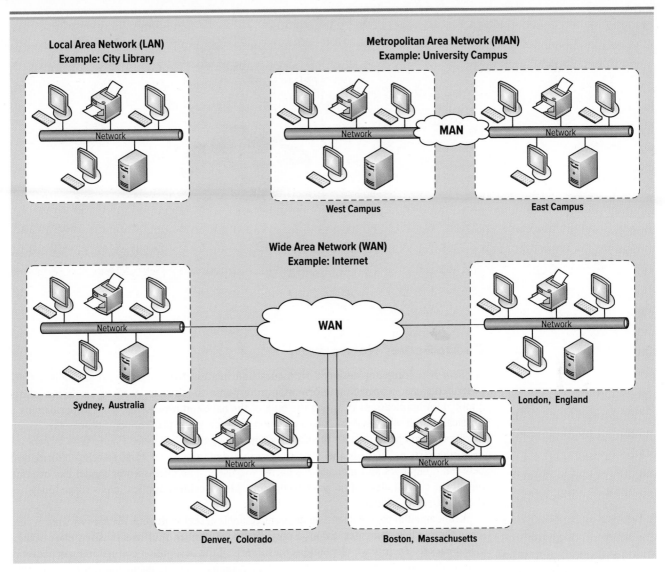

FIGURE B.2

LAN, WAN, and MAN

ARCHITECTURE

The two primary types of network architectures are peer-to-peer networks and client/server networks.

LO B.2: Compare the two types of network architectures.

Peer-to-Peer Networks

A *peer-to-peer (P2P) network* is a computer network that relies on the computing power and bandwidth of the participants in the network rather than a centralized server, as illustrated in Figure B.3. Each networked computer can allow other computers to access its files and use connected printers while it is in use as a workstation without the aid of a server.

Napster may be the most widely known example of a P2P implementation, but it may also be one of the most narrowly focused since the Napster model takes advantage of only one of the many capabilities of P2P computing: file sharing. The technology has far broader capabilities, including sharing processing, memory, and storage, and support of collaboration among vast numbers of distributed computers such as grid computing described in Chapter 5. Peer-to-peer computing enables immediate interaction among people and computer systems.[1]

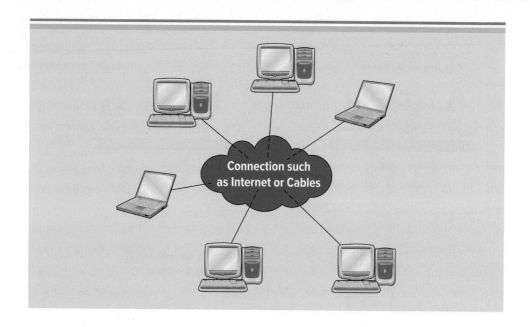

Client/Server Networks

A *client* is a computer designed to request information from a server. A *server* is a computer dedicated to providing information in response to requests. A *client/server network* is a model for applications in which the bulk of the back-end processing, such as performing a physical search of a database, takes place on a server, while the front-end processing, which involves communicating with the users, is handled by the clients (see Figure B.4). A *network operating system (NOS)* is the operating system that runs a network, steering information between computers and managing security and users. The client/server model has become one of the central ideas of network computing. Most business applications written today use the client/server model.

A fundamental part of client/server architecture is packet-switching. *Packet-switching* occurs when the sending computer divides a message into a number of efficiently sized units of data called packets, each of which contains the address of the destination computer. Each packet is sent on the network and intercepted by routers. A *router* is an intelligent connecting device that examines each packet of data it receives and then decides which way to send it onward toward its destination. The packets arrive at their intended destination, although some may have actually traveled by different physical paths, and the receiving computer assembles the packets and delivers the message to the appropriate application.

Network Topologies	
Bus	All devices are connected to a central cable, called the bus or backbone. Bus networks are relatively inexpensive and easy to install for small networks.
Star	All devices are connected to a central device called a hub. Star networks are relatively easy to install and manage, but bottlenecks can occur because all data must pass through a hub.
Ring	All devices are connected to one another in the shape of a closed loop, so that each device is connected directly to two other devices, one on either side of it. Ring topologies are relatively expensive and difficult to install, but they offer high speed and can span large distances.
Hybrid	Groups of star-configured workstations are connected to a linear bus backbone cable, combining the characteristics of the bus and star topologies.
Wireless	Devices are connected by signals between access points and wireless transmitters within a limited range.

TOPOLOGY

LO B.3: Explain topology and the different types found in networks.

Networks are assembled according to certain rules. Cables, for example, have to be a certain length; each cable strand can support only a certain amount of network traffic. A *network topology* refers to the geometric arrangement of the actual physical organization of the computers (and other network devices) in a network. Topologies vary depending on cost and functionality. Figure B.5 highlights the five common topologies used in networks, and Figure B.6 displays each topology.

PROTOCOLS

A *protocol* is a standard that specifies the format of data as well as the rules to be followed during transmission. Simply put, for one computer (or computer program) to talk to another computer (or computer program), they must both be talking the same language, and this language is called a protocol.

A protocol is based on an agreed-upon and established standard, and this way all manufacturers of hardware and software that are using the protocol do so in a similar fashion to allow for interoperability. *Interoperability* is the capability of two or more computer systems to share data and resources, even though they are made by different manufacturers. The most popular network protocols used are Ethernet and transmission control protocol/Internet protocol (TCP/IP).

Ethernet

Ethernet is a physical and data layer technology for LAN networking (see Figure B.7). Ethernet is the most widely installed LAN access method, originally developed by Xerox and then developed further by Xerox, Digital Equipment Corporation, and Intel. When it first began to be widely deployed in the 1980s, Ethernet supported a maximum theoretical data transfer rate of 10 megabits per second (Mbps). More recently, Fast Ethernet has extended traditional Ethernet technology to 100 Mbps peak, and Gigabit Ethernet technology extends performance up to 1,000 Mbps.

Ethernet is one of the most popular LAN technologies for the following reasons:

- Is easy to implement, manage, and maintain.
- Allows low-cost network implementations.
- Provides extensive flexibility for network installation.
- Guarantees interoperability of standards-compliant products, regardless of manufacturer.[2]

FIGURE B.7

Ethernet Protocols

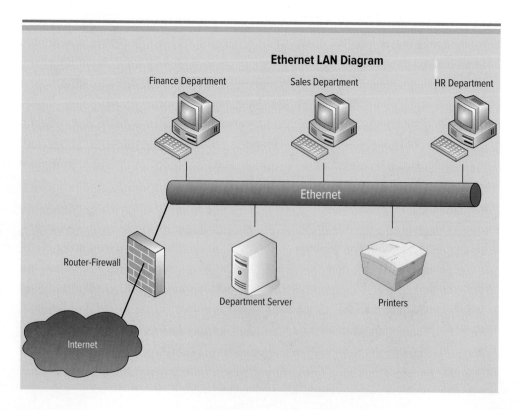

Transmission Control Protocol/Internet Protocol

The most common telecommunication protocol is transmission control protocol/Internet protocol (TCP/IP), which was originally developed by the Department of Defense to connect a system of computer networks that became known as the Internet. *Transmission control protocol/Internet protocol (TCP/IP)* provides the technical foundation for the public Internet as well as for large numbers of private networks. The key achievement of TCP/IP is its flexibility with respect to lower-level protocols. TCP/IP uses a special transmission method that maximizes data transfer and automatically adjusts to slower devices and other delays encountered on a network. Although more than 100 protocols make up the entire TCP/IP protocol suite, the two most important of these are TCP and IP. **TCP** provides transport functions, ensuring, among other things, that the amount of data received is the same as the amount transmitted. **IP** provides the addressing and routing mechanism that acts as a postmaster. Figure B.8 displays TCP/IP's four-layer reference model:

- Application layer—serves as the window for users and application processes to access network services.
- Transport layer—handles end-to-end packet transportation.
- Internet layer—formats the data into packets, adds a header containing the packet sequence and the address of the receiving device, and specifies the services required from the network.
- Network interface layer—places data packets on the network for transmission.[3]

For a computer to communicate with other computers and web servers on the Internet, it must have a unique numeric IP address. IP provides the addressing and routing mechanism that acts as a postmaster. An IP address is a unique 32-bit number that identifies the location of a computer on a network. It works like a street address—as a way to find out exactly where to deliver information.

When IP addressing first came out, everyone thought that there were plenty of addresses to cover any need. Theoretically, you could have 4,294,967,296 unique addresses. The actual number of available addresses is smaller (somewhere between 3.2 and 3.3 billion) due to the way the addresses are separated into classes, and some addresses are set aside for multicasting, testing, or other special uses.[4]

With the explosion of the Internet and the increase in home networks and business networks, the number of available IP addresses is simply not enough. The obvious solution is to redesign the address format to allow for more possible addresses. *Internet protocol version 6 (IPv6)* is the next-generation protocol designed to replace the current version Internet protocol, IP version 4 (IPv4). The main change IPv6 will bring is a much larger address space that allows greater flexibility in assigning addresses. IPv6 uses a 128-bit addressing scheme that produces 3.4×10^{38} addresses.[5]

FIGURE B.8

TCP/IP Four-Layer Reference Model

TCP/IP Applications	
File Transfer Protocol (FTP)	Allows files containing text, programs, graphics, numerical data, and so on to be downloaded off or uploaded onto a network.
Simple Mail Transfer Protocol (SMTP)	TCP/IP's own messaging system for email.
Telnet Protocol	Provides terminal emulation that allows a personal computer or workstation to act as a terminal, or access device, for a server.
Hypertext Transfer Protocol (HTTP)	Allows web browsers and servers to send and receive web pages.
Simple Network Management Protocol (SNMP)	Allows networked nodes to be managed from a single point.

FIGURE B.10

TCP/IP Applications[7]

OSI Model
7. Application
6. Presentation
5. Session
4. Transport
3. Network
2. Data Link
1. Physical

The TCP/IP suite of applications includes five protocols—file transfer, simple mail transfer, telnet, hypertext transfer, and simple network management (see Figures B.9 and B.10).[6]

LO B.5: Identify the different media types found in networks.

MEDIA

Network transmission media refers to the various types of media used to carry the signal between computers. When information is sent across the network, it is converted into electrical signals. These signals are generated as electromagnetic waves (analog signaling) or as a sequence of voltage pulses (digital signaling). To be sent from one location to another, a signal must travel along a physical path. The physical path that is used to carry a signal between a signal transmitter and a signal receiver is called the transmission medium. The two types of transmission media are wire (guided) and wireless (unguided).

Wire Media

Wire media are transmission material manufactured so that signals will be confined to a narrow path and will behave predictably. The three most commonly used types of guided media are (see Figure B.11):

- Twisted-pair cable
- Coaxial cable
- Fiber-optic cable

Twisted-Pair Cable   *Twisted-pair cable* refers to a type of cable composed of four (or more) copper wires twisted around each other within a plastic sheath. The wires are twisted to reduce outside electrical interference. Twisted-pair cables come in shielded and unshielded varieties.

Shielded cables have a metal shield encasing the wires that acts as a ground for electromagnetic interference. Unshielded twisted-pair (UTP) is the most popular and is generally the best option for LAN networks. The quality of UTP may vary from telephone-grade wire to high-speed cable. The cable has four pairs of wires inside the jacket. Each pair is twisted with a different number of twists per inch to help eliminate interference from adjacent pairs and other electrical devices. The connectors (called RF-45) on twisted-pair cables resemble large telephone connectors.[8]

Coaxial Cable   *Coaxial cable* is cable that can carry a wide range of frequencies with low signal loss. It consists of a metallic shield with a single wire placed along the center of a shield and isolated from the shield by an insulator. Coaxial cable is similar to that used for cable television. This type of cable is referred to as coaxial because it contains one copper wire (or physical data channel) that carries the signal and is surrounded by another concentric physical channel consisting of a wire mesh. The outer channel serves as a ground for electrical interference. Because of this grounding feature, several coaxial cables can be placed within a single conduit or sheath without significant loss of data integrity.[9]

Fiber-Optic Cable   *Fiber optic* (or *optical fiber*) refers to the technology associated with the transmission of information as light impulses along a glass wire or fiber. Fiber-optic cable is the same type used by most telephone companies for long-distance service. Fiber-optic cable can transmit data over long distances with little loss in data integrity. In addition, because data are transferred as a pulse of light, fiber optical is not subject to interference. The light pulses travel through a glass wire or fiber encased in an insulating sheath.[10]

Fiber optic's increased maximum effective distance comes at a price. Optical fiber is more fragile than wire, difficult to split, and labor intensive to install. For these reasons, fiber optics is used primarily to transmit data over extended distances where the hardware required to relay the data signal on less expensive media would exceed the cost of fiber-optic installation. It is also used where large amounts of data need to be transmitted on a regular basis.

Wireless Media

Wireless media are natural parts of the Earth's environment that can be used as physical paths to carry electrical signals. The atmosphere and outer space are examples of wireless media that are commonly used to carry these signals. Today, technologies for wireless data transmission include microwave transmission, communication satellites (see Figure B.12), mobile phones, personal digital assistants (PDAs), personal computers (e.g., laptops), and mobile data networks.

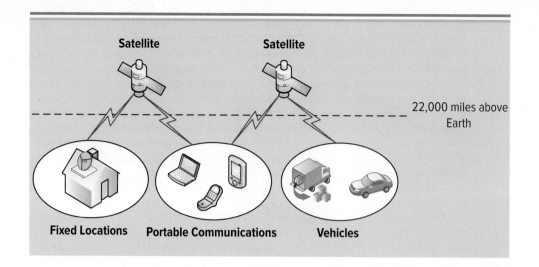

Network signals are transmitted through all media as a type of waveform. When transmitted through wire and cable, the signal is an electrical waveform. When transmitted through fiber-optic cable, the signal is a light wave, either visible or infrared light. When transmitted through the Earth's atmosphere, the signal can take the form of waves in the radio spectrum, including microwaves, infrared, or visible light.

KEY TERMS

Client B.4
Client/server network B.4
Coaxial cable B.9
Ethernet B.6
Fiber optic (or optical
   fiber) B.9
Internet protocol version 6
   (IPv6) B.7
Interoperability B.6
Local area network (LAN) B.2

Metropolitan area network
   (MAN) B.2
Network B.1
Network operating system
   (NOS) B.4
Network topology B.5
Network transmission /
   media B.8
Packet-switching B.4
Peer-to-peer (P2P) network B.3

Protocol B.6
Router B.4
Server B.4
Telecommunication system B.1
Transmission control protocol/
   Internet protocol (TCP/IP) B.7
Twisted-pair cable B.8
Wide area network (WAN) B.2
Wire media B.8
Wireless media B.9

APPLY YOUR KNOWLEDGE

PROJECT # 1. Network Analysis

Global Manufacturing is considering a new technology application. The company wants to process orders in a central location and then assign production to different plants. Each plant will operate its own production scheduling and control system. Data on work in process and completed assemblies will be transmitted back to the central location that processes orders. At each plant, Global uses personal computers that perform routine tasks such as payroll and accounting. The production scheduling and control systems will be a package program running on a new computer dedicated to this application.

The MIS personnel at Global have retained you as a consultant to help with further analysis. What kind of network configuration seems most appropriate? How much bandwidth is needed? What data should be collected? Prepare a plan showing the information Global must develop to establish this network system. Should Global use a private network or can it accomplish its objectives through the Internet?

PROJECT #   2. Secure Access

Organizations that have traditionally maintained private, closed systems have begun to look at the potential of the Internet as a ready-made network resource. The Internet is inexpensive and globally pervasive—every phone jack is a potential connection. However, the Internet lacks security. What obstacles must organizations overcome to allow secure network connections?

PROJECT #   3. Telecommunications Options

Research the telecommunications options that currently exist for you to link to the Internet from where you live. Prepare a list of criteria on which to compare the different technologies, such as price (is there tiered pricing depending on speed and amount you can download?), start-up cost (do you need to buy a special modem, or is there an installation fee?), maximum data transfer rate, and so on. Compare your responses with several classmates and then develop a summary of all telecommunications options that you identified, including the criteria and your group comparison based on the criteria.

PROJECT #   4. Frying Your Brains?

Radio waves, microwaves, and infrared all belong to the electromagnetic radiation spectrum. These terms reference ranges of radiation frequencies we use every day in our wireless networking environments. However, the very word *radiation* strikes fear in many people. Cell towers have sprouted from fields all along highways. Tall rooftops harbor many more cell stations in cities. Millions of cell phone users place microwave transmitters/receivers next to their heads each time they make a call. With all this radiation zapping around, should we be concerned? Research the Internet to find out what the World Health Organization has had to say about this.

PROJECT #   5. Home Network Experience

If you maintain a home computer network (or have set one up in the past), create a document that describes the benefits that the network provides, along with the difficulties that you have experienced. Include in your document a network topology, a detailed description of the type of network you have, and the equipment you use. If you have no experience with home networking, interview someone who does and write up his or her comments. Compare this with several classmates and discuss the benefits and challenges.

Designing Databases

C

APPENDIX

LEARNING OUTCOMES

C.1 Identify the relational database model's basic components.

C.2 Explain the importance of documenting entity relationship diagrams.

C.3 Explain the need for an entity-relationship diagram in a database management system.

INTRODUCTION

LO C.1: Identify the relational database model's basic components.

Businesses rely on databases for accurate, up-to-date information. Without access to mission critical data, most businesses are unable to perform their normal daily functions, much less create queries and reports that help make strategic decisions. For those decisions to be useful, the database must have data that are accurate, complete, consistent, timely, and unique. However, without a good underlying database design, decisions will be inaccurate and inconstant.

A *database* maintains information about various types of objects (inventory), events (transactions), people (employees), and places (warehouses). A *database management system (DBMS)* creates, reads, updates, and deletes data in a database while controlling access and security. A DBMS provides a way to create, update, delete, store, and retrieve data in the database.

Using a data model offers a method for designing a database correctly that will help in meeting the needs of the users in a DBMS environment.

THE RELATIONAL DATABASE MODEL

Numerous elements in a business environment need to store data, and those elements are related to one another in a variety of ways. In fact, a database must contain not only the data but also information about the relationships between those data. Designing a database properly is fundamental to establishing a solid foundation on which to base business decisions. This is done by using a *data model,* or the logical data structures that detail the relationships among data elements using graphics or pictures. A *relational database model* stores information in the form of logically related two-dimensional tables. Tables, or entities as they are formally referred to, will be discussed later.

In developing the relational database model to design a database, an entity-relationship diagram is used. An *entity-relationship diagram (ERD)* is a technique for documenting the entities and relationships in a database environment. Before describing the notation used for developing an ERD, it is important to understand what entities and attributes are.

Entities and Attributes

An *entity* stores information about a person, place, thing, transaction, or event. A customer is an entity, as is a product and an appointment. An *attribute* is the data elements associated with an entity. For example, consider Mega-Video, a physical and online retail store that sells movie DVDs. The company would need to store information about its customers (especially for online purchases) by creating an entity called *CUSTOMER* that contained many attributes such as *Customer Number, First Name, Last Name, Street, City, State, Zip Code, Phone Number,* and *Email* (refer to Figure C.1).

Type of Attributes   There are several types of attributes, including:

- **Simple versus composite.** A simple attribute cannot be broken down into a smaller component. For example, a customer's first name and last name are simple. A composite attribute can be divided into smaller components, which represent more basic attributes that have their own meanings. A common example of a composite attribute is *Address* (see Figure C.2). *Address* can be broken down into a number of subparts, such as *Street, City, State, Zip Code.*

- **Single-valued versus multivalued.** When creating a relational database, the attributes in the data model must be single-valued. *Single-valued attribute* means having only a single value of each attribute of an entity. A person's age is an example of a single-valued attribute because a person cannot have more than one age. *Multivalued attribute* means having the potential to contain more than one value for an attribute. For example, an educational degree of a person is a multivalued attribute because a person can have more than one degree. An entity in a relational database cannot have multivalued attributes; those attributes must be handled by creating another entity to hold them. Therefore, in the example given previously, in designing the database, there would be two entities, one called *PERSON* (or something similar) and one called *DEGREE*. If a multivalued attribute has been identified, it typically is a clue that another entity is needed.

FIGURE C.1

Entities and Attributes Examples

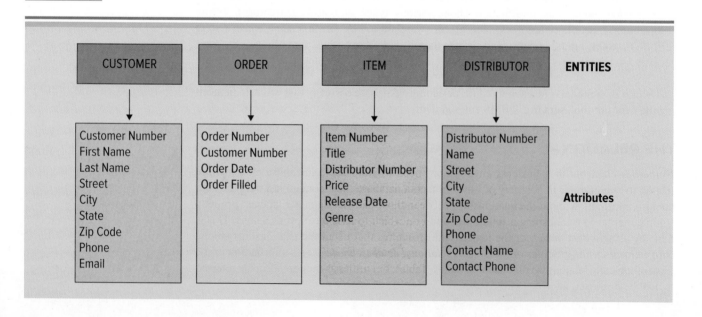

FIGURE C.2

Composite Attributes

- **Stored versus derived.** If an attribute can be calculated using the value of another attribute, it is called a derived attribute. The attribute that is used to derive the attribute is called a stored attribute. Derived attributes are not stored in the file but can be derived when needed from the stored attributes. One example of a derived and stored attribute is a person's age. If the database has a stored attribute such as the person's *Date of Birth,* then a derived attribute called *Age* can be created by subtracting the *Current Date* (this is retrieved from the DBMS) from the *Date of Birth* to get the age.
- **Null-valued.** Sometimes an attribute does not have an applicable value for an attribute. For these situations, the null-valued attribute is created. *Null-valued attribute* is assigned to an attribute when no other value applies or when a value is unknown. A person who does not have a mobile phone would have null stored for the value for the *Mobile Phone Number* attribute. Null can also be used when the attribute value is unknown, such as *Hair Color.* Every person has a hair color, but the information may be missing.

Business Rules

The "correct" design for a specific business depends on the business rules; what is correct for one organization may not be correct for another. A *business rule* is a statement that defines an aspect of a business. It is intended to convey the behavior and rules of a business. The following statements are examples of possible business rules for Mega-Video:

- A customer can purchase many DVDs.
- DVDs can be purchased by many customers.
- A DVD title can have many copies.

A typical business may have hundreds of business rules. Each business rule will have entities and sometimes even attributes in the statements. For instance, in the preceding example, *CUSTOMER* and *DVD* would be entities according to this business rule. Identifying the business rules will help to create a more accurate and complete database design. In addition, the business rules also assist with identifying relationships between entities. This is very useful in creating ERDs.

DOCUMENTING ENTITY RELATIONSHIP DIAGRAMS

LO C.2: Explain the importance of documenting entity relationship diagrams.

Once entities, attributes, and business rules have been identified, the ERD can be documented. The two most commonly used models of ERD documentation are Chen, named after the originator of entity-relationship modeling, Dr. Peter Chen, and information engineering, which grew out of work by James Martin and Clive Finkelstein. It does not matter which is used as long as everyone who is using the diagram understands the notation. For purposes of simplicity, only the Chen model will be described here.

FIGURE C.3

Chen Model with Attributes

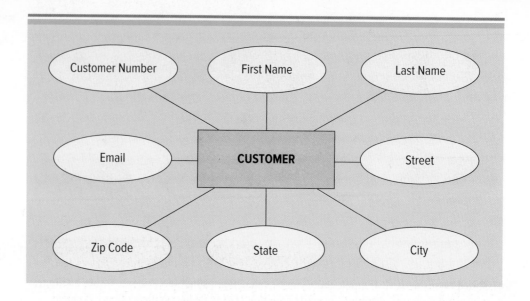

The Chen model notation uses very specific symbols in representing entities and attributes. Rectangles represent entities. Each entity's name appears in the rectangle, is expressed in the singular, and is capitalized, as in *CUSTOMER*. Originally, attributes were not part of the Chen model; however, many database designers have extended it to include the attributes in ovals as illustrated in Figure C.3.

Basic Entity Relationships

One of the main reasons for creating an ERD is to identify and represent the relationships between entities. If the business rules for Mega-Video state that a customer can order many videos (in this case, an item), then a relationship needs to be created between *CUSTOMER, ORDER,* and *ITEM.* This is a purely conceptual representation of what the database will look like and is completely unrelated to the physical storage of the data. Again, what the ERD is doing is creating a model in which to design the database.

The Chen model uses diamonds for relationships and lines to connect relationships between entities. Figure C.4 displays the relationship between a Mega-Video *CUSTOMER* and *ORDER* using this notation. The word within the relationship gives some indication of the meaning of the relationship.

Once the basic entities and their attributes have been defined, the next task is to identify the relationships among those entities. There are three basic types of relationships: (1) one-to-one, (2) one-to-many, and (3) many-to-many.

One-to-One Relationship   A *one-to-one relationship (1:1)* is between two entities in which an instance of one entity can be related to only one instance of a related entity. Consider Mega-Video, which has many stores with several employees and one manager. According to the company's business rules, the manager, who is an employee, can manage only one store. The relationship then becomes 1:1 between *EMPLOYEE* and *STORE.* Using the Chen model notation, as shown in Figure C.5, the relationships between the two instances can then be expressed as "An employee can manage one store and one store has one manager." The

FIGURE C.4

Chen Method with Relationship

FIGURE C.5

A One-to-One Relationship

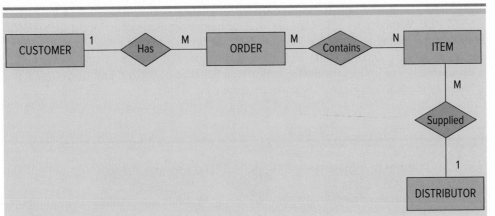

number "1" next to the *EMPLOYEE* and *STORE* entities indicates that only one *EMPLOYEE* manages one *STORE*.

One-to-Many Relationship   Most relational databases are constructed from one-to-many relationships. A ***one-to-many relationship (1:M)*** is between two entities in which an instance of one entity can be related to many instances of a related entity. For example, Mega-Video receives many *ITEM*(s) from one *DISTRIBUTOR,* and each *DISTRIBUTOR* supplies many *ITEM*(s), as Figure C.6 illustrates. Similarly, a *CUSTOMER* can have many *ORDER*(s), but an *ORDER* has only one *CUSTOMER*. These are both examples of a one-to-many relationship. The "M" next to the *ORDER* entity indicates that a *CUSTOMER* can place one or more *ORDER*(s). That notation is also used with *ITEM,* because an *ORDER* can contain one or more *ITEM*(s).

Many-to-Many Relationship   Identifying and removing many-to-many relationships will help to create an accurate and consistent database. A ***many-to-many relationship (M:N)*** is between two entities in which an instance of one entity is related to many instances of another and one instance of the other can be related to many instances of the first entity. There is a many-to-many relationship between a Mega-Video *ORDER* and *ITEM* (refer back to Figure C.6). An *ORDER* can contain many *ITEM*(s), and each *ITEM* can be on many *ORDER*(s). The letter "N" next to *ITEM* in Figure C.6 indicates the many-to-many relationship between *ORDER* and *ITEM.*

However, there are problems with many-to-many relationships. First, the relational data model was not designed to handle many-to-many relationships. This means they need to be replaced with a one-to-many relationship to be used in a relational DBMS. Second, many-to-many relationships will create redundancy in the data that are stored. This then has a negative impact on the accuracy and consistency that a database needs. To understand this problem better, consider the relationship between *ITEM* and *ORDER*. There is a many-to-many relationship between the *ORDER* and the *ITEM* because each *ORDER* can contain many *ITEM*(s) and, over time, each *ITEM* will be on many *ORDER*(s). Whenever a *CUSTOMER* places an *ORDER* for an *ITEM,* the number of *ITEM*(s) varies, depending on how many DVDs the *CUSTOMER* is buying. To break the many-to-many relationship, a composite entity is needed.

FIGURE C.6

A One-to-Many Relationship

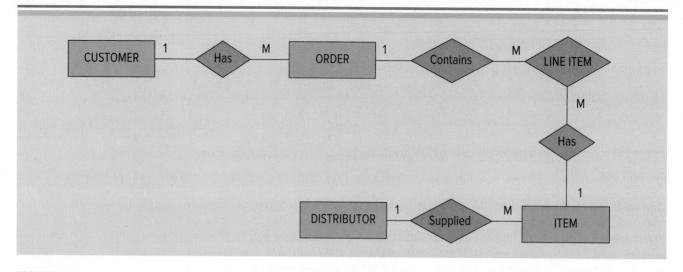

FIGURE C.7

A Composite Entity

Entities that exist to represent the relationship between two other entities are known as *composite entities.* The preceding example needs another entity that breaks up the many-to-many relationship between *ORDER* and *ITEM*. Figure C.7 displays the new relationship.

Creating a composite entity called *LINE ITEM* (think of it as a line item on an invoice slip) breaks up the many-to-many relationship between *ORDER* and *ITEM,* which then eliminates redundancy and other anomalies when deleting or updating information. Using the Chen model, composite entities are documented with a combination of a rectangle and a diamond.

Given the new ERD in Figure C.7, each *ORDER* can contain many *LINE ITEM*(s), but a *LINE ITEM* can belong to only one *ORDER*. As a result, the relationship between *ORDER* and *LINE ITEM* is one-to-many (one order has one or more line items), and the relationship between *LINE ITEM* and *ITEM* is one-to-many (one item can be in many line items). The composite entity has removed the original many-to-many relationship and turned it into two one-to-many relationships.

Relationship Cardinality

Cardinality expresses the specific number of instances in an entity. In the Chen model, the cardinality is indicated by placing numbers beside the entities in the format of (x, y). The first number in the cardinality represents the minimum value and the second number is for the maximum value.

Mega-Video can store data about a *CUSTOMER* in its database before the *CUSTOMER* places an *ORDER*. An instance of the *CUSTOMER* entity does not have to be related to any instance of the *ORDER* entity, meaning there is an optional cardinality.

However, the reverse is not true for the Mega-Video database; an *ORDER must* be related to a *CUSTOMER*. Without a *CUSTOMER,* an *ORDER* cannot exist. An instance of the *CUSTOMER* entity can be related to zero, one, or more *ORDER*(s) using the cardinality notation (0,N). An instance of the *ORDER* entity must be related to one and only one *CUSTOMER,* having a cardinality of (1,1). The relationship between an instance of *ORDER* and *CUSTOMER* is a mandatory relationship. Figure C.8 illustrates these cardinalities.

FIGURE C.8

Example of Cardinalities

RELATIONAL DATA MODEL AND THE DATABASE

LO C.3: Explain the need for an entity-relationship diagram in a database management system.

Once the ERD is completed, it can be translated from a conceptual logical model into the formal data model required by the DBMS. The relational data model is the result of the work of Edgar (E. F.) Codd, a mathematician. During the 1960s, Dr. Codd was working with existing data models when he noticed that data relationships were very inefficient. Using his experience and knowledge in mathematics, he created the relational data model. Most databases, such as Access 2010 and SQL Server 2010, are based on the relational data model.

From Entities to Tables

In creating an ERD for the conceptual model, the focus was on identifying entities and attributes. For the logical relational data model, the attention is on tables and fields. Using the ERD, the entities become tables and attributes turn into fields. A *table* is composed of rows and columns that represent an entity. A *field* is a characteristic of a table. A *record* is a collection of related data elements. The columns in the table definition represent the field, and a row is a record.

At first glance, a table along with the fields and records looks much like information in a spreadsheet, such as that displayed in Figure C.9 of a *CUSTOMER* table.

Fields　Figure C.9 has four fields, *Customer Number, First Name, Last Name,* and *Phone Number.* Two or more tables within the same relational data model may have fields with the same names, but a single table must have unique field names. Using the relational data model notation, the table names are capitalized (e.g., *CUSTOMER*) and all columns are in title case (e.g., Customer Number), as in:
　　CUSTOMER (Customer Number, First Name, Last Name, Phone Number)

Records　A record in a table has the following properties:

- A table cannot have multivalued attributes (as mentioned previously); therefore, only one value is allowed at the intersection of a field and record.
- Each record needs to be unique; there are no duplicate records in a table.
- A record must have an entity identifier, or *primary key,* which is a field (or group of fields), that uniquely identifies a given record in a table.

Primary Key　A primary key makes it possible to identify every record uniquely in a table. The primary key is important to retrieve data accurately from the database.

Using a *Customer Number* as a primary key states that no two customers will ever have the same number. The primary key will be used to identify records associated with it. For example, if someone was searching the Mega-Video database for all the *ITEMS* that a *CUSTOMER* with a *Customer Number* of "112299" bought, he would retrieve only those records and not those associated with another customer.

Along with being unique, a primary key must not contain the value *null.* Recall that null is a special value meaning unknown; however, it is not the same as a field being blank or set to the

FIGURE C.9

A Sample Customer Table

CUSTOMER			
Customer Number	First Name	Last Name	Phone Number
0001	Bill	Miller	777-777-7777
0505	Jane	Cook	444-444-4444
1111	Sam	Smith	555-555-5555
1212	John	Doe	666-666-6666

value of zero. If one record has a null primary key, then the data structure is not in violation. But once a second null value for another record is introduced, the uniqueness of the primary key is lost. Therefore, nulls are forbidden when establishing primary keys.

The proper notation to use when documenting the primary key is to underline it, such as:
CUSTOMER (Customer Number, First Name, Last Name, Phone Number)

Logically Relating Tables

Once the primary key has been defined, tables can be logically related. Each table in Figure C.10 is directly analogous to the entities of the same name in the Mega-Video ERD presented in Figure C.8, excluding the *DISTRIBUTOR*. The *CUSTOMER* table is identified by a Customer Number, a randomly generated unique primary key. The *ORDER* table is identified by an Order Number, another arbitrary unique primary key assigned by Mega-Video. The table *ORDER LINE* tells the company which *ITEM*(s) are part of which *ORDER*. This table requires a concatenated primary key (that is to say, joining two fields that act as one primary key) because multiple *ITEM*(s) can appear on multiple *ORDER*(s). The selection of this primary key, however, has more significance than simply identifying each record; it also represents a relationship among the *ORDER LINES*, the *ORDER* on which they appear, and the *ITEM*(s) being ordered. The primary key for the *ITEM* table is identified by the *Item Number*.

FIGURE C.10

Logically Relating Tables

CUSTOMER

Customer Number	First Name	Last Name	Phone
1111	Sam	Smith	555-555-5555
0505	Jane	Cook	444-444-4444

Primary key →

ORDER   Foreign key

Order Number	Customer Number	Order Date
1000	1111	11/1/2011
1001	1111	11/10/2011
1002	0505	12/11/2011

Primary key

LINE ITEM   Foreign key

Order Number	Item Number	Quantity	Shipped?
1000	9244	1	Y
1001	9244	1	Y
1002	9250	1	Y
1002	9255	1	Y

Foreign key

ITEM

Item Number	Title	Distributor Number	Price
9244	Iron Man 2	002	4.95
9250	Twilight Zone	002	4.95
9255	Avatar	004	5.95

Primary key →

The *Item Number* field in the *ORDER LINE* table is the same as the primary key in the *ITEM* table. This indicates a one-to-many relationship between the two tables. Similarly, there is also a one-to-many relationship between the *ORDER* and *ORDER LINE* tables because the *Order Number* column in the *ORDER LINE* table is the same as the primary key of the *ORDER* table.

When a table contains a field that is the same as the primary key of another table, it is called a foreign key. A *foreign key* is a primary key of one table that appears as an attribute in another table and acts to provide a logical relationship between the two tables. The matching of foreign keys to primary keys represents data relationships in a relational database.

Foreign keys may be a part of a concatenated primary key, as is the case in the *LINE ITEM* table in Figure C.10. By concatenating, or combining, both *Order Number* and *Item Number* in the *LINE ITEM* table as foreign keys, they then become primary keys. However, most foreign keys are not part of the table's primary key. Consider the relation between Mega-Video's *CUSTOMER* and *ORDER* in Figure C.10. The *Customer Number* field in the *ORDER* table is a foreign key that matches the primary key of the *CUSTOMER* table. It represents the one-to-many relationship between *CUSTOMER* and *ORDER*. However, the *Customer Number* is not part of the primary key of the *ORDER* table; it is simply used to create a relationship between the two tables, *CUSTOMER* and *ORDER*.

A relational database uses the relationships indicated by matching data between primary and foreign keys. Assume that a Mega-Video employee wanted to see what *Titles* had been ordered with *Order Number* 1002. First, the database identifies the records in the *LINE ITEM* table that contain an *Order Number* of 1002. Then, it matches them to the *Item Number*(s) in the *ITEM* table. The results are those that match the records from each table.

KEY TERMS

Attributes C.2	Entity C.2	Null-valued attribute C.3
Business rule C.3	Entity-relationship diagram	One-to-many relationship (1:M) C.5
Cardinality C.6	(ERD) C.2	One-to-one relationship (1:1) C.4
Composite entity C.6	Field C.7	Primary key C.7
Data model C.1	Foreign key C.9	Record C.7
Database C.1	Many-to-many relationship	Relational database model C.1
Database management system	(M:N) C.5	Single-valued attribute C.2
(DBMS) C.1	Multivalued attribute C.2	Table C.7

APPLY YOUR KNOWLEDGE

PROJECT #   1. SportTech Events

SportTech Events puts on athletic events for local high school athletes. The company needs a database designed to keep track of the sponsor for the event and where the event is located. Each event needs a description, date, and cost. Separate costs are negotiated for each event. The company would also like to have a list of potential sponsors that includes each sponsor's contact information, such as the name, phone number, and address.

Each event will have a single sponsor, but a particular sponsor may sponsor more than one event. Each location will need an ID, contact person, and phone number. A particular event will use only one location, but a location may be used for multiple events. SportTech asks you to create an ERD from the information described here.

PROJECT #   2. Course and Student Schedules

Paul Bauer, the chair for the information technology (IT) department at the University of Denver, needs to create a database to keep track of all the courses the department offers. In addition to the course information, Bauer would like the database to include each instructor's basic contact information, such as ID number, name, office location, and phone number. Currently, the department has nine instructors (seven full-time faculty and two adjuncts). For each course, Bauer would like to keep track of the course ID, title, and number of credit hours. When courses are offered, the section of the course receives an ID number, and with that number, the department keeps track of which instructor is teaching the course. There is only one instructor per course.

Finally, Bauer needs to be able to keep track of the IT students and to know which courses each student has taken. The information he would like to know about each student includes ID number, name, and phone number. He also needs to know what grade the student receives in each course.

He has asked you to create an ERD from the information described here using the Chen model.

PROJECT #   3. Foothills Athletics

Foothills Athletics is an athletic facility offering services in Highlands Ranch, Colorado. All property owners living in Highlands Ranch are members of the Highlands Ranch Community Association (HRCA), which has partnered with Foothills Athletics to provide recreation facilities for its residents. Foothills Athletics has been using a spreadsheet to keep track of its personnel, facilities, equipment, and the HRCA members. The spreadsheet has created many redundancies along with several anomalies in adding, modifying, and deleting information. One of the HRCA members has suggested that the athletic facility should create a database to improve data collection that will also remove many of the difficulties that the spreadsheet is creating.

Foothills Athletics primary business operations are based on the following:

- **Personnel:** Foothills Athletics has a number of employees, primarily fitness instructors and administrative personnel. Records are kept on each employee, detailing employee name, address, phone number, date of hire, position, and status as either a current or former employee. Employees are assigned a unique four-digit employee ID number when they are hired.

- **Members:** When joining Foothills Athletics, HRCA members are assigned a unique four-digit member ID number. This information along with their name, address, phone number, gender, birth date, and date of membership are recorded. At the time of enrollment, each member decides on one of three available membership types along with a fixed membership fee: Platinum ($400), Gold ($300), and Silver ($200). This is a one-time fee that establishes a lifetime membership.

- **Facilities and equipment:** Foothills Athletics has a variety of facilities and equipment choices. Each facility has a unique room number and a size limitation associated with it. Some of the rooms contain a variety of exercise equipment; all have a serial number that is used for inventory and maintenance purposes. In addition, for each piece of equipment, the purchase date and the date of its last maintenance are recorded. Each piece of equipment belongs to a specific equipment type, such as elliptical machine, and is assigned a unique three-digit identification number. The description, the manufacturer's model number, and the recommended maintenance interval for that model of equipment are also kept on file. Each equipment type is associated with a single manufacturer that is referenced by a unique two-digit manufacturer ID number.

You have been hired to assist Foothills Athletics to create an ERD from the information described here using the Chen model.

PROJECT #   4. Slopeside Ski Rentals

Vail Resort in Vail, Colorado, is internationally known as one of the best places in North America for skiing. Since 1973, Slopeside Ski Rentals has been a tradition in the area. At Slopeside Ski Rentals, customers will find the largest selection of skis, boots, snowboards, clothing, helmets, eyewear, and a variety of other accessories needed for the slopes.

You have been employed by the company for the past three winters. Recently, there has been a surge in business, and the owners need a more accurate way to manage the rental business. You have decided to create a database to help the owners keep track of the ski rentals, who the customers are, amount paid, and any damage to the skis when they are rented. The skis and snowboards vary in type, size, and bindings. When customers rent equipment, they are required to leave their driver's license number and to give a home address, phone number, and credit card number.

A few business rules that you are aware of include:

- A customer can rent one or more skis or snowboards at one time.
- Skis and snowboards can be rented by many customers.
- A ski or snowboard need not be assigned to any customer.

Your job is to develop an ERD from the business rules mentioned here.

Emerging Trends and Technologies

D
APPENDIX

LEARNING OUTCOMES

D.1 Identify the global trends that will have the greatest impact on future business.

D.2 Explain why businesses use trends to assess the future.

D.3 Identify the technologies that will have the greatest impact on future business.

INTRODUCTION

LO D.1: Identify the global trends that will have the greatest impact on future business.

Organizations anticipate, forecast, and assess future events using a variety of rational, scientific methods including:

- *Trend analysis:* A trend is examined to identify its nature, causes, speed of development, and potential impacts.
- *Trend monitoring:* Trends viewed as particularly important in a specific community, industry, or sector are carefully monitored, watched, and reported to key decision makers.
- *Trend projection:* When numerical data are available, a trend can be plotted to display changes through time and into the future.
- *Computer simulation:* Complex systems, such as the U.S. economy, can be modeled by means of mathematical equations, and different scenarios can be run against the model to conduct "what-if" analysis.
- *Historical analysis:* Historical events are studied to anticipate the outcome of current developments.

Foresight is one of the secret ingredients of business success. Foresight, however, is increasingly in short supply because almost everything in our world is changing at a faster pace than ever before. Many organizations have little idea what type of future they should prepare for in this world of hyperchange. Figure D.1 displays the top reasons organizations should look to the future and study trends.

	Top Reasons to Study Trends	
1.	Generate ideas and identify opportunities	Find new ideas and innovations by studying trends and analyzing publications.
2.	Identify early warning signals	Scan the environment for potential threats and risks.
3.	Gain confidence	A solid foundation of awareness about trends can provide an organization with the confidence to take risks.
4.	Beat the competition	Seeing what is coming before others can give an organization the lead time it requires to establish a foothold in the new market.
5.	Understand a trend	Analyzing the details within a trend can help separate truly significant developments from rapidly appearing and disappearing fads.
6.	Balance strategic goals	Thinking about the future is an antidote to a "profit now, worry later" mentality that can lead to trouble in the long term.
7.	Understand the future of specific industries	Organizations must understand everything inside and outside their industry.
8.	Prepare for the future	Any organization that wants to compete in this hyperchanging world needs to make every effort to forecast the future.

LO D.2: Explain why businesses use trends to assess the future.

TRENDS SHAPING OUR FUTURE

According to the World Future Society, the following trends have the potential to change our world, our future, and our lives.

- The world's population will double in the next 40 years.
- People in developed countries are living longer.
- The growth in information industries is creating a knowledge-dependent global society.
- The global economy is becoming more integrated.
- The economy and society are dominated by technology.
- The pace of technological innovation is increasing.
- Time is becoming one of the world's most precious commodities.

The World's Population Will Double in the Next 40 Years

The countries that are expected to have the largest increases in population between 2000 and 2050 are:

- Palestinian Territory—217 percent increase.
- Niger—205 percent increase.
- Yemen—168 percent increase.
- Angola—162 percent increase.
- Democratic Republic of the Congo—161 percent increase.
- Uganda—133 percent increase.

In contrast, developed and industrialized countries are expected to see fertility rates decrease below population replacement levels, leading to significant declines in population (see Figure D.2).

Potential Business Impact

- Global agriculture will be required to supply as much food as has been produced during all of human history to meet human nutritional needs over the next 40 years.
- Developed nations will find that retirees will have to remain on the job to remain competitive and continue economic growth.
- Developed nations will begin to increase immigration limits.

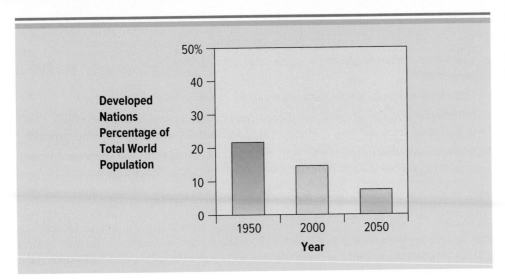

FIGURE D.2

Expected Population Decreases in Developed and Industrialized Nations.

People in Developed Countries Are Living Longer

New pharmaceuticals and medical technologies are making it possible to prevent and cure diseases that would have been fatal to past generations. This is one reason that each generation lives longer and remains healthier than the previous generation. On average, each generation in the United States lives 3 years longer than the previous one. An 80-year-old in 1950 could expect to live 6.5 years longer today. Many developed countries are now experiencing life expectancy over 75 years for males and over 80 years for females (see Figure D.3).

Potential Business Impact

- Global demand for products and services for the elderly will grow quickly in the coming decades.
- The cost of health care is destined to skyrocket.
- Pharmaceutical companies will be pushed for advances in geriatric medicine.

The Growth in Information Industries Is Creating a Knowledge-Dependent Global Society

Estimates indicate that 90 percent of American management personnel are knowledge workers. Estimates for knowledge workers in Europe and Japan are not far behind. Soon, large organizations will be composed of specialists who rely on information from co-workers, customers, and suppliers to guide their actions. Employees will gain new power as they are provided with the authority to make decisions based on the information they acquire.

FIGURE D.3

Rising Life Expectancy in Developed Countries.

Rising Life Expectancy in Developed Countries		
Country	Life Expectancy (Born 1950–1955)	Life Expectancy (Born 1995–2020)
United States	68.9	76.5
United Kingdom	69.2	77.2
Germany	67.5	77.3
France	66.5	78.1
Italy	66.0	78.2
Canada	69.1	78.5
Japan	63.9	80.5

Potential Business Impact

- Top managers must be computer-literate to retain their jobs and achieve success.

- Knowledge workers are generally higher paid, and their proliferation is increasing overall prosperity.

- Entry-level and unskilled positions are requiring a growing level of education.

- Information now flows from front-office workers to higher management for analysis. Thus, in the future, fewer mid-level managers will be required, flattening the corporate pyramid.

- Downsizing, restructuring, reorganization, outsourcing, and layoffs will continue as typical large organizations struggle to reinvent and restructure themselves for greater flexibility.

The Global Economy Is Becoming More Integrated

International outsourcing is on the rise as organizations refuse to pay high salaries for activities that do not contribute directly to the bottom line. The European Union has relaxed its borders and capital controls, making it easier for companies to outsource support functions throughout the continent.

The Internet is one of the primary tools enabling our global economy. One of the primary reasons for the increase in Internet use is the increase in connectivity technology. The increase in Internet use is increasing revenues for ebusinesses.

Potential Business Impact

- Demand for personnel in distant countries will increase the need for foreign-language training, employee incentives suited to other cultures, and many other aspects of performing business globally.

- The growth of ebusiness and the use of the Internet to shop globally for raw materials and supplies will reduce the cost of doing business.

- The Internet will continue to enable small companies to compete with worldwide giants with relatively little investment.

- Internet-based operations require sophisticated knowledge workers, and thus people with the right technical skills will be heavily recruited over the next 15 years.

The Economy and Society Are Dominated by Technology

Computers are becoming a part of our environment. Mundane commercial and service jobs, environmentally dangerous jobs, standard assembly jobs, and even the repair of inaccessible equipment such as space stations will be increasingly performed by robots. Artificial intelligence and expert systems will help most companies and government agencies assimilate data and solve problems beyond the range of today's computers including energy prospecting, automotive diagnostics, insurance underwriting, and law enforcement.

Superconductors operating at economically viable temperatures are now in commercial use. Products eventually will include supercomputers the size of a 3-pound coffee can, electronic motors 75 percent smaller and lighter than those in use today, and power plants.

Potential Business Impact

- New technologies provide dozens of new opportunities to create businesses and jobs.

- Automation will continue to decrease the cost of products and services, making it possible to reduce prices while improving profits.

- The Internet is expected to push prices of most products to the commodity level.

- The demand for scientists, engineers, and technicians will continue to grow.

Pace of Technological Innovation Is Increasing

Technology is advancing at a phenomenal pace. Medical knowledge is doubling every 8 years. Half of what students learn in their freshman year of college about innovative technology is obsolete, revised, or taken for granted by their senior year. In fact, all of today's technical knowledge will represent only 1 percent of the knowledge that will be available in 2050.

Potential Business Impact

- The time to get products and services to market is being shortened by technology. Products must capture their market quickly before the competition can copy them. During the 1940s, the average time to get a product to market was 40 weeks. Today, a product's entire life cycle seldom lasts 40 weeks.

- Industries will face tighter competition based on new technologies. Those who adopt state-of-the-art technology first will prosper, while those who ignore it eventually will fail.

Time Is Becoming One of the World's Most Precious Commodities   In the United States, workers today spend around 10 percent more time on the job than they did a decade ago. European executives and nonunionized workers face the same trend. This high-pressure environment is increasing the need for any product or service that saves time or simplifies life.

Potential Business Impact

- Companies must take an active role in helping their employees balance their time at work with their family lives and need for leisure.

- Stress-related problems affecting employee morale and wellness will continue to grow.

- As time for shopping continues to evaporate, Internet and mail-order marketers will have a growing advantage over traditional stores.

TECHNOLOGIES SHAPING OUR FUTURE

LO D.3: Identify the technologies that will have the greatest impact on future business.

We sit at the center of an expanding set of devices, other people, information, and services that are fluidly and dynamically interconnected. This "digital mesh" surrounds the individual, and new, continuous and ambient experiences will emerge to exploit it. In his session revealing Gartner's Top Strategic Technology Trends at Gartner/Symposium ITxpo 2015 in Orlando, David Cearley, vice president and Gartner Fellow, shared three categories for technology trends: the digital mesh, smart machines, and the new IT reality.

The Digital Mesh

Trend No. 1: The Device Mesh   All devices such as cars, smart phones, appliances, and more are connecting people all over the globe, enabling them to access data, applications, social communities, governments, and businesses. As the mesh of these smart devices continues to evolve, Gartner expects connection models to expand and greater cooperative interaction between devices to emerge. Recall that *virtual reality* is a computer-simulated environment that can be a simulation of the real world or an imaginary world. *Augmented reality* is the viewing of the physical world with computer-generated layers of information added to it. Expect to see amazing developments in wearables and augmented reality, especially, virtual reality.

Trend No. 2: Ambient User Experience   The *ambient digital experience* is a blend of the physical, virtual, and electronic environments creating a real-time ambient environment that changes as the user moves from one place to another. All of our digital interactions can become synchronized into a continuous and ambient digital experience. Users will be able to interact with applications for extended periods of time. Organizations will need to consider their customers' behavior journeys to shift the focus on design from applications to the entire mesh of products and services involved in the user experience.

Trend No. 3: 3D-Printing Materials   *3D printing* builds—layer by layer in an additive process—a three-dimensional solid object from a digital model. To date, 3D printers are generally capable of only printing one type of material at a time. Expect the next generation of 3D printers to be able to mix multiple materials together in one build. Other advances for 3D printing include a wide range of materials such as advanced nickel alloys, carbon fiber, glass, conductive ink, electronics, and even pharmaceuticals and biological materials. *Biological 3D printing* includes the printing of skin and organs and is progressing from theory to reality; however, politicians and the public do not have a full understanding of the implications.

Smart Machines

Trend No. 4: Information of Everything

The *Internet of Things (IoT)* is a world where interconnected Internet-enabled devices or "things" have the ability to collect and share data without human intervention. The *Information of Everything (IoE)* is a concept that extends the Internet of Things emphasis on machine-to-machine communications to describe a more complex system that also encompasses people and processes. IoE encompasses the huge surge of information produced by the digital mesh, including textual, audio, video, sensory and contextual information along with strategies and technologies to link data from all these disparate data sources. The digital mesh surrounds us virtually producing unmeasurable amounts of information. Organizations must learn how to identify what information provides strategic value, how to access data from different sources, and explore how algorithms leverage the information of everything to fuel new business designs.

Trend No. 5: Advanced Machine Learning

Machine learning is a type of artificial intelligence that enables computers to both understand concepts in the environment and also to learn. Machine learning focuses on the development of computer programs that can teach themselves to grow and change when exposed to new data and is responsible for making smart devices appear intelligent. For example, by analyzing vast databases of medical case histories, "learning" machines can reveal previously unknown insights in treatment effectiveness. This area is evolving quickly, and organizations must assess how they can apply these technologies to gain competitive advantage.

Trend No. 6: Autonomous Agents and Things

In the future, people will move through a constant stream of information summoned at the touch of a finger. They will interact with life-size images, data, and text in homes and offices. The days of hunching over a computer will be gone. A *virtual assistant (VA)* will be a small program stored on a PC or portable device that monitors emails, faxes, messages, and phone calls. Virtual assistants will help individuals solve problems in the same way a real assistant would. In time, the VA will take over routine tasks such as writing a letter, retrieving a file, and making a phone call.

An *autonomous agent* is software that carries out some set of operations on behalf of a user or another program with some degree of independence or autonomy and employs some knowledge or representation of the user's goals or desires. Autonomous agent robotic salespeople will take on human appearances and have the ability to perform all tasks associated with a sales job. Robots, vehicles, virtual assistants, and smart advisers acting autonomously feed into the ambient user experience in which an autonomous agent becomes the main user interface. Instead of interacting with a tablet or a smart phone, users will talk directly to an autonomous application, which is really an intelligent agent.

The New IT Reality

Trend No. 7: Adaptive Security Architecture

Real-time adaptive security is the network security model necessary to accommodate the emergence of multiple perimeters and moving parts on the network, and increasingly advanced threats targeting enterprises. The emerging "hacker industry," along with cyberwar and cyberterrorism, have significantly increased the threat surface for an organization. Technology leaders must increase their focus on detecting and responding to threats, as well as more traditional blocking and other measures to prevent attacks.

Trend No. 8: Advanced System Architecture

Autonomic computing is a self-managing computing model named after, and patterned on, the human body's autonomic nervous system. Autonomic computing is one of the building blocks of widespread computing, an anticipated future computing model in which small—even invisible—computers will be all around us, communicating through increasingly interconnected networks. The digital mesh and smart machines require autonomic computing architectures that function more like human brains that are particularly suited to be applied to deep learning and other pattern-matching algorithms. Autonomic architectures will allow distribution with less power into the tiniest IoT endpoints, such as homes, cars, wristwatches, and even human beings.[1]

KEY TERMS

3D printing D.5
Ambient digital experience D.5
Augmented reality D.5
Autonomic computing D.6
Autonomous agent D.6
Biological 3D printing D.6

Computer simulation D.1
Historical analysis D.1
Information of Everything (IoE) D.6
Internet of Things (IoT) D.6
Machine learning D.6
Real-time adaptive security D.6

Trend analysis D.1
Trend monitoring D.1
Trend projection D.1
Virtual assistant (VA) D.6
Virtual reality D.5

APPLY YOUR KNOWLEDGE

PROJECT #   1. Identifying and Following Trends

Hot.com is a new business that specializes in helping companies identify and follow significant trends in their industries. You have recently been hired as a business analyst, and your first task is to highlight current trends in the ebusiness industry. Using the Internet and any other resources you have available, highlight five significant trends not discussed in this text. Prepare a PowerPoint presentation that lists the trends and discusses the potential business impacts for each trend.

PROJECT #   2. NAO Robots

NAO (pronounced *now*) robots are about as cute as anything ever created, and boy, can they dance. A NAO robot is an autonomous, programmable, humanoid robot developed by Aldebaran Robotics, a French robotics company headquartered in Paris. NAO robots have been used for research and education purposes in numerous academic institutions worldwide. As of 2015, over 5,000 NAO units were in use in more than 50 countries. Visit the web to search NAO robot videos and create a new product or service for a NAO robot.

PROJECT #   3. Educational Robots

Robots have always grabbed the attention and imagination of kids (of all ages)! RobotLAB uses this attention to build core 21st century skills such as programming and computational thinking. Using advanced robots, RobotLAB makes abstract math and computer science real by focusing lessons around complex problems that become intuitive through interaction and manipulation of the robots. Visit http://www.robotlab.com/ and review the many robots they are creating to help education. Create a new robot that could help you with your college experience.

PROJECT #   4. Less Is More

Your organization is teetering on the edge of systems chaos. Your systems administrator is stressed beyond tolerance by too many systems, too many applications, too few resources, and too little time. The scope, frequency, and diversity of demand are causing greater risk than anyone dares to admit. Automating (and reducing complexity of) the operating environment is critical for your business to survive. Research autonomic computing and write a report discussing how this technology can help an organization gain control over its systems.

PROJECT #   5. Real-Time Adaptive Security

BusinessED specializes in creating new and innovative software for education in the business market. Danny Henningson, founder and president of BusinessED, is interested in developing educational products for elementary and high schools around the globe. Danny has hired you as the vice president of research and development and is excited to hear your ideas for new products. Your first assignment is to study the many threats and security issues facing public schools today and explain how real-time adaptive security measure could help BusinessED succeed.

PROJECT #   6. Alternative Energy

With energy costs on the rise, many U.S. homes are turning to homegrown energy solutions. Your friend Cole Lazarus has decided to start a business offering such solutions. Cole would like your help developing his business. Begin by researching the Internet and find different ways that you could design a home with its own energy sources. Create a document listing the different sources, along with advantages and disadvantages of each source.

Apply Your Knowledge Project Overview

Project Number	Project Name	Project Type	Plug-In	Focus Area	Project Level	Skill Set	Page Number
1	Financial Destiny	Excel	T2	Personal Budget	Introductory	Formulas	AYK.4
2	Cash Flow	Excel	T2	Cash Flow	Introductory	Formulas	AYK.4
3	Technology Budget	Excel	T1, T2	Hardware and Software	Introductory	Formulas	AYK.4
4	Tracking Donations	Excel	T2	Employee Relationships	Introductory	Formulas	AYK.4
5	Convert Currency	Excel	T2	Global Commerce	Introductory	Formulas	AYK.5
6	Cost Comparison	Excel	T2	Total Cost of Ownership	Introductory	Formulas	AYK.5
7	Time Management	Excel or Project	T12	Project Management	Introductory	Gantt Charts	AYK.6
8	Maximize Profit	Excel	T2, T4	Strategic Analysis	Intermediate	Formulas or Solver	AYK.6
9	Security Analysis	Excel	T3	Filtering Data	Intermediate	Conditional Formatting, Autofilter, Subtotal	AYK.7
10	Gathering Data	Excel	T3	Data Analysis	Intermediate	Conditional Formatting	AYK.8
11	Scanner System	Excel	T2	Strategic Analysis	Intermediate	Formulas	AYK.8
12	Competitive Pricing	Excel	T2	Profit Maximization	Intermediate	Formulas	AYK.9
13	Adequate Acquisitions	Excel	T2	Break-Even Analysis	Intermediate	Formulas	AYK.9
14	Customer Relations	Excel	T3	CRM	Intermediate	PivotTable	AYK.9
15	Assessing the Value of Information	Excel	T3	Data Analysis	Intermediate	PivotTable	AYK.10
16	Growth, Trends, and Forecasts	Excel	T2, T3	Data Forecasting	Advanced	Average, Trend, Growth	AYK.11
17	Shipping Costs	Excel	T4	SCM	Advanced	Solver	AYK.12
18	Formatting Grades	Excel	T3	Data Analysis	Advanced	If, LookUp	AYK.12

(Continued)

Project Number	Project Name	Project Type	Plug-In	Focus Area	Project Level	Skill Set	Page Number
19	Moving Dilemma	Excel	T2, T3	SCM	Advanced	Absolute vs. Relative Values	AYK.13
20	Operational Efficiencies	Excel	T3	SCM	Advanced	PivotTable	AYK.14
21	Too Much Information	Excel	T3	CRM	Advanced	PivotTable	AYK.14
22	Turnover Rates	Excel	T3	Data Mining	Advanced	PivotTable	AYK.15
23	Vital Information	Excel	T3	Data Mining	Advanced	PivotTable	AYK.15
24	Breaking Even	Excel	T4	Business Analysis	Advanced	Goal Seek	AYK.16
25	Profit Scenario	Excel	T4	Sales Analysis	Advanced	Scenario Manager	AYK.16
26	Electronic Résumés	HTML	T9, T10, T11	Electronic Personal Marketing	Introductory	Structural Tags	AYK.17
27	Gathering Feedback	Dreamweaver	T9, T10, T11	Data Collection	Intermediate	Organization of Information	AYK.17
28	Daily Invoice	Access	T5, T6, T7, T8	Business Analysis	Introductory	Entities, Relationships, and Databases	AYK.17
29	Billing Data	Access	T5, T6, T7, T8	Business Intelligence	Introductory	Entities, Relationships, and Databases	AYK.19
30	Inventory Data	Access	T5, T6, T7, T8	SCM	Intermediate	Entities, Relationships, and Databases	AYK.20
31	Call Center	Access	T5, T6, T7, T8	CRM	Intermediate	Entities, Relationships, and Databases	AYK.21
32	Sales Pipeline	Access	T5, T6, T7, T8	Business Intelligence	Advanced	Entities, Relationships, and Databases	AYK.23
33	Online Classified Ads	Access	T5, T6, T7, T8	Ecommerce	Advanced	Entities, Relationships, and Databases	AYK.23

NOTE: Many of the Excel projects support multiple data files. Therefore, the naming convention that you see in the text may not be the same as what you see in a data folder. As an example, in the text we reference data files as AYK1_Data.xlsx; however, you may see a file named AYK1_Data_Version_1.xlsx, or AYK1_Data_Version_2.xlsx.

Project 1:

Financial Destiny

You have been introduced to Microsoft Excel and are ready to begin using it to help track your monthly expenses and take charge of your financial destiny. The first step is to create a personal budget so you can see where you are spending money and whether you need to decrease your monthly expenses or increase your monthly income.

Create a template for a monthly budget of your income and expenditures, with some money set aside for savings (or you can use the data file, AYK1_Data.xlsx, we created). Create variations of this budget to show how much you could save if you cut back on certain expenses, found a roommate, or got a part-time job. Compare the costs of a meal plan to costs of groceries. Consider how much interest would be earned if you saved $100 a month or how much debt would be paid on student loans or credit card bills. To expand your data set, make a fantasy budget for 10 years from now, when you might own a home, have student loan payments, and have a good salary.

Data file: AYK1_Data.xlsx

Project 2:

Cash Flow

Gears is a 5-year-old company that specializes in bike components. The company is having trouble paying for its monthly supplies and would like to perform a cash flow analysis so it can understand its financial position. Cash flow represents the money an investment produces after subtracting cash expenses from income. The statement of cash flows summarizes sources and uses of cash, indicates whether enough cash is available to carry on routine operations, and offers an analysis of all business transactions, reporting where the firm obtained its cash and how it chose to allocate the cash. The cash flow statement shows where money comes from, how the company will spend it, and when the company will require additional cash. Gears would like to project a cash flow statement for the next month.

Using the AYK2_Data.xlsx data file, complete the cash flow statement for Gears, using Excel. Be sure to create formulas so the company can simply input numbers in the future to determine cash flow.

Data file: AYK2_Data.xlsx

Project 3:

Technology Budget

Tally is a start-up website development company located in Seattle, Washington. The company currently has seven employees and is looking to hire six new employees in the next month.

You are in charge of purchasing for Tally. Your first task is to purchase computers for the new employees. Your budget is $250,000 to buy the best computer systems with a scanner, three color printers, and business software. Use the web to research various products and calculate the costs of different systems, using Excel. Use a variety of Excel formulas as you analyze costs and compare prices. Use the AYK3_Data.xlsx data file as a template.

Data file: AYK3_Data.xlsx

Project 4:

Tracking Donations

Lazarus Consulting is a large computer consulting company in New York. Pete Lazarus, the CEO and founder, is well known for his philanthropic efforts. Pete knows that most of his employees contribute to nonprofit organizations and wants to reward them for their efforts while encouraging others to contribute to charities. Pete began a program that matches 50 percent of each employee donation. The only stipulations are that the charity must be a nonprofit organization and the company will match only up to $2,000 per year per employee.

Open the AYK4_Data.xlsx data file and determine the following:

- What was the total donation amount per organization?
- What were the average donations per organization?

Data file: AYK4_Data.xlsx

Project 5:

Convert Currency

You have decided to spend the summer traveling abroad with your friends. Your trip will take you to France, England, Italy, Switzerland, Germany, Norway, and Ireland. You want to use Excel to convert currencies as you travel around the world.

Locate one of the exchange rate calculators on the Internet (www.xe.com or www.x-rates.com). Find the exchange rates for each of the listed countries and create formulas in Excel to convert $100, $500, and $1,000. Use the AYK5_Data.xlsx data file as a template.

Data file: AYK5_Data.xls

Project 6:

Cost Comparison

You are thinking about purchasing a new computer since the machine you are using now is 4 years old, slow, not always reliable, and does not support the latest operating system. Your needs for the new computer are simple: antivirus software, email, web browsing, word processing, spreadsheet, database, iTunes, and some lightweight graphical tools. Your concern is what the total cost of ownership will be for the next 3 years. You have to factor in a few added costs beyond just the initial purchase price for the computer itself, such as added hardware (this could include a new printer, docking station, or scanner), software (purchase of a new operating system), training (you're thinking about pursuing web training to get an internship next term), subsequent software upgrades, and maintenance.

- It is useful to think about costs over time—both direct as well as indirect costs. Part of the reason this distinction is important is that a decision should rest not on the nominal sum of the purchase but, rather, on the present value of the purchase.
- A dollar today is worth more than a dollar one year from now.
- The relevant discount rate (interest rate) is your marginal cost of capital corresponding to a level of risk equal with the purchase.
- Use the AYK6_Data.xlsx data file as a template.

Data file: AYK6_Data.xlsx

FIGURE AYK.1

Sample Layout of New Computer Spreadsheet

	A	B	C	D	E	F
1	COST OF NEW COMPUTER					
2	Discount Rate	1	0.9325	0.9109	0.7051	
3		Time 0	Year 1	Year 2	Year 3	Present Value Costs
4	Computer					
5	Software					
6	Additional Hardware					
7	Training					
8	Software upgrades					
9	Maintenance					
10						
11	Total Costs					
12						

Project 7:

Time Management

You have just been hired as a business analyst by a new start-up company called Multi-Media. Multi-Media is an interactive agency that creates phased and affordable website marketing, providing its clients with real and measurable solutions that are supported by easy-to-use tools. Since the company is very new to the business arena, it needs help in creating a project management plan for developing its own website. The major tasks for the development team have been identified, but you need to create the timeline.

1. The task names, durations, and any prerequisites are:

   - Analyze and plan—two weeks. Cannot start anything else until done.
   - Create and organize content—four weeks. Can start to develop look and feel before this is done.
   - Develop the look and feel—four weeks. Start working on graphics and HTML at the same time.
   - Produce graphics and HTML documents—two weeks. Create working prototype after the first week.
   - Create a working prototype—two weeks. Give to test team when complete.
   - Test, test, test—four weeks.
   - Upload to a web server and test again—one week.
   - Maintain.

2. Using Microsoft Excel or Microsoft Project, create a Gantt chart using the information provided.

Project 8:

Maximize Profit

Books, Books, Books is a wholesale distributor of popular books. The business buys overstocked books and sells them for a discount of more than 50 percent to local area bookstores. The owner of the company, B. K. Kane, would like to determine the best approach to boxing books so he can make the most profit possible. The local bookstores accept all shipments from Books, Books, Books because of B. K.'s incredibly low prices. B. K. can order as many overstocked books as he requires, and this week's options include:

Title	Weight	Cost	Sale Price
Harry Potter and the Deathly Hallows, J. K. Rowling	5 lb	$9	$17
The Children of Húrin, J. R. R. Tolkien	4 lb	$8	$13
The Time Traveler's Wife, Audrey Niffenegger	3.5 lb	$7	$11
The Dark River, John Twelve Hawks	3 lb	$6	$ 9
The Road, Cormac McCarthy	2.5 lb	$5	$ 7
Slaughterhouse-Five, Kurt Vonnegut	1 lb	$4	$ 5

When packing a single box, B. K. must adhere to the following:

- 20 books or fewer.
- Books by three authors.
- Between four and eight books from each author.
- Weight equal to or less than 50 pounds.

BK has come to you to help him determine which books he should order to maximize his profit based on this information. Using the AYK8_Data.xlsx data file, determine the optimal book order for a single box of books.

Data file: AYK8_Data.xlsx

Project 9:

Security Analysis

SecureWorks, Inc., is a small computer security contractor that provides computer security analysis, design, and software implementation for the U.S. government and commercial clients. SecureWorks competes for both private and U.S. government computer security contract work by submitting detailed bids outlining the work the company will perform if awarded the contracts. Because all of the work involves computer security, a highly sensitive area, almost all of SecureWorks tasks require access to classified material or company confidential documents. Consequently, all of the security engineers (simply known as "engineers" within the company) have U.S. government clearances of either secret or top secret. Some have even higher clearances for the 2 percent of SecureWorks work that involves so-called black-box security work. Most of the employees also hold clearances because they must handle classified documents.

Leslie Mamalis is SecureWorks' human resources (HR) manager. She maintains all employee records and is responsible for semiannual review reports, payroll processing, personnel records, recruiting data, employee training, and pension option information. At the heart of an HR system are personnel records. Personnel record maintenance includes activities such as maintaining employee records, tracking cost center data, recording and maintaining pension information, and absence and sick leave record keeping. Although most of this information resides in sophisticated database systems, Leslie maintains a basic employee worksheet for quick calculations and ad hoc report generation. Because SecureWorks is a small company, Leslie can take advantage of Excel's excellent list management capabilities to satisfy many of her personnel information management needs.

Leslie has asked you to assist with a number of functions (she has provided you with a copy of her trusted personnel data file, AYK9_Data.xlsx):

1. Copy the data worksheet to a new worksheet called Sort. Sort the employee list in ascending order by department, then by last name, then by first name.

2. Copy the data worksheet to a new worksheet called Autofilter. Using the Autofilter feature, create a custom filter that will display employees whose birth date is greater than or equal to 1/1/1965 and less than or equal to 12/31/1975.

3. Copy the data worksheet to a new worksheet called Subtotal. Using the subtotal feature, create a sum of the salary for each department.

4. Copy the data worksheet to a new worksheet called Formatting. Using the salary column, change the font color to red if the cell value is greater than or equal to 55000. You must use the conditional formatting feature to complete this step.

Data file: AYK9_Data.xlsx

Project 10:

Gathering Data

You have just accepted a new job offer from a firm that has offices in San Diego, Los Angeles, and San Francisco. You need to decide which location to move to. Because you have not visited any of these three cities and want to get in a lot of golf time, you determine that the main factor that will affect your decision is weather.

Go to www.weather.com and locate the box in which you can enter the city or zip code for which you want information. Enter San Diego, CA, and when the data appear, click the Averages and Records tab. Print this page and repeat this for Los Angeles and San Francisco. You will want to focus on the Monthly Average and Records section on the top of the page.

1. Create a spreadsheet to summarize the information you find.

2. Record the temperature and rainfall in columns and group the cities into four groups of rows labeled Average High, Average Low, Mean, and Average Precipitation.

3. Fill in the appropriate data for each city and month.

4. Because rain is your greatest concern, use conditional formatting to display the months with an average precipitation below 2.5 inches in blue and apply boldface.

5. You also want to be in the warmest weather possible while in California. Use conditional formatting to display the months with average high temperatures above 65 degrees in green and apply an italic font face.

6. Looking at the average high temperatures above 65 degrees and average precipitation below 2 inches, to which city do you think you should relocate? Explain your answer.

Project 11:

Scanner System

FunTown is a popular amusement park filled with roller coasters, games, and water features. Boasting 24 roller coasters, 10 of which exceed 200 feet and 70 miles per hour, and five water parks, the park's attendance remains steady throughout the season. Due to the park's popularity, it is not uncommon for entrance lines to exceed one hour on busy days. FunTown would like your help to find a solution to decrease park entrance lines.

FunTown would like to implement a handheld scanner system that can allow employees to walk around the front gates and accept credit card purchases and print tickets on the spot. The park anticipates an overall increase in sales of 4 percent per year with online ticketing, with an expense of 6 percent of total sales for the scanning equipment. FunTown has created a data file for you to use, AYK11_Data.xlsx, that compares scanning sales and traditional sales. You will need to create the necessary formulas to calculate all the assumptions, including:

- Tickets sold at the booth.
- Tickets sold by the scanner.
- Revenues generated by booth sales.
- Revenues generated by scanner sales.
- Scanner ticket expense.
- Revenue with and without scanner sales.
- Three-year row totals.

Data file: AYK11_Data.xlsx

Project 12:

Competitive Pricing

Bill Schultz is thinking of starting a store that specializes in handmade cowboy boots. Bill is a longtime rancher in the town of Taos, New Mexico. Bill's reputation for honesty and integrity is well-known around town, and he is positive that his new store will be highly successful.

Before opening his store, Bill is curious about how his profit, revenue, and variable costs will change depending on the amount he charges for his boots. Bill would like you to perform the work required for this analysis and has given you the AYK12_Data.xlsx data file. Here are a few things to consider while you perform your analysis:

- Current competitive prices for custom cowboy boots are between $225 and $275 a pair.
- Variable costs will be either $100 or $150 a pair, depending on the types of material Bill chooses to use.
- Fixed costs are $10,000 a month.

Data file: AYK12_Data.xlsx

Project 13:

Adequate Acquisitions

XMark.com is a major Internet company specializing in organic food. XMark.com is thinking of purchasing GoodGrow, another organic food Internet company. GoodGrow has current revenues of $100 million, with expenses of $150 million. Current projections indicate that GoodGrow's revenues are increasing at 35 percent per year and its expenses are increasing by 10 percent per year. XMark.

com understands that projections can be erroneous, however; the company must determine the number of years before GoodGrow will return a profit.

You need to help XMark.com determine the number of years required to break even, using annual growth rates in revenue between 20 percent and 60 percent and annual expense growth rates between 10 percent and 30 percent. You have been provided with a template, AYK13_Data.xlsx, to assist with your analysis.

Data file: AYK13_Data.xlsx

Project 14:
Customer Relations

Schweizer Distribution specializes in distributing fresh produce to local restaurants in the Chicago area. The company currently sells 12 products through the efforts of three sales representatives to 10 restaurants. The company, like all small businesses, is always interested in finding ways to increase revenues and decrease expenses.

The company's founder, Bob Schweizer, has recently hired you as a business analyst. You have just graduated from college with a degree in marketing and a specialization in customer relationship management. Bob is eager to hear your thoughts and ideas on how to improve the business and help the company build strong lasting relationships with its customers.

Bob has provided you with last year's sales information in the AYK14_Data.xlsx data file. Help Bob analyze his distribution company by using a PivotTable to determine the following:

1. Who is Bob's best customer by total sales?

2. Who is Bob's worst customer by total sales?

3. Who is Bob's best customer by total profit?

4. Who is Bob's worst customer by total profit?

5. What is Bob's best-selling product by total sales?

6. What is Bob's worst-selling product by total sales?

7. What is Bob's best-selling product by total profit?

8. What is Bob's worst-selling product by total profit?

9. Who is Bob's best sales representative by total profit?

10. Who is Bob's worst sales representative by total profit?

11. What is the best sales representative's best-selling product (by total profit)?

12. Who is the best sales representative's best customer (by total profit)?

13. What is the best sales representative's worst-selling product (by total profit)?

14. Who is the best sales representative's worst customer (by total profit)?

Data file: AYK14_Data.xlsx

Project 15:
Assessing the Value of Information

Recently Santa Fe, New Mexico, was named one of the safest places to live in the United States. Since then, housing development projects have been springing up all around Santa Fe. Six housing development projects are currently dominating the local market: Pinon Pine, Rancho Hondo, Creek Side, Vista Del Monte, Forest View, and Santa Fe South. These six projects each started with 100 homes, have sold all of them, and are currently developing phase two.

As one of the three partners and real estate agents of Affordable Homes Real Estate, you are responsible for analyzing the information concerning the past 600 home sales and choosing which development project to focus on for selling homes in phase two. Because your real estate firm is so small, you and your partners have decided that the firm should focus on selling homes in only one of the development projects.

From the New Mexico Real Estate Association, you have obtained a spreadsheet file that contains information concerning each of the sales for the first 600 homes. It contains the following fields:

Column	Name	Description
A	LOT #	The number assigned to a specific home within each project.
B	PROJECT #	A unique number assigned to each of the six housing development projects (see the following table).
C	ASK PRICE	The initial posted asking price for the home.
D	SELL PRICE	The actual price for which the home was sold.
E	LIST DATE	The date the home was listed for sale.
F	SALE DATE	The date on which the final contract closed and the home was sold.
G	SQ. FT.	The total square footage for the home.
H	# BATH.	The number of bathrooms in the home.
I	# BDRMS	The number of bedrooms in the home.

The following numbers have been assigned to each of the housing development projects:

Project Number	Project Name
23	Pinon Pine
47	Rancho Hondo
61	Creek Side
78	Vista Del Monte
92	Forest View
97	Santa Fe South

It is your responsibility to analyze the sales list and prepare a report that details which housing development project your real estate firm should focus on. Your analysis should be from as many angles as possible.

1. You do not know how many other real estate firms will also be competing for sales in each of the housing development projects.

2. Phase two for each housing development project will develop homes similar in style, price, and square footage to their respective first phases.

3. As you consider the information provided to you, think in terms of what information is important and what information is not important. Be prepared to justify how you went about your analysis.

4. Upon completing your analysis, please provide concise, yet detailed and thorough documentation (in narrative, numeric, and graphic forms) that justifies your decision.

Data file: AYK15_Data.xlsx

Project 16:

Growth, Trends, and Forecasts

Founded in 2002, Analytics Software provides innovative search software, website accessibility testing software, and usability testing software. All serve as part of its desktop and enterprise content management solutions for government, corporate, educational, and consumer markets. The company's solutions are used by website publishers, digital media publishers, content managers, document managers, business users, consumers, software companies, and consulting services companies. Analytics Software solutions help organizations develop long-term strategies to achieve web content accessibility, enhance usability, and comply with U.S. and international accessibility and search standards.

You manage the customer service group for the company and have just received an email from CIO Sue Downs that the number of phone calls from customers having problems with one of your newer applications is on the increase. This company has a 10-year history of approximately 1 percent in turnover a year, and its focus had always been on customer service. With the informal motto of "Grow big, but stay small," it takes pride in 100 percent callbacks in customer care, knowing that its personal service was one thing that made it outstanding.

The rapid growth to six times its original customer-base size has forced the company to deal with difficult questions for the first time, such as, "How do we serve this many customers?"

One option might be for the company to outsource its customer service department. Before deciding to do that, Analytics Software needs to create a growth, trend, and forecast analysis for future predictions.

1. Create a weekly analysis from the data provided in AYK16_Data.xlsx.

2. The price of the products, the actual product type, and any warranty information are irrelevant.

3. Develop a growth, trend, and forecast analysis. You should use a three-day moving average; a shorter moving average might not display the trend well, and a much longer moving average would shorten the trend too much.

4. Upon completing your analysis, please provide concise yet detailed and thorough documentation (in narrative, numeric, and graphic forms) that justifies your recommendations.

   Data file: AYK16_Data.xlsx

Project 17:
Shipping Costs

One of the main products of the Fairway Woods Company is custom-made golf clubs. The clubs are manufactured at three plants (Denver, Colorado; Phoenix, Arizona; and Dallas, Texas) and are then shipped by truck to five distribution warehouses in Sacramento, California; Salt Lake City, Utah; Chicago, Illinois; Albuquerque, New Mexico; and New York City, New York. Since shipping costs are a major expense, management has begun an analysis to determine ways to reduce them. For the upcoming golf season, the output from each manufacturing plant and how much each warehouse will require to satisfy its customers have been estimated.

The CIO from Fairway Woods Company has created a data file for you, AYK17_Data.xlsx, of the shipping costs from each manufacturing plant to each warehouse as a baseline analysis. Some business rules and requirements you should be aware of include:

- The problem presented, which involves the shipment of goods from three plants to five regional warehouses.

- Goods, which can be shipped from any plant to any warehouse, cost more to ship over long distances than over short distances.

1. Your goal is to minimize the costs of shipping goods from production plants to warehouses, thereby meeting the demand from each metropolitan area while not exceeding the supply available from each plant. To complete this project, it is recommended that you use the Solver function in Excel to assist with the analysis.

2. Specifically, you want to focus on:

   - Minimizing the total shipping costs.

   - Total shipped being less than or equal to supply at a plant.

   - Total shipped to warehouses being greater than or equal to the warehouse demand.

   - Number to ship being greater than or equal to 0.

   Data file: AYK17_Data.xlsx

Project 18:

Formatting Grades

Professor Streterstein is a bit absentminded. His instructor's grade book is a mess, and he would like your help cleaning it up and making it easier to use. In Professor Streterstein's course, the maximum possible points a student can earn is 750. The following table displays the grade equivalent to total points for the course.

Total Points	Calculated Grade
675	A
635	A–
600	B
560	B–
535	C
490	C–
450	D
0	F

Help Professor Streterstein rework his grade book. Open the AYK18_Data.xlsx data file and perform the following:

1. Reformat the workbook so it is readable, understandable, and consistent. Replace column labels, format and align the headings, and add borders and shading as appropriate.

2. Add a column in the grade book for final grade next to the total points earned column.

3. Use the VLookup function to automatically assess final grades automatically, based on the total points column.

4. Using the If function, format the workbook so each student's grade shows a pass or fail—P for pass, F for fail—based on the total points.

Data file: AYK18_Data.xlsx

Project 19:

Moving Dilemma

Pony Espresso is a small business that sells specialty coffee drinks at office buildings. Each morning and afternoon, Pony Espresso trucks arrive at offices' front entrances, and the office employees purchase various beverages such as Java du Jour and Café de Colombia. The business is profitable. Pony Espresso offices, however, are located north of town, where lease rates are less expensive, and the principal sales area is south of town. This means the trucks must drive across town four times each day.

The cost of transportation to and from the sales area plus the power demands of the trucks' coffee brewing equipment are a significant portion of variable costs. Pony Espresso could reduce the amount of driving and, therefore, the variable costs, if it moved the offices closer to the sales area.

Pony Espresso presently has fixed costs of $10,000 per month. The lease of a new office, closer to the sales area, would cost an additional $2,200 per month. This would increase the fixed costs to $12,200 per month.

Although the lease of new offices would increase the fixed costs, a careful estimate of the potential savings in gasoline and vehicle maintenance indicates that Pony Espresso could reduce the variable costs from $0.60 per unit to $0.35 per unit. Total sales are unlikely to increase as a result of the move, but the savings in variable costs should increase the annual profit.

Consider the information provided to you from the owner in the AYK19_Data.xlsx data file. Especially look at the change in the variability of the profit from month to month. From November through January, when it is much more difficult to lure office workers out into the cold to purchase coffee, Pony Espresso barely breaks even. In fact, in December, the business lost money.

1. Develop the cost analysis on the existing lease information using the monthly sales figures provided to you in the data file.
2. Develop the cost analysis from the new lease information provided.
3. Calculate the variability that is reflected in the month-to-month standard deviation of earnings for the current cost structure and the projected cost structure.
4. Do not consider any association with downsizing such as overhead—simply focus on the information provided to you.
5. You will need to calculate the EBIT (earnings before interest and taxes).

Data file: AYK19_Data.xlsx

Project 20:

Operational Efficiencies

Hoover Transportation, Inc., is a large distribution company located in Denver, Colorado. The company is currently seeking to gain operational efficiencies in its supply chain by reducing the number of transportation carriers it is using to outsource. Operational efficiencies for Hoover Transportation, Inc., suggest that reducing the number of carriers from the Denver distribution center to warehouses in the selected states will lead to reduced costs. Brian Hoover, the CEO of Hoover Transportation, requests the number of carriers transporting products from its Denver distribution center to wholesalers in Arizona, Arkansas, Iowa, Missouri, Montana, Oklahoma, Oregon, and Washington be reduced from the current five carriers to two carriers.

Carrier selection should be based on the assumptions that all environmental factors are equal and historical cost trends will continue. Review the historical data from the past several years to determine your recommendation for the top two carriers that Hoover Transportation should continue to use.

1. Analyze the last 24 months of Hoover's Transportation carrier transactions found in the AYK20_Data.xlsx data file.
2. Create a report detailing your recommendation for the top two carriers with which Hoover Transportation should continue to do business. Be sure to use PivotTables and PivotCharts in your report. A few questions to get you started include:
   - What is the average cost per carrier?
   - What are the total shipping costs per state?
   - What are the total shipping weights per state?
   - What are the average shipping costs per pound?
   - What is the average cost per carrier?

Data file: AYK20_Data.xlsx

Project 21:

Too Much Information

You have just landed the job of vice president of operations for The Pitt Stop Restaurants, a national chain of full-service, casual-themed restaurants. During your first week on the job, Suzanne Graham, your boss and CEO of the company, has asked you to provide an analysis of how well the company's restaurants are performing. Specifically, she would like to know which units and regions are performing extremely well, which are performing moderately well, and which are underperforming. Her goal is to identify where to spend time and focus efforts to improve the overall health of the company.

Review the AYK21_Data.xlsx data file and determine how best to analyze and interpret the data. Create a formal presentation of your findings. A few things to consider include the following:

- Should underperforming restaurants be closed or sold?
- Should high-performing restaurants be expanded to accommodate more seats?
- Should the company spend more or less on advertising?

- In which markets should the advertising budget be adjusted?
- How is The Pitt Stop Restaurants performing compared to the competition?
- How are units of like size performing relative to each other?

Data file: AYK21_Data.xlsx

Project 22:

Turnover Rates

Employee turnover rates are at an all-time high at Gizmo Manufacturing's plants. The company is experiencing severe worker retention issues, which are leading to productivity and quality control problems. The majority of the company's workers perform a variety of tasks and are paid by the hour. The company currently tests potential applicants to ensure that they have the skills necessary for the intense mental concentration and dexterity required to fill the positions. Since significant costs are associated with employee turnover, Gizmo Manufacturing wants to find a way to predict which applicants have the characteristics of being a short-term versus a long-term employee.

1. Review the information that Gizmo Manufacturing has collected from two of its data sources. The first data file, AYK22_Data_A.xlsx, contains information regarding employee wages. The second data file, AYK22_Data_B.xlsx, contains information regarding employee retention.

2. Using Excel analysis functions, determine the employee characteristics that you would recommend Gizmo Manufacturing look for when hiring new personnel. It is highly recommended that you use PivotTables as part of your analysis.

3. Prepare a report based on your findings (which should include several forms of graphical representation) for your recommendations.

Data files: AYK22_Data_A.xlsx and AYK22_Data_B.xlsx

Project 23:

Vital Information

Martin Resorts, Inc., owns and operates four spa and golf resorts in Colorado. The company has five traditional lines of business: (1) golf sales; (2) golf lessons; (3) restaurants; (4) retail and rentals; and (5) hotels. David Logan, director of marketing technology at Martin Resorts, Inc., and Donald Mayer, the lead strategic analyst for Martin Resorts, are soliciting your input for their CRM strategic initiative.

Martin Resorts' IT infrastructure is pieced together with various systems and applications. Currently, the company has a difficult time with CRM because its systems are not integrated. The company cannot determine vital information such as which customers are golfing and staying at the hotel or which customers are staying at the hotel and not golfing.

For example, the three details showing that the customer Diego Titus (1) stayed four nights at a Martin Resorts' managed hotel, (2) golfed three days, and (3) took an all-day spa treatment the first day are discrete facts housed in separate systems. Martin Resorts hopes that by using data warehousing technology to integrate its data, the next time Diego reserves lodging for another trip, sales associates may ask him if he would like to book a spa treatment as well and even if he would like the same masseuse that he had on his prior trip.

Martin Resorts is excited about the possibility of taking advantage of customer segmentation and CRM strategies to help increase its business.

The company wants to use CRM and data warehouse technologies to improve service and personalization at each customer touch point. Using a data warehousing tool, important customer information can be accessed from all of its systems daily, weekly, monthly, or once or twice per year. Analyze the sample data in AYK23_Data.xlsx for the following:

1. Currently, the quality of the data within the preceding disparate systems is low. Develop a report for David and Donald discussing the importance of high-quality information and how low-quality information can affect Martin Resorts' business.

2. Review the data that David and Donald are working with from the data warehouse in the AYK23_Data.xlsx data file.

    a. Give examples from the data showing the kind of information Martin Resorts might be able to use to gain a better understanding of its customers. Include the types of data quality issues the company can anticipate and the strategies it can use to help avoid such issues.

    b. Determine who Martin Resorts' best customers are and provide examples of the types of marketing campaigns the company should offer these valuable customers.

    c. Prepare a report that summarizes the benefits Martin Resorts can receive from using business intelligence to mine the data warehouse. Include a financial analysis of the costs and benefits.

        Data file: AYK23_Data.xlsx

Project 24:
Breaking Even

Mountain Cycle specializes in making custom mountain bikes. The company founder, P. J. Steffan, is having a hard time making the business profitable. Knowing that you have great business knowledge and solid financial sense, P. J. has come to you for advice.

    P. J. would like you to determine how many bikes Mountain Cycle needs to sell per year to break even. Using Goal Seek in Excel, solve using the following:

- Fixed cost equals $65,000
- Variable cost equals $1,575
- Bike price equals $2,500

Project 25:
Profit Scenario

Murray Lutz owns a small shop, Lutz Motors, that sells and services vintage motorcycles. Murray is curious how his profit will be affected by his sales over the next year.

    Murray would like your help creating best, worst, and most-likely scenarios for his motorcycle sales over the next year. Using Scenario Manager, help Murray analyze the information in the AYK25_Data.xlsx data file.

        Data file: AYK25_Data.xlsx

Project 26:
Electronic Résumés

Résumés are the currency of the recruitment industry. They are the cornerstone of communication between candidates, recruiters, and employers. Technology is automating elements of the recruitment process, but a complete solution requires proper handling of the actual development of all the pieces and parts that comprise not just a résumé but also an erésumé. Electronic résumés, or erésumés, have moved into the mainstream of today's job market at lightning speed. Erésumés have stepped up the efficiency of job placement to such a point that you could get a call from a recruiter just hours after submitting your erésumé. With this kind of opportunity, you cannot afford to be left in the dark ages of using only a paper résumé.

    In the text or HTML editor of your choice, write your erésumé as though you were putting it online and inviting prospective employers to see it. We recommend typing in all the text and then later adding the HTML tags (rather than trying to type in the tags as you go).

    Use the following checklist to make sure you're covering the basics. You do not need to match it exactly; it just shows what can be done.

- Add structural tags.
- Add paragraphs and headings.
- Find an opportunity to include a list.

- Add inline styles.
- Play with the alignment of elements.
- Add appropriate font selection, font size, and color.

Project 27:

Gathering Feedback

Gathering feedback from a website's visitors can be a valuable way of assessing a site's success, and it can help build a customer or subscriber database. For example, a business could collect the addresses of people who are interested in receiving product samples, email newsletters, or notifications of special offers.

Adding form elements to a web page is simple; they are created using a set of HTML form tags that define menus, text fields, buttons, and so on. Form elements are generally used to collect information from a web page.

In the text or HTML editor of your choice, create a web page form that would collect information for a customer ordering a customized bicycle. Use proper web page design and HTML tools to understand the process and function of form elements. Be sure to pay attention to:

- Form layout and design.
- Visual elements, including labels, alignment, font selection, font size, color.
- Required versus nonrequired fields.
- Drop-down boxes, text fields, and radio buttons.

Project 28:

Daily Invoice

Foothills Animal Hospital is a full-service small animal veterinary hospital located in Morrison, Colorado, specializing in routine medical care, vaccinations, laboratory testing, and surgery. The hospital has experienced tremendous growth over the past six months due to customer referrals. Although Foothills Animal Hospital has typically kept its daily service records in a workbook format, it feels the need to expand its reporting capabilities to develop a relational database as a more functional structure.

Foothills Animal Hospital needs help developing a database, specifically to:

- Create a customer table—name, address, phone, and date of entrance.
- Create a pet table—pet name, type of animal, breed, gender, color, neutered/spayed, weight, and comments.
- Create a medications table—medication code, name of medication, and cost of medication.
- Create a visit table—details of treatments performed, medications dispensed, and date of the visit.
- Produce a daily invoice report.

Figure AYK.2 displays a sample daily invoice report that the Foothills Animal Hospital accountants have requested. Foothills Animal Hospital organizes its treatments using the codes displayed in Figure AYK.3. The entities and primary keys for the database have been identified in Figure AYK.4.

The following business rules have been identified:

1. A customer can have many pets but must have at least one.
2. A pet must be assigned to one and only one customer.
3. A pet can have one or more treatments per visit but must have at least one.
4. A pet can have one or more medications but need not have any.

Your job is to complete the following tasks:

1. Develop and describe the entity-relationship diagram.
2. Use normalization to ensure the correctness of the tables (relations).

3. Create the database by using a personal DBMS package (preferably Microsoft Access).
4. Use the data in Figure AYK.3 to populate your tables. Feel free to enter your own personal information.
5. Use the DBMS package to create the basic report in Figure AYK.2.

FIGURE AYK.2

Foothills Animal Hospital Daily Invoice Report

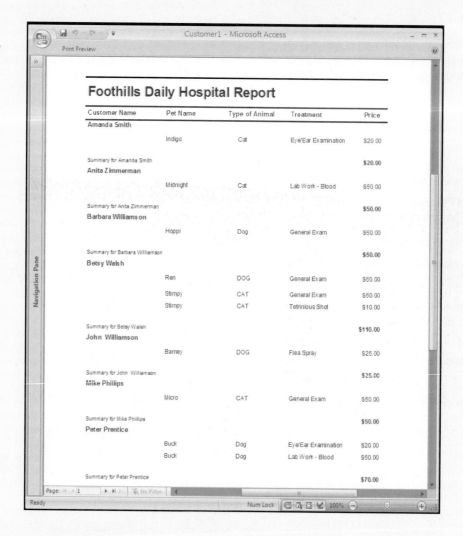

Foothills Daily Hospital Report

Customer Name	Pet Name	Type of Animal	Treatment	Price
Amanda Smith				
	Indigo	Cat	Eye/Ear Examination	$20.00
Summary for Amanda Smith				$20.00
Anita Zimmerman				
	Midnight	Cat	Lab Work - Blood	$50.00
Summary for Anita Zimmerman				$50.00
Barbara Williamson				
	Hoppi	Dog	General Exam	$50.00
Summary for Barbara Williamson				$50.00
Betsy Walsh				
	Ren	DOG	General Exam	$50.00
	Stimpy	CAT	General Exam	$50.00
	Stimpy	CAT	Tetrinious Shot	$10.00
Summary for Betsy Walsh				$110.00
John Williamson				
	Barney	DOG	Flea Spray	$25.00
Summary for John Williamson				$25.00
Mike Phillips				
	Micro	CAT	General Exam	$50.00
Summary for Mike Phillips				$50.00
Peter Prentice				
	Buck	Dog	Eye/Ear Examination	$20.00
	Buck	Dog	Lab Work - Blood	$50.00
Summary for Peter Prentice				$70.00

FIGURE AYK.3

Treatment Codes, Treatments, and Price Descriptions

Treatment Code	Treatment	Price
0100	Tetrinious Shot	$10.00
0201	Rabonius Shot	$20.00
0300	General Exam	$50.00
0303	Eye/Ear Examination	$20.00
0400	Spay/Neuter	$225.00
0405	Reset Dislocation	$165.00
0406	Amputation of Limb	$450.00
0407	Wrap Affected Area	$15.00
0408	Cast Affected Area	$120.00
1000	Lab Work—Blood	$50.00
1003	Lab Work—Misc	$35.00
2003	Flea Spray	$25.00
9999	Other Not Listed	$10.00

FIGURE AYK.4

Entity Names and Primary Keys Foothills Animal Hospital

Entity	Primary Key
CUSTOMER	Customer Number
PET	Pet Number
VISIT	Visit Number
VISIT DETAIL	Visit Number and Line Number (a composite key)
TREATMENT	Treatment Code
MEDICATION	Medication Code

Project 29:

Billing Data

On-The-Level Construction Company is a Denver-based construction company that specializes in subcontracting the development of single-family homes. In business since 1998, On-The-Level Construction has maintained a talented pool of certified staff and independent consultants providing the flexibility and combined experience required to meet the needs of its nearly 300 completed projects in the Denver metropolitan area. The field of operation methods that On-The-Level Construction is responsible for includes structural development, heating and cooling, plumbing, and electricity.

The company charges its clients by billing the hours spent on each contract. The hourly billing rate depends on the employee's position according to the field of operations (as noted previously). Figure AYK.5 shows a basic report that On-The-Level Construction foremen would like to see every week concerning what projects are being assigned, the overall assignment hours, and the charges for the assignment. On-The-Level Construction organizes its internal structure in four operations—Structure (500), Plumbing (501), Electrical (502), and Heating and Ventilation (503). Each of these operational departments can and should have many subcontractors who specialize in that area. On-The-Level Construction has decided to implement a relational database model to track project details according to project name, hours assigned, and charges per hour for each job description. Originally, On-The-Level Construction decided to let one of its employees handle the construction of the database. However, that employee has not had the time to implement the project completely. On-The-Level Construction has asked you to take over and complete the development of the database.

The entities and primary keys for the database have been identified in Figure AYK.6.

The following business rules have been identified:

1. A job can have many employees assigned but must have at least one.

2. An employee must be assigned to one and only one job number.

3. An employee can be assigned to work on one or more projects.

4. A project can be assigned to only one employee but need not be assigned to any employee.

Your job is to complete the following tasks:

1. Develop and describe the entity relationship diagram.

2. Use normalization to ensure the correctness of the tables (relations).

3. Create the database using a personal DBMS package (preferably Microsoft Access).

4. Use the DBMS package to create the basic report in Figure AYK.5.

FIGURE AYK.5

On-The-Level-Construction Detail Report

ON-THE-LEVEL CONSTRUCTION PROJECT DETAIL

PROJECT NAME	ASSIGN DATE	EMPLOYEE LAST NAME	FIRST NAME	JOB DESCRIPTION	ASSIGN HOUR	CHARGE/HOUR
Chatfield						
	6/10/2011	Olenkoski	Glenn	Structure	2.1	$35.75
	6/10/2011	Sullivan	David	Electrical	1.2	$105.00
	6/10/2011	Ramora	Anne	Plumbing	2.6	$96.75
	6/11/2011	Frommer	Matt	Plumbing	1.4	$96.75
Summary of Assignment Hours and Charges					7.30	$588.08
Evergreen						
	6/10/2011	Sullivan	David	Electrical	1.8	$105.00
	6/10/2011	Jones	Anne	Heating and Ventilation	3.4	$84.50
	6/11/2011	Frommer	Matt	Plumbing	4.1	$96.75
	6/16/2011	Bawangi	Terry	Plumbing	4.1	$96.75
	6/16/2011	Newman	John	Electrical	1.7	$105.00
Summary of Assignment Hours and Charges					15.10	$1,448.15
Roxborough						
	6/10/2011	Washberg	Jeff	Plumbing	3.9	$96.75
	6/10/2011	Ramora	Anne	Plumbing	2.6	$96.75
	6/11/2011	Smithfield	William	Structure	2.4	$35.75
	6/11/2011	Bawangi	Terry	Plumbing	2.7	$96.75
	6/16/2011	Johnson	Peter	Electrical	5.2	$105.00
	6/16/2011	Joen	Denise	Plumbing	2.5	$96.75
Summary of Assignment Hours and Charges					19.30	$1,763.78

Entity	Primary Key
PROJECT	Project Number
EMPLOYEE	Employee Number
JOB	Job Number
ASSIGNMENT	Assignment Number

FIGURE AYK.6

Entity Classes and Primary Keys for On-The-Level Construction

5. You may not be able to develop a report that looks exactly like the one in Figure AYK.5. However, your report should include the same information.

6. Complete personnel information is tracked by another database. For this application, include only the minimum: employee number, last name, and first name.

7. Information concerning all projects, employees, and jobs is not readily available. You should create information for several fictitious projects, employees, and jobs to include in your database.

Project 30:

Inventory Data

An independent retailer of mobile entertainment and wireless phones, iToys.com has built its business on offering the widest selection, expert advice, and outstanding customer service. However, iToys.com does not use a formal, consistent inventory tracking system. Periodically, an iToys.com employee visually checks to see what items are in stock. Although iToys.com does try to keep a certain level of each top seller in stock, the lack of a formal inventory tracking system has led to overstocking some items and understocking other items. On occasion, a customer will request a hot item, and it is only then that iToys.com realizes that the item is out of stock. If an item is not available, iToys.com risks losing a customer to a competitor.

Lately, iToys.com has become concerned with its inventory management methods. The owner of iToys.com, Dan Connolly, wants to manage his inventory better. The company receives orders by mail, by telephone, or through its website. Regardless of how the orders are received, Dan needs a database to automate the inventory checking and ordering process.

Dan has provided you with a simplified version of the company's current system (an Excel workbook) for recording inventory and orders in an Excel spreadsheet data file, AYK30_Data.xlsx.

1. Develop an ERD diagram before you begin to create the database. You will need to use the information provided here as well as the data given in the Excel workbook.

2. Create the database using a personal DBMS package (preferably Microsoft Access) that will track items (i.e., products), orders, order details, categories, suppliers, and shipping methods.

3. In addition to what is already mentioned, the database needs to track the inventory levels for each product, according to a reorder level and lead time.

4. At this time, Dan does not need to store information about the customer; he simply needs you to focus on the inventory structure.

5. Develop a query that will display the products that need to be ordered from their supplier. To complete this, you will want to compare a reorder level with how many units are in stock.

6. Develop several reports that display:

   a. Each product ordered by its supplier. The report should include the product name, quantity on hand, and reorder level.

   b. Each supplier ordered by shipping method.

   c. Each product that requires more than five days lead time. (Hint: You will want to create a query for this first.)

   d. Each product ordered by category.

7. Here are some additional business rules to assist you in completing this task:

   a. An order must have at least one product but can contain more than one product.

   b. A product can have one or more orders but need not have any orders.

   c. A product must belong to one and only one category, but a category may contain many products.

   d. A product can only be stocked by one supplier, but a supplier can provide more than one product.

   e. A supplier will use one type of shipping method, but shipping methods can be used by more than one supplier.

   Data file: AYK30_Data.xlsx

Project 31:

Call Center

A manufacturing company, Teleworks, has been a market leader in the wireless telephone business for the past 10 years. Other firms have imitated its product with some degree of success, but Teleworks occupies a dominant position in the marketplace because it has a first-mover advantage with a quality product.

Recently Teleworks began selling a new, enhanced wireless phone. This new phone does not replace its current product but offers additional features, greater durability, and better performance for a somewhat higher price. Offering this enhanced phone has established a new revenue stream for the company.

Many sales executives at Teleworks seem to subscribe to the-more-you-have, the-more-you-want theory of managing customer data. That is, they believe they can never accumulate too much information about their customers and that they can do their jobs more effectively by collecting infinite numbers of customer details. Having a firm grasp on a wide range of customer-focused details—specifically reports summarizing call center information—can be critical in enabling your company to manage a customer relationship management (CRM) solution successfully that creates a positive impact.

To continue to provide excellent customer support and in anticipation of increased calls due to the release of its new product, Teleworks needs a database that it can use to record, track, and query call center information. Teleworks CIO Ken Davisson has hired you to develop this database.

1. Teleworks has provided you with a data file, AYK31_Data.xlsx; its current approach for recording cell center information is a spreadsheet file.

2. Develop an ERD diagram before you begin to create the database.

3. Create the database using a personal DBMS package (preferably Microsoft Access) that will allow data analysts to enter call center data according to the type of issue and the customer, assign each call to a consultant, and prioritize the call.

4. Develop a query that will display all issues that are open.

5. Develop a screen form to browse all issues.

6. Develop several reports that display:

   a. All closed issues.

   b. Each issue in detail ordered by issue ID.

   c. Each issue in detail ordered by consultant.

   d. Each issue in detail ordered by category.

   e. Each issue in detail ordered by status.

7. Here are some additional business rules to assist you in completing this task:

   a. An issue must have at least one customer.

   b. A customer can have more than one issue.

   c. Each issue must be assigned to one consultant.

   d. Each consultant can be assigned to more than one issue.

   e. An issue can only belong to one category.

   f. An issue must be assigned only one status code.

   g. An issue must be assigned a priority code.

8. Priorities are assigned accordingly:

Priority Level
Critical
High
Moderate
Standard
Low

9. Status is recorded as either open or closed.

10. The categories of each issue need to be recorded as:

Category
Hardware/Phone
Software/Voice mail
Internet/Web

Data file: AYK31_Data.xlsx

Project 32:

Sales Pipeline

Sales drive any organization. This is true for every for-profit business, irrespective of size or industry type. If customers are not buying your goods or services, you run the risk of not having a business. This is when tough decisions have to be made, such as whether to slash budgets, lay off staff, or seek additional financing.

Unfortunately, you do not wield ultimate power over your customers' buying habits. Although you can attempt to influence buying behavior through strategic marketing, smart businesses remain one step ahead by collecting and analyzing historical and current customer information from a range of internal and external sources to forecast future sales. In other words, managing the sales pipeline is an essential ingredient of business success.

You have recently been hired by RealTime Solutions, a new company that collects information to understand, manage, and predict specific sales cycles (including the supply chain and lead times) in the automobile business. Having an accurate forecast of future sales will allow the company to increase or decrease the production cycle as required and manage personnel levels, inventory, and cash flow.

Using a personal DBMS package (preferably Microsoft Access), create a sales pipeline database that will:

1. Track opportunities from employees to customers.

- Opportunities should have a ranking, category, source of opportunity, open date, closed date, description.

2. Create a form for inputting customer, employee, and opportunity data.

3. Create a few reports that display:

- All open opportunities, including relevant customer and employee information.
- Closed opportunities, including relevant customer and employee information.
- All customers.

4. Create your own data to test the integrity of the relationships. Use approximately 10 records per table.

Project 33:

Online Classified Ads

With the emergence of the Internet as a worldwide standard for communicating information, *The Morrison Post,* a medium-sized community newspaper in central Colorado, is creating an electronic version of its paper-based classified ads.

Advertisers can place a small ad that lists items that they wish to sell and provide a means (e.g., telephone number and email) by which prospective buyers can contact them.

The nature of a sale via the newspaper's classified system goes as follows:

- During the course of the sale, the information flows in different directions at different stages.
- First, there is a downstream flow of information (from seller to buyer): the listing in print in the newspaper. (Thus, the classified ad listing is just a way of bringing a buyer and seller together.)

- When a potential purchaser's interest has been raised, that interest must be relayed upstream, usually by telephone or by email.
- Finally, a meeting should result that uses face-to-face negotiation to finalize the sale if the sale can be agreed on.

By placing the entire system on the Internet, the upstream and downstream communications are accomplished using a web browser. The sale becomes more of an auction because many potential buyers, all with equal status, can bid for the same item. So it is fairer for all purchasers and gets a better deal for the seller.

Any user who is trying to buy an item can:

- View items for sale.
- Bid on an item he or she wishes to purchase.

Any user who is trying to sell an item can:

- Place a new item for sale.
- Browse a list of the items that he or she is trying to sell, and examine the bids that have been made on each of those items.
- Accept a bid on an item that he or she is selling.

Your job is to complete the following:

1. Develop and describe the entity-relationship diagram for the database that will support the listed activities.
2. Use normalization to ensure the correctness of the tables.
3. Create the database by using a personal DBMS package.
4. Use Figure AYK.7 as a baseline for your database design.

   Data file: AYK33_Data.xlsx

FIGURE AYK.7

3D printing (additive manufacturing) A process that builds—layer by layer in an additive process—a three-dimensional solid object from a digital model.

4D printing Additive manufacturing that prints objects capable of transformation and self-assembly.

A

acceptable use policy (AUP) A policy that a user must agree to follow to be provided access to corporate email, information systems, and the Internet.

access point (AP) The computer or network device that serves as an interface between devices and the network.

accessibility Refers to the varying levels that define what a user can access, view, or perform when operating a system.

accounting and finance ERP component Manages accounting data and financial processes within the enterprise with functions such as general ledger, accounts payable, accounts receivable, budgeting, and asset management.

active RFID tags Have their own transmitter and a power source (typically a battery).

adaptive computer devices Input devices designed for special applications for use by people with different types of special needs.

administrator access Unrestricted access to the entire system.

advanced encryption standard (AES) Introduced by the National Institute of Standards and Technology (NIST), AES is an encryption standard designed to keep government information secure.

adware Software, while purporting to serve some useful function and often fulfilling that function, also allows Internet advertisers to display advertisements without the consent of the computer user.

adwords Keywords that advertisers choose to pay for and appear as sponsored links on the Google results pages.

affiliate program Allows a business to generate commissions or referral fees when a customer visiting its website clicks a link to another merchant's website.

affinity grouping analysis Reveals the relationship between variables along with the nature and frequency of the relationships.

agile methodology Aims for customer satisfaction through early and continuous delivery of useful software components developed by an iterative process using the bare minimum requirements.

agile MIS infrastructure Includes the hardware, software, and telecommunications equipment that, when combined, provides the underlying foundation to support the organization's goals.

algorithms Mathematical formulas placed in software that performs an analysis on a data set.

alpha testing Assessment to determine if the entire system meets the design requirements of the users.

ambient digital experience A blend of the physical, virtual, and electronic environments creating a real-time ambient environment that changes as the user moves from one place to another.

analysis paralysis Occurs when the user goes into an emotional state of overanalyzing (or overthinking) a situation so that a decision or action is never taken, in effect paralyzing the outcome.

analysis phase The firm analyzes its end-user business requirements and refines project goals into defined functions and operations of the intended system.

analytical CRM Supports back-office operations and strategic analysis and includes all systems that do not deal directly with the customers.

analytical information Encompasses all organizational information, and its primary purpose is to support the performance of managerial analysis or semistructured decisions.

analytics The science of fact-based decision making.

anomaly detection The process of identifying rare or unexpected items or events in a data set that do not conform to other items in the data set.

anti-spam policy Simply states that email users will not send unsolicited emails (or spam).

antivirus software Scans and searches hard drives to prevent, detect, and remove known viruses, adware, and spyware.

applet A program that runs within another application such as a website.

appliance A computer dedicated to a single function, such as a calculator or computer game.

application integration The integration of a company's existing management information systems with each other.

application programming interface (API) A set of routines, protocols, and tools for building software applications.

application service provider license Specialty software paid for on a license basis or per-use basis or usage-based licensing.

application software Used for specific information processing needs, including payroll, customer relationship management, project management, training, and many others.

arithmetic-logic unit (ALU) Performs all arithmetic operations (for example, addition and subtraction) and all logic operations (such as sorting and comparing numbers).

artificial intelligence (AI) Simulates human thinking and behavior such as the ability to reason and learn.

As-Is process model Represents the current state of the operation that has been mapped, without any specific improvements or changes to existing processes.

asset tracking Occurs when a company places active or semipassive RFID tags on expensive products or assets to gather data on the items' location with little or no manual intervention.

astroturfing The practice of artificially stimulating online conversation and positive reviews about a product, service, or brand.

asynchronous communication Communication such as email in which the message and the response do not occur at the same time.

attenuation Represents the loss of a network signal strength measured in decibels (dB) and occurs because the transmissions gradually dissipate in strength over longer distances or because of radio interference or physical obstructions such as walls.

attribute   The data elements associated with an entity.

augmented reality   View of the physical world with computer-generated layers of information added to it.

authentication   A method for confirming users' identities.

authorization   The process of providing a user with permission, including access levels and abilities such as file access, hours of access, and amount of allocated storage space.

automatic vehicle location (AVL)   Uses GPS tracking to track vehicles.

automation   Involves computerizing manual tasks making them more efficient and effective and dramatically lowering operational costs.

autonomic computing   A self-managing computing model named after, and patterned on, the human body's autonomic nervous system.

autonomous agent   Software that carries out some set of operations on behalf of a user or another program with some degree of independence or autonomy and employs some knowledge or representation of the user's goals or desires.

availability   Refers to the time frames when the system is operational.

B

backup   An exact copy of a system's information.

backward integration   Sends information entered into a given system automatically to all upstream systems and processes.

balanced scorecard   A management system, as well as a measurement system, that a firm uses to translate business strategies into executable tasks.

bandwidth   The maximum amount of data that can pass from one point to another in a unit of time.

bar chart   A chart or graph that presents grouped data with rectangular bars with lengths proportional to the values that they represent.

benchmark   Baseline values the system seeks to attain.

benchmarking   A process of continuously measuring system results, comparing those results to optimal system performance (benchmark values), and identifying steps and procedures to improve system performance.

best practice   The most successful solutions or problem-solving methods that have been developed by a specific organization or industry.

big data   A collection of large complex data sets, including structured and unstructured data, which cannot be analyzed using traditional database methods and tools.

Big Data as a Service (BDaaS)   Offers a cloud-based big data service to help organizations analyze massive amounts of data to solve business dilemmas.

biological 3D printing   Includes the printing of skin and organs and is progressing from theory to reality; however, politicians and the public do not have a full understanding of the implications.

biometrics   The identification of a user based on a physical characteristic, such as a fingerprint, iris, face, voice, or handwriting.

bit   The smallest element of data and has a value of either 0 or 1.

bit rate (or data rate)   The number of bits transferred or received per unit of time.

black-hat hacker   Breaks into other people's computer systems and may just look around or may steal and destroy information.

blog, or web log   An online journal that allows users to post their own comments, graphics, and video.

Bluetooth   Wireless PAN technology that transmits signals over short distances between cell phones, computers, and other devices.

bottleneck   Occurs when resources reach full capacity and cannot handle any additional demands; it limits throughput and impedes operations.

BPMN activity   A task in a business process.

BPMN event   Anything that happens during the course of a business process.

BPMN flow   Displays the path the process flows.

BPMN gateway   Used to control the flow of a process.

brainstorming   A technique for generating ideas by encouraging participants to offer as many ideas as possible in a short period of time without any analysis until all the ideas have been exhausted.

bring your own device (BYOD)   Policy allowing employees to use their personal mobile devices and computers to access enterprise data and applications.

broadband over power line (BPL)   Technology that makes possible high-speed Internet access over ordinary residential electrical lines and offers an alternative to DSL or high-speed cable modems.

broadband   A high-speed Internet connection that is always connected.

bug bounty program   A crowdsourcing initiative that rewards individuals for discovering and reporting software bugs.

bugs   Defects in the code of an information system.

bullwhip effect   Occurs when distorted product-demand information ripples from one partner to the next throughout the supply chain.

business analytics   The scientific process of transforming data into insight for making better decisions.

business continuity planning (BCP)   Details how a company recovers and restores critical business operations and systems after a disaster or extended disruption.

business-facing processes   Invisible to the external customer but essential to the effective management of the business; they include goal setting, day-to-day planning, giving performance feedback and rewards, and allocating resources.

business impact analysis   A process that identifies all critical business functions and the effect that a specific disaster may have on them.

business intelligence (BI)   Information collected from multiple sources such as suppliers, customers, competitors, partners, and industries that analyze patterns, trends, and relationships for strategic decision making.

business intelligence dashboards   Track corporate metrics such as critical success factors and key performance indicators and include advanced capabilities such as interactive controls, allowing users to manipulate data for analysis.

business model   A plan that details how a company creates, delivers, and generates revenues.

business process   Standardized set of activities that accomplish a specific task.

business process improvement   Attempts to understand and measure the current process and make performance improvements accordingly.

Business Process Model and Notation (BPMN)   A graphical notation that depicts the steps in a business process.

business process modeling (or mapping)   The activity of creating a detailed flowchart or process map of a work process that shows its inputs, tasks, and activities in a structured sequence.

business process model   A graphic description of a process, showing the sequence of process tasks, which is developed for a specific purpose and from a selected viewpoint.

business process patent   A patent that protects a specific set of procedures for conducting a particular business activity.

business process reengineering (BPR) The analysis and redesign of workflow within and between enterprises.

business requirement The specific business requests the system must meet to be successful.

business rule Defines how a company performs a certain aspect of its business and typically results in either a yes/no or true/false answer.

business strategy A leadership plan that achieves a specific set of goals or objectives.

business-critical integrity constraint Enforces business rules vital to an organization's success and often requires more insight and knowledge than relational integrity constraints.

business-to-business (B2B) Applies to businesses buying from and selling to each other over the Internet.

business-to-consumer (B2C) Applies to any business that sells its products or services directly to consumers online.

buyer power One of Porter's five forces; measures the ability of buyers to directly affect the price they are willing to pay for an item.

C

cable modem (or broadband modem) A type of digital modem used with high-speed cable Internet service.

cache memory A small unit of ultra-fast memory that is used to store recently accessed or frequently accessed data so that the CPU does not have to retrieve this data from slower memory circuits such as RAM.

call scripting system Gathers product details and issue resolution information that can be automatically generated into a script for the representative to read to the customer.

campaign management system Guides users through marketing campaigns by performing such tasks as campaign definition, planning, scheduling, segmentation, and success analysis.

candidate relationship management A proactive approach to building, filling, and maintaining a company's talent pipeline for recruiting and hiring.

capacity Represents the maximum throughput a system can deliver; for example, the capacity of a hard drive represents the size or volume.

capacity planning Determines future environmental infrastructure requirements to ensure high-quality system performance.

carbon emissions Includes the carbon dioxide and carbon monoxide in the atmosphere produced by business processes and systems.

cardinality Expresses the specific number of instances in an entity.

cartography The science and art of making an illustrated map or chart.

case-based reasoning A method whereby new problems are solved based on the solutions from similar cases solved in the past.

central processing unit (CPU) (or microprocessor) The actual hardware that interprets and executes the program (software) instructions and coordinates how all the other hardware devices work together.

certificate authority A trusted third party, such as VeriSign, that validates user identities by means of digital certificates.

change agent A person or event that is the catalyst for implementing major changes for a system to meet business changes.

chief automation officer Determines if a person or business process can be replaced by a robot or software.

chief data officer (CDO) Responsible for determining the types of information the enterprise will capture, retain, analyze, and share.

chief information officer (CIO) Responsible for (1) overseeing all uses of MIS and (2) ensuring that MIS strategically aligns with business goals and objectives.

chief intellectual property officer Manages and defends intellectual property, copyrights, and patents.

chief knowledge officer (CKO) Responsible for collecting, maintaining, and distributing company knowledge.

chief privacy officer (CPO) Responsible for ensuring the ethical and legal use of information within a company.

chief security officer (CSO) Responsible for ensuring the security of MIS systems and developing strategies and MIS safeguards against attacks from hackers and viruses.

chief technology officer (CTO) Responsible for ensuring the speed, accuracy, availability, and reliability for an organization's information technology.

chief user experience officer Creates the optimal relationship between user and technology.

Child Online Protection Act (COPA) A law that protects minors from accessing inappropriate material on the Internet.

chipless RFID tags Use plastic or conductive polymers instead of silicon-based microchips, allowing them to be washed or exposed to water without damaging the chip.

classification analysis The process of organizing data into categories or groups for its most effective and efficient use.

clean computing Refers to the environmentally responsible use, manufacture, and disposal of technology products and computer equipment.

click-fraud The practice of artificially inflating traffic statistics for online advertisements.

click-to-talk Allows customers to click a button and talk with a representative via the Internet.

clickstream analytics The process of collecting, analyzing and reporting aggregate data about which pages a website visitor visits—and in what order.

clickstream data Exact pattern of a consumer's navigation through a site.

client A computer designed to request information from a server.

client/server network A model for applications in which the bulk of the back-end processing, such as performing a physical search of a database, takes place on a server, whereas the front-end processing, which involves communicating with the users, is handled by the clients.

closed source Any proprietary software licensed under exclusive legal right of the copyright holder.

cloud audit Creates a standard way for cloud providers to simplify the process of gathering audit data and communicate how they address security, governance, and compliance.

cloud bursting When a company uses its own computing infrastructure for normal usage and accesses the cloud when it needs to scale for high/peak load requirements, ensuring that a sudden spike in usage does not result in poor performance or system crashes.

cloud computing Stores, manages, and processes data and applications over the Internet rather than on a personal computer or server.

cloud fabric The software that makes the benefits of cloud computing possible, such as multi-tenancy.

cloud fabric controller An individual who monitors and provisions cloud resources, similar to a server administrator at an individual company.

Cloud Security Alliance (CSA) A nonprofit organization that promotes research into best practices for securing cloud computing and cloud delivery models.

cluster analysis A technique used to divide an information set into mutually exclusive groups such that the members of each group are as close together as possible to one another and the different groups are as far apart as possible.

coaxial cable   Cable that can carry a wide range of frequencies with low signal loss.

cold site   A separate facility that does not have any computer equipment but is a place where employees can move after a disaster.

collaboration system   A set of tools that supports the work of teams or groups by facilitating the sharing and flow of information.

collective intelligence   Collaborating and tapping into the core knowledge of all employees, partners, and customers.

common data repository   Allows every department of a company to store and retrieve information in real time, allowing information to be more reliable and accessible.

communication device   Equipment used to send information and receive it from one location to another.

communication plan   Defines the how, what, when, and who regarding the flow of project information to stakeholders and is key for managing expectations.

community cloud   Serves a specific community with common business models, security requirements, and compliance considerations.

comparative analysis   Can compare two or more data sets to identify patterns and trends.

competitive advantage   A feature of a product or service on which customers place a greater value than on similar offerings from competitors.

competitive click-fraud   A computer crime in which a competitor or disgruntled employee increases a company's search advertising costs by repeatedly clicking the advertiser's link.

competitive intelligence   The process of gathering information about the competitive environment, including competitors' plans, activities, and products, to improve a company's ability to succeed.

competitive monitoring   Occurs when a company keeps tabs of its competitor's activities on the web using software that automatically tracks all competitor website activities such as discounts and new products.

complex instruction set computer (CISC) chip   Type of CPU that can recognize as many as 100 or more instructions, enough to carry out most computations directly.

composite entities   Entities that exist to represent the relationship between two other entities.

computer   An electronic device operating under the control of instructions stored in its own memory that can accept, manipulate, and store data.

computer simulation   Complex systems, such as the U.S. economy, can be modeled by means of mathematical equations, and different scenarios can be run against the model to conduct "what-if" analysis.

computer-aided design /computer-aided manufacturing (CAD/CAM)   Used to create the digital designs and then manufacture the products.

computer-aided software engineering (CASE)   Software tools that provide automated support for the development of the system.

confidentiality   The assurance that messages and information remain available only to those authorized to view them.

consolidation   The aggregation of data from simple roll-ups to complex groupings of interrelated information.

consumer-to-business (C2B)   Applies to any consumer who sells a product or service to a business on the Internet.

consumer-to-consumer (C2C)   Applies to customers offering goods and services to each other on the Internet.

contact center or call center   Where customer service representatives answer customer inquiries and solve problems, usually by email, chat, or phone.

contact management CRM system   Maintains customer contact information and identifies prospective customers for future sales, using tools such as organizational charts, detailed customer notes, and supplemental sales information.

content creator   The person responsible for creating the original website content.

content editor   The person responsible for updating and maintaining website content.

content filtering   Occurs when organizations use software that filters content, such as emails, to prevent the accidental or malicious transmission of unauthorized information.

content management system (CMS)   Helps companies manage the creation, storage, editing, and publication of their website content.

control objectives for information and related technology (COBIT) A set of best practices that helps an organization to maximize the benefits of an information system, at the same time establishing appropriate controls to ensure minimum errors.

control panel   A Windows feature that provides a group of options that sets default values for the Windows operating system.

control unit   Interprets software instructions and literally tells the other hardware devices what to do, based on the software instructions.

conversion   The process of transferring information from a legacy system to a new system.

copyright   The legal protection afforded an expression of an idea, such as a song, book, or video game.

core ERP components   The traditional components that are included in most ERP systems and primarily focus on internal operations.

core processes   Business processes, such as manufacturing goods, selling products, and providing service, that make up the primary activities in a value chain.

corporate social responsibility   Companies' acknowledged responsibility to society.

corrective maintenance   Makes system changes to repair design flaws, coding errors, or implementation issues.

counterfeit software   Software that is manufactured to look like the real thing and sold as such.

course management software   Contains course information such as a syllabus and assignments and offers drop boxes for quizzes and homework, along with a grade book.

cracker   A hacker with criminal intent.

cradle to grave   Provides logistics support throughout the entire system or life of the product.

critical path   The series of activities that determine the earliest time by which the project can be completed.

critical path analysis   A project diagramming method used to predict total project duration.

critical success factors (CSFs)   Crucial steps companies perform to achieve their goals and objectives and implement their strategies.

CRM analysis technologies   Help organizations segment their customers into categories such as best and worst customers.

CRM predicting technologies   Help organizations predict customer behavior, such as which customers are at risk of leaving.

CRM reporting technologies Help organizations identify their customers across other applications.

cross-selling Selling additional products or services to an existing customer.

crowdfunding Sources capital for a project by raising many small amounts from a large number of individuals, typically via the Internet.

crowdsourcing Refers to the wisdom of the crowd.

cryptography The science that studies encryption, which is the hiding of messages so that only the sender and receiver can read them.

customer analytics Involves gathering, classifying, comparing, and studying customer data to identify buying trends, at-risk customers, and potential future opportunities.

customer relationship management (CRM) A means of managing all aspects of a customer's relationship with an organization to increase customer loyalty and retention and an organization's profitability.

customer segmentation Divides a market into categories that share similar attributes such as age, location, gender, habits, and so on.

customer service and support (CSS) A part of operational CRM that automates service requests, complaints, product returns, and information requests.

customer-facing process Results in a product or service that is received by an organization's external customer.

cyber-espionage Includes governments that are after some form of information about other governments.

cyber-vigilantes Include individuals that seek notoriety or want to make a social or political point such as WikiLeaks.

cyberbullying Threats, negative remarks, or defamatory comments transmitted via the Internet or posted on a website.

cybermediation Refers to the creation of new kinds of intermediaries that simply could not have existed before the advent of ebusiness.

cyberterrorism The use of computer and networking technologies against persons or property to intimidate or coerce governments, individuals, or any segment of society to attain political, religious, or ideological goals.

cyberterrorists Seek to cause harm to people or to destroy critical systems or information and use the Internet as a weapon of mass destruction.

cybervandalism The electronic defacement of an existing website.

cyberwar An organized attempt by a country's military to disrupt or destroy information and communication systems of another country.

cyborg anthropologist An individual who studies the interaction between humans and technology, observing how technology can shape humans' lives.

cycle time The time required to process an order.

D

dark web The portion of the Internet that is intentionally hidden from search engines, uses masked IP addresses, and is accessible only with a special web browser: part of the deep web.

data Raw facts that describe the characteristics of an event or object.

data aggregation The collection of data from various sources for the purpose of data processing.

data artist A business analytics specialist who uses visual tools to help people understand complex data.

Data as a Service (DaaS) Facilitates the accessibility of business-critical data in a timely, secure, and affordable manner.

data broker A business that collects personal information about consumers and sells that information to other organizations.

data center A facility used to house management information systems and associated components, such as telecommunications and storage systems.

data dictionary Compiles all of the metadata about the data elements in the data model.

data element (or data field) The smallest or basic unit of information.

data flow diagram (DFD) Illustrates the movement of information between external entities and the processes and data stores within the system.

data gap analysis Occurs when a company examines its data to determine if it can meet business expectations, while identifying possible data gaps or where missing data might exist.

data governance Refers to the overall management of the availability, usability, integrity, and security of company data.

data integration The integration of data from multiple sources, which provides a unified view of all data.

data lake A storage repository that holds a vast amount of raw data in its original format until the business needs it.

data latency The time it takes for data to be stored or retrieved.

data map A technique for establishing a match, or balance, between the source data and the target data warehouse.

data mart Contains a subset of data warehouse information.

data mining The process of analyzing data to extract information not offered by the raw data alone.

data mining tool Uses a variety of techniques to find patterns and relationships in large volumes of information that predict future behavior and guide decision making.

data model Logical data structures that detail the relationships among data elements using graphics or pictures.

data point An individual item on a graph or a chart.

data profiling The process of collecting statistics and information about data in an existing source.

data quality audit Determines the accuracy and completeness of its data.

data replication The process of sharing information to ensure consistency between multiple data sources.

data scientist Extracts knowledge from data by performing statistical analysis, data mining, and advanced analytics on big data to identify trends, market changes, and other relevant information.

data set An organized collection of data.

data steward Responsible for ensuring the policies and procedures are implemented across the organization and acts as a liaison between the MIS department and the business.

data stewardship The management and oversight of an organization's data assets to help provide business users with high-quality data that is easily accessible in a consistent manner.

data validation Includes the tests and evaluations used to determine compliance with data governance polices to ensure correctness of data.

data visualization tools Move beyond Excel graphs and charts into sophisticated analysis techniques such as pie charts, controls, instruments, maps, time-series graphs, etc.

data visualization Describes technologies that allow users to "see" or visualize data to transform information into a business perspective.

data warehouse   A logical collection of information, gathered from many operational databases, that supports business analysis activities and decision-making tasks.

data-driven decision management   An approach to business governance that values decisions that can be backed up with verifiable data.

data-driven website   An interactive website kept constantly updated and relevant to the needs of its customers using a database.

database   Maintains information about various types of objects (inventory), events (transactions), people (employees), and places (warehouses).

database management system (DBMS)   Creates, reads, updates, and deletes data in a database while controlling access and security.

decision support system (DSS)   Model information using OLAP, which provides assistance in evaluating and choosing among different courses of action.

decrypt   Decodes information and is the opposite of encrypt.

deep learning   A process that employs specialized algorithms to model and study complex datasets; the method is also used to establish relationships among data and datasets.

deep web   The large part of the Internet that is inaccessible to conventional search engines.

dependency   A logical relationship that exists between the project tasks or between a project task and a milestone.

descriptive analytics   Analytical techniques that describe past performance and history.

design phase   Establishes descriptions of the desired features and operations of the system including screen layouts, business rules, process diagrams, pseudocode, and other documentation.

destructive agents   Malicious agents designed by spammers and other Internet attackers to farm email addresses off websites or deposit spyware on machines.

development phase   Transforms all the detailed design documents from the design phase into the actual system.

development testing   Testing the system to ensure it is bug-free.

digital certificate   A data file that identifies individuals or organizations online and is comparable to a digital signature.

digital Darwinism   Implies that organizations that cannot adapt to the new demands placed on them for surviving in the information age are doomed to extinction.

digital dashboard   Tracks KPIs and CSFs by compiling information from multiple sources and tailoring it to meet user needs.

digital divide   A worldwide gap giving advantage to those with access to technology.

digital rights management   A technological solution that allows publishers to control their digital media to discourage, limit, or prevent illegal copying and distribution.

digital subscriber line (DSL)   Provides high-speed digital data transmission over standard telephone lines using broadband modem technology, allowing both Internet and telephone services to work over the same phone lines.

dirty data   Erroneous or flawed data.

Disaster Recovery as a Service (DRaaS)   Offers backup services that use cloud resources to protect applications and data from disruption caused by disaster.

disaster recovery cost curve   Charts (1) the cost to the company of the unavailability of information and technology and (2) the cost to the company of recovering from a disaster over time.

disaster recovery plan   A detailed process for recovering information or a system in the event of a catastrophic disaster.

discovery prototyping   Building a small-scale representation or working model of the system to ensure that it meets the user and business requirements.

disintermediation   Occurs when a business sells direct to the customer online and cuts out the intermediary.

disruptive technology   A new way of doing things that initially does not meet the needs of existing customers.

distributed computing   Processes and manages algorithms across many machines in a computing environment.

domain name hosting (web hosting)   A service that allows the owner of a domain name to maintain a simple website and provide email capacity.

domain name system (DNS)   Converts IP address into domains, or identifying labels that use a variety of recognizable naming conventions.

dot-com   The original term for a company operating on the Internet.

downtime   Refers to a period of time when a system is unavailable.

drill-down   Enables users to view details, and details of details, of information. This is the reverse of consolidation.

drive-by hacking   A computer attack by which an attacker accesses a wireless computer network, intercepts data, uses network services, and/or sends attack instructions without entering the office or organization that owns the network.

drone   An unmanned aircraft that can fly autonomously, or without a human. Amazon.com is piloting drone aircraft for package deliveries.

dual boot   Provides the user with the option of choosing the operating system when the computer is turned on.

dumpster diving   Looking through people's trash; another way hackers obtain information.

dynamic catalog   An area of a website that stores information about products in a database.

dynamic host configuration protocol (DHCP)   Allows dynamic IP address allocation so users do not have to have a preconfigured IP address to use the network.

dynamic information   Includes data that change based on user actions.

dynamic process   A continuously changing process used to provide business solutions to ever-changing business operations.

dynamic report   A report that changes automatically during creation.

dynamic scaling   Means that the MIS infrastructure can be automatically scaled up or down based on needed requirements.

E

ebook   An electronic book that can be read on a computer or special reading device.

ebusiness   Includes ecommerce along with all activities related to internal and external business operations such as servicing customer accounts, collaborating with partners, and exchanging real-time information.

ebusiness model   A plan that details how a company creates, delivers, and generates revenues on the Internet.

ecommerce   The buying and selling of goods and services over the Internet.

edge matching (warping, rubber sheeting)   Occurs when paper maps are laid edge to edge, and items that run across maps but do not match are reconfigured to match.

ediscovery (or electronic discovery)   Refers to the ability of a company to identify, search, gather, seize, or export digital information in responding to a litigation, audit, investigation, or information inquiry.

effectiveness MIS metrics   Measure the impact MIS has on business processes and activities, including customer satisfaction and customer conversion rates.

efficiency MIS metrics   Measure the performance of MIS itself such as throughput, transaction speed, and system availability.

egovernment   Involves the use of strategies and technologies to transform government(s) by improving the delivery of services and enhancing the quality of interaction between the citizen-consumer and all branches of government.

eintegration   The use of the Internet to provide customers with the ability to gain personalized information by querying corporate databases and their information sources.

electronic data interchange (EDI)   A standard format for the electronic exchange of information between supply chain participants.

elogistics   Manages the transportation and storage of goods.

email privacy policy   Details the extent to which email messages may be read by others.

embedded operating system   Used for a single purpose in computer appliances and special-purpose applications, such as an automobile, ATM, or media player.

emergency   A sudden, unexpected event requiring immediate action due to potential threat to health and safety, the environment, or property.

emergency notification service   An infrastructure built for notifying people in the event of an emergency.

emergency preparedness   Ensures that a company is ready to respond to an emergency in an organized, timely, and effective manner.

employee monitoring policy   States explicitly how, when, and where the company monitors its employees.

employee relationship management (ERM)   Provides web-based self-service tools that streamline and automate the human resources department.

encryption   Scrambles information into an alternative form that requires a key or password to decrypt.

energy consumption   The amount of energy consumed by business processes and systems.

enterprise application integration (EAI)   Connects the plans, methods, and tools aimed at integrating separate enterprise systems.

enterprise application integration (EAI) middleware   Takes a new approach to middleware by packaging commonly used applications together, reducing the time needed to integrate applications from multiple vendors.

enterprise architect   A person grounded in technology, fluent in business, and able to provide the important bridge between MIS and the business.

enterprise resource planning (ERP)   Integrates all departments and functions throughout an organization into a single IT system (or integrated set of IT systems) so employees can make decisions by viewing enterprisewide information about all business operations.

enterprise system   Provides enterprisewide support and data access for a firm's operations and business processes.

entity   Stores information about a person, place, thing, transaction, or event.

entity-relationship diagram (ERD)   A technique for documenting the entities and relationships in a database environment.

entry barrier   A feature of a product or service that customers have come to expect and entering competitors must offer the same for survival.

epolicies   Policies and procedures that address information management along with the ethical use of computers and the Internet in the business environment.

eprocurement   The business-to-business (B2B) online purchase and sale of supplies and services.

eshop (estore or etailer)   An online version of a retail store where customers can shop at any hour.

estimated time en route (ETE)   The time remaining before reaching a destination using the present speed; typically used for navigation applications.

estimated time of arrival (ETA)   The time of day of an expected arrival at a certain destination; typically used for navigation applications.

estimation analysis   Determines values for an unknown continuous variable behavior or estimated future value.

ethernet   A physical and data layer technology for LAN networking.

ethical computer use policy   Contains general principles to guide computer user behavior.

ethics   The principles and standards that guide our behavior toward other people.

ewaste   Refers to discarded, obsolete, or broken electronic devices.

executive information system (EIS)   A specialized DSS that supports senior-level executives and unstructured, long-term, nonroutine decisions requiring judgment, evaluation, and insight.

executive sponsor   The person or group who provides the financial resources for the project.

expert system   Computerized advisory programs that imitate the reasoning processes of experts in solving difficult problems.

explicit knowledge   Consists of anything that can be documented, archived, and codified, often with the help of MIS.

extended ERP component   The extra components that meet organizational needs not covered by the core components and primarily focus on external operations.

Extensible Markup Language (XML)   A markup language for documents containing structured information.

extraction, transformation, and loading (ETL)   A process that extracts information from internal and external databases, transforms it using a common set of enterprise definitions, and loads it into a data warehouse.

extranet   An extension of an intranet that is only available to authorized outsiders, such as customers, partners, and suppliers.

extreme programming (XP) methodology   Breaks a project into four phases, and developers cannot continue to the next phase until the previous phase is complete.

ezine   A magazine published only in electronic form on a computer network.

F

fact   The confirmation or validation of an event or object.

failback   Occurs when the primary machine recovers and resumes operations, taking over from the secondary server.

failover   A specific type of fault tolerance, occurs when a redundant storage server offers an exact replica of the real-time data, and if the primary server crashes, the users are automatically directed to the secondary server or backup server.

fair information practices (FIP)   A general term for a set of standards governing the collection and use of personal data and addressing issues of privacy and accuracy.

fast data   The application of big data analytics to smaller data sets in near-real or real-time in order to solve a problem or create business value.

fault tolerance   A general concept that a system has the ability to respond to unexpected failures or system crashes as the backup system immediately and automatically takes over with no loss of service.

feasibility   The measure of the tangible and intangible benefits of an information system.

feedback   Information that returns to its original transmitter (input, transform, or output) and modifies the transmitter's actions.

fiber optic (or optical fiber)   Refers to the technology associated with the transmission of information as light impulses along a glass wire or fiber.

field   A characteristic of a table.

file transfer protocol (FTP)   A simple network protocol that allows the transfer of files between two computers on the Internet.

firewall   Hardware and/or software that guard a private network by analyzing incoming and outgoing information for the correct markings.

first-mover advantage   An advantage that occurs when a company can significantly increase its market share by being first to market with a competitive advantage.

flash memory   A special type of rewritable read-only memory (ROM) that is compact and portable.

folksonomy   Similar to taxonomy except that crowdsourcing determines the tags or keyword-based classification system.

forecasting model   Predictions based on time-series information allowing users to manipulate the time series for forecasting activities.

foreign key   A primary key of one table that appears as an attribute in another table and acts to provide a logical relationship between the two tables.

forward integration   Sends information entered in a given system automatically to all downstream systems and processes.

fourth-generation languages (4GL)   Programming languages that look similar to human languages.

fuzzy logic   A mathematical method of handling imprecise or subjective information.

G

Gantt chart   A simple bar chart that lists project tasks vertically against the project's time frame, listed horizontally.

genetic algorithm   An artificial intelligence system that mimics the evolutionary, survival-of-the-fittest process to generate increasingly better solutions to a problem.

geocache   A GPS technology adventure game that posts on the Internet the longitude and latitude location of an item for users to find.

geocoding   A coding process in spatial databases that assigns a digital map feature an attribute that serves as a unique ID (tract number, node number) or classification (soil type, zoning category).

geocoin   A round coin-sized object that is uniquely numbered and hidden in geocache.

geographic information system (GIS)   Stores, views, and analyzes geographic data, creating multidimensional charts or maps.

gigabyte (GB)   Roughly 1 billion bytes.

gigahertz (GHz)   The number of billions of CPU cycles per second.

GIS map automation   Links business assets to a centralized system where they can be tracked and monitored over time.

global positioning system (GPS)   A satellite-based navigation system providing extremely accurate position, time, and speed information.

goal-seeking analysis   Finds the inputs necessary to achieve a goal such as a desired level of output. It is the reverse of what-if and sensitivity analysis.

goods   Material items or products that customers will buy to satisfy a want or need. Clothing, groceries, cell phones, and cars are all examples of goods that people buy to fulfill their needs.

Google Glass   A wearable computer with an optical head-mounted display (OHMD).

granularity   Refers to the level of detail in the model or the decision-making process.

green personal computer (green PC)   A computer built using environmentally friendly materials and designed to save energy.

grid computing   A collection of computers, often geographically dispersed, that are coordinated to solve a common problem.

H

hackers   Experts in technology who use their knowledge to break into computers and computer networks, either for profit or motivated by the challenge.

hactivists   Have philosophical and political reasons for breaking into systems and will often deface the website as a protest.

haptic interface   Uses technology allowing humans to interact with a computer through bodily sensations and movements.

hard drive   A secondary storage medium that uses several rigid disks coated with a magnetically sensitive material and housed together with the recording heads in a hermetically sealed mechanism.

hardware   Consists of the physical devices associated with a computer system.

hashtag   A keyword or phrase used to identify a topic and preceded by a hash or pound sign (#).

heat map   A two-dimensional representation of data in which values are represented by colors.

help desk   A group of people who respond to users' questions.

high availability   Occurs when a system is continuously operational at all times.

high-speed Internet cable connection   Provides Internet access by using a cable television company's infrastructure and a special cable modem.

HIPAA Security Rule   Ensures national standards for securing patient data that is stored or transferred electronically.

histogram   A graphical display of data using bars of different heights.

historical analysis   Historical events are studied to anticipate the outcome of current developments.

hitbots   Create the illusion that a large number of potential customers are clicking the advertiser's links, when in fact there is no likelihood that any of the clicks will lead to profit for the advertiser.

horizontal privilege escalation   Attackers grant themselves the same access levels they already have but assume the identity of another user.

hot site   A separate and fully equipped facility where the company can move immediately after a disaster and resume business.

hotspots   Designated locations where Wi-Fi access points are publicly available.

HTML 5   The current version of HTML; delivers everything from animation to graphics, music to movies. Can be used to build complicated web applications and works across platforms, including a PC, tablet, smart phone, or smart TV.

human resources ERP component   Tracks employee information, including payroll, benefits, compensation, and performance assessment and ensures compliance with all laws.

human-generated data   Data that humans, in interaction with computers, generate.

hybrid cloud   Includes two or more private, public, or community clouds, but each cloud remains separate and is only linked by technology that enables data and application portability.

hybrid cloud storage   Uses both on-site and off-site resources to store corporate data.

hybrid ERP   Splits the ERP functions between an on-premises ERP system and one or more functions handled as Software as a Service (SaaS) in the cloud.

hypertext markup language (HTML)   Publishes hypertext on the WWW, which allows users to move from one document to another simply by clicking a hot spot or link.

hypertext transport protocol (HTTP)   The Internet protocol web browsers use to request and display web pages using universal resource locators.

I

identity management   A broad administrative area that deals with identifying individuals in a system (such as a country, a network, or an enterprise) and controlling their access to resources within that system by associating user rights and restrictions with the established identity.

identity theft   Forging someone's identity for the purpose of fraud.

IEEE 802.11n (or Wireless-N)   The newest standard for wireless networking.

implementation phase   When the organization places the system into production so users can begin to perform actual business operations with it.

in-sourcing (in-house development)   Uses the professional expertise within an organization to develop and maintain its information technology systems.

incident   Unplanned interruption of a service.

incident management   The process responsible for managing how incidents are identified and corrected.

incident record   Contains all of the details of an incident.

infographics (information graphics)   A representation of information in a graphic format designed to make the data easily understandable at a glance.

information age   The present time, during which infinite quantities of facts are widely available to anyone who can use a computer.

information cleansing or scrubbing   A process that weeds out and fixes or discards inconsistent, incorrect, or incomplete information.

information compliance   The act of conforming, acquiescing, or yielding information.

information cube   The common term for the representation of multidimensional information.

information ethics   Govern the ethical and moral issues arising from the development and use of information technologies as well as the creation, collection, duplication, distribution, and processing of information itself (with or without the aid of computer technologies).

information governance   A method or system of government for information management or control.

information granularity   The extent of detail within the information (fine and detailed or coarse and abstract).

information inconsistency   Occurs when the same data element has different values.

information integrity   A measure of the quality of information.

information integrity issue   Occurs when a system produces incorrect, inconsistent, or duplicate data.

information management   Examines the organizational resource of information and regulates its definitions, uses, value, and distribution, ensuring that it has the types of data/information required to function and grow effectively.

information MIS infrastructure   Identifies where and how important information, such as customer records, is maintained and secured.

Information of Everything (IoE)   A concept that extends the Internet of Things (IoT) emphasis on machine-to-machine communications to describe a more complex system that also encompasses people and processes.

information privacy policy   Contains general principles regarding information privacy.

information property   An ethical issue that focuses on who owns information about individuals and how information can be sold and exchanged.

information reach   Measures the number of people a firm can communicate with all over the world.

information redundancy   The duplication of data, or the storage of the same data in multiple places.

information richness   Refers to the depth and breadth of details contained in a piece of textual, graphic, audio, or video information.

information secrecy   The category of computer security that addresses the protection of data from unauthorized disclosure and confirmation of data source authenticity.

information security   A broad term encompassing the protection of information from accidental or intentional misuse by persons inside or outside an organization.

information security plan   Details how an organization will implement the information security policies.

information security policies   Identify the rules required to maintain information security, such as requiring users to log off before leaving for lunch or meetings, never sharing passwords with anyone, and changing passwords every 30 days.

information   Data converted into a meaningful and useful context.

Infrastructure as a Service (IaaS)   The delivery of computer hardware capability, including the use of servers, networking, and storage, as a service.

input device   Equipment used to capture information and commands.

insiders   Legitimate users who purposely or accidentally misuse their access to the environment and cause some kind of business-affecting incident.

instant messaging (sometimes called IM or IMing)   A service that enables instant or real-time communication between people.

Institute of Electrical and Electronics Engineers (IEEE)   An organization that researches and institutes electrical standards for communication and other technologies.

intangible benefits   Difficult to quantify or measure.

integration Allows separate systems to communicate directly with each other, eliminating the need for manual entry into multiple systems.

integration testing Verifying that separate systems can work together, passing data back and forth correctly.

integrity constraint Rules that help ensure the quality of information.

intellectual property Intangible creative work that is embodied in physical form and includes copyrights, trademarks, and patents.

intelligent agent A special-purpose knowledge-based information system that accomplishes specific tasks on behalf of its users.

intelligent system Various commercial applications of artificial intelligence.

interactivity Measures advertising effectiveness by counting visitor interactions with the target ad, including time spent viewing the ad, number of pages viewed, and number of repeat visits to the advertisement.

intermediaries Agents, software, or businesses that provide a trading infrastructure to bring buyers and sellers together.

Internet A massive network that connects computers all over the world and allows them to communicate with one another.

Internet censorship Government attempts to control Internet traffic, thus preventing some material from being viewed by a country's citizens.

Internet Corporation for Assigned Names and Numbers (ICANN) A nonprofit organization that has assumed the responsibility for IP address space allocation, protocol parameter assignment, domain name system management, and root server system management functions previously performed under U.S. government contract.

Internet of Things (IoT) A world in which interconnected, Internet-enabled devices or things can collect and share data without human intervention.

Internet Protocol TV (IPTV) Distributes digital video content by using IP across the Internet and private IP networks.

Internet protocol version 6 (IPv6) The next-generation protocol, designed to replace the current version Internet protocol, IP version 4 (IPv4).

Internet service provider (ISP) A company that provides access to the Internet for a monthly fee.

Internet use policy Contains general principles to guide the proper use of the Internet.

interoperability The capability of two or more computer systems to share data and resources, even though they are made by different manufacturers.

intranet A restricted network that relies on Internet technologies to provide an Internet-like environment within the company for information sharing, communications, collaboration, web publishing, and the support of business processes.

intrusion detection software (IDS) Features full-time monitoring tools that search for patterns in network traffic to identify intruders.

IP address A unique number that identifies where computers are located on the network.

IT consumerization The blending of personal and business use of technology devices and applications.

iterative development Consists of a series of tiny projects.

J

joint application development Session in which employees meet to define or review the business requirements for the system.

K

key performance indicators (KPIs) Quantifiable metrics a company uses to evaluate progress toward critical success factors.

kill switch A trigger that enables a project manager to close the project before completion.

knowledge assets The human, structural, and recorded resources available to the organization.

knowledge facilitator A person that helps harness the wealth of knowledge in the organization.

knowledge management (KM) Involves capturing, classifying, evaluating, retrieving, and sharing information assets in a way that provides context for effective decisions and actions.

knowledge management system (KMS) Supports the capture, organization, and dissemination of knowledge (i.e., know-how) throughout an organization.

knowledge Skills, experience, and expertise coupled with information and intelligence that creates a person's intellectual resources.

knowledge workers Individuals valued for their ability to interpret and analyze information.

L

latitude Represents a north/south measurement of position.

legacy system An old system that is fast approaching or beyond the end of its useful life within an organization.

list generator Compiles customer information from a variety of sources and segments it for different marketing campaigns.

local area network (LAN) Connects a group of computers in proximity, such as in an office building, school, or home.

location-based services (LBS) Applications that use location information to provide a service.

logical view of information Shows how individual users logically access information to meet their own particular business needs.

logistics Includes the processes that control the distribution, maintenance, and replacement of materials and personnel to support the supply chain.

long tail Referring to the tail of a typical sales curve.

longitude Represents an east/west measurement of position.

loose coupling The capability of services to be joined on demand to create composite services or disassembled just as easily into their functional components.

loyalty program A program to reward customers based on spending.

M

machine learning A type of artificial intelligence that enables computers to both understand concepts in the environment and also to learn.

machine vision The ability of a computer to "see" by digitizing an image, processing the data it contains and taking some kind of action.

machine vision resolution The extent to which a machine can differentiate between objects.

machine vision sensitivity The ability of a machine to see in dim light, or to detect weak impulses at invisible wavelengths.

machine-generated data Created by a machine without human intervention.

machine-to-machine (M2M) Devices that connect directly to other devices.

magnetic medium   A secondary storage medium that uses magnetic techniques to store and retrieve data on disks or tapes coated with magnetically sensitive materials.

magnetic tape   An older secondary storage medium that uses a strip of thin plastic coated with a magnetically sensitive recording medium.

mail bomb   Sends a massive amount of email to a specific person or system that can cause that user's server to stop functioning.

maintainability (or flexibility)   Refers to how quickly a system can transform to support environmental changes.

maintenance phase   When the organization performs changes, corrections, additions, and upgrades to ensure that the system continues to meet its business goals.

maker movement   A cultural trend that places value on an individual's ability to be a creator of things as well as a consumer of things.

makerspace   A community center that provides technology, manufacturing equipment, and educational opportunities to the public that would otherwise be inaccessible or unaffordable.

malware   Software that is intended to damage or disable computers and computer systems.

management information systems (MIS)   A business function, like accounting and human resources, that moves information about people, products, and processes across the company to facilitate decision making and problem solving.

managerial business process   Semidynamic, semiroutine, monthly business processes such as resource allocation, sales strategy, or manufacturing process improvements.

managerial decisions   Concern how the organization should achieve the goals and objectives set by its strategy, and they are usually the responsibility of mid-level management.

managerial level   Employees are continuously evaluating company operations to hone the firm's abilities to identify, adapt to, and leverage change.

many-to-many relationship (M:N)   Between two entities in which an instance of one entity is related to many instances of another and one instance of the other can be related to many instances of the first entity.

market basket analysis   Evaluates such items as websites and checkout scanner information to detect customers' buying behavior and predict future behavior by identifying affinities among customers' choices of products and services.

market share   The proportion of the market that a firm captures.

mashup   Website or web application that uses content from more than one source to create a completely new product or service.

mashup editor   WYSIWYG, or what-you-see-is-what-you-get tools.

mass customization   The ability of an organization to tailor its products or services to the customers' specifications.

master data management (MDM)   The practice of gathering data and ensuring that it is uniform, accurate, consistent, and complete, including such entities as customers, suppliers, products, sales, employees, and other critical entities that are commonly integrated across organizational systems.

materials management   Includes activities that govern the flow of tangible, physical materials through the supply chain such as shipping, transport, distribution, and warehousing.

megabyte (MB or M or Meg)   Roughly 1 million bytes.

megahertz (MHz)   The number of millions of CPU cycles per second.

memory cards   Contain high-capacity storage that holds data such as captured images, music, or text files.

memory sticks   Provide nonvolatile memory for a range of portable devices including computers, digital cameras, MP3 players, and PDAs.

metadata   Details about data.

methodology   A set of policies, procedures, standards, processes, practices, tools, techniques, and tasks that people apply to technical and management challenges.

metrics   Measurements that evaluate results to determine whether a project is meeting its goals.

metropolitan area network (MAN)   A large computer network usually spanning a city.

microblogging   The practice of sending brief posts (140 to 200 characters) to a personal blog, either publicly or to a private group of subscribers who can read the posts as IMs or as text messages.

middleware   Several types of software that sit between and provide connectivity for two or more software applications.

MIS infrastructure   Includes the plans for how a firm will build, deploy, use, and share its data, processes, and MIS assets.

MIS skills gap   The difference between existing MIS workplace knowledge and the knowledge required to fulfill the business goals and strategies.

mobile application management (MAM)   Administers and delivers applications to corporate and personal smart phones and tablets.

mobile business (or mbusiness, mcommerce)   The ability to purchase goods and services through a wireless Internet-enabled device.

mobile device management (MDM)   Remotely controls smart phones and tablets, ensuring data security.

model   A simplified representation or abstraction of reality.

modem   A device that enables a computer to transmit and receive data.

module software design   Divides the system into a set of functional units (named modules) that can be used independently or combined with other modules for increased business flexibility.

Moore's Law   Refers to the computer chip performance per dollar doubling every 18 months.

multi-tenancy   A single instance of a system serves multiple customers.

multifactor authentication   Requires more than two means of authentication such as what the user knows (password), what the user has (security token), and what the user is (biometric verification).

multiple-in/multiple-out (MIMO) technology   Multiple transmitters and receivers allow sending and receiving greater amounts of data than traditional networking devices.

multitasking   Allows more than one piece of software to be used at a time.

multivalued attribute   Having the potential to contain more than one value for an attribute.

mutation   The process within a genetic algorithm of randomly trying combinations and evaluating the success (or failure) of the outcome.

N

national service providers (NSPs)   Private companies that own and maintain the worldwide backbone that supports the Internet.

native advertising   Online marketing concept in which the advertiser attempts to gain attention by providing content in the context of the user's experience in terms of its content, format, style, or placement.

nearshore outsourcing Contracting an outsourcing arrangement with a company in a nearby country.

network A communications system created by linking two or more devices and establishing a standard methodology in which they can communicate.

network behavior analysis Gathers an organization's computer network traffic patterns to identify unusual or suspicious operations

network convergence The efficient coexistence of telephone, video, and data communication within a single network, offering convenience and flexibility not possible with separate infrastructures.

network effect Describes how products in a network increase in value to users as the number of users increases.

network operating system (NOS) Operating system that runs a network, steering information between computers and managing security and users.

network topology Refers to the geometric arrangement of the actual physical organization of the computers (and other network devices) in a network.

network transmission media Refers to the various types of media used to carry the signal between computers.

network user license Enables anyone on the network to install and use the software.

network virtualization Combines networks by splitting the available bandwidth into independent channels that can be assigned in real time to a specific device.

neural network A category of AI that attempts to emulate the way the human brain works.

noisy neighbor Refers to a multi-tenancy co-tenant that monopolizes bandwidth, servers, CPUs, and other resources that cause network performance issues.

nonrepudiation A contractual stipulation to ensure that ebusiness participants do not deny (repudiate) their online actions.

nonsensitive PII Information transmitted without encryption and includes information collected from public records, phone books, corporate directories, websites, etc.

nonvolatile Does not require constant power to function.

null-valued attribute Assigned to an attribute when no other value applies or when a value is unknown.

O

object-oriented language Groups data and corresponding processes into objects.

off-the-shelf application software Supports general business processes and does not require any specific software customization to meet the organization's needs.

offshore outsourcing Using organizations from developing countries to write code and develop systems.

on-premise system Includes a server at a physical location using an internal network for internal access and firewalls for remote users' access.

one-to-many relationship (1:M) A relationship between two entities in which an instance of one entity can be related to many instances of a related entity.

one-to-one relationship (1:1) A relationship between two entities in which an instance of one entity can be related to only one instance of a related entity.

online analytical processing (OLAP) The manipulation of information to create business intelligence in support of strategic decision making.

online training Runs over the Internet or on a CD or DVD, and employees complete the training on their own time at their own pace.

online transaction processing (OLTP) The capture of transaction and event information by using technology to (1) process the information according to defined business rules, (2) store the information, and (3) update existing information to reflect the new information.

onshore outsourcing Engaging another company within the same country for services.

open source Refers to any software whose source code is made available free for any third party to review and modify.

open system Consists of nonproprietary hardware and software based on publicly known standards that allow third parties to create add-on products to plug into or interoperate with the system.

operating system software Controls the application software and manages how the hardware devices work together.

operational business process Static, routine, daily business processes such as stocking inventory, checking out customers, or daily opening/closing processes.

operational CRM Supports traditional transactional processing for day-to-day front-office operations or systems that deal directly with the customers.

operational decisions Affect how the firm is run from day to day; they are the domain of operations managers, who are the closest to the customer.

operational level Employees develop, control, and maintain core business activities required to run the day-to-day operations.

operationalized analytics Makes analytics part of a business process.

opportunity management CRM system Targets sales opportunities by finding new customers or companies for future sales.

opt in Receiving emails by choosing to allow permissions to incoming emails.

opt out Customer specifically chooses to deny permission to incoming emails.

optimization analysis An extension of goal-seeking analysis, finds the optimum value for a target variable by repeatedly changing other variables, subject to specified constraints.

optimization model A statistical process that finds the way to make a design, system, or decision as effective as possible, for example, finding the values of controllable variables that determine maximal productivity or minimal waste.

outlier A data value that is numerically distant from most of the other data points in a set of data.

output device Equipment used to see, hear, or otherwise accept the results of information processing requests.

outsourcing An arrangement by which one organization provides a service or services for another organization that chooses not to perform them in-house.

P

packet A single unit of binary data routed through a network.

packet footer Represents the end of the packet or transmission end.

packet header Lists the destination (for example, in IP packets the destination is the IP address) along with the length of the message data.

packet-switching Occurs when the sending computer divides a message into a number of efficiently sized units of data called packets, each of which contains the address of the destination computer.

paradigm shift Occurs when a new radical form of business enters the market that reshapes the way companies and organizations behave.

parallel implementation Use of both a legacy system and a new system until all users verify that the new system functions correctly.

partner relationship management (PRM) Discovers optimal sales channels by selecting the right partners and identifying mutual customers.

passive RFID tags Do not have a power source.

patent An exclusive right to make, use, and sell an invention; granted by a government to the inventor.

pay-per-call Generates revenue each time users click on a link that takes them directly to an online agent waiting for a call.

pay-per-click Generates revenue each time a user clicks on a link to a retailer's website.

pay-per-conversion Generates revenue each time a website visitor is converted to a customer.

peer-to-peer (P2P) network A computer network that relies on the computing power and bandwidth of the participants in the network rather than on a centralized server.

performance Measures how quickly a system performs a process or transaction.

personal area network (PAN) Provides communication over a short distance that is intended for use with devices that are owned and operated by a single user.

personal information management (PIM) software Software that handles contact information, appointments, task lists, and email.

personalization Occurs when a company knows enough about a customer's likes and dislikes that it can fashion offers more likely to appeal to that person, say by tailoring its website to individuals or groups based on profile information, demographics, or prior transactions.

personally identifiable information (PII) Any data that could potentially identify a specific individual.

PERT (Program Evaluation and Review Technique) chart A graphical network model that depicts a project's tasks and the relationships between them.

pharming attack Uses a zombie farm, often by an organized crime association, to launch a massive phishing attack.

pharming Reroutes requests for legitimate websites to false websites.

phased implementation Installation of the new system in phases (for example, by department) until it is verified to work correctly.

phishing A technique to gain personal information for the purpose of identity theft, usually by means of fraudulent emails that look as though they came from legitimate sources.

phishing expedition A masquerading attack that combines spam with spoofing.

physical security Tangible protection such as alarms, guards, fireproof doors, fences, and vaults.

physical view of information The physical storage of information on a storage device.

pie chart A type of graph in which a circle is divided into sectors that each represent a proportion of the whole.

pilot implementation Assignment of a small group of people to use the new system until it is verified to work correctly; then the remaining users migrate to the new system.

pirated software The unauthorized use, duplication, distribution, or sale of copyrighted software.

planning phase Establishes a high-level plan of the intended project and determines project goals.

Platform as a Service (PaaS) Supports the deployment of entire systems, including hardware, networking, and applications, using a pay-per-use revenue model.

plunge implementation Discarding the legacy system and immediately migrating all users to the new system.

podcasting Converts an audio broadcast to a digital music player.

portability Refers to the ability of an application to operate on different devices or software platforms, such as different operating systems.

Porter's Five Forces Model A model for analyzing the competitive forces within the environment in which a company operates to assess the potential for profitability in an industry.

Porter's three generic strategies Generic business strategies that are neither organization nor industry specific and can be applied to any business, product, or service.

prediction A statement about what will happen or might happen in the future; for example, predicting future sales or employee turnover.

predictive analytics Analytical techniques that extract information from data and use it to predict future trends and identify behavioral patterns.

prescriptive analytics Analytical techniques that create models indicating the best decision to make or course of action to take.

pretexting A form of social engineering in which one individual lies to obtain confidential data about another individual.

preventive maintenance Makes system changes to reduce the chance of future system failure.

primary key A field (or group of fields) that uniquely identifies a given record in a table.

primary storage Computer's main memory, which consists of the random access memory (RAM), cache memory, and read-only memory (ROM) that is directly accessible to the CPU.

primary value activities Found at the bottom of the value chain, these include business processes that acquire raw materials and manufacture, deliver, market, sell, and provide after-sales services.

privacy The right to be left alone when you want to be, to have control over your personal possessions, and not to be observed without your consent.

private cloud Serves only one customer or organization and can be located on the customers' premises or off the customer's premises.

privilege escalation A network intrusion attack that takes advantage of programming errors or design flaws to grant the attacker elevated access to the network and its associated data and applications.

process modeling Graphical representation of the processes that capture, manipulate, store, and distribute information between a system and its environment.

procurement The purchase of goods and services to meet the needs of the supply chain.

product differentiation An advantage that occurs when a company develops unique differences in its products with the intent to influence demand.

production The process by which a business processes raw materials and or converts them into a finished product for its goods or services.

production and materials management ERP component Handles production planning and execution tasks such as demand forecasting, production scheduling, job cost accounting, and quality control.

productivity The rate at which goods and services are produced based on total output given total inputs.

programming language   A unique set of keywords (words that it understands) along with a special syntax for organizing program instructions that execute computer commands.

project   Temporary activity a company undertakes to create a unique product, service, or result.

project assumption   Factors considered to be true, real, or certain without proof or demonstration.

project constraint   Specific factors that can limit options, including budget, delivery dates, available skilled resources, and organizational policies.

project deliverable   Any measurable, tangible, verifiable outcome, result, or item that is produced to complete a project or part of a project.

project management office (PMO)   An internal department that oversees all organizational projects.

project management   The application of knowledge, skills, tools, and techniques to project activities to meet project requirements.

project manager   An individual who is an expert in project planning and management, defines and develops the project plan, and tracks the plan to ensure that the project is completed on time and on budget.

project milestones   Represent key dates when a certain group of activities must be performed.

project objectives   Quantifiable criteria that must be met for the project to be considered a success.

project plan   A formal, approved document that manages and controls project execution.

project requirements document   Defines the specifications for product/output of the project and is key for managing expectations, controlling scope, and completing other planning efforts.

project scope   Describes the business needs and the justification, requirements, and current boundaries for the project.

project scope statement   Links the project to the organization's overall business goals.

project stakeholder   Individuals and organizations actively involved in the project or whose interests might be affected as a result of project execution or project completion.

protocol   A standard that specifies the format of data as well as the rules to be followed during transmission.

prototyping   A modern design approach by which the designers and system users use an iterative approach to building the system.

proxy   Software that prevents direct communication between a sending and a receiving computer and is used to monitor packets for security reasons.

pseudocode   An informal description of how the computer program should work.

public cloud   Promotes massive, global, industrywide applications offered to the general public.

public key encryption (PKE)   Uses two keys: a public key that everyone can have and a private key for only the recipient.

Q

query-by-example (QBE) tool   Helps users graphically design the answer to a question against a database.

R

radio-frequency identification (RFID)   Uses electronic tags and labels to identify objects wirelessly over short distances.

random access memory (RAM)   The computer's primary working memory, in which program instructions and data are stored so that they can be accessed directly by the CPU via the processor's high-speed external data bus.

ransomware   A form of malicious software that infects your computer and asks for money.

rapid application development (RAD) methodology (also called rapid prototyping)   Emphasizes extensive user involvement in the rapid and evolutionary construction of working prototypes of a system to accelerate the systems development process.

rational unified process (RUP) methodology   Provides a framework for breaking down the development of software into four gates.

read-only memory (ROM)   The portion of a computer's primary storage that does not lose its contents when one switches off the power.

real simple syndication (RSS)   A web format used to publish frequently updated works, such as blogs, news headlines, audio, and video in a standardized format.

real-time adaptive security   The network security model necessary to accommodate the emergence of multiple perimeters and moving parts on the network, and increasingly advanced threats targeting enterprises.

real-time communication   Occurs when a system updates information at the same rate it receives it.

real-time information   Immediate, up-to-date information.

real-time system   Provides real-time information in response to requests.

recommendation engine   A data-mining algorithm that analyzes a customer's purchases and actions on a website and then uses the data to recommend complementary products.

record   A collection of related data elements.

recovery   The ability to get a system up and running in the event of a system crash or failure that includes restoring the information backup.

reduced instruction set computer (RISC) chip   Limits the number of instructions the CPU can execute to increase processing speed.

redundancy   Occurs when a task or activity is unnecessarily repeated.

regional service providers (RSPs)   Offer Internet service by connecting to NSPs, but they also can connect directly to each other.

regression model   A statistical process for estimating the relationships among variables.

reintermediation   Steps are added to the value chain as new players find ways to add value to the business process.

relational database management system   Allows users to create, read, update, and delete data in a relational database.

relational database model   Stores information in the form of logically related two-dimensional tables.

relational integrity constraint   Rules that enforce basic and fundamental information-based constraints.

reliability (or accuracy)   Ensures that a system is functioning correctly and providing accurate information.

repeater   Receives and repeats a signal to reduce its attenuation and extend its range.

report   A document containing data organized in a table, matrix, or graphical format allowing users to easily comprehend and understand information.

repository   A central location in which data is stored and managed.

reputation system   Where buyers post feedback on sellers.

requirements definition document   Prioritizes all of the business requirements by order of importance to the company.

requirements management The process of managing changes to the business requirements throughout the project.

responsibility matrix Defines all project roles and indicates what responsibilities are associated with each role.

return on investment (ROI) Indicates the earning power of a project.

RFID accelerometer A device that measures the acceleration (the rate of change of velocity) of an item and is used to track truck speeds or taxi cab speeds.

RFID reader (RFID interrogator) A transmitter/receiver that reads the contents of RFID tags in the area.

RFID tag An electronic identification device that is made up of a chip and antenna.

RFID's electronic product code (RFID EPC) Promotes serialization or the ability to track individual items by using the unique serial number associated with each RFID tag.

rivalry among existing competitors One of Porter's five forces; high when competition is fierce in a market and low when competitors are more complacent.

robotic process automation (RPA) The use of software with artificial intelligence (AI) and machine learning capabilities to handle high-volume, repeatable tasks that previously required a human to perform.

robotics Focuses on creating artificial intelligence devices that can move and react to sensory input.

router An intelligent connecting device that examines each packet of data it receives and then decides which way to send it toward its destination.

Rule 41 The part of the United States Federal Rules of Criminal Procedure that covers the search and seizure of physical and digital evidence.

S

safe mode Occurs if the system is failing and will load only the most essential parts of the operating system and will not run many of the background operating utilities.

sales analytics Involves gathering, classifying, comparing, and studying company sales data to analyze product cycles, sales pipelines, and competitive intelligence.

sales force automation (SFA) Automatically tracks all the steps in the sales process.

sales management CRM system Automates each phase of the sales process, helping individual sales representatives coordinate and organize all their accounts.

satellite A space station that orbits Earth receiving and transmitting signals from Earth-based stations over a wide area.

scalability Describes how well a system can scale up or adapt to the increased demands of growth.

scareware A type of malware designed to trick victims into giving up personal information to purchase or download useless and potentially dangerous software.

script kiddies or script bunnies Find hacking code on the Internet and click-and-point their way into systems to cause damage or spread viruses.

scripting language A programming method that provides for interactive modules to a website.

scrum methodology Uses small teams to produce small pieces of software using a series of sprints, or 30-day intervals, to achieve an appointed goal.

search engine Website software that finds other pages based on keyword matching.

search engine optimization (SEO) Combines art along with science to determine how to make URLs more attractive to search engines, resulting in higher search engine ranking.

search engine ranking Evaluates variables that search engines use to determine where a URL appears on the list of search results.

secondary storage Consists of equipment designed to store large volumes of data for long-term storage.

secure hypertext transfer protocol (SHTTP or HTTPS) A combination of HTTP and SSL to provide encryption and secure identification of an Internet server.

secure sockets layer (SSL) A standard security technology for establishing an encrypted link between a web server and a browser, ensuring that all data passed between them remains private.

Security as a Service (SaaS) Involves applications such as anti-virus software delivered over the Internet with constant virus definition updates that are not reliant on user compliance.

selfie A self-photograph placed on a social media website.

semantic web A component of Web 3.0 that describes things in a way that computers can understand.

semi-passive RFID tags Include a battery to run the microchip's circuitry but communicate by drawing power from the RFID reader.

semistructured decision Occurs in situations in which a few established processes help to evaluate potential solutions, but not enough to lead to a definite recommended decision.

sensitive PII Information transmitted with encryption and, when disclosed, results in a breach of an individual's privacy and can potentially cause the individual harm.

sensitivity analysis A special case of what-if analysis; the study of the impact on other variables when one variable is changed repeatedly.

server A computer dedicated to providing information in response to requests.

server virtualization Combines the physical resources, such as servers, processors and operating systems, from the applications.

service-oriented architecture (SOA) A business-driven enterprise architecture that supports integrating a business as linked, repeatable activities, tasks, or services

serviceability How quickly a third party or vendor can change a system to ensure that it meets user needs and the terms of any contracts, including agreed levels of reliability, maintainability, or availability.

services Tasks that customers will buy to satisfy a want or need.

shopping bot Software that will search several retailer websites and provide a comparison of each retailer's offerings, including price and availability.

sign-off Users' actual signatures, indicating they approve all of the business requirements.

single-factor authentication The traditional security process that requires a user name and password.

single-tenancy Each customer or tenant must purchase and maintain an individual system.

single-user license Restricts the use of the software to one user at a time.

single-valued attribute Having only a single value of each attribute of an entity.

site license Enables any qualified users within the organization to install the software, regardless of whether the computer is on a network. Some employees might install the software on a home computer for working remotely.

slack   The amount of time an activity may be delayed without delaying a succeeding activity or the project finish date.

slice-and-dice   The ability to look at information from different perspectives; often performed along a time axis to analyze trends and find time-based patterns in the information.

smart card   A device about the size of a credit card containing embedded technologies that can store information and small amounts of software to perform some limited processing.

smart grid   Delivers electricity using two-way digital technology.

smart phones   Offer more advanced computing ability and connectivity than basic cell phones.

snackable content   Website content that is designed to be easy for readers to consume and to share.

snapshot   A view of data at a particular moment in time.

social bookmarking   Allows users to share, organize, search, and manage bookmarks.

social engineering   Hackers use their social skills to trick people into revealing access credentials or other valuable information.

social graphs   Represent the interconnection of relationships in a social network.

social media   Refers to websites that rely on user participation and user-contributed content.

social media manager   A person within the organization who is trusted to monitor, contribute, filter, and guide the social media presence of a company, individual, product, or brand.

social media monitoring   The process of monitoring and responding to what is being said about a company, individual, product, or brand.

social media policy   Outlines the corporate guidelines or principles governing employee online communications.

social network   An application that connects people by matching profile information.

social networking analysis (SNA)   Maps group contacts identifying who knows each other and who works together.

social networking   The practice of expanding your business and/or social contacts by constructing a personal network.

social tagging   Describes the collaborative activity of marking shared online content with keywords or tags as a way to organize it for future navigation, filtering, or searching.

sock puppet marketing   The use of a false identity to artificially stimulate demand for a product, brand, or service.

software   The set of instructions the hardware executes to carry out specific tasks.

Software as a Service (SaaS)   Delivers applications over the cloud using a pay-per-use revenue model.

software customization   Modifies software to meet specific user or business requirements.

software engineering   A disciplined approach for constructing information systems through the use of common methods, techniques, or tools.

software updates (software patch)   Occurs when the software vendor releases updates to software to fix problems or enhance features.

software upgrade   Occurs when the software vendor releases a new version of the software, making significant changes to the program.

solid state drive   An all-electronic storage device that is an alternative to a hard disk and is faster than a hard disk because there is zero latency (no read/write head to move).

source code   Contains instructions written by a programmer specifying the actions to be performed by computer software.

source data   Identifies the primary location where data is collected.

source document   The original transaction record.

spam   Unsolicited email.

sparkline   A small embedded line graph that illustrates a single trend.

spatial data (geospatial data or geographic information)   Identifies the geographic location of features and boundaries on Earth, such as natural or constructed features, oceans, and more.

spear phishing   A phishing expedition in which the emails are carefully designed to target a particular person or organization.

spyware   A special class of adware that collects data about the user and transmits it over the Internet without the user's knowledge or permission.

SSL certificate   An electronic document that confirms the identity of a website or server and verifies that a public key belongs to a trustworthy individual or company.

stakeholder   A person or group that has an interest or concern in an organization.

standard packet format   Includes a packet header, packet body containing the original message, and packet footer.

static information   Includes fixed data that are not capable of change in the event of a user action.

static process   Process that uses a systematic approach in an attempt to improve business effectiveness and efficiency continuously.

static report   A report created once based on data that does not change.

status report   Periodic review of actual performance versus expected performance.

storage virtualization   Combines multiple network storage devices so they appear to be a single storage device.

strategic business process   Dynamic, nonroutine, long-term business process such as financial planning, expansion strategies, and stakeholder interactions.

strategic decisions   Involve higher level issues concerned with the overall direction of the organization; these decisions define the organization's overall goals and aspirations for the future.

strategic level   Managers develop overall business strategies, goals, and objectives as part of the company's strategic plan.

streaming   A method of sending audio and video files over the Internet in such a way that the user can view the file while it is being transferred.

streamlining   Improves business process efficiencies, simplifying or eliminating unnecessary steps.

structured data   Data that has a defined length, type, and format and includes numbers, dates, or strings such as Customer Address.

structured decision   Involves situations in which established processes offer potential solutions.

structured query language (SQL)   Users write lines of code to answer questions against a database.

stylus   A penlike device used to tap the screen to enter commands.

supplier power   One of Porter's five forces; measures the suppliers' ability to influence the prices they charge for supplies (including materials, labor, and services).

supplier relationship management (SRM)   Focuses on keeping suppliers satisfied by evaluating and categorizing suppliers for different projects.

supply chain All parties involved, directly or indirectly, in obtaining raw materials or a product.

supply chain design Determines how to structure a supply chain, including the product, selection of partners, the location and capacity of warehouses, transportation methods, and supporting management information systems.

supply chain execution system Ensures supply chain cohesion by automating the different activities of the supply chain.

supply chain management (SCM) The management of information flows between and among activities in a supply chain to maximize total supply chain effectiveness and corporate profitability.

supply chain planning system Uses advanced mathematical algorithms to improve the flow and efficiency of the supply chain while reducing inventory.

supply chain visibility The ability to view all areas up and down the supply chain in real time.

support value activities Found along the top of the value chain and includes business processes, such as firm infrastructure, human resource management, technology development, and procurement, that support the primary value activities.

sustainable MIS disposal Refers to the safe disposal of MIS assets at the end of their life cycle.

sustainable MIS infrastructure Identifies ways that a company can grow in terms of computing resources while simultaneously becoming less dependent on hardware and energy consumption.

sustainable, or green, MIS Describes the production, management, use, and disposal of technology in a way that minimizes damage to the environment.

sustaining technology Produces an improved product customers are eager to buy, such as a faster car or larger hard drive.

swim lane Layout arranges the steps of a business process into a set of rows depicting the various elements.

switching costs Costs that make customers reluctant to switch to another product or service.

SWOT analysis Evaluates an organization's **s**trengths, **w**eaknesses, **o**pportunities, and **t**hreats to identify significant influences that work for or against business strategies.

synchronous communication Communications that occur at the same time such as IM or chat.

system A collection of parts that link to achieve a common purpose.

system clock Works like a wristwatch and uses a battery mounted on the motherboard to provide power when the computer is turned off.

system restore Enables a user to return to the previous operating system.

system software Controls how the various technology tools work together along with the application software.

system testing Verification that the units or pieces of code function correctly when integrated.

system virtualization The ability to present the resources of a single computer as if it is a collection of separate computers ("virtual machines"), each with its own virtual CPUs, network interfaces, storage, and operating system.

systems development life cycle (SDLC) The overall process for developing information systems, from planning and analysis through implementation and maintenance.

systems thinking A way of monitoring the entire system by viewing multiple inputs being processed or transformed to produce outputs while continuously gathering feedback on each part.

T

table Composed of rows and columns that represent an entity.

tacit knowledge The knowledge contained in people's heads.

tag Specific keyword or phrase incorporated into website content for means of classification or taxonomy.

tangible benefits Easy to quantify and typically measured to determine the success or failure of a project.

taxonomy The scientific classification of organisms into groups based on similarities of structure or origin.

technology failure Occurs when the ability of a company to operate is impaired because of a hardware, software, or data outage.

technology recovery strategies Focus specifically on prioritizing the order for restoring hardware, software, and data across the organization that best meets business recovery requirements.

teergrubing Anti-spamming approach by which the receiving computer launches a return attack against the spammer, sending email messages back to the computer that originated the suspected spam.

telecommunication system Enables the transmission of data over public or private networks.

telecommuting (virtual workforce) Allows users to work from remote locations such as a home or hotel, using high-speed Internet to access business applications and data.

telepresence robot A remote-controlled, wheeled device with a display to enable video chat and videoconferencing.

terabyte (TB) Roughly 1 trillion bytes.

test condition Details the steps the system must perform along with the expected result of each step.

testing phase Brings all the project pieces together into a special testing environment to eliminate errors and bugs and verify that the system meets all the business requirements defined in the analysis phase.

threat An act or object that poses a danger to assets.

threat of new entrants One of Porter's five forces; high when it is easy for new competitors to enter a market and low when there are significant entry barriers to joining a market.

threat of substitute products or services One of Porter's five forces; high when there are many alternatives to a product or service and low when there are few alternatives from which to choose.

time bombs Computer viruses that wait for a specific date before executing instructions.

time-series chart A graphical representation showing change of a variable over time.

time-series information Time-stamped information collected at a particular frequency.

To-Be process model Shows the results of applying change improvement opportunities to the current (As-Is) process model.

tokens Small electronic devices that change user passwords automatically.

traceroute A utility application that monitors the network path of packet data sent to a remote computer.

transaction processing system (TPS) The basic business system that serves the operational level (analysts) and assists in making structured decisions.

transactional information Encompasses all of the information contained within a single business process or unit of work, and its primary purpose is to support the performance of daily operational or structured decisions.

transmission control protocol/Internet protocol (TCP/IP)   Provides the technical foundation for the public Internet as well as for large numbers of private networks.

trend analysis   A trend is examined to identify its nature, causes, speed of development, and potential impacts.

trend monitoring   Trends viewed as particularly important in a specific community, industry, or sector are carefully monitored, watched, and reported to key decision makers.

trend projection   When numerical data are available, a trend can be plotted to display changes through time and into the future.

twisted-pair cable   Refers to a type of cable composed of four (or more) copper wires twisted around each other within a plastic sheath.

two-factor authentication   Requires the user to provide two means of authentication: what the user knows (password) and what the user has (security token).

typosquatting   A problem that occurs when someone registers purposely misspelled variations of well-known domain names.

U

unavailable   When a system is not operating or cannot be used.

unified communications (UC)   The integration of communication channels into a single service.

Unified Communications as a Service (UCaaS)   Offers enterprise communication and collaboration services over the Internet such as instant messaging systems, online meetings, and video conferencing.

unit testing   Testing individual units or pieces of code for a system.

universal resource locator (URL)   The address of a file or resource on the web such as www.apple.com.

unstructured data   Data that is not defined, does not follow a specified format, and is typically free-form text such as emails, Twitter tweets, and text messages.

unstructured decision   Occurs when no procedures or rules exist to guide decision makers toward the correct choice.

up-selling   Increasing the value of the sale.

upcycle   Reuses or refurbishes ewaste and creates a new product.

uplift modeling   A form of predictive analytics for marketing campaigns that attempts to identify target markets or people who could be convinced to buy products.

URL shortening   The translation of a long URL into an abbreviated alternative that redirects to the longer URL.

usability   The degree to which a system is easy to learn and efficient and satisfying to use.

user acceptance testing (UAT)   The determination if the system satisfies user and business requirements.

user documentation   Highlights how to use the system and how to troubleshoot issues or problems.

user-contributed content (also referred to as user-generated content)   Content created and updated by many users for many users.

utility computing   Offers a pay-per-use revenue model similar to a metered service such as gas or electricity.

utility software   Provides additional functionality to the operating system.

V

variable   A data characteristic that stands for a value that changes or varies over time.

value chain analysis   Views a firm as a series of business processes that each add value to the product or service.

vertical privilege escalation   Attackers grant themselves a higher access level such as administrator, allowing the attacker to perform illegal actions such as running unauthorized code or deleting data.

videoconference   Allows people at two or more locations to interact via two-way video and audio transmissions simultaneously as well as share documents, data, computer displays, and whiteboards.

virtual assistant (VA)   A small program stored on a PC or portable device that monitors emails, faxes, messages, and phone calls.

virtual private network (VPN)   Companies can establish direct private network links among themselves or create private, secure Internet access, in effect a private tunnel within the Internet.

virtual reality   A computer-simulated environment that can be a simulation of the real world or an imaginary world.

virtual workplace   A workplace that is not located in any one physical space.

virtualization   Creates multiple virtual machines on a single computing device.

virus   Software written with malicious intent to cause annoyance or damage.

vishing (voice phishing)   A phone scam that attempts to defraud people by asking them to call a bogus telephone number to confirm their account information.

visualization   Produces graphical displays of patterns and complex relationships in large amounts of data.

Voice over IP (VoIP)   Uses IP technology to transmit telephone calls.

Voice over LTE (VoLTE)   Allows mobile voice calls to be made over broadband networks, creating—under the right network conditions—clearer audio and fewer dropped calls.

voiceprint   A set of measurable characteristics of a human voice that uniquely identifies an individual.

volatile   Must have constant power to function; contents are lost when the computer's electric supply fails.

volatility   Refers to a device's ability to function with or without power.

vulnerability   A system weakness that can be exploited by a threat; for example, a password that is never changed or a system left on while an employee goes to lunch.

W

war chalking   The practice of tagging pavement with codes displaying where Wi-Fi access is available.

war driving   Deliberately searching for Wi-Fi signals from a vehicle.

warm site   A separate facility with computer equipment that requires installation and configuration.

waterfall methodology   A sequence of phases in which the output of each phase becomes the input for the next.

Web 1.0 (or Business 1.0)   Refers to the World Wide Web during its first few years of operation between 1991 and 2003.

Web 2.0 (or Business 2.0) The next generation of Internet use—a more mature, distinctive communications platform characterized by new qualities such as collaboration and sharing, and being free.

web accessibility Means that people with disabilities—including visual, auditory, physical, speech, cognitive, and neurological disabilities—can use the web.

web accessibility initiative (WAI) Brings together people from industry, disability organizations, government, and research labs from around the world to develop guidelines and resources to help make the web accessible to people with disabilities, including auditory, cognitive, neurological, physical, speech, and visual disabilities.

web browser Allows users to access the WWW.

web conferencing (webinar) Blends videoconferencing with document-sharing and allows the user to deliver a presentation over the web to a group of geographically dispersed participants.

Web Real-Time Communications (WebRTC) An open source project that seeks to embed real-time voice, text, and video communications capabilities in web browsers.

web service An open-standards way of supporting interoperability.

web-based self-service system Allows customers to use the web to find answers to their questions or solutions to their problems.

website bookmark A locally stored URL or the address of a file or Internet page saved as a shortcut.

website ebusiness analytics Uses clickstream data to determine the effectiveness of the site as a channel-to-market.

website name stealing The theft of a website's name that occurs when someone, posing as a site's administrator, changes the ownership of the domain name assigned to the website to another website owner.

website personalization Occurs when a website has stored enough data about a person's likes and dislikes to fashion offers more likely to appeal to that person.

website traffic analytics Uses clickstream data to determine the efficiency of the site for the users and operates at the server level.

What-if analysis Checks the impact of a change in a variable or assumption on the model. Users repeat this analysis with different variables until they understand all the effects of various situations.

white-hat hackers Work at the request of the system owners to find system vulnerabilities and plug the holes.

Wi-Fi infrastructure Includes the inner workings of a Wi-Fi service or utility, including the signal transmitters, towers, or poles, along with additional equipment required to send a Wi-Fi signal.

Wi-Fi protected access (WPA) A wireless security protocol to protect Wi-Fi networks.

wide area network (WAN) Spans a large geographic area such as a state, province, or country.

wiki A type of collaborative web page that allows users to add, remove, and change content, which can be easily organized and reorganized as required.

wire media Transmission material manufactured so that signals will be confined to a narrow path and will behave predictably.

wired equivalent privacy (WEP) An encryption algorithm designed to protect wireless transmission data.

wireless access point (WAP) Enables devices to connect to a wireless network to communicate with each other.

wireless fidelity (Wi-Fi) A means by which portable devices can connect wirelessly to a local area network, using access points that send and receive data via radio waves.

wireless LAN (WLAN) A local area network that uses radio signals to transmit and receive data over distances of a few hundred feet.

wireless MAN (WMAN) A metropolitan area network that uses radio signals to transmit and receive data.

wireless media Natural parts of Earth's environment that can be used as physical paths to carry electrical signals.

wireless WAN (WWAN) A wide area network that uses radio signals to transmit and receive data.

workflow Includes the tasks, activities, and responsibilities required to execute each step in a business process.

workflow control system Monitors processes to ensure that tasks, activities, and responsibilities are executed as specified.

workplace MIS monitoring Tracks people's activities by such measures as number of keystrokes, error rate, and number of transactions processed.

workshop training Held in a classroom environment and led by an instructor.

World Wide Web (WWW) Provides access to Internet information through documents, including text, graphics, audio, and video files that use a special formatting language called HTML.

World Wide Web Consortium (W3C) An international community that develops open standards to ensure the long-term growth of the web (www.w3.org).

Worldwide Interoperability for Microwave Access (WiMAX) A communications technology aimed at providing high-speed wireless data over metropolitan area networks.

worm Malware computer program that spreads itself not only from file to file but also from computer to computer.

Z

zombie A program that secretly takes over another computer for the purpose of launching attacks on other computers.

zombie farm A group of computers on which a hacker has planted zombie programs.

Chapter 1

1. Sources: "Internet of Things Applications Across Industries," Intel. http://www.intel.com; Chui, Michael, Markus Löffler, and Roberts, Roger, "The Internet of Things," *Mckinsey Quarterly*, March 2010. http://www.mckinsey.com; Ferber, Stefan, "How the Internet of Things Changes Everything," *Harvard Business Review*, May 2013.

2. Source: *Interesting Facts*. www.interestingfacts.org.

3. Source: Risen, Tom, "Futurology: Bill Gates Predicts a Prosperous Africa in 2030," *US News and World Report*, January 22, 2014. http://www.usnews.com.

4. http://www.intel.com/content/www/us/en/internet-of-things/industry solutions.html, accessed May 2014; Michael Chui, Markus Löffler, and Roger Roberts, "The Internet of Things," *Mckinsey Quarterly*, March 2010 (site now discontinued), http://www.mckinsey.com/insights/high_tech_ telecoms_internet/the_internet_of_things; Stefan Ferber, "How the Internet of Things Changes Everything," *Harvard Business Review*, May 2013.

5. http://www.intel.com/content/www/us/en/internet-of-things/industry solutions.html, accessed May 2014; Michael Chui, Markus Löffler, and Roger Roberts, "The Internet of Things," *Mckinsey Quarterly*, March 2010, http://www.mckinsey.com/insights/high_tech_telecoms_ internet/the_internet_of_things; Stefan Ferber, "How the Internet of Things Changes Everything," *Harvard Business Review*, May 2013.

6. Ina Fried, "Apple Earnings Top Estimates," *CNET News*, October 11, 2005, http://news.cnet.com/Apple-earnings-topestimates/2100-1041_3-5893289.html?tag 5 lia;rcol, accessed January 18, 2010. (site now discontinued)

7. www.investopedia.com/terms/s/swot.asp, accessed June 2015

8. Sources: Porter, Michael E., "The Five Competitive Forces That Shape Strategy," The Harvard Business Review Book Series, *Harvard Business Review*, January 2008; Porter, Michael E., "Competitive Strategy: Techniques for Analyzing Industries and Competitors," *Harvard Business Review*, January 2002; Porter, Michael E., "On Competition," The Harvard Business Review Book Series. Boston: Harvard Business School Publishing, 1985; Harvard Institute for Strategy and Competitiveness. http://www.isc.hbs.edu/.

9. Ibid.

10. Ibid.

11. Sources: Porter, Michael E., "The Five Competitive Forces That Shape Strategy," The Harvard Business Review Book Series, *Harvard Business Review*, January 2008; Porter, Michael E., "Competitive Strategy: Techniques for Analyzing Industries and Competitors," *Harvard Business Review*, January 2002; Porter, Michael E., "On Competition," The Harvard Business Review Book Series. Boston: Harvard Business School Publishing, 1985; Harvard Institute for Strategy and Competitiveness. http://www.isc.hbs.edu/.

12. Ibid.

13. Ibid.

14. Ibid.

15. Sources: Porter, Michael E., "The Five Competitive Forces That Shape Strategy," The Harvard Business Review Book Series, *Harvard Business Review*, January 2008; Porter, Michael E., "Competitive Strategy: Techniques for Analyzing Industries and Competitors,"

Harvard Business Review, January 2002; Porter, Michael E., "On Competition," The Harvard Business Review Book Series. Boston: Harvard Business School Publishing, 1985; Harvard Institute for Strategy and Competitiveness. http://www.isc.hbs.edu/.

16. Sources: Porter, Michael E., "The Five Competitive Forces That Shape Strategy," The Harvard Business Review Book Series, *Harvard Business Review*, January 2008; Porter, Michael E., "Competitive Strategy: Techniques for Analyzing Industries and Competitors," *Harvard Business Review*, January 2002; Porter, Michael E., "On Competition," The Harvard Business Review Book Series. Boston: Harvard Business School Publishing, 1985; Harvard Institute for Strategy and Competitiveness. http://www.isc.hbs.edu/.

17. Sources: Porter, Michael E., "The Five Competitive Forces That Shape Strategy," The Harvard Business Review Book Series, *Harvard Business Review*, January 2008; Porter, Michael E., "Competitive Strategy: Techniques for Analyzing Industries and Competitors," *Harvard Business Review*, January 2002; Porter, Michael E., "On Competition," The Harvard Business Review Book Series. Boston: Harvard Business School Publishing, 1985; Harvard Institute for Strategy and Competitiveness. http://www.isc.hbs.edu/.

18. Source: "Harvard Business Review on Managing the Value Chain," *Harvard Business School Press*, January 2000.

19. Source: Ransom, Diana, "America's Coolest College Startups 2014," *Inc.*, May 2014. http://www.inc.com.

20. "Harvard Business Review on Managing the Value Chain," *Harvard Business School Press*, January 2000.

21. Sources: Hiroko Tabuchi, "Stores Suffer From a Shift of Behavior in Buyers," *NY Times*, August 13, 2015, accessed 4/15/2016. Travis Bradberry, "You Should Spend Your Money on Experiences, Not Things," *Entrepreneur*, March 1, 2016, accessed 4/14/2016.

22. Sources: Friedman, Thomas L., *The World Is Flat*. New York: Farrar, Straus and Giroux, 2005; Friedman, Thomas L., "The World Is Flat," www.thomaslfriedman.com; Friedman, Thomas L., "The Opinion Pages," *The New York Times*. topics.nytimes.com.

23. Sources: Friedman, Thomas L., *The World Is Flat*. New York: Farrar, Straus and Giroux, 2005.

24. Thomas L. Friedman, *Hot, Flat, and Crowded: Why We Need a Green Revolution—and How It Can Renew America* (New York: Farrar, Straus and Giroux, 2008).

25. Clive Thompson, "Do You Speak Statistics?" *Wired*, May 2010, p. 36.

26. Ina Fried, "Adobe to Buy Omniture for $1.8 Billion," *CNET News*, September 15, 2009, http://news.cnet.com/8301-13860_3-10353733-56.html.

27. Seidell, Streeter, "10 Best Things We'll Say to Our Grandkids," *Wired*, September, 21, 2009, www.wired.com/culture/culturereviews/magazine/17-10/st_best#ixzz0s65fFq1t.

28. http://www.sochi2014.com/en/medal-standings, accessed January 2014.

29. Source: Friedman, Thomas L., *Hot, Flat, and Crowded: Why We Need a Green Revolution—and How It Can Renew America*. New York: Farrar, Straus and Giroux, 2008.

30. Source: "TED: Ideas Worth Spreading." http://www.ted.com/pages/view/id/5.

Chapter 2

1. Bill Wasik, "Why Wearable Tech Will Be as Big as the Smartphone," *Wired Magazine,* December 17, 2013. http://www.wired.com/2013/12/wearable-computers/.

2. Source: Wasik, Bill, "Why Wearable Tech Will Be as Big as the Smartphone," *Wired Magazine,* December 17, 2013. http://www.wired.com.

3. Source: Wasik, Bill, "Why Wearable Tech Will Be as Big as the Smartphone," *Wired Magazine,* December 17, 2013. http://www.wired.com.

4. Source: Davenport, Tom, "Tom Davenport: Back to Decision-Making Basics," *BusinessWeek,* March 11, 2008. http://www.businessweek.com.

5. Source: Blanchard, Ken, "Effectiveness vs. Efficiency," *Wachovia Small Business.* www.wachovia.com.

6. Source: "What Is Systems Thinking," *SearchCIO.com.* http://searchcio.techtarget.com/.

7. "French Trader in Scandal Ordered behind Bars," MSNBC, February 8, 2008, http://www.msnbc.msn.com/id/23065812/.

8. Sources: Begley, Sharon, "Software au Naturel," *Newsweek*, May 7, 1995; McManus, Neil, "Robots at Your Service," *Wired*, January 2003; Santa Fe Institute; Arbib, Michael A., ed., *The Handbook of Brain Theory and Neural Networks.* Cambridge, MA: MIT Press, 2003; Biacino, L., and Gerla, G., "Fuzzy Logic, Continuity and Effectiveness," *Archive for Mathematical Logic*, vol. 41, no. 7.

9. Sources: "Business Process Reengineering Six Sigma," iSixSigma. www.isixsigma.com/me/bpr/; Hammer, Michael, *Beyond Reengineering: How the Process-Centered Organization Is Changing Our Work and Our Lives.* New York: HarperCollins Publishers, 1996; Chang, Richard, *Process Reengineering in Action: A Practical Guide to Achieving Breakthrough Results*, Quality Improvement Series. San Francisco: Pfeiffer, 1996.

10. Source: "Object Management Group Business Process Model and Notation," *BPMN.* www.bpmn.org.

11. Source: "Object Management Group Business Process Model and Notation," *BPMN.* www.bpmn.org.

12. Sources: "Business Process Reengineering Six Sigma," iSixSigma. www.isixsigma.com/me/bpr/; Hammer, Michael, *Beyond Reengineering: How the Process-Centered Organization Is Changing Our Work and Our Lives.* New York: HarperCollins Publishers, 1996; Chang, Richard, *Process Reengineering in Action: A Practical Guide to Achieving Breakthrough Results*, Quality Improvement Series. San Francisco: Pfeiffer, 1996.

13. Sources: "Business Process Reengineering Six Sigma," iSixSigma. www.isixsigma.com/me/bpr/; Hammer, Michael, *Beyond Reengineering: How the Process-Centered Organization Is Changing Our Work and Our Lives.* New York: HarperCollins Publishers, 1996; Chang, Richard, Process Reengineering in Action: A Practical Guide to Achieving Breakthrough Results, Quality Improvement Series. San Francisco: Pfeiffer, 1996.

14. www.ibm.com/Watson, accessed January 2017

15. Sources: "Business Process Reengineering Six Sigma," iSixSigma. www.isixsigma.com/me/bpr/; Hammer, Michael, *Beyond Reengineering: How the Process-Centered Organization Is Changing Our Work and Our Lives.* New York: HarperCollins Publishers, 1996; Chang, Richard, *Process Reengineering in Action: A Practical Guide to Achieving Breakthrough Results*, Quality Improvement Series. San Francisco: Pfeiffer, 1996.

16. Source: Robbins, Steven, "Tips for Mastering E-Mail Overload," *Harvard Business School,* October 25, 2009. http://hbswk.hbs.edu/archive/4438.html.

17. Sources: "Business Process Reengineering Six Sigma," iSixSigma. www.isixsigma.com/me/bpr/; Hammer, Michael, *Beyond Reengineering: How the Process-Centered Organization Is Changing Our Work and Our Lives.* New York: HarperCollins Publishers, 1996; Chang, Richard, *Process Reengineering in Action: A Practical Guide to Achieving Breakthrough Results*, Quality Improvement Series. San Francisco: Pfeiffer, 1996.

18. Source: "Wearables," *Electronics Weekly,* March 2014. http://www.electronicsweekly.com.

19. Sources: Harrington, H. James, *Business Process Improvement Workbook: Documentation, Analysis, Design, and Management of Business Process Improvement.* New York: McGraw-Hill, 1997; Hammer, Michael, *Beyond Reengineering*; Hammer, Michael, and Champy, James, *Reengineering the Corporation: A Manifesto for Business Revolution.* New York: HarperCollins Publishers, 1993.

20. Source: Wasik, Bill, "Why Wearable Tech Will Be as Big as the Smartphone," *Wired Magazine,* December 17, 2013. http://www.wired.com.

21. Source: www.darpa.mil, accessed 5/12/2017.

22. Sources: Voth, Jeff, "Texting and Other Bad Driving Decisions," *Yahoo Autos,* http://ca.autos.yahoo.com/; Belkin, Lisa, "Breastfeeding While Driving," *The New York Times,* March 2, 2009. http://parenting.blogs.nytimes.com.

23. Source: Jaroslovsky, Rich, "Your Own Private Help Desk," *Bloomberg Businessweek,* March 11, 2010.

24. Source: Buchanan, Leigh, "Letting Employees Battle It Out," *Inc.,* October 1, 2009. http://www.inc.com.

25. Rachel King, "Soon That Nearby Worker Might Be a Robot," *Bloomberg Businessweek*, June 1, 2010, http://www.businessweek.Com/Technology/content/jun2010/tc2010061_798891.htm.

26. Phil Mansfield, "Bronx Graduate Trina Thompson Sues Monroe College for $70,000 over Unemployment," *Daily News,* August 3, 2009, http://www.nydailynews.com/ny_local/2009/08/03/2009083_student_.html#ixzz1174LU5KS.

27. Caroline Winter, "Fitbit for Testosterone Junkies: Health-Tracking Gadgets Reach the Molecular Level," *BusinessWeek,* June 6, 2014. http://www.businessweek.com/articles/2014-06-06/fitbit-fortestosterone-junkies-health-tracking-gadgets-reach-the-molecular-level.

Chapter 3

1. www.hellofresh.com, accessed January 15, 2016.

2. Adam Lashinsky, "Kodak's Developing Situation," *Fortune,* January 20, 2003, p. 176.

3. Source: Christensen, Clayton, *The Innovator's Dilemma.* Boston: Harvard Business School, 1997.

4. Clayton Christensen, *The Innovator's Dilemma* (Boston: Harvard Business School, 1997).

5. Internet World Statistics, www.internetworldstats.com, January 2010.

6. info.cern.ch, accessed March 1, 2005. (site now discontinued)

7. Source: Dudley, Brier, "Changes in Technology Almost Too Fast to Follow," *The Seattle Times,* October 13, 2005.

8. Source: Chafkin, Max, "Good Domain Names Grow Scarce," *Inc.,* July 1, 2009. http://www.inc.com.

9. Source: Anderson, Chris, "The Long Tail: Why the Future of Business Is Selling Less of More," *The Long Tail,* 2006. http://www.longtail.com.

10. Source: "Disintermediation," *TechTarget,* http://whatis.techtarget.com.

11. "Reintermediation," PCMag.com, http://www.pcmag.com/ encyclopedia_term/0, 2542,t 5 reintermediation&i 5 50364,00.asp, accessed April 4, 2010. (site now discontinued)

12. Scott McCartney, "You Paid What for That Flight?" *The Wall Street Journal,* August 26, 2010, http://online.wsj.com/article/SB100014240 52748704540904575451653489562606.html.

13. Sources: The Complete Web 2.0 Directory," *All About Casino Hold 'Em.* www.go2web20.net; "Web 2.0 for CIOs," *CIO Magazine.* www.cio.com/ article/16807; www.emarketer.com.

14. Ibid.

15. Sources: O'Reilly, Tim, "What Is Web 2.0: Design Patterns and Business Models for the Next Generation of Software," *O'Reilly.* www.oreillynet.com; "Web 2.0 for CIOs," *CIO Magazine.* www.cio. com/article/16807.

16. Ibid.

17. Sources: O'Reilly, Tim, "What Is Web 2.0: Design Patterns and Business Models for the Next Generation of Software," *O'Reilly.* www.oreillynet.com; "Web 2.0 for CIOs," *CIO Magazine.* www.cio. com/article/16807.

18. Sources: O'Reilly, Tim, "What Is Web 2.0: Design Patterns and Business Models for the Next Generation of Software," *O'Reilly;* "Web 2.0 for CIOs," *CIO Magazine.* www.cio.com/article/16807.

19. "Kiva—Loans That Change Lives," www.kiva.org, accessed April 10, 2010.

20. Sources: O'Reilly, Tim, "What Is Web 2.0: Design Patterns and Business Models for the Next Generation of Software," *O'Reilly;* "Web 2.0 for CIOs," *CIO Magazine.* www.cio.com/article/16807.

21. Tony Bradley, "Firefox 3.6 Becomes Number Two Browser as IE6 Declines," *PCWorld,* September 1, 2010, http://www.pcworld.com/ businesscenter/article/204698/firefox_36_becomes_number_two_ browser_as_ie6_declines.html.

22. Source: Google Images. http://www.google.com/images?.

23. "About Us," LinkedIn, http://press.linkedin.com/, accessed April 3, 2010.

24. Source: Pink, Daniel, "Folksonomy," *The New York Times,* December 11, 2005. http://www.nytimes.com.

25. Daniel Nations, "What Is Social Bookmarking," About.com : Web Trends, http://webtrends.about.com/od/socialbookmarking101/p/ aboutsocialtags.htm, accessed April 5, 2010.

26. Gary Matuszak, "Enterprise 2.0: Fad or Future," KPMG International, www.kpmg.com/Global/en/. . ./Enterprise. . ./Enterprise-2-Fador-Future.pdf, accessed April 10, 2010.

27. Rachel Metz, "Changing at the Push of a Button," *Wired,* September 27, 2004.

28. Wikipedia Statistics, http://en.wikipedia.org/wiki/Statistics, accessed April 15, 2010.

29. Wikipedia: The Free Encyclopedia, http://en.wikipedia.org/wiki/ Wikipedia:About, accessed April 15, 2010.

30. Source: Smith, Cooper, "Shopping Cart Abandonment: Online Retailers' Biggest Headache Is Actually A Huge Opportunity," *Business Insider,* July 13, 2014. http://www.businessinsider.com.

31. Read more: http://www.businessinsider.com/heres-how-retailerscan-reduce-shopping-cart-abandonment-and-recoup-billions-ofdollars-in-lost-sales-2014-4#ixzz38OdzCraQ. (site now discontinued)

32. John Seigenthaler, "A False Wikipedia Biography," *USA Today,* November 29, 2005, http://www.usatoday.com/news/opinion/ editorials/2005-11-29-wikipedia-edit_x.htm.

33. Source: Berners-Lee, Tim, "Semantic Web Road Map," *W3,* October 14, 1998. http://www.w3.org.

34. Sources: Hamburger, Ellis, "Slack is killing email," *The Verge,* August 12, 2014. http://www.theverge.com/2014/8/12/5991005/slack-is-killing-email-yes-really, www.slack.com, accessed April 2016.

35. Sources: www.actionaly.com, accessed April 2012; www.socialmedia. biz/2011/01/12/top-20-social-media-monitoring-vendors-forbusiness, accessed April 2012; www.radian6.com, accessed April 2012; www.collectiveintellect.com, accessed April 2012.

36. Jenna Ross, "Toughest College Test: No Cell Phone, No Facebook," *StarTribune,* March 13, 2010, http://www.startribune.com/ entertainment/tv/87598062.html.

Chapter 4

1. Source: Brandon, John, "Five Ways Hackers Can Get Your Business," *Inc. Magazine,* December 2013. http://www.inc.com.

2. Source: Schrage, Michael, "Build the Business Case," *CIO Magazine,* March 15, 2003. http://www.cio.com.

3. Scott Berinato, "The CIO Code of Ethical Data Management," *CIO Magazine,* July 1, 2002, www.cio.com, accessed April 17, 2010.

4. https://www.law.cornell.edu/rules/frcp/rule_41, accessed 2/14/2017.

5. Peter S. Green, "Take the Data Pledge," *Bloomberg Businessweek,* April 23, 2009.

6. Mike Brunker, "Online Poker Cheating Blamed on Employee," MSNBC. com, October 19, 2007, http://www.msnbc.msn.com/id/21381022/, accessed April 15, 2010.

7. Organisation of Economic Cooperation and Development, www.oecd. org/unitedstates, accessed April 2014.

8. Dave Lee, "Google to Face Data Watchdogs over 'Right to Be Forgotten'," BBCNews.com, April 2014, http://www.bbc.com/news/ technology-28458194.

9. Source: "Consumer Information: Identity Theft," *Federal Trade Commission.* www.consumer.ftc.gov/features.

10. Andy McCue, "Bank Boss Quits after Porn Found on PC," *Bloomberg Businessweek,* www.businessweek.com, accessed June 2004.

11. Sources: AMA Research, "Workplace Monitoring and Surveillance," *AMA.* www.amanet.org; "2005 CSI/FBI Computer Crime and Security," *FBI.* https://www.fbi.gov.

12. Source: "Survey," *GoCSI.* www.gocsi.com.

13. Thomas Claburn, "Web 2.0. Internet Too Dangerous for Normal People," *InformationWeek,* April 1, 2009, http://www.information week.com/news/internet/web2.0/showArticle.jhtml?articleID 5 2 16402352&query Text5 web%202.0%20security%20concerns. (site now discontinued)

14. Paige Baltzan, email received May 21, 2010.

15. Source: Zetter, Kim, "Lifelock's CEO Identity Stolen 13 Times," *Wired,* May 28, 2010. http://www.wired.com.

16. Source: Bertrand, Natasha, "Here's What Happened To Your Target Data That Was Hacked," *Business Insider,* October 2014. http://www.businessinsider.com.

17. Source: Bryant, Charles, "Top 10 Things You Should Not Share on Social Networks," *HowStuffWorks.* howstuffworks.com.

18. David Kravets, "Former Teen Cheerleader Dinged $27,750 for File Sharing 37 Songs," *Wired,* February 26, 2010, http://www.wired.com/threatlevel/2010/02/ former-teen-cheerleader-dinged-27750-for-infringing-37-songs/.

19. Armen Keteyian "Digital Photocopier Loaded with Secrets," CBSnews. com, April 15, 2010, http://www.cbsnews.com/stories/2010/04/19/ eveningnews/main6412439.shtml.

20. Zetter, Kim, "Lifelock's CEO Identity Stolen 13 Times," *Wired,* May 28, 2010. http://www.wired.com.

Chapter 5

1. Source: King, Rachel, "How Aaron Levie and his childhood friends built Box into a $2 billion business, without stabbing each other in the back," *Tech Republic,* October 2014. http://www.techrepublic.com.

2. Source: *TechTarget.com,* http://events.techtarget.com/html/topic-disaster_recovery.html, accessed May 2014.

3. U.S. Geological Service, "The Great 1906 San Francisco Earthquake," http://earthquake.usgs.gov/regional/nca/1906/18april/index.php, accessed July 14, 2010.

4. Source: TechTarget.com, http://events.techtarget.com/html/topic-disaster_recovery.html, accessed May 2014.

5. "Moore's Law," www.intel.com/technology/mooreslaw, accessed April 2, 2010; Electronics TakeBack Coalition, "Facts and Figures on E-Waste and Recycling," www.electronicstakeback.com, accessed April 3, 2010; U.S. Environmental Protection Agency, "EPA Report to Congress on Server and Data Center Energy Efficiency," www.energystar.gov/ia/partners/prod_development/downloads/EPA_Report_Exec_Summary_Final.pdf, accessed January 23, 2008.

6. "Moore's Law," www.intel.com/technology/mooreslaw, accessed April 2, 2010; Electronics TakeBack Coalition, "Facts and Figures on E-Waste and Recycling," www.electronicstakeback.com, accessed April 3, 2010; U.S. Environmental Protection Agency, "EPA Report to Congress on Server and Data Center Energy Efficiency,"www.energystar.gov/ia/partners/prod_development/downloads/EPA_Report_Exec_Summary_Final.pdf, accessed January 23, 2008.

7. "Moore's Law," www.intel.com/technology/mooreslaw, accessed April 2, 2010; Electronics TakeBack Coalition, "Facts and Figures on E-Waste and Recycling," www.electronicstakeback.com, accessed April 3, 2010; U.S. Environmental Protection Agency, "EPA Report to Congress on Server and Data Center Energy Efficiency,"www.energystar.gov/ia/partners/prod_development/downloads/EPA_Report_Exec_Summary_Final.pdf, accessed January 23, 2008.

8. Sources: "Switch on the Benefits of Grid Computing," h20338.www2.hp.com/enterprise/downloads/7_Benefits%20of%20grid%20computing.pdf, accessed April 2, 2010; "Talking to the Grid," www.technologyreview.com/energy/23706/, accessed April 3, 2010; "Tech Update: What's All the Smart Grid Buzz About?" www.fieldtechnologiesonline.com/download.mvc/Whats-All-The-Smart-Grid-Buzz-About-0001, accessed April 3, 2010.

9. www.nature.org/greenliving/carboncalculator/, accessed May 2014.

10. Sources: "Switch on the Benefits of Grid Computing," h20338.www2.hp.com/enterprise/downloads/7_Benefits%20of%20grid%20computing.pdf, accessed April 2, 2010; "Talking to the Grid," www.technologyreview.com/energy/23706/, accessed April 3, 2010; "Tech Update: What's All the Smart Grid Buzz About?" www.fieldtechnologiesonline.com/download.mvc/Whats-All-The-Smart-Grid-Buzz-About-0001, accessed April 3, 2010.

11. "Switch on the Benefits of Grid Computing,"h20338.www2.hp.com/enterprise/downloads/7_Benefits%20of%20grid%20computing.pdf, accessed April 2, 2010; "Talking to the Grid,"www.technologyreview.com/energy/23706/, accessed April 3, 2010; "Tech Update: What's All the Smart Grid Buzz About?"www.fieldtechnologiesonline.com/download.mvc/Whats-All-The-Smart-Grid-Buzz-About-0001, accessed April 3, 2010.

12. Rich Miller, "Google Data Center FAQ," Data Center Knowledge, www.datacenterknowledge.com/archives/2008/03/27/google-data-center-faq/, accessed April 1, 2010.

13. Source: McKendrick, Joe, "20 Most Popular Cloud-Based Apps Downloaded into Enterprises," *Forbes,* March 2013. http://www.forbes.com/fdc/welcome_mjx.shtml.

14. http://www.livescience.com/41967-world-e-waste-to-grow-33-percent-2017.html; http://www.entrepreneur.com/article/226675, accessed March 2014.

15. Source: Carey Dunne, "How One Knitter Makes Almost $1 Million A Year On Etsy," *Fastcodesign.com,* February 12, 2015.

16. Source: Pinterest.com

17. Source: Ingrid Lunden, "Pinterest Updates Terms of Service as It Preps an API and Private Pinboards: More Copyright Friendly," Tech Crunch, April 2012; Chad McCloud, "What Pinterest Teaches Us About Innovation in Business," *Bloomberg Businessweek*, May 2012; Courteney Palis, "Pinterest Traffic Growth Soars to New Heights: Experian Report," *The Huffington Post*, April 6, 2012.

18. Goodwill Industries International, "Dell and Goodwill Expand Free Recycling Program to Include Microsoft Product," April 21, 2010, http://www.goodwill.org/press-releases/dell-goodwill-expandfree consumer-recycling-program-to-include-microsoft-products/, accessed June 3, 2010.

19. One Laptop Per Child, http://laptop.org/en/, accessed June 5, 2010.

20. "VMware—History of Virtualization." www.virtualizationworks.com/Virtualization-History.asp, accessed January 23, 2008.

21. Rich Miller, "Google Data Center FAQ," www.datacenterknowledge.com/archives/2008/03/27/google-data-center-faq/, accessed April 1, 2010.

Chapter 6

1. Source: "The Complete Beginners Guide to Big Data in 2017," *Forbes.* https://www.forbes.com/sites/bernardmarr/2017/03/14/the-complete-beginners-guide-to-big-data-in-2017/#568cdf847365, accessed January 2017.

2. Julia Kiling, "OLAP Gains Fans among Data-Hungry Firms," *ComputerWorld,* January 8, 2001, p. 54.

3. www.tableau.com, accessed March 2014.

4. Mitch Betts, "Unexpected Insights," *ComputerWorld,* April 14, 2003, www.computerworld.com, accessed September 4, 2003.

5. Source: Schlangenstein, Mary, "Facebook Manipulated User Feeds," *Bloomberg Businessweek,* June 29, 2012. http://www.bloomberg.com.

6. Source: www.zappos.com, accessed April 9, 2010.

7. "Data, Data Everywhere," *The Economist,* www.economist.com/specialreports/displayStory.cfm?story_id 5 15557443. (site now discontinued)

8. Kiling, "OLAP Gains Fans among Data-Hungry Firms." *ComputerWorld,* January 8, 2001, p. 54

9. Source: Popova, Maria, "Data Visualization: Stories for the Information Age," *Bloomberg Businessweek,* August 12, 2009. http://www.businessweek.com.

10. Source: www.webdesignerdepot.com, accessed April 2012; flowingdata.com/2011/12/21/the-best-data-visualization-projects-of-2011/, accessed April 2012.

Chapter 7

1. Stone, Brad, "Invasion of the Taxi Snatchers: Uber Leads an Industry's Disruption," *Bloomberg Businessweek*, February 2014. http://www.businessweek.com/. Copyright © 2014 by Bloomberg Business. All rights reserved. Used with permission of YGS Group.

2. "Top 23 U.S. ISPs by Subscriber: Q3 2010," *ISP Planet,* http://www.isp-planet.com/research/rankings/usa.html. (site now discontinued)

3. Source: "Top 23 U.S. ISPs by Subscriber: Q3 2010," *ISP Planet.* http://www.isp-planet.com/research/rankings/usa.html.

4. "Bandwidth Meter Online Speed Test," *CNET Reviews*, http://reviews.cnet.com/internet-speed-test/, accessed June 2010; "Broadband Technology Overview," www.corning.com/docs/opticalfiber/wp6321.pdf, accessed February 1, 2008. (site now discontinued)

5. Ibid.

6. Ibid.

7. Ibid.

8. Sources: "Bandwidth Meter Online Speed Test," *CNET Reviews,* http://reviews.cnet.com/internet-speed-test/, accessed June 2010; "Broadband Technology Overview," www.corning.com/docs/opticalfiber/wp6321.pdf, accessed February 1, 2008.

9. Source: Selyukh, Alina, and David Ingram, "U.S. appeals court strikes down FCC net neutrality rules," *Reuters,* February 2014. http://www.reuters.com.

10. http://www.savetheinternet.com/, accessed May 15, 2010.

11. Source: http://www.networksolutions.com/, accessed May 16, 2010.

12. www.godaddy.com, accessed May 16, 2010.

13. Source: "IP Telephony/Voice over IP (VoIP): An Introduction," *Cisco,* http://www.cisco.com; "VoIP Business Solutions," www.vocalocity.com, accessed January 21, 2008.

14. Ibid.

15. Source: Cooper, Aaron, "FCC to consider allowing cell phone calls on flights," *CNN.com,* November 2014. http://www.cnn.com.

16. Source: "IP Telephony/Voice over IP (VoIP): An Introduction," *Cisco,* http://www.cisco.com; "VoIP Business Solutions," www.vocalocity.com, accessed January 21, 2008.

17. Source: *Internet 101,* http://www.internet101.org/, accessed April 5, 2010.

18. Source: Ingersoll, Geoffrey, "Trainer Straps GoPro to an Eagle, Awesomeness Ensues," *Business Insider.* http://www.businessinsider.com.

19. Boston Digital Bridge Foundation, http://www.digitalbridgefoundation.org/, accessed May 18, 2010. (site now discontinued)

20. The Liberty Coalition, "Carnivore—DCS 1000," July 27, 2006, http://www.libertycoalition.net/node/247. (site now discontinued)

21. "A Science Odyssey," PBS, http://www.pbs.org/wgbh/aso/databank/entries/btmarc.html.

22. "Rip Curl Turns to Skype for Global Communications," www.voipinbusiness.co.uk/rip_curl_turns_to_skype_for_gl.asp July 07, 2006, accessed January 21, 2008; "Navigating the Mobility Wave," www.busmanagement.com, accessed February 2, 2008; "Sprint Plans Launch of Commercial WiMAX Service in Q2 2008," www.intomobile.com, accessed February 10, 2008; Deepak Pareek, *WiMAX: Taking Wireless to the MAX* (Boca Raton, FL: CRC Press, 2006), wimax.com, accessed February 9, 2008. (site now discontinued)

23. Ibid.

24. Source: Ferris, Stephan, "This High-Tech Tennis Racket Comes With a Built-In Digital Coach," *Bloomberg Businessweek,* June 2014. http://www.businessweek.com.

25. Sources: "Rip Curl Turns to Skype for Global Communications," www.voipinbusiness.co.uk/rip_curl_turns_to_skype_for_gl.asp July 07, 2006, accessed January 21, 2008; "Navigating the Mobility Wave," www.busmanagement.com, accessed February 2, 2008; "Sprint Plans Launch of Commercial WiMAX Service in Q2 2008," www.intomobile.com, accessed February 10, 2008; Deepak Pareek, *WiMAX: Taking Wireless to the MAX,* Boca Raton, FL: CRC Press, 2006. wimax.com, accessed February 9, 2008.

26. Rip Curl Turns to Skype for Global Communications," www.voipinbusiness.co.uk/rip_curl_turns_to_skype_for_gl.asp July 07, 2006, accessed January 21, 2008; "Navigating the Mobility Wave," www.busmanagement.com, accessed February 2, 2008; "Sprint Plans Launch of Commercial WiMAX Service in Q2 2008," www.intomobile.com, accessed February 10, 2008; Deepak Pareek, *WiMAX: Taking Wireless to the MAX* (Boca Raton, FL: CRC Press, 2006), wimax.com, accessed February 9, 2008. (site now discontinued)

27. Sources: "Rip Curl Turns to Skype for Global Communications," www.voipinbusiness.co.uk/rip_curl_turns_to_skype_for_gl.asp July 07, 2006, accessed January 21, 2008; "Navigating the Mobility Wave," www.busmanagement.com, accessed February 2, 2008; "Sprint Plans Launch of Commercial WiMAX Service in Q2 2008," www.intomobile.com, accessed February 10, 2008; Deepak Pareek, *WiMAX: Taking Wireless to the MAX,* Boca Raton, FL: CRC Press, 2006. wimax.com, accessed February 9, 2008.

28. Ibid.

29. Sources: "Rip Curl Turns to Skype for Global Communications," www.voipinbusiness.co.uk/rip_curl_turns_to_skype_for_gl.asp July 07, 2006, accessed January 21, 2008; "Navigating the Mobility Wave," www.busmanagement.com, accessed February 2, 2008; "Sprint Plans Launch of Commercial WiMAX Service in Q2 2008," www.intomobile.com, accessed February 10, 2008; Deepak Pareek, *WiMAX: Taking Wireless to the MAX,* Boca Raton, FL: CRC Press, 2006. wimax.com, accessed February 9, 2008.

30. Ibid.

31. Ibid.

32. Source: Gungor, V. C., Lambert, F. C., "A Survey on Communication Networks for Electric System Automation, Computer Networks," *The International Journal of Computer and Telecommunications Networking,* May 15, 2006, 877–97.

33. Melissa Delaney, "How Businesses Make the Most of Wireless Networks," *BizTech,* August 2013. http://www.biztechmagazine.com/article/2013/08/how-businesses-make-most-wireless-networks.

34. Sources: Attaran, Mohsen, "RFID: an Enabler of Supply Chain Operations," *Supply Chain Management: An International Journal,* vol. 12, 2007, 249–57; Dortch, Michael, "Winning RFID Strategies for 2008," *Benchmark Report,* December 31, 2007.

35. Damian Joseph, "The GPS Revolution," *Bloomberg BusinessWeek,* May 27, 2009, http://www.businessweek.com/innovate/content/may2009/id20090526_735316.htm. (site now discontinued)

36. Source: Lomas, Natasha, "Location Based Services to Boom in 2008," *Bloomberg Businessweek,* February 11, 2008. http://www.businessweek.com.

37. Natasha Lomas, "Location Based Services to Boom in 2008," *Bloomberg Businessweek,* February 11, 2008, http://www.businessweek.com/globalbiz/content/feb2008/gb20080211_420894.htm. (site now discontinued)

38. Source: Walker, Alissa, "The Technology Driving Denver's B-cycle Bike Sharing System," *Fast Company,* June 3, 2010. http://www.fastcompany.com.

39. Source: Cohen, Noam, "In Allowing Ad Blockers, a Test for Google," *The New York Times,* January 3, 2010. http://www.nytimes.com.

40. Source: Genachowski, Julius, "America's 2020 Broadband Vision," *The Official Blog of The Federal Communication Commission,* February 17, 2010. http://reboot.fcc.gov/blog/?entryId 5 172819.

41. Al Sacco, "Foursquare Addresses Cheating Issue, Frustrates Legit Users," *CIO Magazine,* April 8, 2010, http://advice.cio.com/al_sacco/10000/foursquare_addresses_cheating_issue_frustrates_legit_users.

42. Ryan Singel, "FYI, Pandora Makes Your Music Public," *Wired*, May 14, 2010, http://www.wired.com/epicenter/2010/05/pandora-privacy/#ixzz118uMDaUa.

43. Rob Flickenger, "Antenna On the Cheap," O'Reilly Wireless DevCenter, July 2001, http://www.oreillynet.com/cs/weblog/view/wlg/448.

44. Robert McMillian, "Domain Name Record Altered to Hack Comcast.net," *PC World*, May 28, 2009, http://www.pcworld.com/businesscenter/article/146461/domain_name_record_altered_to_hack_comcastnet.html.

45. Clint Boulton, "Google Street View Accidentally Collected User Data via WiFi," *eWeek*, May 16, 2010, http://www.eweek.com/c/a/Search-Engines/Google-Street-View-Accidentally-Violates-User-Privacy-Via-WiFi-290159/.

46. Source: http://top10.com/broadband/news/2010/02/top_10_broadband_gadgets/, accessed June 2010.

47. C. G. Lynch, "GPS Innovation Gives Weather Bots a New Ride," *CIO Magazine*, May 9, 2007, http://www.cio.com/article/108500/GPS_Innovation_Gives_Weather_Bots_a_New_Ride.

48. Austin Carr, "Kayak.com Cofounder Paul English Plans to Blanket Africa in Free Wireless Internet," *Fast Company*, May 12, 2010, http://www.fastcompany.com/1645485/kayak-cofounder-starting-initativeto-blanket-africa-in-free-wirelessinternet.

49. Chris Matyszczyk "Marathon Winner Disqualified for Wearing iPod," *CNET News*, October 11, 2009, http://news.cnet.com/8301-17852_3-10372586-71.html.

50. Bob Sullivan, "Ding A Ling Took My $400," MSNBC.com, October 2, 2009, http://redtape.msnbc.com/2009/10/mary-coxs-consumer-nightmare-began-with-poor-satellite-television-receptionbut-ended-up-costing-her-a-430-early-terminatio/comments/page/2/.

51. Associated Press, "Woman Has 911 Meltdown over McNuggets," MSNBC.com, March 4, 2009, http://www.msnbc.msn.com/id/29498350/.

52. http://www.citysense.net/, accessed June 2010.

Chapter 8

1. Maker Media, "MAKE: Ultimate Guide to 3D Printing," *Make Magazine*, May 2014.

2. Source: Helen Foley, "15 of the Best 3D Printed Products," *The Next Web*, November 2013. http://thenextweb.com/dd/2013/11/06/15-best-3d-printed-items-year/.

3. http://www.isc.hbs.edu/strategy/business-strategy/pages/the-five-forces.aspx

4. Source: James P. Womack, Daniel Jones, and Daniel Roos, *The Machine That Changed the World*, New York: Harper Perennial, 1991.

5. Source: Maker Media, "MAKE: Ultimate Guide to 3D Printing," *Make Magazine*, May 2014.

6. "The Future of 3D Printing and Manufacturing," *Forbes*, January 2014, http://www.forbes.com/fdc/welcome_mjx.shtml. (site now discontinued)

7. "The Future of 3D Printing and Manufacturing," *Forbes*, January 2014, http://www.forbes.com/fdc/welcome_mjx.shtml.

8. Source: Maker Media, "MAKE: Ultimate Guide to 3D Printing," *Make Magazine*, May 2014.

9. Source: Gregory S. McNeal, "Six Things You Should Know about Amazon's Drones," *Forbes*, July 2014. http://www.forbes.com/sites/gregorymcneal/2014/07/11/six-things-you-need-to-know-about-amazons-drones/.

10. Source: Mervyn Rothstein, "Isaac Asimov, Whose Thoughts and Books Traveled the Universe, Is Dead at 72," *The New York Times*, http://www.nytimes.com/books/97/03/23/lifetimes/asi-v-obit.html.

11. https://www.therobotreport.com/news/filling-the-void-left-by-kiva-systems-acquisition-by-amazon, accessed April 10, 2010.

12. www.rubyreceptions.com, accessed April 2014. (site now discontinued)

13. "Nice Emotions," http://www.nice.com/smartcenter-suite, accessed March 10, 2010. (site now discontinued)

14. "Customer Success," www.rackspace.com, accessed June 2005.

15. Source: *The Balanced Scorecard*, www.balancedscorecard.org, accessed February 2008.

16. Amazon Reveals Impressive Prime Air Drone, www.247supplychain.com, accessed November 2015.

17. Fruhlinger, Josh, and Wailgum, Thomas, "15 famous ERP disasters, dustups and disappointments," *CIO*, July 10, 2017. http://www.cio.com/. Copyright © 2017 by CIO. All rights reserved. Used with permission of YGS Group.

18. Frank Quinn, "The Payoff Potential in Supply Chain Management"; William Copacino and Jonathan Byrnes, "How to Become a Supply Chain Master," *Supply Chain Management Review*, September/October, 2001; www.manufacturing.net, accessed June 12, 2003.

19. "Bridgestone/Firestone Tire Recall," About.com, August 9, 2000, http://usgovinfo.about.com/blfirestone.htm.

20. http://www.walmart.com/cp/An-Introduction-to-Walmart.com/542413, accessed May 2010.

21. Source: Carmine Gallo, "Delivering Happiness the Zappos Way," *Bloomberg Businessweek*, May 12, 2009, http://www.business week.com/smallbiz/content/may2009/sb20090512_831040.htm.

Chapter 9

1. Source: Jason W. Bay, "Video Game Programmer Salary for 2016," *Game Industry Career Guide*. http://www.gameindustrycareerguide.com/video-game-programmer-salary/, accessed 4/15/2016.

2. "Overcoming Software Development Problems," www.sams publishing.com, accessed October 2005. (site now discontinued)

3. Source: www.ted.com, accessed June 15, 2010.

4. Antony Savvas, "Oklahoma Department of Corrections Leaks Personal Data from Website," ComputerWeekly.com, April 2008, http://www.computerweekly.com/Articles/2008/04/18/230353/Oklahoma-Department-of-Corrections-leaks-personal-data-from.htm.

5. Sources: *CIO Magazine*, June 1, 2006; "The Project Manager in the IT Industry," www.si2.com, accessed December 15, 2003; Jim Johnson, *My Life Is Failure*, Boston: Standish Group International, 2006, 46; Gary McGraw, "Making Essential Software Work," *Software Quality Management*, April 2003, www.sqmmagazine.com, accessed November 14, 2003.

6. Agile Alliance Manifesto, www.agile.com, accessed November 1, 2003.

7. "Software Costs," *CIO Magazine*, www.cio.com, accessed December 5, 2003.

8. IBM Rational Unified Process, http://www-01.ibm.com/software/awdtools/rup/, accessed January 2010.

9. Source: "SharePoint," *Microsoft*. http://products.office.com/en-us/sharepoint/collaboration, accessed June 2014.

10. https://scratch.mit.edu/, accessed August 2014.

11. Sources: *CIO Magazine,* June 1, 2006; "The Project Manager in the IT Industry," www.standishgroup.com; Johnson, *My Life Is Failure;* McGraw, "Making Essential Software Work."

12. Source: Karl Ritter, "Bill Murray Faces DUI after Golf-Cart Escapade in Sweden," *The Seattle Times,* August 22, 2007, http://seattletimes.nwsource.com/html/entertainment/2003848077_webmurray22.html.

13. Source: Edward Yourdon, *Death March: The Complete Software Developer's Guide to Surviving "Mission Impossible" Projects.* Upper Saddle River, NJ: Prentice Hall PTR, 1999.

14. Source: "Baggage Handling System Errors," www.flavors.com, accessed November 16, 2003.

15. Source: "Overcoming Software Development Problems," www.samspublishing.com, accessed October 2005.

Appendix A

1. "Electronic Breaking Points," *PC World,* August 2005.

2. Tom Davenport, "Playing Catch-Up," *CIO Magazine,* May 1, 2001.

3. Source: "Hector Ruiz, Advanced Micro Devices," *BusinessWeek,* January 10, 2005.

4. www.powergridfitness.com, accessed October 2005.

5. Denise Brehm, "Sloan Students Pedal Exercise," www.mit.edu, accessed May 5, 2003.

6. Margaret Locher, "Hands That Speak," *CIO Magazine,* June 1, 2005.

7. www.needapresent.com, accessed October 2005.

8. Aaron Ricadela, "Seismic Shift," *Information Week,* March 14, 2005.

9. www.mit.com, accessed October 2005.

10. "The Linux Counter," counter.li.org, accessed October 2005.

Appendix B

1. Andy Patrizio, "Peer-to-Peer Goes Beyond Napster," *Wired,* February, 14, 2001, http://www.wired.com/science/discoveries/news/2001/02/41768, accessed January 2009.

2. Source: Intel in Communications, "10 Gigabit Ethernet Technology Overview," http://www.intel.com/network/connectivity/resources/doc_library/white_papers/pro10gbe_lr_sa_wp.pdf, accessed January 2009.

3. Source: Cisco, "TCP/IP Overview," http://www.cisco.com/en/US/tech/tk365/technologies_white_paper09186a008014f8a9.shtml, accessed January 2009.

4. Ibid.

5. "IPv6," www.ipv6.org, accessed January 2009.

6. Source: Cisco, "TCP/IP Overview," http://www.cisco.com/en/US/tech/tk365/technologies_white_paper09186a008014f8a9.shtml, accessed January 2009.

7. Source: Cisco, "TCP/IP Overview," http://www.cisco.com/en/US/tech/tk365/technologies_white_paper09186a008014f8a9.shtml, accessed January 2009.

8. Cisco, "Network Media Types," http://www.ciscopress.com/articles/article.asp?p 5 31276, accessed January 2009.

9. Ibid.

10. Ibid.

Appendix D

1. https://www.forbes.com/sites/bernardmarr/2017/03/14/the-complete-beginners-guide-to-big-data-in-2017/#568cdf847365, accessed January 2017

A

ABC, 136
Aberman, Rich, 138
AbsolutePoker.com, 147
Acceptable use policy (AUP), 148–149
Accessibility, 190–191
Accounting, 13–15, 71
Accounting and finance ERP components, 355
Accuracy, 192
Actionly.com, 133
Active RFID tags, 304
Adaptive computer devices, A.8
Administrator access, 191
Advanced encryption standard (AES), 163
Advanced Micro Devices (AMD), A.2
Adware, 156, 164
AdWords, 112
AES (advanced encryption standard), 163
Affiliate programs, 112
Affinity grouping analysis, 255
Africa, 316
Agent-based modeling systems, 69
Agile methodologies (software development),
    390–391
Agile MIS infrastructure, 183, 189–194
A Hundred Monkeys, 104
Airline industry, 26–27
Albertsons, 25
Algorithms, 65, 259
Altman, Eli, 104
ALU (Arithmetic-logic unit), A.2
Amazon.com, 5, 26, 45, 96, 105, 109, 118,
    124, 333, 373
Amazon EC2 (Elastic Compute Cloud), 211
Amazon Web Services (AWS), 209
Ambient digital experience, D.5
AMD (Advanced Micro Devices), A.2
American Express, 68, 104, 304
American Family Immigration History Center, 237
Analysis paralysis, 260
Analysis phase (SDLC), 381–382
Analytical CRM, 342
Analytical information, 59, 227–228
Analytics, 259
Anderson, Chris, 105, 381
Anomaly detection, 259
Anti-spam policy, 150
Antivirus software, 164
AOL, 114, 282
API (Application programming interface), 124
Apple Inc., 222
Apple's iPod, 21
Applets, 103
Apple TV, 313

Appliance, A.10
Application programming interface (API), 124
Application service provider license, A.14
Application software, A.13
Aristotle, 115
Arithmetic-logic unit (ALU), A.2
ARPANET, 102
Artificial intelligence, 48, 64–70, 87
Artificial neural networks, 67–68
Asia, 404
As-Is process models, 73–75, 87
Asset tracking, 304
Associate programs, 108
Association detection, 256
Asynchronous communications, 120
AT&T, 114, 144, 282, 285, A.11, A.12
Attributes, 234, 256, 271, C.2–C.3
AT&T Wireless, 144
Audi, 43
Augmented reality, 69, D.5
AUP (acceptable use policy), 148–149
Authentication, 159–162
Authorization, 159–162
Auto insurance claims processes, 82
Automated teller machines (ATMs), 57
Automatic vehicle location (AVL), 304
Automation, 78, 87
Autonomic computing, D.6
Autonomous agent, D.6
AutoTrader.com, 104
Availability, 191–192
Avatar (film), 5
AVL (automatic vehicle location), 304
AWS (Amazon Web Services), 209
Axelbank, Gary, 96

B

Backdoor programs, 157
Background Draw-a-Secret (BDAS), 176
Back orders, 327
Backup, 214
Backup and recovery plan, 219
Backward integration, 323
BAE, 410
Balanced scorecard, 356
Bandwidth, 283
Banner ad, 107, 108
Bar chart, 62, 65
Bar code scanner, A.7
Barnes & Noble, 110
B2B (Business-to-business), 110
BBN Technologies, 317
B2C (Business-to-consumer), 110
BCP (Business continuity planning), 186

BDAS (Background Draw-a-Secret), 176
Benchmarking, 58
Benchmarks, 58
Berners-Lee, Tim, 191, 381
Best Buy, 371
Bezos, Jeff, 5, 381
BI; see Business intelligence
Big data, 7, 250
Bike-sharing programs, 310
Binary digit, 283
Biological 3D printing, D.6
Biometrics, 176
Bit, 283
Bit rate, 283
Bizrate.com, 111
BlackBerrys, 297, 300
Black-hat hackers, 156
Blockbuster, 106
Blogs and blogging, 125, 129
Bloomberg, 137
Bloomberg Businessweek, 168
Bloomberg.com, 111
Bluetooth, 295
Book'em, 135
Bookmarking, 121
Boston Digital Bridge Foundation, 293
Botti, Chris, 312
Bottlenecks, 79, 80
Box, 273
Boxee, 313
Box sites, 207
Box storage, 180–181
BPL (Broadband over power line), 285
BPMN (Business process model and notation),
    73, 74
BPR (Business process reengineering), 80
Bradesco, 314
Brainstorming, 379
Brand Keys, 133
Branson, Richard, 381
Brazil, 314, A.10
Brick-and-mortar business, 110
Bring your own device (BYOD) policy, 148
Brin, Sergey, 381
Broadband, 284
Broadband modem, 285
Broadband over power line (BPL), 285
Browser software, A.13
Buffalo, New York, Police Dept., 173
Bugs, 385
Bullwhip effect, 329
Burton, Tim, 344
Business 2.0; see Web 2.0 (Business 2.0)
Business analytics, 10

Business continuity planning (BCP), 186, 188–189
Business continuity strategies, 189
Business-critical integrity constraints, 238
Business decisions
    artificial intelligence, 64–70
    MIS, 58–64
    organizational, 53–58
Business driven ethics and security, 147; *see also* Ethics; Information security
    domain squatting/cyber squatting, 104
    ewaste, 195
    and Jobs' obituary, 137
    planning for the unexpected, 392
    at *Real People* magazine, 231
Business driven MIS, 5–19
    business intelligence, 10–11
    car black box hacking, 313
    classic car company, 353
    data, 6–8
    data manipulation, 38
    and departmental companies, 13–19
    at Google, 193
    information, 9–10
    and information age, 5–13
    knowledge, 11–13
    streamlining email, 79
Business focus, choosing, 27–28
Business impact analysis, 188
Business intelligence (BI), 10–11, 241–250
    data marts, 243–244
    data mining, 253–258
    data warehousing, 242
    ERP components for, 356
    supporting decisions with, 241–250
Business intelligence dashboards, 262–263
Business models
    defined, 108
    for ebusiness, 110
Business-office processes, 72
Business processes, 29, 70–85, 87
    management, 70–75
    MIS for improving, 75–85
    models, 73–75
Business process improvement, 76, 77
Business process model and notation (BPMN), 73, 74
Business process modeling, 73–75
Business process patent, 72
Business process reengineering (BPR), 80
Business requirements, 381, 382, 396
Business rule, 238
Business rules, C.3
Business strategy, 20
    choosing business focus, 27–28
    generic, 27–28
    identifying competitive advantages, 20–23
    Porter's Five Forces Model, 23–27
    value chain analysis, 29–32
Business-to-business (B2B), 110
Business-to-consumer (B2C), 110
Bus topology, B.5
Bus width, A.4
Butterfly effects, 245

Buyer power, 23–24
BYOD (Bring your own device) policy, 148

C

Cable, 285, A.9, B.5, B.8–B.9
Cable modems, 285
Cable & Wireless Worldwide, 282
Cache memory, A.5
CAD (Computer aided design), 332
Call centers, 345
Call scripting systems, 345
Campaign management systems, 343
Canada, 305
Canadian Broadcasting Company (CBC), 174
Capacity, 193
Capacity planning, 193
Carbon emissions, 196
Carbon footprint calculator, 199
Cardinalities, C.6
Carfax, 110
Carnivore, 294
Cartography, 305
CASE (Computer-aided software engineering), 382
Case-based reasoning, 67
C2B (Consumer-to-business), 110
CBC (Canadian Broadcasting Company), 174
CBS, 136
C2C (Consumer-to-consumer), 110–111
CDO (Chief data officer), 17
CD-ROM (Compact disk-read-only memory) drives, A.6
CD-RW (Compact disk-read-write) drives, A.6
Celebrities, social media used by, 109
Cell phones, 218, A.1
Cellular communication systems, 298–300
Center for American Progress, 39
Central processing unit (CPU), A.2–A.3
Certificate authority, 163
Change agent, 379
Charlesschwab.com, 111
Chen, Peter, C.3
Chief automation officer, 19
Chief data officer (CDO), 17
Chief information officer (CIO), 17
Chief intellectual property officer, 19
Chief knowledge officer (CKO), 18
Chief privacy officer (CPO), 18
Chief security officer (CSO), 18
Chief technology officer (CTO), 17
Chief user experience officer, 19
China, 37, 44, 174, 371, 403, A.10
Chipless RFID tags, 304
Chip line width, A.4
Christensen, Clayton M., 135
Cicero, 175
CinemaNow, 313
CIO (Chief information officer), 17
CISC (Complex instruction set computer) chips, A.3
Cisco, 95, 104
Citibank, 68, 107

CitySense, 317
CKO (Chief knowledge officer), 18
Classification analysis, 257
Clearwire, 298
Clerico, Bill, 138
Click-and-mortar business, 110
Clickstream data, 107, 152
Click-through, 108
Click-to-talk, 345
Client, 183, B.4
Client/server networks, B.4
Climate change, 39
Clinton, Bill, 381
Clock speed, A.4
Cloud applications, 207
Cloud bursting, 210
Cloud computing, 204–205
Cloud data, 171, 180
Cloud fabric controller, 206
Cloud providers, 205
Cluster analysis, 256
CMS (Content management systems), 115
CNN.com, 111
Coaxial cable, B.9
COBIT (Control objects for information and related technology), 385
Codd, Edgar (E. F.), C.7
Cold sites, 187
Collaboration, 118–120
Collaboration systems, 118
Collaborative engineering, 336
Collective intelligence, 118
College Hunks Hauling Junk, 95
Columbus, Christopher, 37
Comcast, 114, 282, 287
Commerce Department, 36
Communication devices, A.8
Communications, asynchronous *vs.* synchronous, 120
Communication software, A.13
Community cloud, 209
Compact disk-read-only memory (CD-ROM) drives, A.6
Compact disk-read-write (CD-RW) drives, A.6
Comparative analysis, 248
Competitive advantage, 21, 33
Competitive advantages, 393
Competitive click-fraud, 147
Competitive intelligence, 21
Competitive monitoring, 248
Complex instruction set computer (CISC) chips, A.3
Composite entities, C.6
Computer aided design (CAD), 332
Computer-aided software engineering (CASE), 382
Computers, 197
    categories of, A.10
    defined, A.2
Computer simulation, D.1
Confidentiality, 143, 405
Connectivity services, 138; *see also* Networks
Consolidation, 65

Consumer protection, with ebusiness, 116
Consumer-to-business (C2B), 110
Consumer-to-consumer (C2C), 110–111
Contact centers, 345
Contact management CRM systems, 345
Content creator, 239
Content editor, 239
Content filtering, 162
Content management systems (CMS), 115
Content providers, 111
Contracts, outsourcing, 405
Control objects for information and related
    technology (COBIT), 385
Control panel, A.12
Control unit, A.2
Convergence, network, 288
Conversion, 379
Conversion rates, 56
Cookies, 108, 152
Copyright, 125–126, 143
Core ERP components, 353–355
Core processes, 72
Corporate social responsibility, 195
Corrective maintenance, 388
Costco Wholesale, 35
Cost leadership, 27
Counterfeit software, 143
Course management software, A.13
CPO (Chief privacy officer), 18
CPU (Central processing unit), A.2–A.3
Crackers, 156
Craigslist, 45, 137
Crash-proof software, A.13
Critical path, 401
Critical success factors (CSFs), 53, 55, 86
CRM; see Customer relationship management
CRM analysis technologies, 339
CRM communication channels, 325, 338
CRM predicting technologies, 339
CRM reporting technologies, 339
Cross-selling, 344
Crowdfunding, 120
Crowdsourcing, 119
Cryptography, 163
CSO (Chief security officer), 18
CTO (Chief technology officer), 17
Cubes (data), 277
Customer contact points, 338
Customer-facing processes, 72, 87
Customer order cycle time, 327
Customer phone calls, 93
Customer power, 371
Customer relationship management (CRM),
    336–347
    customer power, 338
    customer segmentation, 346
    ERP components for, 356
    extension of, 347–348
Customer satisfaction, 56
Customer segmentation, 346
Cyberbullying, 164
Cyber squatting, 104
Cyberterrorism, 156

Cyberterrorists, 156
Cyberwar, 164
Cyborgs, 82
Cycle time, 79

D

3D printers, 321–322
    computer aided design, 332
    disruptive business technologies, 332
    ewaste and scrap metal, 331
    financial times, 332
    maker movement, 332
    weapons, 335
3D printing, D.5
Dallas, 45
DARPA (Defense Advanced Research Projects
    Agency), 102
Data, 6–8
    for business driven MIS, 6–8
    inappropriate data handling, 39
    manipulation, 38
Data analytics, 250–253
Data artist, 260
Database management system (DBMS),
    232, C.1; see also Relational database
    management systems
Databases, 232
    defined, C.1
    designing, C.1–C.9
    relational, C.1–C.3
Data centers, 203–204
Data dictionary, 233
Data-driven websites, 239
Data element, 233
Data field, 233
Data flow diagram (DFD), 382
Data governance, 232
Data inconsistency, 229
Data integrity issues, 229
Data management software, A.14
Data marts, 243–244
Data mining, 253–258
Data-mining tools, 257
Data models, 233, C.1
Data point, 247
Data profiling, 254
Data quality audits, 247
Data rate, 283
Data redundancy, 238
Data replication, 254
Data scientist, 260
Data set, 248
Data steward, 232
Data stewardship, 232
Data storage, 272–273
Data visualization, 260–263
Data warehouses, 242
Davis, Todd, 176–177
DBMS (Database management system),
    232, C.1
DCS1000, 294
DDoS (Distributed denial-of-service attack), 157

Death March (Edward Yourdon), 406
DEC (Digital Equipment Corporation), 101, B.6
Decision making, 50–70
    and artificial intelligence, 64–70
    business intelligence support for, 241–249
    challenges in, 50–53
    managerial, 59–63
    measuring organizational business decisions,
        53–58
    metrics for, 53–58
    MIS, 58–64
    operational, 59, 60
    strategic, 61–64
Decision support systems (DSSs), 59–63
Decryption, 157
Deep learning, 68
Defense Advanced Research Projects Agency
    (DARPA), 102
Defense Advanced Research Projects Agency
    (DARPA) Grand Challenge, 91
Dell Computers, 5, 42, 106, 222, 369,
    A.12, A.14
Denial-of-service attack (DoS), 157
Dentix, 93
Denver B-cycle, 310
Denver International Airport (DIA), 410–411
Dependency, 401
Descriptive analytics, 10–11
Design phase (SDLC), 382
Desktop computers, A.11
Desktop publishing software, A.13
Development phase (SDLC), 384
Device Mesh, D.5
DFD (Data flow diagram), 382
DIA (Denver International Airport), 410
Dial-up access, 284, A.9
Diamandis, Peter, 381
Digg, 120
Digital certificates, 163
Digital Darwinism, 101
Digital dashboards, 63–65
    design, 94
Digital divide, 293
Digital Equipment Corporation (DEC), 101, B.6
Digital rights management, 143
Digital subscriber line (DSL), 284–285, A.9
Digital video disk (DVD), A.6
Digital video disk-read/write (DVD-RW), A.6
Ding-A-Ling, 317
Dirty data, 244
Disaster recovery cost curve, 187
Disaster recovery plans, 188
Disaster recovery strategies, 188
Discovery prototyping, 389
Disintermediation, 106
Disk image software for data recovery, A.12
Disk optimization software, A.13
Disruptive technologies, 101–102, 128
Distributed computing, 250
Distributed denial-of-service attack (DDoS), 157
DivX, 313
DNS (domain name system), 287, 313–314
DNS cache poisoning, 313

DoD; *see* U.S. Department of Defense
Dole Organic, 125
Domain name hosting (web hosting), 103
Domain name system (DNS), 287, 313–314
Domain squatting, 104
Domino's Pizza, 150
DoS (denial-of-service attack), 157
Dot-com, 109
Downtime, 154
DPW (Dubai Ports World), 368
DreamWorks Animation, 198
Drill-down, 65
Driving decisions, 95
Drones, 333, 335
DropBox, 273
Drucker, Peter, 53, 56
DSL (digital subscriber line), 284–285, A.9
Dual boot, A.12
Dubai Ports World (DPW), 368
Dumpster diving, 158
Dunn, Elizabeth, 36
DVD (Digital video disk), A.6
DVD-ROM drives, A.6
DVD-RW (Digital video disk-read/write), A.6
Dynamic catalog, 239
Dynamic information, 239
Dynamic process, 72
Dynamic report, 9
Dynamic scaling, 211

E

EAI (Enterprise application integration), 324
EAI (Enterprise application integration) middleware, 324
Earthlink, 114, 282
EB (Exabyte), A.6
eBay, 45, 57, 85, 118, 124
Ebooks, A.10
Ebusiness, 101–116
    advantages of, 105–107
    business models for, 108–112
    challenges of, 114–115
    disruptive technologies and, 101–102
    ERP components for, 356
    MIS tools for, 112–116
Ebusiness model, 108–112
Ecommerce, 103
Edge matching, 305
EDI (Electronic data interchange), 328
Ediscovery, 145
Edmunds, 111
Effectiveness
    with ebusiness, 107–108
    MIS metrics, 56–58
Efficiency MIS metrics, 56–58
Egovernment, 127–128
802.11 (Wi-Fi standard), 296
EIS (Executive information system), 61
Elastic Compute Cloud (Amazon EC2), 211
Electronic data interchange (EDI), 328
Electronic discovery, 145
Electronic waste; *see* Ewaste

Elevation of privilege, 158
Elogistics, 356
Email, 45, 114
Email privacy policy, 149–150
Email software, A.11, A.13
Embedded operating system, A.12
Emergency, 188
Emergency Alert System, 189
Emergency notification services, 189
Emergency preparedness, 188
Emerson, 270
Emotion-detection software, 346
Employee monitoring policy, 152–154
Employee relationship management (ERM), 348
Encrypt data software, A.13
Encryption, 162
Energy consumption, 196
English, Paul, 316
Enterprise application integration (EAI), 324
Enterprise application integration (EAI) middleware, 324
Enterprise architect, 183
Enterprise MIS, 321–361, 376–405
    customer relationship management, 337–342
    developing software, 379–402
    enterprise resource planning, 348–357
    outsourcing projects, 403–405
    project planning, 399–402
    supply chain management, 325–329
    and systems development life cycle, 379–388
Enterprise Rent-A-Car, 371
Enterprise resource planning (ERP), 348–361
    benefits of, 354–355
    cloud/SaaS, 358–361
    costs, 356
    hybrid, 361
    on-premise ERP, 358
    software customization, 356
    vendors, 361
Enterprise systems, 324
Entities, 271, C.2
Entity-relationship diagrams (ERDs), C.2, C.3–C.6
Entry barrier, 25
Epolicies, 146–147
Eprocurement, 356
Equifax, 144
ERDs (Entity-relationship diagrams), C.2, C.3–C.6
ERM (Employee relationship management), 348
ERP; *see* Enterprise resource planning
Eshops, 109
Estimated time enroute (ETE), 305
Estimated time of arrival (ETA), 305
Estores, 110
ETA (estimated time of arrival), 305
Etailers, 110
ETE (estimated time enroute), 305
Ethernet, B.6
Ethical computer use policy, 146–148

Ethics, 143–154; *see also* Business driven ethics and security
    developing information management policies, 145–154
    information ethics, 143–145
    setting boundaries, 175
ETL (Extraction, transformation, and loading), 243
Etrade, 111
Europe, 404
European Union, D.4
Ewaste, 195, 219
Exabyte (EB), A.6
Excel, 232, 233
Executive information system (EIS), 61
Expedia.com, 104
Expert systems, 67
Explicit knowledge, 118
Extended ERP components, 353, 355–356
Extensible Markup Language (XML), 394
Extraction, transformation, and loading (ETL), 243
Extranets, 291
Extreme programming (XP) methodology, 394
ExxonMobil, 369
Ezine, 124

F

Facebook, 133, 169, 170, 219, 239, 263, 294, 307
Fact, 5
Failback, 185
Failover, 185
Fair Credit Reporting Act (FCRA), 144
Fair information practices, 148
Fast data, 259
Fast Ethernet, B.6
Fault tolerance, 185
FBI (Federal Bureau of Investigation), 294
FCC; *see* Federal Communications Commission
FCRA (Fair Credit Reporting Act), 144
Feasibility, 395
Federal Bureau of Investigation (FBI), 294
Federal Communications Commission (FCC), 287
FedEx, 21, 79–80
Feedback, 16
Fiber-optic cable, B.9
Fidelity, 111
Fields, C.7
Fiero, Sandy, 92
50 Cent, 138
File and data recovery software, A.13
File Transfer Protocol (FTP), B.8
Finance, 13–15, 71
Financial metrics, 56
Financial times, 331
Find It, 93
Finkelstein, Clive, C.3
Firestone Tire Company, 369
Firewalls, 163

Firm infrastructure, 29
FirstGov.gov, 127
First-mover advantage, 21
Five Forces Model; see Porter's Five
    Forces Model
Flash memory, A.5
Flexibility, 192
Flickr, 132
Flipboard, 124
Focused business strategies, 27–28
Folksonomy, 121
Ford, 369
Forecasts, 254, 257
Foreign key, 235, C.9
Forrester Research, 104
Fortune magazine, 38, 45
Forward integration, 323
Foursquare, 307, 312
Fourth-generation languages (4GL), 385
Friedman, Nick, 95
Friedman, Thomas, 37–38, 44
Frito-Lay, 21, A.1
Front-office processes, 72
FTP (File Transfer Protocol), B.8
Fuzzy logic, 68

G

3G (Third-generation), 300
Gantt chart, 401
The Gap, 109
Gates, Bill, 137, 381
GB (Gigabyte), A.5
Genachowski, Julius, 312
General Motors Corporation, 102, A.11
Genetic algorithm, 68
Geocache, 304
Geocoding, 305
Geocoin, 304
Geographic information, 305
Geographic information system (GIS), 305–307
Geospatial data, 305
Germany, 410
GHz (Gigahertz), A.3
Gigabit Ethernet, B.6
Gigabyte (GB), A.5
Gigahertz (GHz), A.3
Gilovich, Thomas, 36
GIS (geographic information system), 305–307
GIS map automation, 305
Gladwell, Malcolm, 381
Globalization, 37–38
    cultural blunders, 405
    floating data centers, 223
    global databases, 261
    Google's China operations, 174
    iYogi.net help desk, 95
    nonprofits, 117
Global positioning systems (GPS), 304
Goal seeking analysis, 61
Godin, Seth, 381
Goebel, Jennifer, 316
Goldman, Eric, 134

Goods, 14, 15
Goodwill Industries International, 222
Google, 110, 111, 112, 125, 126, 132, 136,
    149, 156, 161, 173, 174, 223, 287
Google Cloud Connect, 209
Google Docs, 136, 273
Google Earth, 306
Google Glass, 69, 82
Google Maps, 314
Gore, 137
Gowalla, 307
GPS (global positioning systems), 304
Granularity, 61
Great Britain, 294
Green MIS, 194
Grid computing, 197
Groupware, A.13
The Guardian, 266

H

Hackers, 155
Hactivists, 156
Handheld computers, A.11
Haptic interface, 69
Haptic technology, 92
Hard drives, A.6
Hardware, 183, A.1–A.12
    central processing unit, A.2–A.3
    communication devices, A.9
    computer categories, A–10
    input devices, A.7–A.8
    output devices, A.8–A.9
    primary storage, A.3–A.5
    secondary storage, A.5–A.6
Hardware key logger, 152
Harvard Business School, 356
Harvard University, 317
Hashtags, 119
Hawking, Stephen, 48
Help desk, 387
Hernandez-Rebollar, Jose L., A.9
Hetz, Pam, 94
Hewlett-Packard, 95, 152, A.12
High availability, 191
High-speed Internet cable connections, 284
Histogram, 62, 65
Historical analysis, D.1
Hoaxes, 158
Hogan, Hulk, 369
Home Depot, 102
Hotels.com, 269
Hotmail, 108
Hot sites, 187
Hotspots, 296
Hsieh, Tony, 372
HTC EVO 4G phones, 314
HTML (Hypertext markup language), 103
HTTP (Hypertext transfer protocol), 103, B.8
HTTPS (Secure hypertext transfer protocol),
    293
Hub (switch or router), B.2
Hug shirt, 92

Human-generated data, 7
Human resource management, 29
Human resources, 13–15, 71
Human resources ERP components, 355
Hummer, 43
Hybrid cloud, 210
Hybrid ERP, 361
Hybrid topology, B.5
Hypertext markup language (HTML), 103
Hypertext transfer protocol (HTTP), 103, B.8
Hyundai, 43

I

i2, 379
IaaS (Infrastructure as a Service), 211
IBM, 101, 106, 391, 403, A.12
ICANN (Internet Corporation for
    Assigning Names and Numbers), 288
Identity management, 238
Identity theft, 159
IDS (Intrusion detection software), 164–165
IMing (Instant messaging), 114
Implementation phase (SDLC), 386
Inbound logistics, 29
Incident management, 189
Incident records, 189
Incidents, 189
Inc. magazine, 30
India, 37, 44
Infographics, 61–62
Infographics (Information graphics), 260
Infomediaries, 111
Information, 9–10
    age, 5, 32
    analytical, 59
    architecture, 115
    cleansing, 243–248
    compliance, 146
    on decision support systems, 94
    ethics, 143–145
    governance, 146, 232
    granularity, 227
    inconsistency, 229
    integrity, 238
    integrity issues, 229
    management, 146
    property, 146
    quality of, 227–232
    reach, 105
    richness, 105
    secrecy, 159
    setting boundaries, 175
    transactional, 59, 60
    vandalism, 125
Information accuracy, 56
Information cleansing/scrubbing, 244
Information cube, 258
Information granularity, 227
Information graphics (Infographics), 260
Information inconsistency, 229
Information integrity, 238
Information integrity issues, 229

Information management policies, 145–154
  acceptable use, 148
  email privacy, 149
  ethical computer use, 147
  information privacy, 148
  social media, 151
  workplace monitoring, 151–154
Information MIS infrastructure, 183
Information of Everything (IoE), D.6
Information privacy policy, 148
Information quality, 271
Information redundancy, 238
Information security, 154–165, 238; see also
    Business driven ethics and security
  databases, 238
  for networks, 293
  and Oklahoma state database, 383
  people for, 159
  protecting intellectual assets, 154–158
  technology for, 159–164
Information security plan, 159
Information security policies, 159
Information technology monitoring, 150, 151
Information timeliness, 271
Infosys, 404
Infrastructure
  firm, 29
  MIS; see MIS infrastructure
Infrastructure as a Service (IaaS), 211
In-house development, 403
Innovation
  emotion-detection software, 346
  News Dots, 249
  password doodling, 176
  robots, 96
  scratch, 404
  virtualization, 222–223
  and Web 1.0 vs. 2.0, 137
The Innovator's Dilemma (Christensen), 135
Input devices, A.7
Insiders, 158
In-sourcing, 403
Instant messaging (IMing), 114
Intangible benefits, 395
Integrations, 353
Integrity constraint, 238
Integrity constraints, 238
Intel, 136, 194, 298, 313, A.2, B.6
Intellectual assets, protecting, 154–158
Intellectual capital, 11
Intellectual property, 143
Intelligent agents, 69
Intelligent systems, 65–66
Interactivity, 107
Intermediaries, 106
Internet, 102–105, D.4
Internet cable connections, 284, 308
Internet Corporation for Assigning Names and
    Numbers (ICANN), 288
Internet of Things (IoT), 3–7, D.6
  time management, 41
Internet protocol (IP), B.7–B.8
Internet Protocol TV (IPTV), 289

Internet protocol version 6 (IPv6), B.7
Internet service providers (ISPs), 114
Internet use policy, 148
Interoperability, B.6
Intranets, 291
Intrusion detection software (IDS), 164–165
Inventory cycle time, 327
Inventory turnover, 327
IoE (Information of Everything), D.6
IoT (Internet of Things), 3–7, D.6
IP (Internet protocol), B.7–B.8
iPad, 298
iPhones, 297
iPods, 194, 316–317
IPTV (Internet Protocol TV), 289
IPv6 (Internet protocol version 6), B.7
Ireland, 404
iRobots, 66
ISPs (Internet service providers), 114
Israel, 404
IT consumerization, 302
Iterative development, 390
iTunes, 21, 287
iYogi.net, 95

J

Jackson, Warren, 316
Jagger, Mick, 369
James, Josh, 39
Jeopardy (game show), 93
JetBlue, 42
JetBlue Airways, 37, 371–372
Jobs, Steve, 21, 137
Johnson & Johnson, 102
JoinAfrica, 316
Jordan, Chris, 267
Joystick, A.7

K

Kaplan, Robert, 356
Kayak.com, 316
KB (Kilobyte), A.6
Kelkoo, 107
Kennedy, John F., 125
Kennedy, Robert F., 125
Keyboard, A.7
Key logger software, 152
Key performance indicators (KPIs), 53–55, 86
Key trapper software, 152
Kia, 43
Kill switch, 400
Kilobyte (KB), A.6
Kilowatt Sport input device, A.7
Kiva, 117
Kiva Systems, 96
KM (Knowledge management), 118
KMS (Knowledge management system), 118
Knight, Philip, 379
Knowledge, 11–13
  assets, 11
  explicit and tacit, 119

  facilitator, 11–12
  workers, 11
Knowledge management (KM), 118
Knowledge management system (KMS), 118
Knowledge workers, 118
Koblin, Aaron, 266
Kroger, 25

L

LANs; see Local area networks
Laptop computers, A.10
Latitude, 304
LBS; see Location-based services
Legacy systems, 358, 379
Lending Tree, 104
Level3, 282
Levi Strauss, 107
Levitt, Steven, 381
LifeLock, 176–177
Lin, Alfred, 372
LinkedIn, 120, 133, 169, 171, 174
LinkExchange, 372
Linux, A.12
List generators, 343
Live Help, 107
Local area networks (LANs), 282, B.2
Location-based services (LBS), 306
Logical view (databases), 237
Logistics, inbound and outbound, 29
Longitude, 304
Long tail, 105, 135
Loopt, 307
Loyalty program, 24
Lulu.com, 106
Lutz, Bob, 123

M

M (Megabyte), A.5
Machine-generated data, 6
Machine learning, 66, D.6
Machine-to-machine (M2M), 5
Machine vision, 67
Machine vision resolution, 67
Machine vision sensitivity, 67
Mac OS X, A.12
Madoff, Bernard, 45
Magnetic medium, A.5
Magnetic tape, A.6
Mail bombs, 150
Mainframe computers, A.11
Maintainability, 192
Maintenance phase (SDLC), 388
Maker movement, 332
Malicious code, 158
MAM (Mobile application management), 302
Management information systems (MIS), 17, 32
  business driven; see also Business
      driven MIS
  efficiency and effectiveness metrics, 56–58
  to enhance DSS, 58–64
  enterprise, 183; see also Enterprise MIS
  to improve business processes, 75–85

roles and responsibilities, 17–19
sustainable, 194–196; *see also* Sustainable
    MIS infrastructure
in value chain, 29–30
Managerial business processes, 79–80
Managerial decisions, 53, 86
Managerial level, 53
Managerial support systems, 59–63, 87
MANs; *see* Metropolitan area networks
Many-to-many relationship (M:N), C.5
Mapping, 73; *see also* Business process modeling
Mapquest, 111
Marconi, Guglielmo, 294
Marcus, Neiman, 27
Market basket analysis, 256
Marketing, 13–15, 29, 71, 343, 373–374
Market share, 54
Markovich, Ray, 279
Martin, James, C.3
Mashup editors, 124
Mashups, 124–125
Mass customization, 105
MasterCard, 304
Master data management (MDM), 232
MB (Megabyte), A.5
Mbusiness, 105
McDonald's, 317, 329, 344
MCI, 282
MDM (Master data management), 232
MDM (Mobile device management), 302
Megabyte (MB, M, Meg), A.5
Megahertz (MHz), A.3
Memory cards, A.5
Memory sticks, A.5
Mercedes-Benz, 43
Metadata, 233
Methodology, 388–389
Metrics, 53–58, 86
    critical success factors, 53, 55
    efficiency and effectiveness, 56–58
    key performance indicators, 53–55
Metropolitan area networks (MANs), 282, B.2
Mexico, 369
MHz (Megahertz), A.3
Microblogging, 123
Microcomputers, A.11
Microprocessors, A.2
Microsoft, 95, 202, 203, 204, 372, 401, 402
Microsoft Windows, A.12
Minicomputers, A.11
MIS; *see* Management information systems
MIS infrastructure, 183–210
    agile, 189–194
    and the environment, 194–196
    information, 184–189
    sustainable, 196–210
MIS skills gap, 19
MIS systems, 245
M:N (Many-to-many relationship), C.5
Mobile application management (MAM), 302
Mobile device management (MDM), 302
Mobile technologies, 294–295
Model, 58

Modem, 307–308
Monroe College, 96
Moore, Gordon, 194–195
Moore's Law, 194
Mosaic, A.10
Motorola, 136, 298
Mouse, A.7
Mozilla, 118
MS-DOS, A.12
MSN.com, 111
Mulcahy, Anne, 45
Multiagent system, 69
Multifactor authentication, 162
Multitasking, A.12
Multi-tenancy, 206
Multi-valued attribute, C.2
Murray, Bill, 405
Mutation, 68
MySpace, 137

N

NAPs (Network access points), 282
Napster, 21, B.3
NASA, A.11
Nasty Gal, 136
National Aeronautics and Space
    Administration, 302
National Institute of Standards and Technology
    (NIST), 204
National service providers (NSPs), 282
National Weather Service, 316
Nearshore outsourcing, 403
Needapresent.com, A.9
Neeleman, David, 371
Nelson, Willie, 312
Nestlé, 230
Netflix Inc., 5, 38, 45, 106, 255, 263, 273,
    287, 313
Net neutrality, 287
Netscape, A.10
NET Virtua, 313
Network access points (NAPs), 282
Network access technologies, 283–286
Network convergence, 288–290
Network effect, 124
Networking, with Business, 120–122; *see also*
    Social networking
Network interface card (NIC), B.2
Network operating system (NOS), B.4
Network protocols, 286–288
Network providers, 282–283
Networks, 183, B.1–B.5
    access technologies, 283–286
    architecture, B.3–B.5
    benefits of, 291–293
    categories of, 294–302
    challenges with
    convergence, 288–290
    Ethernet, B.6
    network providers, 282–283
    neural, 67–68
    protocols, 286–288, B.6–B.8

    topology, B.5
    wireless, 294–302
Network topologies, B.5
Network transmission media, B.8
Network user license, A.14
Network virtualization, 202
NetZero, 114, 283
Neural networks, 67–68
News dots, 249
The New York Times, 266
NIC (Network interface card), B.2
Nice Systems, 346
Niche markets, 105
NIIT, 404
Nike, 379
NIST (National Institute of Standards and
    Technology), 204
Nokia, 298
Nonrepudiation, 148
Nonvolatile, A.5
Norton, David, 356
NOS (Network operating system), B.4
NSPs (national service providers), 282
NTT, 282
Null-valued attributes, C.3

O

Obama, Barack, 249
Object-oriented languages, 385
Office Depot, 222
Offshore outsourcing (offshoring), 403
Off-the-shelf application software, 379
Oklahoma state database, 383
OLAP (Online analytical processing), 60
OLPC (One Laptop Per Child), 222
OLTP (Online transaction processing), 59
One Laptop Per Child (OLPC), 222
One-to-many relationship (1:M), C.5
One-to-one relationship (1:1), C.4
Online analytical processing (OLAP), 60
Online banking process model, 83
Online fulfillment process model, 84
Online marketplaces, 111
Online sales process model, 83
Online training, 387
Online transaction processing (OLTP), 59
Onshore outsourcing, 403
Oooooc, 104
Open source, 117–118
Open system, 117
Operating system software, A.12
Operational business processes, 76–79
Operational CRM, 342–347
Operational decisions, 51, 86
Operationalized analytics, 76
Operational level, 51
Operational support systems, 59, 60, 86
Operations, 29
Operations management, 13–15, 71
Opportunity management CRM systems, 344
Optical fiber, B.9
Optical medium, A.6

Optimization analysis, 61
Oracle, 100, 110
Oracle Financials, 42
Order-to-delivery process, 71, 72
Osbourne, Ozzy, 369
Outbound logistics, 29
Outlier, 259
Output devices, A.8–A.9
Outsourcing, 37, 403–405

P

PaaS (Platform as a Service), 212
PacifiCorp, 219
Packet, 286
Packet footers, 286
Packet headers, 286
Packet-switching, B.4
Packet tampering, 158
Page, Larry, 380
Palmer, Shelly, 48
Pandora, 312
PANs (personal area networks), 296
Paradigm shift, 103
Partner relationship management (PRM),
    347, 348
Passive RFID tags, 304
Passwords, 161–162, 170
Payless, 28
PayPal, 137
Pay-per-call, 112
Pay-per-click, 112
Pay-per-conversion, 112
Payroll process, 78
PB (Petabyte), A.6
PDA (Personal digital assistant), A.11
Peer-to-peer (P2P) networks, 289, B.3
Pentagon, 168
Perform, 346
Performance, 193
Personal area networks (PANs), 296
Personal computers, A.11
Personal digital assistant (PDA), A.11
Personal information management (PIM)
    software, A.13
Personalization, 105, 346
PERT (Program Evaluation and Review
    Technique) chart, 401
Petabyte (PB), A.6
Petraeus, David, 45
P&G (Procter & Gamble), 102, 325–326
Pharming, 160
Pharming attacks, 161
Philippines, 404
Phishing, 160
Phishing expedition, 160
Physical security, 152
Physical view of information, 237
Pie chart, 62, 65
PIM (Personal information management)
    software, A.13
Pirated software, 143
Pivot, 65

PKE (Public key encryption), 163
Plagiarism, 125–126
Planning phase (SDLC), 379
Platform as a Service (PaaS), 212
PMI (Project Management Institute), 380
P&O, 368
Podcasting, 114
Point-of-sale (POS), A.7
Polaroid, 101
Polymorphic viruses and worms, 157
Popbox, 313
Pop-up ads, 108
Portability, 192
Portals, 111
Porter, Michael, 29, 38, 44
Porter's Five Forces Model, 33, 40
    in airline industry, 26–27
    buyer power in, 23–24
    rivalry among existing competitors in, 25–26
    supplier power in, 24–25
    and supply chain management, 326–327
    threat of new entrants in, 25
    threat of substitute products/services in, 25
    in value chain analysis, 30, 32, 33
Porter's three generic strategies, 27, 28, 33, 41
Portland, 340
POS (Point-of-sale), A.7
Powergrid Fitness, A.7
P2P (peer-to-peer) networks, 289, B.3
Predictive analytics, 11
Premier One, 372
Prescriptive analytics, 11
Presentation graphics software, A.13
Preventive maintenance, 388
Priceline.com, 110
Primary key, 234–235, C.7–C.8
Primary value activities, 29
Privacy, 143
Private cloud, 209
PRM (Partner relationship management),
    347, 348
Process modeling, 382
Procter & Gamble (P&G), 102, 325–326
Procurement, 29
Product differentiation, 26
Production, 16
Production and materials management ERP
    components, 355
Productivity, 16
Program Evaluation and Review Technique
    (PERT) chart, 401
Programming software, A.13
Progressive insurance, 82
Project, 53, 380
Project management, 380, 394–406
Project Management Institute (PMI), 380
Project manager, 381
Project plan, 381
Project planning, 399–402
Project planning diagrams, 399–402
Project scope, 381
Project stakeholders, 399
Protocols, 286, B.6

Prototypes, 389
Prototyping, 389
Proxy, 286
Public cloud, 209
Public key encryption (PKE), 163
Pure-play businesses, 110

Q

QBE (Query-by-example) tool, 233
Query-by-example (QBE) tool, 233

R

Rackspace, 347
Radio-frequency identification (RFID), 303, 333
RAD (Rapid application development)
    methodology, 390
RAM (Random access memory), A.4
Random access memory (RAM), A.4
Rapid application development (RAD)
    methodology, 390
Rapid prototyping, 389
Rational unified process (RUP)
    methodology, 391
Read-only memory (ROM), A.5
Real People magazine, 231
Real Simple Syndication (RSS), 123
Real-time adaptive security, D.6
Real-time communication, 114
Real-time information, 229
Real-time systems, 229
Recording Industry Association of America, 173
Records, 234, C.7
Recovery, 185
    backup and recovery plan, 219
    disaster recovery plan, 219
Redbox, 38
Reduced instruction set computer (RISC)
    chips, A.3
Redundancy, 79
Reengineering, 80–85, 87, 94
Regional service providers (RSPs), 282
Reidenberg, Joe, 144
Reintermediation, 107
Relational database management systems, 234
Relational database model, 234, C.1–C.3,
    C.7–C.9
Relational databases, 271
Relational integrity constraints, 238
Reliability, 192
Report, 9
Reputation system, 118
Requirements definition document, 381
Requirements management, 381
Resource sharing, 291
Response time, 56
Retail, 35
Return on investment (ROI), 54
Revamping accounts, 92
RFID (Radio-frequency identification), 303, 333
RFID accelerometer, 304
RFID EPC (RFID's electronic product code), 333
RFID reader/RFID interrogator, 303

RFID's Electronic product code (RFID EPC), 333
RFID tags, 303–304
RIM, 300
Ring topology, B.5
RISC (Reduced instruction set computer) chips, A.3
Rivalry among existing competitors, 25–26
Robotic process automation (RPA), 79
Robotics, 335
Robots, 48–49, 96, 335
Roku, 313
ROM (Read-only memory), A.5
Rosen, Dr., 93
Routers, B.4
Rovi, 313
Rowdii, 104
RSPs (Regional service providers), 282
RSS (Real Simple Syndication), 123
Rubber sheeting, 305
RUP (Rational unified process) methodology, 391
Russia, 168, 174, 404
Ruth, Babe, 369

S

SaaS (Software as a Service), 211–212
SABRE Airline Solutions, B.2
Safe mode, A.13
Safeway, 25
Sales, 13–15, 29, 71
Sales force automation (SFA), 344
Salesforce.com, 211
Sales management CRM systems, 345
Samsung, 298, 314
SAP, 110
Satellite access, A.9
Satellite communication systems, 298, 300, B.10
Satellites, 300, 304
Satyam, 404
Scalability, 193
SCEM (Supply chain event management), 336
Schick, David, 35
Schmidt, Eric, 137
Schwartz, Jonathan, 123
SCM; see Supply chain management
Scripting language, 385
Script kiddies (Script bunnies), 156
Scrubbing, information, 244–248
Scrum methodology, 391
SDLC (Systems development life cycle), 379
Search engine optimization (SEO), 112
Search engine ranking, 112
Search engines, 112
Sears, 101
Secondary storage, A.5
Secure hypertext transfer protocol (SHTPP, HTTPS), 293
Secure sockets layer (SSL), 293
Security; see Information security
Seigenthaler, John, Sr., 125
Selling chain management, 336

Semantic web, 126
Semi-passive RFID tags, 304
Semistructured decisions, 53
Sensitive data, 26
Sensitivity analysis, 61
SEO (Search engine optimization), 112
Servers, 183, A.12, B.4
Server virtualization, 202
Serviceabilty, 194
Service-oriented architecture (SOA), 391–394
  interoperability, 393
  loose coupling, 394
  SOA service, 393
  web service, 394
  XML, 394
Service providers, 114, 282
Services, 14, 15, 29
SFA (Sales force automation), 344
SharePoint, 401
Shopping bot, 69
Shrek films, 198
SHTPP (Secure hypertext transfer protocol), 293
Sign-off, 381
Simple Mail Transfer Protocol (SMTP), B.8
Simple Network Management Protocol (SNMP), B.8
Single-factor authentication, 162
Single tenancy, 206
Single user license, A.12
Single-valued attribute, C.2
Site license, A.14
Skype, 289, 297
Slack, 131–132
Slate, 249
Slice-and-dice, 65
Smart cards, 162
Smart grids, 200–201
Smart machines, D.6
Smartphones, 300, A.11
SMTP (Simple Mail Transfer Protocol), B.8
SNA (Social networking analysis), 120
Snapshot, 7
Sneakware, 152
Sniffer, 158
SNMP (Simple Network Management Protocol), B.8
SOA (Service-oriented architecture), 391–394
Socializr, 104
Social media, 120
Social media manager, 151
Social media monitoring, 151
Social media policy, 151
Social networking; see also specific networking sites
  safety tips for using, 144–148
Social networking analysis (SNA), 120
Social networks, 120, 169–171, 174
Social tagging, 121
Soden, Michael, 151
Software, 183, A.12–A.14
  application, A.13
  developing, 379–402

pirated, 143
  system, A.12–A.13
Software as a Service (SaaS), 211–212
Software customization, 356, 357, 379
Software engineering, 385
Software patches, A.13
Software updates, A.13
Software upgrades, A.13
Solving the Ewaste Problem (StEP), 207
Sony, 101, 136, 313, 314
Source code, 118
Source documents, 59
South Africa, 404
Soviet Union, 37
Spam, 150
Spam blogs, 158
Sparkline, 63
Spatial data, 305
Spear phishing, 160
Speech analytics, 260
Splogs (Spam blogs), 158
Spoofing, 158
Spreadsheet software, A.13
Sprint, 282, 298
Spyware, 158
SQL (Structured query language), 233
Square, 311
SRM (Supplier relationship management), 347, 348
SSL (Secure sockets layer), 293
SSL Certificate, 293
Stakeholder, 20
Stamps.com, 43
Standard packet formats, 286
Staples, 96, 222, 336
Starbucks, 44, 123
Star topology, B.5
Start-ups
  College Hunks Hauling Junk, 95
Start-ups:
  Rackspace, 346
  Ruby receptionists, 340
  TED, 381
  viruses, 218
  WePay, 138
Static information, 239
Static process, 72
Static report, 9
Stealthware, 152
StEP (Solving the Ewaste Problem), 207
Storage:
  primary, A.3
  secondary, A.5
Storage virtualization, 201
Strategic business processes, 80–85
Strategic decisions, 53, 86
Strategic level, 53
Strategic support systems, 61–64, 87
Streaming, 300
Streamlining, 79–80, 87
Structured data, 6, 247
Structured decisions, 51, 86
Structured query language (SQL), 233

Study Trends, D.2
StumbleUpon, 121
Stylus, A.7
Supercomputers, A.10
Supplier power, 24–25
Supplier relationship management (SRM), 347, 348
Supply chain, 24, 325–329
Supply chain event management (SCEM), 336
Supply chain execution systems, 328
Supply chain management (SCM), 325–329
  ERP components for, 354–355
Supply chain planning systems, 328
Supply chain technologies, 329–336
  logistics, 329–330
  materials management, 331
  procurement, 329
Supply chain visibility, 328
Support value activities, 29
Surge pricing, 280
Sustainable MIS, 194
Sustainable MIS disposal, 195
Sustainable MIS infrastructure, 196–210
  cloud computing, 204–208
  grid computing, 197–201
  virtualized computing, 201–204
Sustaining technologies, 128
Sweitzer, Heather, 44
Swim lane, 75
Switching costs, 24
SWOT analysis, 22–23, 33
Synchronous communications, 120
Syntax, A.12, A.13
System, 14
System availability, 56
System clock, A.12
System restore, A.13
Systems; see also specific systems
Systems development life cycle (SDLC), 379
System software, A.12
Systems thinking, 16–17
System thinking, 81

T

T1 lines, 285, 308
Tableau, 235
Tables, C.7–C.9
Tablet computers, A.11
Tacit knowledge, 119
Tags, 121
Tangible benefits, 395
Taxonomies, 115
Tax policies, 116
TB (Terabyte), A.5
TCP (Transmission control protocol), B.7–B.8
TCP/IP; see Transmission control protocol/
  Internet protocol
Technological innovation, D.4–D.5
Technology, 45

Technology:
  dependence on, 125
  for information security, 154–165
Technology development, 29
Technology, Entertainment, Design (TED), 45, 380
Technology failures, 189
Technology recovery strategies, 189
TED (Technology, Entertainment, Design), 45, 380
Telecommunication protocols, B.7–B.8
Telecommunication systems, B.1
  media for, B.9–B.10
  protocols for, B.6–B.8
Telecommuting, 285
Telepresence robot, 66
Telnet Protocol, B.8
Telstar, 295
Terabyte (TB), A.5
Terminator movie, 48
Test conditions, 385
Testing phase (SDLC), 385
Texting, 45
Text mining, 260
The Gap, 96
The World Is Flat (Friedman), 37–38, 44
Third-generation (3G), 300
Thompson, Trina, 96
Threat of new entrants, 25
Threat of substitute products/services, 25
Throughput, 56
Tiffany & Co., 28
Tiffany-style, 36
Timeliness of information, 271
Time-series chart, 63, 65
Time-series information, 258
T.J. Maxx, 110
T-Mobile, 136, 315
To-Be process models, 73, 74, 87
Tokens, 162
Torvalds Linus, A.12
Toshiba, 314
Touch pad, A.7
Touch screen, A.7
Toys "R" Us, 369
TPS (Transaction processing system), 59, 60
Traceroute, 286
Trackur.com, 151
Transactional information, 59, 227
Transaction brokers, 111
Transaction processing system (TPS), 59, 60
Transaction speed, 56
Transmission control protocol (TCP), B.7–B.8
Transmission control protocol/Internet protocol
  (TCP/IP), 286, B.7
Trek, 310
Trend analysis, D.1
Trend monitoring, D.1
Trend projection, D.1
Triple constraint, 398–399
Trojan-horse virus, 157

Trust, consumer, 116
Twisted-pair cable, B.8
Twitter, 102, 123, 131–133, 150, 151, 247, 273, 307
Two-factor authentication, 162

U

UAE (United Arab Emirates), 368–369
UC (Unified communications), 288
Unavailable systems, 191
Unified communications (UC), 288
Uninstaller software, A.13
Union Bank of California, 187
United Arab Emirates (UAE), 368–369
United States, 41, 310, 312, 330, 368, 369, 403
Universal resource locators (URLs), 102
University of Pennsylvania, 316
UNIX, A.13
Unstructured communications, 92
Unstructured data, 7, 247, 250
Unstructured decisions, 53
Uplift modeling, 346
Up-selling, 344
URLs (Universal resource locators), 102
Usability, 56, 194
U.S. Bureau of Labor Statistics, 273
U.S. Department of Defense (DoD), 304, B.7
User-contributed (-generated) content, 118
User documentation, 386
U.S. Postal Service, 43
U.S. Secret Service, 62
Utility software, A.12–A.13
UUNet/WorldCom, 282

V

Value chain, 29, 30, 32
Value chain analysis, 29–32
Variable, 10
Verisign, 293
Verizon, 282
Videoconferencing, 114
Viral marketing, 108, 127
Virtual abandonment, 124
Virtual assistant, D.6
Virtual businesses, 110
Virtual data centers, 203–204
Virtualization, 201, 218, 222–223, 291
Virtual private networks (VPNs), 291
Virtual reality, 69–70, D.5
Virtual workforces, 285
Virtual workplace, 69
Viruses, 156–158
Visa, 68, 148
Vishing (Voice phishing), 160
Visual images, 268
Visualization, 61, 260, 266–267
Visualization tools, 235, 249
Voice over IP (VoIP), 289

Voice phishing, 160
VoIP (Voice over IP), 289
Volatile, A.5
Volatility, A.5
VPNs (Virtual private networks), 291
VUDU, 313

W

Walgreens, 96, 333
The Wall Street Journal, 411
Walmart, 27, 28, 35, 42, 135, 227–228,
    304, 367
Walton, Sam, 369
WANs; *see* Wide area networks
WAPs (Wireless access points), 295
War chalking, 302
War driving, 302
Warm sites, 187
Warping, 305
Waterfall methodology, 388
Watson supercomputer process, 78
Watson, Thomas J., 78
Wearable technologies, 89–90
Web 1.0, 137; *see also* Ebusiness
Web 2.0 (Business 2.0), 116–120
    advantages of, 116–120
    for capacity planning, 193
    challenges of, 125–126
    collaboration tools with, 122–125
    networking communities with, 120–122
Web 3.0, 126–128
Web-based self-service systems, 345
Web browsers, 114
Web conferencing, 114–115
Webinars, 134
Web logs, 122, 152
Website bookmarks, 121
Website personalization, 346
Websites
    data-driven, 239–241

Website traffic analytics, 108
WEP (wired equivalent privacy), 302
WePay, 138
What-if analysis, 61
White-hat hackers, 156
WHO (World Health Organization), B.11
Wide area networks (WANs), 282, B.2
Wi-Fi (Wireless fidelity), 295
Wi-Fi networks, 296–297, 316
Wi-Fi Protected Access (WPA), 302
Wikipedia, 118, 123–124, 192
Wikis, 123–124
WiMAX (Worldwide Interoperability for
    Microwave Access), 298
WiMAX technology, 314
Windows Azure, 209
Wipro, 404
Wired equivalent privacy (WEP), 302
Wired magazine, 40
Wireless (LMCS), A.9
Wireless access points (WAPs), 295
Wireless fidelity (Wi-Fi), 295
Wireless LANs (WLANs), 295–297
Wireless MANs (WMANs), 298
Wireless media, B.9–B.10
Wireless networking standard 802.11, 296
Wireless networks, 294–309, B.5
    business applications of, 302–307
    categories of, 281, 294–302
    security of, 312
Wireless technologies, 294
Wireless WANs (WWANs), 295, 298–300
Wire media, B.8–B.9
WLANs (wireless LANs), 295–297
WMANs (wireless MANs), 298
Word length, A.4
Word processing software, A.13
Workflow, 75
Workflow control systems, 75
Workplace MIS monitoring, 152
Workplace monitoring policy, 151–154

Workshop training, 387
Workstation computers, A.11
Workstations, A.11
World Future Society, D.2
World Health Organization (WHO), B.11
Worldwide Interoperability for Microwave
    Access (WiMAX), 298
World Wide Web (WWW), 103
World Wide Web Consortium (W3C), 108
Worms, 156, 157
WPA (Wi-Fi Protected Access), 302
WTC (World Triathlon Corporation), 284
WWANs (wireless WANs), 295, 298–300
WWW (World Wide Web), 103

X

Xbox, 313
Xcel Energy, 201
Xerox, 101, B.6
XML (Extensible Markup Language), 394
XP (Extreme programming) methodology, 391

Y

Yahoo!, 111, 124, 126, 203
Yahoo! Connected TV, 313
Yale University, 218
Yourdon, Edward, 406
YouTube, 111, 118, 133, 150, 173, 287, 292,
    294, 371–372
Yuuguu, 104

Z

Zappos, 5, 96, 240, 241, 372–373
Zillow.com, 111
Zombie farms, 160
Zombies, 161
Zoomr, 104
Zuckerberg, Mark, 5